**Edited and designed by**
**Time Out Guides Limited**
**Universal House**
**251 Tottenham Court Road**
**London W1T 7AB**
**Tel + 44 (020) 7813 3000**
**Fax + 44 (020) 7813 6001**
**Email guides@timeout.com**
**www.timeout.com**

## Editorial

**Editor** Jonathan Cox
**Deputy Editor** Sue Heady
**Researcher** Carol Lu
**Listings Checker** Bernice Chan
**Proofreader** Rachel Sawyer
**Indexer** Selena Cox

**Editorial Director** Peter Fiennes
**Series Editor** Ruth Jarvis
**Deputy Series Editor** Jonathan Cox
**Guides Co-ordinator** Jenny Noden

## Design

**Art Director** John Oakey
**Art Editor** Mandy Martin
**Senior Designer** Scott Moore
**Designers** Benjamin de Lotz, Lucy Grant,
Kate Vincent-Smith
**Scanning/Imaging** Dan Conway
**Picture Editor** Kerri Miles
**Deputy Picture Editor** Olivia Duncan-Jones
**Ad Make-up** Glen Impey

## Advertising

**Group Commercial Director** Lesley Gill
**Sales Director** Mark Phillips
**International Sales Co-ordinator** Ross Canadé
**Advertisement Sales (Hong Kong)** Sammy A Hussain
**Advertising Assistant** Catherine Shepherd

## Administration

**Publisher** Tony Elliott
**Managing Director** Mike Hardwick
**Group Financial Director** Kevin Ellis
**Marketing Director** Christine Cort
**Marketing Manager** Mandy Martinez
**Group General Manager** Nichola Coulthard
**Production Manager** Mark Lamond
**Production Controller** Samantha Furniss
**Accountant** Sarah Bostock

### Features in this guide were written and researched by:

**Introduction** Jason Wordie. **History** Jason Wordie. **Hong Kong Today** Jason Wordie. **HK Culture & Customs** Neil Western, Andrew Dembina, Mark Graham. **Wild Hong Kong** Joanne Bunker (*Pink dolphins* Jonathan Cox). **Accommodation** Neil Western. **Sightseeing** Andrew Stone, Jonathan Cox, Christi Daugherty, Sue Heady (*HK profiles* Neil Western; *The lost world of Suzie Wong* Adam Nebbs; *Will Hong Kong lose its shirt?* Matthew Scott; *Tin Hau, sea goddess* Sue Heady; *Kadoorie Farm & Botanic Garden* Jonathan Cox; *Expat strongholds* Mark Graham). **Restaurants** Neil Western (*Chinese cuisines* Andrew Dembina). **Pubs & Bars** Neil Western. **Shops & Services** Kirsten Beith, Hiram To (*The art of bargaining* Jonathan Cox; *HK profiles* Neil Western). **By Season** Chris Baker. **Children** Benjamin Blain. **Film** Adam Nebbs. **Galleries** Hiram To. **Gay & Lesbian** Hiram To. **Nightlife** Neil Western (*Everybody salsa!* Cliff Hall). **Performing Arts** Chris Baker (*Chinese performing arts* Andrew Dembina). **Sport & Fitness** Catharine Nicol. **Trips Out of Town: Macau** Matthew Scott, Jason Wordie, Christi Daugherty, Sue Heady; **Guangzhou** Mark Kitto. **Directory** Rehana Sheikh, Jonathan Cox, Sue Heady, Catharine Nicol.

### The Editor would like to thank:

Christi Daugherty, Sian Griffiths, Mark Kitto, Annabel Mackie, Neil Western, Jason Wordie and Shelley Yip.

**Maps by** J. S. Graphics, 17 Beadles Lane, Old Oxted, Surrey, RH8 9JG. Digital data for maps on pages 62, 110, 126, 256, 268-9, 310-1 and 316 supplied by Apa Publications GmbH & Co. Verlag KG (Singapore branch).

**All photography by** Amanda Edwards except: page 7, 9, 11, 22 AKG; page 24, 105 Associated Press; page iii, 5, 26, 32, 46, 55, 56, 63, 68, 69, 71, 72, 73, 75, 77, 78, 81, 84, 85, 88, 92, 93, 94, 99, 100, 102, 103, 106, 107, 111, 139, 209, 211, 254, 281 Jonathan Cox; page 35 Hong Kong Dolphin Watch; page 83, 101 The Kobal Collection; page 216 The Ronald Grant Archive; page 16, 58, 59, 60, 61, 121, 137, 205, 206, 208, 243, 251, 252 Hong Kong Tourism Board; page 232 Popperfoto; page 275 Thats Guangzhou.

The following images were provided by the featured establishments: pages 39, 41, 70, 219, 221, 239.

# Contents

Introduction                              2

## In Context

History                                   7
Hong Kong Today                          26
HK Culture & Customs                     28
Wild Hong Kong                           34

## Accommodation

Accommodation                            40

## Sightseeing

Introduction                             56
Hong Kong Skyline                        58
Hong Kong Island                         63
  Central                                63
  Sheung Wan & Mid-Levels                75
  Wan Chai & Causeway Bay                81
  The Peak                               88
  South & east coast                     91
Kowloon                                  97
  Tsim Sha Tsui                          99
  Yau Ma Tei & Mong Kok                 108
  New Kowloon                           112
The New Territories                     114
  Central New Territories               114
  West New Territories                  120
  East New Territories                  123
The Outlying Islands                    127
  Lamma                                 127
  Lantau                                130
  Cheung Chau                           135
  Other islands                         137

## Eat, Drink, Shop

Restaurants                             141
Pubs & Bars                             166
Shops & Services                        175

## Arts & Entertainment

By Season                               204
Children                                209
Film                                    215
Galleries                               220
Gay & Lesbian                           223

Nightlife                               228
Performing Arts                         238
Sport & Fitness                         247

## Trips Out of Town

Macau                                   254
Guangzhou                               267

## Directory

Getting Around                          282
Resources A-Z                           286
The Language                            298
Further Reference                       299
Index                                   302
Advertisers' Index                      308

## Maps

Hong Kong                               310
Hong Kong, Macau & Guangzhou            313
Street Index                            314
Rail Transport                          316

# Introduction

A vibrant, cosmopolitan, international 'world' city blending the best of East and West; English-speaking ex-British colony; a shopping and gourmet paradise; and a teeming concrete jungle, with more people per square kilometre than anywhere else on Earth.

These are just some of the stereotypical images of Hong Kong, which, as most visitors stay for only a few days, are the impressions they generally leave with. But there is much more to the place, and for those who stay a couple of weeks or so, a different picture starts to emerge. The key to appreciating Hong Kong for what it is (as opposed to what it is supposed to be) is to strip out the clichés and enjoy what lies beneath.

Hong Kong is an overwhelmingly Chinese city, albeit with an international gloss. Ninety six per cent of the population is ethnic Chinese, with two per cent of the remaining four made up of Filipino and Indonesian domestic servants, Indians, Pakistanis and Nepalese, and the final two per cent representing just about every race, creed and nationality on earth. And, contrary to expectation, many of these people don't speak much, if any, English.

Hong Kong's reputation as a shoppers' nirvana is now very dated. During the 1960s and 1970s, there were bargains aplenty. But as wages, rents and the general cost of living rose, the days when Hong Kong could offer the world's best deals on the likes of electronics and cameras are long over. Still, there is a terrific range of goods on offer and some items, such as clothes, remain cheaper than in many other parts of the world.

The region's reputation for fine dining is likewise overhyped. Yes, there are plenty of good Chinese and other Asian restaurants – though the better ones are usually quite pricey and the cheaper back-street establishments can be daunting for the non-Cantonese speaker – but the range of international restaurants is still limited when compared with the likes of London, Sydney or San Francisco.

What the tourist board literature fails to mention is that Hong Kong's nightlife is hotting up. This is a city in which lax licensing laws have meant that it's always been possible to drink 24/7, but now it's become one of the best cities in Asia for clubbing.

Not that people in Hong Kong are only into playing hard; they work hard, too. The result? A city of phenomenal energy. And, when you are lost within the concrete canyons and snaking walkways of Central, the image of the city as a pulsing urban jungle seems only too real. But stand on the waterfront promenade at Tsim Sha Tsui and look across to Hong Kong Island, and a different picture emerges – one of towering buildings backed by deep green, thickly forested mountainsides. Take the Peak Tram up the hillside and, after a few minutes, the tower-blocks of the Mid-Levels give way to stunning vistas of harbour, islands and the sea.

This is the place to come when you need to put the frenzied city into context, and there can be few other cities with the incredible juxtaposition of urban and wild landscapes as Hong Kong. This wildly lovely 'other' Hong Kong is perhaps its most unexplored – and, therefore, most surprising and enjoyable – side. Over 60 per cent of the total land area is designated as Country Park, and there are places where it is possible to hike for hours and see almost nobody.

See it, explore it, and enjoy it. For many people, Hong Kong is like nowhere else they have ever been or imagined, and more than a few who originally came intending to stay a year or two are still here, still addicted, sometimes hating it, but mostly loving all that Hong Kong has to offer.

## ABOUT THE TIME OUT CITY GUIDES

The *Time Out Hong Kong Guide* is one of an expanding series of *Time Out* City Guides, now numbering over 35, produced by the people behind London and New York's successful listings magazines. Our guides are all written and updated by resident experts who have striven to provide you with all the most up-to-date information you'll need to explore the city or read up on its background, whether you're a local or a first-time visitor.

## THE LOWDOWN ON THE LISTINGS

Above all, we've tried to make this book as useful as possible. Addresses, telephone numbers, websites, transport information, opening times, admission prices and credit card details have all been included in the listings.

And, as far as possible, we've given details of facilities, services and events, all checked and correct as we went to press. However, owners and managers can change their arrangements at any time. Before you go out of your way, we'd advise you to telephone and check opening times, ticket prices and other particulars. While every effort has been made to ensure the accuracy of the information contained in this guide, the publishers cannot accept responsibility for any errors it may contain.

### PRICES AND PAYMENT
We have noted where venues such as shops, hotels and restaurants accept the following credit cards: American Express (AmEx), Diners Club (DC), MasterCard (MC) and Visa (V). Many will also accept travellers' cheques.

The prices we've supplied should be treated as guidelines, not gospel. If prices vary wildly from those we've quoted, please write and let us know. We aim to give the best and most up-to-date advice, so we always want to know if you've been badly treated or overcharged.

### THE LIE OF THE LAND
Hong Kong falls fairly neatly into four basic areas: Hong Kong Island, the Kowloon peninsula (across Victoria Harbour), the New Territories (the vast swathe of land ballooning out from the north of Kowloon up to the border with Guangdong province and the rest of China) and the Outlying Islands. Each of these areas has its own chapter within the Sightseeing chapter, and each is further subdivided into districts (these districts are included within all addresses in this guide). The great majority of places listed also include a map reference.

### TELEPHONE NUMBERS
The international code for Hong Kong is 852; there is no area code. All phone numbers are eight digits. For more on telephones, see p294.

### ESSENTIAL INFORMATION
For all the practical information you might need for visiting Hong Kong, including visa and customs information, advice on disabled facilities and access, emergency telephone numbers and local transport, turn to the **Directory** chapter at the back of the guide.

### MAPS
The maps section at the back of this book includes overview maps of Hong Kong, the region and of the public transport system.

There is an online version of this guide, as well as weekly events listings for over 30 international cities, at www.timeout.com.

In addition, there are detailed street maps within the relevant sections of the Sightseeing chapter. Wherever possible, a map reference is provided for places listed.

### LET US KNOW WHAT YOU THINK
We hope you enjoy the *Time Out Hong Kong Guide*, and we'd like to know what you think of it. We welcome tips for places that you consider we should include in future editions and take note of your criticism of our choices. There's a reader's reply card at the back of this book for your feedback, or you can email us at hongkongguide@timeout.com.

## Advertisers
We would like to stress that no establishment has been included in this guide because it has advertised in any of our publications and no payment of any kind has influenced any review. The opinions given in this book are those of *Time Out* writers and entirely independent.

**TimeOut** international agenda

The best weekly entertainment listings from around the world.
Every Wednesday in
**Time Out•Time Out New York•El País**

Amsterdam•Barcelona•Berlin•Boston•Brussels•Budapest•Chicago
Dublin•Edinburgh•Florence•Glasgow•Hong Kong•Johannesburg
Las Vegas•Lisbon•London•Los Angeles•Madrid•Miami•Moscow
New Orleans•New York•Paris•Philadelphia•Prague•Rome•San Francisco
Shanghai•Sydney•Tokyo•Venice•Vienna•Washington, DC

**www.timeout.com**

# Time Out

# Hong Kong

**timeout.com/hongkong**

**Penguin Books**

PENGUIN BOOKS

Published by the Penguin Group
Penguin Books Ltd, 27 Wrights Lane, London W8 5TZ, England
Penguin Books USA Inc., 375 Hudson Street, New York, New York 10014, USA
Penguin Books Australia Ltd, Ringwood, Victoria, Australia
Penguin Books Canada Ltd, 10 Alcorn Avenue, Toronto, Ontario, Canada M4V 3B2
Penguin Books (NZ) Ltd, 182-190 Wairau Road, Auckland 10, New Zealand

Penguin Books Ltd, Registered Offices: Harmondsworth, Middlesex, England

First published 2001
10 9 8 7 6 5 4 3 2 1

Copyright © Time Out Group Ltd, 2001
All rights reserved

Colour reprographics by Icon, Crown House, 56-58 Southwark Street, London SE1
and Precise Litho, 34-35 Great Sutton Street, London EC1
Printed and bound by Cayfosa-Quebecor, Ctra. de Caldes, Km 3 08 130 Sta, Perpètua de Mogoda, Barcelona, Spain

# In Context

| History | 7 |
| Hong Kong Today | 26 |
| HK Culture & Customs | 28 |
| Wild Hong Kong | 34 |

## Feature boxes

| Where the streets have old names | 8 |
| History? What history? | 13 |
| Plague! | 14 |
| **HK profiles** Sir Cecil Clementi | 18 |
| The decline of pidgin English | 21 |
| Key events | 25 |
| Pink dolphins | 35 |
| **HK walks** Across the Dragon's Back | 36 |

Truly Original

Time Out
LONDON'S
LIVING GUIDE
EVERY WEEK
timeout.com

PHOTO: JONATHON FOSTER WILLIAMS

# History

From pirates and opium traders to pirate software and bond traders in 160 years.

The Portuguese mariner Jorge Alvares was the first European to visit the area surrounding Hong Kong. In 1513, he landed on the island of Lintin, which lies west of the New Territories in the middle of the Pearl River Delta.

## WEST MEETS EAST

Alvares' mission had started in Malacca, now in Malaysia, which the Portuguese had captured in 1511. He was intent on establishing a sea route to China, so that greater profit could be made on goods purchased direct from their source, rather than through Chinese traders. Chinese porcelain, for example, fetched extremely high prices in Europe, with good quality ceramics commanding twice their own weight in silver when re-sold in Goa.

When Alvares arrived on Lintin, the local mandarinate received him in a friendly manner and trade commenced. As a result, Alvares spent most of the next ten months on Lintin (which is known as 'Solitary Nail' in Chinese, due to its sharply-pointed shape), before returning to Malacca when the south-west

monsoon winds permitted his little flotilla to sail. While not given much freedom of movement, the traders visiting Lintin were not as closely confined by the Chinese authorities as in later centuries, and, while it is not recorded, it is highly likely that Alvares and his men visited the nearby mainland.

While on Lintin, they erected a *padrão* (or stone) carved with the Portuguese cross and crest, though nothing of it survives today. These stones functioned more as markers of passage for later seafarers than as territorial claims, and were erected wherever Portuguese mariners sailed, from Mombasa and Ormuz to western India and the Moluccas. They can still be seen in some of these places today. Alvares's young son accompanied him on the voyage from Malacca, but he died at Lintin and was buried at the base of the *padrão* erected by his father. Alvares himself made two more voyages to China, in 1519 and in 1521. During the latter, he died and was buried beneath the *padrão* in the same spot as his son.

# Where the streets have old names

Amnesia comes naturally to go-ahead Hong Kong – the territory's colonial past already seems a distant memory for many. Yet there is one remaining aspect of Hong Kong that still maps its colonial history, and that is the names of its streets.

For the first 100 or so years of the colony's history, almost every British Prime Minister, Foreign Secretary and Governor ended up with a street named after him. Below, you'll find a potted who's who.

## CENTRAL

**Aberdeen Street, Aberdeen**
Lord Aberdeen: Secretary of State for the Colonies 1834-35; Foreign Secretary 1841-46; Prime Minister 1852-55

**Bonham Road/Strand East & West**
Sir George Bonham: Governor 1848-54

**Caine Road/Lane**
William Caine: Chief Magistrate and, later, Secretary of State for the Colonies from the early 1840s to the mid 1850s

**Chater Road/Garden**
Sir Paul Chater: financier and member of the Legislative Council and Executive Council 1887-1926

**D'Aguilar Street/Peak, Cape D'Aguilar**
Major-General Charles D'Aguilar: led raid on Canton in 1847

**Des Voeux Road**
Sir William Des Voeux: Governor 1887-91

**Elgin Street**
Lord Elgin: Envoy extraordinaire during the Second Opium War (1857-60)

**Pedder Street**
Lieutenant William Pedder: Harbour Master in the 1840s

**Peel Street**
Robert Peel: Prime Minister 1834, 1841-46

**Pottinger Street/Peak**
Sir Henry Pottinger: Administrator 1841-43; Governor 1843-44

**Robinson Road**
Sir Hercules Robinson: Governor 1859-65

**Stanley Street**
Lord Stanley (later 14th Lord Derby): Secretary of State for the Colonies 1833-34, 1841-45; Prime Minister 1852, 1858-59, 1866-68

**Wellington Street**
Duke of Wellington: Foreign Secretary 1834-35

## MID-LEVELS & THE PEAK

**Bowen Road**
Sir George F Bowen: Governor 1883-85

**Kennedy Road**
Sir Arthur E Kennedy: Governor 1872-77

**Lugard Road**
Sir Frederick Lugard: Governor 1907-12

**MacDonnell Road**
Sir Richard G MacDonnell: Governor 1866-72

**Mount Davis**
Sir John F Davis: Governor 1844-48

## WAN CHAI & CAUSEWAY BAY

**Harcourt Road**
Sir Cecil Harcourt: led fleet back home in 1945

**Hennessy Road**
Sir John Pope Hennessy: Governor 1877-82

**Jardine's Bazaar/Crescent, Matheson Street**
Jardine Matheson: the trading house.

**Lockhart Road**
James Stewart Lockhart: Colonial Secretary in the 1890s

**Stubbs Road**
Sir Reginald E Stubbs: Governor 1919-25

## TSIM SHA TSUI

**Bowring Street**
Sir John Bowring: Governor 1854-59

**Cameron Road, Mount Cameron**
Major-General NG Cameron: General Officer Commanding 1887

**Carnarvon Road**
Lord Carnarvon: Secretary of State for the Colonies 1866-67, 1874-78

**Granville Road**
Lord Granville: Foreign Secretary 1851-52, 1870-74, 1880-85; Secretary of State for the Colonies 1868-70, 1886

**Hart Avenue**
Sir Robert Hart: Inspector-General of the Customs Service 1861-1906

**Kimberley Road**
Lord Kimberley: Secretary of State for the Colonies 1870-74; Foreign Secretary 1894-95

**Knutsford Terrace**
Lord Knutsford: Secretary of State for the Colonies 1887-92

**Nathan Road**
Sir Matthew Nathan: Governor 1904-07

**Salisbury Road**
Lord Salisbury: Foreign Secretary 1878-80; Prime Minister 1885-86, 1886-92, 1895-1902

**Victoria Harbour** as seen from Central, circa 1900.

Other navigators followed in Alvares's wake in the succeeding five decades. Periodic trade developed between the Portuguese and Chinese at various locations up and down the coast. These changed from season to season, but one of the most regularly used was the island of Lampacao (for several years in the 1540s and 1550s). It was here that the Catholic missionary St Francis Xavier died and was buried, later being exhumed and re-buried in Malacca, before being removed at a later date to Goa.

At this time, the prevalence of pirates on the islands around the mouth of the Pearl River Delta led to them being dubbed the *Ilhas Ladrones* or Islands of Robbers. In fact, piracy remained a major problem in these waters up to the mid 20th century. But that did not stop trading ships from all over Asia anchoring in the triangle between Lintin, the northern side of Deep Bay and present-day Tuen Mun, in the hope of trading with south China. The Siamese, in particular, had quite a large seasonal presence, mooring further out along the northern coast of Lantau.

### THE GROWTH OF MACAU
However, when the Portuguese established Macau as a permanent trading settlement with the permission of the local Chinese mandarinate in about 1557, the face of South China trade changed. The tiny port rapidly developed as a centre of entrepôt trade between China and Japan, using Portuguese vessels and mariners as carriers. Repeated piratical raids by the Japanese had led to their prohibition from Chinese ports. This, together with Ming Dynasty restrictions on the movement of Chinese abroad, meant that the Portuguese were in the perfect position to act as middle men, bringing mainly raw Chinese silk to Japan, and returning with silver and copper (though

there was some trade in high-quality porcelain as well). A virtual monopoly of the carrying trade resulted for the Portuguese, ushering in a period of wealth and prosperity that Macau has never seen since – the period from 1560 to 1640 is often referred to as the Golden Age of Macau.

In addition to trade, the Portuguese played a major role in exporting Catholic missionaries to Japan, an unwelcome activity that eventually led to the complete closure of Japan to Portuguese trade in 1639. (The Calvinist Dutch, however, were still allowed to trade at Deshima, near Nagasaki, as their cargoes were conspicuously free of priests.)

> '**The closure of Japan to Portuguese trade was an important factor in both Macau's period of slow decline... and the subsequent rise of British and Dutch colonial power in Asia.**'

Around this time, the first British navigator to reach the China Coast, Captain Weddell, had landed at Macau in 1637, and, in spite of orders by the Chinese not to approach, tried to enter the city of Canton (now Guangzhou). He was driven away and no further British vessels visited these waters for several decades.

The closure of Japan to Portuguese trade was an important factor in both Macau's period of slow decline (which continued until the late 18th century) and the subsequent rise of British and Dutch colonial power in Asia. Throughout this period, Hong Kong remained unnoticed on the other side of the Pearl River Delta, just one more island among hundreds up and down the Guangdong coast, inhabited by a few fishermen, subsistence farmers and pirates.

## CANTON TRADE

For centuries after the establishment of Macau, European traders were not permitted any permanent trading station in China other than Macau itself. Seasonal trade at the port of Canton was permitted, but merchants had to leave the city at the end of the trading season and return to Macau. While in Canton, they were prohibited from bringing their wives and families with them, forbidden to learn Chinese and had their movement around town restricted. Few were allowed to venture beyond their trading compounds or 'factories', as they were known. Gradually, these restrictions became increasingly irksome, accompanied as they were by bribery, corruption and constantly changing standards and expectations.

## 'The key to unlocking the Chinese treasure chest was opium.'

The mid 18th century witnessed a growing passion in Europe for tea, silk and other luxury goods, thanks to a long period of steadily rising prosperity. Tea, especially, was in enormous demand and, at this time, China enjoyed a world monopoly on supply. The Chinese insisted that everything be paid for in silver specie (China remained on the silver standard until the early 1930s), which, in due course, led to serious balance of trade deficits in favour of China, as it had little use for European trade goods at the time, other than a few clocks, trinkets and curios. The key to unlocking the Chinese treasure chest was opium.

## BRITISH EAST INDIA COMPANY

The British East India Company grew opium under government monopoly in India and sold it at public auction in Calcutta every year. As the Company was officially opposed to the opium trade, and opium was not to be carried in Company ships or traded by Company officials, a system of private traders (known as the 'Country Trade') developed. These merchants bought opium at the Calcutta auctions and smuggled it to China aboard specially built vessels. Numerous early trading houses, which later became big names on the China Coast, such as Jardine Matheson, Dent's and Russell's, were heavily involved in the opium trade.

While it is the British who are usually vilified for introducing opium to China, it is worth remembering that numerous Scandinavian and American firms were heavily involved as well. The major opium-smuggling depot was located on Lintin, where Alvares (*see p7*) had made his China landfall in 1513. Although a series of opium bans were introduced by the Chinese Government, they were largely ineffectual due mainly to localised corruption and the active involvement of Chinese officials in the illicit opium trade. What's more, a couple of attempts by British East India Company officials to formalise diplomatic relations between Britain and China were rebuffed by the Chinese.

However, the ever-increasing volume of foreign merchant shipping in the region did alarm the Chinese authorities and they constructed a range of coastal defences, including forts at Fan Lau and Tung Chung on Lantau island, at the Bocca Tigris (Bogue) and elsewhere in the Pearl River Delta, some of which still stand today.

## THE FIRST OPIUM WAR

From 1830, there was a gradual increase in tension between the British merchants and the Chinese authorities in Canton over the opium question. As a result, in 1834, Lord William John Napier was appointed as Commissioner of Trade, with the intention of regularising trade and, eventually, establishing diplomatic relations between the two empires. (Napier's name, unpromisingly, transliterated into Chinese as 'laboriously vile'.)

When Napier died while on official duty, he was succeeded by Captain Charles Elliot. Elliot was in the unenviable position of having to support a trade of which (subsequent correspondence has shown) he did not personally approve, and negotiate with the Chinese, who – at this time – had no experience of dealing with other nations except as tributaries.

In 1839, Commissioner Lin Tse-hsu was appointed to completely suppress the opium trade. Lin did his work well, and his campaign resulted in the surrender and destruction of over 20,000 chests of (mostly British-owned) opium at Canton. This action provided the *causus belli* for military action, for which many of the merchants had long been agitating in the British Parliament, and a British fleet dispatched from India attacked the Bogue forts on the Pearl River approaches to Canton.

Various attempts at conciliation between the two parties failed, but eventually the Convention of Chuen Pi (signed in 1841) ended hostilities. The subsequent Treaty of Nanking, signed in 1842, arranged for the opening of five Chinese ports to foreign trade (the first Treaty Ports) and for the cession of Hong Kong Island 'in perpetuity' to the British Crown, as a place of permanent, stable, safe British trade.

A wet day in the heart of **Central** in the early 1950s.

## WHY HONG KONG ISLAND?

Hong Kong Island was chosen, over other larger and more prosperous locations (such as the island of Chusan at the entrance to the Yangtze in eastern China), because it was well known to mariners and possessed an excellent, well-sheltered natural harbour. Ships travelling to Canton or further up and down the coast would usually call at Waterfall Bay (near where you'll now find Wah Fu Estate on the western side of Hong Kong Island) for fresh drinking water; they also took shelter from stormy weather and typhoons at Shek Pai Wan (modern Aberdeen). The name Hong Kong is a corruption of Heung Gong, meaning 'fragrant harbour', which is a reference to the sandalwood incense mills then found at Aberdeen that could be smelled from out at sea.

Hong Kong Island was formally occupied on 26 January 1841, and developed rapidly as merchants and traders who had previously been based in Canton and Macau moved to the island.

## EARLY HONG KONG

Central district was the first area of planned urban development in Hong Kong. At land sales held in June 1841 (five months after the British flag was raised at Possession Point), 51 lots of land were sold to 23 merchant houses for the purpose of building offices and godowns (as warehouses are known in Asia). These firms included Jardine Matheson, which is still prominent today, and its then-rival Dent's, which was wiped out in the slump of 1867. Office buildings in a style very reminiscent of Macau were constructed between the waterfront and Queen's Road as far as Central Market, the site of which was designated a public market in 1842.

In November 1841, the ridge of land between Albany Nullah (now Garden Road) and Glenealy Nullah (now Glenealy) was set aside for Crown use, and subsequently became known as Government Hill. The Colonial Secretariat, Government House, Albany

Government Quarters and St John's Cathedral were all built on this slope. The area extending between Government Hill and Wan Chai was designated for military use. Victoria and Wellington Barracks were built, and the area remained on the defence estate until the late 1970s. This officially created division between the districts of Central and Wan Chai meant, in effect, that additional residential and commercial areas could only be developed to the east of the military cantonment.

In 1843, after Hong Kong officially became a Crown Colony and, thus, a permanent settlement, the rapidly developing city was named Victoria; it extended over what is now Sheung Wan, Central and Wan Chai. Central, however, became the principal business district and centre of administration – it remains so today. In addition to the military cantonments established to the east of Government Hill, a military camp was established at Stanley soon after the British arrival.

> 'The Crown Colony's
> first 20 years were very
> buccaneering in spirit,
> characterised by corruption,
> lawlessness, brutality and
> a generalised sense of
> 'make-it-quick, make-it-now,
> then-get-out-fast'.'

From the 1840s, the area around Lyndhurst Terrace, Hollywood Road and Aberdeen Street was a European residential area. From the 1870s onwards, however, increasing numbers of Chinese merchants bought properties in this area, converting the buildings into tenements. From this time onwards, therefore, the Europeans moved up the hill to the area of Caine and Robinson roads, marking the beginnings of residential development in the Mid-Levels.

The Crown Colony's first 20 years were very buccaneering in spirit, characterised by corruption, lawlessness, brutality and a generalised sense of 'make-it-quick, make-it-now, then-get-out-fast', which – some would say – has persisted ever since.

A key problem at the beginning was the lack of an efficient civil service, as almost no Government officers for the first 20 or so years of the colony's existence were able to either speak or read Chinese. Policing and the legal system were hopelessly inadequate, with many government posts filled by almost anyone who happened to be in Hong Kong when a job was going.

There was little interaction between the Chinese and European communities – outside the bedrooms of a few – leading to a great deal of fear, bigotry and misunderstanding on both sides. An attempted poisoning of the main European bread supply in 1857 caused widespread panic and further hastened the process of racial alienation and polarisation.

The first specially recruited Hong Kong Government administrative cadets (who all learned about Chinese culture and how to speak Cantonese) were appointed in 1862, and this led gradually to an improvement in government standards. In general terms, Hong Kong witnessed a gradual and steady improvement throughout the 1860s and 1870s.

## THE SECOND OPIUM WAR AND THE DEVELOPMENT OF KOWLOON

A Chinese-led raid on a British registered vessel – the *Arrow* – led to what became known as the Second Opium (or Arrow) War (1857-60). During this conflict, the Summer Palace in Beijing was sacked, looted and burned, and an Anglo-French force governed Canton from 1858 to 1860.

Locally, the conflict led to the cession of the Kowloon peninsula and nearby Stonecutter's Island to Britain in 1859. The new extent of the territory stretched northwards to what eventually became Boundary Street, and included the entire Tsim Sha Tsui area. The majority of the residents were Hakka, engaged in stonecutting in the surrounding hills – the stone was ferried across the harbour and used in construction projects.

The first European settlers in Kowloon were the local Portuguese community, who moved across the harbour from the late 19th century. By the 1920s, Tsim Sha Tsui was almost a Portuguese district, and, until the 1950s, the Portuguese represented the largest non-British, non-Chinese section of the population.

From the 1860s onwards, the commercial and residential opportunities of the new area became apparent, leading to the gradual expansion of Kowloon. At around the same time, Hong Kong experienced a prolonged period of economic boom.

The original (ie pre-1859) land area of Tsim Sha Tsui and the Kowloon peninsula has been greatly enlarged by numerous phases of reclamation over the years; many of which have been infilled using the tops of the hills that used to dominate the area. The result is that the topography of the area has changed completely. The location of some Kowloon streets today, such as Reclamation Street in Yau Ma Tei, provide some of the best clues to the peninsula's former coastlines and hills.

# History? What history?

Something that often strikes newcomers to Hong Kong is how extraordinarily little knowledge – or even curiosity – most people born and brought up here seem to have about the place they've inhabited all their lives. Cynics frequently sneer that if Hong Kong people can't make money out of something, sing into it, eat it or hang a designer label off it, then they feel it's not worth knowing about. The underlying reasons why so many have ended up knowing so little are deep-rooted and complex.

Before 1949 (and the founding of the People's Republic of China), very few people of any race *were* local, in the sense of being lifelong residents, born, raised and educated in Hong Kong. The overwhelming majority – both Chinese and Europeans – were in the territory to make a living, not a home, so to speak of 'Hong Kong people' before that time, in the sense that the term would be understood by many today, had virtually no meaning. Almost everyone was from somewhere else (and, in many cases, a refugee of some sort) and all intended to go back from whence they came one day.

With little shared heritage, and so much discontinuity after World War II, what was here before 1949 was largely irrelevant to those who came afterwards. In the 1950s, almost no sense of a shared Hong Kong community existed. Instead, there was a collection of different nationalities who lived side by side but seldom – if ever – mingled. Thus, cultivating a common, Hong Kong-based heritage through the study of local history (and encouraging the sense of patrimony that develops as a result) was a non-starter when, for most residents, there was simply no common legacy to begin with.

Given this situation, why should anyone bother to care for the place, or want to know more about it than they needed to for day-to-day living? If graceful old buildings were heedlessly destroyed, beautiful vistas irretrievably ruined, the harbour and beaches fouled almost beyond redemption, and the New Territories countryside squandered and lost, well, ultimately it didn't matter – or so the flawed reasoning went. After all, Hong Kong wasn't really home; it was just a place to make enough money to buy an emigrant's visa to Canada or Australia, just as two generations earlier Hong Kong represented

little more than the opportunity to save up for a comfortable retirement elsewhere in the Pearl River Delta or in a picturesque English village, depending from where one had originally hailed.

The conscious development of a distinct Hong Kong identity was never encouraged, largely because it would have been interpreted by the mainland government – a fact it has admitted – as the colonial authorities trying to create a separate, ultimately self-governing, entity. The same sentiment very much applies today, as the concept of 'One Country' is paramount – whatever the rider about 'Two Systems' might once have been taken to mean. The result is that a Hong Kong identity has evolved by default – and somehow managed to flourish against the odds.

Of course, many of the thoughts of the Hong Kong people today on the SAR's history have been formed by their education. In the early post-war period, a number of schools opened up that catered to the immigrant population, with decidedly political considerations. Nationalist-inspired disturbances in 1956 and Communist-fomented ones in 1966-67 showed that the ideological divisions after the end of the civil war were still too bitter to discuss rationally. If the events in China after the end of the Manchu Dynasty and establishment of the Republic were simply not taught, then the potential strife caused by differing interpretations would not arise – or so the argument went.

A further barrier to teaching local history was the scarcity of resource materials. No authoritatively written, comprehensive history of Hong Kong – in either English or Chinese – existed until the GB Endacott wrote *A History of Hong Kong*, which was published in 1958. In 1965, John Stokes (headmaster of Queen's College) and his wife's *Hong Kong In History* – published in both English and Chinese – demonstrated that local history could be both interesting and worthwhile.

By the mid 1990s, the study of Hong Kong had finally made its way into mainstream school curricula, thanks to Ko Tim Keung's superb *Heung Kong Kam Sik* (Hong Kong Past and Present; 1994), which is now standard issue in secondary schools. But in spite of a steadily growing interest in Hong Kong studies, not one of Hong Kong's universities has yet established a Chair in Hong Kong History.

# Plague!

Even today, living in Hong Kong can be a threat to one's health. Cholera sometimes appears in the summer months, but the principal concern is from insidious air-borne pollution.

In the late 19th century, disease outbreaks had more sudden, and fatal, consequences. Bubonic plague first made its appearance in the spring of 1894, after the coldest winter then recorded in Hong Kong. It was to be a recurrent menace for the next 30 years.

Although there was little scientific knowledge of epidemics and their causes at the time, a connection between filthy conditions and pandemics had been made, and, in 1881, a full-scale inquiry into sanitary conditions had been ordered by the Secretary of State for the Colonies. The Chadwick Report, made public in 1882, recommended numerous sweeping changes, including the establishment of a much-needed Sanitary Board (from which today's Urban Council would eventually develop). However, when the plague broke out 12 years later, most of the reforms had still to be implemented.

It was no surprise that the areas most badly affected by this disease were the grossly overcrowded tenements of Tai Ping Shan, located just to the west of the city of Victoria. In this closely packed area, humans shared water supplies and living space with cattle, pigs and poultry – perfect conditions for a serious outbreak of plague.

Much of Tai Ping Shan was cordoned off. Three hundred soldiers were brought in to help cleanse and disinfect the area, but their presence was felt to be intrusive by local residents and anti-foreign unrest grew. Five of the servicemen became plague victims themselves and were buried in the Colonial Cemetery at Happy Valley, where their graves can still be seen.

The Government Civil Hospital was overwhelmed by the number of victims, so the Kennedy Town glassworks, a recently completed pig depot and the Royal Navy hospital ship *Hygeia* were all pressed into action. Disinfecting stations were erected at Tai Ping Shan and Mong Kok, and public bath-houses built at Pound Lane and Wan Chai. After the plague, the latter became a feature of the city, and remain to this day in parts of Hong Kong. One is still in use in Sai Ying Poon, next to the old Tsan Yuk Hospital (now the Western District Community Centre).

The human cost of the plague was very high. As the Chinese believed it was inauspicious for the sick to die at home, many of the diseased were simply thrown out on to the streets to die. On just one day in June 1894, 109 plague victims were collected from where they had been abandoned. With no laws requiring the registration of deaths among the Chinese population, it proved impossible to accurately count the number of plague deaths.

Business also suffered as a result of the disease. Ships avoided a known plague port, so the volume of trade rapidly declined. By the same token, as the colony relied on imports of virtually everything (as it still does), prices soon began to rise, further fuelling local unrest.

Events in Hong Kong were also used for political means across the border, and wild tales abounded. For example, inflammatory placards appeared in Canton accusing European doctors in the British colony of scooping out the eyes of new-born Chinese children to use in anti-plague medicines.

When these rumours spread to Hong Kong, thousands of people decamped to the mainland. Contemporary reports allege that over 100,000 people – half the population of the colony – left for the mainland. However, the official figure, given in the Governor's dispatch to the Secretary of State, indicated that 80,000 people left.

The governor at the time, Sir William Robinson, felt the only effective long-term remedy was razing and rebuilding all insanitary property. Despite the predictable objections of those with vested property interests, the worst and most decrepit tenements were subsequently demolished. Some of the new space was used to create Blake Garden. Construction of the Government Bacteriological Laboratory was also authorised; it was eventually erected nearby in 1906. One of the most attractive buildings in the area to have survived, it now houses the Hong Kong Museum of Medical Sciences (*see p78*).

The last significant outbreak of bubonic plague in Hong Kong occurred in the late 1920s. By this time, appropriate measures were in place to control infectious diseases, and fatalities were few. Hong Kong's reputation for filth, however, persisted for many years to come.

The early settlement comprised a British military encampment at Tsim Sha Tsui and a few scattered Chinese hamlets, the most significant being Tai Hang, which was located near the present-day Granville Road (at the Chatham Road South end). The military presence continued for many years, with permanent barracks being established at Gun Club Hill on Austin Road and Whitfield Barracks (now Kowloon Park) on Nathan Road. From the mid 1920s, another large barracks was built on the new reclamation at Sham Shui Po, which was used as a military prisoner-of-war camp during the World War II.

Some replication of Victoria's street names occurred when Tsim Sha Tsui was first laid out. The present Nathan Road was at one time called Robinson Road, Chatham Road was named Des Voeux Road and Canton Road was known as MacDonnell Road. To avoid confusion with the city across the harbour, they were later changed.

**'The first European settlers in Kowloon were the local Portuguese community, who moved across the harbour from the late 19th century.'**

In time, as development spread northwards, the area south of Boundary Street became known as Old Kowloon, whilst the area to the north (which includes modern Sham Shui Po) was referred to as New Kowloon. Hung Hom further to the east and Sham Shui Po were both early industrial areas, and were established long before the post-war boom in industry that led to Hong Kong's phenomenal growth and resounding international success. The industry that developed here was light manufacturing and included the production of plimsolls, torches and other low technology goods, as well as food processing.

The Peak district, Hong Kong's answer to the other British hill stations in Asia, from Simla in India to Penang in Malaysia, gradually became more popular as a retreat from hot weather, and the first houses were built there in the 1860s. The hillside funicular Peak Tram commenced operations in 1888, and has been popular with both visitors and residents ever since.

Reclamation work aimed at extending the business district started in 1890 and finished in 1904, adding a large new area. Statue Square, in modern Central, is part of that early scheme.

Industry started its initially tentative development at this time with the construction of commercial dockyards at Aberdeen, Hung

Hom and Taikoo. These catered to the annually increasing volume of shipping that frequented the colony's harbour. All major and many minor shipping lines called at Hong Kong.

Hong Kong's streets were gaslit from the 1880s (there are still four gas lamps from that time operating in Central today), and electric light was introduced in the 1890s.

Communications with the world's markets were swift and efficient, with Hong Kong becoming a major telecommunications hub; telegraph cables linking Britain and Hong Kong Island's southern coast (the cable house can still be seen today at Deep Water Bay) were laid in 1870.

## HEALTH AND THE TUNG WAH HOSPITAL

For its first 30 years as a British colony, Hong Kong lacked a general hospital. The Government Civil Hospital was established in 1850, and at first catered mainly for the police force and the destitutes they picked up; around 1864 it became accessible to private paying patients as well. The then-expensive fees of HK$1 were a discouragement for most, and very few Chinese wished to use it anyway. Part of this reluctance was due to a general distrust of foreigners, and a deeply held belief that their intentions – however noble they might seem on the surface – were ultimately evil. Western medicine, in particular, emphasised surgery and post-mortem examinations at a time when most Chinese devoutly believed that after death one should return to one's ancestors with an unmutilated body. And 19th-century Western medical science, with its dirty, badly administered hospitals, poorly trained nurses and few specific cures for diseases did little to inspire public confidence – even among those familiar with its practices.

The closest thing that the Chinese had to a hospital was an I Ts'z (a death house or hospice), where the terminally ill were sent to die because death at home was reckoned to render the house unclean. For those who did die elsewhere, the I Ts'z was a place where corpses could be kept before they were returned to their home towns in China. In 1869, however, the then Governor Sir Richard MacDonnell closed the I Ts'z on account of the appalling conditions, and the idea of a hospital (to be funded and administered by Chinese) was proposed. Consequently, the Tung Wah Hospital was established with Chinese community donations of over HK$40,000 and a Government contribution of HK$115,000.

The Tung Wah Hospital Ordinance defined the hospital as 'a Chinese hospital for the care and treatment of the indigent sick to be supported by voluntary contributions', which

The **Peak Tram** opened for business in 1888. *See p88.*

is how it has largely remained until this day. Sir Richard MacDonnell laid the foundation stone in 1870 on a site granted on Po Yan Street in Western district, and the hospital opened to patients two years later. It is still located there today, and the old stone can be seen near the entrance to the modern building.

The hospital was run by a committee, the members of which were drawn from the comprador (mercantile middle-man) class. Compradors at this time were at the height of their wealth, power and influence in Hong Kong and the Treaty Ports, but, in time, their influence declined as Chinese independently engaged in business, medicine or the law took their place. Later still, the compradors were further pushed aside by bankers, department store owners, rich overseas Chinese and émigrés from the 1911 Revolution. This latter group formed a more diversified Chinese elite than existed in the 19th century, and eventually replaced the compradors as arbiters of power and influence within the Tung Wah.

Another important component of the Tung Wah Hospital Committee were the representatives of the various merchant guilds, such as the Nam Pak Hong (dealing mainly with the import of rice and South-East Asian products), the California Merchant's Guild (which dealt with the lucrative West Coast trade) and the Chinese Medicine Guild. The guilds, which were also prominent and influential elsewhere in China at this time,

elected representative members to the Tung Wah Hospital Committee from among their own number – a forerunner of today's functional constituencies.

> **'The first tentative steps at involving representatives of the Chinese community more actively in government affairs in Hong Kong started in the late 1870s.'**

Kaifongs (street committees), which were found all over Hong Kong, also elected members to the Tung Wah Hospital Committee. Kaifong members were simply groups of civic-minded, status-seeking citizens resident in a particular area of the city, who set themselves up and voted themselves in as a public body. Accepted – or at least tolerated – by the general public because they were either affluent or 'fixers', none of their 'constituents' ever actually picked them; they chose themselves. Elections to the Tung Wah Hospital Committee were conducted from among these closed ranks.

The Committee wielded so much influence among the Chinese community that in time it became a sort of 'shadow' Legislative Council, and was often resented and criticised by the Hong Kong government for its wide-ranging power over the Chinese community. However, much later, the more senior members of the Committee would be appointed unofficial Chinese members of the Legislative Council, with the result that their influence was regularised and channelled into the administration.

## POLITICAL DEVELOPMENT FOR THE CHINESE COMMUNITY

The first tentative steps at involving representatives of the Chinese community more actively in government affairs in Hong Kong started in the late 1870s. The experiment, which did not actually prove to be a great success, involved the forward-thinking governor Sir John Pope Hennessy and one Ng Choy, also known as Wu Ting Fang.

When Pope Hennessy arrived in Hong Kong in 1877, one of his first thoughts was that the time had come to accord more representation to the Chinese community and their interests on the Legislative Council. The Chinese community had already begun to demand such representation, and, in January 1879, sent a memorandum to London arguing that as there were ten times more Chinese than foreigners in Hong Kong, 'it would be but fair to allow the Chinese community a share in the management of the affairs of the colony'. Regional precedents for such a move existed – Singapore had appointed a Chinese member to the Legislative Council in 1869, and Pope Hennessy had made a similar appointment when he was Governor on Labuan, an island off the Borneo coast that was then administered separately from the rest of the Straits Settlements.

Pope Hennessy's sympathetic attitude to Asiatics was partially coloured by his marriage to Kitty, the vivacious and very attractive Eurasian daughter of the early Malayan administrator Sir Hugh Low. He certainly had no problem with appointing Ng Choy, a British subject born in Singapore in 1842 into the famous Canton merchant family of Howqua, to the Legislative Council. Educated from an early age in England, Ng Choy trained as a barrister, becoming the first Chinese to be called to the English bar, and subsequently practised in Hong Kong.

The appointment was strongly criticised by European merchants, who felt the move was too conciliatory to the Chinese, and would only encourage further demands for participation in public life. They also questioned how it was possible for a Chinese to be loyal to Britain, as questions of race and nationality were so closely intertwined. Following financial difficulties, Ng Choy finally resigned from the Legislative Council in 1883.

As Wu Ting Fang, Ng Choy later became a national figure on the mainland, serving at various times as Chinese Ambassador to the United States, Peru, Mexico and Cuba, and as Chinese Foreign Minister. He became senior vice-president of the Chinese Ministry of Commerce in 1903, but left after a few months, and died in 1922.

As a British subject, Ng Choy (who certainly became more intensely nationalistic as he grew older) represented the dilemma of the 'overseas' Chinese. Where did their ultimate loyalties lie? With China or with the countries in which they were born and raised? This question is still faced by overseas Chinese communities, in places such as Indonesia, today. As was later demonstrated, Ng Choy's first loyalty was with China, which credits the point of those who protested so vigorously against his appointment to the Legislative Council in Hong Kong.

## LEASING OF THE NEW TERRITORIES

Towards the end of the 19th century, tensions increased between the various European powers with interests in China. The Germans were heavily involved in Shantung province in north China, where the city of Tsing Tao, still world famous for its brewery, remained a Teutonic enclave until the Germans were expelled by the Japanese in 1915. The French leased the port of Kwangchowwan, half-way between Hong Kong and Haiphong on the Guangdong coast in 1898 (at the same time as the British leased the New Territories), and remained there until 1943.

It was also in 1898 that the British leased the tiny port of Weihaiwei in Shantung, where they remained until 1930. Used as a cool weather station for the Royal Navy, Weihaiwei later played a role in recruiting Shantung men into the Hong Kong Police force.

The principal reason behind the lease of the New Territories was the British belief that it would be impossible to defend Hong Kong Island and Kowloon against attack (which at that time was thought might come from the French or the Russians) without having possession of the hills that lay north of the Kowloon peninsula.

Unlike the two previous cessions of land from China to Britain (which were essentially the spoils of war and 'unequal treaty'), the New Territories (and around 230 islands) were obtained on a 99-year lease through the 1898 Convention of Peking, sparking off the entire 1997 issue. Without this additional expansion, Hong Kong and Kowloon might still be British today.

# HK profiles Sir Cecil Clementi

It is widely (if incorrectly) believed that the tentative beginnings of more representative government in Hong Kong only began in the 1980s, to be accelerated by the Patten reforms of the early 1990s. Those with slightly longer memories (still wrongly) might quote the Young Plan of 1946, which was abandoned in the 1950s, as the first step towards political development.

Although Sir John Pope Hennessy made an unsuccessful attempt to integrate the Chinese into the Legislative Council in 1889 (*see p17*), it was a quiet achiever by the name of **Sir Cecil Clementi** who instigated wider community representation on the ruling body while Governor of Hong Kong (1925-30).

Unlike many governors who were posted to Hong Kong after years of service in other colonies, Clementi started his career in Hong Kong in 1899. From 1903-06, he was a Land Officer and Police Magistrate in the New Territories. During that time, he was responsible for the cadastral surveys conducted in the New Territories, establishing and validating over 300,000 individual land claims. The decisions he made then helped establish a system of land tenure that persists until this day.

The benevolent concern that he showed towards the villagers of the New Territories, which was based on an intimate working knowledge of their customs and affairs, was continued by generations of officials posted to the New Territories. Clementi also realised that control in the newly leased areas was best exercised by British officials who behaved as much like traditional Chinese officials as possible. Thus, although the local magistrate's race changed, nothing much else in the villagers' daily lives did. This minimised disruption and kept local unrest to a minimum, greatly reducing the need for a strong military or police presence. This pattern of close personal rule, typical in district administration in the rest of the British Empire, continued largely unchanged in the New Territories until very recently.

After postings in other British colonies, Clementi returned to Hong Kong as Governor in late 1925. Although speaking fluent Cantonese and Mandarin and being a sinologist of some note were useful to him when dealing with the Chinese, he soon came to realise that this affinity also made him an object of some suspicion among the racially conscious merchants of his day. For example, when Clementi proposed amending the seal of the colony to include the Chinese characters for Hong Kong, the Jardine Matheson representative on the Legislative Council decried the notion, contemptuously saying that there would not be ten Europeans in the entire colony who would even know what they meant.

However, it was at Clementi's instigation in 1926 that the number of unofficial members of the Legislative Council was increased to eight, three of whom were to be Chinese, and one local Portuguese. In the same year, a Chinese was appointed to the Executive Council for the first time. While by no means a full democracy, the appointments marked the beginning of a realisation that local people (and not just the Chinese), as well as the British, had a stake in Hong Kong. Furthermore, they recognised that this stake had to be channelled and addressed if the loyalty of the local people to both Britain and Hong Kong was to be maintained.

Unfortunately, Clementi was governor during a period of rising nationalist aspirations that frequently spilled over into Hong Kong, disturbing what had hitherto been a very tranquil settlement. The devastating General Strike of 1925 was barely over when he arrived and further labour unrest, fomented by the Kuomintang, then in power in Canton, made his time in office a vexing period of continual political turmoil.

Clementi, being a great admirer of traditional Chinese culture and the Confucian values embodied within it, certainly did not like the political changes being brought about by the Kuomintang – and he felt they would be disastrous for China in the long term. He, therefore, attempted to swim against the tide in the area under his control.

However, he is remembered by very few today (although his keen appreciation of the Hong Kong countryside is marked by the name of a trail above Quarry Bay, Sir Cecil's Ride). It is a great shame, for Sir Cecil Clementi was that rare and exceptional find in the Hong Kong administration – a far-sighted visionary, many decades ahead of his time.

Another key element of Hong Kong's relationship with the New Territories has always been fresh water. From the earliest days of British settlement, demand has continually outstripped supply, due to the steady increase in population that the colony's politically stable environment encouraged. Tank streams were quickly over-utilised, and wells in urban areas rapidly became contaminated and unsafe.

In the 19th century, a number of reservoirs were built on Hong Kong Island and, for a while, they were adequate for the needs of the growing city. By the late 1920s, however, the growth of urban Hong Kong, both on the island and beyond the boundary of Kowloon, made the need for a new reservoir extremely urgent. The only viable location was in the Kowloon hills, at the head of the Shing Mun valley. The project was opposed by the Colonial Office for a long period on the grounds that the reservoir would be built in the New Territories, which were leased and would, therefore, revert to China in around 70 years. Building a capital-intensive scheme on someone else's land, as it were, was, they felt, a great waste of money.

This was a view strongly countered by Sir Cecil Clementi (*see p18* **HK profiles: Sir Cecil Clementi**), one of Hong Kong's most able and visionary – and least remembered – colonial administrators. A possible solution to the problem of the Shing Mun reservoirs, in Clementi's view, lay over a thousand miles to the north of Hong Kong.

The small settlement of Weihaiwei on the coast of Shantung had been leased at the same time as the New Territories. Clementi's proposal involved offering to return Weihaiwei to Chinese control – as it was a disposable backwater that had never really prospered – in return for outright cession by China of the New Territories, which were vital to Hong Kong's continued growth.

His proposal was rejected by the Foreign Office as unnecessary and unworkable, and likely to stir up demands from the Nanking Government for further abandonment of British concessions and privileges elsewhere in China. Yet, in 1930, as a gesture of goodwill, Weihaiwei was returned to Chinese rule.

The Shing Mun reservoirs were eventually built anyway, as the growing demand for reliable water supplies overrode any objections concerning their theoretical return to China in the seemingly distant future. At the time of its construction, the scheme in the Shing Mun valley was the largest water scheme taking place in the British Empire. Extensive reforestation was undertaken to safeguard the water catchments. Photographs of the Shing Mun area taken in the late 1930s show large areas of thriving new forestry, in stark contrast to the treeless grassy hills in much of the rest of the New Territories. The villages in the valley were removed and their inhabitants were resettled in Kam Tin in the north-west New Territories.

Rural people displaced from their villages by development were always resettled and well compensated from early times, something that is not generally recognised today. The village built for them at Kam Tin was named Shing Mun San Tsuen, or Shing Mun New Village. Located between Tai Hong Wai and Wing Lung Wai, the resettlement village – and its inhabitants – still maintains a distinct and separate identity from the rest of the village. There are numerous old people who remember the move from the old village, now under water for decades. Even after more than 60 years, the Shing Mun people are still outsiders at Kam Tin.

## GROWTH OF CHINESE NATIONALISM

In 1900, two years after the New Territories lease was ratified, the Boxer Rebellion broke out in China. Overspill into the Hong Kong region was limited, with the areas most affected being in north China.

> **'A tramways strike and boycott in 1912-13, a seamen's strike in 1922 and a General Strike in 1925 all caused lengthy disruption and affected trade.'**

Support for radical change in China during this period was generated in southern China by Dr Sun Yat-sen and the earlier reformer Kang Yu-hwei (both of whom were Cantonese). Sun Yat-sen attended school in Hong Kong and was a graduate of the Hong Kong College of Medicine. At a lecture he gave at Hong Kong University in 1923, he said that it was the pace, prosperity and good government that he had experienced in the British colony, which – contrasted with the chaos and corruption in China itself – had turned him into a revolutionary.

Gradually, escalating periods of Chinese nationalist agitation during the years following the fall of the Ching (or Manchu) Dynasty and beginning of the Republican period spilled over into Hong Kong. A tramways strike and boycott in 1912-13, a seamen's strike in 1922 and a General Strike in 1925 all caused lengthy disruption and affected trade. The Nationalist (or Kuomintang) Government was based during this period at Canton, and China was divided into numerous feuding warlord fiefdoms. The country was unified under the Nationalists after Chiang Kai-Shek led the Northern Expedition in 1927-28, and subsequently removed the capital to Nanking. China and domestic Chinese politics were always a matter for concern among British diplomats and the Hong Kong Government from this period onwards.

## THE SPECTRE OF JAPAN

Around 1853-4, Japan emerged from a period of self-imposed isolation (during which time it was known as *sakoku* or the Closed Country). Rapidly opening itself up to the West, it modernised every aspect of government, industrialised rapidly and started encroaching on foreign borders.

To begin with, Japan went to war with – and defeated – the Chinese in 1894-95. Then, while fighting on the Allied side during World War I, it occupied German ports, mines, railway concessions and other enterprises in China, most of which were granted to Japan in the 1919 Versailles Peace Conference. The intellectual ferment of the student-led May 4th Movement was largely a response to Japanese aggression and the perceived betrayal of China by the Western powers. Throughout the 1920s, there was continued Japanese expansion throughout the north-east of China.

The rise to power of Chang Hsueh-liang (known as the Young Marshal) – who only came to power after the Japanese assassinated his father, Manchurian warlord Chang Tso-lin (known as the Old Marshal), at Mukden in 1928 – stemmed the Japanese advance for a time. However, in 1934, Pu Yi, the last Manchu Emperor of China, was made the puppet Emperor of Manchukuo by the Japanese, formalising their annexation of China's north-eastern provinces.

All-out war between Japan and China began in July 1937. The Japanese quickly captured Chinese coastal cities (surrounding Shanghai's International Settlement in the process) and advanced up the Yangtze Valley where they perpetrated the notorious Rape of Nanking. In October 1938, the city of Canton fell to the Japanese, who advanced to the Shum Chun River (forming the border between the Chinese mainland and Hong Kong) a week or so later.

The Japanese advance led to a massive influx of refugees into Hong Kong, which would eventually lead to a post-war housing crisis. Gradually forested from the 1860s to the 1930s, mainly to protect watercourses and catchment areas, Hong Kong's once-bare hills were swiftly deforested by refugees searching for fuel and somewhere to build huts.

The late 1930s marked the start of Hong Kong's small-scale industrialisation in Sham Shui Po in northern Kowloon and elsewhere in the colony, a process that continued into the 1950s, and lasted until the late 1980s.

In spite of – or perhaps because of – the unsettled conditions on the Chinese mainland, Hong Kong experienced a prolonged period of economic boom. Japanese territorial incursions, which included on one occasion the overflying of Hong Kong territory and the strafing of a packed refugee train near Fanling, led to a steady strengthening of defensive measures and a gradual increase in the size of the garrison.

## OCCUPATION

In 1941, at the same time as they launched attacks on Pearl Harbor, the Philippines and north Malaya, the Japanese crossed the border into the New Territories and bombed the airport at Kai Tak. Hong Kong's garrison, while prepared for war, was small and hopelessly outnumbered by the Japanese.

**'After 18 days of hostilities, the British finally surrendered on Christmas afternoon 1941, the first British colony to surrender to Japan during the Pacific War.'**

In the late 1930s, a string of defensive tunnels, bunkers and machine-gun emplacements had been built in the Kowloon hills as Hong Kong's answer to the Maginot Line. Known then as the Inner Line, post-war it was referred to as the Gin Drinker's Line, due to its geographical position, extending between Gin Drinker's Bay (now reclaimed and part of modern Kwai Chung) and Port Shelter. Unfortunately, it did not stand for long. After three days of fighting, the Line fell and Kowloon was evacuated, crowding Hong Kong Island with refugees. This further added to existing accommodation shortages and caused a water supply crisis that eventually played a large part in forcing the British to surrender.

After waiting for almost a week, during which time they sent across two peace missions, the Japanese landed on Hong Kong Island on 18 December 1941. There followed a period of heavy fighting on the eastern side of Hong Kong Island, in the centre of the island at and around Wong Nai Chung Gap, and at Stanley.

# The decline of pidgin English

Go into an upmarket café in Central and ask the head waiter 'Boy, can do two more piecee man?' ('Would you happen to have a table for two?') and chances are he will stare blankly at you and then giggle, in either embarrassed incomprehension or secret derision. Sixty years ago, though, the question would have been immediately understood, and followed by the swift response of either 'can do' ('certainly!') or 'no can do' ('sorry, we're fully booked'). Almost universal 50 years ago, that old China Coast standby – pidgin English – is now completely extinct.

Sometimes described as 'English meat on Chinese bones', pidgin closely resembles literal translations of spoken Cantonese. Thus '*seung-been*' became 'top-side' and '*ha-been*' changed to 'bottom-side', while '*tai-ha*' came out as 'lookee-see'. The origin of other terms such as '*maskee*' (never mind) and '*chop-chop*' (faster) are more obscure, but may have been derived from Portuguese. But all these words, along with once-common phrases such as 'small chow' ('canapés') and 'bye-m-bye' ('sooner or later') have now become linguistic dinosaurs.

The Macau Portuguese, longer on the China Coast than other Europeans, and by far the best integrated, also developed pidgin Portuguese, known as *patoá*. Metropolitan Portuguese was rendered down to the simplest constructions and peppered with Cantonese phrases, as well as corrupted Malay, English and Japanese words. Like pidgin English, *patoá* is effectively a dead language.

By the mid 19th century, pidgin had become a well-established means of communication between foreigner and Chinese, and knowledge of it became a highly marketable skill, for which employees could charge considerably more for their labour.

To the uninitiated, pidgin remained an almost incomprehensible – and somewhat irritating – form of baby-talk. 'Hobson-Jobson', Henry Yule and AC Burnell's extremely detailed glossary of words and phrases, which was first published in 1886, describes pidgin English as 'the vile jargon which forms the means of communication at the Chinese ports between Englishmen who do not speak Chinese and those Chinese with whom they are in the habit of communicating'.

The intrepid Victorian traveller Isabella Bird, never very reticent with her opinions,

described China Coast pidgin in *The Golden Chersonese and the Way Thither*, her classic account of Victorian-era Asian travel. 'The Pidjun English is revolting, and the most dignified persons demean themselves by speaking it. How the whole English-speaking community, without the distinction of rank, has come to communicate with the Chinese in this baby-talk is extraordinary.'

For all its faults though, pidgin served its primary purpose; it enabled people from completely different worlds to communicate to mutual advantage. Some linguists even take the view that, in addition to overcoming superficial communication difficulties, pidgin performed the subtle function of bringing together people from totally alien backgrounds. And by speaking in a language that was native to neither, and therefore neutral, they also avoided, to some extent, the minefield of cultural conventions that appear when speaking a 'real' language.

Pidgin – like any language – followed rules of its own and had to be picked up, so one sometimes wonders why more Europeans didn't simply learn proper Chinese in the first place. Questioned on this subject recently, one very elderly ex-Hong Kong resident, now in his 90s, replied after reflecting for a few moments, 'Well, it wasn't really necessary to learn, as we didn't mix with the Chinese all that much, but I suppose the real reason was that talking Chinese was something one just didn't really *do* – and weren't really expected to do either. Those who did make too much of an effort were seen as cranks somehow, come to think of it. And no-one wanted to be thought of as a crank!'

Perhaps strangely, given these prejudices, pidgin was almost exclusively a China Coast phenomena. In Malaya and the Straits Settlements, Malay was used to communicate between Europeans and Chinese – often ungrammatical 'kitchen Malay', but Malay nonetheless – and pidgin English never really caught on.

Pidgin eventually declined in Hong Kong, thanks to better education and the wider use of standard English, and was almost obsolete by the late 1960s. With the retirement of the last professional Cantonese domestic servants, replaced in most cases by English-speaking Filipinos, this entertaining, infuriating language finally died a natural death.

After 18 days of hostilities, the British finally surrendered on Christmas afternoon 1941, the first British colony to surrender to Japan during the Pacific War.

In part as a measure of controlling Hong Kong Island's housing, food and fuel problems, the Japanese immediately initiated a policy of depopulation by forcing the local Chinese to evacuate to their mainland homes. Given the difficult conditions in Hong Kong, many Chinese residents in the urban areas voluntarily returned to their ancestral villages in the hinterland, where – although conditions may have been difficult – there was at least enough to eat.

Following the British surrender, there was widespread cooperation between the erstwhile local elite and the Japanese occupation authorities; events which eventually prompted a post-war enquiry into collaboration, the findings of which were, perhaps unsurprisingly, never released.

Almost the entire Allied civilian population – men, women and children – were interned in a concentration camp at Stanley. Male military prisoners of war, meanwhile, were imprisoned in their former barracks in Kowloon; many were later transported to Japan to work as slaves in the mines and on the docks.

One of the most aesthetically pleasing legacies of Japanese rule in Hong Kong is Government House (*see p71*). The original, built in the mid 19th century in Georgian style, was in desperate need of repair when it was renovated by the Japanese. An attractive building with a tower, it still stands on Upper Albert Road in Central today, even though it has not been used as an official residence since 1997. The gardens can be visited by the general public once a year when the stunning azaleas are in bloom.

Throughout their occupation, Chinese guerrillas operating from Kwangtung's East River district harried the Japanese and mounted a number of operations within Hong Kong, including a daring raid on the railway bridge in central Kowloon, but otherwise there was little resistance and the city was remarkably safe and peaceful.

Following the Hiroshima and Nagasaki atomic bombs, the Japanese surrendered on 15 August 1945, much earlier than the Allies had anticipated. This left a brief power vacuum, which was filled by British officials coming out from internment and assuming control from the Japanese.

A British fleet was dispatched from Sydney (where it had been undergoing a refit) when the surrender came through; it arrived in Hong Kong on 30 August 1945. A period of

Commercial **Central** around 1970.

British Military Administration followed, but civilian government was restored in May 1946 under Sir Mark Young, the pre-war governor, who returned to the role having been a prisoner of war.

## POSTWAR RECOVERY

As business – and more especially the entrepôt trade – had always been Hong Kong's lifeblood, the port was back in full operation very soon after the British returned. The fact that Hong Kong operated on the dollar bloc rather than sterling, and was able to buy supplies direct from the United States, without having to wait for quotas to be approved from London, meant that the local economy was back on an even footing very swiftly.

> **'Rapid and highly efficient industrialisation... took place by the mid 1950s.'**

Sir Mark Young left Hong Kong in 1947, and was succeeded as governor by Sir Alexander Grantham, a former cadet who had started his administrative career in Hong Kong. For the next ten years, Grantham oversaw a prolonged period of uncertainty.

In 1949, civil war and the Communist takeover took place on the mainland. A year later, the Korean War broke out and the subsequent American embargo on trade with China – which as far as they were concerned included Hong Kong – stifled the colony's traditional reliance on the entrepôt trade.

However, much was also achieved during the decade (including the extension of Kai Tak airport). Rapid and highly efficient industrialisation, mainly utilising Shanghainese entrepreneurs (and their capital) who had fled the Communists, took place by the mid 1950s, using the large pool of refugee labour that the aftermath of the civil war had made available and willing to work for almost any wage.

It was around this time that formerly marginal areas, such as Kwun Tong and Tsuen Wan on the outskirts of Kowloon, rapidly developed into industrial towns, full of spinning, dyeing and weaving mills, toy and plastics factories, and other labour-intensive light industries. Industry of this kind remained a mainstay of the Hong Kong economy until the late 1980s, when the re-opening of China to foreign and overseas investment made manufacturing on the mainland, with its low wages and lax controls, much more economical than in Hong Kong.

In the immediate post-war period, it was thought that many of the refugees who had fled to Hong Kong following the end of the civil war and the Communist takeover would return to the mainland as the dust settled, much as waves of refugees had done in the past. Gradually, however, it became apparent that this latest influx had no intention of returning, and, eventually, provision had to be made for their integration into Hong Kong.

Housing policy (which hitherto had been to tolerate the theoretically temporary squatter settlements that had grown up in various parts of urban Hong Kong) changed dramatically following a massive fire in one of the largest squatter settlements, Shek Kip Mei in the northern part of Kowloon, which made 53,000 people homeless on Christmas Day 1953. The Government's response was to develop a public housing programme that is probably post-war Hong Kong's most notable success. The largest single commercial landlord in the world, Hong Kong's Housing Authority provides subsidised housing to over half the population – at well below market rates.

There were other problems around this time. The aftermath of civil war on the mainland often spilled over into Hong Kong, and low-level Nationalist/Communist confrontations continued throughout the 1950s. Kowloon had serious Nationalist-inspired riots in 1956, while the **Star Ferry Riots** in 1966 were Communist-fomented (ironically, considering they were over the increase in price of first-class ferry tickets). Finally, in the summer of 1967, the Cultural Revolution overspilled into Hong Kong and Macau – bombs were thrown and a number of people were killed, but, in the end, the people of Hong Kong came out firmly in favour of the local government.

In addition, rapid industrialisation, massive population movements and a get-rich-quick refugee mentality (largely caused by the uncertainties of the Communist regime over the border) all led to a spectacular growth of official corruption, especially within the Hong Kong Police. Eventually, the situation became so bad that a special Independent Commission Against Corruption (ICAC), with wide-ranging powers, was introduced in 1974. The Commission was remarkably effective – by the 1980s Hong Kong, formerly known as one of the most corrupt places in Asia, was one of the most straight and transparent.

For a long time, Hong Kong University was the only university in the territory, thus putting limits on the scope of education available locally to youngsters. This situation was only partially rectified in the early 1960s with the establishment of a second university; in the late 1980s, however, widespread tertiary education became available.

## MACLEHOSE AND A CHANGE OF DIRECTION

Under Governor Sir Murray MacLehose, who was in Hong Kong from 1971 to 1981, Hong Kong expanded into a regional financial centre. This resulted in a gradual move away from its traditional entrepôt role and the industrial reliance it had developed since the early 1950s.

**'In 1979, MacLehose visited Beijing, where he was told by Deng Xiaoping to tell Hong Kong investors to 'put their hearts at ease'.'**

After the domestic turmoil of the Cultural Revolution (1966-76), China re-emerged as a major consideration, especially as the time for the expiry of the New Territories lease drew closer. By the late 1970s, big business interests were beginning to press for a closer examination of the future of Hong Kong, as the issue of major developmental loans that would still be operational after 1997 needed to be addressed.

Last governor **Chris Patten** and current Chief Executive **Tung Chee-hwa**.

In 1979, MacLehose visited Beijing, where he was told by Deng Xiaoping to tell Hong Kong investors to 'put their hearts at ease'. Confidence in the future of Hong Kong soared, as many took this statement to be tacit approval for Hong Kong remaining under British rule beyond 1997. Behind the scenes, however, diplomatic moves were made to determine exactly what the situation was, and, following Margaret Thatcher's visit to Beijing in 1982, both governments moved towards what eventually became the Joint Declaration, signed in 1984.

The Joint Declaration guaranteed that Hong Kong would revert to full Chinese administration (China had, after all, never admitted any British sovereignty) in 1997, with legal guarantees and safeguards for the future 'stability and prosperity' of Hong Kong.

Confidence, badly eroded in the early 1980s, was restored and Hong Kong continued to prosper. The professional classes, many of whom – or whose families – had fled China in the aftermath of the Communist takeover, had no desire to become Chinese subjects, and the 1980s and 1990s saw over 50,000 a year emigrate to Australia, Canada, New Zealand and the United States. Many have since returned, having acquired a foreign passport or permanent residence, creating a returnee backwash with mixed – and at times confused – loyalties, that has numerous interesting implications for the future of Hong Kong.

## RUN-UP TO THE HANDOVER

June 1989 saw the violent suppression of student-led protests in Beijing's Tiananmen Square and, for a while, a deteriorated confidence in Hong Kong. Government policy at the time was not to further antagonise the Chinese Government in any way, but this attitude radically altered with the appointment of Chris Patten as the last British governor in 1992.

Patten launched a series of wide-reaching electoral reforms without the backing of the Chinese Government, and a long period ensued when very little that was constructive was achieved. The small flurry of popular interest in democracy kicked up at the time subsided back into general political apathy within a few years. Environmental and education reforms, in urgent need of implementation, were sidelined due to politicking and are only being introduced now.

June 1997 saw the long-awaited Handover, a media feeding frenzy for the world press, which nevertheless turned into something of a non-event. The riots and unrest that the film crews were not-so-secretly hoping for didn't happen, the People's Liberation Army didn't have any opportunity for an immediate crackdown on the streets of Central (they still haven't, at the time of writing), it rained continually for weeks and, finally, on the night of 30 June, the last governor boarded the *Britannia* and sailed away in a flood of his own tears.

# Key events

**1513** First maritime contact between Portugal and China.

**1557** Macau settled by the Portuguese as a base from which to control the trade between China and Japan.

**1637** First British ship to reach China is driven back from Canton (Guangzhou).

**1639** Japan closed to the Portuguese.

**1685** Limited trade to Canton permitted; the British East India Company starts trading.

**1773** British ships unload opium in Canton.

**1793** Macartney mission to normalise relations between Britain and China fails.

**1799** The spread of opium addiction causes Beijing to ban it, driving the trade underground.

**1816-17** Amherst mission to improve relations with Beijing fails.

**1834** British East India Company loses its opium trade monopoly; Lord Napier aims to regularise Sino-British trade and diplomatic relations.

**1839** Lin Tse-hsu tries to stamp out the opium trade; he confiscates 20,000 chests of opium in Canton, sparking the First Opium (or Anglo-Chinese) War.

**1841** The British attack Canton and occupy its forts. The dispute is settled by the Convention of Chuen Pi, which cedes the island of Hong Kong to Britain, although neither side ratifies the treaty.

**1842** The Treaty of Nanking finally ends the war, confirming British sovereignty over Hong Kong 'in perpetuity' and opening up five Chinese cities to British trade.

**1859** Kowloon and Stonecutter's Island are ceded by China to Britain during the Second Opium (or Arrow) War.

**1862** China signs over Macau to Portugal.

**1870** Founding of the Tung Wah Hospital.

**1894** Plague outbreak in Hong Kong.

**1898** The British lease the New Territories from China for 99 years.

**1911** Sun Yat-sen overthrows the Ching Dynasty and establishes the Republic of China.

**1922** Seamen's strike in Hong Kong.

**1925** General Strike in Hong Kong.

**1945** China's civil war between continues as World War II ends.

**1949** The Communists triumph, founding the People's Republic of China; the Nationalists flee to Taiwan.

**1966** Rioting in Hong Kong over the increase of first-class tickets on the Star Ferry; the start of the Cultural Revolution.

**1971** Taiwan is replaced in the United Nations General Assembly by the People's Republic of China; Sir Murray MacLehose appointed as governor.

**1973** Opening of the first New Town: Tuen Mun.

**1974** Independent Commission Against Corruption (ICAC) formed to combat crime and corruption.

**1979** Opening of Hong Kong's Mass Transit Railway (MTR).

**1982** British Prime Minister Margaret Thatcher visits Hong Kong and Beijing, beginning talks on the future of Hong Kong. China starts to develop the town of Shenzhen as a special economic zone, just over Hong Kong's northern border.

**1983** China announces that Hong Kong will become a Special Administrative Region (SAR) after the 1997 Handover, retaining capitalism, its police and judiciary.

**1984** A Sino-British 'Draft Agreement on the Future of Hong Kong' (aka the 'Joint Declaration') is announced.

**1985** The Agreement is ratified and a joint liaison group is set up to co-ordinate the transition. The first democratic elections to the Legislative Council are criticised by China.

**1988** Publication of the Basic Law, Hong Kong's post-Handover constitution.

**1989** The Tiananmen Square massacre provokes a huge demonstration in Hong Kong. Hong Kong Government plans for a new airport, made without consulting the Chinese, are attacked by Beijing.

**1991** Britain and China reach agreement over the new airport.

**1992** Chris Patten, Hong Kong's 28th and last governor, arrives. His proposed reforms of the political system are criticised by Beijing.

**1994** Legislative Council passes Patten's proposed electoral reforms; arguments with Beijing continue for three more years.

**1997** Handover of sovereignty from Britain to China at midnight on 30 June. Swearing in of new government of the Hong Kong Special Administrative Region (SAR); the Beijing-appointed provisional legislature supplants the Legislative Council; Tung Chee-hwa is appointed as Chief Executive.

**1998** Opening of the new international airport on Chek Lap Kok.

# Hong Kong Today

As energetic as ever it was, the post-colonial city,
nevertheless, has its fair share of problems.

Without doubt one of the first questions
asked of long-time residents by visitors is
'What has changed since 1997?' The short
answer is – not a great deal.

There have been changes, but not ones that
the casual visitor will stay long enough to
notice. Perhaps the most alarming development
is a decline in government accountability.
The Legislative Council, which remains
partly elected, partly appointed, is effectively
powerless, and regularly derided in the local
press (both English- and Chinese-language) as a
time-wasting 'talking shop'. Ultimate authority
resides with the Chief Executive – as in colonial
days it was vested in the governor. But when
the Government gets things wrong – as it does
with tiresome regularity – no-one steps forward
to take the blame.

Called buck-passing elsewhere, here in
Hong Kong it's more like passing the ice cube.
The ice cube goes round and round, slowly
melting and getting smaller all the time,
until finally it dissolves altogether and those
involved look around, throw up their arms

and loudly exclaim 'Ice cube? What ice cube?' –
with only their damp hands and a rapidly
evaporating puddle on the floor to betray
the truth.

But some things haven't altered at all.
All the clichéd images of Hong Kong still
abound and the local tourist literature is
full of them. All loudly proclaim that right
here in Hong Kong, East meets West (whatever
that is supposed to mean), Old meets New –
that sort of thing. The reality is a bit different.
Perhaps the most commonly purveyed image
that visitors to Hong Kong expect to see
when they arrive are Chinese junks sailing
through Victoria Harbour against the amazing
backdrop of Hong Kong Island's Manhattan-
like skyline. Featured in everything from
airline advertisements to trailers for the local
television news, these vessels are one example
of an icon long past its natural date. Don't
expect to see too many – if any – batwing
junks in Victoria Harbour today.

Such sights were common in Hong Kong
waters up to the 1950s, but with the gradual

introduction of motorised vessels, and the decline of inshore fishing in the 1960s due to pollution and massive overfishing, the numbers of junks rapidly declined. By the early 1980s, only a few remained. Yet the image persists, the ultimate Hong Kong stereotype.

Likewise shopping. The time has long past when every visitor staggered to the airport laden down with goodies. There are still bargains to be had, but you need to know prices in your own country, where to look in Hong Kong and precisely what you're looking for.

During the 1980s and 1990s, pre-Handover Hong Kong had what must have been one of the longest of long goodbyes ever. While the extended transition period certainly made for stability, administrative continuity and prosperity – all those essential elements so lacking in most ex-colonial situations – the attenuated transition also caused many problems which still await imaginative solutions.

> **'Victoria Harbour, beautiful though it is, is little more than an open sewer, and standing at the edge of it on a hot summer's day, it certainly smells like it.'**

Desperately needed reform measures in many areas of Hong Kong life, which were first up for discussion in the 1980s, were greatly delayed by the Handover complications, or just never happened. Widespread environmental deterioration, especially apparent in the New Territories, and the steadily worsening air quality were already important issues by the early 1990s; both were allowed to drift due to the last governor Chris Patten's insistence on implementing political 'reforms', however doomed to ultimate failure they were. In direct consequence, Victoria Harbour, beautiful though it is, is little more than an open sewer and, standing at the edge of it on a hot summer's day, it certainly smells like it. The overwhelming natural beauty of Hong Kong still remains, however, and the skyline is as stunning as ever, even though much of it is veiled in a cloud of smog most days.

Hong Kong's local education system, which in the 1960s was one of the best in the world – albeit of an elite, narrow-margin type – had deteriorated to such an alarming extent that by the late 1990s many local graduates could leave university – after their entire education had been 'English-medium' – barely able to string a sentence together.

The happy mantra has it that China is becoming more like Hong Kong, and, certainly in terms of material prosperity, that is very obvious. But since the Handover, Hong Kong, in many respects, has become more like China – more monocultural. Hong Kong's veneer of cosmopolitanism was always ice-thin, but it has thinned further over the last few years. It remains to be seen how long aspects that have never really grafted on, like widespread use of English, decline in importance.

> **'Since the Handover, Hong Kong, in many respects, has become more like China – more monocultural.'**

The four per cent of the total population that comprises non-Chinese Hong Kongers has become steadily more expatriate, in the sense that foreigners increasingly tend to come to Hong Kong to work on relatively short-term contracts. Formerly, especially with government, many foreigners came to Hong Kong intending to remain for their entire working lifetime, and quite a few stayed on after retirement. This is one new aspect of Hong Kong that seems set to continue into the future. Hang out in the bar area of Lan Kwai Fong in Central, or the nearby burgeoning nightlife area of SoHo and you could well believe the 'cosmopolitan' spin on things; but go a few blocks and the reality is very different. And expect to attract a few stares in more outlying areas.

Probably the most elemental part of the change is related to the change itself. Since June 1997, Hong Kong has been a Special Administrative Region of the People's Republic of China. Like it or not, the inescapable fact remains that Hong Kong was a British Crown Colony for 156 years, and it is no longer one today. Many of the aspects that made it so unique were intrinsically related to its colonial status, lingering – if not positively thriving – decades after all that ended everywhere else. And now that it has passed, something of the specialness that made Hong Kong such a unique place has gone, too. Hong Kong is still a great place to live and work, and remains a destination of a lifetime, but it is a very different place to how it was before the Handover.

If you came before the Handover, come back to enjoy what you loved about the place last time. If you have never been to Hong Kong before, come to experience one of the world's most remarkable cities. And be assured that the doomsday scenario writers got it all terribly wrong; Hong Kong didn't come to an end in 1997.

**Kwan Kung Pavilion** on Cheung Chau. *See p135.*

# HK Culture & Customs

Race and face, *feng shui* and festivals, arts and astrology – unravel the complex cultural make-up of Hong Kong people.

Hong Kong is usually regarded as a multicultural, cosmopolitan city, yet 96 per cent of its population is Chinese. Most of these are **Punti**, or **Cantonese**, who built their power base through land ownership. In the 19th century, for example, the five great Cantonese clans (Tang, Hau, Pang, Liu and Man) had their own areas over which they ruled. However, there are still pockets of three other Chinese races – namely **Hakkas**, **Hoklos** and **Tankas**. The Hakkas are the largest of these minority groups, living together in villages in the New Territories. The first inhabitants of the region were **Yao** and **Maio** peoples (racially similar to Taiwan's aboriginals and Filipinos) – although pockets of them still survive in Guangdong and Guangxi provinces, no trace of them remains in Hong Kong.

These days, there is an even greater mix, with immigrants, both legal and illegal, having flooded into Hong Kong from other parts of China over the last four decades. Most of them, however, have tended to come from neighbouring provinces such as Guangdong and Fujian, as well as many from Shanghai.

The remaining four per cent of the population is composed of foreigners, who – despite their small numbers – form highly visible groups (in central areas, at least). Unsurprisingly, Hong Kong's former colonial status means that the **British** form a significant minority. Pre-1997, British citizens did not need a work visa to get a job in the territory, so it was easy for young Brits on the backpacker trail to stop off in Hong Kong for a few months and earn a few bucks working in a bar, before heading around Asia or on to Australia. That's not possible these days, but there are still around 30,000 British people working in Hong Kong (many of these are Chinese with British passports).

**Americans** have also had a strong presence for several decades, mainly thanks to the large number of businesses with regional head offices in Hong Kong, which has long been seen as the gateway to China. For much the same reason, there's also a strong mix of Europeans.

All 'white' foreigners are dubbed *'gweilo'* (*'gweipor'* for women) by the Cantonese, which roughly translates as 'foreign devil'. Despite the fact that the term is unashamedly offensive, most *gweilos* happily accept the tag and use it freely themselves.

Over the last couple of decades, however, the largest immigrant group has been from the Philippines. There are currently more than 100,000 **Filipinos** (nearly all female), based here working as maids (or amahs) for Chinese or Western employers. Indonesia and Thailand also provides many thousands of domestic helpers. They are poorly paid by local standards (earning an average HK$3,200 per month) and often work 14 hours a day, six days a week. Claims of mistreatment regularly crop up in the newspapers and courts, and there's no doubt they are treated as a subservient class. Every Sunday and public holiday, thousands gather in the squares of Central to sit on the pavement, eat, chat, sing, worship and generally relax. Many have no choice, having been thrown out of their employers' home for the day.

There is a small, but important, **Indian** population, as well as a number of **Nepalese**, most of whom are the children of Gurkhas who had served in the British army. More than 15,000 **Vietnamese** refugees also call Hong Kong home. They are part of the 200,000 plus 'boat people' who escaped their war-torn country from the late 1970s. While 67,000 were repatriated and 143,000 resettled overseas, the remainder have been allowed to stay in Hong Kong. The majority survive on casual construction jobs.

### KEEPING THE FAITH

While it may appear that Mammon is the object of worship for most Hong Kong people, religion plays an important, and often indispensable, role in many people's lives.

Most of Hong Kong's near seven million population are either Buddhists or Taoists, but there are also about half a million Christians, up to 100,000 Muslims and a smattering of Hindus, Sikhs and Jews. Religion is evident throughout the city, from ornate cathedrals and temples to tiny shrines outside residents' homes and even

inside staff quarters of nightclubs (check the ones in the Wan Chai girlie bars for irony).

The earliest religious beliefs are tied to the area's first needs – those of the fishing community. The protector of seafarers, Tin Hau (*see p94* **Tin Hau, sea goddess**), was honoured with temples that used to overlook the South China Sea, but, due to reclamation, now mostly lie inland. The 40 or more Tin Hau temples that are still standing overflow when the **Birthday of Tin Hau** (*see p204*) is celebrated annually; the best spot to be is Joss House Bay, where the temple, still perched above the water, is visited by scores of fishing boats adorned with brightly coloured flags. Like many local deities, Tin Hau is of Taoist origin. But as the faiths of Taoism and Buddhism often blur into one integrated belief system, both deities are often honoured in the same temple.

**Taoism**, based on the writings of Lao Tse, aims to put mankind in context with nature. Its esoteric philosophies are in perpetual debate and defy in-a-nutshell explanations: Tao itself is usually translated as 'The Way'. Best known to the world is the Taoist yin-yang pictogram, in which all existence struggles infinitely to find harmony.

**Buddhism**, originally from India, is based on principles of dharma; these include spiritual and moral codes that are little known outside Hong Kong's monk and nun fraternities, which are found in monasteries in the New Territories and on Lantau (the **Po Lin Monastery** being the best known; *see p132*). Buddha's birthday is celebrated on the eighth day of the fourth moon (he was 2,545 in 2001).

For all the religious dictums, the average Hong Konger goes to Taoist or Buddhist temples to appease the deities and, almost without exception, to ask for some compassion or good fortune. Gifts of food and fruit are presented, and incense and special paper offerings are burned in respect. Donations are also given for the upkeep of the temple. Unlike many other religions, individuals visit temples independently, rather than attend services held by priests; the exception to this rule is when special ceremonies, such as weddings and funerals, take place.

Temples often have one or more fortune teller in residence, who (for a fee) will interpret a visitor's palm, face, foot or the symbol written on a *chim* stick, which is selected by gently shaking a bamboo beaker full of *chim* in front of a temple altar until one rises up above the rest of the pack.

**Wong Tai Sin** (*see p113*) and **Che Kung** (*see p117*), found in temples named after them, are approached for general matters of health, while **Kam Fa** – a saint from nearby

Guangdong – is said to protect pregnant women. Two of Hong Kong's most popular deities are the polar opposites of **Kwun Yum**, goddess of mercy, and **Kwan Kung**, god of war. The former is regarded as a compassionate protector of all, while the fearsome-looking latter is, bizarrely, the god of choice for both police officers and triads. Porcelain representations of the two deities adorn many homes, often in altars.

> **'Popular paper offerings to be burned these days include meticulously crafted mobile phones, home entertainment systems and cars.'**

Besides idols, domestic altars often carry a memorial plaque to departed relatives, which is regarded as one way of maintaining a spiritual link between ancestors and the living; some families who own space in rural parts of the territory also have ancestral temples in memory of several generations. During the **Ching Ming** and **Chuen Yun** festivals, families will flock to these temples (or, alternatively, cemeteries and crematoriums) to clean the memorials of their loved ones and present offerings to be symbolically enjoyed in the afterlife. Popular paper offerings to be burned these days include meticulously crafted mobile phones, home entertainment systems and cars, which join the old staples of money, silver and gold ingots, and smart clothes. Even papier mâché models of domestic helpers are known to have been burned!

Western missionaries did an efficient job of promoting **Christianity** from the 19th century onwards. There is a pretty even split between Catholic and Anglican/Protestant congregations, with the highest proliferation of churches being in Kowloon Tong, Tsim Sha Tsui – look out for the palm trees outside the Rosary Church on Chatham Road South (built by the local Portuguese) – and Central, where the Anglican cathedral, St John's, stands (*see p71*).

The **Muslim** community is 50 per cent Chinese, while faiths with smaller numbers have predominantly non-Chinese congregations. The mosque on Shelley Street, Mid-Levels is older and more charming than the main one next to Kowloon Park; not far away from it, you'll find that the Ohel Leah Synagogue, in the shadow of the Jewish Community Centre, also has old-world appeal. A more orthodox interpretation of **Judaism** is practised by the Chabad strain at their temple in the Furama Hotel. An impressive **Hindu** temple in Happy Valley caters to a

mostly Indian congregation, and smaller places of worship for Methodists, Mormons, Quakers, Scientologists and Sikhs are scattered around the territory, which, unlike the mainland, enjoys total freedom of religious practice. There are some fears, though, that intimidation from Beijing may interfere with this in future, particularly in light of the crackdown on the Falun Gong, a quasi-religious group.

### FACE: HOW TO KEEP IT... AND LOSE IT

You've just enjoyed a lovely meal in a restaurant with your local host and the time has arrived to pay. Your host takes the bill and reaches for his credit card. 'No,' you say, 'I'll get it.' The usual 'No, I'll pay' to-and-froing then ensues. To end the discussion, you grab the bill and take it to the cashier's desk, where you pay, believing your generosity will be greatly appreciated. Wrong. You've just committed a serious faux pas. Your host has lost face and that's just about *the* cardinal sin in Hong Kong. You won't be invited again, and if you were hoping to seal a business deal, you can forget it.

> **'Confrontation and criticism are guaranteed face-destroyers.'**

Face is a peculiar Chinese value and its importance in Hong Kong can never be underestimated. It can lead to arguments, broken friendships and even fights, so a little care is needed to avoid stepping on people's toes. The concept is like pride in other countries (and everyone has that to a degree), but in Hong Kong face is accorded the utmost seriousness and people are judged by it. Some folk go to great lengths to acquire it by displays of wealth or generosity. It confirms social status. The big shot in the restaurant wearing the chunky Rolex and handing around the expensive brandy may look and talk like a billionaire, but he could be a small-time entrepreneur blowing more money than he can really afford to gain face in front of potential clients.

But issues of face are not always so obvious. Subtlety and sensitivity are needed, since the concept of giving face is easier to explain than the potential for losing it. Complimenting someone on their clothes, hairstyle and business nous – especially in front of their pals or colleagues – is a sure-fire winner. People try to avoid unduly damaging the prestige and self-respect of others, as well as themselves, in public. Confrontation and criticism are guaranteed face-destroyers. Yet arguing with shopkeepers and waiters is, sadly, sometimes necessary.

But in general, in both China and Hong Kong, Western-style bluntness is not appreciated or expected: a polite and gentle approach is more likely to endear guests to their hosts. That might seem at odds with Hong Kong's very visible boldness and brashness and displays of public rudeness, but behind closed doors, or with friends and acquaintances, manners matter.

Common sense, as ever, goes a long way in dealing with the issue. When in doubt, lavish those compliments. There is no race of people in the world – from Chinese to Chileans – that does not respond warmly to praise for its culture and traditions.

### FENG SHUI

*Feng shui* may be seen in the West as little more than a trendy fad, but in China this ancient art is serious business. Although Hong Kong is a commercial, modern city, it still pays great heed to this time-honoured art. *Feng shui* is more than another quirk of a superstitious culture – many of its principle tenets are the basics of good and effective design. The main aim (of aligning oneself and one's home or work place within an environment) has been followed by successive generations of Chinese in Hong Kong. There is a general belief that businesses and personal health will flourish if this age-old practice, sometimes called geomancy in the West, is employed under the direction of an experienced master. Even the biggest multi-nationals pay heed to it when laying out an office or constructing a building, partly out of deference to their staff and partly out of honouring Chinese custom.

The term *feng shui* is Mandarin (it is known as *fung shui* in Cantonese) for 'wind water', but this philosophy of how to live in harmony with nature taps into more than just these two elements alone. Experts in the field claim that the interplay of wood, fire, earth and even gold also have to be taken into account and balanced to obtain the optimum result, which is harmony in all areas of one's life. Believers are convinced good fortune is not determined by chance, but by correct *feng shui*.

The basic tools of the *feng shui* practitioner's trade are a multi-ringed compass, astronomical charts and ancient texts on the processes of divination. The master will note the natural and man-made features in the building's environs, and will then decide the direction that certain rooms and furniture should face, and the features that should be introduced to enhance positivity. Often these features include mirrors, engraved coins and bamboo flutes, hung on walls, from beams or in the corner of rooms.

Water features, such as small babbling electric mini-fountains or fish aquariums, are also used regularly. Even the number and colour of fish has to be right – if they die over time, this is said to be a sign that the fish have absorbed bad luck that would otherwise have wreaked havoc on human occupants. Dead fish therefore need to be replaced, to maintain the fortuitous number in the tank.

## 'The angular Bank of China Tower... is said to shoot out poison arrows.'

Typically, *feng shui* has been more strongly adhered to in Hong Kong's rural areas. When tunnelling for the Kowloon–Canton Railway began early last century, for example, no Chinese labourers could be persuaded to work on the project for fear of disturbing the earth spirits. Even in 2001, the Kowloon–Canton Railway Corporation (KCRC) called in a *feng shui* expert for input in a feasibility study for a proposed new rail link in the New Territories. (Although, strangely enough, villagers' *feng shui* problems often seem to disappear when compensation terms are raised.)

Some buildings, although built in accordance with a geomancer's instructions, are said to give off bad *feng shui*. The angular Bank of China Tower (*see p69*), for example, with its prominent criss-cross cladding, is said to shoot out poison arrows from the apex of these exterior panels, some say targeting former Government House (which was one reason why Chief Executive Tung Chee-hwa declined to live there). A weeping willow is said to have been planted in the grounds of Government House to deflect the negative influence. Other buildings include a large hole in their structure or are built on stilts, in order to prevent energy flows being blocked.

Like partially blocked Chinese temple doorways, which are used to bar the entry of bad spirits, it is quite common for building entrances to be built at an angle – The Mandarin Oriental hotel has one of many angled entrances around town. Some home owners opt for a staggered entrance into their flat for the same reason.

However, there is some debate between *feng shui* practitioners over how the traditional rules of the art apply to modern-day residential buildings that can be full of hundreds of apartments. For instance, should traditional entrance treatments apply to today's internal front doors, when they were originally designed for the external entrances of antiquated courtyard dwellings?

With space at such a premium, these days murals are sometimes used as a substitute for natural environments. They will often feature components such as rivers and waterfalls emptying into a lake, surrounded by ripe rice fields and fruit-bearing trees, against a backdrop of hills that are populated by birds and butterflies. These elements read logically: water stands for money and the full lake ensures it stays plentiful; the rice and fruit symbolise full dinner tables; the hills offer protection; and the fauna represents harmony.

Whether *feng shui* works or not is a matter for debate. But enough people put store by it to make it a significant business, as well as a preoccupation for many. Scoff if you like, but put it this way: who wouldn't want to live in a home next to a waterfall, a lake and flourishing fields?

## TRADITIONAL FESTIVALS

While Christian festivals like Easter and Christmas are acknowledged with holidays, they are not really celebrated. Given that the Chinese have five major festivals of their own, it's probably just as well, but it does add up to a lot of public holidays. As with Christmas in the West, the Chinese festivals provide families with an opportunity to come together to eat well and exchange gifts. For details of the festivals, *see* chapter **By Season**.

## CHINESE ARTS

Despite being one of the most modern cities in the world, it is still possible to witness traditional Chinese arts in Hong Kong. You'll find ancient tea ware at the **Flagstaff House Museum of Tea Ware** (*see p72*), classic calligraphy at the **Hong Kong Museum of Art** (*see p102*) and (the most basic) Chinese opera at **Temple Street Night Market** (*see p108*). But the Hong Kong arts scene is also international and in touch with contemporary global trends, so don't be surprised if the latest West End theatre production is enjoying a short term run as well.

For more on traditional music, opera and dance, *see p242* **Chinese performing arts**.

## PASTIMES

Besides eating, Hong Kongers traditionally spend their leisure time playing games (from the board to finger guessing variety), singing karaoke (which borders on an obsession), gambling on horses, games or at the casinos in Macau, and keeping fit through martial arts and breathing exercises – think Falun Gong without all the fuss.

Wherever you are in Hong Kong, chances are you will hear a furious clatter accompanied by lots of shouting and raucous behaviour emanating from flats and village homes,

**Man Mo Temple.** *See p76.*

especially during holidays. The cause of this racket? **Mah jong** – Hong Kong's favourite game. Tracing its origins as far back as 2350BC (although some say it was only invented by Confucius in 500BC), it is played with 144 tiles made up of three suits (bamboo, Chinese characters and circles), numbered from 1 to 9, of which there are four of each kind, meaning that there are 36 tiles per suit – and 108 suit tiles in total. The remaining 36 tiles are composed of three groups (flowers, winds and dragons), which have different functions depending on the house rules. It's as complex as bridge in terms of explaining the rules, but there are two certainties – the game will last a long time (with many rounds over several hours) and as much noise as possible will be made clattering the tiles on the table.

**Chinese chess**, or *xiangqi*, is more sedate. The game is one of the four Chinese arts along with *qin* (music), *hua* (brush painting) and *shu* (calligraphy). It involves two players, each of whom is assigned 16 pieces: one king, two chariots, two horses, two elephants, two guards, two cannons and five soldiers. The object, like in Western chess, is to capture the king. Games can be seen being played by men (most of them elderly) in public areas across Hong Kong – they will usually be surrounded by crowds and don't be surprised if wagers are being placed.

Even more sedate is the martial art of *tai chi*. As dawn breaks, folk (again most of whom are elderly) head for the hills, parks and beaches to bend, stretch and meditate in silence. It's an awesome sight. Because *tai chi* emphasises correct form and feeling in each movement, with the aim being to improve the flow of internal energy within the body, it is practised very slowly and gently. At the end of the day, *tai chi* promotes strength, stamina and flexibility, cultivating the link between mind and body, and enhancing balance and coordination.

If you'd like to give it a go, the Hong Kong Tourism Board conducts free *tai chi* classes for tourists (*see p248*).

## CHINESE MEDICINE

Almost every district you visit in Hong Kong has old-fashioned shops selling Chinese medicines and herbal treatments, either loose or in jars. There is a large concentration of these shops in Sheung Wan, where you will see row after row of wooden chests with tiny drawers containing all manner of powders, pills, plants and animal parts, each of which is purported to play a distinctive role in the health of human beings.

Westerners may scoff at their healing powers, and animal rights activists rightly protest at the use of bear gall bladders, tiger penis and seahorses to boost such functions as sexual virility and hair growth, but there's more to Chinese medicine than age-old myths. And an extremely high percentage of Hong Kong people still turn to Chinese medics either before, or along with Western doctors, when illness strikes.

The origin of Chinese medicine dates back five millennia to the genesis of Chinese civilization, but the first recorded case of diagnosing and treating disease dates back to about 1500BC during the Shang dynasty. The concept is holistic – both in treating and preventing illness – and is as relevant today as it ever was. While Chinese medicine can remedy ailments and alter states of mind, it can also reportedly enhance recuperative power, immunity, and the capacity for pleasure, work, and creativity.

Within Chinese Cosmology, all of creation is born from the marriage of two polar principles, yin and yang: earth and heaven, winter and summer, night and day, cold and hot, wet and dry, inner and outer, body and mind. Harmony of this union means health, good weather and good fortune, while disharmony leads to disease, disaster and bad luck. The strategy of Chinese medicine is to restore harmony.

Each human is seen as a world in miniature. Every person has a unique terrain to be mapped, a resilient yet sensitive ecology to be maintained. Practitioners assess a person's health by feeling the pulse at each wrist, and by observing the colour and form of the face, tongue and body. This information is interpreted in the context of a patient's present and past complaints, work and living habits, physical environment, family health history, and emotional life.

Treatment varies from acupuncture and acupressure to herbal remedies, exercise, massage and diet (tonic soups are drunk by everyone and essence of chicken broth is a top-seller – head to Sheung Wan on Hong Kong Island if you fancy trying one; *see p76*).

## CHINESE ASTROLOGY

The Chinese lunar calendar is the longest chronological record in history, dating from 2637BC when the first cycle of the zodiac was introduced. An entire cycle takes 60 years to complete and is made up of five simple cycles of 12 years each. The 78th cycle started in February 1984 and will end in February 2044.

## 'Belief in the Chinese zodiac remains strong in Hong Kong today.'

According to legend, the Lord Buddha summoned all the animals in the world to him before he departed from earth. As only 12 animals appeared to bid him farewell, he named a year after each one – in the order that they arrived to see him. First came the rat, then the ox, the tiger, rabbit, dragon, snake, horse, sheep, monkey, rooster, dog and boar. Thus the 12 animal signs of today came into being. The animal ruling the year in which you were born is said to exercise a profound influence on your life and determine your character.

Belief in the Chinese zodiac remains strong in Hong Kong today. In the lunar year straddling 2000-2001, pregnancies increased because of the desire of parents to have children born in the Year of the Dragon, believed to be the most powerful of all animals.

During the complete 60-year cycle, each of the animal signs (sometimes also referred to as the 12 earth branches) is combined with the five elements of wood, fire, earth, metal and water. The element of your lunar sign will also exercise its influence on your life. No element is called the strongest or weakest – they are forever dependent on one another.

The lunar year is divided into twelve months of 29 days. Every two and a half years, an intercalary month is added to adjust the calendar. The addition of this month every third year produces the Lunar Leap Year. For easy reference, the beginning of each lunar month is the date of the New Moon marked on the Western calendar.

The importance of the lunar calendar remains significant in Hong Kong to this day, and particular care is taken to ensure certain events like marriages, business openings and ancestral worship take place on the most auspicious days. Some prospective newlyweds queue for days to ensure they can land a ceremony in one of the city's register offices on the right day.

# Wild Hong Kong

Mountains, forests, remote beaches and wonderful hiking – there's life in abundance beyond the metropolis.

Hong Kong's dramatic urban geography is famed the world over, but few people are aware of the extraordinary natural beauty that lies just beyond the skyscrapers. No less than 40 per cent of its territory falls within 22 country parks, and the wide open spaces of the New Territories and the countless outlying islands offer endless opportunities for enjoying nature. Even on Hong Kong Island, you don't need to travel far to escape the crowds and understand the seductive beauty of the other side of Hong Kong.

### HIKERS' PARADISE

Strange as it sounds, this is one of the best cities in the world for walkers. In fact, it's a hiker's dream: you can escape urbana and walk for up to eight hours without seeing another of the 6.7 million human beings who live here. An added rambler's godsend is that no matter

where you're standing in Hong Kong, you are usually within 30 minutes of reaching lush countryside, which criminally few tourists (and almost as few residents) take the time to enjoy.

So what's to see? You name it, Hong Kong has it. Panoramic hiking trails for beginners and adventurers alike, jungle trekking, remote, pristine sandy beaches, hidden valleys, deserted traditional villages, waterfalls and crystal plunge pools ripe for swimming, and – best of all – solitude.

Hong Kong has an endless combination of hikes. The best-known trails are clearly mapped, and can stretch for 100 kilometres. The four big ones follow.

The 100-kilometre (62-mile) **MacLehose Trail** in the New Territories, named after Sir Murray MacLehose (a hill-loving former governor; *see p23*), is divided into ten stages, taking in around 20 mountains and stretching east to west across almost the breadth of the New Territories, starting from Sai Kung and ending in Tuen Mun. It is one of the most diverse and beautiful trails that Hong Kong has to offer. Each November, about 5,000 hikers compete to finish the 'Big Mac' in less than 48 hours (*see p206* **Trailwalker**). The current record is 13 hours and 18 minutes.

The 70-kilometre (44-mile) **Wilson Trail** (named after another ex-governor) is divided into several different sections. It starts at Stanley on Hong Kong Island and heads across Tai Tam Country Park, before hopping over the harbour to the New Territories (crossing the MacLehose Trail in several points) and finally ending at the stunning Pat Seng Leng mountain range, not far from Plover Cove Reservoir.

> **'It's a hiker's dream: you can escape urbana and walk for up to eight hours without seeing another of the 6.7 million human beings who live here.'**

The 50-kilometre (31-mile) **Hong Kong Trail** is the most 'gentle' alternative trail to the other routes, with fewer mountains and inclines, more shade, and an easier and more accessible route that snakes across the length of Hong Kong Island. An annual hiking competition takes place along the trail (usually in February or March) called the Green Power Hike. Hikers aim to complete the trail in 18 hours or less.

The 70-kilometre (44-mile) **Lantau Trail** curls around the whole of Lantau island. Considerably bigger than Hong Kong Island, Lantau offers some of Hong Kong's highest and most scenic mountains. The two most popular mountains to walk are Lantau Peak and Sunset Peak, both challenging and best avoided during the stifling summer months. However, the island is not just hills. There are plenty of beach hikes (Cheung Sha), hidden waterfalls (outside Tai O), and stunning reservoir and island views (Shek Pik and Fan Lau). The Lantau Trail is another annual hiking challenge.

The best two pieces of advice you'll ever receive about hiking in Hong Kong are to take a map and as much water as you can physically carry. Maps are easily found in the hiking and book shops around town, and the Government Publications Office (*see p180*). Water is another matter. Each year, a handful of people die when hiking in Hong Kong due to dehydration. By the time you feel thirsty, it's too late – you're in the early stages of dehydration. Along with lots of

# Pink dolphins

Of all Hong Kong's diverse fauna, one species has captured the public imagination more than any other: the rare pink dolphin. Properly known as *sousa chinesis*, the Indo-Pacific humpback dolphin is found around South Africa, India and Australia, but only along the Chinese coast does it have this unique colouration – and no-one really knows why. It is born almost black, which quickly fades to pale grey, before progressing to white and pink.

The Pearl River Delta supports a population of around 1,000 dolphins, but pollution and habitat erosion is posing a serious threat to the dolphins' survival. Around 190,000 cubic metres of raw sewage is dumped into the western harbour every day (and this is due to increase to 700,000 per day by 2010); organochlorines (such as DDT) have been found in dolphin tissue samples in very high doses; overfishing is depleting the dolphins' food supply; and heavy boat traffic causes injury and further pollution.

**Hong Kong Dolphinwatch** (GPO Box 4102, 1528A Star House, Tsim Sha Tsui, Kowloon; 2984 1414/www.zianet.com/ dolphins/dolphins@hk.super.net) runs trips to see the dolphins every Wednesday, Friday, Saturday and Sunday (HK$320 per person; HK$160 for under-12s); call them for details, or look at their website.

The trips, hosted by knowledgeable guides, are well worth the money and provide a valuable insight into some of the major problems facing Hong Kong today. Don't, however, expect to see the dolphins jumping over the bow of the boat and snatching fish out of your hands – this is a shy species and sightings tend to be relatively distant. But, after all the abuse man has heaped on their habitat, who can blame them for being wary.

# HK walks Across the Dragon's Back

The **Dragon's Back** is one of Hong Kong Island's easiest and most popular hiking routes. Although the very beginning of the walk is at Big Wave Bay, this shorter version is a perfect beginner's hike and one that you can take kids on, too.

Starting near Mount Collinson (named after the maker of the first detailed topographical map of Hong Kong Island), this walk ends in the former fishing village of Shek O on the island's east coast. The eight-kilometre (five-mile) yomp takes about two hours, even at a leisurely pace, and is easy to reach via public transport.

Walking along the gentle ridge reveals unrivalled views of the South China Sea, the outlying islands, Tai Tam Country Park's reservoirs, Mounts Parker and Butler, and Violet Hill, as well as clear views of Stanley, the Red Hill Peninsula and some parts of Kowloon. On most weekend afternoons, you can spot at least a handful of keen paragliders leaping off the Dragon's Back, enjoying some of Asia's finest thermals and then floating down to land on one of Shek O's smaller beaches.

The reward at the end of the hike is the laid-back village of Shek O, which has a great beach, plenty of restaurants and a small headland to explore.

### GETTING THERE

Catch the MTR to Shau Kei Wan station (exit A3) and take the number 9 bus to Shek O from the bus station outside. Stay on the bus for about five kilometres (three miles) and ring the bell as soon as you see a mini roundabout (the only one along this road), so that you can get off at the next stop.

water, pick up some iodine tablets (from any pharmacy or hiking shop), which you can use to purify stream/reservoir water if your own supply runs out. Carrying a first aid kit is also advisable. Many people underestimate just how remote parts of Hong Kong are – you can easily be around six to eight hours from the nearest road or telephone.

### FLORA AND FAUNA

The diversity of landscapes within Hong Kong means that there is an impressive range of plant- and wildlife to be discovered. The territory divides roughly into three types of vegetation – woodland, brushland and scrubland – boasting more than 2,000 different species of plants, including over 200 types of fern and 120 types of orchid. Early summer is the best time to enjoy blossoming trees and flowers, many of which have heady scents.

Oaks and laurels are the two main species of trees in Hong Kong, while the most common trees are the odoriferous camphor and yellow camphor (there is a theory that their pungent smell led to the adoption of the name 'Hong Kong', meaning 'fragrant harbour'). The largest

# Resources & contacts

The following are all useful contacts and information sources for those wanting to explore Hong Kong's wildernesses.

**Country & Marine Parks Authority**
www.afdparks.gov.hk
**Friends of the Country Parks**
focp@hongkong.com
**Friends of the Earth**
foe@foe.org.hk
**Green Power**
www.greenpower.org.hk
**Hong Kong Women's Walking Group**
jbunker@netvigator.com
**Hong Kong YWCA**

www.esmdywca.com
**Kadoorie Farm & Botanical Garden**
www.kfbg.org.hk

### Recommended books

*Exploring Hong Kong's Countryside: A Visitor's Companion* Edward Stokes (HKTB)
*Hong Kong Pathfinder* Martin Williams (Asia 2000)
*Hong Kong's Wild Places* Edward Stokes (OUP)
*Lantau Island Explorer's Guide* (HKTB)
*The MacLehose Trail* (CUP)
*Magic Walks* Kaarlo Schepel (The Alternative Press)
*Trailwalker* (Oxfam Hong Kong)

## THE HIKE

Remain on the same side of the road as the bus stop. Walk straight ahead and you will see a set of steps. Climb the steps and turn right at the top by the women's detention centre. Walk past the centre (there may be some gates) and up a concrete road. At the top, the road forks. A sign indicates a path to the left that leads to Big Wave Bay (a surfer hang out), but continue ahead for Shek O along a mud-worn path lined by trees and bushes. (Don't worry about getting lost; there are no turn offs.)

After about 30-40 minutes, look for a knee-high wooden post (no.90). Shortly after this, you'll see another post next to a right-hand turn off. Take this right turn, and walk uphill for about five minutes (off path).

When you reach the top, you are officially at the start of the Dragon's Back. Turn right at the top (the sea is on your left) and walk along the whole of the Dragon's Back.

Looking down the hill, you will see the village of Shek O on your left side and Tai Tam Harbour on your right.

The path runs out after about 30-40 minutes of ridge walking (a seat marks the end of the trail) and you'll notice a path and steps that lead downhill. Follow them for about 15 minutes and you'll reach the main road (Shek O Road) next to a bus stop.

Rather than walk on the main road (there is no path and traffic is fast), hop back on to the number 9 bus – it is a five-minute journey into Shek O, where the bus terminates.

## THE AFTER-HIKE REWARDS

Once in Shek O, there are plenty of good, informal restaurants. A couple of delicious hiker hangouts are the Thai-Chinese Restaurant, specialising in seafood (and a popular haunt of Hong Kong's last governor, Chris Patten), and a funkier place, with superb home-made food, the Black Sheep (see p172). Reservations are recommended.

expanses of montane forest can be found in the country parks of Tai Lam, Tai Mo Shan and Shing Mun, and the Tai Po Kau Special Area.

> ## 'Hong Kong supports an incredible 2,000 species of moths and 225 of butterflies.'

A shortage of wood during the Japanese occupation in World War II means that few very old trees survive in Hong Kong (except for the occasional preserved banyan), but re-forested valleys boast groves of rhodoleia, Chinese red pine, American slash pine and Brisbane pine. A smell you get used to in the forests is that of the Australian gum tree (eucalyptus).

Wildlife is similarly diverse, and includes 47 species of mammals, 27 of reptiles and 445 of birds. The best spot for wildlife sightings are the rich woodlands of Tai Mo Shan, Shing Mun and Tai Po Kau, where you can see (especially in the early morning or at dusk) larger native mammals, such as small wild boar, pangolin, Chinese porcupine, civet, ferret badger and the small barking deer. Hong Kong's reservoirs and waterways support healthy populations of fresh water turtle, terrapin, snapping turtle and carp.

The 49 species of snakes (generally seen in Tai Po Kau and Tai Mo Shan) include the Chinese cobra, the red-necked keelback, the

coral snake and the banded krait – all these are poisonous, but the vast majority of snakes found in Hong Kong are harmless.

On a more fur-friendly note, if you're a monkey fan and want to see primates in their natural habitat (in their troops), the places to hike are Kam Shan and Lion Rock Country Park. Rhesus and long-tailed macaques are numerous, cheeky and used to visitors. They are deceptively tame, but do take care as they can turn nasty if provoked.

Hong Kong supports an incredible 2,000 species of moths and 225 of butterflies. Some pretty spring butterflies to watch out for (in March and April) are the great orange tip, the grey pansy, the mottled migrant, the bamboo tree brown and the banana skipper. The ever-present background noise of the spotted black cicada also becomes inescapable in the parks.

Two of the best places to go to appreciate the diversity of Hong Kong's flora and fauna are the **Kadoorie Farm & Botanic Garden** (see p119) and **Mai Po Marshes** (see p122), both in the New Territories.

▶ For more on walks, both urban and rural, see p90 **Peak perambulations**, p127 **Lamma** and p210 **Jungles, concrete & otherwise**.
▶ For more on Hong Kong's natural attractions, see p91 **Hong Kong Island: South & east coast**, p127 **Outlying islands** and p114 **New Territories**.

# East Meets West

## Kowloon Shangri-La

64 Mody Road, Kowloon (tel: 2721 2111/
fax 2723 8686)
Tsimshatsui MTR (exit D2)

### A deluxe hotel in the heart of Tsimshatsui East's bustling shopping and nightlife districts

*For a feast of global flavours under one roof, check
out two of our dining options:*

## Shang Palace Chinese Restauarant
(tel: 2733 8754)
**Open** 12-3pm, 6.30-11pm Mon-Sat; 10am-3pm,
6.30-11pm Sun, PH  **Average** lunch HK$150,
dinner HK$400.  **Credit** all major credit cards

- The finest Cantonese cuisine in Hong Kong in a lavish, Chinese imperial-influenced setting

- Vast menu of seasonal delicacies

- Dim sum, bird's, nest shark's fin and abalone all served

## Napa Califorian Restaurant
(tel: 2733 8752)
**Open** 12-3pm, 6.30-12pm cocktails 11pm-1am
daily  **Average** lunch HK$200,
dinner HK$450.  **Credit** all major credit cards

- A top floor loocation with sweeping views of Victoria Harbour and Island skyline

- European, Asian and American-influenced cuisine

- Semi -buffet lunch & à la carte dinner menus

- The city's most comprehensive selction of Californian vintages

# Accommodation

**Accommodation**      **40**

**Feature boxes**

The best hotels      47
Charlie Mansions?      51
Youth hostels      52

# Accommodation

From glitz to the pits – there's no shortage of places to lay your head.

Be prepared: this is an expensive city. Hong Kong boasts some of the top hotels in the world, offering five-star luxury, fine dining and business facilities par excellence. All this comes at a hefty price, of course, with rack rates likely to frighten off all but the expenses-paid business traveller. This is, perhaps, inevitable in a city that thrives on its role as a commercial centre and trading entrepôt. Nevertheless, many hotels offer great package, low-season and weekend deals – sometimes less than half the published standard rates, so shopping around can pay big dividends. And value can still be found, particularly if you're not put off by names. The YMCAs here, for example, outclass some 'premium hotels' found in other major cities in terms of facilities, comfort and service.

The main luxury hotel districts include Admiralty's Supreme Court Road, Central's Chater Road, and the Tsim Sha Tsui and Wan Chai harboursides. Tsim Sha Tsui and Wan Chai also have lots of budget accommodation nestled cheek by jowl with five-star hotels. For example, the extremely cheap Chungking and Mirador Mansions guesthouses (see p51 **Charlie Mansions?**) are a dumpling's throw away from the Peninsula, arguably the city's top hotel. While the guesthouses may lack swimming pools and Internet access, they are often clean, tidy and highly affordable. Hotels in areas outside the main districts, like Western, North Point and parts of Kowloon other than Tsim Sha Tsui, usually provide the same level of luxury as that offered in top hotels for less money. And as public transport is cheap and easy (with most hotels operating free shuttle buses anyway), don't put too much store in geography if you want to stretch your money. However, this is all relative – you can certainly cast aside any thoughts that you're in Asia now and everything is cheap.

The late autumn months through to Christmas and Chinese New Year (three days between late January and mid March) usually denote high season, while many good deals can be found in spring and early summer. Check whether hotel prices are inclusive or exclusive of taxes – the current government surcharge is 13 per cent, and an additional service charge may also be levied. Unless otherwise indicated, rates are exclusive of taxes and of breakfast.

# Hong Kong Island

## Central & Mid-Levels

As the business heart of the city, it's no surprise that Central is (almost without exception) a phenomenally expensive place to stay. Many of the city's premier luxury hotels are located here.

### Deluxe

#### Conrad Hong Kong

*Pacific Place, 88 Queensway, Central, HK Island (2521 3838/fax 2521 3888/www.conrad.com.hk). Admiralty MTR (exit C1)/buses & trams along Queensway.* **Rates** from HK$2,950 single; from HK$3,150 double; from HK$5,600 suite. **Credit** AmEx, DC, MC, V. **Map** p67 F5.

Three of the towers piercing the Admiralty skyline are deluxe hotels (the others being the Island Shangri-La, *see below*; and the JW Marriott), creating Hong Kong's most exclusive hotel neighbourhood. All three rise out of the flashy, pricey Pacific Place shopping and entertainment mall (*see p182*), and are a short walk from the haven of Hong Kong Park (*see p72*). With the Conrad's 509 rooms (including 46 suites) comes a spectacular view – either of the harbour or the Peak – and each is luxuriously decorated, including wooden writing table and comfortable armchairs. The hotel's restaurants include Nicholini's (probably the best Italian in Asia; *see p144*) and the Garden Café by the heated outdoor pool. The hotel also hosts regular theatre and dinner performances.

**Hotel services** *Air-conditioning. Babysitting. Bar. Beauty salon. Business services. Concierge. Disabled rooms. Garden. Gym. Laundry. Limousine service. No-smoking floors. Restaurants. Swimming pool (outdoor).* **Room services** *Dataport. Iron. Mini-bar. Room service (24hrs). Telephone. Turndown. TV: cable/pay movies/satellite.*

#### Island Shangri-La

*Pacific Place, Supreme Court Road, Central, HK Island (2877 3838/fax 2521 8742/www.shangri-la.com). Admiralty MTR (exit C1)/buses & trams along Queensway.* **Rates** HK$2,400-$3,550 double/twin; HK$5,800-$26,000 suite. **Credit** AmEx, DC, MC, V. **Map** p67 F5.

Opened in 1991, the 56-storey Island Shangri-La is the tallest hotel in Hong Kong, and boasts the largest guest rooms on Hong Kong Island (which offer marvellous views of either the harbour or the Peak). The opulent lobby is dominated by architectural

The **Mandarin Oriental**... and the lofty atrium at the **Island Shangri-La**. *See p40.*

flower arrangements and three outrageously huge chandeliers, while the atrium (running from the 39th to 55th floors) is distinguished by a gargantuan 51-metre (167-foot) tall silk landscape painting. This is primarily a business hotel, as might be expected given its location close to Hong Kong's financial centre, but sitting atop the 200-outlet Pacific Place mega-mall (*see p182*), it is also well-located for hard core shoppers, and the lovely Hong Kong Park (*see p72*) is also on its doorstep. The 565 rooms and suites all have in-room Internet access, lashings of dark wood and marble bathrooms. Of the raft of restaurants within the hotel, the most distinguished is the top-floor French restaurant Petrus (*see p143*). The wonderful views from the bar, Cyrano (*see p168, p237*), are also well worth checking out. There's also a large outdoor pool with its own bar and a good-sized 24-hour gym. Nice extra touches for guests paying the tariff rates are free limousine transfer from the airport, free laundry and dry cleaning, complimentary breakfast, cost-price phone calls and 6pm checkout. The hotel is also notable for its pioneering environmental policy.

## Mandarin Oriental

*5 Connaught Road, Central, HK Island (2522 0111/ fax 2810 6190/www.mandarinoriental.com). Central MTR (exit F, H)/buses to Central Star Ferry/Central Star Ferry Pier.* **Rates** HK$2,950-$4,200 single; HK$3,200-$4,200 double; HK$5,500-$5,750 suite. **Credit** AmEx, DC, MC, V. **Map** p67 E3.

One of the world's best-known hotels, the multi-award-winning Mandarin Oriental doesn't have to prove anything to anybody. Given its prime location in the heart of the financial district, it's no surprise that it pulls in a primarily business clientele – many a deal has been struck over breakfast, or lunch at the Mandarin Grill. The building dates from 1963, at which time it dominated the surrounding area. Now the hotel is, in turn, dwarfed by modern towers. The scale of the 542 guest rooms and suites and public areas is, consequently, more modest than in some of Hong Kong's younger luxury hotels. Bedrooms are decorated in neutral tones with Oriental influences and plenty of wood, and most have balconies – a rarity in Hong Kong – the reason being clear when you step out on to them and are enveloped in traffic noise

# Stay in the Heart
# of Hong Kong

For over 27 years, the Furama - as it is affectionately known locally - has been one of Hong Kong's most trusted hotels.

In prime position near the waterfront in Central, the Furama is close to everything this exciting city has to offer - from the nightlife of Lan Kwai Fong to major banks and businesses, the famed Star Ferry and the Peak Tram.

During your stay, the Furama is your home away from home. 517 rooms and suites overlooking either Victoria Harbour or The Peak, feature all the modern conveniences you would expect from deluxe hotel including broadband wirele internet access and electronic safe.

With five restaurants and bars including th famous La Ronda Revolving Restauran banquet and conference facilities caterin up to 1,000 people; Business Centre; full equipped Fitness Club complete with Sauna Spas and Steam Rooms; Hairdresser; Flow Shop; Cake Shop and Shopping Arcade, yo can rest assured your stay will meet all you expectations.

(the double glazing offers excellent sound-proofing). Impressively, all rooms have broadband Internet access. If you want to splash out, the 12 individually themed suites are decorated with imagination and style. Hotel facilities include a health centre, a compact indoor pool and gym. The top-floor French-Asian fusion restaurant Vong (see p147) is one of the hotel's highlights, as is the surprisingly relaxed and buzzy attached bar.

**Hotel services** *Air-conditioning. Babysitting. Bars. Beauty salon. Business services. Concierge. Gym. Laundry. Limousine service. No-smoking rooms. Payphone. Restaurants. Swimming pool (indoor).* **Room services** *Dataport. Iron. Mini-bar. Room service (24hrs). Telephone. Turndown. TV: cable/pay movies/satellite.*

## Expensive

### Ritz-Carlton

*3 Connaught Road, Central, HK Island (2877 6666/ fax 2877 6778/www.ritzcarlton.com). Central MTR (exit J3)/buses through Central/Central Star Ferry Pier.* **Rates** *from HK$1,650 single/double; from HK$2,850 suite.* **Credit** AmEx, DC, MC, V. **Map** p67 E4.

**Garden View International House.**

With just 216 rooms, the Ritz-Carlton is one of Hong Kong's smaller, more intimate luxury hotels. Its Central location makes it ideal to explore the nearby entertainment areas on foot or to travel anywhere by day. Elegance best sums up the style of this narrow, tall hotel, which offers views of the harbour. Rooms are excellent, and feature Italian marble bathrooms. The Ritz-Carlton is known for delivering high-quality service in a no-fuss manner, as you will discover if you frequent its bars and restaurants, from the basement Shanghainese restaurant to the stately, yet cosy, Chater Lounge (see p237). Its outdoor pool is one of the best in Hong Kong.

**Hotel services** *Air-conditioning. Babysitting. Bar. Beauty salon. Business services. Concierge. Disabled rooms. Garden. Gym. Laundry. Limousine service. No-smoking floors. Restaurants. Swimming pool (outdoor).* **Room services** *Dataport. Iron. Mini-bar. Room service (24hrs). Telephone. Turndown. TV: cable/pay movies/satellite.*

## Cheap

### Garden View International House

*1 MacDonnell Road, Mid-Levels, HK Island (2877 3737). Taxi from Hong Kong Airport Express Station.* **Rates** HK$550 standard; HK$650 superior. **Credit** AmEx, DC, MC, V.

Want to know what it's like living in the upmarket Mid-Levels residential area of Hong Kong? Here's your chance, at a remarkably low price for the area. Garden View International House is located close to Hong Kong Park, the Botanical Gardens and the Peak Tram, though a bus or taxi ride away from shopping and entertainment centres. It's a quiet place, with good facilities, but only certain superior rooms have a harbour view. Fast food is available, and there's also a Chinese restaurant on site. Minibuses run down to Central every few minutes.

**Hotel services** *Air-conditioning. Bar. Gym. Laundry. Restaurant. Swimming pool (outdoor).* **Room services** *TV: Star.*

## Wan Chai & Causeway Bay

Wan Chai and Causeway Bay, just east of Central, offer a wide choice of accommodation. The districts – jammed with people and traffic – aren't exactly pretty or havens of calm, but there's a huge range of shops, bars and restaurants, and transport links are excellent.

## Deluxe

### Grand Hyatt

*1 Harbour Road, Wan Chai, HK Island (2588 1234/ fax 2802 0677/http://hongkong.hyatt.com). Wan Chai MTR (exit A1)/buses along Gloucester Road & Harbour Road/Wan Chai Star Ferry Pier.* **Rates** from HK$2,900 single; from HK$3,150 double; from HK$5,500 suite. **Credit** AmEx, DC, MC, V. **Map** p80 B1.

Grand by name and grand by nature, this hotel is the apogee of luxury. A high-ceilinged, opulent lobby sets the tone for the interior, which extends to the (572) superb rooms, the best of which have a harbour view. A recent redesign of the guest rooms has left them with sleekly modern soft furnishings and packed with technological know-how, including Internet access. Situated adjacent to the Hong Kong Convention and Exhibition Centre, the Grand Hyatt has played host to a continuous stream of rich and powerful guests, including Bill and Hillary Clinton. Its Italian restaurant, Grissini (see p153), offers great cuisine in a magnificent setting (former governor Chris Patten was a satisfied regular) and the lobby bar is ideal for a view of Tsim Sha Tsui across the harbour. The immediate surrounding area of Wan Chai waterfront provides a good place for a stroll.
**Hotel services** *Air-conditioning. Babysitting. Bar. Beauty salon. Business services. Concierge. Disabled rooms. Garden. Gym. Laundry. Limousine service. No-smoking floors. Restaurants. Swimming pool (outdoor).* **Room services** *Dataport. Iron. Mini-bar. Room service (24hrs). Telephone. Turndown. TV: cable/pay movies/satellite.*

## Expensive

### Empire Hotel

*33 Hennessy Road, Wan Chai, HK Island (2866 9111/fax 2863 3121/ehhresa@asiastandard.com). Wan Chai MTR (exit B1)/shuttle bus H1 from Hong Kong Airport Express Station or buses along Hennessy Road.* **Rates** (including tax & service charge) HK$1,482-$2,000 single/double. **Credit** AmEx, DC, V. **Map** p80 A2.
At the Empire you are paying mainly for its prime location, between Wan Chai and Central, with excellent links. Although not far from the harbourfront, there is no seaview, but it's within easy reach of the shopping and entertainment facilities of Pacific Place, and the nightlife of Wan Chai. The hotel would not win any style awards, but the small rooms are all comfortable, clean and decently decorated.
**Hotel services** *Air-conditioning. Babysitting. Bar. Business services. Concierge. Disabled rooms. Gym. Laundry. No-smoking rooms. Restaurants. Swimming pool (outdoor).* **Room services** *Dataport. Mini-bar. Room service. Telephone. TV: cable.*

### The Excelsior

*281 Gloucester Road, Causeway Bay, HK Island (2894 8888/fax 2895 6459/www.mandarin-oriental.com/excelsior). Causeway Bay MTR (exit C)/buses along Gloucester Road.* **Rates** from HK$1,800 single/double; from HK$3,800 suite. **Credit** AmEx, DC, MC, V. **Map** p80 D1.
Rooms 866, plus 21 suites.
Located in the heart of thronging Causeway Bay, the Excelsior is a similarly busy hotel (many airlines use it for their staff). Both locals and guests frequent its bars and restaurants, including the

basement Dickens Bar, a lively sports pub and a great place to start a night out. Weekend dim sum in the Marina Rooms (used as conference venues during the week) is a must, desserts in the first-floor café are enjoyed well past midnight, while kitschy Tott's Asian Grill & Bar (see p172) is a good spot for a drink and a snack. Close to the waterfront (although a busy highway intervenes), the Excelsior offers good views of the harbour and the famous Royal Hong Kong Yacht Club. An ideal place to stay for shoppers and those who want to experience Hong Kong's 24/7 culture.
**Hotel services** *Air-conditioning. Babysitting. Bar. Beauty salon. Business services. Concierge. Disabled rooms. Garden. Gym. Laundry. Limousine service. No-smoking floors. Restaurants. Swimming pool (outdoor).* **Room services** *Dataport. Iron. Mini-bar. Room service (24hrs). Telephone. Turndown. TV: cable/pay movies/satellite.*

## Moderate

### The Wharney

*57-73 Lockhart Road, Wan Chai, HK Island (2861 1000/fax 2865 6023/http://wharney.gdhotels.net/en/home). Wan Chai MTR (exit C)/shuttle bus from Hong Kong Airport Express Station, E11 bus from the airport or buses along Hennessy Road.* **Rates** HK$800-$1,600 single/double. **Credit** AmEx, MC, DC, V. **Map** p80 B2.
Although the Wharney has a good location – it's easy to reach by public transport, close to the malls and shops of Causeway Bay and lies in the heart of Wan Chai's busy nightlife zone – it's not the friendliest of places, and facilities are no better than standard. Rooms are spacious compared to many hotels in the area at this price, but the furnishings are rather frilly and cheesy.
**Hotel services** *Air-conditioning. Babysitting. Bar. Business services. Concierge. Gym. Laundry (self-service). Limousine service. No-smoking rooms. Restaurant.* **Room services** *Mini-bar. Room service. Telephone. TV: satellite.*

## Cheap

### Harbour View International House

*4 Harbour Road, Wan Chai, HK Island (2802 0111). Wan Chai MTR (exit A1, C)/ taxi from Hong Kong Airport Express Station.* **Rates** HK$715 standard; HK$880 harbour view twin; HK$990 double. **Credit** AmEx, MC, V. **Map** p80 B1.
Not cheap for a hostel, perhaps, but you're paying for the downtown location at Harbour View International House. If you don't want to spend a fortune, but want to be by the harbour and in the hub of the city's buzzing nightlife, then this place is hard to beat. Set in a sizeable tower, there are great views from many rooms – all of which are of a reasonable standard, with simple and tasteful furniture and decoration. Although close to Wan Chai's bars and

clubs, this place is actually located in a quieter area, next to the Arts Centre and Academy for Performing Arts – and just across the road from the glitzy Grand Hyatt (*see p43*).

**Hotel services** *Air-conditioning.* **Room services** *Mini-bar. TV: cable.*

### The Wesley

*22 Hennessy Road, Wan Chai, HK Island (2866 6688/fax 2866 6633/www.grandhotel.com.hk/ wesley/index.htm). Wan Chai MTR (exit B1)/shuttle bus from Hong Kong (Airport Express) station or buses along Hennessy Road.* **Rates** HK$700-$1,800 single/double. **Credit** AmEx, MC, DC, V. **Map** p80 A2.
A real bargain for a hotel located in the heart of the city, the Wesley caters mainly to business travellers, and there is nothing too fancy about it. It has one Western and one Chinese restaurant, neither of which is particularly special, but when you are in the heart of the Wan Chai nightlife area, that shouldn't pose too much of a problem.

**Hotel services** *Air-conditioning. Babysitting. Bar. Business services. Concierge. Disabled rooms. Laundry. Restaurants.* **Room services** *Dataport. Mini-bar. TV: cable/satellite.*

## Guesthouse

### Hwa Seng Guesthouse

*Block B1, 5/F, Great George Building, 27 Paterson Street, Causeway Bay, HK Island (2895 6859/fax 2838 7052/info@guesthouse.com.hk). Causeway MTR (exit E)/buses along Yee Wo Street.* **Rates** from HK$400 single/double. **No credit cards.** **Map** p80 D1.
Hwa Seng offers good quality rooms at keen rates in a clean family-run guesthouse. Situated near Causeway Bay MTR station, this place is extremely convenient and in the heart of Hong Kong's shopping mecca. Some rooms include private toilet and bathroom.

**Room services** *Air-conditioning. TV.*

## West coast

## Hostel

### Jockey Club Mount Davis Youth Hostel

*Mount Davis Path, Mount Davis, Kennedy Town, HK Island (2817 5715). Taxi or shuttle bus from Shun Tak Centre (opposite 7/11 store) from Sheung Wan MTR.* **Rates** HK$65 dorm bed; HK$220 2-bed room; HK$260 3-bed room. **No credit cards.** **Map** p62.
Formerly known as Ma Wui Hall, this 111-bed hostel is located on top of Mount Davis at the west end of Hong Kong Island, and enjoys magnificent views of the Tsing Ma Bridge and the harbour. It offers mainly dorm rooms, and, like all youth hostels, everything is DIY. There's a kitchen, dining room, TV room and a friendly atmosphere. This is the best hostel to stay at if you want to explore Hong

The lobby at the **Peninsula**. *See p46.*

Kong Island as cheaply as possible – but be warned that it's not simple to reach. The shuttle bus from Sheung Wan MTR to the hostel runs at 9.30am, 7pm, 9pm and 10.30pm daily.

**Hotel services** *Kitchen. TV room.*
**Room services** *Air-conditioning.*

# Kowloon

## Tsim Sha Tsui

The southern tip of the Kowloon peninsula contains probably the greatest concentration of visitor accommodation in Hong Kong. Alongside some of the territory's glitziest hotels are some of the cheapest guesthouses in the city. The area might not be as chic as some on Hong Kong Island, but there are museums and shops aplenty, and great transport links – plus Hong Kong's finest view from the waterfront.

Same view, rather different prices: the **Salisbury YMCA** (*see p49*) and the **Peninsula**.

## Deluxe

### The Peninsula

*Salisbury Road, Tsim Sha Tsui, Kowloon (2920 2888/www.peninsula.com). Tsim Sha Tsui MTR (exit E)/shuttle bus K3 from Kowloon Airport Express Station or buses along Nathan Road & Salisbury Road/Tsim Sha Tsui Star Ferry Pier.* **Rates** HK$3,000-$4,900 double/twin; HK$5,600-$39,000 suite. **Credit** AmEx, DC, MC, V. **Map** p98 B3.

Still the crème de la crème of Hong Kong hotels, the Peninsula wears its luxury and tradition lightly. Founded in 1928, it exudes a breezy confidence that only comes in a place where both staff and guests feel they're at the top of the tree. Where some of the city's top-end hotels give off the air that gaudy is good, the Peninsula shows its class by going for the 'less is more' approach. The restrained colonial-style elegance starts in the famous lofty-ceilinged lobby – open to all for a drink, breakfast or afternoon tea (to the accompaniment of live music). The 300 bedrooms are all spacious, decorated in soothing East-meets-West style and kitted out with the latest technology (including fax machine with personal numbers, laser disc/CD player, mood lighting, current temperature and humidity level displays, hands-free phones with two lines and ISDN lines). The marble bathrooms all have two sinks, big tubs, separate shower stalls and TVs. The suites are even more luxurious – many have stunning 180-degree-plus panoramic views. Hotel facilities are also first-rate – there's a small but well-equipped gym, a health spa and a lovely faux-Roman swimming pool with a bar and views out through floor-to-ceiling retractable windows towards Hong Kong Island. The eight restaurants and bars within the hotel are

all excellent, and include the classic French Gaddi's (*see p156*), Japanese Imasa, Cantonese Spring Moon (*see p155*), Swiss Chesa and the audacious Philippe Starck-designed Felix (*see p156*) at the top of the tower. Even if you can't afford to stay or eat here, you have to fork out for a drink at the characteristically bizarre bar at the latter. The impish design is impressive enough, but the views out across to Hong Kong island and over Kowloon are simply jaw-dropping. Add to this, service that is unsurpassed, a fleet of Rolls-Royce Silver Spur IIIs at guests' disposal and the unique Peninsula Academy programme offering insights into Chinese culture and cuisine, and you have a undisputed winner.

**Hotel services** *Air-conditioning. Bars. Beauty salon. Business services. Concierge. Gym. Laundry. Limousine service. No-smoking floors. Payphone. Restaurants. Swimming pool (indoor).* **Room services** *Dataport. Iron. Mini-bar. Room service (24hrs). Telephone. Turndown. TV: cable/pay movies/satellite.*

### The Regent

*18 Salisbury Road, Tsim Sha Tsui, Kowloon (2721 1211/fax 2739 4546/www.fourseasons.com). Tsim Sha Tsui MTR (exit E)/buses along Salisbury Road/Tsim Sha Tsui Star Ferry Pier.* **Rates** from HK$2,600 single/double; from HK$4,650 suite. **Credit** AmEx, DC, MC, V. **Map** p98 C3.

The Regent has a reputation for splendour – and parties. This was the setting for the most extravagant public parties held to celebrate the 1997 Handover and the Millennium, taking up several of the hotel's huge ballrooms. Its location on the waterfront guarantees fabulous views of Hong Kong Island from many rooms. While it falls short of the grace and charm of its nearby rival, the Peninsula (*see above*), the Regent has modern grandeur. Rooms

here are luxuriously comfortable and have plenty of space, enough room in fact for sunken Jacuzzis and steam-showers. The restaurants are good, but do not enjoy the same reputation as many of their five-star competitors. Even if you're not staying here, it's worth having a drink at the bar in order to enjoy the stunning views.
**Hotel services** *Air-conditioning. Babysitting. Bar. Beauty salon. Business services. Concierge. Disabled rooms. Garden. Gym. Laundry. Limousine service. No-smoking floors. Restaurants. Swimming pool (outdoor).* **Room services** *Dataport. Iron. Mini-bar. Room service (24hrs). Telephone. Turndown. TV: cable/pay movies/satellite.*

## Expensive

### Holiday Inn Golden Mile

*50 Nathan Road, Tsim Sha Tsui, Kowloon (2369 3111/fax 2369 8016/www.goldenmile.com). Tsim Sha Tsui MTR (exit C1, C2)/buses along Nathan Road.* **Rates** from HK$2,200 single; from HK$2,300 double; from HK$5,500 suite. **Credit** AmEx, DC, MC, V. **Map** p98 C2.
Nathan Road's 'Golden Mile' is the heart of Kowloon's shopping mecca, and no hotel is better placed to exploit it than the Holiday Inn. Its style is more upfront than grandiose, with a web of escalators and elevators taking you between its thriving bars and restaurants (which offer good value, if not outstanding quality). The location makes it more popular with tourists than the business suits who dominate many other hotels, giving it a more relaxed atmosphere. Rooms are not large, but are perfectly comfortable.
**Hotel services** *Air-conditioning. Babysitting. Bar. Beauty salon. Business services. Concierge. Disabled rooms. Garden. Gym. Laundry. Limousine service. No-smoking floors. Restaurants. Swimming pool (outdoor).* **Room services** *Dataport. Iron. Mini-bar. Room service (24hrs). Telephone. Turndown. TV: cable/pay movies/satellite.*

### Kowloon Shangri-La

*64 Mody Road, Tsim Sha Tsui East, Kowloon (2721 1111/fax 2723 8686/www.shangri-la.com). Tsim Sha Tsui MTR (exit C1)/203, 973 bus & buses along Chatham Road South & Salisbury Road.* **Rates** from HK$1,980 single; from HK$2,180 double; from HK$4,200 suite. **Credit** AmEx, DC, MC, V. **Map** p98 D2.
Its sister hotel on Hong Kong Island (see p40) may have all the finesse and get all the glory, but this older sibling is no slouch. While not as shiny and new, it still has the trademark Shangri-La luxury. The location is, perhaps, better for tourists who want to see some serious shopping action, and it's close to the Tsim Sha Tsui waterfront, which provides the best urban promenade in the city for viewing the island's skyline. The six restaurants here are excellent – the food is often as good as many more expensive establishments. The sizeable rooms offer everything in the way of comfort you would expect from a reputable upmarket chain hotel.

**The best** Hotels

### For affordable rooms in Central
The **Garden View International House** (see p43) is one of the few cheap places close to Hong Kong's business district.

### For location, location, location – at a bargain price
The **Salisbury YMCA** (see p49) is without compare in this price bracket – excellent rooms, facilities and service, and views to die for.

### For rose-tinted colonial grandeur
The **Peninsula** (see p46) has class oozing out of every pore, and some of the best restaurants in town.

### For hostelling with a view
The **Jockey Club Mount Davis Youth Hostel** (see p45), Hong Kong Island's only youth hostel, offers fabulous views over the harbour.

### For unabashed glitz
The **Grand Hyatt** (see p43) makes opulence an art form, and its rooms are feature- and technology-packed.

### For services beyond its price bracket
The **Kowloon Hotel** (see p48) is well connected on every level.

**Hotel services** *Air-conditioning. Babysitting. Bar. Beauty salon. Business services. Concierge. Disabled rooms. Garden. Gym. Laundry. Limousine service. No-smoking floors. Restaurants. Swimming pool (outdoor).* **Room services** *Dataport. Iron. Mini-bar. Room service (24hrs). Telephone. Turndown. TV: cable/pay movies/satellite.*

### Royal Garden Hong Kong

*69 Mody Road, Tsim Sha Tsui, Kowloon (2721 5215/fax 2369 9976/www.theroyalgardenhotel. com.hk). Tsim Sha Tsui MTR (exit C1)/203, 973 bus & buses along Chatham Road South & Salisbury Road.* **Rates** HK$2,100-$2,600 single; HK$2,250-$2,750 double; HK$3,850-$13,700 suite. **Credit** AmEx, DC, MC, V. **Map** p98 D2.
The garden atrium at the Royal Garden sums up the feel of the whole hotel – a green oasis in a concrete jungle. Trees, tropical plants and running water features create a tranquil oasis. The 422 spacious, comfortable rooms are built around the garden. Hotel facilities include a sky lounge and good dining options.

Hotel services *Air-conditioning. Babysitting. Bar. Beauty salon. Business services. Concierge. Disabled rooms. Garden. Gym. Laundry. Limousine service. No-smoking floors. Restaurants. Swimming pool (outdoor).* **Room services** *Dataport. Iron. Mini-bar. Room service (24hrs). Telephone. Turndown. TV: cable/pay movies/satellite.*

## Stanford Hillview

*13-17 Observatory Road, Tsim Sha Tsui, Kowloon (2722 7822/fax 2723 3718/ www.stanfordhillview.com). Tsim Sha Tsui MTR (exit B2)/shuttle bus from Kowloon Airport Express Station or buses along Nathan Road.* **Rates** *(including tax & service charge) from HK$1,450 single/double.* **Credit** *AmEx, DC, MC, V.* **Map** *p98 C1.*

There is little to mark the Stanford Hillview out from any other hotel. There's friendly service, reasonably comfortable rooms and standard facilities. If you are not familiar with Hong Kong, it is quite difficult to find, but once you get here, it's very convenient for the bars and restaurants in 'Kowloon's Lan Kwai Fong' – Knutsford Terrace. With only a coffee shop and a lounge in the hotel, these place prove an invaluable enhancement to your stay.

**Hotel services** *Air-conditioning. Babysitting. Business services. Laundry (self-service). Restaurant.* **Room services** *Dataport. Mini-bar. Telephone. TV: cable.*

# Moderate

## BP International House

*8 Austin Road, Tsim Sha Tsui, Kowloon (2376 1111/fax 2376 1333/www.megahotels.com.hk/hotel/ bp_int_house/con2.html). Jordan MTR (exit D)/ shuttle bus K5 from Kowloon Airport Express Station or bus A21 from the airport or buses along Austin Road.* **Rates** *(including breakfast) HK$990-$1,800 single/double.* **Credit** *AmEx, DC, MC, V.* **Map** *p110 A5.*

Despite its name, this hotel has nothing to do with the oil multinational. Located next to the Hong Kong Boy Scouts Headquarters, BP International House is ideally situated for shopping and dining. It lies between the consumer mecca of Tsim Sha Tsui, and Jordan, where numerous shops and restaurants are open at almost any hour of day or night. Rooms are not particularly spacious, but they are clean and satisfactory. If you're lucky, you might be able to get one overlooking Victoria Harbour. This is one of Hong Kong's better value hotels, given its location.

**Hotel services** *Air-conditioning. Babysitting. Bar. Business services. Disabled room. Gym. Laundry (self-service).* **Room services** *Mini-bar. Refrigerator. TV: satellite.*

## Imperial Hotel

*30-34 Nathan Road, Tsim Sha Tsui, Kowloon (2366 2201). Tsim Sha Tsui MTR (exit E)/A21 bus from the airport or buses along Nathan Road/Tsim Sha Tsui Ferry Pier.* **Rates** *HK$850 single; HK$950 double.* **Credit** *AmEx, MC, V.* **Map** *p98.*

The **Royal Garden Hong Kong**. *See p47.*

The Imperial is dwarfed by surrounding high-rises, which block the view from its rooms, which are tiny, but good enough for a short stay. It's a handy base for exploring Kowloon as its at the centre of the shopping and party action of Nathan Road. Noise levels rising after dark is the biggest worry for light sleepers, but those who want to have fun will be happy.

**Hotel services** *Air-conditioning.* **Room services** *TV: cable/Star.*

## Kowloon Hotel

*19 Nathan Road, Tsim Sha Tsui, Kowloon (2369 8698/fax 2739 9811/www.peninsula.com/ hotels/kowloon/kowloon.html). Tsim Sha Tsui MTR (exit E)/shuttle bus K3 from Kowloon Airport Express Station or buses along Nathan Road & Salisbury Road/Tsim Sha Tsui Star Ferry Pier.* **Rates** *(including tax & service charge) HK$1,100-$2,500 single/double.* **Credit** *AmEx, DC, MC, V.* **Map** *p98 B2.*

Tech-savvy or business travellers should make this a first choice. The Kowloon was the first hotel in Asia to install personal email and fax services for guests. Each room has its own computer, and when you check in you will be assigned an email address under the hotel's network; the same applies to the fax service. The 736 'streamlined' rooms (including 17 suites), however, are relatively small, although some offer a harbour view, and the location is great, with easy access to Tsim Sha Tsui's shops and waterfront. The Star Ferry pier is only a few minutes' walk away. Right next door is the exemplary Peninsula (*see p46*), and, as part of the same group as its big sister, staff at the Kowloon are trained to the same high standards.

**Hotel services** *Air-conditioning. Babysitting. Bar. Beauty salon. Business services. Concierge. Laundry. No-smoking rooms. Restaurants.* **Room services** *Dataport. Mini-bar. Telephone. TV: cable/pay movies/satellite.*

**48** Time Out Hong Kong Guide

## Nathan Hotel

*378 Nathan Road, Tsim Sha Tsui, Kowloon (2388 5141). Jordan MTR (exit B1)/A21 bus from the airport or buses along Nathan Road.* **Rates** HK$882 single; HK$995 double. **Credit** AmEx, DC, MC, V. **Map** p110 B5.

A cheapish alternative on the 'Golden Mile', the Nathan is a good place to crash out and use as an exploration base. Rooms are pretty small and dim, but there's a restaurant and an Internet service is available in the hotel's business centre. A short walk will take you to the nightspots of Tsim Sha Tsui or a number of tourist attractions.

**Hotel services** *Air-conditioning. Babysitting. Business centre. Laundry.* **Room services** *TV.*

## Park Hotel

*61-65 Chatham Road South, Tsim Sha Tsui (2366 1371/fax 2739 7259/www.parkhotel.com.hk). Tsim Sha Tsui MTR (exit B2)/shuttle bus K5 from Kowloon Airport Express Station or buses along Chatham Road South.* **Rates** HK$880-$1,580 double; HK$2,380 suite. **Credit** AmEx, DC, MC, V. **Map** p98 D1.

The rooms here may be spacious, but they don't really justify the prices, especially as the location is rather inconvenient compared to other hotels in the same district. The Park is not in the centre of Tsim Sha Tsui, but towards the grubbier east end, although it is handy for Granville Road, where lots of shops selling manufacturing surpluses (and copies) of designer clothes labels can be found. It's also near the Museum of Science (*see p106*) and the new Museum of History (*see p106*), but Tsim Sha Tsui MTR station is a ten-minute walk away. In terms of facilities, there is a mediocre bar, a restaurant and a coffee shop. The hotel even charges HK$50 per 15 minutes for Internet access. On the positive side, the service here is good.

**Hotel services** *Air-conditioning. Babysitting. Bar. Beauty salon. Business services. Concierge. Disabled rooms. Laundry (self-service). No-smoking rooms. Restaurant.* **Room services** *Mini-bar. TV: cable/pay movies/satellite.*

## Cheap

### Salisbury YMCA

*41 Salisbury Road, Tsim Sha Tsui, Kowloon (2369 2211/fax 2739 9315/www.ymcahk.org.hk). Tsim Sha Tsui MTR (exit E)/buses along Salisbury Road/Tsim Sha Tsui Ferry Pier.* **Rates** HK$675 single; HK$745-$940 double; HK$1,200-$1,400 suite. **Credit** AmEx, DC, MC, V. **Map** p98 B3.

What is probably the most expensive YMCA in the world just might also be the best value hotel in Hong Kong. Banish your preconceptions: there are dorm rooms here (and they're a tremendous bargain), but this is essentially a hotel, and a surprisingly slick one. The spotlessly clean rooms are kitted out in soothing neutral tones, with plenty of light wood and a good range of facilities (including free fruit and tea/coffee). It's definitely worth shelling out a little more for a Harbour View Room (and ask for

one on a high floor) – the panorama of the towers of Hong Kong Island and the Peak is one of the finest you'll get from a hotel room anywhere in the world (and it's exactly the same as that of the swanky Peninsula next door (*see p146*), but for a fraction of the cost). Add in an excellent range of hotel facilities, including a well-equipped gym (extra cost) and swimming pool, and it's no surprise that this is Hong Kong's least best-kept secret. The Hong Kong Cultural Centre, Star Ferry Terminal and the shops of Nathan Road are only a minute's walk away.

**Hotel services** *Air-conditioning. Babysitting. Concierge. Business services. Disabled facilities. Gym. Hair salon. Laundry (both hotel & self-service). No-smoking rooms. Restaurants. Swimming pool (indoor). Wellness Centre.* **Room services** *Dataport. Mini-bar. Room service. Tea/coffee. Telephone. TV: cable/satellite.*

## Guesthouses

Many visitors on serious budgets stay in guesthouses within immense mansion blocks, such as Chungking Mansions and Mirador Mansions. Below is a selection of the more salubrious options therein. *See p51* **Charlie Mansions?**

### Apollo Guest House

*Flat F3, 6/F, Mirador Mansions, 54-64 Nathan Road, Tsim Sha Tsui, Kowloon (2366 8588). Tsim Sha Tsui MTR (exit E)/buses along Nathan Road & Salisbury Road/Tsim Sha Tsui Star Ferry Pier.* **Rates** from HK$300 per person. **No credit cards**. **Map** p98 C2.

One of Mirador's better accommodation options. Rooms are not as small as in many other guesthouses, and are clean and relatively quiet.

### Chungking House

*Block A 4F & 5F, Chungking Mansions, 40 Nathan Road, Tsim Sha Tsui, Kowloon (2366 5362/fax 2721 3570). Tsim Sha Tsui MTR (exit E)/buses along Nathan Road/Tsim Sha Tsui Star Ferry Pier.* **Rates** HK$280-$380 single; HK$380-$400 double; HK$480-$500 triple. **No credit cards**. **Map** p98 C2.

With more than 100 rooms this is the biggest and probably best place to settle in at Chungking Mansions. Rooms are comfortable, reasonably spacious compared to many smaller hostelries and staff are trained and attentive. Try here first.

**Hotel services** *Coffee shop. Laundry. Smoke-free dining area. Tour Desk.*

### Delhi Guest House

*Block B, Flat B2, 5/F, Chungking Mansions, 36-44 Nathan Road, Tsim Sha Tsui, Kowloon (2723 6985). Tsim Sha Tsui MTR (exit E)/buses along Nathan Road & Salisbury Road/Tsim Sha Tsui Star Ferry Pier.* **Rates** from HK$300 single/double. **No credit cards**. **Map** p98 C2.

Typical of the dozens of small guesthouses within the labyrinth of Chungking Mansions, the Delhi has six small rooms, with sparse furnishings and no-frills decor. But it's clean enough, and cheap.

timeout.com

The World's Living Guide

# Charlie Mansions?

Nestling cheek-by-jowl with some of Tsim Sha Tsui's flashiest hotels are scores of guesthouses offering Hong Kong's most affordable accommodation. These places are cheap and extremely basic, so they're not for those seeking home comforts. But they are usually conveniently located, like Mirador Mansions and Chungking Mansions on Nathan Road, in the shadow of the posh Peninsula hotel. Others are dotted further along Nathan Road towards Yau Ma Tei and Jordan. If you're considering staying at one of these leviathans, the best thing to do is look at a few places, haggle over price (the longer you commit to staying the cheaper the daily rate will be) and have a look at the surrounding areas.

## Chungking Mansions

This rundown, ramshackle building is a rabbit warren of guesthouses, tiny shops and curry houses, but for all its faults, Chungking Mansions has its charm. It's a pot pourri of races, ages and characters and has been the backdrop for more stories within its walls than Irvine Welsh could imagine in a lifetime.

This is where most backpackers start out. The environment is filthy and there is a risk of crime. By its very nature, the transient population includes thieves, drug dealers and all manner of rogues. Always be alert to who is around you, and try to avoid dark corners when alone. Inside the guesthouses there are normally staff on duty, so it should be safe, but lock doors and never leave valuables in your rooms. It's still the cheapest and most down-to-earth way to get to know Hong Kong. For a handful of the better guesthouses within Chungking, *see p49*. *See also p101* **Fear and lodging in Kowloon**.

## Mirador Mansions

Mirador is Chungking's poorer relation in that it neither has the infamy or is anywhere near as celebrated for its faults as its next-door neighbour. But there are great similarities. Guesthouses here tend to be a little less shabby and the environment slightly less dingy. But don't expect a room with a view. For a few dollars more, you may feel slightly more comfortable. For a couple of decent places within Mirador, *see p49*.

---

### Holy Carpenter Guesthouse

*1 Dyer Avenue, Hung Hom, Kowloon (2362 0301/ fax 2362 2193). Buses along Hung Hom Road.*
**Rates** from HK$350 single/double. **No credit cards**.
Bigger and brighter than the guesthouses down the road at Chungking and Mirador, there are even conference facilities here (although not the plushest).

### New Chung King House

*Block A, Flat 5, 3/F, Chungking Mansions, 40 Nathan Road, Tsim Sha Tsui, Kowloon (2366 7468). Tsim Sha Tsui MTR (exit E)/buses along Nathan Road & Salisbury Road/Tsim Sha Tsui Star Ferry Pier.* **Rates** from HK$320 single/double. **No credit cards**. Map p98 C2.
Not a patch on the old Chung King House, but this place is brighter than most. It's small (nine rooms), though, and service is minimal.

### SA SA Guest House

*Flat A11, 9/F, Mirador Mansions, 54-64 Nathan Road, Tsim Sha Tsui, Kowloon (2739 6331/fax 2311 7057). Tsim Sha Tsui MTR (exit E)/buses along Nathan Road & Salisbury Road/Tsim Sha Tsui Star Ferry Pier.* **Rates** from HK$350 single/double. **No credit cards**. Map p98 C2.

As with most guesthouses, this is nothing more than a flat divided into small rooms, but it's comfortable and tidy enough for a short stay.

## Yau Ma Tei & Mong Kok

### Moderate

### Eaton Hotel

*380 Nathan Road, Yau Ma Tei (2782 1818/ www.eaton-hotel.com). Jordan MTR (exit A, B1)/A21 bus from the airport or buses along Nathan Road.* **Rates** (including tax and service charge) HK$900-$1,800 single/double. **Credit** AmEx, DC, MC, V. **Map** p110 B4.
No harbour views here, but the Eaton Hotel's staff offer such friendly and helpful service that a good stay is guaranteed. While the rooms are not particularly large, they do have all the necessities (as well as some impressive facilities, like broadband Internet access). Decoration is pragmatic but comfortable. The hotel is a fair distance from Tsim Sha Tsui, the main shopping area in Kowloon, but the MTR station is only a few minutes' walk away, and there's plenty of life in the area.

# Youth hostels

Hong Kong is far more than a concrete jungle. There are youth hostels located in beautiful countryside in the New Territories and on the islands. Many are in isolated areas, which make them great for exploring nature, but not so suitable for using as a base for seeing the city. Transport links to some hostels can be slow and infrequent; be sure to check when booking.

There are seven hostels in Hong Kong: four in the New Territories, two on Lantau and one on Hong Kong Island (see the relevant sections of this chapter for details).

Rates are usually HK$35 for a dormitory bed. Air-conditioning is available in some hostels (for an extra charge in most) from May to October. You'll need to be a YHA member to stay at a hostel; membership cards can be bought from YHA offices in your home country, the Hong Kong head office (*see below*) or any hostel. A e-mail booking form is available on the HKYHA website (*see below*). Reservations can also be made by fax or mail (note that phone reservations are only taken within ten days of the time of your intended stay).

## Hong Kong Youth Hostels Association

*Rm 225-226, Block 19, Shek Kip Mei Estate, Sham Shui Po, Kowloon (2788 1638/fax 2788 3105/www.yha.org.hk). Sham Shui Po MTR.* **Open** *9.30am-5.30pm Mon, Wed, Fri; 9.30am-7pm Tue, Thur, Sat; 9.30am-1pm Sun.*

**Hotel services** *Air-conditioning. Babysitting. Bar. Business services. Disabled rooms. Gym. Laundry. Limousine service. No-smoking rooms. Restaurants. Swimming pool (outdoor).* **Room services** *Dataport. Iron. Mini-bar. Telephone. TV: cable/satellite.*

## Cheap

### Anne Black Guest House (YWCA)

*5 Man Fuk Road, Mong Kok, Kowloon (2713 9211). Yau Ma Tei MTR, then taxi or 20-min walk/shuttle bus from airport.* **Rates** *(including tax and service charge) single/double HK$484.* **Credit** *AmEx, DC, MC, V.*

This is an ideal place to stay for those travelling on a budget who don't mind being a little out of the action. Rooms, although not luxuriously decorated, are tidy and have en-suite facilities. There is a

restaurant on the ground floor and many good and cheap local restaurants nearby. Shopping and dining is also available in Mong Kok and Ho Man Tin.
**Hotel services** *Air-conditioning. Restaurant.* **Room services** *Refrigerator. TV.*

### Booth Lodge

*11 Wing Sing Lane, Yau Ma Tei, Kowloon (2771 9266). Yau Ma Tei MTR (exit D), then 10-min walk/ A21 bus from the airport.* **Rates** *(including breakfast) HK$462 single/double.* **Credit** *AmEx, MC, V.*

The distinctive sloping front of Booth Lodge makes it a distinctive landmark in Yau Ma Tei. Run by the Salvation Army, it offers clean and tidy rooms for backpackers, most of them with en-suite bathroom, though its location is rather inconvenient. An advantage of its remoteness, however, is that it is isolated from the most crowded areas of Yau Ma Tei, so you can enjoy a good night's sleep without the worry of noise from traffic and karaoke clubs or the glare of neon signs. There are only 54 rooms, so it can get booked up quickly.
**Hotel services** *Air-conditioning. Laundry. Restaurant.* **Room services** *Telephone. TV: satellite.*

### Caritas Bianchi Lodge

*4 Cliff Road, Yau Ma Tei, Kowloon (2388 1111). Yau Ma Tei MTR (exit C)/A21 bus from the airport or buses along Nathan Road.* **Rates** *from HK$396 single/double/triple.* **Credit** *AmEx, MC, V.* **Map** *p110 B4.*

It's very basic, but then it's very cheap. Cleaner and in better condition than many of the other hostels in the area, this place is relatively safe, clean and accessible. Triple rooms are available for those traveling in groups or families. Perched on top of the Caritas Bianchi adult school facing Nathan Road, the lodge is convenient for shopping and is popular among young tourists and businessmen who often stay for one or two days on their way to mainland China.
**Hotel services** *Air-conditioning.* **Room services** *TV: Star.*

### New Kings Hotel

*473 Nathan Road, Yau Ma Tei, Kowloon (2780 1281). Yau Ma Tei MTR (exit C)/A21 bus from the airport or buses along Nathan Road.* **Rates** *HK$450 single; HK$493 double.* **Credit** *AmEx, MC, V.* **Map** *p110 A4.*

Situated on Nathan Road, New Kings Hotel is convenient for getting around Kowloon, but the immediate surroundings leave something to be desired. The area's noisy and crowded, and circling high rises block out any views. The rooms are tidy but small, while service is not bad for such a cheap place.
**Hotel services** *Air-conditioning.* **Room services** *TV: satellite.*

### YMCA International House

*23 Waterloo Road, Mong Kok, Kowloon (2771 9111). Yau Ma Tei MTR (exit D)/bus A21 from the airport/buses along Nathan Road.* **Rates** *HK$616 single; HK$748 double.* **Credit** *AmEx, DC, MC, V.* **Map** *p110 B3.*

This 391-room tower has all the amenities of a top hotel, but for a third the price. Besides a bar, coffee shop and banqueting facilities, it boasts tennis and squash courts, a health centre and sauna. The best feature is a swimming pool – a great attraction on a muggy summer's day. There's also a Western-style restaurant and a lounge to relax in. Rooms are decent-sized and each has simple and comfortable furnishings.

**Hotel services** *Air-conditioning. Bar. Gym. Laundry. Restaurant. Swimming pool (outdoor).* **Room services** *TV: cable.*

# The New Territories

## Hostel

### Sze Lok Yuen Hostel

*Tai Mo Shan, Tsuen Wan, New Territories (2488 8188). Bus 51 from Tsuen Wan MTR (call for onward directions).* **Rates** HK$35 dorm bed; HK$16 tent pitch. **No credit cards.** **Map** p311.

Sze Lok Yuen is dedicated to hikers. It perches on the top of Tai Mo Shan (Hong Kong's tallest mountain) and the only way to get there is on foot. There is no air-conditioning, and not even an electric fan, which means summer nights would be close to unbearable.

## Hostels

### Bradbury Hall Hostel

*Chek Keng, Sai Kung, New Territories (2328 2458). Minibus from Choi Hung MTR (call for onward directions).* **Rates** HK$35 dorm bed; HK$16 tent pitch. **No credit cards.** **Map** p311.

This 100-bed hostel mainly takes in hikers in mid hike; thus, the facilities and decoration are rather basic. It does, however, have a nice view of the neighbouring hillside.

### Bradbury Lodge

*Tai Mei Tuk, New Territories (2662 5123). Bus 75 going from Tai Po Market KCR.* **Rates** HK$45 dorm bed; HK$200 2-bed room; HK$260 4-bed room. **No credit cards.** **Map** p311.

The facilities of 94-bed Bradbury Lodge are better than other hostels. Staying here gives you a feeling of being on holiday, not just having a brief stop on your hiking route. It is near the waterfront and has a watersports centre nearby for windsurfing, kayaking, etc. Air-conditioning is included in the cost of the two- and four-bed rooms, but costs HK$10 per night in the dorms.

### Pak Sha O Hostel

*Pak Sha O, Hoi Ha Road, New Territories (2328 2327). Bus 92 from Choi Hung MTR to Sai Kung (call for onward directions).* **Rates** HK$35 dorm bed; HK$16 tent pitch. **No credit cards.** **Map** p311.

This hard-to-reach 112-bed hostel is located in the heart of a country park. Outside the dormitory there is a huge barbeque area and a basketball court. Views are spectacular. Camping permitted

# The Outlying Islands

## Cheap

### Cheung Chau Warwick

*East Bay, Cheung Chau (2981 0081). Cheung Chau Ferry Pier, then 15-min walk.* **Rates** from HK$680 single/double. **Credit** AmEx, MC, V. **Map** p126.

A hotel close to the beach and with a sea view for under HK$1,000 is hard to find, which is why it takes a 40-minute ferry ride to get to this one on Cheung Chau. It's a busy island, packed with weekenders throughout the summer, but if you do not need to be at the centre of it all, offers a solid getaway. It's a bit dilapidated, looks a horrible concrete mess from the outside, and furnishings are on the budget side, but check the view. Although the building is quite old, the rooms are tidy and clean. There are two restaurants and a bar in the hotel, but it's best to visit the many seafood restaurants located on the island.

**Hotel services** *Air-conditioning.* **Room services** *Laundry. Mini-bar. TV: Star.*

## Hostels

### Jockey Club Mong Tung Wan Hostel

*Mong Tung Wan, Lantau (2984 1389). Taxi from Mui Wo Ferry Pier or sampan to Mong Tung Wan jetty.* **Rates** HK$35 dorm bed; HK$16 tent pitch. **No credit cards.** **Map** p126.

This 88-bed hostel lies close to the beach of Mong Tung Wan, but is difficult to reach by public transport. There is a good sea view from the hostel and a communal kitchen. Camping permitted.

### SG Davis Hostel

*Ngong Ping, Lantau (2985 5610). Bus 23 from Tung Chung or bus 2 from Mui Wo ferry pier.* **Rates** HK$35 dorm bed; HK$16 tent pitch. **No credit cards.** **Map** p126.

SG Davis is near to Lantau's Big Buddha (*see p132*), high in Lantau's beautiful mountains, and the quaint Tai O fishing village is just about within walking distance. The hostel is rather small, with only 52 beds, but the decoration is homely and facilities of a high standard. You can also camp here.

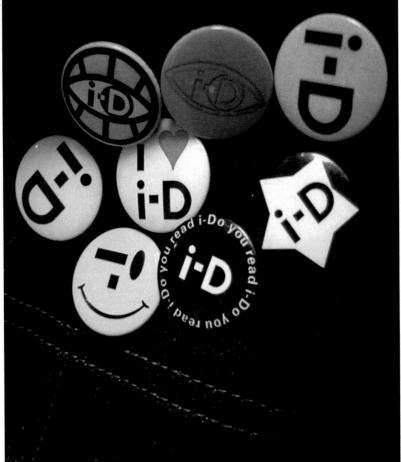

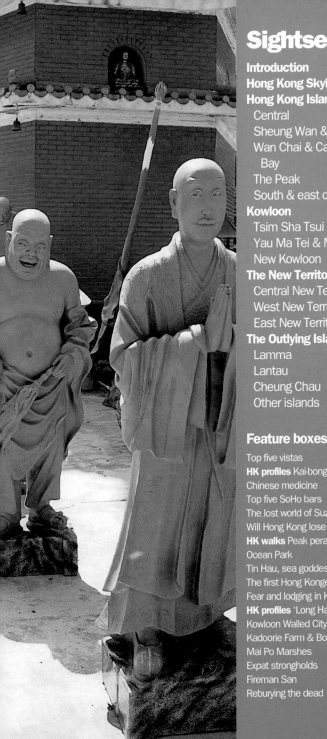

# Sightseeing

| | |
|---|---|
| **Introduction** | **56** |
| **Hong Kong Skyline** | **58** |
| **Hong Kong Island** | **63** |
| Central | 63 |
| Sheung Wan & Mid-Levels | 75 |
| Wan Chai & Causeway Bay | 81 |
| The Peak | 88 |
| South & east coast | 91 |
| **Kowloon** | **97** |
| Tsim Sha Tsui | 99 |
| Yau Ma Tei & Mong Kok | 108 |
| New Kowloon | 112 |
| **The New Territories** | **114** |
| Central New Territories | 114 |
| West New Territories | 120 |
| East New Territories | 123 |
| **The Outlying Islands** | **127** |
| Lamma | 127 |
| Lantau | 130 |
| Cheung Chau | 135 |
| Other islands | 137 |

## Feature boxes

| | |
|---|---|
| Top five vistas | 65 |
| **HK profiles** Kai-bong & Brenda | 70 |
| Chinese medicine | 76 |
| Top five SoHo bars | 79 |
| The lost world of Suzie Wong | 82 |
| Will Hong Kong lose its shirt? | 87 |
| **HK walks** Peak perambulations | 90 |
| Ocean Park | 92 |
| Tin Hau, sea goddess | 94 |
| The first Hong Kongers? | 96 |
| Fear and lodging in Kowloon | 101 |
| **HK profiles** 'Long Hair' | 105 |
| Kowloon Walled City | 113 |
| Kadoorie Farm & Botanic Garden | 119 |
| Mai Po Marshes | 121 |
| Expat strongholds | 124 |
| Fireman San | 128 |
| Reburying the dead | 136 |

# Introduction

Enjoy a unique collision of metropolitan excitement and rural relaxation.

Although on the surface much of Hong Kong may appear to be a homogeneous mass of skyscrapers, there are many distinct districts within the Special Administrative Region (as the former colony is now known), each with its own character and points of interest for visitors.

Depending on where you are staying, the first areas you are likely to explore are those that line Hong Kong harbour. **Central**, on the northern coast of **Hong Kong Island**, is a natural starting point, being home to the seat of government and the all-important financial district. Its highlights include glamorous shopping, some striking modern architecture, a lovely park and a thriving nightlife.

**Sheung Wan** may only be minutes to the west of Central, but it is worlds apart in terms of atmosphere. This is where you'll get a feel for an older, and distinctly more Chinese, Hong Kong. Antiques, Chinese medicine, dried food and funeral shops aren't found in these numbers anywhere else in the SAR.

To the east of Central, **Wan Chai** and **Causeway Bay** are primarily dedicated to nightlife and shopping, respectively. Heavily

built up, the urban crush is relieved by the large open space of Victoria Park and Happy Valley Racecourse, just to the south.

Towering above Central is the **Peak**, which, with its fantastic panoramas, should not be missed. Hong Kong Island's highest point is best reached via the Peak Tram. There are fine walks up here, too.

Most visitors also enjoy a trip to the comparatively rural parts in the the centre of the island and along the **south and east coast**. Here, you can hike, relax on a beach, potter around a market or have fun in a theme park.

Across the harbour from Central, **Kowloon** – particularly the district of **Tsim Sha Tsui** on the peninsula's tip – contains the greatest concentration of museums, as well as the Cultural Centre (the largest performing arts venue). It's also a great place from which to admire Hong Kong Island's stunning skyline (*see p58*). Shop-lined Nathan Road, forming the spine of Kowloon, starts here and extends north through the districts of **Yau Ma Tei** and **Mong Kok**, home to some of Hong Kong's most interesting specialist markets.

Once you've spent a couple of days exploring the more built-up areas of the city (which can be hard and unhealthy work due to the crowds and pollution), travel out into the **New Territories** to discover a side of Hong Kong that few visitors experience. There's a fair amount of unsightly industrial and urban sprawl in places (particularly in the west), but also some interesting museums, walled villages and ancestral halls, plus – and this is the biggest and most surprising attraction – great swathes of unspoiled countryside criss-crossed by hiking trails, and some wonderfully remote, pristine beaches (in the east, especially).

An alternative is to head for one (or more) of the **outlying islands**. Having chugged through the harbour on a ferry, you'll get a real sense of being well away from the city. Depending on your own interests, you can explore the peaceful monasteries of huge, hilly Lantau, the laid-back charm and seafood restaurants of Lamma or villagey Cheung Chau.

And if you have the time, a visit to the characterful former Portuguese colony of **Macau** or the dynamic city of **Guangzhou** is well worthwhile.

# Essential Hong Kong

## ... in 24 hours

● Take a tram to Western Market (*see p75*), mooch around Sheung Wan (*see p75*), then walk up to the many antiques shops on Upper Lascar Row (*see p76*) and along Hollywood Road.

● Head to Hong Kong Park (*see p72*) for an al fresco lunch.

● Take the Peak Tram (*see p89*) up to Victoria Peak.

● Stroll around Lugard and Harlech roads (*see p90*), and up to the Peak itself, taking in the stunning panoramas.

● Return to Central by the Peak Tram and walk down to the Star Ferry pier, crossing over to Tsim Sha Tsui to admire the Hong Kong Island skyline.

● Enjoy afternoon tea in the Peninsula hotel (*see p46*) or early evening drinks in the hotel's sky-high Felix bar and restaurant (*see p156*).

● Either ride the MTR to Temple Street Night Market (*see p108*) and chance your luck at a street-side *dai pai dong* food stall, or return via the Star Ferry for dinner in Lan Kwai Fong (*see p71*) or SoHo (*see p78*).

## ... in 48 hours

Day two:

● Spend the morning walking the Dragon's Back (*see p36*) or, if you are here with kids, at Ocean Park (*see p92*).

● If you do the walk, lunch in Shek O (*see p95*), then relax on the beach for a couple of hours; if you take the Ocean Park option, then, afterwards, catch the bus into Stanley to eat and peruse the market (*see p93*).

● Take the bus and MTR to Causeway Bay (*see p85*) for a bit of late afternoon shopping.

● End the day by exploring Wan Chai's nightlife (*see p171*) or, if the day and season are right, go to Happy Valley for a night at the races (*see p251*).

## ... in 72 hours

Day three:

● Rise early to practise *tai chi* on the Tsim Sha Tsui waterfront (*see p248*).

● Spend the morning visiting whichever museum in Tsim Sha Tsui is of interest, be it Science, Space, Art or History (*see p102 & p106*).

● Take the Star Ferry across Victoria harbour for an early dim sum lunch at City Hall (*see p142*).

● Walk to the nearby Outlying Islands Ferry Piers and catch a ferry to Yung Shue Wan on Lamma (*see p127*).

● Walk across the island to Sok Kwu Wan, stopping off at a beach along the way; eat an early seafood dinner and catch the ferry back to Central.

## ... in 96 hours

Day four:

● Early in the morning, take the KCR to Sha Tin and visit the Hong Kong Heritage Museum (*see p115*) and the Ten Thousand Buddhas Monastery (*see p114*).

● Grab a bite to eat in Sha Tin, before taking a taxi to the Sai Kung peninsula.

● Hire a sampan from Sai Kung's main ferry pier if you wish to spend the afternoon on a secluded beach (*see p123*) or, if you're feeling more energetic, hike through Sai Kung Country Park from Pak Tam Chung (*see p124*).

● Dine in one of the many good restaurants in Sai Kung (*see p163*), before heading back to the city.

## ... in 120 hours or more

● Venture further afield, with a day or two in the ex-Portuguese colony of Macau (*see p254*) or the city of Guangzhou (*see p267*).

Sightseeing

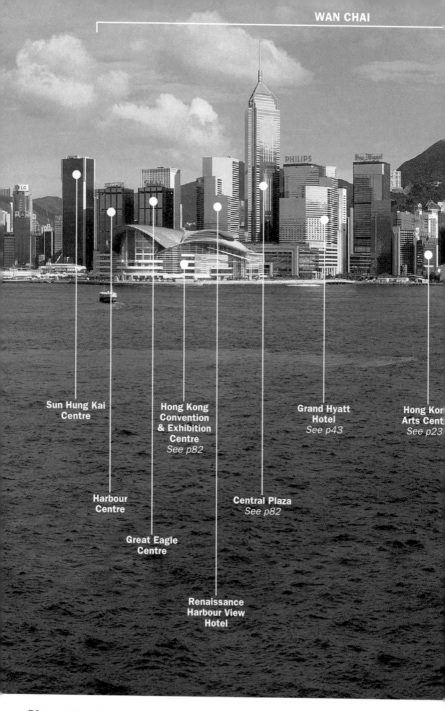

Sun Hung Kai
Centre

Hong Kong
Convention
& Exhibition
Centre
*See p82*

Grand Hyatt
Hotel
*See p43*

Hong Kong
Arts Centre
*See p23*

Harbour
Centre

Central Plaza
*See p82*

Great Eagle
Centre

Renaissance
Harbour View
Hotel

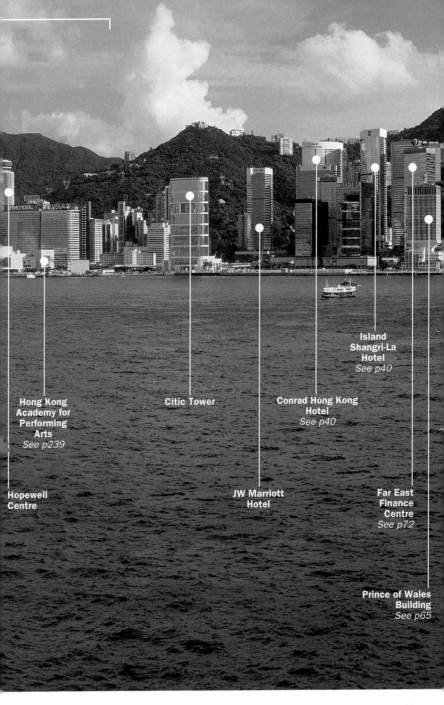

Hong Kong
Academy for
Performing
Arts
*See p239*

Citic Tower

Conrad Hong Kong
Hotel
*See p40*

Island
Shangri-La
Hotel
*See p40*

Hopewell
Centre

JW Marriott
Hotel

Far East
Finance
Centre
*See p72*

Prince of Wales
Building
*See p65*

Conrad
Hong Kong
Hotel
*See p40*

Ritz-
Carlton
Hotel
*See p43*

Hong
Kong
Club

Island
Shangri-La
Hotel
*See p40*

Hutchison
House

Cheung
Kong
Centre
*See p69*

Bank
of America
Tower

Furama
Hotel

HSBC
Building
*See p*

Far East
Finance
Centre
*See p72*

Bank of China
Tower
*See p69*

Hong
Kong
City Hall
(High Block)
*See p65*

Lippo Centre
*See p72*

Hong Kong
City Hall
(Low Block)
*See p65*

Prince of Wales
Building
*See p65*

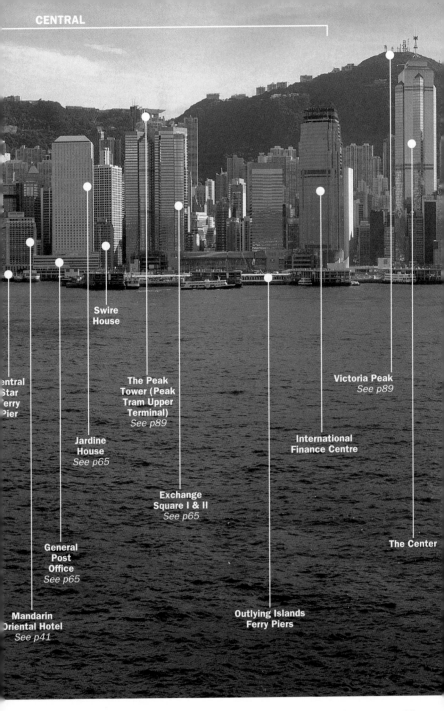

Swire
House

entral
Star
erry
Pier

The Peak
Tower (Peak
Tram Upper
Terminal)
*See p89*

Victoria Peak
*See p89*

Jardine
House
*See p65*

International
Finance Centre

Exchange
Square I & II
*See p65*

General
Post
Office
*See p65*

The Center

Mandarin
Oriental Hotel
*See p41*

Outlying Islands
Ferry Piers

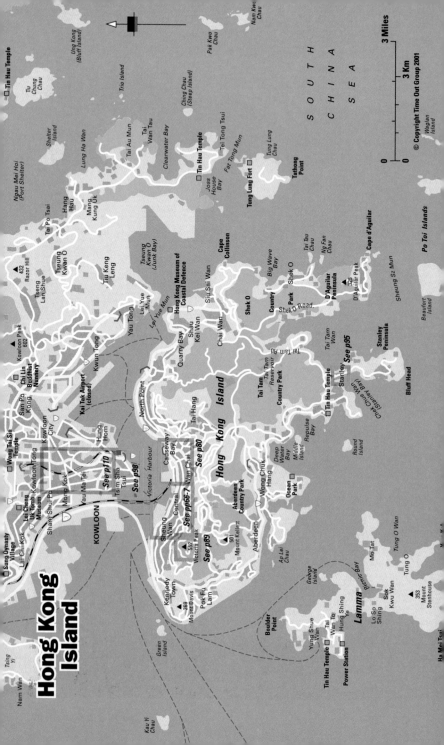

# Hong Kong Island

Shopping, eating and drinking in spades: just don't expect too many 'sights'.

It's a funny thing, given that the two districts are less than a couple of kilometres of water apart, but those who live on Hong Kong Island rarely visit Kowloon, and vice versa. Residents of the island, however, definitely consider themselves superior to their counterparts across the harbour.

A lot of this perceived superiority has to do with the fact that Victoria, the official capital, and all the associated kudos that goes with that, is on Hong Kong Island. But it is also because the smartest shopping centres, social clubs and residential areas are all on the island. In fact, most island residents wouldn't bat an eyelid if Kowloon suddenly disappeared in a puff of smoke – although they might worry about how they were going to get to the airport.

Hong Kong Island certainly has it all: plenty of business opportunities, shops galore, its fair share of sights, the SAR's only theme park, some good beaches, several country parks and a thriving nightlife to rival the best in the world.

**Connaught Road**: Central's own highway.

## Central

Vertiginous skyscrapers, impatient crowds, streaming traffic, disorientating tangles of raised pedestrian walkways: Hong Kong's political, financial and commercial centre is an undeniably exciting, if occasionally overwhelming, place. Squeezed into a narrow strip between harbour and hills, towards the western end of Hong Kong Island's north side, this is, and has always been, the territory's ground zero.

Today, **Central** is a temple to conspicuous consumption, and fashionistas will have no problem finding endless high-class malls in which to worship. Culturally speaking, pickings are far more meagre – compared with almost any other city of its size (certainly in the West), there are relatively few museums and galleries in Hong Kong. Constantly re-inventing itself, and without the slightest vestige of sentimentality (or sense of history, its critics would argue; *see p13* **History? What history?**), Central is the epitome of here-and-now Hong Kong – the few remnants of its colonial past that survive are little more than scraps, which inexorable development and land reclamation have left marooned among the towers of steel and glass.

Despite this, there is plenty to see in Central. Some of its most impressive modern buildings can be examined up close, Lan Kwai Fong (the main drinking, eating and partying enclave) is a lively lunch- and night-time destination, and there are a couple of green oases in which to recuperate.

### FIRST CONTACT

By far the most thrilling way to approach Central is to take the eight-minute **Star Ferry** ride across Victoria Harbour from Kowloon (costing a mere HK$2.20 for a seat on the first-class, upper deck). The tub-like, green-and-cream Star Ferries have been running this route since 1874, and it's no exaggeration to say (and it has been said many, many times before) that this is one of the world's greatest ferry journeys.

Comparisons with the Manhattan skyline aren't entirely fanciful, the north side of Hong Kong Island having the added element of a backing of deep green, thickly wooded hills, seemingly on the verge of barging the tightly huddled strip of towers into the harbour.

# TRATTORIA
## ★ RESTAURANT & BAR ★

Ground Floor, The Landmark, 15 Queen's Road Central
Tel: 2524 0111   Fax: 2524 0855

**BREAKFAST 7:30 - 10:30**
A choice of traditional hot dishes and pastries served in both of our Italian Cafes.

**LUNCH 11:30 - 2:30**
Reservations recommended
Daily Set Lunches at $180 for 2 courses and $220 for 3 courses plus our extensive a la carte menu with classic and modern dishes available.

**AFTERNOON TEA 2:30 - 6:00**
Tea Sets at $55.00 or $80.00 with a wide selection of home made desserts.

**HAPPY HOUR 5:00 - 8:00**
All drinks available at reduced Happy Hour prices.

**DINNER 6:00 - 11:00**
Set Dinners of 2 or 3 courses With or without wine from $195 to $295 plus our extensive a la carte menu.

It's the most astonishingly improbable view of the world's most astonishingly improbable city.

Although undeniably the most romantic approach to Central, the Star Ferry is just one spoke in the district's transport hub. The **Airport Express** train line terminates at **Hong Kong Station**, just west of the Central Star Ferry Pier. North of the station stand the piers from where ferries to the outlying islands leave. In addition, there's the busy **Central MTR** (metro) station, and almost every bus and tram along the north side of the island passes along one of the three parallel roads that define Central's lateral layout: Connaught Road/Harcourt Road, Des Voeux Road/Chater Road and Queen's Road/Queensway.

**ON THE WATERFRONT**
Central's most interesting 'sights' are architectural. The district has changed out of all recognition since the 1970s, and the profusion of modern towers that have sprung up in the last 20 or so years – some markedly more successful than others – define modern Hong Kong.

Just west of the Star Ferry Pier is the **General Post Office** and beyond that, accessible by elevated walkway, stands the **Exchange Square** complex (1985), where Hong Kong's Stock Exchange has operated since the merger of its previous four exchanges in 1986. Swiss architect Remo Riva's strategy of 'architecture as sculpture' only really works from a distance, which means that his building is best appreciated from mid harbour on the Star Ferry. Up close, the scale and layout of the three interlinked buildings is somewhat confusing and inhuman. More pleasing is its open piazza, with its fountains and Henry Moore's *Single Oval* sculpture, Dame Elizabeth Frink's bronzes and Taiwanese artist Zhu Ming's stylised human figure in *tai chi* pose. It's an agreeable spot to sit out with a snack or a drink (there are plenty of bars, cafés and restaurants nearby).

Just east of Exchange Square, opposite the General Post Office, stands **Jardine House** (1973), known locally as the 'House of a Thousand Arseholes' (partly due to its 1,700-plus porthole-style windows, partly as a comment on those who work behind them). This 52-storey structure, once the tallest building in Asia, is the HQ of **Jardine Matheson**, one of the major trading houses that virtually founded commerce in Hong Kong (*see p10*). Another Henry Moore piece, *Double Oval,* can be seen in a small outdoor area to the east of the building.

On a prime waterfront site east of the Star Ferry Pier stands the remarkably undistinguished low-rise **Hong Kong City Hall** (*see p239*). Its two blocks reflect the general disregard for aesthetics in much 1960s civic architecture, especially when you compare them with (a picture of) the original – a rather grand mid 19th-century French classical style incarnation. The Low Block contains a theatre and a concert hall, as well as an enclosed garden through which wedding parties regularly parade. The High Block, to the rear, houses a succession of libraries, a recital hall and various committee rooms. The Chinese restaurant on the second floor, with views out over Kowloon, is rightly famed for its dim sum (*see p142*).

Further to the east is the **Prince of Wales Building** (sometimes compared to an upturned gin bottle). Formerly known as HMS Tamar (after the frigate that was moored here and used as a floating naval base until it was scuttled in World War II), this former British naval HQ in Hong Kong is now occupied, in a low-key way, by the People's Liberation Army.

**BANKS AND GARDENS**
Crossing the car-streaming conduit of Connaught Road Central (by elevated walkway or subway), the old colonial heart of Hong Kong centres around the unremarkable **Statue Square**, which was once flanked by granite colonial buildings with columned verandas. At one time, the square was filled

**Top five** Vistas

**Bowen Road**
A favourite with joggers, this car-free road winds along the hillside above Wan Chai. See p249.

**The Peak**
Enjoy spectacular views over Central and across the harbour to Kowloon from the Peak Tower, the Peak itself, and along shady Harlech Road and Lugard Road. See p88.

**Bank of China Tower**
Take in Central from the viewing gallery on the 47th floor of Hong Kong's most spectacular modern building. See p69.

**Felix, The Peninsula**
Go to Philippe Starck's ultra-cool bar and restaurant in the evening and gape at Hong Kong Island ablaze with light. See p156.

**Star Ferry**
The quintessential Hong Kong experience – approach the stunning cityscape of the Island from the water.

*Sightseeing*

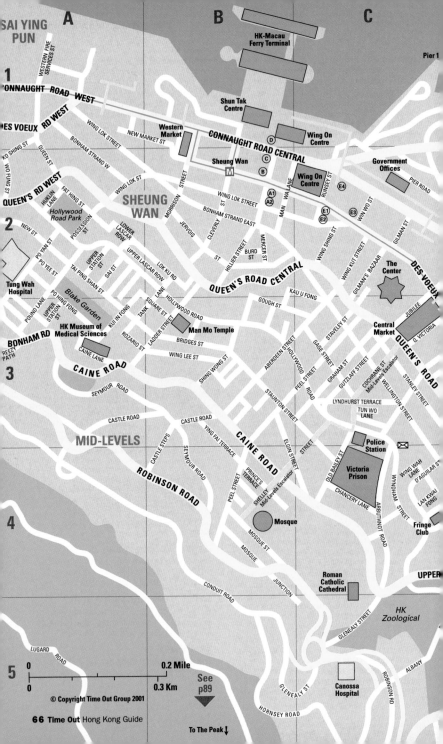

© Copyright Time Out Group 2001

# Central, Sheung Wan & Mid-Levels

See p98

Pier 2

Pier 3

Pier 4

To Tuen Mun (New Territories)

To Yung Shue Wan (Lamma)

To Tsuen Wan/Tsing Yi (New Territories)

Pier 5

To Sok Kwu Wan (Lamma)

Pier 6

To Cheung Chau

Pier 7

To Peng Chau

To Mui Wo (Lantau)

MAN KWONG STREET

MAN PO STREET

Bus Terminal

To Tsim Sha Tsui Star Ferry Pier

To Discovery Bay (Lantau)

Victoria Harbour

To Tsim Sha Tsui East

International Finance Centre

MAN CHEUNG ST

Hong Kong Airport Express Station

HARBOUR VIEW ST

CONNAUGHT ROAD CENTRAL

ROAD CENTRAL

STREET

POTTINGER STREET

YUEN ST W

LI YUEN ST E

Exchange Square

MAN YIU STREET

General Post Office

CONNAUGHT

Central Star Ferry Pier

Queen's Pier

EDINBURGH PLACE

LUNG WUI ROAD

CONNAUGHT PLACE

Jardine House

Bus Terminal

City Hall

Prince of Wales Building

See p80

DOUGLAS ST

Queen's Theatre

CHIU LUNG ST

THEATRE LANE

Swire House

STREET

Mandarin Oriental Hotel

CLUB ST

CONNAUGHT ROAD CENTRAL

TIM WA AVE

To Wan Chai & Causeway Bay

Central

Central Building

PEDDER

The Landmark

Prince's Building

HOUSE

CHATER ROAD

Leg. Co. Building

Statue Square

Furama Hotel

Ritz-Carlton Hotel

Bank of America Tower

LAMBETH WALK

ADMIRALTY

HARCOURT ROAD

CENTRAL

VAN SHAU LA ON LAN ST

ZETLAND ST

Henley House (Hanart TZ Gallery)

ICE

HSBC Building

JACKSON RD

BANK ST

Chater Garden

Former Bank of China

MURRAY RD

Far East Finance Centre

Admiralty Centre

New World Tower

DUDDELL ST

QUEEN'S ROAD CENTRAL

BATTERY PATH

Court of Final Appeal

Cheung Kong Centre

Lippo Centre

Admiralty

DRAKE STREET

Queensway Plaza

HKC Hospital

ICE HOUSE STREET

LOWER ALBERT ROAD

St John's Cathedral

Bank of China Tower

QUEENSWAY

Pacific Place

ALBERT ROAD

Li Hall

GARDEN ROAD

Asia Pacific Financial Tower

High Court

Island Shangri-La Hotel

JW Marriott Hotel

& Botanical Gardens

Former Government House

Lower Peak Tram Terminal

COTTON TREE DRIVE

ST JOSEPH'S PATH

Hong Kong Visual Arts Centre

GARDEN ROAD

Hong Kong Park

Edward Youde Aviary

Flagstaff House Museum of Tea Ware

KENNEDY ROAD

SUPREME COURT RD

Conrad Hong Kong Hotel

The **Bank of China Tower** (*see p69*)...

... the **Lippo Centre** (*see p72*)...

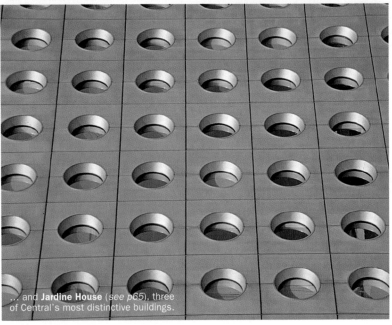

... and **Jardine House** (*see p65*), three of Central's most distinctive buildings.

with statues of English royals, but the occupying Japanese removed during World War II. Today, Statue Square has just one statue; appropriately, if somewhat blandly, that of the besuited former HSBC Chief Manager Sir Thomas Jackson. Its lack of artistic inspiration doesn't seem to bother the scores of Filipina maids, who gather here on Sundays (and in every open space between here and the Star Ferry) to enjoy their day off.

On the eastern edge of the square stands one of the few remaining colonial buildings, the neo-classical **Legislative Council Building**. It originally served as the Supreme Court and now houses the Hong Kong Legislative Council, making it the closest thing the SAR has to a parliamentary building. The eastern side of the Legislative Council Building faces **Chater Garden**, which was the site of the Hong Kong Cricket Club until the 1960s. A pleasant enough public park, it has been a popular gathering place for political activists and pressure groups.

Along Statue Square's southern side, Hong Kong's ancient, and unfeasibly narrow, trams have trundled for almost a century. With a HK$2 flat fare, these wood-panelled relics are a cheap and enjoyable way to travel along the northern side of the island.

Dominating the south side of Statue Square is Norman Foster's phenomenally expensive (HK$5.2 billion) **HSBC Building**. The world's most expensive building when it was completed in 1985, this financial cathedral of cross struts and glass rests on four tall pillars, creating a huge, airy atrium. It is worth taking the escalator up to the quietly business-like first floor for a sense of the scale of the place, and to feel for a moment like nothing more than one of the stick people in an architectural concept drawing.

According to those in the know, the building has some of the best *feng shui* in Hong Kong. Its unencumbered views of the harbour and the hills behind it are favourable, but – more significantly – it sits at the only local junction of five dragon lines (magnetic fields thought to follow the direction of underground water flows, which carry powerful channels of positive *chi*, or life-force energy). This energy is said to be sucked inside the huge atrium of the bank by the angled escalators and the undulating floor. The two huge lions guarding the entrance help block negative energy, and are also supposed to confer good luck on passers-by who rub their paws.

Corporate competition between the HSBC and the Bank of China extended to a *feng shui* war when the **Bank of China Tower** was built. Its knife-like structure and dominant position undid much of the HSBC's good *feng shui*, until local tycoon Li Ka-shing built the **Cheung Kong Centre** between them,

restoring much of the harmony and energy flow. The Bank of China Tower is also one of the buildings that encroached on the *feng shui* of the old Government House (no one believes accidentally) and was one of the reasons that the Chief Executive Tung Chee-hwa gave for preferring not to move into the traditional seat of power.

When the Bank of China outgrew its former home (a small but perfectly formed 1950s stone gem) alongside the HSBC Building, Chinese-American architectural superstar IM Pei was commissioned to build the new HQ. The result is Hong Kong's most striking modern building. Completed in 1990, its elegant, dynamic, asymmetrical geometry, resembling black, triangular building blocks, presents a fascinating aspect from every angle. It's well worth going up to the 47th floor viewing gallery.

### COLONIAL FRAGMENTS

South of the HSBC Building, up the hill, lie a few reminders of Hong Kong's dwindling colonial heritage. Climb the steps up to Battery Path and you'll come across the **Court of Final Appeal**, housed in the charming red-brick, green-shuttered, neo-classical **French Mission Building**, dating from the 1860s. French Catholic missionaries added a chapel to the original building. Ironically, the Court

**St John's Cathedral.** *See p71.*

# HK profiles Kai-bong & Brenda

The social scene in Hong Kong is an outrageously opulent whirl of billionaires, socialites, minor celebrities, power-brokers, starlets, hangers-on and desperate wannabes. It has enough gossip and flaky characters to keep a novelist like Jackie Collins wiping out forests for years. But, whatever the occasion, a party isn't really considered a party unless self-confessed 'draculas' **Kai-bong** and **Brenda Chau** turn out. And they normally do.

While it takes them hours to don their make-up and co-ordinate clothes (they usually wear matching outfits), the prince and princess of darkness usually manage to attend more than one bash a night. In the 1997 Handover days, when anyone who was anyone had to throw a party, they would attend at least six in the same evening. But they drink little and behave more as royalty on a meet-and-greet mission than true party animals.

Despite their social ubiquity, paparazzi bulbs flash wherever the couple go, reflecting not just their glamour, but also the fact that they're more than a tad eccentric. For a start, the couple know how to arrive in style... of a sort. Kai-bong and Brenda are hard to miss when their chauffeur-driven pink Rolls Royce pulls up, but you know that it's a really grand occasion if they show up in their gold Rolls; the humble beige-coloured Rolls is simply kept for dress-down days.

The Chaus' love, almost need, to be seen. From scores of interviews given to journalists and television crews around the world, it appears their raison d'être is simply that. By which standards, they are supremely successful. When talking about their life, they are always candid. 'We are draculas, we only go out after dark' is their most common refrain. It is true – you will rarely see them during the day. And, given the fact that many Chinese believe sun tans represent poverty, the pallid Chaus are truly the richest people on earth. The couple run a law firm, but work does tend to get in the way of the real business of socialising.

It is unlikely you will ever get an invite to their pad on Mount Davis Road, a wealthy residential area on the north-western tip of Hong Kong Island, but pictures of it abound. Palatial is not quite the right word – think

Barbara Cartland meets the last days of imperial Russia, as the couple's fetish for pink and gold runs riot. Beyond the gold front door lie lavish living and entertaining rooms. Dinner is eaten off a golden dinner service, with ornate golden cutlery. Lamps and ornaments are, of course, gold or jewel encrusted. And when it comes to using the toilet... yes, you've guessed it. The word ostentatious could have been coined for the Chaus.

Their philosophy of 'if you've got it, flaunt it' was a perfect metaphor for the excess of Hong Kong in the 1980s and 1990s. But, even after the Asian financial crash sobered a few minds and altered a few perceptions, the ethos lives on. However, the Chaus are far from resented and remain far more than objects of curiosity. The Hong Kong public regards them with considerable affection, and high society sees them as flag bearers. It's as if they are the Gene Kelly and Fred Astaire of the social scene. They may be ageing (they'd never tell you their exact age), but their style is timeless. When the time comes for the pink Rolls to be parked up for the last time, they could never be replaced. For, in essence, the Chaus are the spirit of Hong Kong's golden (and pink) era.

**Former Government House.**

of Final Appeal has recently let Beijing courts have the final say on certain controversial issues, such as the rights of abode for mainland immigrants.

Opposite the Court stands **St John's Cathedral** (*see p74*), completed in 1849, which is, in terms of size and grandeur, more akin to a sizeable English parish church than a cathedral. Its entrance doors are made from the wood of HMS Tamar, the British Navy's floating HQ that was scuttled during World War II to prevent the Japanese invaders using it.

Across Lower Albert Road and further up the hill stands **former Government House**, residence of Hong Kong's British governors (since 1855). Originally constructed in Georgian style, the building was rebuilt by the occupying Japanese. It was they who added its distinctive central tower and gave the exterior a more *shinto* look. The building (closed to the public) is still used for official functions. The pretty gardens are opened to the public once a year (call the HKTB for details). While it used to enjoy a prime location, with uninterrupted views of the harbour, the building is now hemmed in from all sides by corporate towers – neatly illustrating how quickly Hong Kong turns its back on its past.

Not far away, at the junction of Ice House Street and Lower Albert Road, stands the early 20th-century, brown-and-cream brick old **Dairy Farm Building**, which now houses the Fringe Club (*see p241*), a restaurant and the Foreign Correspondents' Club. Ice House Street gained its name from the ice storage facility that stood nearby in the days when ice was imported from North America.

### EATING, DRINKING AND SHOPPING
The portion of Central west of the Old Dairy Farm Building is largely devoted to restaurants, bars and shops. The best concentration of drinking and eating joints is on and around **Lan Kwai Fong**, off D'Aguilar Street. During the day, it's not much to look at, but after work hours, the neon shines brightly above a raucous

procession of diners, drinkers, demob-happy suits and pre-clubbers, particularly on Fridays. For a quintessential Hong Kong experience, be sure to grab a plastic stool, a bottle of Singha and a fine curry outside **Good Luck Thai Café** on Wing Wah Lane (*see p145*) and enjoy the street life. These days, however, the hipper and more discerning expats tend to favour the burgeoning drinking and dining scene of the area (west of here) informally known as SoHo, short for 'south of Hollywood Road' (*see p78*).

Close by, north of Queen's Road Central, stands one of Central's biggest up-market malls: **The Landmark**, containing most of the area's swankiest boutiques (with prices to match). If it's bargains you're after, head for Pedder Street and explore the unpromising-looking **Pedder Building**, which houses a series of small shops selling a mixture of genuine, cut-price and fake labels, beautiful embroidered shawls and a fair helping of tat. Most of it is womenswear, but there is one decent shop selling cut-price men's labels. Also on the first floor of the Pedder Building, looking down on the throng of Pedder Street, is the China Tee Club, a cool, quiet restaurant and café with a faux colonial air, thanks to the old ceiling fans, dark wood furniture and trilling song birds in antique cages.

Neon nights in **Lan Kwai Fong**.

On the ground floor is **Shanghai Tang** (*see p189*), a stylishly retro and tongue-in-cheek kitsch boutique, selling some beautiful fabrics, Chinese style clothes (such as *cheongsams* and silk pyjamas), ornaments and chic, fun gifts (like embroidered silk jewellery boxes and Chairman Mao watches). It's not cheap, though.

Running between Des Voeux Road Central and Queen's Road Central, a few minutes' walk north-west, are Li Yuen Street East and Li Yuen Street West (known as 'The Lanes'), which are crowded with cheap clothing, beads, handbag stalls and shoppers. It's a place to come as much for the spectacle as for the bargain hunting. Similar fare is also on offer in nearby Pottinger Street. A little further beyond, at the foot of the Mid-Levels Escalator (*see p76*) stands **Central Market**. For many years, this lively fruit and veg, meat and fish market has provided a lively contrast to Central's homogeneous shopping streets and malls, but it is presently under threat of redevelopment.

### SANCTUARY

When the maelstrom of Central gets too much, there are, unexpectedly, a couple of green havens in which to recuperate. The Victorian-style **Hong Kong Zoological & Botanical Gardens** (*see p74*) sit overlooking the former Government House across Upper Albert Road.

The **Zoological & Botanical Gardens**.

Featuring dozens of animal (mainly primate) and bird species, and more than 1,000 types of flora, the gardens are small but full of interest, as well as being peaceful and blissfully shaded (don't underestimate the importance of that on a sweltering summer day).

To the east of the gardens, beyond the Peak Tram Lower Terminal is **Hong Kong Park** (*see p74*). Spread across one square kilometre (0.38 square miles) of prime real estate, here is proof that Hong Kong doesn't *always* put money before everything else. Spectacularly bordered by some of Central's most striking towers, this unusual park contains landscaped gardens, an artificial lake (complete with multi-coloured fish and sunbathing terrapins), a children's playground, a *tai chi* garden, an amphitheatre, a restaurant and bar (Park Inn, great for al fresco imbibing; *see p170*), and the architecturally stunning **Edward Youde Aviary** (*see p74*). This elegant expanse of undulating mesh, stretched over a series of arches, manages to be both spectacular and discreet, and provides a perfect setting in which to wander along the raised wooden walkway, trying to spot the 150 species of South-East Asian birdlife therein.

Also in the park is the **Flagstaff House Museum of Tea Ware** (*see p74*), occupying an elegant colonial building constructed between 1844 and 1846, which, until 1978, served as official residence of the Commander of British Forces in Hong Kong. Now, it is devoted to telling the story of Chinese tea and tea ware.

One of Britain's most enduring legacies in Hong Kong would appear to be the traditional flouncy white wedding dress, judging by the remarkable number of identikit brides taking photo calls in the park most afternoons (the Register Office is within the park's boundaries).

If all this space and greenery proves overwhelming, shopping junkies can cross Supreme Court Road and duck into the immense **Pacific Place** (*see p182*), a colourless multi-floor mall. It's a dull place, even for shopping, but a food hall and restaurants provide plenty of decent eating and drinking choices, although most are on the pricey side.

This area, linking Central and Wan Chai, is known as **Admiralty**, thanks to its proximity to the former HMS Tamar naval base (*see p65*). Its most interesting buildings are the two glittering silver towers of the **Lippo Centre** (made all the more startling by their proximity to the golden **Far East Finance Centre**) overlooking Hong Kong Park. Designed by American architect Paul Rudolph in 1988, the Centre has something of an aura of bad luck, having seen three large corporate occupants go bankrupt, including the Australian entrepreneur Alan Bond, after whom the building was originally named.

**OSightseeing**

Four sides of
**Hong Kong Park.**
*See p72.*

An habitué of the **Edward Youde Aviary**.

### Edward Youde Aviary
*Hong Kong Park, Cotton Tree Drive, Central, HK Island (2521 5041). Admiralty MTR (exit B)/buses & trams along Queensway & buses along Cotton Tree Drive.* **Open** *9am-5pm daily.* **Admission** *free.* **Map** p67 E5.
The undoubted highlight of Hong Kong Park, the aviary's spectacular expanse of steel netting contains a swathe of woods and streams created to resemble rainforest. A long wooden aerial walkway snakes through the aviary, offering an excellent branch-high vantage point from which to spot some exotically coloured and flamboyantly named species, such as the bronzed tree pie, the chestnut-backed scimitar babbler and the greater racquet-tailed drongo. All the birds are indigenous to an evolutionarily distinct region known as Malesia, which stretches from the Malay Archipelago to Indonesia and New Guinea. You don't have to be an ornithologist or naturalist, though, to enjoy this terrific, well-designed haven.

### Flagstaff House Museum of Tea Ware
*Hong Kong Park, 10 Cotton Tree Drive, Central, HK Island (2869 0690/2869 6690). Admiralty MTR (exit B)/buses & trams along Queensway & buses along Cotton Tree Drive.* **Open** *10am-5pm daily.* **Admission** *free.* **Map** p67 F5.
This museum offers a fairly staid, unexciting display of tea ware and the different types of tea and tea preparation, but there are some beautiful and extra-

ordinarily well-crafted antique and modern pieces. A couple of dozen different teas are for sale in the museum shop – some are rare and expensive, costing as much as HK$480 for a small pack. There are also plenty of teapots for sale. The best reason to visit, though, is the building itself.

### Hong Kong Park
*19 Cotton Tree Drive, Central, HK Island (2521 5041). Admiralty MTR (exit B, C1)/buses & trams along Queensway & buses along Cotton Tree Drive.* **Open** *6.30am-11pm daily.* **Admission** *free.* **Map** p67 E5.
Opened in 1991, on the site of the old Victoria Barracks, this delightful, unusual park, dwarfed by surrounding corporate towers, centres around a large artificial lake, replete with multi-hued fish. Among its numerous attractions are a bar/café, a conservatory (open 9am-5pm daily), a *tai chi* garden, a children's playground and the impressive Edward Youde Aviary (*see above*).

### Hong Kong Zoological & Botanical Gardens
*Albany Road, Central, HK Island (no phone). Buses along Upper Albert Road.* **Open** *7am-7pm daily.* **Admission** *free.* **Map** p66 C5/p67 D5.
Founded in 1864, the western side of the gardens is where you'll find most of the animal enclosures. There's an impressive collection of primates, including macaques, tamarins and a family of bored looking orang-utans, including Datu, an immense, pot-bellied and impressively grumpy male. Other exotic residents are a tree kangaroo and a family of improbably cute ring-tailed lemurs. It's not a place for those who object to seeing caged animals as the enclosures are not huge, although most of the creatures look well enough (with the exception of a miserable jaguar). In the eastern half of the gardens, on the other side of Albany Road, there are several bird enclosures, housing the likes of American flamingos and a flock of vivid scarlet ibis. You'll also find a large fountain, lawns and well-tended flowerbeds.

### St John's Cathedral
*4-8 Garden Road, Central, HK Island (2523 4157/ www.stjohnscathedral.org.hk). Central MTR (exit K)/buses along Garden Road.* **Open** *8am-6pm daily.* **Admission** *free.* **Map** p67 E4.
This gleaming neo-gothic edifice, now marooned by ultra-modern towers, is one of the oldest Anglican churches in Asia (its foundation stone was laid in 1847 and it was completed in 1849 – and later extended in 1873). Within, it's pleasingly airy and light, but there is little evidence of its former parishioners – the memorial stones that marked the deaths of prominent expats and Chinese were removed during World War II by occupying Japanese forces (who used the church as a social club). One of the few memorials that remain is to the memory of Captain Thornton Bate RN, who died when British forces stormed Canton in 1857.

## Sheung Wan & Mid-Levels

Blending into Central on its western side, Sheung Wan (also known as Western) is the Chinese heart of old Hong Kong. It's a vibrant, colourful area that's best explored on foot. Although development has levelled many of the older, more ramshackle apartment blocks, there's still a distinctly old-fashioned, Chinese character to the area, and none of the bland mega-malls that dominate so much of the north side of the island.

As you climb the hill – or ride the world's longest escalator – you'll cross over Hollywood Road (the main centre for Hong Kong's antiques and curio trade, and the location of the atmospheric Man Mo Temple) and reach the trendy bar and restaurant enclave of SoHo, prior to the up-market residential district of Mid-Levels.

### Sheung Wan

The area around **Sheung Wan** MTR makes for some of the most colourful and interesting sightseeing in Hong Kong.

Many of the streets around here specialise in specific trades. For instance, head to Man Wa Lane for name chop stalls. Chops are usually made from pieces of wood, bamboo or bone, onto which Chinese names are carved. You can watch them being carved and have one made with a Chinese translation of your name for about HK$100.

Wing Lok Street, Queen's Road West and many of the neighbouring streets are filled with shops piled high with sacks of dried seafood and unidentifiable ingredients for Chinese medicine (*see p76* **Chinese medicine**). If you know what to look for, you can uncover entire desiccated deer foetuses, deer penises, dinosaur teeth (suspend that disbelief) and horse bezoars (hard balls of hair or vegetable fibre that collect in their stomachs; said to make an excellent antidote to poison).

This is also the centre of the uncontrolled shark fin trade, which is decimating shark numbers. Good shark's fin soup sells for about HK$300 a bowl, and the import trade was estimated to have been worth HK$2.5 billion in 2000. Several shops in the area also seem to base their businesses entirely on the sale of ginseng roots or swallows' nests, the latter gathered at great risk from the frighteningly high walls of Malay sea caves. Constructed entirely of swallows' spittle, they are used in a number of Chinese dishes, but most commonly for bird's nest soup, which is often served as a starter at formal dinners. (If you want to sample some, check out the snappily-named Golden

Sightseeing

Ship Swallow Nests and Sea Products Restaurant at 78 Bonham Strand East; 2541 5837 – a dish with an entire bird's nest will cost about HK$260.)

Another popular ingredient in both Chinese medicine and cuisine can be found sleeping in a rather dingy shop at 13 Hillier Street: snakes. Their blood, flesh and, particularly, their bile are favoured as a warming food, and are very popular during the winter months.

A good place to browse for tacky knick-knacks is the handsome Edwardian-style **Western Market**, just west of Sheung Wan MTR. It's a light, airy three-floor building, built in 1906 and renovated in the 1990s (after 80 or so years as a food market). On the ground floor are stalls selling jade trinkets, Hong Kong memorabilia, opium pipes, antique cameras and clocks. The second floor is dedicated to the sale of fabrics and the third floor is home to the Treasure Inn Restaurant, a popular lunch venue.

Continuing westward from Sheung Wan, the tram line terminates at **Kennedy Town** (named after 19th-century governor Sir Arthur Kennedy). Few visitors make it this far, as there is little to see other than an authentic working district of Hong Kong. **Mount Davis** rises 269 metres (883 feet) behind Kennedy Town, its summit crowned by the ruins of a 1910 fort.

## The Mid-Levels Escalator

In 1993, in a (not very successful) attempt to ease traffic congestion, a 792-metre (2,600-foot) long escalator opened between Central Market and the residential area of Mid-Levels. It is actually a series of 20 escalators and three travelators, with exits to all of the streets across which it cuts. It's a good way to reach the hip bars and restaurants of SoHo (**So**uth of **Ho**llywood Road; see p78). The Escalator heads downwards from 6am to 10.20am (taking commuters to work in Central), but then changes direction and remains running uphill until midnight.

## Hollywood Road & Tai Ping Shan

As the Escalator ascends, it crosses one of the area's defining arteries: **Hollywood Road**. Snaking around the contours of the Peak's lower slopes, this lengthy strand, along with many of its side streets, is almost entirely taken up by shops selling real and replica antique furniture, ornaments, statues, trinkets and curios. The posher stores tend to congregate at its eastern end, where you'll also find a couple of surviving colonial structures: **Hollywood Road Police Station** and the adjacent **Victoria Prison**.

Running parallel to Hollywood Road, but further west, is Upper Lascar Row, also known as Cat Street (from its once numerous brothels), which is a well-known hunting ground for cheap antiques, bric-a-brac and plain junk. Although its days as the place to find bargain antiques have long past, there is plenty to look at and you might even find something worth buying, such as jade, jewellery, old photos of Hong Kong and plenty of kitsch memorabilia, like Chairman Mao ashtrays, ornaments and badges. More antique shops can be found in the Cat Street Galleries on the north side of the road. (For more on antique shops, see p176.)

Close by, at the corner of Hollywood Road and Ladder Street, stands **Man Mo Temple** (see p79), one of the most atmospheric places on Hong Kong Island. Dating from the 1840s, and still a popular place of worship, its gloomy red and gold interior is dimly lit by red lanterns. Sandalwood smoke hangs thick in the air from

# Chinese medicine

Baffling though it might appear to outsiders, the philosophy and techniques of Chinese medicine have been built up over 4,000 years in China, Korea, Japan, Tibet and Vietnam, with roots in Buddhism, Confucianism and Taoism. Chinese medicine is practised throughout China alongside conventional medicine.

According to Chinese medical theory, each person has his own mix of the five elements: water, wood, fire, earth and metal. The other central tenet of Chinese medicine is the theory of *chi*, the body's energy, which has six main functions, including producing motion, transporting nutrients to the muscles and transforming foods and fluids. Illness disturbs the flow of energy and treatments are, therefore, designed to restore the body's balance. These include massage, acupuncture, acupressure, moxibustion (involving a cigar-shaped herb that is lit and held over specific parts of the patient to warm key energy points in the body) and cupping (similar to acupuncture, but involving small vacuum cups instead of needles).

If you fancy trying out the efficacy of Chinese medication, you could sample the general health tonic dispensed from a brass urn at the Good Spring Company on Cochrane Street, directly beneath the Mid-Levels Escalator. The herbalists here can also prescribe a more tailored health tonic, and most of the day an English-speaking herbalist is available for a consultation. He will ask a few questions, take your pulse, look at your tongue and pronounce how balanced your humours are and whether you have too much heat or cold in your constitution. According to the prognosis, he will prescribe a specially made tea that will probably taste as evil as it looks and smells, served with sweets to try to mask its bitter taste. The ingredients are usually herbs, but reading the labels on the items in the window will reveal some more unusual ingredients, such as deer's horn, monkey's visceral organs (for 'removing excessive sputum') and deer's tail (for 'strengthening sinews and treating the seminal emission').

**Man Mo Temple**. *See p76.*

the coils of incense suspended from the ceiling, the largest of which take a couple of weeks to burn through. To propitiate the spirits of the dead, locals burn paper offerings in two huge iron urns. There's quite a choice of spirit world combustibles available in specialist shops. The most popular are 'Bank of Hell' banknotes, but you can also send up in flames complete mini-sets of kitchenware, cars, and gold and silver ingots, as well as computers and portable compact disc players.

The temple became a cultural and political focal point for the Chinese community soon after it opened. Meetings were held, grievances aired and a customary tribunal established by and for Chinese residents. If you've seen the film of Richard Mason's Hong Kong novel *The World of Suzie Wong* (*see p82 & p216*), then this part of town may look familiar, as several scenes were filmed around here. Although visiting the temple is free, any donations made go towards local charities.

More temples can be found a little further west at the junction of Tai Ping Shan Street with Pound Lane (which lies just south of Hollywood Road). The district of **Tai Ping Shan** (meaning 'peaceful mountain') was one of the first areas to be settled by the Chinese after

the colony was founded. It was anything but peaceful, being notorious for its overcrowded housing and outbreaks of plague, and as an early haunt of the Hong Kong triad societies. Above street level, the temples are easily missed, resembling parts of homes rather than places of worship, an impression that persists until you see the incense sticks.

The **Kuan Yin Temple** is dedicated to the Buddhist goddess of mercy (very popular with prostitutes), while the **Sui Tsing Pak Temple** next door holds a statue of the god Sui Tsing Pak, known as the 'pacifying general' and revered for his ability to cure illnesses – the statue was brought here in 1894 during a particularly virulent outbreak of plague (*see p14* **Plague!**). One of the rooms is used by fortune tellers, and there are rows of *tai sui* – statues of the 60 different gods, each relating to a specific year in the 60-year cycle of the Chinese calendar. In times of strife, or to avert trouble, people make offerings to the god of their year of birth.

There are a number of shrines nearby, the most interesting of which is the **Pak Sing** ('hundred names') **Ancestral Hall**. Originally created in the mid 19th century, it was rebuilt in 1895, when all the buildings in the area were razed because of the plague. Used to store the bodies of those awaiting burial back in China, it still houses ancestral tablets (little wooden boards bearing the name and date of birth of dead people, and sometimes a photograph, too). Some of these tablets are hardly recognisable, they have been so completely blackened by years of incense and smoke. The incinerator in the courtyard behind the altar is for burning the usual paper offerings to the dead.

Nearby is the not particularly impressive **Hong Kong Museum of Medical Sciences** (*see below*), although the building itself is an attractive reminder of how the Mid-Levels looked before the tower blocks.

Across Hollywood Road from Pound Lane is Possession Street. It was here, above the one-time shoreline, that the British planted the Union Jack and officially took possession of Hong Kong Island in 1841. No memorial marks the occasion or the location. The distance from here to today's harbour-front illustrates the extent of land reclamation in Hong Kong.

At the far western end of Hollywood Road is **Hollywood Road Park**, a small but charming place with pagoda-style tiled walls and roofs, running water, goldfish ponds and plenty of shade under venerable old trees. Opposite are several coffin makers, with some huge and expensive looking caskets on display.

**Western Market.** See p75.

## SoHo

The Mid-Levels Escalator may have done little to decrease traffic congestion, but it has opened up a previously hard-to-access tangle of streets between Hollywood Road and the swanky Mid-Levels residential blocks. This area, informally known as **SoHo** (**So**uth of **Ho**llywood Road), has become the hippest place to hang out in Hong Kong over the past few years. On Staunton, Elgin, Shelley and surrounding streets, a cool bar or restaurant seems to be opening almost every week. Whereas once Hong Kong's main nightlife options were a cheap bowl of noodles, a pretentious Italian or French meal or a pie and a pint in a beery expat boozer, you can now eat and imbibe in fashionable bars and cosmopolitan eateries that wouldn't look out of place in London or New York. (For details of specific places, *see p142* and *p168*.) And – for the moment at least – SoHo is one of Hong Kong's most mixed and characterful areas, with traditional Chinese businesses operating beside DJ bars and cutting-edge restaurants.

A red sign on Staunton Street marks the former headquarters of Xing Zhong Hui (Revive China Society), the revolutionary organisation established by Dr Sun Yat-sen in 1895, and dedicated to overthrowing the Qing Dynasty in China. It marks the start of the **Sun Yat-sen Historial Trail**, an easy-to-follow walk around 13 sites related to the revolutionary's life, all in and around Hollywood Road, where he lived briefly during the 1890s.

Much further west, in Mid-Levels, is the entrance to the main campus of **Hong Kong University** (founded in 1912) on Bonham Road (Sun Yat-sen was a student of the college of medicine that preceded it). If you have any interest in Chinese art and archaeology, it's worth visiting the **University Museum & Art Gallery** (*see p79*) – its collection of antique bronzes, ceramics and paintings are exquisite.

### Hong Kong Museum of Medical Sciences

*2 Caine Lane, off Caine Road, Mid-Levels, HK Island (2549 5123). Bus 26/8, 22 minibus.* **Open** 10am-5pm Tue-Sat; 1-5pm Sun. **Admission** free. **Map** p66 A3. Located in the Old Bacteriological Institute (established in 1906; later known as the Pathological Institute), the three floors of this rather disappointing museum are taken up with desultory displays of old medical equipment, and some half-hearted information on health and the treatment of disease. A handful of exhibits make it worth a quick visit, though; most notably, the story of the 1894 outbreak and treatment of the bubonic plague in Hong Kong (*see p14* **Plague!**). Another potentially interesting section on Chinese medicine is, alas, only labelled in Chinese.

Sightseeing

**Staunton's** wine bar and café (*see p170*), in the heart of burgeoning SoHo.

## Man Mo Temple

*126 Hollywood Road, Central, HK Island
(2540 0350). Sheung Wan MTR (exit A2)/26 bus.*
**Open** 9am-6pm daily. **Admission** free;
donations appreciated. **Map** p66 B3.
This popular, atmospheric temple is dedicated to
Man, the god of literature and civil servants, and Mo,
the god of war. They are reputed to have been real
men, who were deified by later emperors. Cheung
Ah-tse (Man) was a celebrated administrator from
the third century, while Kwan Wan-chung (Mo) was
a successful military leader from the second century. The statues of Man and Mo sit at the far end of
the temple. Against the eastern wall rest the elaborately carved, gold-plated sedan chairs on which the
statues are taken out on processions.

## University Museum & Art Gallery

*University of Hong Kong, 94 Bonham Road, Pok Fu
Lam, HK Island (2975 5600/www.hku.hk/hkumag).
Bus 3B, 23, 40, 40M, 43, 103.* **Open** 9.30am-6pm
Mon-Sat; 1.30pm-5.30pm Sun. **Admission** free.
This collection of Chinese pottery, paintings and
artefacts spanning 5,000 years is small, but contains
some beautiful exhibits from the Han Dynasty,
including terracotta horses and blue and white Ming
porcelain. It also features the world's largest collection of bronze crosses belonging to the Christian
Nestorian church. The museum hosts art exhibitions, which change every couple of months.

**Top
five** SoHo bars

**Boca**
Tapas, both traditional and fusion, and
wonderful wines in a slick, modern setting.
*See p145.*

**Club Feather Boa**
Imbibe in style from ornate glasses in
an elegant, friendly ex-antiques shop.
*See p168.*

**Empire Bar**
A velvety womb of a bar, popular with
thirtysomethings. Hard to locate, but worth
the trouble. *See p169.*

**Liquid**
Ultra-cool lounge bar/night club with
different vibes on different floors.
*See p230.*

**phi-b**
Undoubtedly the smallest DJ bar in town,
and unquestionably one of the hippest.
*See p231.*

## Wan Chai & Causeway Bay

Wan Chai and Causeway Bay hug the northern edge of the island to the east of Central. Wan Chai's colourful 1950s and 1960s past, evoked in Richard Mason's novel *The World of Suzy Wong*, has faded as it has become more of an extension of Central (*see p82* **The lost world of Suzy Wong** *& p167* **Sex in the city**). The seedy streets of a once-considerable red light district have given way to new development.

Two of Wan Chai's least attractive aspects are its pollution and an almost total lack of open space. There are proposals to make more of the area's features, create some green spaces and al fresco dining and drinking areas, but the planners have their work cut out. For relief, though, a stiff climb up towards Wan Chai Gap up to traffic-free Bowen Road affords pleasant walking and some fine views out through the crowded towers and out over the harbour.

At first sight, Causeway Bay's huge – and numerous – department stores make it just another mercantile mecca. There are other points of interest, however. Victoria Park, Hong Kong's largest – and one of its best – public parks, lies at the far end of Causeway Bay. And there are a few relics from its colonial past, most notably the Noonday Gun, fired daily from the edge of the Typhoon Shelter.

South of these two districts, you'll find the island's celebrated horse racing track at Happy Valley, a terrifically atmospheric place during mid-week race nights.

## Wan Chai

East of Central, **Wan Chai** is easily accessible by foot, tram, bus, MTR or taxi. Wan Chai MTR is a good starting point for a tour on foot. Crudely speaking, Wan Chai can be divided into the area of land reclamation north of Hennessy Road, crowned by the massive and grandiose Convention & Exhibition Centre, and the warren of narrow streets of 'old' Wan Chai between Johnston Road and Queen's Road East, where you'll still find a few interesting nooks.

### NORTH OF HENNESSY ROAD

A walk along Lockhart Road, which runs east to west parallel to the waterfront, reveals the area's few remaining ties with *The World of Suzy Wong*. Along a 100-metre strip, you'll find a handful of sorry-looking topless bars rejoicing in classy names, such as Club Lady and Club Romance; this is where Mason's muses plied their trade. These seedy places are notorious for their extortionate, sometimes invisible, extra charges just for entering and ordering a drink, but then having a drink is not the point of going. A better place to sample some of the area's character without being ripped off is the Old China Hand, a rakish but friendly pub in the midst of all the seedier joints (though a refurbishment has left it far less dingy than previously; *see p167* **Sex in the city**). Local denizens, sometimes with working girls in tow, frequent the pub. Happy hour lasts all afternoon.

Sightseeing

The **Convention & Exhibition Centre** dominates the Wan Chai waterfront. *See p82.*

# The lost world of Suzie Wong

*'Suzie... that's a very pretty name...that's a scintillating sound... it buzzes... Suzie!'*
Michael Wilding meets Nancy Kwan in *The World of Suzie Wong* (1960).

Created in the imagination of British author Richard Mason more than four decades ago, Suzie Wong is a name that in Western minds still evokes wistful images of the exotic orient, and of the women who belong here. In her time she was one of very few fictional Asian characters to sympathetically capture the English-speaking imagination; today she is, sadly, little more than a byword for the Asian sex trade. Among the Chinese population in Hong Kong – a city that she helped to make a major tourist attraction – she is well-known, but by name, reputation and little else. The film is never shown on local television, and the book – a runaway bestseller in its day – is certainly not widely regarded as required reading.

Not surprisingly, the subject of a Chinese prostitute finding liberation in the arms of an English artist is not one widely appreciated by many in Hong Kong; and the book and film are often thought of as demeaning to the local population. The edge of this subjective point of view is, though, somewhat balanced by the fact that both were banned in apartheid-era South Africa for recognising and romanticising the possibilities of inter-racial harmony.

Arguably the classic Hong Kong novel, *The World of Suzie Wong* was published in 1957 and immediately became an international bestseller. (Despite the efforts of Paul Theroux, James Clavell and others, its vivid characters and engaging narrative still stand head and shoulders above anything else set in the territory.) Such was the book's popularity that in the following year it was transferred to the Broadway stage, and then to London's West End in 1959.

Loved by audiences but loathed by critics, the Broadway production, written by Paul Osborn and produced by Joshua Logan, opened at the Broadhurst Theatre in 1958. Nineteen-year-old newcomer France Nuyen, a striking, half-French, half-Vietnamese model from Marseilles played the role of Suzie, while the part of her lover, Robert Lomax, was played by a young William Shatner. (The two would star opposite each other again ten years later, with Nuyen playing the title role in the *Star Trek* episode, 'Elaan of Troysius'.)

In the West End, Shanghainese actress Tsai Chin, the first Chinese actress to study at RADA, played Suzie for two years at the Prince of Wales Theatre. More than three decades later, France Nuyen and Tsai Chin would act together for the first time: both played principal roles in *The Joy Luck Club* (1993) – a film that roundly dismisses the screen version of the Suzie Wong story as being 'racist'.

Suzie reached the climax of her whirlwind rise to fame in 1960 with the release of the Paramount film, also entitled *The World of Suzie Wong*. France Nuyen was originally slated to bring her role to the screen, and even came to Hong Kong with leading man William Holden to shoot the location scenes, but she was fired on her return to London. According to Holden's biographer, Bob Thomas, she put on so much weight while

A five-minute walk north of the MTR exit on Lockhart Road is **Central Plaza**, the tallest skyscraper in Hong Kong at the time of its construction in 1992 (374 metres/1,227 feet). Apart from its height, Central Plaza is undistinguished, but it does at least allow visitors to enjoy its views. Walk through the lofty, marble-clad lobby and take the escalator up to the lift lobby. The vantage point on the 46th floor has tall plate glass windows, offering spectacular views of the city's streets and harbour.

Facing Central Plaza across Harbour Road is the **Hong Kong Convention & Exhibition Centre** (*see p240*). Its new wing, which juts out into the harbour and marks the most northerly section of the extensive land reclamation in Wan Chai, is one of the city's most striking buildings. Costing HK$4.8 billion, the sweeping lines of the extension are intended to create the impression of a bird taking flight. This was the appropriately impressive venue for the 1997 Handover ceremony. Although most of the building is given up to exhibition space, it's definitely worth a wander round. Gaze at the harbour through high glass windows, sip coffee or eat at one of several cafés and restaurants, or surf the Internet for free at a couple of access points. Outside, there's a large promenade around the edge of the building and a sitting out area that's perfect for making the most of the breeze. There's also a black obelisk marking the Handover, which is inscribed with a rhetorical celebration of the SAR's return to Chinese rule.

four-time Oscar winner John Box went on to be David Lean's production designer for films such as *Lawrence of Arabia*, *Dr Zhivago* and *Passage to India*. Phyliss Dalton, who also dressed Peter O'Toole and Omar Shariff in *Lawrence of Arabia* and *Dr Zhivago*, designed the fabulous *cheongsams* worn by Suzie Wong and her giggling coterie. The remarkable portraits of Suzie and her child were painted by Liz Moore, who ten years later produced the sculptures and paintings for Stanley Kubrick's *A Clockwork Orange*.

Mason researched his material in 1955, at the old Luk Kwok hotel in Wan Chai (demolished in 1988; replaced with another of the same name). He tells his story with a sympathetic voice for his subject – essentially, the Chinese bargirls of the 1950s – and is surprisingly candid and informed in his views on prostitution and its subculture. The peripheral characters

pining for boyfriend Marlon Brando, who was playing the field in Hollywood, that she could no longer fit into her trademark *cheongsam*. (Holden gallantly insisted on giving Nuyen a part in his next film, *Satan Never Sleeps*.)

Instead the job was given to Nancy Kwan, a then unknown Hong Kong-born Eurasian who had trained with the Royal Ballet. Neither she nor Holden were very convincing in their roles, and the film, which does little justice to the book, is interesting today mainly for its location shots around Hong Kong. All the interiors, while quite realistic, were filmed at Elstree Studios in England.

Still, it remains an underrated film, and one with a strong crew pedigree. Art director and

are supposedly fictitious, but, like Suzie Wong, they seem rather too real to be products of pure imagination. But while Mason has some fun with the girls' characters and foibles, he never judges their profession or questions their integrity or reasons. For, as he points out, it was all just a matter of circumstance and ill-fortune – and a situation in which any young woman of the time might find herself:

'It would surprise the nice girls how easily they could get used to it if it came to the push; how soon they'd be chattering about positions and prices; how quickly they'd know a sailor who was out for a free fumble from a sailor good for a short-time. How quickly it became their world.'

The **Hong Kong Arts Centre** and the **Hong Kong Academy for Performing Arts** (for both, *see p239*) are both a couple of minutes' walk west of here. The Arts Centre on Harbour Road hosts regular exhibitions of art and photography (*see p221*), while *Artslink*, its monthly magazine, contains full listings for, and reviews of, the local arts scene. It also has a café.

## SOUTH OF HENNESSY ROAD

The narrow streets and older tenement buildings between Johnston Road and Queen's Road East offer a flavour of older Wan Chai. Wander along any one of these streets and you're sure to stumble across something a little out of the ordinary – be it a market stall, shop or small factory turning out anything from

metalwork and printed matter to furniture. Queen's Road East is the furniture centre of Hong Kong; a bevy of shops specialise in rattan, mahogany and dark, reddish rosewood.

The **Hung Shing Temple**, a small sooty shrine dating to the 1860s, stands at 129 Queen's Road East. It is dedicated to a government official from the Tang dynasty who became a patron saint of seafarers due to his excellent weather forecasting skills. It used to look out onto the sea, before land reclamation marooned it far inland.

The revolving restaurant on the top (and 62nd) floor of the tall, tubular **Hopewell Centre** on Queen's Road East makes a scenic lunch stop, with particularly good views over the harbour and east towards Happy Valley. Even if

Sightseeing

Street life in Wan Chai – by day...                 ... and night.

you don't want to eat, the ride up the glass
escalators on the outside of the building is a good
way to get a glimpse of the surrounding area.

Further east along Queen's Road East, under
a venerable old mango tree, is the **Old Wan
Chai Post Office**, built in 1912-13. This small,
one-storey building ceased service in 1992, and
now houses an Environmental Resources Centre.
It also marks the start of the steep 1.5-kilometre
(one-mile) Green Trail. The early stage consists
of a rather pitiful selection of plaques pointing
out unremarkable, but in Wan Chai rare, trees.
The second section is rather better as it winds
up Wan Chai Gap Road into the woods. It ends
close to Wan Chai Gap, near one of the entrances
to Aberdeen Country Park and the small **Police
Museum** (*see p87*) at Coombe Road. (For a walk
that takes in this area, *see p210*.)

Further along Queen's Road East, close to
Happy Valley and just past the entrance to the
Ruttonjee Hospital, is Wan Chai Park, a small,
unremarkable but precious speck of green space.

### BOWRINGTON ROAD MARKET

There are several dingy concrete buildings in
Hong Kong housing busy marketplaces, but the
one at Bowrington Road is a particularly fine
example. On the borders of Causeway Bay, by
the busy Canal Road flyover, it has separate
floors for fruit and veg, fish and meat. Walk
along the side streets nearby and you'll find
similar fare. The colourful produce, including
fresh steaming white bean curd being scooped
from old wooden tubs, makes for great photos.

There's also more gore here than in a
gladiatorial arena. All manner of seafood,

including writhing eels and fidgeting
crustaceans, is picked live from its tub and
dismembered before your eyes, while frogs and
turtles blink nonchalantly in baskets nearby.
Hanging from hooks overhead, meanwhile, is
every imaginable cut of cow and pig, including
whole heads, tails, lungs and brains.

For sensitive souls, it's probably not a good
idea to linger too long around the poultry stalls,
where live birds are dispatched with a casual
flick of a blade and stuffed still twitching into
a boiler after which they are tossed into a
plucking machine. Perhaps the most absorbing
and grisly sight, though, is the spectacle of live
fish being deftly sliced lengthways and expertly
gutted, while the exposed heart keeps beating.

## Causeway Bay

Across Canal Road, the huge **Times Square**
mall (*see p185*) marks the start of Hong
Kong's busiest shopping district. Packed with
boutiques of every description, you'll find it
has upmarket stores as well as less expensive
chains. There are also a number of department
stores, including the Japanese giant **Sogo** (*see
p183*) and the local **Wing On** (*see p185*) selling
everyday household goods.

East of Times Square, close to Causeway
Bay MTR station, there are two small streets,
Jardine's Bazaar and Jardine's Crescent, which
are crammed with market stalls selling food
and bargain-priced clothes.

From here, it's a couple of minutes' walk east
to sprawling **Victoria Park**, Hong Kong's
largest public park. Aside from plenty of open

The morning *tai chi* session in **Victoria Park**.

space, it contains a running track, a 50-metre (164-foot) swimming pool, basketball and tennis courts, and a model boating lake. This deservedly popular park is the venue for large gatherings, such as at Chinese New Year (*see p208*). Beyond the park, on Tin Hau Temple Road, is a small and fairly typical temple to Tin Hau, the goddess of the sea. As one of Hong Kong's most popular Taoist gods, there are at least 24 temples in the SAR dedicated to her (*see p94* **Tin Hau, sea goddess**).

A major road separates the northern side of Victoria Park from the **Causeway Bay Typhoon Shelter**. By the side of the shelter, roughly in front of the Excelsior Hotel, stands the **Noon Day Gun**, fired daily since the 1850s and celebrated in the song *Mad Dogs and Englishmen* by Noël Coward. A small plaque details the (apocryphal) story of the gun. According to legend, Jardine Matheson, one of the largest and oldest trading houses in Hong Kong, often fired the gun to salute the arrival of its senior managers in port, which so incensed a naval officer's sense of protocol that he ordered Jardine's to fire the gun daily as a punishment for its presumption.

The firing of the gun is now something of a charity fund-raising event, with Jardine's distributing the money that people pay to fire it to local charities. If no one has paid, then the brightly polished three pounder is fired with a terrific report by an elderly retainer in Jardine's livery. The small enclosure housing the gun is open for half an hour after noon. From Victoria Park, the gun is best reached via the walkway crossing Victoria Park Road, or from Causeway Bay via a badly signposted underpass, the entrance to which is in the multi-storey car park below the World Trade Centre Mall.

In the Typhoon Shelter, there are about a dozen tiny houseboats, which are essentially sampans converted into neatly kept floating residences, with flower boxes on their porches. On a promontory at the western end of the typhoon shelter stands the **Hong Kong Yacht Club**. Keen or aspiring sailors should leave their details on a notice-board outside the club's bar if they wish to join the crew of any yacht sailing out of Hong Kong. There's more chance of those with experience being signed on, but it's not unheard of for an inexperienced but willing deckhand to hitch a ride.

## Happy Valley

From Causeway Bay, one of Hong Kong's most venerated institutions, **Happy Valley Racecourse** (*see p251*; closed July/Aug), is just to the south. The easiest way to get to the racecourse is to hop on a tram to Happy Valley.

Although smaller than its sister site at Sha Tin (*see p207*), the Happy Valley Racecourse, in use since 1846, is the traditional home of horse racing in Hong Kong. An evening's racing here, with the stands packed out with more than 55,000 spectators, still offers one of the quintessential Hong Kong experiences.

Ironically named Happy Valley when still a mosquito and malaria-ridden marsh, the site was chosen because it was the only piece of flat ground on the island large enough for a race track. Wednesday evenings are the best time to visit the brightly floodlit track. With the lights of apartments twinkling in the high-rises beyond the track, the excitement is palpable. It seems that every second person is a chain smoker and, if you stand at the bottom of the huge racing stand, you will see, caught in the glare, a thick smoke plume rising from the cigarettes of thousands of nervous punters.

The small, well laid out **Hong Kong Racing Museum** (*see p87*), on the second floor of the stand, records the history of racing in Hong Kong. You can stop off for a bite to eat at the Moon Koon (2966 7111) next door, a reasonably priced Chinese restaurant with good food and terrific views onto the racetrack through the large plate glass windows.

# Will Hong Kong lose its shirt?

Horse racing is by far the most popular sport in Hong Kong. But for the local populace, gambling is the name of the game. It's not unheard of for the money in a single race to surpass the entire amount taken in a week's racing in the UK. The Jockey Club is the only body legally allowed to take bets in Hong Kong. It is a non-profit organisation that pays surplus earnings from racing and the lottery, which it also runs, to charity. A significant proportion of the takings also flows into government coffers (HK$11.9 billion in 2000). The club's betting turnover totalled HK$83.4 billion in 1999/2000. Of that money, 14 per cent went to the government in betting duty and profits tax (an incredible 5.3 per cent of the government's entire income), and two per cent to charities.

The Internet is casting a shadow over all this easy income, however. Offshore betting businesses are making a nonsense of the SAR's strict gambling laws and threaten to decimate the Jockey Club's turnover. The Jockey Club has been protesting in vain against the syndicates based in international tax havens, which offer discounted online

betting to race fans in Hong Kong. Despite the fact that legitimate and non-legitimate gambling is taking off at a breakneck pace in Asia, almost unbelievably at the start of 2001, Hong Kong residents were not allowed to bet on anything other than horse racing. Unsurprisingly, an estimated HK$40 billion will have been bet illegally in the territory in 2001. Despite the rapid growth of online gambling, the Hong Kong authorities and the Jockey Club have been slow to tackle the threats or embrace the opportunities offered by the Internet.

## Further east

Beyond Causeway Bay, the residential and commercial towers continue to stretch east through North Point and Quarry Bay to Shau Kei Wan, where one of Hong Kong's newest museums, the **Hong Kong Museum of Coastal Defence** (*see below*) is situated.

### Hong Kong Museum of Coastal Defence

*175 Tung Hei Road, Shau Kei Wan, HK Island (2569 1500/www.lcsd.gov.hk/CE/Museum/History/e-hkmocd/body.html). Shau Kei Wan MTR (exit B2)/84, 85 bus.* **Open** 10am-5pm Mon-Wed, Fri-Sun. **Admission** HK$10; HK$5 concessions. **No credit cards. Map** p62.
This HK$300 million branch of the Hong Kong Museum of History (*see p106*) opened in 2000 within the 100-year-old Lei Yue Mun Fort. The core of the museum is the Redoubt, featuring an exhibition on '600 Years of Hong Kong's Coastal Defence', which is supplemented by a range of artefacts and multimedia displays. Other historic military structures on the site, such as the gun batteries and the Brennan Torpedo, have been restored to form a Historical Trail. The museum is a 15-minute walk from Shau Kei Wan MTR; there's also a free shuttle bus to the museum from Heng Fa Chuen MTR at weekends.

### Hong Kong Racing Museum

*2/F, Happy Valley Stand, Happy Valley, HK Island (2966 8065/www.hkjockeyclub.com). Trams to Happy Valley.* **Open** 10am-5pm Tue-Sun. **Admission** free. **Map** p80 C3.
Hong Kong's racing history and Chinese depictions of the horse in art are the focus of this museum. Through eight galleries, it tells the story of racing in Hong Kong from the early days of Happy Valley in the 1840s, and of horse breeding and trading in China and Mongolia, where the most prized ponies were raised. The skeleton of Hong Kong's legendary champion racehorse Silver Lining is mounted in pride of place.

### Police Museum

*27 Coombe Road, Wan Chai Gap, HK Island (2849 7019). Bus 15, 15B.* **Open** 2-5pm Tue; 9am-5pm Wed-Sun. **Admission** free.
This smallish museum at the top of Wan Chai Gap Road is rather disappointing, but – as it's free – is worth dropping into if you are walking past, particularly if you have children in tow. The displays are all static, being encased in glass cabinets, and seemingly random; they certainly tell no coherent story of the Hong Kong Police. Unfortunately, a small, but potentially interesting, section containing ritual items from triad criminal societies is left entirely unexplained.

Sightseeing

## The Peak

Towering above the commercial heart of Hong
Kong Island, Victoria Peak – otherwise simply
known as the Peak – offers the most spectacular
views in Hong Kong. On a clear day (which
you can never take for granted), the 552-metre
(1,810-foot) summit overlooks not just the
improbable towers of the north side of
Hong Kong Island, but also Victoria Harbour,
Kowloon and the hills of the New Territories
beyond. To the south, the lush vegetation of
the south side of Hong Kong Island leads down
towards Lamma island (the chimneys of its
power station prominent); while to the west
lie the islands of Cheung Chau, Peng Chau
and massive Lantau. The vistas are just as
spectacular by night.

The Peak is also the starting point for
a number of fine walks, ranging from the
gentle to the arduous (*see p90* **HK Walks:
Peak Perambulations**).

Since the 1860s, those Hong Kong residents
with the means headed up to the Peak to escape
the heat and humidity of the city streets. Its
milder temperatures (an average 5°C lower
than at sea level) and extraordinary vantage
point have long made the Peak the most
sought after address in Hong Kong. Governor
Sir Richard MacDonnell built a summer
house here around 1868, when the trip from
Central, by horse, sedan chair or on foot, took
around an hour.

The commencement of the **Peak Tram**
(*see p90*) services in 1888 cut the arduous
journey down to just under ten minutes.
Remarkably, the Tram (actually a funicular
railway) has never suffered any fatal accidents
– its most serious setback occurred during a
severe typhoon in the 1960s, when much of
the track was washed away. The arrival of the
tram also opened the Peak up to substantial
development (it's as well to remember that
the Tram was designed as a commuter, not
a tourist, service). Today, it is among the

View from **the Peak** by day...

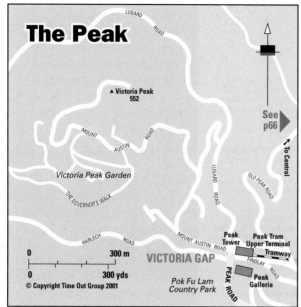

# The Peak

▲ Victoria Peak
552

See p66 ▶

Victoria Peak Garden

THE GOVERNOR'S WALK

HARLECH ROAD

0 _____ 300 m
0 _____ 300 yds
© Copyright Time Out Group 2001

VICTORIA GAP

MOUNT AUSTIN ROAD

Pok Fu Lam Country Park

Peak Tower

Peak Tram Upper Terminal

Tramway

FINDLAY ROAD

Peak Galleria

To Central

LUGARD ROAD

OLD PEAK ROAD

MOUNT AUSTIN ROAD

PEAK ROAD

*Sightseeing*

right-hand side going up for the best views.

The tram empties into Terry Farrell's **Peak Tower** (2849 7654), an ugly development of largely pointless shops and tourist attractions that opened in 1996. On its seven floors, you'll find restaurants, cafés, a motion simulator ride called the **Peak Explorer** (HK$35; HK$32 concessions), the **Rise of the Dragon** dark ride ('experience the sights, smells and sounds of old Hong Kong'), the local **Madame Tussaud's** and **Ripley's Believe It or Not! Odditorium** (for both, *see p90*). The viewing terrace on level five affords some excellent views (Hong Kong's fickle weather permitting), as does the outdoor seating at Eat Noodles on level two, which is also a good place to enjoy an inexpensive drink and some decent, cheap noodles.

Next to the Peak Tower is the **Peak Galleria**, another blight on the hillside, with mostly tacky tourist shops, more cafés, restaurants and a supermarket. For westward views towards the outlying islands, head across the road to the **Peak Café** (*see p149*), a comfortable, well-appointed but pricier place for refreshments (due to change ownership in June 2001).

most expensive places in the world to buy property, and many of Hong Kong's movers and shakers live here.

At their height in 1997, Hong Kong's property prices were briefly the highest (square foot for square foot) in the world. Houses on the Peak regularly went for more than HK$100 million, and their purchase was thought to have been a popular way for triads to launder large amounts of money. A subsequent property slump led to prices per square foot dropping by up to half, typically from about HK$20,000 to HK$10,000. Property has long been the base on which tycoons, triads and middle-class folk in Hong Kong have built their wealth and long-term prosperity. The severe drop of the market has, therefore, plunged many citizens into negative equity, a legacy which is likely to linger, and a major source of discontent in the territory.

## Victoria Gap

Bus number 15 and minibus number 1 run from the Central Star Ferry Pier up to the Peak, but the classic ascent is to take the Peak Tram from its Lower Terminal on Garden Road (reached by taking the number 15C shuttle bus from the ferry pier). Victoria Gap – not the Peak itself – is the final stop on the 373-metre (1,224-foot) gut-churningly steep (up to 27°) tram ride up from Mid-Levels – make sure you sit on the

## Victoria Peak

Surprisingly, the buildings at Victoria Gap offer no information about, or signposts to, the summit of Victoria Peak, although the tourist board does intend to rectify this in a proposed revamp of the area.

The Peak itself, immediately to the west of Victoria Gap, is a steep 15-minute walk up Mount Austin Road. For a gentler and longer stroll, head along Harlech Road (until its junction with Lugard Road on the south-west side of the Peak) and up the Governor's Walk, which threads a gently rising path up to the small, but well-tended **Victoria Peak Garden**. Located on the site of the old Governor's lodge, which was destroyed after

World War II, it offers viewing areas looking west, south and east. Disappointingly, the very summit of the Peak is occupied by telephone masts and surrounded by a large fenced-off area belonging to Cable & Wireless.

### Madame Tussaud's

*Level 2, Peak Tower, 128 Peak Road, The Peak, HK Island (Ticketek advance booking 31 288 288/ www.madame-tussauds.com). Peak Tram/15 bus or 1 minibus.* **Open** noon-8pm daily. **Admission** HK$75; HK$50 concessions. **Credit** AmEx, MC, V. **Map** p89.

Madame T's first venture into Asia opened in summer 2000, with more than 100 waxy celebs. The credulous can hang out with Sly, Arnie, Jacko and friends, or be snapped with local heroes Jackie Chan, Olympic gold-winning windsurfer Lee Lai-shan and (only in Hong Kong) top business supremo Li Ka-shing.

### Peak Tram

*Lower Terminal, Garden Road, Central, HK Island; Upper Terminal, Lugard Road, The Peak, HK Island (2849 7654/www.thepeak.com.hk). Bus 15C.* **Open** 7am-midnight daily (every 15 minutes). **Tickets** *single* HK$20, HK$6 concessions; *return* HK$30, HK$9 concessions. **Credit** (minimum HK$350) MC, V. **Map** p67 E5 & p69.

### Ripley's Believe It or Not! Odditorium

*Level 3, Peak Tower, 128 Peak Road, The Peak, HK Island (2849 0818/www.ripleys.com). Peak Tram/15 bus or 1 minibus.* **Open** 9am-10pm daily. **Admission** HK$65; HK$40 concessions. **Credit** (minimum HK$350) AmEx, DC, MC, V. **Map** p69.

This inexplicable freak show chain offers a haphazard collection of strange facts and anthropological bric-a-brac, some of it truly gruesome.

... and by night.

# HK walks Peak perambulations

One of the best ways to enjoy the Peak area is to meander along the paved, pushchair-friendly three-kilometre (two-mile) circular walk around the base of the Peak, along Lugard Road and back along Harlech Road. It's a pretty, tree-shaded route affording spectacular panoramic views of land and sea, and some tantalising glimpses of some of the Peak's most expensive properties. At night, it is fully lit, and the views are particularly impressive.

Another easy five-kilometre (three-mile) walk starts from outside the Peak Galleria and heads down Pok Fu Lam Reservoir Road, through the wooded **Pok Fu Lam Country Park**, to the reservoir and back. If you can't face the trudge back up the hill, you can always walk

down to Pok Fu Lam Road, from where there are plenty of buses back into Central.

More adventurous ramblers can also walk to Aberdeen, turning left halfway down Reservoir Road, and along the side of Mount Kellett. Victoria Gap is also the starting point for the 50-kilometre (31-mile) **Hong Kong Trail**, which passes through the island's four country parks, ending at Shek O.

A short circular tour of **Mount Gough**, along Findlay Road, east from the Peak Tower, will take you past some more of the area's swankiest properties and more superb views. Be aware, though, you'll have to walk along the road itself for much of its length, and some of the corners are very tight. Traffic will be busiest at the weekend.

## South & east coast

When the hustle and hassle of the north side of Hong Kong Island become too much, jump on a bus and head over to the more relaxed south and east coasts, where the pace of life is slower and a variety of man-made and natural attractions await.

Aberdeen is a vibrant commercial fishing town with a busy harbour. Close to it is Ocean Park, a sprawling, varied and spectacularly situated amusement park. Further south are the golden beaches of Repulse and Deep Water Bays and the pretty seaside town of Stanley. To really get away from it all, the sleepy village of Shek O at the far south-eastern end of the island offers a striking coastline and great beaches. And don't neglect the hilly interior of the island, which features great hiking and superb views (*see chapter* **Wild Hong Kong**).

### Aberdeen

Drab high-rise blocks edge **Aberdeen** harbour. Ignore the ugly town centre and head to the typhoon shelter, which is always jammed with dozens, if not hundreds, of fishing boats – most of them the old-fashioned, high-prowed wooden type. Tyre-festooned sampans dodge deftly among them and at the harbour edge small-scale shipyards refit ageing vessels. Towards the western end of the harbour is the large, and often frantically busy, wholesale fish and seafood market. During the day, it's crowded with merchants and restaurateurs buying all kinds of seafood and loading up their trucks.

Sampan tours of the harbour are available from pushy elderly women lying in wait for meandering tourists or from the Aberdeen Sampan Company, prominently signposted east of the wholesale market. HK$60 (less if there's more than one passenger – be prepared to haggle) will buy a 15-minute tour of the harbour. You won't get much out of your guide – unless you speak Cantonese – but she will point out the few remaining houseboats, which used to be a common sight here. Most of the older folk who once lived on their fishing boats have moved into the new developments around Aberdeen.

The ferry that constantly shuttles diners from the quayside to the three giant floating seafood restaurants moored out towards the southern end of the typhoon shelter will provide you with a slightly less extensive, but free, tour of the harbour. These floating restaurants are what put Aberdeen on the map for many tourists.

A sampan ride across **Aberdeen** harbour.

The most famous, and by far the most elaborate and garish, of them is the red and gold hulk of the **Jumbo Floating Restaurant**, resembling something between a technicolour pagoda and a Mississippi paddle steamer-turned-casino. There's a production line approach to business at the Jumbo, with the result that an estimated 30 million people have dined here since it opened in the 1970s. The impersonal approach extends to the assigning of tables (for which you are issued with a ticket at busy times), the service and the food itself, which does not have a particularly great reputation and is by no means cheap. None of this seems to deter diners – tourists and locals alike pack it out at weekends. The Jumbo also organises a number of tours that usually involve a cruise and meal – details are available at any HKTB centre.

If the Jumbo experience does not appeal, and time permits, you can always catch a ferry from Aberdeen to the much better seafood restaurants on Lamma island (*see p127*). Go either to Yung Shue Wan, the main settlement, or the quieter (and closer) Sok Kwu Wan on the east side of the island.

Incidentally, Aberdeen has no connection with the Scottish city of the same name. It's named after Lord Aberdeen – Secretary of State for the Colonies in the mid 19th-century.

Sightseeing

# Ocean Park

Sightseeing

Stretched over a peninsula close to Aberdeen, **Ocean Park** is Hong Kong's answer to Disneyland, at least until its own Disneyland opens on Lantau island in 2005. With plenty to do and see, families can probably fill most of a day at this enjoyable theme park.

Ocean Park is divided into seven sections. If you enter the park through the main entrance, you'll find yourself in the **Lowland Gardens**, which is home to the stars of Ocean Park – two pandas An An and Jia Jia. Other attractions include the Goldfish Pagoda, the Butterfly House, the Dinosaur Discovery Trail, the Meteor Attack simulator ride and Discovery of the Ancient World – a walk through extensive recreated 'ruins of an ancient civilization', complete with lifesize replicas of gorillas and other jungle dwellers.

Adjacent to the Lowland Gardens is **Kids' World**, packed with gentle child-centric rides, as well as Dolphin University, where you can learn more about everyone's favourite marine mammal, and about the five dolphins who have been born at the park.

The Lowland is linked to the Headland by a sedate cable car ride across a hillside that drops steeply to the shore a hundred or so feet below. The eerily quiet ride is an experience in itself, offering a terrific view over the South China Sea and across Deep Water Bay. The **Headland Rides** are relatively modest thrill-wise by modern standards, and include two reasonably scary rollercoasters.

Nearby are the more impressive draws of **Marine Land**. At the Ocean Theatre there are several shows a day featuring performing dolphins and sea lions – very entertaining if you don't have any moral objections. A recent addition is Pacific Pier, where visitors can watch dolphins and sea lions swimming underwater, and feed them, too. The sea theme continues in the rather disappointing Shark Aquarium and the excellent Atoll Reef, a huge, well stocked and well explained water tank that recreates the habitat of a coral lagoon and has underwater viewing points on four levels. The 4,000 fish here represent 400 different species and include an 80-year-old, two-metre (six-foot) long giant grouper.

Further around the headland is **Adventure Land**, where you'll find Ocean Park's best rides. The Mine Train rollercoaster is genuinely thrilling, while the Space Wheel and Raging River water ride offer slightly less stomach-churning pleasures. In 2001, the

Abyss Turbo Drop opened, promising visitors a freefall plunge of 60 metres (197 feet).

From here, Asia's 'second largest outdoor escalator' (225 metres/738 feet) takes you down to the aviaries of **Bird Paradise**, and the slightly tacky **Middle Kingdom**, a supposed recreation of historic China (due to be replaced by another attraction soon).

A water fun park, **Water World**, is located by the Lowland Gardens entrance to Ocean Park, but it was closed for refurbishment at the time of going to press, and no details about when it will re-open were available.

*Aberdeen, HK Island (2552 0291/ www.oceanpark.com.hk). Bus 6, 70, 75, 90, 97, 260 from Central.* **Open** 10am-6pm daily. **Admission** HK$150; $75 concessions; free under-3s. **Credit** AmEx, DC, MC, V. **Map** p62. In addition to the buses above, the Ocean Park CityBus runs from the Central Star Ferry Pier (10am-3pm daily, every 30 minutes) and Admiralty MTR (9am-3.30pm daily, every ten minutes). The fare includes round trip transportation and admission to the park, and costs HK$174 for adults and HK$87 for kids.

## Deep Water & Repulse Bays

Travelling east along the south coast from
Aberdeen towards Stanley takes you past
Ocean Park (*see p92*) and a number of decent
beaches. **Deep Water Bay** is a pretty spot
favoured by the wealthy – as the number of
plush houses in the area testify. The long
stretch of beach, lined by trees, has an almost
Riviera air. As with most major beaches in
Hong Kong, there are barbecue areas, but be
warned that on Sundays local Chinese, Filipina
and Indonesian domestic workers on their day
off are likely to have staked their claim to every
barbecue pit very early in the morning.

Just around a headland to the south, huge,
upmarket and expensive apartment blocks,
populated by well-paid executives, surround the
long, well-tended beach at **Repulse Bay**. The
beach is a popular destination in the summer
and gets very crowded. Above it, the Verandah
restaurant (*see p154*) is a lovely, if expensive,
place for a drink or afternoon tea. Behind the
Verandah, there's a supermarket, and a couple
of cafés.

At the southern end of the beach is the Hong
Kong Life Guards' Club, which resembles a
Chinese temple. Among the canoes and
lifesaving equipment, you'll find scores of
statues of gods, animals and fabulous beasts
dotted around its grounds. For example, there

are huge statues of Kwun Yam, the goddess of
mercy, and Tin Hau (*see p94* **Tin Hau, sea
goddess**), plus several bronze Buddhas, their
bald heads and ample bellies polished bright
by hundreds of human hands.

## Stanley

The pretty town and sandy beaches of
**Stanley** are a 25-minute bus ride from Central
(take bus 6, 6A, 6X or 260) or ten minutes by
minibus from Aberdeen. Stanley was one of
the early destinations for the first colonial
settlers and a Chinese settlement long before
that. Until relatively recently, it was a thriving
fishing village. Today, it feels more like an
English seaside town, complete with pubs.
Despite extensive development, Stanley still
retains considerable charm and it's possible
to spend a leisurely day wandering around
the town.

The extensive sprawl of **Stanley Market**'s
'stalls' (many of them now smart shops) is one
of the main reasons for Stanley's continued
popularity. There are perhaps a couple of
hundred outlets selling clothes, beachwear, silk,
accessories, jewellery, jade, trinkets, paintings,
DVDs and furniture, usually cheaper than in
central Hong Kong or Kowloon (though the
days of real bargains are long gone). The
market is open from 10am to 6.30pm daily.

**Sightseeing**

Incense coils inside **Stanley**'s **Tin Hau Temple**. *See p94.*

A pleasant promenade links the market area with the quiet seafront, populated by several restaurants serving Italian, Thai, Spanish, Vietnamese and Chinese food, as well as the friendly Smugglers Inn (*see p172*) on Stanley Main Road. This is also where you'll find the **Old Police Station**, a historical landmark and the oldest surviving police station in Hong Kong (built 1859), which has been converted into a restaurant. A new shopping development at the western end of the promenade has, by Hong Kong standards at least, been introduced with some sensitivity. Five storeys high, it is tucked unobtrusively away and includes a supermarket, car park and attractive square facing the sea, which is covered by a large canopy with seating for public events.

The large neo-classical building beside the square is **Murray House**. It contains some smart but reasonably-priced restaurants with views over the bay. The building originally stood in Central (at the spot now occupied by the Bank of China Tower) until 1982, when it was dismantled, the granite details numbered

and put into storage. It was only recently that it was reassembled here over a concrete shell; look closely and you'll see that some of the numbers labelling each block for the move are visible. One of the earliest colonial structures in Hong Kong, it dates to 1843, when it was used as quarters for British army officers.

Nearby is Stanley's **Tin Hau Temple**, which can trace its origins back to 1767, making it one of the oldest – and, inside at least, most evocative – temples on the island. Incense coils fill it with scented smoke, while the altar is populated by elaborate statuary, depicting Tin Hau (*see below* **Tin Hau, sea goddess**) and a bodyguard of grimacing warriors.

On the other side of town is **Stanley Cemetery**, a beautifully kept place in which you can trace the earliest colonial days through the gravestones of military personnel and their families. The toll taken by disease is shocking, particularly on young children and babies, but perhaps most moving is the profusion of stones marking the deaths of some 4,500 British and Commonwealth servicemen (buried

# Tin Hau, sea goddess

Tin Hau, the goddess of the sea, is one of the most popular deities in Hong Kong, which is not surprising, given the historical importance of fishing to local people. The SAR has at least 40 Tin Hau temples, all of them originally built on the waterfront, but most now far inland thanks to ongoing land reclamation.

The compassionate Taoist goddess Tin Hau was the saintly daughter of a tenth-century fisherman from Fukian province who was said to be able to forecast the weather, calm the waves and generally help fishermen to land a decent catch. However, she died at an early age trying to save the lives of her two brothers. Several years later, fishermen started claiming that her apparition had appeared to save them from death at sea. As a result, ships began carrying her image, and numerous shrines to Tin Hau were built along the South China coast. In the 12th century, she was canonised as a 'Saintly and Diligent Saviour', and in 1683, she

was promoted to the exulted rank of 'Queen of Heaven' ('Tin Hau' in Cantonese).

The festival held to celebrate the **birthday of Tin Hau** (*see also p204*) is usually held in late April or early May (the 23rd day of the 3rd lunar month). One of Hong Kong's most colourful festivals, events take place at all the Tin Hau temples scattered throughout Hong Kong, but the festival focuses on those in Joss House Bay and Yuen Long. The goddess herself is supposed to visit the temple at Joss House Bay during the festival, so around 20,000 people usually turn up to experience her presence. In tribute to Tin Hau, fishing boats are decorated with colourful flags, there are parades, opera performances and lion dances, and family shrines are carried to the shore to be blessed by Taoist priests. In addition, offerings in the form of different kinds of food, including pink dumplings, are made – particularly by fishermen – as a mark of respect.

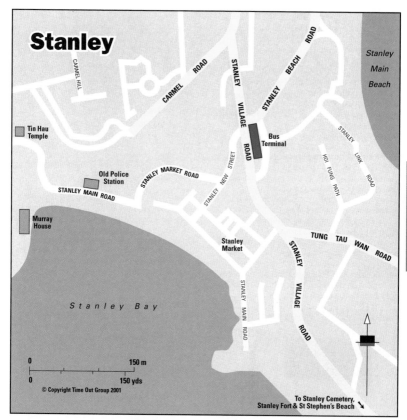

# Stanley

Tin Hau
Temple

Old Police
Station

STANLEY MAIN ROAD

STANLEY MARKET ROAD

Murray
House

CARMEL HILL

CARMEL ROAD

STANLEY VILLAGE ROAD

STANLEY BEACH ROAD

Stanley
Main
Beach

STANLEY NEW STREET

Bus
Terminal

HOI FUNG PATH

STANLEY LINK ROAD

Stanley
Market

TUNG TAU WAN ROAD

STANLEY VILLAGE ROAD

STANLEY MAIN ROAD

*S t a n l e y   B a y*

0           150 m

0           150 yds

© Copyright Time Out Group 2001

To Stanley Cemetery,
Stanley Fort & St Stephen's Beach

**Sightseeing**

according to contingent), who perished
during the fall of Hong Kong in 1941 and,
subsequently, while Japanese prisoners of
war. A memorial at the entrance details the
desperate defence of the New Territories and
the island by British-led forces, who finally
surrendered on Christmas Day 1941.

Below the cemetery is the relatively clean
**St Stephen's Beach**, with views towards
the town and across to Lamma island. South
of the beach lies Stanley Peninsula, which
is home to **Stanley Fort**, previously
occupied by the British Army and now a
sparsely populated outpost for the People's
Liberation Army. It is not accessible without
a permit.

On the other side of the peninsula, a short
distance from the bus terminus in the centre of
town is **Stanley Main Beach**, a good long
stretch of sand and the venue for the local
dragon boat race in June (*see p205*).

## Shek O

The tiny, sleepy village of **Shek O**, which
clusters on a small headland at the far south-
eastern corner of Hong Kong Island, has so far
escaped any unsightly development. This is
the place to go for a day of sea breezes, great
beaches and peace (especially on weekdays).
It's a thoroughly relaxing place with some
dramatic shoreline and great South China
Sea views.

Shek O is also one of the finishing points for
the Dragon's Back Trail (*see p36*) and the Hong
Kong Trail. It is most easily reached by taking
the number 9 bus, which runs every 15 minutes
from the bus terminus just outside Shau Kei
Wan MTR. At the end of the long, winding and
scenic route, the bus drops you in the centre
of the village. From the bus stop, turn right at
the mini roundabout for the main beach, an
immaculately kept stretch of golden sand with

changing facilities and lifeguards. It's also worth taking a walk to the small rocky islet at the tip of the headland (straight ahead across the roundabout from the bus stop). The five-minute walk will take you past Shek O's mix of small, pretty, weather-beaten dwellings and the larger mansions on the edges of the headland. On the shoreline, there's usually a strong, fresh breeze blowing and large waves crashing against the strikingly pitted and fissured rocks.

From the headland, there's a footbridge to a small island called **Tai Tau Chau**, from where there are great views across to the New Territories. Eating and drinking choices are limited in Shek O to the restaurants that circle the mini-roundabout. The largest is the Shek O Chinese & Thailand Seafood Restaurant, which offers average prices and quality but an extensive menu, including the theatrical 'Chicken on Fire', which is flambéed in brandy at your table. Close to the roundabout, tucked down a narrow alley off Headland Road, there is a small but immaculately kept and very pretty temple dedicated to Tin Hau (*see p94* **Tin Hau, sea goddess**). The flowers decked outside and the smiles on the faces of the statues make it one of the most cheerful on the island.

A warm day on **Shek O** beach. *See p95.*

# The first Hong Kongers?

The carving at Big Wave Bay, found by a policeman in 1970, is one of eight similar carvings that have been discovered on Hong Kong island and some of the outlying islands. Next to nothing is known of the people who made these carvings, except that they probably lived in the Bronze Age and depended on the sea for their livelihood. The geometric patterns of the carvings are certainly consistent with those seen on Bronze Age vessels found in southern and northern China. And the fact that most are sited on rocky outcrops overlooking bays suggests that the carvings may have been intended to propitiate the power of the sea and protect the communities who made them. The stylised semi-human or animal images may have represented tribal totems, gods or goddesses, and the ledges or platforms often found in front of the carvings may have been the sites of ritual gatherings or offerings. The carved designs were probably produced through laborious hammering using stone picks, which have been found in many archaeological sites in Hong Kong.

**Big Wave Bay**, a couple of kilometres to the north, has a good sandy beach set between ruggedly beautiful cliffs and rocks. It's almost the only place Hong Kong's small surfing community can go to catch a wave. It's an easy, but not particularly pleasant, walk from Shek O along the road to Big Wave Bay; there's no pavement so watch out for passing traffic. The road cuts through the golf course of the upmarket Shek O Country Club and passes several large mansions set in extensive grounds, homes to some of the Hong Kong elite.

If surfing is the idea, there are two hire shops by the beach, although they are closed at quiet times of year. Long and short boards can be hired for about HK$50 a day, plus a HK$100 deposit. At the far north-eastern end of the bay, close to the furthest lifeguard's station, is one of Hong Kong's ancient rock carvings (*see above* **The first Hong Kongers?**), thought to date back to the Bronze Age between 2,500 and 3,000BC. Faint geometric designs and stylised animal figures can just be made out on a small area of rock inside the small protective shelter.

# Kowloon

Though separated by only a short stretch of water, Central and Kowloon represent two very different sides to Hong Kong.

**Nathan Road –** spine of Kowloon.

The view of Hong Kong Island from the tip of the Kowloon peninsula is one of the most stirring sights in the territory. It is the source of dozens of guidebook covers, hundreds of postcards and millions of holiday photographs. But Kowloon offers much more than just a look back at Hong Kong Island. It may not carry the cachet and high sheen of Central, but when it comes to shopping and sightseeing, Kowloon is one of the area's top destinations. The 12-square kilometre (four-and-a-half-square mile) peninsula is tightly packed with shops, bars, hotels and housing in an untidy jumble of new skyscrapers and old low-rise tenements. Within this small space, there are half a dozen temples and museums, the Cultural Centre and, tucked away on its side streets, old Chinese neighbourhoods and busy street markets.

Exploring on foot is less of a hassle in Kowloon than it is in Central – although its streets are never-less-than busy, traffic and buildings do not encroach on pedestrian space as much as they do over the water, and virtually everything is accessible by foot. Public transport is convenient, as the MTR and numerous buses follow the line of Nathan Road, which forms the spine of Kowloon, from Tsim Sha Tsui through the districts of Yau Ma Tei and Mong Kok.

The name Kowloon comes from the Cantonese phrase *gau lung* or 'nine dragons'. Its derivation is one of the area's favourite legends. According to lore, Kowloon was named eight centuries ago when the boy emperor Ping, the last of the Song emperors, arrived in the area while fleeing from invading Mongols. It is said that he pointed to the eight hills above the peninsula and announced that eight dragons must dwell here – one for each hill. But he was swiftly reminded that, as emperors were also considered dragons, his own presence meant that there were nine dragons in the area. No giant lizards saved the little emperor, though, as he met his end nearby, throwing himself into the sea to escape the approaching Mongols. Today, the dragons of the Kowloon hills look down upon row after row of anonymous buildings.

When the British claimed Hong Kong Island in 1841, Kowloon was not part of the deal, but the colonists soon realised that its proximity represented a potential threat to the fledgling colony, and forced the Chinese to cede the peninsula to them in 1860. Around three kilometres (two miles) inland, Boundary Street, which runs west to east in a ruler-straight line, once defined the frontier between Hong Kong and China.

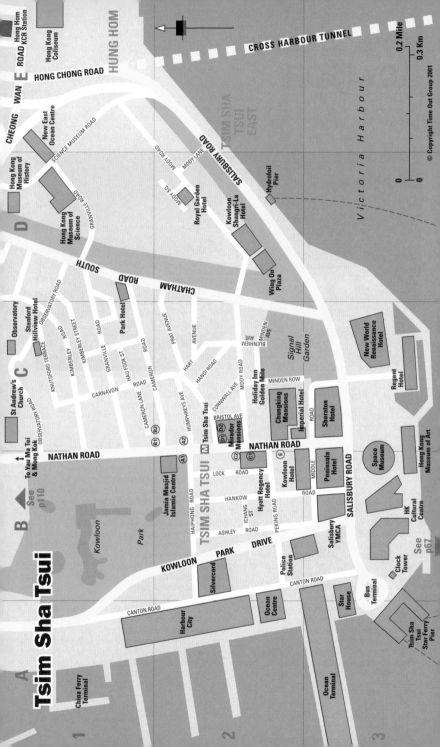

The **Peninsula** hotel (*see p103*) and the **Clock Tower** from the old railway station.

## Tsim Sha Tsui

**Tsim Sha Tsui**, the southern tip of Kowloon, is the grubbier cousin of Central, which it faces across the harbour. Its major thoroughfare, shop-lined **Nathan Road**, is a wide, straight highway that has attempted to adopt the nickname 'the Golden Mile'. (In truth, the epithet is overly flattering – shops here are far less glitzy as a rule than those of Central – and inaccurate – it's considerably longer than one mile). Hundreds of electronics stores, clothing shops, a handful of topless bars and, every few yards it seems, tailors touting their services, are found on Nathan Road and its bustling tributaries.

Tsim Sha Tsui isn't entirely devoted to commercial activities, however; it also contains most of Hong Kong's museums and its Cultural Centre. This area of the city is also a major tourist accommodation area, with hotels available from the cheapest dosshouse to the ritziest five-star.

When setting out to explore, a natural starting point is the **Tsim Sha Tsui Star Ferry Pier** – where ferries arrive from Central and Wan Chai. Within the Star Ferry Pier building, there is a **Hong Kong Tourism Board** office. Stop in here to pick up free maps, brochures, and information on tours and upcoming events.

Next to the Star Ferry Pier is the old **Clock Tower**. Overlooking the tip of the peninsula, the 44-metre (144-foot) tower is all that remains of the southern terminus of the Kowloon–Canton Railway (and of the Orient Express service from London), which stood here from 1915 until it was short-sightedly demolished in 1978.

Near the Star Ferry Pier are two shopping arcades. The nearer (and smaller) one, **Star House**, is known for its extensive offerings of Asian arts and crafts, and is home to a massive China Arts & Crafts (*see p196*), selling an impressive array of jewellery, ornaments, furniture, embroidered tablecloths, clothing and jade. The larger, and more up-market, **Harbour City** (incorporating Ocean Terminal and Ocean Centre; *see p181*) features an enormous number of shops, alongside a handy first-floor café with free Internet access.

From the pier, sweeping past the clock and beyond, there is a long waterfront promenade, offering fabulous views by day and night over the water towards Hong Kong Island. Such a prime site would seem made for outdoor cafés and waterfront bars – but there are none.

Hong Kong Island, as seen from the **Tsim Sha Tsui** waterfront... and the **Star Ferry**.

# Fear and lodging in Kowloon

If you spend much time in Hong Kong, you are bound to meet somebody who has stayed – or is staying – in the massive, shambolic **Chungking Mansions** (*see also p51* **Charlie Mansions?**). Maybe you're even staying there yourself... This grim high-rise at 36-44 Nathan Road is the cheapest place to stay in Hong Kong – and one of the dirtiest. The contrast with the luxury of the Peninsula (*see p46*), which stands just a minute's walk away, could not be greater. Yet, despite its less than salubrious reputation, Chungking is legendary among budget travellers for its tiny, gritty rooms that can cost less than HK$150 per night, and dorm beds for HK$70.

Although known collectively as the Mansions, Chungking is actually home to dozens of guest-houses, which are located in blocks lettered like prison wings. The section fronting Nathan Road advertising 'Chungking House De Luxe Hotel' in filthy, ancient lettering is deceptively small, as the complex stretches back all the way to Minden Row. In here, you'll find a variety of guest-houses: some are about as bad as it gets, while others are really quite decent – it just takes a fair amount of research to track them down.

However, accounts of its decrepit lifts, defunct air conditioners and grim dormitory rooms shared with strangers and cockroaches are legion. Certainly, a trip up one of the inside staircases and out onto one of the back exits (even though there are signs forbidding it) is a real eye-opener – if you have not already had your fill of squalor. Graffiti-covered staircases open onto a landscape of never-washed windows, wheezing air conditioning units, leaking pipes, open drains and discarded food and rubbish.

Be warned, however, that with the squalor comes crime. Hong Kong is an extremely safe city, and so is Chungking for most visitors, but there are occasional problems. Not so long ago, a gang of robbers was found to be targeting Chungking residents, and drug dealing and prostitution are low-key but endemic. There are also occasional stories of drug addicts passing out, or even expiring, on the stairwells. Of course, when it comes to Chungking, some of the stories are myth, some are truth; they're all part of the legend.

In a way, Chungking is a city in its own right, as – in addition to accommodation – it is home to a number of restaurants and shops. In fact, the food places on the bottom two floors of Chungking's front block are pretty decent, and include inexpensive Indian and Chinese restaurants, as well as dirt cheap food stalls. You can also find bargains galore on these floors: luggage, clothing and fabrics cost peanuts here. Just watch out for the lurid look and feel of the synthetic shirts and ties – and stay away from open flames.

If you're staying elsewhere, and aren't intending to change your plans, then at least take a few moments to wander through the crumbling fortress. If even this is too much to contemplate, you can experience the place on screen via Wong Kar-wai's superb 1994 film *Chungking Express* (*pictured*), which is based on activities that take place in its lengthy, winding corridors and tiny, dirty rooms.

Just to the east of the Star Ferry Pier (along the promenade), you'll find the **Hong Kong Cultural Centre** (*see p240*), one of the territory's greatest missed architectural opportunities. When the Kowloon–Canton railway station was demolished in 1978 it freed up one of Hong Kong's, and indeed the world's, most spectacular sites. Facing the incomparable vista of the north side of Hong Kong Island, what was built? A structure without any windows, clad in insipid pinky-beige tiles, resembling an outsize public convenience crossed with a ski jump. It's only saving grace is that it at least provides a wide-ranging cultural programme within its concert hall and two theatres.

On the waterfront next door to the Cultural Centre, the **Hong Kong Museum of Art** (*see p104 & p220*) plays host to some excellent permanent exhibitions of Asian ceramics and a pictorial history of Chinese art, with an emphasis on classic and contemporary Hong Kong art.

Between the Museum of Art and the Peninsula hotel, you'll find the **Hong Kong Space Museum** (*see p106*), which has clearly seen better days, but does have a few interesting interactive displays. Inside a tiled hemisphere within the museum's lobby is the Space Theatre. At regular intervals, so-called 'sky shows' are projected onto its domed ceiling; these are 30-minute films on outer space, natural history and the like. While the idea might be good, the films tend to be underwhelming and the content of many is sleep-inducingly dull.

At the opposite end of the architectural universe, and directly across Salisbury Road, is the handsome, neo-classical exterior of the **Peninsula** hotel (*see p46*), with its sympathetic tower extension. Arguably the grandest remaining symbol of Hong Kong's colonial days, this effortlessly classy place is a must-see. Even if you can't stretch to staying the night, don't miss the chance to take afternoon tea in the elegant, high-ceilinged and pillar-bedecked lobby (served between 2pm and 7pm, a full tea for one costs HK$165). And if you think the Pen is stuck in the past, take the elevator up to the top floor and step out into the Philippe Starck-designed **Felix** restaurant and bar (*see p156*). Floor-to-ceiling windows deliver astonishing views over the harbour to Hong Kong Island on one side and towards the New Territories on the other. Gents shouldn't miss going to the loos – the urinals are placed in front of vast windows, giving the user the somewhat god-like feeling that he is relieving himself over all Kowloon.

A couple of minutes' walk east of the Peninsula along Salisbury Road is the tiny, but charming, **Signal Hill Garden**. This little-appreciated green nook contains a steep hill topped by a tower (open 9-11am, 4-6pm daily) offering a good vantage point. The tower was originally built to send signals to ships in the harbour, thus enabling seafarers to verify the accuracy of their chronographs. But advanced technology, particularly radio time signals, ultimately rendered it redundant.

The **Hong Kong Cultural Centre**.

香港文化中心
Hong Kong Cultural Centre

香港藝術館
Hong Kong Museum Of Art

香港太空館
Hong Kong Space Museum

梳士巴利花園
Salisbury Garden

沙咀婚姻登記
shatsui Marriage Regi

展覽
Exhibition Ga

If you crave further greenery, walk up Nathan Road to **Kowloon Park** (open 6am-midnight daily). This is one of Hong Kong's larger and most precious open spaces. The park was previously the site of the Whitfield Barracks for British (mostly Indian) soldiers. It is well designed, so there's plenty to see, as well as lots of space in which to stroll or just sit and relax. A large, attractive swimming area (open April to October) takes up the northern section of the park – be warned: it gets very busy. Just south of the pools, there is an aviary alive with birdlife and a pond crowded with flamingos and waterfowl, alongside a secluded Chinese garden. On the park's eastern edge is a small, waist-high maze in which to get marginally disoriented, a lovely sculpture garden and a number of fountains and other water features.

Just past the south-eastern edge of the park, the minarets of the **Jamia Masjid Islamic Centre** rise near the intersection of Nathan and Cameron roads. Hong Kong's largest mosque, it was built in the early 1980s to replace a late 19th-century mosque that had been constructed for the use of British Indian troops. Note, however, that visitors are not allowed to wander in off the street and look around, so keep your distance.

For a choice of places to eat and drink, head down Kimberley Road opposite the park. Tucked away off the street is **Knutsford Terrace**, a short strip of restaurants and bars. It may not rival Lan Kwai Fong in Central, but it is one of the few areas in Kowloon with al fresco dining.

East of here, across Chatham Road South, are two major museums: the **Hong Kong Museum of History** (*see p106*) and the excellent, hands-on **Hong Kong Museum of Science** (*see p106*).

## Hung Hom

East of the museums lies the area of **Hung Hom**. At its southern end stands the 12,500-seater **Hong Kong Coliseum**, an inverted pyramid that plays host to major sporting events and music concerts. Next door is **Hung Hom Station**, the terminus of the Kowloon–Canton Railway (KCR), from where trains depart to the New Territories, Guangzhou, Shanghai and Beijing.

The reclaimed land on the eastern edge of Hung Hom belongs to mega-tycoon Li Ka-shing and has been developed into a largely utilitarian area of housing, shops and offices. A mirage rises in the midst of the thicket of retail outlets on Hung Hom Road – you can't miss the massive hull of the **Whampoa** (visible from the path to Tsim Sha Tsui; on Shung King Street at

Tak Fung Street), a ship-shaped hunk of concrete that will never set sail, as it is, in fact, a shopping mall. With four levels (or 'decks'), the 100-metre (328-foot) long ship houses upmarket shops, restaurants, a playground and a cinema. The nautical theme is due to the site previously being home to the Hong Kong and Whampoa dockyard.

Aside from the Whampoa, there are only a couple of other parts of Hung Hom worth visiting. Close by, on the waterfront near the bus terminus, is the impressive five-star **Harbour Plaza**. The bar restaurant outside is a relaxed, if expensive, place for snacks in an al fresco setting with easterly views of the harbour. Conveniently, a Star Ferry sails frequently from the Hung Hom Ferry Pier (just in front of the bus terminus) to Wan Chai and Central.

One of the hidden gems of Hung Hom is Sung Kit Street, a pedestrian alley off Bailey Street that is crowded with cheap and unpretentious Japanese restaurants.

### Hong Kong Museum of Art
*Hong Kong Cultural Centre, 10 Salisbury Road, Tsim Sha Tsui, Kowloon (2721 0116/ www.lcsd.gov.hk/CE/Museum/Arts). Tsim Sha Tsui MTR (exit E)/buses to Tsim Sha Tsui Star Ferry Pier*

**Nathan Road** neon.

# HK profiles 'Long Hair'

'**Long Hair**' **Leung Kwok-hung** is a rare breed. He's a full-time protester in a city that doesn't really protest. On the Richter scale of protests, street demonstrations on Hong Kong would score 0.1 – a ripple unlikely to shake a squirrel out a tree, let alone uproot the government. A turnout of more than 20 flag-waving, banner-carrying, slogan-chanting refuseniks is normally counted as a pretty solid showing of dissent.

But none of this deters Leung. He has protested against his former colonial masters, Chinese leaders, Japanese 'imperialists', local government officials… in fact, pretty much anyone who's in authority.

Leung remembers when days were different. The 1966 Star Ferry riots over a tiny increase in the cross-harbour fare was the closest the local populace ever came to overthrowing their British colonial rulers. In 1989, up to a million rallied against the massacre that ruthlessly crushed the Tiananmen Square demonstration. Both were rare moments of solidarity. At the time of the 1997 Handover, the world's media converged expecting battles on the street, but nothing erupted. The police played Beethoven over loudspeakers, saying it was to add to the festive atmosphere, but it handily drowned out the cries of the few protesters who had gathered outside the ceremony, too. Since then, the onset of the Asian financial crisis has fuelled a trend towards street rallies against unpopular government policies, but they have failed to swell.

None of this is for lack of effort by 'Long Hair'. His trademark locks, penchant for Che Guevara T-shirts and scruffy jeans, and his willingness to join the cause – any cause for that matter – means he is rarely out of the news. Leung believes in democracy, as in real democracy and not the sham the British ushered in during the death throes of colonial government. He is also a member of the radical April 5th Action Group – named after the day of mourning dead ancestors in Chinese culture, and the date of a 1976 Tiananmen solidarity gathering.

Put more bluntly, he's a revolutionary trapped in a capitalist haven where hardly anyone gives a damn. His rallying cry is 'power to the people', but the people hardly seem to care. Voter turnout at the limited elections held is risible. 'Show me the money' would be a more unifying call to arms.

Leung likes to be seen and heard. He's on the streets one day denouncing the latest 'outrage' of the Chinese Government, the next he's in the public gallery of the Legislative Council shouting for Chief Executive Tung Chee-hwa to resign. And, of course, he spends much of his time in between in court. If you suggest he is a rent-a-protester he won't demur. There are so many causes worth fighting for after all. And he's only ever a phone call away.

At night, he can be found in more restrained mode at the Club 64 bar (*see p168*) in Lan Kwai Fong, where he will happily explain his beliefs to you if you buy him a pint or two. He's not hard to spot.

But recently Long Hair's been missing from his usual bar stool. After countless brushes with the law, he has twice found himself slung behind bars. Not for his views, but for interrupting such trivial matters as the SAR leader giving his budget speech. Leung recently served his second seven-day sentence in less than a year. On both occasions, shock waves reverberated through the local media. And what caused the uproar? Indignation at such high-handed treatment? Outrage at the infringement of freedom of speech? No, the press were horrified by the fact that Long Hair would be forced to have a prison hair cut.

Such a response suggests Leung is not only far from achieving his ambitions, he's not even getting them on the agenda. But one thing's certain: they can remove his hair, but they'll never take his pride.

The **Hong Kong Space Museum**.

& along Salisbury Road/Tsim Sha Tsui Star Ferry Pier. **Open** 10am-6pm Mon-Wed, Fri-Sun. **Admission** HK$10; HK$5 concessions; free Wed. **No credit cards**. **Map** p98 B3.

Although not large by Western standards, this museum has much to offer. Works are arranged in six galleries, five of which house permanent displays, and one of which is a constantly changing exhibition of international art. Among the permanent displays are an extensive collection of crafts from southern China and Asia dating from Neolithic times to the present day. Featured are more than 3,000 objects in ceramic, bronze, jade, lacquer, enamel, glass, wood, ivory and rhinoceros horn, as well as pieces of furniture.

While the exhibitions are wide-ranging, porcelain forms the museum's core, with an extensive collection of extraordinarily fine pieces, and a useful explanation of the manufacturing process and the development of porcelain-making techniques. There is also a permanent exhibition of historical paintings and lithographs of Kong Kong, Macau and Canton in colonial and pre-colonial days, and a small collection of contemporary art from China and Hong Kong, which tends to be an interesting, albeit patchy mix of abstract and figurative works.

An audio guide (HK$10) explains some of the exhibits, but much of the content is blandly factual and fails to put the subjects into a wider context, which can be baffling for those without background knowledge. There's also a frustrating lack of infor-

mation or context about Chinese calligraphy or the artists featured in the exhibition. However, overall, the museum's pros outweigh its cons. On the ground floor, there's a well-stocked shop selling art books, prints and postcards. *See also p220.*

## Hong Kong Museum of History

*100 Chatham Road South, Tsim Sha Tsui East, Kowloon (2724 9042/www.lcsd.gov.hk/CE/Museum/ History). Buses along Chatham Road South.* **Open** 10am-6pm Tue-Sat; 1-6pm Sun. **Admission** HK$10; HK$5 concessions; free Wed. **No credit cards**. **Map** p98 D1.

At the time of going to press, this museum, which recently moved to its current location from its former site in Kowloon Park, was still under construction (at a cost of HK$390 million). The small display area open during construction contains a few interesting nuggets, and plenty of less compelling odds and ends. However, the plans to create separate themed areas look ambitious and impressive; they include displays on the region's geological formation, its natural history, pre-historic and pre-dynastic eras, as well as its folk history and more recent cultural past. Certainly, the museum has some unusual artefacts, including Bronze Age daggers, pottery and arrow heads found on Lamma and Lantau islands.

## Hong Kong Museum of Science

*2 Science Museum Road, Tsim Sha Tsui East, Kowloon (2732 3232/www.lcsd.gov.hk/CE/Museum/ Science/eindex.htm). Buses along Chatham Road South.* **Open** 1-9pm Tue-Fri; 10am-9pm Sat, Sun. **Admission** HK$25; HK$12.50 concessions; free Thur. **No credit cards**. **Map** p98 D1.

The four floors of the Science Museum are almost entirely filled with excellent interactive displays neatly demonstrating the basic principles of physics, electricity, chemistry and everyday technology. A popular destination for parents and children of all ages, the museum is a fun, boisterous place, often filled with excitable school parties.

## Hong Kong Space Museum

*10 Salisbury Road, Tsim Sha Tsui, Kowloon (2721 0226/www.lcsd.gov.hk/CE/Museum/Space/ e_index.htm). Tsim Sha Tsui MTR (exit E)/buses to Kowloon Star Ferry Pier & along Salisbury Road/Kowloon Star Ferry Pier.* **Open** 1-9pm Mon, Wed-Fri; 10am-9pm Sat, Sun. **Admission** *Space Museum* free. *Sky Show* HK$24; HK$12 concessions. **No credit cards**. **Map** p98 B3.

Not the most thrilling museum in Hong Kong, but kids might like the four or five good interactive exhibits, including a virtual jetpack, a ride simulating the gravity on the moon, a centrifuge, a gyroscope and a game simulating the landing of the lunar module. The displays explaining the workings of rockets, the solar system and stars are reasonably well put together. Some of the exhibits have seen better days, however, and many are poorly explained. The same goes for the Sculpture Garden outside; some of its dozen or so pieces are labelled, but there's little other information about the works or their creators.

## Yau Ma Tei & Mong Kok

North of Kowloon Park, Tsim Sha Tsui melds imperceptibly into the district of Yau Ma Tei. Further north still is Mong Kok. Yau Ma Tei means 'land of the sesame plants' in Cantonese, although you'd be hard-pressed to find any such plants growing in this very urban area today. Instead, you'll discover a colourful hunting ground for sightseers and bargain lovers. Both Yau Ma Tei and Mong Kok are crammed with markets, including the Jade Market in Yau Ma Tei and the Flower Market in Mong Kok.

## Yau Ma Tei

Jordan MTR is a good starting point from which to explore Yau Ma Tei. To find the heart of the district, take exit A out of the MTR station and head west along Jordan Road to Temple Street and walk north. This is where you'll find the heart of the **Temple Street Night Market** (*see p194*), at its best, naturally, during the evening. There is a good deal of tat on sale here, but you can find decent buys, particularly cheap designer fakes of name-brand watches. On the corner of Temple and Pak Hoi Streets, half a dozen or so inexpensive canteen-style restaurants operate out of a small covered area, serving food until quite late at night. The squeamish may want to avoid it, however, as the table etiquette here regards spitting gristle and bone fragments onto the plastic table tops as entirely acceptable.

If you haven't already seen a Chinese food and produce market, **Reclamation Street**, which runs parallel with Temple Street (two blocks to the west), hosts a large food market during the day. Virtually the entire area around Reclamation Street, stretching between Argyle Street to the north, Ferry Street to the west and Nathan Road to the east is full of interesting Chinese shops and businesses, including funeral parlours, herbalists and health tea shops. Ning Po Street is particularly interesting – check out the shop at No.21 that specialises in snake products; its walls are lined with jars of pickled reptiles. You'll also find a number of paper shops here, selling the likes of colourful kites and fragile paper houses.

At the end of Temple Street (on Kansu Street under the flyover just west of the top end of Temple Street) is the famous **Jade Market** (*see p194*). Inside the small covered market, around 50 stalls sell jade ornaments and jewellery, as well as carved bone trinkets. Be prepared for some heavy-duty bargaining, and know how much the items cost elsewhere before you buy. Unless you're a jade expert (or have one handily in tow), don't part with any significant sums –

it's all too easy for novices to be ripped off. The market is open from 9am to 6pm, but is best visited early in the day as some vendors close up shop around lunchtime.

A minute's walk north-east of the Jade Market is Yau Ma Tei's sizeable **Tin Hau Temple** (open 8am-6pm daily), divided into three separate areas for the worship of Hong Kong's favourite goddess, Tin Hau (*see p94* **Tin Hau, sea goddess**), Shing Wong, the god of the city, and To Tei, the god of the earth. It costs nothing to enter and look around, but it is considered polite to make a small contribution. Photography is frowned upon, if not forbidden. In the evenings, fortune tellers gather outside the temple to offer their services. There are a choice of face and palm readers, as well as 'birds of fortune' (small birds in cages that tell your fortune by picking out tarot-style cards). A couple of fortune tellers, one of them advertising fortunes told in English, also operate from the annexe at the far end of the temple building during the day.

## Mong Kok

Most of the sights and shopping in Mong Kok are just east of Mong Kok MTR. One of its busiest markets is known as the **Ladies' Market** (running the length of Tung Choi Street), even though it sells a huge range of goods not necessarily restricted to female tastes. Clothes, CDs, luggage, sandals, boas and wigs are all here in abundance, along with other essentials like fluff removers and grape peelers. Running parallel to the market is Fa Yuen Street, where dozens of shops sell trainers and other sports goods, while at the northern end of the market is the **Goldfish Market**, which is more a cluster of goldfish shops than a market. Goldfish are extremely popular among the Chinese (they are believed to bring good luck and to help absorb bad *chi* – and are good pets for small flats), and there is a fascinating variety of breeds – the Goldfish Pagoda in Ocean Park explains them in full; *see p92*.

A short walk north of here along Prince Edward Road West brings you to the **Flower Market**. At its best in the early morning, it consists of a long line of shops and stalls selling a huge array of exotic flowers and budding branches. This vivid street teems with customers year round, but is particularly crowded around Chinese New Year.

A stretch of garden running alongside Yuen Po Street at the far end of Flower Market Road is a gathering place for local bird lovers. The **Bird Market** (*see p194*) is alive with the twitter and chirp of many species of songbird (many illegally smuggled). Many enthusiasts

Three sides to the food market in and around Reclamation Street, Yau Ma Tei.

take their own birds along, usually in delicately wrought – and often wretchedly tiny – cages. A dozen or so stalls sell birds, bird food and accessories, including bags of grasshoppers that are often fed to the birds using chopsticks. The ornate cages make fine souvenirs.

At the top end of the garden runs **Boundary Street**, the old Kowloon-China border. After the British forced China to cede the Kowloon Peninsula to them in 1860, they then became worried that it wasn't enough. As fears over the growing influence of other Western powers over China grew (particularly considering new gunnery technology that increased the range of artillery) and concerns about the lack of a fresh water supply for the colony were raised, the British persuaded the Chinese government into leasing the New Territories to them for 99 years in 1898.

The decision to take only a temporary lease was Britain's big mistake. Hong Kong Island and Kowloon had been permanently ceded, but the necessity of returning the New Territories to China in 1997 made the retention of the rest of the colony untenable.

Mong Kok's **Bird Market**...

... and the nearby **Flower Market**. *See p108.*

# New Kowloon

Although the area just north of Boundary Street is officially part of the New Territories, it has become known locally as New Kowloon. Much of it is of little interest to tourists, but there are several places worth visiting. To the east along the Quarry Bay MTR line are the large, busy Wong Tai Sin temple and the beautiful, strange, Kowloon Walled City Park, while to the west along the Tsuen Wan MTR line is the cheap clothes and goods market of Sham Shui Po.

## East along the Quarry Bay line

When you arrive in New Kowloon, you are likely to feel that you've wandered into a massive construction site – much of it is in the process of being torn down and replaced by newer, taller tower blocks, shopping centres and office blocks. (The strict height restrictions in Kowloon, necessary while the old Kai Tak airport was in use, have now been lifted.)

The construction is easily avoided, however, and a good starting point for exploring the area on foot is the Lok Fu MTR station. When you come out of the station, walk down Wang Tau Hom East Road and turn left at the T-junction along Junction Road. On the left-hand side of the road, you'll see the **Chinese Christian Cemetery**, with its graves stacked up and squeezed into every available piece of ground. Nearby is the traditional, tiny and very lovely **Hau Wong Temple** (open 8am-5pm daily), built in 1737, and dedicated to one of the exiled boy-emperor Ping's most loyal generals.

Close to the temple, you'll find an oasis of fountains, elaborate topiary, sculptures and meandering walkways in the **Kowloon Walled City Park** (open 6.30am-11pm daily). Inside the old almshouse, facing the main entrance on Tung Tsing Road, is a history of the Walled City (*see p113* **Kowloon Walled City**), which once stood where the garden is today.

Another New Kowloon site worth visiting is the **Wong Tai Sin Temple** (*see p113*). Located close to the Wong Tai Sin MTR station, one stop from Lok Fu, the temple is one of Hong Kong's largest, busiest and most interesting places of worship. The complex contains altars and shrines to several Buddhist, Confucian and Taoist deities, and is regularly filled with worshippers, noise and swirling incense. Near the main temple is a large covered area containing more than 100 fortune teller stalls. Several of these soothsayers can reveal your fortune in English, mostly through palm and face reading. You're likely to be

quoted about HK$200 for a five-minute consultation, but it should be possible to haggle them down to HK$100 or less. Kneeling in front of the main temple's altar, many locals can be seen and heard solemnly shaking small canisters of bamboo sticks until one emerges from the can. Each stick is marked with a numeral and a corresponding meaning. Many users immediately head to the fortune tellers to have their stick interpreted. An alternative method of divination to the fortune sticks are *bui*, two pieces of wood shaped like orange segments. This fortune telling process is known as *sing pei* or 'Buddha's lips'. A question is asked, the *bui* are thrown and the 'lips' answer 'yes' or 'no', depending on which way they land.

The next stop on the MTR line is **Diamond Hill**, from where it is a short and well-signposted walk to the **Chi Lin Buddhist Nunnery** (*see p113*), a larger but more serene place than Wong Tai Sin Temple. Its yellow cedar timbers and elegantly tiled roof are new, although built in the ancient Tang style of architecture, while the carefully contrived layout of the large courtyard, temple and gardens all contribute to a sense of order and calm. The temples hold large and finely sculpted golden statues of various incarnations of Buddha.

The small, charming village of **Lei Yue Mun**, which has long been a favourite destination for seafood lovers, lies at the very southern tip of Kowloon in the eastern part of Victoria harbour. (To get there, take the MTR to Kwun Tong station, and then the number 14C bus to its terminus at Sam Ka Tsuen typhoon shelter.) Once you arrive in the village, walk east from the edge of the small harbour (past the large modern library building) and turn right around the edge of the harbour to find the heart of the village. Here, there are dark narrow alleyways, hemmed in by hundreds of tanks filled with sea life, and, further into the village, several seafood restaurants. Prices aren't cheap – most people are attracted by the experience of eating in the village's bucolic environs. And there's the advantage of being able to choose and buy your dinner from one of the seafood vendors; the restaurants will then cook it for a fee. Make sure you agree on a price first.

Aside from the seafood restaurants, Lei Yue Mun is a thriving village and there's plenty going on throughout the week. If you make it out here on a weekday, it's worth wandering further into the village, past the boisterously playing children in the primary school, and along the shore to see the dozens of rod fishermen crouching on the rocks, catching your dinner.

# Kowloon Walled City

Built by the Chinese in 1847 as part of the empire's southern coastal defences, the Walled City was always a strange place. When the British leased the New Territories in 1898, an inexplicable slip left the fortress under Chinese jurisdiction. A year later, it was quietly taken over by the British police, but jurisdiction of the area remained ambiguous, with the result that the Walled City was left as an unregulated plot of Chinese soil within British territory. It became known as 'City of Darkness'.

After World War II, when much of the fort was levelled by Japanese forces, squatters moved into this legal and physical no man's land. High-rise apartments sprang up and the settlement mushroomed. At its height, 40,000 souls were estimated to live on this tiny stretch of land within a dark maze of narrow, medieval-esque streets, many of them

in ramshackle rooms with no plumbing. The entire city was served by a solitary postman. The advantages of living in this underworld were no taxes and its ambiguous legal status, but the absence of regulation soon attracted the triad gangs who virtually ruled here in the 1950s and 1960s, when peep shows, brothels and opium dens flourished. Kowloon police still tell stories of the crime, filth and enormous rats of the Walled City, which was not pulled down until 1992.

Among the displays in the almshouse (close to the Park's main entrance) are intriguing photos of the dense, brooding, post-war slum that rose on the grounds of the Walled City. Things are very different today. Following the demolition of the Walled City, a stunning park was created; it is one of the best parks in Hong Kong in which to find the bauhinia (the official flower of the territory), when it blooms between November and March.

## West along the Tsuen Wan line

Travelling west through New Kowloon, one of the first worthwhile stops is **Sham Shui Po Market**, which is close to Sham Shui Po MTR station. Although this open-air market and its surrounding shops are not unique, they do sell a diverse range of goods and the prices are very low. Outside the Apliu Street exit of the MTR, the extensive street market stretches away in all directions. Here, luggage and clothes are probably as cheap as they get this side of the Chinese border, although the choice is not as great as in Shenzhen (*see p201*).

To the north-west of the MTR station, there's a large computer market in the upstairs section of the **Golden Shopping Centre** on Yen Chow Street; prices are marginally better than in Kowloon. A few metres away at 100 Yen Chow Street, a good VCD and DVD shop has one of the most comprehensive selections of US and UK TV series, as well as hundreds of films.

After perusing the wares on offer, get back onto the MTR and head one stop west to **Cheung Sha Wan**, home of the **Lei Cheng Uk Han Tomb Museum** (*see below*). It is an easy and well signposted walk from the MTR station. Turn left up Tonkin Street and the museum is just off Po On Road, past the public garden. Uncovered by workmen in 1955, this burial tomb is not the world's most riveting museum, but it's worth a quick look if you are in the area.

## Chi Lin Buddhist Nunnery

*Chi Lin Drive, Diamond Hill, Kowloon (2354 1730). Diamond Hill MTR (exit C2).* **Open** 9am-3.30pm Mon, Tue, Thur-Sun. **Admission** free. **Map** p62. An elegant and peaceful complex erected in the 1930s in the style and using the techniques of the Tang Dynasty (618-907AD). The Nunnery contains some fine statues of the Sakyamuni Buddha.

## Lei Cheng Uk Han Tomb Museum

*41 Tonkin Street, Cheung Sha Wan, Kowloon (2386 2863/www.lcsd.gov.hk/CE/Museum/History). Cheung Sha Wan MTR (exit A2, A3)/buses along Tonkin Street.* **Open** 10am-1pm, 2-6pm Mon-Wed, Fri, Sat; 1-6pm Sun. **Admission** free. **Map** p62. This Han burial tomb has been dated to the Eastern Han Dynasty (AD24-220). There's a small display of the (mostly pottery) finds excavated from the tomb. The tomb itself, only visible through a misted-up Perspex sheet and resembling a small brick kiln, is outside in the courtyard. Alas, there's very little information about who built the tomb and for whom.

## Wong Tai Sin Temple

*Wong Tai Sin, Kowloon (2328 0270). Wong Tai Sin MTR (exit B2).* **Open** 7am-5.30pm daily. **Admission** free. **Map** p62. Dedicated primarily to the god Wong Tai Sin, the protector of the surrounding settlement. Wong Tai Sin was a shepherd from Zhejiang Province who was taught how to make a healing potion by an immortal. He then went on to perform many miracles among the sick. The temple is not limited strictly to Wong Tai Sin, however, as it also takes in a broad sweep of Taoist, Confucian and Buddhist deities.

Sightseeing

# The New Territories

New towns and wild country – discover the least known side of Hong Kong.

When the British extended the colony of Hong Kong beyond the Kowloon peninsula in 1898, leasing from China 794 square kilometres (306 square miles) of steep hills, mountains and jagged coastline north of what is now Boundary Street at the edge of New Kowloon, they dubbed this ancient land the New Territories.

Today, more than three million people (just over 40 per cent of Hong Kong's population) live in this extensive, diverse region, yet, despite some extremely unsightly and badly planned urban, commercial and industrial developments (particularly in the west), there are large tracts of unspoiled countryside, hundreds of square kilometres of which are given over to country parks. There is wonderful hiking and wildlife-watching to be had along the New Territories' many mountainous trails and within its thick forest (see chapter **Wild Hong Kong**), while many of Hong Kong's finest beaches are to be found in the remote east.

In addition, because significant settlements have existed here for hundreds of years, the New Territories have more Chinese heritage on offer than Hong Kong Island and Kowloon put together. Dozens of temples, ancestral halls and walled villages – some dating back to long distant Chinese dynasties – are dotted around the countryside.

Adding to the New Territories' attraction is the fact that, despite its lingering rural feel and considerable extent, travel is very easy. The central Kowloon–Canton Railway (KCR), the Light Rail Transit in the west, and excellent bus services and ferries elsewhere, all make even the remote areas accessible.

Before you head out here, pay a visit to the Government Publications Centre (see p180) and pick up the *Countryside* series of maps, which cover the New Territories.

## Central New Territories

If your time in the area is tight, a day or two spent exploring along the KCR offers the most convenience and reward.

On the route towards the Chinese border, you'll find temples, the new Heritage Museum at Sha Tin, old ancestral halls and, in the far north, glimpses through the smog to Shenzhen, one of China's economic powerhouses.

## Tai Wai

The first stop made by the KCR after Kowloon Tong is **Tai Wai** (which today virtually merges into Sha Tin; see below). **Amah Rock**, said to resemble a woman who was turned to stone by the gods after her husband failed to return from a fishing expedition (though it's actually a pre-Chinese phallic symbol), is the most prominent sight in the area. It can be reached from the station via Hung Miu Kuk Road and a subsequent path.

Closer to the station on Che Kung Miu Road is the popular **Che Kung Temple** (see p117), while another ten minutes walk up the road is the impressive walled village known as **Tsang Tai Uk**. Translated as 'Tsang's big house', this mid 19th-century structure was built for members of the Tsang clan and retains a powerfully evocative atmosphere.

## Sha Tin

Like so many towns in the New Territories, **Sha Tin** is large and government-planned. But don't let that scare you. Despite its bureaucratic roots, it is, in fact, an attractive and interesting place. Among its many offerings, Sha Tin features generous expanses of parkland running along its river front.

The Sha Tin KCR station empties into the sprawling **New Town Plaza**, a popular shopping destination that is perpetually heaving. For visitors, there are far better places to shop, but if you can bear trudging through its vast length, and don't mind the constant press of people, there are a passable number of dining options within its depths.

A 15-minute walk from the northern exit of the KCR is the outlandish **Ten Thousand Buddhas Monastery** (see p119). To reach it, cross the road in front of the station and follow the signposts to the temple at the top of a wooded hill. You'll know you're on the right path when, after about five or so minutes, you begin to see the large, golden, scarlet-lipped Buddhas lining the steep route. More than 400 steps must be climbed to reach the temple, but it's worth the work – there are actually more than 10,000 Buddha statues inside (as well as the mummified corpse of a former abbot).

Ten Thousand Buddhas
Monastery. *See p114.*

Sightseeing

If you go to only one museum while you are in Hong Kong, go to the brand new, HK$390 million **Hong Kong Heritage Museum** (*see p118*). Located on the outskirts of Sha Tin (next to the Shing Mun River), the museum offers a fascinating and comprehensive history of Hong Kong – dating back to the region's geological formation. Its extensive displays cover more than 6,000 years of human existence in the region. The museum's displays, audio-visual exhibits and interactive terminals are impressive.

The town's other main draw is **Sha Tin Racecourse** (*see p118*). Built in 1980, at a reported cost of HK$500 million plus, this huge, high-tech stadium looks striking against the scenic backdrop of nearby hills. *See also p251.*

## University

A couple of stops north of Sha Tin on the KCR is University station, serving the **Chinese University of Hong Kong**. Depending on what is on display at the **Chinese University Art Museum** (*see p118*), it may be worth the trip to this small gallery. While many of the paintings are unimpressive, the museum has a good – and extensive – collection that includes gold jewellery and jade ornaments, which it

**Che Kung Temple**: another piece of the New Territories' cultural jigsaw. *See p114.*

displays on rotation. To reach the museum, exit the KCR on the campus (west) side, turn right and board the free campus shuttle bus. Get off at the second stop – the museum is close to the library and the administration building. The buildings are on the south side of the road, but are not immediately obvious and are badly signposted, so you may have to ask one of the students to point it out if you're in doubt.

The area around the University KCR station is a prime location for boat trips to the islands of Tap Mun Chau and Ping Chau, as well as remoter parts of the Sai Kung Peninsula (*see p123*) at the mouth of Tolo Harbour. Ferries to the islands can be caught at **Ma Liu Shui**, a 15-minute walk from the station. **Tap Mun Chau** (*see also p138*) is notable for its rugged peacefulness, beautiful beaches, caves along its shores and rural fishing village. It is also home to a **Tin Hau Temple** (*see p94* **Tin Hau, sea goddess**), which was built during

the Ching dynasty. The smaller **Ping Chau** is also treasured for its white sand beaches and excellent swimming.

## Tai Po

A further stop north on the KCR and you're at Tai Po Market station. **Tai Po** is another of the newly created towns that dot the New Territories countryside, though not one of the region's most interesting communities. It does have a few quirks though: take the **Wishing Tree**. This mystical object, a short bus ride from the station (take the number 64K bus to the Fong Ma Po stop), is worth the ride, if only for the potential good luck involved – not to mention the strange ceremony of it all. For a few dollars, the stallholders around the tree – you can't miss it, it's covered in oranges and paper streamers – will sell you an orange with a vividly coloured streamer attached to it. You then write your wish on the streamer and hurl the orange at the tree. If the fruit lodges among the branches, your wish will come true. Odd to think one's fate could hinge on the strength of one's pitching arm, but there it is. Of course, if you're still doubtful about how well your wish has been received by the tree, you can always consult a fortune teller just down the road at the small **Tin Hau Temple** – they'll tell you how you have done, and how you will do, apparently.

**Tai Po Market** itself is worth a peruse. Nearby is the vaguely disappointing **Hong Kong Railway Museum** (*see p118*), which probably won't even quicken the pulse of railway junkies. And, on Fu Shin Street, you'll find the handsome, if unspectacular, 19th-century **Man Mo Temple**.

Luckily, once you've had your fill of Tai Po's limited offerings, you're in an ideal location to catch a bus bound for the wilderness and walking trails of the **Plover Cove Country Park** (*see p123*).

## Fanling

Continuing north along the KCR, the biggest attraction for most visitors to the small town of **Fanling** is the Lung Yuek Tau Heritage Trail. But before setting off on the hike, it is worth taking a few minutes to visit the **Fung Ying Sin Koon Temple** (open 9am-5pm daily), located a three-minute walk from the west exit of the station. A large, modern Taoist temple, it includes a section dedicated to the deities of particular years (past, current and future) and their corresponding Chinese birth signs. Worshippers pray, bow and make offerings to their own relevant statues. This temple is also dedicated to the dead, so the ashen remains of those who have passed away are stored in small tombs, each bearing a photograph of its occupant. As with other temples, this is not a museum and is, therefore, often filled with believers – move carefully among them so as not to cause offence.

A ten-minute ride on the number 54K bus from the eastern side of the KCR will bring you to the **Tang Chung Ling Ancestral Hall** (*see p119*), one of the largest of its kind in the New Territories. The hall lies along the **Lung Yuek Tau Heritage Trail**, which passes five *wai tsuens* (walled villages) and six *tsuens* (villages), all within a couple of kilometres of each other.

The hall is the best starting point for hitting the trail – it is on a bus route and there's a detailed map posted outside. The trail is not terribly long, so walking its entire length is easily accomplished in a morning or afternoon, but make sure you take a good map as the signposting is patchy along the way.

Interestingly, far from being deserted monuments, the *wais* on this trail are still inhabited. In fact, they are very much modern communities straddling historic lines. Some, such as **Tong Kok Wai** (just north of the ancestral hall), have dozens of houses inside their crumbling walls and, while most are old dwellings, some are very recent.

One of the better-preserved walled villages highlighted on the trail is **Lo Wai**. Here, the village entrance, the watchtower above it, and the thick, sturdy walls surrounding it, are all still intact. Walk within the walls and you'll get a real feel for the place as it was generations ago. Another worthwhile stop on the trail is **Ma Wat Wai**. Built in the 1700s, the watchtowers that once stood at each corner have long since disappeared, but the main entrance (including its ancient iron chain-link gate) is well preserved.

## Sheung Shui & beyond

**Sheung Shui** is the last stop on the KCR before it reaches the border at Lo Wu. This is the most convenient stop for trips to the **Mai Po Marshes** (*see p122* **Mai Po Marshes**). But before wandering out into the damp and mud, the **Tai Fu Tai** residence (*see p119*) just north of the village of Wing Ping Tsuen is worth a quick look. This stately home was built in 1865 by a senior member of the Man clan. To get here, take the number 76K bus from outside Sheung Shui KCR station to Wing Ping Tsuen – alight when you see San Tin post office. Signs mark the way to Tai Fu Tai, a couple of minutes' walk north of the post office.

Two kilometres (1.25 miles) to the north-east of Tai Fu Tai is the old border lookout of **Lok Ma Chau** (it's possible to walk the route from Tai Fu Tai, but simpler, not to mention faster, to take a taxi). The lookout is just a few hundred metres from the Chinese city of **Shenzhen** (*see p201* **Break for the border: Shenzhen**), which is considered (by China) to be one of its economic success stories. Shenzhen has grown rapidly over the past two decades, changing from a quiet country village into the bustling modern city it is today. Whether or not that's a good thing, of course, depends on your perspective. The view of Shenzhen's crowded skyline and its traffic-choked streets was more exciting in the days when China and Hong Kong were divided and it represented a view into the forbidden Communist country.

### Che Kung Temple

*Che Kung Miu Road, Tai Wai, New Territories (no phone). Tai Wai KCR.* **Open** 9am-5pm daily. **Admission** free. **Map** p311.

Dedicated to Che Kung, a general who reputedly rid the area of plague, this is a popular local temple.

Tsang Tai Uk walled village. See p114.

### Chinese University Art Museum

*Chinese University of Hong Kong, Tai Po Road, Sha Tin, New Territories (2609 7416/ www.cuhk.edu.hk/ics/amm). University KCR, then free shuttle bus.* **Open** 10am-4.45pm Mon-Sat; 12.30-5.30pm Sun. **Admission** free. **Map** p311.

The Hong Kong Museum of Art in Kowloon (*see p104*) and the Hong Kong Heritage Museum in Sha Tin (*see below*) both have more interesting traditional Chinese paintings than the permanent collection on display here. However, the Art Museum owns a large and impressive collection of decorative arts, including fine ceramics, sculptures and jade. Some of the more than 7,000 items displayed date back to Neolithic times. These, and other special collections, are shown on rotation, so, if you want to see something specific, it's advisable to check beforehand what's on display before setting out.

### Hong Kong Heritage Museum

*1 Man Lam Road, Sha Tin, New Territories (2180 8188/www.heritagemuseum.gov.hk). Sha Tin KCR, then bus 68K or free shuttle bus (Sat, Sun).* **Open** 10am-6pm Tue-Thur, Sat, Sun; 10am-9pm Fri. **Admission** HK$10; concessions HK$5; free Wed. **No credit cards. Map** p311.

It only opened in December 2000, but the Hong Kong Heritage Museum has already established itself as by far the best museum in the territory. There are six excellent permanent exhibitions, plus plenty of space for temporary displays. The best, and largest, of the permanent exhibitions is the New Territories Heritage Hall. It explains how the landscape was formed, and illustrates the arrival of animal and prehistoric human life, the rise of the traditional village society, eventual colonial rule and the large-scale development of the New Territories towns. While you could spend all day in this one gallery, there's much more to see. Beautiful calligraphy and renderings of plants and animals by the acclaimed artist Chao Shao-an hang from scrolls on the first floor, while the TT Tsui Gallery holds a wide range of ceramics dating to Neolithic times. There's also a colourful, educational exhibition on Cantonese opera that explains some of the elaborate ritual involved.

### Hong Kong Railway Museum

*13 Shung Tak Street, Tai Po Market, Tai Po (2653 3455/www.heritagemuseum.gov.uk). Tai Po Market KCR, then minibus 25K.* **Open** 9am-5pm Mon, Wed-Sun. **Admission** free. **Map** p311.

There's not much here, apart from an old narrow-gauge engine, a few rail carriages and some model railways. The photos of the old railway station on the Tsim Sha Tsui waterfront and of Kowloon (before it was so heavily developed) are interesting, though.

### Sha Tin Racecourse

*Sha Tin, New Territories (2966 8111/ www.hkjockeyclub.com). Racecourse KCR (race days only).* **Open** see website or phone for racing calendar. **Admission** HK$10. **No credit cards. Map** p311.

While it does not quite have the atmosphere of the night races at Happy Valley (*see p250*), the scale of Sha Tin is nonetheless impressive. And its backdrop of wide-open spaces and rugged hills is undeniably lovely. Visitors can either pay the regular admission fee, or stump up HK$50 to enter the Members' Enclosure, which guarantees entry to busy race meetings (you must be over 18, have been in Hong Kong for less than 21 days and have a valid passport).

### Tai Fu Tai
*Wing Ping Tsuen, New Territories (no phone).*
*Sheung Shui KCR, then bus 76K.* **Open** 9am-1pm, 2-5pm Mon, Wed-Sun. **Admission** free. **Map** p311.
This large, ornate house, built in about 1865, is one of the New Territories' better restored heritage sites. It was once the home of Man Chung-luen, a senior civil servant, or *dafu*.

### Tang Chung Ling Ancestral Hall
*Lo Wai, Fanling, New Territories (2508 1234).*
*Fanling KCR.* **Open** 9am-5pm daily.
**Admission** free. **Map** p311.
Dating back more than 500 years, this large ancestral hall was founded by the Tang clan, one of the five great New Territories clans. You'll find some ancient and ornate ancestral tablets at the end of the temple, including those of a 12th-century princess

of the southern Song Dynasty. Despite its popularity with tourists, this is still an active clan hall where members worship, pay respects to their ancestors, honour traditions, and hold meetings and celebrations as their families have done for centuries.

### Ten Thousand Buddhas Monastery
*Sha Tin (no phone). Sha Tin KCR.*
**Open** 9am-5pm daily. **Admission** free.
**Map** p311.
It's a long climb up to the monastery's main building, but you are rewarded with the extraordinary sight of thousands of tiny golden Buddhas in hundreds of poses lining shelves that reach to the ceiling. More Buddhas can be found outside – there's Buddha astride a giant white elephant and here he is again atop a huge dog. Nearby, Buddhas peer down from a bright red nine-storey pagoda. In a small annexe above the main temple lies the body of the temple's founding monk, who died in 1965. This annexe was recently closed to the public for repairs, but if it is open when you're here, go in. Like a gilded Buddhist Sleeping Beauty, he lies inside a glass case, covered in gold leaf. If the climb has made you peckish, the spartan vegetarian canteen next to the main temple is cheap (a meal will set you back about HK$30) and pretty good.

*Sightseeing*

# Kadoorie Farm & Botanic Garden

In the years following World War II, Hong Kong was flooded with refugees, many of whom were destitute and did not have the funds to set themselves up working on the land. In response to this situation, the brothers (Lord) Lawrence and (Sir) Horace Kadoorie set up an agricultural aid project, which succeeded in providing around a third of a million people with the means to help themselves.

As farming has declined in Hong Kong, the organisation has developed a new focus towards education and conservation, aiming 'to increase the awareness of our relationship with the environment'. Its showcase is the superb **Kadoorie Farm & Botanic Garden** (KFBG).

More than a half of all the diverse plants found within Hong Kong are now growing at the KFBG, but its activities don't stop with the study and preservation of flora. Many of Hong Kong's larger mammals, as well as amphibians, reptiles and insects, can also be seen here, and there is also a substantial organic farm. One of the KFBG's particular concerns is the protection of native orchids and the rehabilitation of birds of prey.

Attractions on the scenic site include a waterfowl enclosure, a butterfly house and a deer haven. Visitors are welcome, but be sure to phone in advance to book an appointment.

*Lam Kam Road, Tai Po, New Territories (2488 1317/www.kfbg.org.hk). Tai Wo KCR, then taxi, or Tai Po Market KCR, then 64K bus.*
**Open** by appointment 9.30am-5pm Mon-Sat.
**Admission** free. **Map** p311.

## West New Territories

Large, modern satellite towns dominate much of the southern coast and low-lying valleys of the western New Territories. Beyond them are vast expanses of wilderness, much of it contained within the borders of the country parks of Lam Tsuen, Tai Lam and Tai Mo Shan. Mai Po Marshes, one of Hong Kong's most pristine wilderness areas, is also nearby.

### Tsuen Wan & Tai Mo Shan

**Tsuen Wan** was one of the first new settlements to be developed in the New Territories and, like most of the modern towns in the region, it is ugly, crowded and traffic-congested. Although it has little to offer the average tourist, there are a few worthwhile sights. The first is just a five-minute walk east of the MTR (take exit B3 to Sai Lau Kok Road), where you'll find the **Sam Tung Uk Museum** (*see p122*). Actually an 18th-century walled village, it was only recently made into a museum, because it was an active residential site – home to members of the Chan clan who migrated from Fujian province – until 1980, when the last residents finally moved out. Many people feel that much of its authenticity was damaged when the village was subjected to a subsequent restoration programme.

If the intricacies of large-scale engineering projects are your thing, then you'll be interested in the **Airport Core Programme Exhibition Centre** (*see p122*), just west of the Ting Kau bridge. This small exhibition details the huge project of building Hong Kong's new international airport on the levelled island of Chek Lap Kok.

The other sites associated with Tsuen Wan are a 25-minute walk into the hills above the town. Unfortunately, it's not a particularly pleasant stroll, as much of it is along and under busy highways, so it is more sensible to treat yourself to a taxi (which will cost about HK$20). The first site is one of the area's best temple complexes – **Chuk Lam Shim Yuen Monastery** ('Bamboo Forest Monastery'; *see p122*), a working Buddhist retreat, founded in 1927.

A short distance away is another temple facility, the **Yuen Yuen Institute** (*see p122*), which is the one sight that most visitors to Tsuen Wan want to see. A large facility housing Buddhist, Taoist and Confucianist temples, the Yuen Yuen is a fascinating, active complex with a variety of points of interest.

On the hillside just above the institute are footpaths leading up to **Tai Mo Shan**, the SAR's highest peak (its name means 'Big Misty Mountain'). It's a serious climb to the top, and you'll need to be well prepared: equip yourself with a decent map, plenty of water, suitable attire, a good pair of lungs and about four spare hours for a round trip journey. There are no facilities or shops on the way or at the summit, and there's no fast ride down on a funicular if you get tired or bored. The route is pretty, although more spectacular trails to the top lie along the **MacLehose Trail** (*see p34*), which runs roughly east to west on either side of Tai Mo Shan's summit. Sadly, the summit is dominated by a telecommunications complex, but there are still good views of the countryside, and you should be able to take photos that aren't filled with aluminium scaffolding and cables. Despite the direct line of sight across to Hong Kong Island, it is likely to be almost totally obscured, even on a cloudless day, by smog. The best way back to the city is to walk down the road to the edge of **Tai Mo Shan Country Park** and then catch the number 51 bus back to Tsuen Wan MTR station.

### Along the LRT from Tuen Mun

The former pirate port of **Tuen Mun** is now a large new town close to the far western edge of the New Territories. Although it doesn't look promising on first sight (dominated, as it is, by rows of modern buildings), don't give up – the area contains a couple of interesting and accessible temples, as well as the Ping Shan Heritage Trail.

Getting to Tuen Mun is easy – take the number 960 or 962 bus from Central and around an hour later you'll be here. Once you've arrived, it shouldn't take long to get the hang of the excellent Light Rail Transit (LRT), a complex looking but, in practice, very simple and efficient tram network. The LRT links Tuen Mun with Yuen Long to the north and what is turning into the sprawling conurbation between them. (Note that Octopus cards – *see p284* – are accepted on the LRT and must be validated at the correct terminal prior to boarding and again when alighting.)

Your first stop should be the **Ching Chung Koon Temple** (*see p122*), a Taoist temple set in lovely, carefully cultivated grounds. Climbing back onto the LRT and travelling two stops further north to Lam Tei LRT station will bring you to the modern and elaborately endowed **Mui Fat Buddhist Monastery** (*see p122*).

Perhaps the most rewarding place to spend an hour or so in the western New Territories is a few stops further up the line, where the short **Ping Shan Heritage Trail** starts just south

Sightseeing

# Mai Po Marshes

Within sight of the towers of Shenzhen and within earshot of the piledrivers laying foundations for new skyscrapers, wildlife flourishes in Hong Kong's richest habitat: **Mai Po Marshes**. The ponds, shrimp beds and mangrove swamps of this globally significant wetland attract a huge variety of bird and animal life. Cormorants, egrets, kingfishers and herons are just some of the bird species populating the marshes (around 60,000 birds winter here each year).

The 38-square kilometre (15-square mile) reserve is also the New Territories' last haven for otters, and one of the last habitats for the critically endangered black-faced spoonbill and Saunders' gull. Tens of thousands of migratory birds pass through here – some fly from Mai Po to Australia without feeding, a journey of more than 6,500 kilometres (4,000 miles). It is also the only remaining place where *gei wais*, traditional Chinese prawn ponds, are maintained and farmed. Simple to navigate, the flat reserve makes for very easy walking. Several bird hides provide good cover and the main hide is equipped with powerful binoculars.

Mai Po has become more ecologically significant in recent years, due to the disappearance of similar habitats along the Pearl River Delta as development and pollution have taken their toll. Unfortunately, the marsh has not escaped pollution. Sewage and industrial waste flushed into Deep Bay from Hong Kong and mainland China has affected the area's food chain since the 1980s, and is thought to be the reason behind an alarming decline in bird numbers in recent years.

Mai Po is a restricted area. The easiest way to visit is as part of a WWF tour, run every weekend and on public holidays. Tours last about three hours and cost HK$70 per person (binoculars can be hired for HK$20). Be sure to book well in advance – the tours are very popular. To reach Mai Po, take the KCR to Sheung Shui, then bus 76K to Yuen Long, which passes the entrance to the reserve.

For further information, phone the WWF on 2526 4473 or visit their website: www.wwf.org.hk/eng/maipo/index.html.

of Yuen Long. Like the Lung Yuek Tau Heritage Trail outside Fanling (*see p117*), the Ping Shan Heritage Trail features several historic buildings dating back hundreds of years. The first two buildings you'll come across en route are the 18th-century **Hung Shing Temple** and the beautifully painted, high-ceilinged **Kun Ting Study Hall**, which was built in the 19th century as a place where members of the Tang clan could study for their imperial civil service examination.

(Unfortunately, at the time of going to press, the study hall was closed to the public due to a long-running dispute between local villagers and the government.) Also on the trail, you'll find the recently-restored 700-year-old **Tang Ancestral Hall**, one of the finest in Hong Kong, and the 16th-century **Yu Kiu Ancestral Hall**. Keep an eye out, too, for the intriguing narrow alleyways and tiny houses of **Sheung Cheung Wai**, a walled village that is still inhabited today.

To reach the trail, take the LRT to Ping Shan station and walk west from the tram/road crossing for about five minutes. Look on the right side of the road for the map detailing the route of the trail, which begins at the Hung Shing Temple. It's best to be armed with a map from the start, as the signposting from the LRT to the trail is not clear.

Another sight worth visiting in the Tuen Mun area is **Castle Peak Monastery** (*see below*), perched halfway up a steep hillside south-west of town.

## Airport Core Programme Exhibition Centre

*401 Castle Peak Road, Ting Kau, New Territories (2491 9202). Bus 23B, 52, 96, 96M.* **Open** 10am-5pm Tue-Fri; 10am-6.30pm Sat, Sun. **Admission** free. **Map** p310.

This expensively put together exhibition offers plenty of impressively meaningless statistics about the ten large infrastructure projects connected with the new airport (such as how many times the steel cables used to construct the bridges could stretch round the world). There are a few good visuals, but the sum of the exhibition is disappointing, and it doesn't come close to doing justice to the enormity of the civil engineering that went into the creation of the airport. Instead, it devotes a good deal of space to rather boring projects, like land reclamation on the Kowloon peninsula. The best feature is the viewing platform on the roof, which offers good views over the harbour and across to the Tsing Ma and Ting Kau bridges.

## Castle Peak Monastery

*Tsing Shan Tsuen, near Tuen Mun, New Territories (no phone). Bus to Tuen Mun, then taxi.* **Open** 9am-5pm daily. **Admission** free. **Map** p310.

This Buddhist monastery is an eerily quiet place, often buffeted by a strong breeze blowing in from the sea. Inside, chanted prayers seem to come from nowhere (but are actually broadcast by a concealed modern sound system). The nearest LRT stop is Tsing Shan Tsuen, but it's a hard, steep trudge of about 1.5 kilometres (one mile) to the monastery from the station. A better way for those who are not hard core climbers is to take a taxi up the hill (which will cost about HK$20 from the town centre) and then walk back down to the LRT.

## Ching Chung Koon Temple

*Tuen Mun (no phone). Bus to Tuen Mun, then LRT to Ching Chung.* **Open** 9am-5pm daily. **Admission** free. **Map** p310.

This Taoist complex is a peaceful oasis, complete with ponds, sculptures, fountains and hundreds of venerable bonsai trees. In addition, if you happen to be in the area during the third or seventh lunar months, you might stumble upon one of the large-scale religious ceremonies held in its ancestral memorial halls. The temple is located a short walk north from Ching Chung LRT station.

## Chuk Lam Shim Yuen Monastery

*Tsuen Wan, New Territories (no phone). Tsuen Wan KCR, then taxi.* **Open** 7am-4pm daily. **Admission** free. **Map** p310.

The hillside facility houses several large and precious statues of the Buddha. On most days, monks clad in mustard-coloured robes can be seen chanting and offering prayers in the temple at the far end of the complex. With its large grounds and bucolic setting, the site is atmospheric, although some temple aficionados believe it not as impressive as the Po Lin monastery on Lantau (*see p132*). Judge for yourself.

## Mui Fat Buddhist Monastery

*Lam Tei, New Territories (no phone). Bus to Tuen Mun, then LRT to Lam Tei.* **Open** 9am-5pm daily. **Admission** free. **Map** p310.

Two large dragons coil up the pillars by the front door, flanked by two grimacing lions. This is a lavish, active and modern monastery with plenty of gold and marble, huge chandeliers, and the obligatory surfeit of large and small golden Buddha statues. There's also a popular vegetarian canteen on the second floor. The monastery is located a five-minute walk north of the LRT station, on the eastern side of a busy highway – you can see it from the pedestrian bridge at the station.

## Sam Tung Uk Museum

*2 Kwu Uk Lane, Tsuen Wan, New Territories (2411 2001/www.lcsd.gov.hk/stum). Tsuen Wan KCR.* **Open** 9am-5pm Mon, Wed-Sun. **Admission** free. **Map** p310.

Those looking for authenticity may be disappointed, as this walled village was virtually rebuilt from the ground up when the last residents more than 20 years ago, and many of the exhibits and materials used in the reconstruction were sourced from southern China. However, it's an interesting and creditable (if somewhat sanitised) attempt to paint a picture of life in a New Territories walled village 100 or so years ago.

## Yuen Yuen Institute

*Tsuen Wan, New Territories (no phone). Tsuen Wan KCR, then taxi.* **Open** 9am-6pm daily. **Admission** free. **Map** p310.

This highly popular Buddhist, Confucianist and Taoist complex is on most New Territories tourists' agenda. It includes a temple dedicated to the deities in charge of certain years and birth signs (similar to the Fung Ying Sin Koon temple in Fanling; *see p117*). The temple is almost always thronging with worshippers making offerings. The statues of the gods are all lively (and sometimes grotesquely) carved. A sign outside updates believers as to which birth signs might have trouble with the earth god of the current year and suggests making offerings to the relevant deity at the beginning and end of the year to help balance out the potential ill effects. The on-site vegetarian restaurant is popular with worshippers and tourists.

## East New Territories

The eastern New Territories is the most sparsely inhabited and least developed part of the SAR. To the north is the jagged peninsula containing the remote Pat Sing Leng and Plover Cove Country Parks. To the south is the even larger and similarly out of the way Sai Kung Peninsula with its long hiking trails, spectacular scenery and rock formations, and beautiful, isolated beaches.

### Plover Cove & the north-east

Prior to the development of the New Territories, the few incursions by humans into the wilderness of the north-east amounted to little more than small pearl fisheries and tiny Hakka settlements (the Hakka people migrated from north to south China centuries ago, and first settled in Hong Kong in the late 17th century; most are farmers and you will see the women out working in the fields wearing distinctive bamboo hats with black cloth fringes). Even today, there is no significant settlement east of Tai Po (*see p116*) and it remains a haven for adventurous hikers and wildlife enthusiasts. The **Wilson Trail** (*see p35*) winds north of **Plover Cove**, the huge reservoir that was created when a natural seawater bay was sealed with a massive dam. Larger fauna, such as

On the waterfront: **Sai Kung**.

barking deer and wild boar, still thrive in the area, although sightings from the trails are rare.

The best way to reach this area is to take the number 75K bus from Tai Po Market KCR station – it'll take about 40 minutes to reach **Tai Mei Tuk**. There, you will find a youth hostel (Bradbury Lodge; *see p53*) and a water sports centre (which, sadly, does not allow the casual hire of boats or windsurfing equipment). Walking opportunities abound here, ranging from ambitious hikes for the absurdly healthy to easy walks for those with only a modicum of fitness. One of the easiest is the gentle path around **Bride's Pool** – a naturally formed pool with a waterfall at the end of Bride's Pool Road, just under five kilometres (three miles) from Tai Mei Tuk. You can even make a picnic out of it, as there's a barbecue area close to the pool. For stronger walkers, Bride's Pool lies at the end of another walk – the well-marked six-kilometre (four-mile) **Pat Sing Leng Nature Trail**, which begins just above the **Plover Cove Country Park Visitor Centre** (a ten-minute walk east along Ting Kok Road from the Tai Mei Tuk bus stop). The route offers wonderful views of Plover Cove Reservoir and **Tolo Harbour**. For those who just can't bear the thought of walking one more step, a taxi ride from the bus stop back to Tai Po Market KCR station should cost no more than HK$25.

### Sai Kung & the south-east

This more easily accessible area of the New Territories takes in fine parkland, golden beaches, rolling surf and waterfront cafés and bars. You can hire a sampan to see the islands of Sai Kung, or simply wander to the gorgeous beaches near Wong Shek.

**Sai Kung** town is a sweet place with a quiet harbour that has become a popular refuge for expats (*see p124* **Expat strongholds**), who believe the Sai Kung Peninsula has some of Hong Kong's best beaches and loveliest open spaces. But while it's surrounded by a fairly wild area, Sai Kung itself offers a pleasant haven of civilisation, with a reasonable selection of restaurants (*see p163*), cafés, pubs and bars (*see p173*).

If heading out onto the water is your goal, your best bet is to start near the main ferry pier, where middle-aged women offer sampan rides around the harbour. Sampan hire costs about HK$50 per half hour, although it's worth trying to haggle the price down. The sampans are the only way to get to the small, secluded beaches on the islands close to Sai Kung (although the best beaches lie on the south-eastern tip of the peninsula). If you do hire a sampan, the tiny island of **Yim Tin Tsai** is worth a stop.

**Sightseeing**

# Expat strongholds

Visitors walking into the pubs of the fishing village of Sai Kung in the eastern New Territories would be forgiven for thinking the Brits had not departed from Hong Kong after all in 1997. The beer will be Boddington's, the accents ranging from rough Glaswegian to Devonian burr and the conversation about those quintessential British sports of rugby, cricket and football.

Listen carefully and there will probably be the odd Aussie or Kiwi accent piping up, and – occasionally – a Cantonese contribution, invariably from a local who has lived overseas and developed a taste for draught beer, shepherd's pie and blokeish company.

The pubs and bars of Sai Kung and other favoured expat residential areas act as drop-zones for the latest video episode of *Coronation Street* and all-round comfort zones for the homesick. Stroll into any hostelry in Sai Kung, or on Lamma or Lantau islands and the welcome will generally be warm: cliques do not have much time to develop in such a transient place as Hong Kong.

But a hard-core nucleus of expatriates do consider themselves belongers: anyone resident for seven continuous years earns the right to stay put indefinitely, vote in elections and generally enjoy the same rights as the mostly Chinese population.

Many workers involved in the airport construction, or other infrastructural projects, simply remained, picking up enough work to pay their bar bills, travel on the odd trip to Thailand or the Philippines and enjoy a generally cushier and more amenable lifestyle than in Scunthorpe or Southampton.

Others are involved in the full spectrum of professions and blue-collar work. There are pilots for Cathay Pacific on top-notch pay deals, second-hand car salesmen, teachers, scaffolders, musicians, tennis coaches, cops, deep-sea divers, hairdressers, photographers, dog kennel owners... and bartenders. Hong Kong – then and now – is a place where it is relatively easy to start a new life; people fleeing broken

Most of its devout Christian residents have departed, and many of the buildings are dilapidated – including St Joseph's Chapel at the top of the hill – but the remaining community is of interest.

Visiting the beaches at the south-eastern edge of Sai Kung is much more difficult, but it is feasible in a day if you start off early. The number 94 bus passes through Sai Kung every half hour (every hour at weekends) on its way to the coast at **Wong Shek**, a strategic spot from which to head for the beaches, and from which to begin walks to the north and east of the peninsula. One particularly dramatic day-long hike hugs the southern edge of the **High Island Reservoir**, ending at the lovely beach of **Long Ke Wan**. If you want to spend more than a day in the area, you can either camp or stay at the youth hostels in Wong Shek.

If time and/or energy are in short supply, there are walks closer to Sai Kung at **Pak Tam Chung**. For instance, if you take the number 94 bus to the **Pak Tam Chung Visitor Centre**, a short stroll along the nearby nature trail will take you past the well-preserved, but otherwise underwhelming, **Sheung Yiu Folk Museum** (*see p125*), a partially rebuilt 19th-century Hakka village. It's also worth popping into the Visitor Centre, which has some good displays on the wildlife and geology of the area.

Note that getting into, out of and around the wilderness on the Sai Kung Peninsula does take time. Careful planning and an early start will be necessary for all but the shortest walks. The number 92 bus to Sai Kung leaves frequently from Diamond Hill MTR.

The scenery and wilderness of **Clearwater Bay**, ten or so kilometres south of Sai Kung, may be less spectacular than in Sai Kung or Plover Cove, but the area has some good, easily accessible beaches. (Take the number 91 bus, which departs regularly from Diamond Hill MTR station.) The best two are those with the not particularly descriptive names of **Beach**

marriages and dull suburban jobs can reinvent themselves and quickly acquire a new circle of friends.

The largest concentration of long-staying expats is probably in Sai Kung, where four British-style pubs, Oddfellas, Steamers, Cheers and the Duke of York, serve Tetley's beer and fish and chips and stay open until the last man or woman is standing, or rather swaying. The seaside village, a favoured location because of its relatively cheap rents and mountain-fresh air, is an hour away from Central.

Another nucleus of voluntary exiles chooses to live in a similarly rural environment, on Lantau island, where a cluster of British-style pubs await passengers alighting from the ferry. Also a mere 60 minutes from downtown is Lamma island, once the favoured haunt of backpackers en route from Kathmandu to Australia. The whiff of not-so-legal substances used to mingle with the dried fish paste: stricter work visa requirement after 1997 saw many of the neo-hippies pack their frayed rucksacks for more friendly pastures.

Nonetheless, Lamma remains a lifestyle choice for the more laid-back members of the expat community. Stores near the pier sell second-hand books, banana muffins and patchouli oil, items not normally high on the average Cantonese family's shopping list.

The typical Lamma resident's idea of expat hell would be a transfer to the close-by community of Discovery Bay on Lantau island (*see p130*), a sealed-off collection of lookalike high rises straight out of *The Truman Show*. It's a great place for expats who like orderliness and calm – precisely the people who do not, on balance, care over-much for the bustle and buzz of Hong Kong.

Every day, professionals dressed in identical office outfits emerge from identical apartment blocks, board identical buses and step onto identical ferries. Individuality is discouraged: anyone having the temerity to leave so much as a shoe rack outside their apartment door is yellow-carded by the management.

Naturally, this family-oriented artificial creation does not have anything so welcoming or earthy as a pub; those with a thirst and hankering for convivial company hop on a rocking ferry to next-door Peng Chau for a cold Carlsberg.

The ultimate conglomeration of expats is, of course, up on the Peak, but for the most part the residents there are either on expatriate packages or diplomatic postings. And for all its undoubted merits, there is no place up there where a homesick expat can pop his (or her) head around the pub door and get the latest on *East Enders* or Manchester United.

One and **Beach Two**, where the water is clear and the golden sand is clean. They also have lifeguards and good facilities. Perhaps not surprisingly, these beaches are popular and tend to be very busy at weekends. Under no circumstances should you be tempted to stop at **Silverstrand Beach**, which – despite its nicer name – is a small sad place; its shores are lapped by dirty water awash with detritus.

Aside from sunbathing and swimming, there's not much to do at Clearwater Bay, which isn't necessarily a bad thing. However, if you can tear yourself away from the surf for a minute, there is a short excursion worth making. Two kilometres (1.5 miles) from Beach Two is the oldest surviving **Tin Hau Temple** (*see p94* **Tin Hau, sea goddess**) in Hong Kong, which dates back to 1274. Although it has been rebuilt and renovated, it's still one of the most impressive and atmospheric of the many Tin Hau temples in the SAR. The walk to the temple is fairly flat, and follows the

road from the Clearwater Bay bus stop south to Clearwater Bay Country Club. The path from the Club to the temple is not clearly marked, but is immediately to the right of the Club's guardhouse.

When your day in the sun is over, you can either take the number 91 bus all the way back to Diamond Hill MTR station, or as far as the prison on Clearwater Bay Road, where you can change to the number 101 bus that goes to Sai Kung.

### Sheung Yiu Folk Museum

*Pak Tam Chung Nature Trail, Sai Kung, New Territories (2792 6365/www.heritagemuseum.gov.hk/ english/branch.htm). Bus 94.* **Open** 9am-4pm Mon, Wed-Sun. **Admission** free. **Map** p311.
This museum was once a fortified village. Built in the late 19th century, it included dwellings, animal sheds and a watchtower. The displays include farm implements, household goods and everyday belongings of Hakka people. In many ways, it's a smaller version of the Sam Tung Uk Museum (*see p122*).

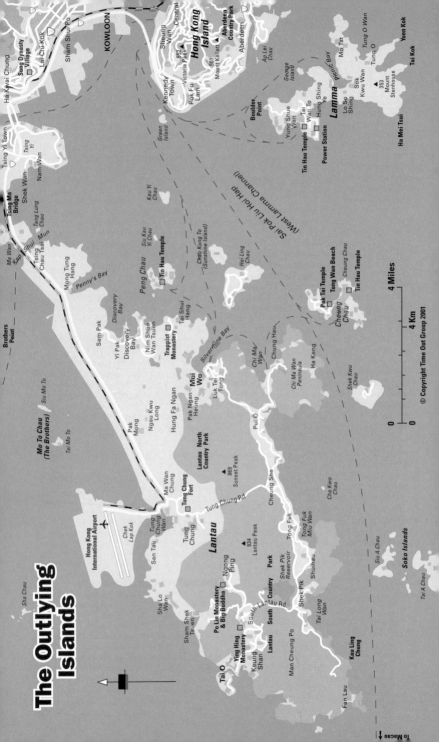

# The Outlying Islands

Secluded coves, great beaches, stunning hiking and fine seafood restaurants are but a boat ride away.

If you want to experience a very different side of Hong Kong to the ultra-modern maelstrom of Central and Tsim Sha Tsui, all you have to do is make for the outlying islands ferry piers in Central and head to one of the many unspoiled islands scattered to the west and south of Hong Kong Island. For pristine wilderness and dramatic mountainous landscapes, try massive Lantau; for gentler walking and superb seafood restaurants, go to Lamma; or sample the subtle charms of some of the smaller islands such as Cheung Chau and Peng Chau.

## Lamma

The third largest island in the SAR at 13 square kilometres (five square miles), **Lamma** is famed for its many open-air seafood restaurants, lack of motorised transport, greenery, abundant hillside trails and a significant, mostly British, expat community. It's certainly worth spending time here walking the trails, loafing on the beach or lounging in one of the many bars, pubs and cafés.

The most frequent ferry departures from Central and Aberdeen on Hong Kong Island head to the main town of **Yung Shue Wan** on the island's north-west tip, but it is also worth taking the boat to **Sok Kwu Wan** (on the south-east coast) for its long stretch of waterside seafood restaurants, and secluded walks and beaches. The best compromise is to go to one destination, then walk the four kilometres (two-and-a-half miles) across the island and leave from the other. The classic route is to start off in Yung Shue Wan, take in some of the cafés or some dim sum and complete the relatively gentle hike (though it is quite draining on a hot day) to Sok Kwu Wan's seafood restaurants, perhaps via one of the small beaches.

As one of the most easily reached pieces of greenery in Hong Kong, many city slickers head to Lamma at weekends, so weekdays offer the best chance to relax and enjoy all the space. And if you want to spend more than a day on Lamma, that's possible too, as there are several modest guesthouses and a youth hostel on the island.

Sok Kwu Wan. *See p129.*

### Yung Shue Wan

The ramshackle town of **Yung Shue Wan** starts around the ferry pier and runs along its harbour. This was a small fishing settlement until after World War II, and thereafter grew only slowly, much of its income earned from the manufacture of plastic goods in the 1970s. Today, it's a busy, charming place with plenty of expats, attracted by lower rents, cleaner air, and a generally friendlier and more relaxed atmosphere than on Hong Kong Island. In the 1990s, it attracted an alternative foreign crowd, including hippies, New Agers and hedonistic Eurotrash partiers, but since the Handover, their

# Fireman San

If you are lucky, you may see Lamma's lilliputian fire brigade performing a drill along the narrow lanes of Yung Shue Wan. Until recently, the fire-fighting force on the island consisted of just three tiny fire engines small enough to pass along paths less than 1.5 metres (five feet) wide. Four fire fighters ride with great solemnity on each of these minute tenders, which crawl through the crowded streets at a snail's pace. However, the force has been bolstered lately by the addition of two quad bikes, which are much more agile and speedier (if considerably less endearing) than the fire tenders.

If you don't get to see a drill, but still want to see Lamma's finest, head east out of Yung Shue Wan past the HSBC branch, then bear left and up the steep hill to Tai Peng village, taking the first right at the top, along the level path. You'll get a good view over the harbour and, after about five minutes, Lamma Fire Station, which will be visible on the right. The tenders are usually parked alongside a fun-size ambulance – the island's only conventional petrol-engined vehicle, which is used to carry the sick or injured to the ferry pier. It's undoubtedly a tough job being a Lamma firefighter and the crack teams here keep their professional edge by playing lengthy games of volleyball in the yard. The brigade does have to earn its keep at certain times of the year, particularly in the late autumn and during grave-visiting festivals, when sparks from burnt offerings or joss sticks start bush fires.

numbers – and the party spirit – have dwindled. However, their influence remains in the form of veggie cafés and the occasional party held on the beach next to the power station.

As you leave the ferry at Yung Shue Wan, look to the left and you'll see a smaller harbour with fishing boats and several traditional stilt houses overhanging the rocks and water. Turn to the right and you'll find the narrow main street. Most of the shops, restaurants, bars and cafés lie on either side of this street. The seafood restaurants are not cheap, as they supposedly source their seafood from outside Hong Kong's polluted waters, but there are a couple of good ones. The Sampan (see p164), which is the most popular with the locals, also serves good, cheap dim sum until about midday. The Green Cottage next door has some outdoor seating and offers health food, including some delicious fresh fruit juice concoctions. There's also a very good, and reasonably priced, sushi restaurant about 20 metres further along the main street. For a drink with a harbour view, head to the superbly named Deli Lamma, just south of the sushi place. The cheerfully alternative Bookworm Café (see p164), towards the far end of the main street, is a lovely, peaceful place to have a drink, eat excellent vegetarian food and read a book (from its mini library). For more on Yung Shue Wan's bars, see p174.

## Beaches

There are two beaches close to Yung Shue Wan, both within a 15-minute walk of the village. The first, **Tai Wan To**, is disconcertingly overlooked by Lamma's huge power station. Despite the view, it's not a bad stretch of sand, and is the site of one Hong Kong's most significant archaeological digs – items belonging to the Bronze Age societies that inhabited Lamma between 1200 and 400 BC have been unearthed here. Some of these artefacts, including finely crafted arrow heads and pottery, are on view in the Museum of History in Tsim Sha Tsui (see p106). Another few minutes' walk further south, just past the main police station, there's an excellent and popular beach at **Hung Shing Ye**. The Concerto Inn overlooking the beach is a cheap and cheerful café with some holiday accommodation.

## Sok Kwu Wan & southern Lamma

Hung Shing Ye beach is just off the main concrete path to Sok Kwu Wan, which is about an hour's steady walk from Yung Shue Wan. The more rugged dirt trail running over the hills, with fantastic views over the harbour and Hong Kong Island, offers a more scenic route to the south of the island, but you'll need a decent map and plenty of time to allow for detours and back tracking.

In the middle of Lamma, at its narrowest point, is **Lo So Shing**, an excellent, secluded beach that is also an archaeological site.

Whichever route you decide to take, you should see signs to the **Kamikaze Caves** on your right as you hit the eastern shore, very close to Sok Kwu Wan. Created by occupying Japanese forces during World War II, the caves were designed to hide small speedboats packed with explosives that were going to be used for suicide attacks on British shipping, but the war ended before they were ever employed.

**Sok Kwu Wan** has about a dozen seafood restaurants, none of which is cheap. All have views over the harbour, and there's not that much to differentiate them, but the Shark's Fin Restaurant is pretty consistent, the Lamma Mandarin Seafood Restaurant is well-known for its pigeon dishes and Rainbow Seafood (*see p164*) is always popular. The only blot on the landscape is the huge quarry facing the restaurants. However, some of it is being landscaped, which will lessen the impact of the ugly gouges taken out of the cliff face.

If you're not ready to eat, there's a fairly flat circular five-kilometre (three-mile) walk to the southern tip of the island that offers good shoreline views. You'll also come across the sleepy hamlet of **Shek Pai Wan**; as far away from stereotypical Hong Kong as it's possible to imagine. The lovely south-facing beach, where some of the older locals sit and play cards or mah jong, is spoiled somewhat by the

glass flotsam that has smashed in the surf and lies half hidden, particularly towards the western end of the beach, so take care if you go paddling or swimming. There's also a small temple to the sea god Hung Shing (who was a Tang Dynasty official credited with developing a basic form of meteorology), sacred to fishermen. **Tung O**, the small, all but deserted village nearby, is where Chow Yun-fat, star of the multi-award-winning *Crouching Tiger, Hidden Dragon*, was born and grew up.

Perhaps the best and most secluded beach on Lamma is just on the other side of the headland at **Sham Wan** – it is only accessible via a very narrow, overgrown track. This is the only beach in Hong Kong where green turtles still lay their eggs. It's also an archaeological site, from which finds dating back 6,000 years to the Stone Age have been dug. The oldest known settlement in Hong Kong, it was inhabited by a tribe of skilled seafarers, warriors and metal workers, known as the Yueh.

A steep climb away to the west, on the circular path back to Sok Kwu Wan, is **Mount Stenhouse**. The 353-metre (1,150-feet) summit is a spectacular vantage-point, offering an almost complete view of Lamma, fine vistas of Hong Kong Island to the north and Lantau to the west, and vertiginous views down to the wave battered rocks below. The route up is a tough scramble along a rocky, overgrown path, but well worth the effort for the reasonably fit.

Tin Hau Temple, **Sok Kwu Wan**.

# Lantau

Although twice the size of Hong Kong Island, Lantau remains, with a couple of exceptions, largely undeveloped. Many areas look much the same as they did when the island was acquired along with the New Territories in 1898. Two huge country parks contain the peaks that form the backbone of the island and numerous hiking trails. On a misty day, the steep wooded hillsides are somewhat reminiscent of the Scottish Highlands. Lantau Peak, the second highest, at 934 metres (3,064 feet) would just qualify as a Scottish Munro.

The development of the new airport on Chek Lap Kok and the Tsing Ma Bridge linking the northern coast of Lantau with the mainland have not had a hugely noticeable impact on the character of the island. However, the opening of the new Disneyland at Penny's Bay in 2005, which is expected to attract 18 million (mostly mainland Chinese) visitors annually, as well as the infrastructure and hotels that will go with it, looks likely to change all that. Today, the main settlements are limited to the wealthy enclave of Discovery Bay, the new airport town of Tung Chung and the ferry terminal at Mui Wo.

This leaves plenty of space, particularly at the south-western end of Lantau, making it a terrific retreat from the clamour of Hong Kong. The seclusion offered on Lantau has made it a popular retreat for (mainly Buddhist) religious orders. The most striking retreat is the Po Lin Monastery, high on the hill next to Lantau Peak, which is home to one of the world's largest outdoor Buddha statues.

There are some good beaches along the southern coast of Lantau, as well as some very wild and inaccessible areas inland. One of the few remaining (and probably the most interesting) traditional fishing settlements in Hong Kong clings to the western coast of Lantau at Tai O. Here, you will still find a large cluster of traditional stilt houses on the muddy banks of the small estuary. Tai O has terrific character and a wander around this sleepy town is definitely recommended.

## Discovery Bay

The purpose-built executive enclave of **Discovery Bay** lies just north-east of the ferry port of Mui Wo. The settlement here has an eery Stepford-meets-Disney feel to it, providing a haven for its Benetton-clad *gweilo* residents, back from their executive offices in Central, in up-market Bay apartment blocks that rejoice in names like Brilliance Court, Bijou Hamlet and Neo Horizon. As cars are banned, the better-off own golf buggies, which are parked all over the place, some with baby seats, others sporting football stickers in their windscreens.

The main reasons for coming here are the long sandy beach, the short walk to the Trappist Monastery and the *kaido* (small ferry) to Peng Chau (*see below*). The fast, smart catamaran ferry to Discovery Bay takes about 25 minutes from Central, costs HK$25 and empties onto the neat square or, as it's known in Discovery Bay, plaza. Needless to say, there are some good, although not outstanding, restaurants here, and a few coffee shops. The clean, man-made beach just north of the ferry pier is tidy and the water looks relatively clean, but if the wind is blowing from behind the beach, it whips up stinging sandstorms.

*Kaidos* to Peng Chau run pretty much hourly from the quayside at the southern edge of the headland that divides Discovery Bay from the small harbour and beach of **Nim Shue Wan**. From the plaza by the Discovery Bay ferry terminal, walk to the far end of the bus station, turn left and then walk along the small quayside, looking out for a very small timetable and steps, from where the *kaidos* depart. If you fancy a short hike, there's a two-kilometre (one-mile) or so route starting at the top of Nim Shue Wan beach, which leads to the **Trappist Monastery**. From there, you can also jump on a *kaido* to Peng Chau, although only ten run each day and none operates between 12.20pm and 3pm. Both *kaido* rides cost HK$4 and take roughly ten minutes. If you don't feel like walking, there are also a few *kaidos* each day that go to Peng Chau via the ferry pier leading to the Trappist Monastery. From there, it's a short, steep trudge up to the monastery, the way lined – appropriately enough – with some sombre stations of the cross.

## Mui Wo & the southern beaches

**Mui Wo** (dubbed **Silvermine Bay** by the British), is the main jumping-off point for Lantau and the place to catch buses to most other destinations on the island. It's 40 minutes and HK$10.50 away on the ferry from Central, and the bus terminus is right outside the Mui Wo ferry terminal. Catch a bus from here to the beaches on Lantau's southern coast, to Ngong Ping for the Big Buddha and Lantau Peak, and to the old fishing village of Tai O.

Mui Wo is a pleasant enough place, but there are more interesting destinations on the island. If you want to – or are forced to – spend time here, there are a few things to do. Mui Wo's long stretch of beach, complete with shark net, is a five-minute walk north along the edge of the bay. There are also a few bars (such as the China Bear and the Hippo Bar; *see p164*) and

Majestic Lantau, as seen from **Po Lin Monastery**. *See p132.*

some restaurants, most of them around the ferry and bus terminals. The cooked food market just above the bus station contains several restaurants serving cheap, but not particularly appetising, canteen fare. The Sea View offers dim sum from 6am to 1pm. A number of pricier, but better, places just west of the bus station serve up everything from curry to pizza. There are also a couple of bars and cafés, including the pub-like Papa Doc's, and a supermarket.

One possible excursion from Mui Wo is the three-kilometre (two-mile) walk to the **Trappist Monastery** to the north-west of the town, although the route is steep and pretty tough in parts. Be sure to take a good map with you.

A number of decent, extensive beaches run along the southern coast of Lantau; two of the best, in terms of cleanliness and facilities, being **Pui O Wan** and **Cheung Sha**. All buses leaving Mui Wo (except for the number 7, which only goes as far as the village of Pui O) pass these two beaches. Cheung Sha is just over two kilometres (one mile) further west of Pui O. Look out for the signs marking Cheung Sha and ring the bell for the stop just after the police station, which you should see on the right. The path to the beach is a few metres further west along the road. The beach here is excellent (long, clean and empty, with changing facilities), while the water is as clean as anywhere in Hong Kong, although there's no shark net. There are a couple of places to eat, including Stoep (*see p165*), which offers a mix of good value Mediterranean and South African food. The house speciality is the barbecue menu, which includes home-made *boerewors*, a type of South African sausage. The pickled Cape fish with curry sauce is also good.

## Ngong Ping, Po Lin Monastery & the Big Buddha

From Mui Wo, it's a bumpy, winding 16-kilometre (ten-mile) journey on the number 2 bus to **Ngong Ping**. En route, the bus passes along the edge of **Lantau South Country Park** and **Shek Pik Reservoir**. If it's a clear day (and you're sitting on the right-hand side of the bus), you will get a good view of the 34-metre (110-foot) high Buddha statue at Ngong Ping as the bus passes the reservoir.

When the bus finally reaches its destination, tourists and devotees (the former usually outnumbering the latter) disgorge and head for the nearby **Po Lin Monastery** (*see p134*) and the **Big Buddha** – the largest bronze outdoor seated Buddha in the world. Monks began arriving on Lantau in the early 20th century,

The fishing village...

but the monastery really developed in the 1920s when the first abbot was appointed and the great hall built. The immense Buddha statue was the location of a mass, month-long demonstration in 2000 by members of the Falun Gong movement who were upset that the abbot of Po Lin had spoken out against them and their beliefs during the National People's Congress in China.

Ngong Ping is also a good starting point from which to tackle the steep slopes of **Fung Wong Shan** or **Lantau Peak**, the second highest summit in the SAR. The route up begins to the east of the monastery past the Tea Farm (which consists of a scruffy café and a meagre tea plantation). Many walkers stay overnight at the SG Davis Youth Hostel (*see p53*) and get up early to make it up the peak in time for sunrise. Call ahead to book a bed and check opening times, as the hostel is often closed during the day.

Other walking options from the monastery include the relatively gentle trek down from the monastery north to **Tung Chung**, which is about 6.5 kilometres (four miles) away. From the town, there is a fast train back into Central – a single ticket costs HK$23. Take care if you do decide to tackle the concrete path, as parts are slick with moss and mulch when it has rained. On the way down, you will pass two Buddhist monasteries. The path takes you through the gardens of the first; these are

... of **Tai O**.

often tended by nuns, and smell of a mix of incense and freshly dug earth. A place of quiet retreat, visitors are not usually permitted to enter the buildings. At the bottom of the path, where it meets the road, you'll find the rather more friendly and welcoming **Lo Hon Monastery** (2988 1419). It serves a vegetarian lunch costing HK$60 daily from 11.30am to 3.30pm.

## The Fan Lau Trail

An excellent day-long hike, taking in old ruins, stunning sea views and beaches, snakes around the edges of the south-western spur of Lantau. There are two possible routes. The first, flatter option is to take the path that starts at the south-western tip of Shek Pik Reservoir and hugs the coastline. The second, steeper and more dramatic route starts from the top of a hill on the Lantau Trail, just to the north-west of the reservoir. The distances covered are both around the 12-14-kilometre (seven-and-a-half-nine-mile) mark, depending on the detours taken. Both trails take between five and six hours to complete, and end up in the village of Tai O. If you take the first option, there are a couple of places to camp along the way.

At enchanting **Fan Lau**, you'll find yourself in the company of an old Tin Hau temple, an old school house and a few elderly residents. There's also an ancient Chinese fort, thought to

have been built some time in the early 1800s, which is a good place to gaze out to sea and watch the Macau-bound jetfoils streak past. The going becomes even easier once you've passed the abandoned village of Yi O San Tsuen on the western side of the spur, as the path has been concreted pretty much all the way into Tai O. A good map and plenty of water are essential if you want to tackle this trail.

## Tai O

**Tai O**, a large but quiet village perched on the far south-western coast of Lantau, is certainly worth a trip. It's one of the last remaining fishing villages with stilt houses, which were first built here by the Tanka people (nomadic boat people who have fished in Hong Kong's waters for centuries) several hundred years ago.

If you're not walking to Tai O, you should take the number 1 bus from Mui Wo – a journey that takes about 40 minutes and costs HK$8 (plus a couple of extra dollars on Sundays).

From the bus station, the village clusters around the mouth of a small estuary. A walk over the short pedestrian bridge will take you into the heart of the settlement. Close to Tai O Market Street, you'll find a temple dedicated to Kwan Tai, the god of war and righteousness, that dates back to the 1530s. The main cluster of stilt houses lies a short walk east along Tai O

Market Street; some of these tiny dwellings are little larger than Wendy houses. Walk behind them and you'll find that there is a small boat moored at almost every house.

The left-hand fork on Tai O Market Street (in front of the Kwan Tai temple) leads to the western edge of Tai O, past the fire station, complete with tiny fire tenders (like those found on Lamma; *see p128* **Fireman San**), and a couple of shrimp paste manufacturers. You will probably pick up the pungent smell of the paste before you see the blue plastic tubs in which it ferments in the sun. You can buy jars of shrimp paste and shrimp sauce here for between HK$15 and HK$30. These sharp, powerful sauces are similar to Thai fish paste and impart a strong fishy flavour – they can even jack up a simple dish like stir-fried vegetables. It's also used to spice up squid in many of the seafood restaurants on the outlying islands.

About 200 metres (650 feet) past the shrimp paste manufacturers, you'll come across the fortress-like Tai O police station, which dominates the edge of the island. The ferries to Sha Lo Wan (further north along the coast) and Tuen Mun (in the New Territories) stop here. There are two sailings each way, one in the morning and one in the afternoon, from Monday to Friday; three sailings on Saturday and five on Sunday. The fare is HK$15 to Sha Lo Wan and HK$28 to Tuen Mun.

Food in Tai O is very traditionally Chinese and, needless to say, seafood dishes dominate. The Fook Moon Lam Restaurant, next door to the Kwan Tai temple to Tai O Market Street, does good seafood and dim sum. The Wing Fat Restaurant close to the bus stop (before you head over the bridge) has a varied menu of simple Cantonese dishes and Western snacks. Prices are very reasonable.

### Po Lin Monastery

*Ngong Ping, Lantau (no phone). Bus from Mui Wo ferry pier.* **Open** 10am-6pm daily. **Admission** free. **Map** p126.

The monastery itself is grand, although somewhat outshone by the statue of the Buddha. Inside the grounds, there are bauhinia and orchid gardens, as well as basic but good, cheap vegetarian food in two canteens inside the grand hall complex. You must buy a meal ticket at the foot of the steps to the Buddha statue – this also grants access to the display rooms underneath the Buddha, which tell the story of Buddha's path to enlightenment. The filling, if somewhat stodgy, snack menu (noodles and dim sum) costs HK$28, while the full vegetarian lunch costs HK$60 for the basic and HK$100 for the deluxe menu. Meals are served between 11.30am and 5pm.

The **Big Buddha**, star attraction at **Po Lin Monastery**.

# Cheung Chau

The tiny former pirate island haven of **Cheung Chau** lies west of Hong Kong Island and close to Lantau. It supports a population of around 20,000, but somehow manages to accommodate them all without ever seeming too crowded – except, of course, when visitors from the rest of Hong Kong flock here at weekends. Even when it's packed, this is an intriguing place to head when you've had enough of the urban jungle. There are plenty of secluded areas and a couple of good beaches. The sheltered cliffside walk on the southern coast passes small rocky bays and elegant, neatly kept houses reminiscent of the Mediterranean. It's a surprising contrast to the deeply Chinese feel of the town's narrow shopping alleys or the temples and mini-shrines dotted around it.

Cheung Chau is perhaps best known for its colourful **Bun Festival** (*see p205*) held every May; it honours the island's patron god and placates the restless spirits of former Cheung Chau souls who met with untimely deaths through plagues or piracy.

It's perfectly feasible to spend a leisurely day here. Orienting yourself on the island is simple: the narrow spine where the ferries dock forms the centre of town, while the blocks of land to the south and north (which were originally two separate islands) contain walking trails and smaller beaches. In terms of going out and eating, Cheung Chau does not have quite the diversity of Lamma, but the seafood here is cheaper (*see p165*).

The ferries from Central or Lantau empty out onto a wide strip running the length of the harbour that is mostly occupied by seafood restaurants. Standards and prices are pretty uniform, but one of the most popular places (with Westerners and Chinese alike) is the Baccarat towards the northern end of the harbour front. The small alleys running off Pak She and San Hing streets contain dozens of small Chinese shops and businesses, selling incense, paper offerings and Chinese medicine.

A couple of minutes walk away from the ferry pier is the **Pak Tai Temple** (being almost completely rebuilt at the time of going to press) opposite the basketball court at the top of Pak She Street. The god Pak Tai is credited with bringing to an end a virulent outbreak of the plague in 1777, prompting the grateful islanders to build an ornate temple in his honour in 1783.

The island comes to a standstill every May during the famous **Cheung Chau Bun Festival** (*see p205*), a religious festival that has evolved into a colourful three-day carnival attracting thousands of visitors. About 100 years ago, after an episode of bad luck and

**Tung Wan** beach. *See p136.*

illness, the islanders started offering lotus-paste buns to the spirits of the dead. Health and prosperity returned to the island, and it was decided to make the ceremony an annual event. Each year, three 13-metre (40-feet) high bamboo towers, covered in thousands of steamed buns, are erected in front of the Pak Tai Temple and left out for three days. Taoist priests hold the requisite ceremonies to encourage the return of all the restless ghosts to the underworld. Before they return, the spirits consume the 'essence' of the buns, while islanders and visitors eat the remains. The chaotic scramble to reach the luckiest buns at the top of the pile was once one of the striking events in the festival, but this mad rush was banned years ago after a serious accident. Today, the focus of the festival is on the procession of floats, lion dancers and the colourful 'floating' children, representing characters from myth and legend, who are strapped to cleverly hidden poles and seemingly waft along above the crowd.

The islanders do not just limit their homage and worship to Pak Tai. Dozens of small temples and shrines dot the island, many of them dedicated to earth spirits. One of the most important is the banyan tree on Tung Wan Road, close to the bottom end of San Hing

Sightseeing

Street. The tree and the spirits said to inhabit it are held in such esteem that when the road needed to be widened, a restaurant opposite was demolished instead of the tree.

One of the best (and most popular) beaches is **Tung Wan**, which you'll find at the eastern end of Tung Wan Road. The beach is fairly large by Hong Kong standards and is well kept. The shark nets are removed and the facilities closed between November and April, but it is still possible to swim.

Although there are some pleasant, secluded paths in the northern section of the island, the southern part of Cheung Chau offers the best walks. From Tung Wan beach, head south around the back of the Warwick Hotel and go past the Kwun Yum temple. The gradients are gentle and it's an easy walk to the south-western tip of the island along Peak Road West. When you reach the cemetery, make a detour down to **Pak Tso Wan**, one of the nicer small beaches in southern Cheung Chau.

Peak Road West heads into the small village of **Sai Wan**, from where it is possible to get the constantly shuttling HK$2.50 sampan back into the centre of Cheung Chau. It's also a good way to see the harbour. Turning sharp left opposite the pier will take you along the path to the far western tip of the island. The signs point to the final destination, a tiny cave with dubious claims to being the place where the 19th-century pirate Cheung Po-tsai hid the plunder from his raids on shipping in the area. There's not much to see, but the rocky outcrop offers good sea views and it's a pleasant walk. The cave itself is really just a small hole; you'll need a torch to see inside it.

# Reburying the dead

It has long been a tradition in Hong Kong and China that the dead are buried with their ancestors and close to family members who are still alive. Many burial plots on Cheung Chau, as with those in other parts of Hong Kong, are leased for seven years, after which the offspring of the deceased disinter the bones, clean them, place them in a large earthenware jar and take it to an ancestral burial ground or memorial.

The practice is particularly popular in Hong Kong, where there is a lack of burial space. Prime cemetery sites (with good *feng shui*) are expensive: a first-rate burial plot can cost several hundred thousand Hong Kong dollars. The belief in family closeness, even after death, is strong and there's even a special day-long festival, **Ching Ming**, when families gather together to show respect to their ancestors. The strength of this belief has led to a small, but flourishing, trade in the transportation of remains from Hong Kong to the USA, Canada, Australia and other places where Hong Kong Chinese have settled abroad, so that the emigrants can pay their respects to their dead relatives more often and with greater ease.

**Cheung Chau**'s main drag.

## Other islands

There are literally hundreds of small islands scattered around Hong Kong's waters, many of them uninhabited and often inaccessible. Unless you hire a boat for the day or evening, you will be bound by the infrequent ferry services to Po Toi and Tap Mun Chau, though access to Peng Chau is easier. Hiring a junk with a crew is not out of the question if you are in a group of five or more. Prices start at about HK$2,000 for a day, although you may be able to haggle the price down on weekdays. The Yellow Pages has extensive junk hire listings.

## Peng Chau

The tiny island of **Peng Chau** lies just across the water from Discovery Bay on Lantau. Partly owing to its size, there's less to do and see here than on the other populated islands. Peng Chau's charm lies in its very traditional Hong Kong character; it's certainly a welcome contrast to the unappealing anodyne orderliness of Discovery Bay (*see p130*).

The main settlement around the ferry pier is a maze of small alleys, shops and tiny temples. The easy pace of life here is maintained to a soundtrack of Chinese crooning leaking from old radio sets and the clatter of mah jong tiles. Given that Peng Chau is less than one square kilometre (half a square mile), you probably won't be surprised to learn either that the island lacks a decent beach or that eating and drinking options are limited.

An hour or two is all that's needed to stroll around the entire island. A good place to head first is south down Wing On Street and Shing Ka Road, then east along Nam Shan Road to **Finger Hill**, Peng Chau's highest point. It's only about ten minutes' walk from the ferry pier, but the final stretch is steep. The reward, however, is to share the view over the island with the black kites that hover lazily around the summit.

The little town, which so far has not been spoiled by development, is the only place to go for food or drink. Although the seafood restaurants here are not especially celebrated, they are relatively cheap, and are popular at weekends. If you crave Western snack food, try the Jungle and the Sea Breeze, next door to each other at 38 and 40 Wing Hing Street. The outside seating at the former looks across to the ferry pier and Lantau, although a new road running between the restaurants

Peng Chau.

and the water (under construction at the time of going to press) may interrupt the peace and quiet.

Similarly, the construction of a new road and rocky breakwater along the edge of the small harbour at Tung Wan on the other side of the island has essentially destroyed the beach. It's not a great loss, however, as both water and beach have long been polluted.

Peng Chau is easily accessible from the outlying islands ferry pier in Central, with ferries leaving every 45 minutes. A single fare on the slow ferry, which takes about 45 minutes, costs HK$10.50. The single fare on the slightly faster express costs HK$21. There are also less frequent ferry and *kaido* (small boat) services from Discovery Bay and Mui Wo on Lantau and from Cheung Chau. Some of the *kaidos* plying their trade between Discovery Bay and Peng Chau also stop at the ferry pier near the Trappist Monastery. If you plan to head back into Discovery Bay, it's worthwhile jumping off at the monastery pier and making the short two-kilometre (one-and-a-half-mile) walk along the well-signposted shoreline path.

## Po Toi

The hills and cliffs of the small rocky island of **Po Toi** shelve steeply into the ocean a few kilometres south of Hong Kong Island. It has some rugged walking trails, from which there are terrific views over the South China Sea and across to Hong Kong Island. The tiny, pretty harbour and beach of Tai Wan contains one good seafood restaurant, the Ming Kee (2849 7038), which is open every day.

Despite its proximity to Hong Kong, Po Toi is remote and sparsely populated. Travelling to the island without chartering a boat is only really practical on Sunday, as there's no return ferry during the week and the island has no accommodation or flat ground on which to camp. However, it's certainly worth considering Po Toi as a destination during the week if you have hired a junk for the day.

There are several walking routes, ranging from concrete paths to rocky, semi-overgrown trails. The most dramatic walking is on the eastern side of the island, on the steep (and often slippery) trail above the Tin Hau temple. One of Hong Kong's ancient rock carvings, thought to date back to the Bronze Age and similar to the one found at Shek O (*see p96* **The first Hong Kongers?**), is found on the western side of the island, but there's not much to see as the carvings have been all but weathered away. In two hours, you should have circumnavigated the island.

The *kaido* from the ferry pier at St Stephen's beach in Stanley takes about 40 minutes and costs HK$40 for the return journey; on the way out, you'll need to tell the operator which afternoon boat you'll be returning on. The *kaido* leaves Stanley on Sunday at 10am and 11am, and returns at 3pm and 4.30pm. A ferry also leaves from Aberdeen (right next to the fish market) at 8am on Sunday and returns at 6pm.

## Tap Mun Chau

**Tap Mun Chau** (*see also p116*) is a tiny island just over two kilometres (one mile) long and about one kilometre (half a mile) wide, located off the north-east tip of the Sai Kung Peninsula. It's a real out of the way place with considerable charm, clean water and some small but good beaches on its east side. There's a surprisingly large and pretty **Tin Hau Temple** in the village of **Tap Mun**, whose few inhabitants still live to a great extent off the sea. It's one of the few places in Hong Kong where you can still see plenty of seafood being dried in the sun.

The short walk past the police post to the eastern shore takes in Tap Mun Chau's strange fern (presumably where the island gets its name, which translates as Grass Island) and cactus-like coastal plant life and, surreally, its small herd of cows. A refreshing breeze blows off the South China Sea and big waves break against the striking rock formations. Typically for Hong Kong, many weekend visitors take the opportunity to dump as much rubbish as possible here and it lies strewn all over this side of the island. In fact, the most rubbish-free places are the island's few bins.

Boats for Tap Mun Chau depart from Ma Liu Shui ferry pier, on the outskirts of Sha Tin. To reach the ferry pier, exit the Sha Tin KCR on the east side and walk north past the station. The path goes over and then under the busy carriageway. As you emerge from the short tunnel, the ferry pier will be visible a couple of hundred metres to the north. As there are only two sailings a day to Tap Mun Chau, it's advisable to plan ahead. Basically, you can either go early and spend the whole day there, or you can take the afternoon cruise, which will give you an hour to look around the island. The journey takes about an hour on the slow old *kaido*, which costs HK$16 each way during the week and HK$25 each way at the weekend. The *kaido* leaves Ma Liu Shui at 8.30am and 3pm, returning at 11.10am and 5.30pm, Monday to Friday. Weekend departures are at 8.30am, 12.30pm and 3pm, with return journeys at 11.10am, 1.45pm and 5.30pm. However, it's recommended to phone the ferry company (2527 2513) to double-check times.

# Eat, Drink, Shop

**Restaurants**     **141**
**Pubs & Bars**     **166**
**Shops & Services**     **175**

**Feature boxes**

| | |
|---|---|
| The best restaurants | 144 |
| Chinese cuisines | 148 |
| Fast food, coffee & snacks | 154 |
| Restaurants by cuisine | 158 |
| Bars with food | 163 |
| Sex in the city | 167 |
| The best bars | 174 |
| The art of bargaining | 177 |
| Hong Kong fashion designers | 183 |
| **HK profiles** David Tang | 189 |
| **HK profiles** Sam the Tailor | 191 |
| Markets of Hong Kong | 194 |
| Break for the border: Shenzhen | 201 |

**Yung Kee Restaurant** Open since 1942, one of the oldest establishments in Hong Kong. Yung Kee acquires fame for its gourmet speciality - Roasted Goose, it becomes well known not only in Hong Kong, and it also attracts many tourists from foreign countries.

Yung Kee Restaurant is famous in the world since the 60's. In 1968, it was the only Chinese restaurant chosen by the FORTUNE MAGAZINE as one of the Top Fifteen Best Restaurant in the World. We have been awarded over 40 prizes including Gold Award and Platinum Award in the international culinary competitions.

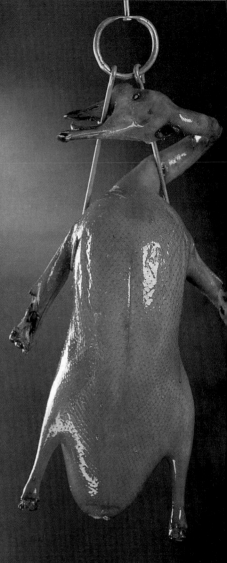

鏞記酒家
YUNG KEE RESTAURANT

**Open Daily** 11:00am ~ 11:30pm
(Dim-sum dining) 2:00 ~ 5:30pm (Monday to Saturday)
11:00am ~ 5:30pm (Sunday and Public Hol
**Reservation and Information** Tel. 2522 1624 Fax. 2840
**Credit Cards** We honour Visa, Mastercard, American Exp
and Diners Club.
**Free Parking Service** 6:30 ~ 11:00pm Daily

32-40 Wellington Street, Central, Hong Kong

# Restaurants

Hong Kong's army of moneymakers certainly marches on its stomach, and it has a wonderful array of Western and Eastern eateries from which to choose.

Passion for food is as strong in Hong Kong as anywhere in the world, including France. The native cuisine is Cantonese, but locals are willing to try anything. Dishes from Sichuan, Chiu Chow and Shanghai are the most popular regional Chinese cuisines (*see p148* **Chinese cuisines**), while Japanese, Vietnamese and Thai top those from Asia. Beyond that, this city has everything from Alsatian to Mexican and Italian to Australian.

Eating out is a central part of Hong Kong life. This has a lot to do with the fact that large, extended families tend to live in cramped flats with tiny kitchens, so it is often easier to eat out up to three meals per day. Noodle shops are ubiquitous. The food is cheap and tasty, though service is often rude and hurried: don't be offended if a waiter grabs your menu, spills your dish when placing it on the table or gives you your bill before you can say '*Mei dan, mgoi*' (bill, please). That's the norm. Choose a place that looks clean, and if there's no English menu, look at what other diners are eating and point. If you don't think you're ready to try

chicken feet, duck tongues or pigs' lungs, there are plenty of simple rice and noodle dishes on offer. Barbecued pork, steamed chicken and roast goose are invariably good.

Many of the top Western restaurants used to be located in the city's five-star hotels, but now a large number of independent world-class eateries have been opened, many by former hotel chefs. In fact, the choice has become so wide it can be bewildering. But, in general, because they are recent additions to the restaurant scene, the trend is towards modern chrome-and-glass decor, with marble surfaces and large windows. Most offer an intriguing new combination of tastes and allow creative chefs to devise original menus, with the emphasis very much on fusion dishes that combine traditional Western ingredients with Asian spices. And the clientele – a mix of expats and Chinese – tends to match the food. The main dining out areas are Central (Lan Kwai Fong and SoHo), Wan Chai, Causeway Bay and Tsim Sha Tsui, along with the outlying islands and coastal areas, which are busy on weekends.

You've got to go for the goose at **Yung Kee**. *See p143.*

## PRICES & TIPPING

Eating out in Hong Kong is not cheap. While local noodle and rice shops and fast food outlets (*see p154* **Fast food, coffee & snacks**) offer inexpensive eats, anywhere that deems itself a restaurant hikes up the price according to its perceived status. Spending HK$1,000 on a meal for two with wine will not mean you are in one of the city's top establishments, merely a middle-range restaurant. Many expats have large disposable incomes, while the rent for premises can be outrageously high, so restaurateurs charge accordingly.

Major credit cards are accepted in most of the city's restaurants (above the basic level) and a ten per cent service charge is automatically added to the bill in most cases. In Hong Kong, however, this rarely goes to the staff, so a further gratuity is normal – the amount is discretionary, depending on the level of service.

# Hong Kong Island

## Central

## American

### The Bayou

*9-13 Shelley Street, Central, HK Island (2526 2118). Mid-Levels Escalator/12M, 13, 12A, 26, 40M, 43 bus.* **Open** 9am-midnight daily. **Main courses** HK$80-$200. **Credit** AmEx, DC, MC, V. **Map** p66 B4.
Authentic cooking from America's deep south, from where the extrovert female owner hails. With dishes like alligator stew, Cajun chicken and prawn creole gumbo, the food is never dull. A bar area next to the main restaurant serves great snack meals and breakfasts for well under HK$100, and it's an ideal place for people watching as the Mid-Levels Escalator slides by outside.

## Asian

### Eating Plus

*Shop 1009, 1/F, International Finance Centre, Central, HK Island (2868 0599). Central MTR Station (exit A)/buses along Connaught Road Central.* **Open** 7.30am-10pm daily. **Main courses** HK$35-$65. **No credit cards**. **Map** p67 D2.
Long wooden tables shared by diners perched on benches mean that this is not a place to linger. But it's always packed as shoppers and office workers wolf down the healthy, palate-tingling dishes. The menu is innovative, with a great selection of fruit and vegetable juices, along with superb fusion food. Ramen noodles served in spicy hot broth are a must. The decor is bright, modern and airy (a no-smoking zone), but the best moment comes when you see how low the bill is.

### Noodle Box

*30-32 Wyndham Street, Central, HK Island (2536 0371). Central MTR (exit D1, G)/13, 26, 43 bus.* **Open** 11.30am-10pm Mon-Sat. **Main courses** HK$25-$40. **No credit cards**. **Map** p66 C4.
The best value meal in town is the happy hour special served between 3.30pm and 6pm every day at this tiny, bright eatery. For HK$25 you can have a piping hot broth with noodles of your choice cooked in the style of various cuisines around Asia. The Thai chicken and the spicy seafood are amazing. Prices in normal hours are pretty cheap anyway, and there are a few other snacks and cakes from which to choose.

## British

### Soho Soho

*9 Old Bailey Street, Central, HK Island (2147 2618). Central MTR (exit D1, D2)/Mid-Levels Escalator/buses along Hollywood Road & Caine Road.* **Main courses** HK$120-$180. **Credit** AmEx, DC, MC, V. **Map** p66 C4.
A fine example of how far British cuisine has developed in world terms. The chefs here take traditional ingredients like beef, pastry and potatoes but serve them up in an aesthetically pleasing, waistline-preserving way. More taste, less fat – until the desserts arrive, like good old bread and butter pudding. Soho Soho's cosy and attracts a mixed Chinese/expat clientele.

## Chinese: Cantonese

### City Hall Chinese Restaurant

*2/F, Low Block, City Hall, 7 Edinburgh Place, Central, HK Island (2521 1303). Central MTR (exit A, J3)/buses along Connaught Road Central/Central Star Ferry Pier.* **Open** noon-10pm daily. **Main courses** HK$30-$80. **No credit cards**. **Map** p67 E3.
Dim sum, the old-fashioned way. The restaurant occupies one huge room with diners jostling for tables, decibel-levels hitting supersonic heights and staff rushing around with little time to take your order. But the dim sum is about the best in town. Ladies push trolleys around – just point to what you fancy. It's easy, simple and a true taste of old Canton.

### Law Fu Kee Noodle Shop

*50 Lyndhurst Terrace, Central, HK Island (2850 6756). Central MTR (exit D1, D2, G)/Mid-Levels Escalator/12M, 13, 23A, 40M, 43 bus.* **Open** 8am-8pm daily. **Main courses** HK$20-$40. **No credit cards**. **Map** p66 C3.
Smart and clean, Law Fu Kee is a good place to sample dishes you may not get back home, like ox brisket soup or pig's kidney and lung congee. For the less adventurous, braised noodles in oyster sauce with ginger and spring onion is a delight. But this is not a place to linger.

## Luk Yu Teahouse

*24-26 Stanley Street, Central, HK Island (2523 5463). Central MTR (exit D1, D2, G)/buses along Queen's Road Central.* **Open** 7am-10pm daily. **Main courses** HK$50-$100. **No credit cards.** **Map** p66 C3.

Luk Yu Teahouse is Hong Kong's downmarket equivalent of the Ritz, where well-to-do locals love to sit, chatter and *yum cha* (drink tea) or nibble on dim sum, which is very good. But don't expect a smile from the generally surly staff if you can catch their attention.

## Yung Kee

*32-40 Wellington Street, Central, HK Island (2522 1624). Central MTR (exit D1, D2, G)/12M, 13, 23A, 40M, 43 bus.* **Open** 11am-11pm daily. **Main courses** HK$60-$180. **Credit** AmEx, DC, MC, V. **Map** p66 C3.

If you only try one local restaurant in Hong Kong, this must be it. Classic Cantonese fare created in an open kitchen where you can see the chefs at work. The 1,000-year-old duck egg (it's not really that old, just preserved) with fresh ginger is given to every table on arrival, but is an acquired taste. The dim sum, roast pork and Yung Kee's legendary roast goose, however, are popular with everyone. The atmosphere is convivial, staff more helpful than most and there's an English-language menu. The restaurant occupies many floors, but it is still best to book.

Classy **Madison's**. *See p144.*

## Chinese: Hunanese

### Hunan Garden

*3/F, The Forum, Exchange Square, Central, HK Island (2868 2880). Central MTR (exit A)/buses along Connaught Road Central.* **Open** 11.30am-3pm, 5.30pm-midnight daily. **Main courses** HK$70-$150. **Credit** AmEx, DC, MC, V. **Map** p67 D3.

Hunanese restaurants aren't common in Hong Kong, but if you want to sample the considerable charms of the cuisine of Chairman Mao's home province, Hunan Garden won't disappoint. It's a large, classy place, where the helpful staff are happy to explain such specialities as Hunan mashed chicken soup in bamboo and flavour-packed eels in garlic sauce.

## French

### Café Des Artistes

*UG/F, California Tower, 30-32 D'Aguilar Street, Central, HK Island (2526 3880). Central MTR (exit D1, G)/12M, 13, 23A, 40M, 43 bus.* **Open** noon-3pm, 7-10.30pm Mon-Thur; noon-3pm, 7-11pm Fri, Sat; 7-10.30pm Sun. **Main courses** HK$160-$280. **Credit** AmEx, DC, MC, V. **Map** p66 C4.

A window on Lan Kwai Fong. Dining here is not for those trying to shun the public glare, but it's not too flash either. The food leans towards Provence, from where the chef hails, and is good solid Gallic fare. Some say it is overpriced, but the prime location may explain that.

### Petrus

*56/F, Island Shangri-La Hotel, Pacific Place, Admiralty, HK Island (2877 3838). Admiralty MTR (exit C1)/buses & trams along Queensway.* **Open** noon-3pm, 7-11pm daily. **Main courses** HK$250-$400. **Credit** AmEx, DC, MC, V. **Map** p67 F5.

The best French restaurant in town, and then some. If you can take your eyes off the food, the view of Kowloon is jaw-dropping. The decor is opulent, but the atmosphere relaxed. If you're prepared to splash out you may as well go for the oysters and foie gras. Another good feature is that the wine list includes New World tipples.

### Le Tire Bouchon

*45A Graham Street, Central, HK Island (2523 5459). Mid-Levels Escalator/26 bus.* **Open** *Bar* 11am-11pm Mon-Sat. *Restaurant* noon-2.30pm, 7-10.30pm Mon-Sat. **Main courses** HK$165-$215. **Credit** AmEx, DC, MC, V. **Map** p66 C3.

A hidden treasure. The entrance is almost cave-like, but the interior is elegant and ideal for a romantic meal or friends' get together. The Gallic staff are knowledgeable about their cuisine, which is classic French, and have been running the restaurant for 15 years. The pièce de resistance is the tournedos rossini (beef fillet in a port and shallot sauce with duck liver). Heavy but delicious. On the lighter side there are a good range of fish dishes, including sole and monkfish. For dessert, the soufflé and profiteroles are wonderful. The wine list has more than 200 choices.

## Indian

### India Today

*1/F, 26-30 Elgin Street, Central, HK Island (2801 5959). Mid-Levels Escalator/26 bus.* **Open** 11.30am-3pm, 6-11pm daily. **Main courses** HK$60-$110. **Credit** AmEx, DC, MC, V. **Map** p66 B3.

India Today is a notch above most Hong Kong Indian restaurants in terms of quality and price. But the exotic creations and fresh ingredients are worth paying the little extra for. The banana chat (fried bananas and potatoes with spices) and sizzling jheera prawns are particularly fine. The atmosphere is more stately than your usual Indian restaurant, too.

## International

### Aqua

*49 Hollywood Road, Central, HK Island (2545 9889). Central MTR (exit D1, D2, G)/Mid-Levels Escalator/12M, 13, 23A, 26, 40M, 43 bus.* **Main courses** HK$140-$250. **Open** noon-2am daily. **Credit** AmEx, DC, MC, V. **Map** p66 C3.

**The best** Restaurants

### For a glimpse of the high life

**Felix** (*see p156*) – where the glitterati go for stunning views, fine food and the coolest interior design.

### For orgasmic gastronomy

**M At The Fringe** (*see p144*) – exquisitely elegant in decor and cuisine.

### For an authentic dim sum experience

**City Hall Chinese Restaurant** (*see p142*) – noisy, chaotic, but simply delicious food.

### For the freshest seafood

Any of the coastal restaurants on Lamma, Cheung Chau or in Sai Kung (*see pp163-5*).

### For a sub-tropical paradise

**Stoep** (*see p165*) – sand, sea and roaming water buffalo.

### For an intimate candlelit dinner with a view

**The Verandah** (*see p154*) – a colonial-style restaurant that oozes romance.

### For back-to-basics street life

**Good Luck Thai Café** (*see p145*) – al fresco dining on great, cheap Thai food.

Hyper-trendy restaurant with a glass-fronted façade allowing diners – mostly high-fliers and the chic set – to see and be seen. If you can stand the gawping, the food is superb with a good selection of fish, seafood, meat and vegetarian dishes cooked simply, but deliciously. From Thursday to Saturday nights it becomes a late lounge, with DJs playing chill-out music and a snack menu available.

### Madison's

*Shop 340, Level 3, Pacific Place, 88 Queensway, Admiralty, HK Island (2523 4772). Admiralty MTR (exit C1)/buses & trams along Queensway.* **Open** noon-10.30pm daily. **Main courses** HK$150-$250. **Credit** AmEx, DC, MC, V. **Map** p67 F5.

Finding top class restaurants inside dining malls is not unusual in Hong Kong – Madison's is one such place. Inside, it's classy, cosy and stylish, and the menu offers classic dishes with a luxurious twist to great effect.

### M At The Fringe

*1/F, 2 Lower Albert Road, Central, HK Island (2877 4000). Central MTR (exit K)/23A bus.* **Open** noon-2.30pm, 7-10pm Mon-Sat. **Main courses** HK$200-$280. **Credit** AmEx, DC, MC, V. **Map** p67 F5.

Undoubtedly one of Hong Kong's finest and best-loved restaurants. The bistro has a hip clientele, quirky decor (including 1970s cutlery and crockery), a menu featuring innovative creations and the best desserts in town. The intimate atmosphere makes it popular for small groups and couples.

## Italian

### Nicholini's

*8/F, Conrad Hotel, Pacific Place, 88 Queensway, Admiralty, HK Island (2521 3838). Admiralty MTR (exit C1)/buses & trams along Queensway.* **Open** noon-3pm, 6.30-11pm Mon-Sat; 11am-3pm, 6.30-11pm Sun. **Main courses** HK$220-$350. **Credit** AmEx, DC, MC, V. **Map** p67 D4.

Repeatedly voted the best Italian restaurant in Asia by Italian globetrotters, and deservedly so. The setting is nothing special, but the food is. Gastronomic delights include truffle dishes and lobster, while the antipasti buffet is a must – but it comes at a price. Lunchtimes are busy with businessmen exploiting their expense accounts, evenings with couples.

### Trattoria

*G/F, The Landmark, 15 Queen's Road, Central (2524 0111). Central MTR (exit D1, D2, G)/buses along Queen's Road Central.* **Open** 11.30am-11pm daily. **Main courses** HK$120-$240. **Credit** AmEx, DC, MC, V. **Map** p67 D4.

On weekdays, this stylish, spacious eaterie throngs with so many power lunchers it's hard to get a seat. In the evening, it's quieter and more relaxed. The baked seafood and spaghetti (served in paper) is irresistible, while its café outlet on the third floor of the same shopping centre serves gorgeous desserts, sandwiches and the best mushroom soup in town.

Eat, Drink, Shop

## Japanese

### Tokio Joe

*16 Lan Kwai Fong, Central, HK Island (2525 1889).*
*Central MTR (exit D1, G)/12M, 13, 23A, 40M, 43
bus.* **Open** noon-3pm, 6.30pm-midnight Mon-Sat;
6.30pm-midnight Sun. **Main courses** HK$160-$300.
**Credit** AmEx, DC, MC, V. **Map** p66 C4.
It's not cheap, but good Japanese restaurants rarely
are, and the food at Tokio Joe is exquisite, with
sushi and sashimi that will have you in raptures.
Try the soft-shell crab roll, or any of the mixed
platters. The ambience is good, with a sushi island
bar having recently been introduced in the middle
of the room.

## Mexican

### I-Caramba

*2 Elgin Street, Central, HK Island (2530 9963).*
*Mid-Levels Escalator/26 bus.* **Open** noon-11pm daily.
**Main courses** HK$80-$150. **Credit** AmEx, DC, MC,
V. **Map** p66 B3.
There's little room to manoeuvre in this narrow
restaurant, unless you land the window seat. But
after a few jugs of the potent margaritas you won't
care about the squeeze. The mango and prawn
salad is a great starter and the burritos are good.
And, if your tongue's made of asbestos, you can
choose to top them with one of more than 100
imported hot sauces.

## Spanish

### Boca

*65 Peel Street, Central, HK Island (2548 1717).*
*Mid-Levels Escalator/buses along Caine Road.*
**Open** noon-3pm, 6-11pm Mon-Fri; 12.30pm-2am Sat,
Sun. **Tapas** HK$50-$80. **Credit** MC, V.
**Map** p66 B3.
The choice of wines by the glass here is among the
best in Hong Kong, and the tapas (both traditional
and fusion) is top-drawer. But perhaps thoroughly
metropolitan Boca's most alluring feature is its
sumptuous couches, into which you can sink and
idle away hours with friends. A perfect lunch stop
or relaxing watering hole after a busy day. Booking
advisable in the evening.

### Olé

*1/F Shun Ho Tower, 24-30 Ice House Street, Central,
HK Island (2523 8624). Central MTR (exit D1, G)
/13, 23A, 26, 43 bus.* **Open** noon-3pm, 6.30-11.30pm
daily. **Main courses** HK$180-$350. **Credit** AmEx,
DC, MC, V. **Map** p67 D4.
The best and most authentic Spanish restaurant
in town. The Spanish owner makes the finest
paella, bursting with flavour, not to mention a
delicate suckling pig, white asparagus and some
mouthwatering regional dishes. Sangria flows,
musicians serenade you and the patron turns out to
be a true amigo.

**Boca** – home of hip tapas.

### Rico's

*44 Robinson Road, Mid-Levels, HK Island (2840
0937). Bus 3B, 12M, 23, 40.* **Open** noon-11pm
daily. **Main courses** HK$125-$180. **Credit** AmEx,
DC, MC, V. **Map** p66 B4.
A cosy restaurant with warm yellow rag-rolled
walls, candle-lit tables and friendly service. The food
is not as good as it once was, but the tapas and
paella are still tasty enough to draw a crowd most
evenings. And the sangria may have you dancing
before the night is out.

## Thai

### Café Siam

*40-42 Lyndhurst Terrace, Central, HK Island
(2851 4803). Central MTR (exit D1, D2, G)/
Mid-Levels Escalator/12M, 13, 23A, 40M, 43 bus.*
**Open** 11.45am-2.30pm, 6-11pm daily. **Main
courses** HK$60-$120. **Credit** AmEx, DC, MC, V.
**Map** p66 C3.
Serving good quality food at reasonable prices, Café
Siam is always busy, with customers sharing large
servings of Thai classics. The red duck curry is
superb, if a little oily, the tom yam soup is refresh-
ingly spicy, and nearly every dish is well cooked
and presented. Friendly staff add to the bustling yet
laid-back ambience.

### Good Luck Thai Café

*13 Wing Wah Lane, Central, HK Island (2877 2971).
Central MTR (exit D1, G)/12M, 13, 23A, 40M, 43
bus.* **Open** 10am-2am Mon-Sat. **Main courses**
HK$40-$70. **No credit cards. Map** p66 C4.
Amazingly popular with locals and tourists, scores
of whom perch on wobbly stools designed for
dwarfs down a dirty alley off Lan Kwai Fong every

**Good Luck Thai Café.** *See p145.*

night. But the food is another matter and explains its popularity – the tom yam and roast chicken are magical. Several rivals have opened in the alley, but this remains the best.

## Vietnamese

### Indochine 1929
*2/F, California Tower, Lan Kwai Fong, Central, HK Island (2869 7399). Central MTR (exit D1, G)/ 12M, 13, 23A, 40M, 43 bus.* **Open** noon-2.30pm, 6.30-10.30pm Mon-Sat; 6.30-10.30pm Sun. **Main courses** HK$110-$200. **Credit** AmEx, DC, MC, V. **Map** p66 C4.
For ambience and culinary craft, this elegant restaurant (circa colonial era Indochina) is hard to beat. It's certainly the finest Vietnamese eaterie in Hong Kong. Sure, it's pricier than the rest, but the quality is exceptional and the atmosphere unrivalled – you may even bump into one of the many local celebrities who hang out here. The soft-shell crab is divine, the chicken with hoi sin sauce irresistible and the wine list impressive.

### Song
*L/G, 75 Hollywood Road, Central, HK Island (2559 0997). Central MTR (exit D1, D2, G)/Mid-Levels Escalator/12M, 13, 23A, 26, 40M, 43 bus.* **Open** noon-3pm, 7pm-midnight Mon-Fri; 7pm-midnight Sat. **Main courses** HK$80-$120. **Credit** AmEx, DC, MC, V. **Map** p66 B3.
Song is hard to track down (spot the sign on Hollywood Road and walk down a few dimly lit steps) but it's worth seeking out. Authentic modern Vietnamese cuisine is ensured by the use of vegetables, herbs and spices imported from Vietnam. The green papaya and green mango salad is startlingly good, and the hot and sour fish soup equally so. The chic eaterie is tiny, so make sure you book.

## West-east fusion

### Vong
*25/F, Mandarin Oriental Hotel, 5 Connaught Road, Central, HK Island (2825 4028/2522 0111) Central MTR (exit F)/buses through Central/Central Star Ferry Pier.* **Open** noon-3pm, 6pm-midnight daily. **Main courses** HK$150-$200. **Credit** AmEx, DC, MC, V. **Map** p67 E3.
Located atop the Mandarin Oriental, Vong opened in 1997, and represents a welcome return to an old stomping ground for Jean-Georges Vongerichten (who worked here during the 1980s). The setting's a stunner – a restrained use of black and gold within and marvellous views without. Anyone who's visited the New York and London Vongs will be familiar with the trademark French-Oriental fusion food, featuring the likes of crab spring roll with tamarind dip and Maine lobster with Thai herbs. If you're new to the experience, go for the black plate selection, which features mini versions of most of the specialities. The bar here is a surprisingly laid-back but buzzy place for a drink, particularly early in the evening when it fills up with demob-happy workers. If you're off the sauce, don't miss the fabulously refreshing home-made ginger ale (with lemongrass and chilli).

## Sheung Wan

### Chinese: vegetarian

### Po Lin Vegetarian Restaurant
*69 Jervois Street, Sheung Wan, HK Island (2543 0823). Sheung Wan MTR (exit A2)/buses along Queen's Road Central.* **Open** 8am-9.30pm Mon-Sat. **Main courses** HK$20-$30. **No credit cards**. **Map** p66 B2.

# Chinese cuisines

One of the great pleasures of a visit to Hong Kong is the opportunity to sample the huge range of Chinese regional cuisines on offer. The following are the most popular, but look out also for restaurants specialising in less commonly found cuisines such as Hainanese, Taiwanese, Yunnanese and Hunanese.

## CANTONESE

The native cuisine of the great majority of local Chinese. There is a saying on the mainland that the Cantonese will eat anything with wings that isn't a plane and anything with legs that isn't a table. While it is true that Hong Kong's Cantonese restaurants may include plenty of ingredients that visitors would not expect to find on menus back home (such as fish lips and snake), endangered animals such as bears and civet cats (as well as dogs) are not allowed to be served in the city. What is more, a growing number of environmentally aware diners in Hong Kong do not eat the (astonishingly expensive) delicacies of shark's fin, abalone (a deep-sea shellfish) and bird's nest, arguing that the consuming of these products will lead to the eradication of certain species.

The one characteristic that sums up Cantonese fare is freshness. Sauces and flavourings are subtle, in order to let the taste of the main ingredient shine. Steamed fish or chicken typify 'the fresher, the better' style of cooking, sprinkled with a little soy sauce and oil and garnished with chopped spring onions and ginger. The most prized fish for steaming is coral trout or garoupa, but any will do.

Many Cantonese restaurants have prominent fish tanks displaying daily-changing produce. The live fish, crustaceans and molluscs are often far more exotic than those available in the West and other parts of Asia, but – for the less adventurous – snapper, prawns, scallops, mussels and clams are usually on offer. When eating seafood, you may want to check its country of origin – for the simple reason that Hong Kong waters are not the world's cleanest. Probably the most enjoyable places to enjoy seafood in Hong Kong are the waterside restaurants at Sai Kung in the New Territories and on Cheung Chau and Lamma islands (*see pp163-5*).

If you are in the New Territories in the cooler months of the year, you should hunt down a restaurant that serves *poon choi*, which literally translates as 'big bowl vegetable', even though vegetables are only a part of the story in this robust dish. The big bowl is about the diameter of an adult-sized bicycle wheel, which means a minimum of eight people should be in your dining party. The bowl is

This is a hidden gem. Like most local eateries, it's busy, noisy and hurried, and the decor isn't going to win any design prizes, but the dim sum, vegetables and noodle dishes are ultra fresh and utterly delicious. There's no English menu, so use the fallback ordering method of keeping your eye on what other diners are eating and pointing at what you fancy.

## International

### IP Café
*Island Pacific Hotel, 152 Connaught Road West, Sheung Wan, HK Island (2131 1188). Buses along Connaught Road West or Des Voeux Road West.* **Open** noon-2.30pm, 6.30-9.30pm daily. **Main courses** HK$80-$160. **Credit** AmEx, DC, MC, V.
Apart from fast food outlets, there's little in this part of town to satisfy hunger pangs, especially in terms of quality. The IP Café, while not a major gastronomic experience, is certainly a decent one. Lunch and dinner buffets are excellent value, while the à la carte menu has an extensive array of dishes from both East and West.

## The Peak

### International

#### Café Deco
*Peak Galleria, 118 Peak Road, The Peak, HK Island (2849 5111). Peak Tram Upper Terminus/15, 15B bus.* **Open** 11am-11pm Mon-Thur, Sun; 11am-11.30pm Fri, Sat. **Main courses** HK$100-$200. **Credit** AmEx, DC, MC, V. **Map** p89.
Considering how tacky many of the 'attractions' around the Peak are, it's a delight to find a place with such slick art deco style and fantastic food. Huge glass windows and a small terrace for pre- or after-meal drinks exploit the magnificent Peak views to their fullest. The interior is just as pleasing to the eye, with an open kitchen running the length of the restaurant. The chefs can cook anything from pizzas to Indian curries, Thai dishes and Cantonese favourites with equal aplomb. Even though the restaurant occupies two floors, you'll still need to book. There's often live jazz laid on. Dress up (this is no café, despite the name) and live it up.

layered with six to ten dishes on a bed of steamed rice. Typically, hearty dishes such as braised chicken, deep-fried beancurd, fried fish, fried prawn with onion, fried air-dried sausage, braised dehydrated mushroom and a few other vegetable dishes make up the feast.

Hong Kong's mild winter is also the time to enjoy *da bin lo* or 'hot pot'. A pot of bubbling broth is placed on a cooker at the centre of a dining table and small dishes of sliced raw ingredients, typically meat, seafood, beancurd and vegetables, are cooked by the diners using small long-handled sieves. At the end of the meal, the broth, having absorbed the flavours of all the cooked ingredients, is enjoyed as a soup – sometimes with noodles or *won ton* dumplings. This very sociable concept bears similarities to a fondue.

Also in winter, you'll sometimes find snake and other reptiles on the menu – eating them supposedly warms the blood. Speciality reptile restaurants are not hard to spot – they're the ones with serpents, lizards and frogs writhing about in street-side cages or shop windows. While snake soup – in which the fairly tasteless shredded flesh is placed in a seasoned chicken broth – is the most popular serpentine dish, snake banquets of up to eight courses allow for a wider investigation.

### DIM SUM

A unique feature of Cantonese cuisine, dim sum, which literally translates as 'touching

the heart', is casually enjoyed for breakfast or lunch (but never dinner). The term *yum cha*, literally meaning 'drink tea', is usually applied to a dim sum meal, as endlessly re-filled pots of tea traditionally accompany the food.

The dim sum selection consists primarily of small dumplings, buns, meatballs, spring rolls, pastries, cakes and tarts. Many of the dishes are steamed – these are the ones that are generally served in little bamboo baskets – while others are fried or deep-fried. Common dishes include shrimp dumplings (*har gao*), shrimp and minced pork dumplings (*siu mai*), pork ribs in black bean sauce (*pai guat*) and buns filled with barbecued pork (*char siu bau*). Less common are curried squid, steamed cow's stomach and braised chicken feet. Rice and noodle dishes, as well as the usual Cantonese staples, can usually be ordered too. Desserts often include egg tarts, deep-fried rice balls with a red bean paste centre and sweet bean soups.

A visit to a sprawling dim sum restaurant, where families and friends go to really let their hair down at weekends – the vibrancy and din in these places is unimaginable – is a true Hong Kong experience. Middle-aged women trundle between tables with trolleys stacked with various dishes; if you can't understand what they're yelling, simply stop the trolley and take a closer peek, until something appeals. Each group of diners has its bill stamped by servers every time they pick a dish. ▶

### Peak Café

*121 Peak Road, The Peak, HK Island (2849 7868). Peak Tram Upper Terminus/15, 15B bus.* **Open** 10.30am-11.30pm Mon-Fri; 8am-midnight Sat, Sun. **Main courses** HK$100-$160. **Credit** AmEx, DC, MC, V. **Map** p89.

The much-loved Peak Café closed in June 2001. The original owners lost out in a government tendering process to a firm that intends to turn the venue into a steakhouse, prompting fears that its quintessential colonial charm will be lost.

## Wan Chai & Causeway Bay

### British

#### Harry Ramsden's

*3-4 Wu Chung House, 213 Queen's Road East, Wan Chai, HK Island (2832 9626). Wan Chai MTR (exit A3)/buses along Queen's Road East.* **Open** 11.30am-11pm Mon-Sat; 8am-11pm Sun. **Main courses** HK$50 (takeaway); HK$110-$150 (eat in). **Credit** AmEx, DC, MC, V. **Map** p80 B3.

Al fresco dining at the **Peak Café**, as it was.

## Chinese cuisines (continued)

### BEIJINGESE

Traditionally, Beijing food is rich and mostly meaty, with preserved meats and 'Beggar's chicken' (*see below* **Shanghainese**) being particularly popular. This is a throw-back to long northern winters past, when vegetables were scarce and there was little else to eat besides Tientsin cabbage and pickled vegetables. Flavours are strong, with garlic, ginger and small leeks regularly used for seasoning. Vinegar from Shanxi Province is highly regarded and often splashed into dishes, or used as a dipping sauce.

Wheat is as much a staple as rice; steamed and fried breads, and all kinds of dumplings and noodles are eaten. In larger restaurants, it is mandatory to have a chef demonstrate the acrobatic art of noodle making.

The most famous restaurant dish is, of course, Peking duck – slivers of crisp skin and meat are rolled up by diners in small thin pancakes with shreds of cucumber, spring onions and a dab of plum sauce.

### CHIU CHOWNESE

The Chiu Chow region of south-east Guangdong province is home to a popular Cantonese splinter cuisine. Meals traditionally start and end with tiny cups of very strong Iron Buddha tea – the Chinese equivalent of an espresso – also known as 'kung fu tea' because of the punch it packs.

Cold pre-cooked dishes – such as cold boiled crab and spiced goose, both served with a vinegary dipping sauce – are popular. You can often recognise a Chiu Chow restaurant by the crabs hanging in the window.

Seafood, duck and goose are accompanied by speciality Chiu Chow sauces and condiments, like preserved limes, shredded olive and fermented bean sauces, that give the cuisine a distinctive flavour. Other highlights include crispy deep-fried crab and prawn balls served with sweet bean sauce, and mullet flavoured with preserved limes, which often arrive at the table on a sizzling iron plate. Omelette containing tiny oysters and coriander is a tasty side dish.

Rather than steamed rice, congee – soupy overcooked rice – frequently accompanies meat and noodles, often of the fine vermicelli variety. Chiu Chow chefs excel at preparing the two expensive delicacies of shark's fin and bird's nest – most often in soups. Bird's nest soup is usually sweet, often combined with coconut milk, but can be savoury, whereas the shark's fin is always savoury, usually served in soup and occasionally fried with egg.

### SHANGHAINESE

Hong Kong's considerable Shanghainese community means that there is a profusion of food redolent of the Yangtze River delta

---

Good old fish and chips cooked the way Brits love them. Mushy peas, pies, fish chowder, rhubarb crumble and custard… you get the idea. The take-away next door, which has a sit-down area, offers full English breakfasts before 11am and massive set meals after, all for under HK$60 – a true bargain. It's a guaranteed fill-up.

## Chinese: Beijingese

### American Restaurant

*20 Lockhart Road, Wan Chai, HK Island (2527 7277). Wan Chai MTR (exit C)/buses along Hennessy Road.* **Open** 11.30am-10.30pm daily. **Main courses** HK$80-$140. **Credit** AmEx, DC, MC, V. **Map** p80 A2.

Critics say the American is too western, and it's true that expats and tourists love it. But there's no denying the food here is rich and sumptuous. The Peking duck, of course, is storming, but the minced pigeon eaten in lettuce leaves is the most outstanding dish. Sweet and sour pork is another winner, and there are more native Chinese options, too. It gets crowded, so book.

## Chinese: Cantonese

### Dim Sum

*63 Sing Woo Road, Happy Valley, HK Island (2834 8893). Bus 1, 19/trams to Happy Valley.* **Open** 11am-3pm, 6-11pm daily. **Main courses** HK$60-$120. **Credit** AmEx, DC, MC, V. **Map** p80 D3.

This eponymous restaurant is more expensive than many dim sum outlets, but it's also a good notch up in terms of elegance, imagination and quality. Luxurious ingredients like abalone and lobster are weaved into the extensive list of traditional dim sum dishes.

## Chinese: Shanghainese

### Lao Ching Hing

*Basement, Century Hong Kong Hotel, 238 Jaffe Road, Wan Chai, HK Island (2598 6080). Wan Chai MTR (exit A1)/buses along Gloucester Road.* **Open** 11am-11pm daily. **Main courses** HK$50-$150. **Credit** AmEx, MC, V. **Map** p80 B2.

region. The cuisine is rich, oily, sweet and luscious. Sumptuous, velvety meat and fish dishes braised with soy sauce, sugar and a touch of vinegar are common. Shaoxing wine, fermented from glutinous rice, is used extensively in cooking and drunk warm – it tastes a bit like sherry. The Shanghainese repertoire includes a number of 'drunken' dishes, in which food is marinated in wine.

A Shanghainese meal usually starts with a selection of cold appetisers, such as 'mock goose' – bean curd sheets rolled and braised to resemble goose – drunken chicken, duck's tongues and shredded jellyfish, tossed in a little sesame oil, as well as various pressed meats and spiced smoked fish.

Stir-fried eel with garlic is popular, as are crunchy tiny freshwater shrimps that may be stir-fried plain or flavoured with tea. Carp, fried or steamed, garnished with a sweet and sour sauce – one of the few times that this sauce, so popular in the West, genuinely appears in Chinese cuisine – is a favourite. In autumn, freshwater Shanghai crabs, also called hairy crabs, are a delicacy and enjoyed for their rich roe. 'Beggar's chicken' sees the fowl wrapped in lotus leaves, and then coated with mud and baked, resulting in tender, lightly flavoured chicken.

As staples, the Shanghainese eat dumplings and noodles as often as rice. For earthy food, try the full-flavoured local dumplings – fried, steamed or in soup, filled with meat and vegetables. You can buy these,

and deep-fried dough sticks, from small restaurants, along with a glass of warm or chilled fresh soya milk.

**SICHUANESE**

Sichuan province may be panda country, but its cuisine is anything but cute and cuddly – more likely fiery and intense. Black Sichuanese peppercorns and potent red chillis flavour most dishes, and garlic and ginger are liberally thrown into the pot.

Crispy rice cakes that crackle and pop are served with a rich, spicy sauce, and hot and sour soup is exactly as its name suggests. The most famous Sichuanese signature dish is *ma po* beancurd – chilli-laced minced pork atop steamed beancurd.

In landlocked Sichuan, freshwater fish is fried or steamed and smothered in – you've guessed it – a chilli sauce, spiked with vinegar and hot bean paste. Carp simmered with turnip makes a popular soup.

A delicacy of the province is smoked duck, marinated with flavourings such as aniseed, cinnamon and pepper, then steamed and smoked over wood chips and tea. Sichuanese hot pot consists of raw slices of meat, fish and vegetables that are self-cooked in a pork-based broth that bubbles away on the table (similar to *da bin lo, see p148* **Cantonese**). The broth is laced with chilli and there are bowls of hand-made, rough-cut *dan dan* noodles that arrive with a minced pork, chilli and garlic sauce.

A roomy, relaxing basement restaurant that offers a good introduction to Shanghainese cuisine. Don't miss some of the more unusual specialities like braised lion-head meatballs or drunken Shanghai crab. Unusually good service.

## Chinese: Sichuanese

### Red Pepper
*7 Lan Fong Road, Causeway Bay, HK Island (2577 3811). Causeway Bay MTR (exit B)/ buses along Percival Street & Leighton Road.* **Open** 11.30am-11.30pm daily. **Main courses** HK$60-$130. **Credit** AmEx, DC, MC, V. **Map** p80 D2.
If you crave fire in your food, look no further than Red Pepper, which specialises in the intensely flavoured, chilli-rich cuisine of Sichuan province – try the sliced pork with garlic chilli sauce, or shredded chicken with sesame sauce. A great accompaniment is fragrant lychee tea (which will come as no surprise to those who know how well lychee-nosed Gewürztraminer matches spicy food). The restaurant is relatively small and always busy.

## Greek/Middle Eastern

### Bacchus
*Basement, Hop Hing Centre, 8-12 Hennessy Road, Wan Chai, HK Island (2529 9032). Wan Chai MTR (exit B1)/buses along Hennessy Road.* **Open** 11.30am-2.30pm, 6-10.30pm Mon-Sat. **Main courses** HK$210. **Credit** AmEx, DC, MC, V. **Map** p80 A2.
Bacchus's relaxed basement setting is a world away from the pollution-choked streets of Wan Chai outside. Rag-rolled walls and spaciously separated tables make for a comfortable lunch or dinner. The lamb moussaka is divine, the meze platter enough to share and game hen superbly roasted. Ideal for romantic occasions.

## Indian

### The Chapel
*27 Yik Yam Street, Happy Valley, HK Island (2834 6565). Bus 1, 5A, 19/trams to Happy Valley.* **Open** 3pm-2am Mon-Fri; noon-5am Sat; noon-2am Sun. **Main courses** HK$60-$80. **Credit** V. **Map** p80 D3.

**Dim Sum**. *See p150.*

Expect top Thai tucker at **Thai Thai**.

The church pews may seem somewhat unusual for a curry house, but the Chapel makes a virtue of its singular decor. The food, however, is as authentic as you get, from the mutton madras to the tandoori chicken. Its best point is the late opening hours, especially on Saturdays.

## International

### Open Kitchen
*6/F, Hong Kong Arts Centre, 2 Harbour Road, Wan Chai, HK Island (2827 2923). Wan Chai MTR (exit A1, C)/A12, 18, 88 bus/Wan Chai Star Ferry Pier.* **Open** 11am-11pm Mon-Fri; 10am-11pm Sat, Sun. **Main courses** HK$50-$120. **Credit** AmEx, MC, V. **Map** p80 B2.
This glass-fronted café is not only situated in a high quality venue, it also serves high quality food. Beyond the usual salad bar and sandwiches, there are a variety of mouth-watering mains, such as steak, kebabs, Southeast Asian specialities like the excellent nonya laksa and local Cantonese fare. Diners are not just arty types, but also those in the know when it comes to eating well for less.

# Restaurants

## Italian

### Fat Angelo's
*414 Jaffe Road, Wan Chai, HK Island (2574 6263). Causeway Bay MTR (exit C)/buses along Gloucester Road.* **Open** noon-midnight daily. **Main courses** HK$220. **Credit** AmEx, DC, MC, V. **Map** p80 C1.
Italian homecooking like mamma used to make it. A complimentary salad and bread basket get you started, then come the plates piled high with enough food to serve either two to four or four to six people, so it's a great place for groups. The food wouldn't win any awards, but it is tasty and filling. Try the lamb osso bucco – it's the best dish. Fat Angelo's also serves wine by the carafe. There are branches at 49 Elgin Street, Central, and 29-43 Ashley Road, Tsim Sha Tsui.

### Grissini
*2/F, Grand Hyatt, 1 Harbour Road, Wan Chai, HK Island (2588 1234, ext 7313). Wan Chai MTR (exit A1, C)/A12, 18, 88 bus/Wan Chai Star Ferry Pier.* **Open** noon-2.30pm, 7-11pm daily. **Main courses** HK$200-$350. **Credit** AmEx, DC, MC, V. **Map** p80 B1.
Grissini serves up as good Italian cuisine as you'll find anywhere outside Italy. The location is spacious and comfortable, while the food will have you in raptures. The menu changes frequently, but whether it's quail, veal or lobster, the dish will be gastronomic perfection. Obviously, this comes at a serious price.

## Thai

### Chili Club
*1/F, 88 Lockhart Road, Wan Chai, HK Island (2527 2872). Wan Chai MTR (exit C)/buses along Hennessy Road.* **Open** noon-3pm, 6-10.30pm daily. **Main courses** HK$80-$150. **Credit** AmEx, DC, MC, V. **Map** p80.
Hot food at cool prices. The steamed fish is one of the best you'll find in town – it arrives simmering in a sauce bubbling with chilli and coriander. The tom yam soup, pad Thai and curries are also good – and made for sharing, so the bill's a nice surprise. However, the staff have a tendency to be unhelpful and sometimes plain rude.

### Thai Thai
*36 Lan Fong Road, Causeway Bay, HK Island (2895 0699). Causeway Bay MTR (exit B)/buses along Percival Street & Leighton Road.* **Open** noon-10.30pm daily. **Main courses** HK$60-$140. **Credit** AmEx, DC, MC, V. **Map** p80 D2.
A spotlessly clean restaurant where colourful combinations of food delight the eye and the taste buds. There are plenty of good, reasonably-priced, filling meals, from pad Thai to red, yellow or green curries, but if you want to go overboard, try the curried crab or steamed fish. Spice heaven.

Eat, Drink, Shop

**Time Out** Hong Kong Guide **153**

# Fast food, coffee & snacks

Legend has it that the average walking pace in Hong Kong is the fastest in the world, even though it's hard to believe when you see shuffling masses held up by jammed roads and dug-up pavements. But there's no doubt Hong Kong is a city on the move. Time is money and in Hong Kong, money is everything. So it's no surprise that fast food outlets are on every corner, offering cheap, but rarely healthy, meals in double-quick time. Everybody, inevitably, uses them now and again, whatever their opinion on mass-market meals. There are many to choose from, but that doesn't mean they're any good.

### THE CHAIN GANG

Among the unfamiliar options for visitors are the local chains, **Maxim's**, **Café de Coral** and **Fairwood**. They all serve simple Cantonese dishes that are not too bad in terms of taste and value, with Maxim's being the best. Try the barbecued pork and rice if you're after a good filling meal. However, if you can find one, you'd be better off in a good noodle shop. Another chain, **Farmhouse**, offers Western and Asian dishes, but the food is generally poor. **Spaghetti House** signs are visible all over town, but don't bother with it if you want authentic Italian food – few homesick Italians will find much they recognise.

Sad though it is to say, **McDonald's** golden arches are the most common sight on Hong Kong's streets. Perhaps part of its appeal is the third lowest Big Mac price in the world (after neighbouring Macau and Romania) There's one every few hundred metres, and

its clever marketeers have tapped into the locals' (yes, even adults') love of cute animals. A recent Snoopy promotion had customers fighting for the last toy. McDonald's reach is so powerful, it has no real rivals in the burger wars, although **Hardee's** has a few branches. The other major Western fast food chain is **KFC**. For better Western options, *see below* **Coffee & cake**.

### GOING NATIVE

Street stalls selling Cantonese snacks have been almost totally outlawed due to safety and sanitary concerns. In their place, small open-fronted shops in heavy pedestrian areas sell the same popular Hong Kong nibbles. The most popular, sold on wooden skewers, are boiled minced fish or pork balls, fried bell pepper stuffed with minced fish and sliced pork sausage. Also popular are bright orange braised chicken feet, pressed and grilled cuttlefish, and the very pungent deep-fried *chow dofu*, literally 'smelly beancurd', which is definitely an acquired taste.

Herbal drinks outlets provide a healthy alternative to junk snacks. As well as the fragrant five flower and bitter 24-ingredient teas, which are designed to regulate the body when it overheats, they often sell turtle jelly and steamed cakes. Turtle is believed to be a cure-all ingredient. These (usually open-fronted) shops are easily recognisable by their over-sized shiny brass urns.

## Vegetarian

### Vegetarian International Paradise

*11/F, Times Square Food Forum, Times Square, 1 Matheson Street, Causeway Bay, HK Island (2808 0333). Causeway Bay MTR (exit A)/buses along Hennessy Road.* **Open** 6pm-midnight daily. **Main courses** HK$75-$125. **Credit** AmEx, DC, MC, V. **Map** p80 D2.

Sound like veggie heaven? Well, almost. There are fish and seafood dishes included on the menu for the not-so-strict vegetarians, but the many vegetable, noodle and rice dishes are tasty and filling. The daily buffet option is good if you want to sample different Western and Asian dishes. Located within the never-less-than-hectic Times Square shopping complex, the restaurant is big, bright and brash, so don't come here expecting to have a romantic meal.

## South & east coast

### International

### The Verandah

*1/F, Repulse Bay Hotel, 109 Repulse Bay Road, Repulse Bay, HK Island (2812 2722). Buses to Repulse Bay.* **Open** noon-2.30pm, 3-5.30pm, 6-10pm Mon-Sat; 11am-2.30pm Sun. **Main courses** HK$200-$300. **Credit** AmEx, DC, MC, V.

The Verandah is one of the most romantic places to dine in Hong Kong, with a colonial setting offering a grand sea view. Smart staff give attentive service and roll a Champagne trolley to your table when you arrive. If not all the dishes live up to expectations, then none disappoint either. The Sunday brunch is legendary, so book weeks in advance if you wish to go.

## COFFEE & CAKE

Coffee culture has only really developed in Hong Kong in the past five years, with **Pacific Century Coffee** leading the way. Its outlets vary in size and comfort, but all have computers for web surfing, a good range of coffees and shakes, and food.

In 2001, **Starbucks** began to make inroads into the market, opening a handful of establishments in major districts and earmarking many more sites. The Seattle-based chain serves better coffee, good cakes and pastries, and prides itself on its environmentally friendly packaging.

Dairy stores, serving up an extraordinary variety of steamed, condensed and evaporated milk drinks, are popular with local children and young people. They are particularly common in Jordan and Yau Ma Tei in Kowloon (try **Yee Shun Milk Co**, 519 Nathan Road, Yau Ma Tei; 2734 5460).

If you feel in need of revitalisation, sample the fine smoothies and super juices served up at **The Mix** (3 Queen's Road, Central, HK Island; 2523 7396/www.themix.com.hk). It also serves salads and healthy snacks, and is an agreeable place to chill out.

Other useful places to stop for a snack, although the coffee in not a highlight in either, are **Delifrance** and **Oliver's**. Delifrance, which sells croissants, fresh fruit custard tarts, sandwiches, quiches and coffee, is everywhere. The food is solid fare (although the French are unlikely to be impressed) and the outlets are comfortable. Oliver's also offers a range of made-to-order sandwiches, toasties, baked potatoes, juices and cheap meals. They can be found in most busy districts.

## Mediterranean

### Lucy's

*64 Stanley Main Street, Stanley, HK Island (2813 9055). Buses to Stanley.* **Open** noon-3pm, 7-10.30pm daily. **Main courses** HK$70-$130. **Credit** AmEx, DC, MC, V. **Map** p95.

Hidden in among Stanley's ever-popular market, crammed with tourists and weekend day-trippers, lies Lucy's, an oasis of calm amid the madness. Inside, it's quiet and unpretentious, with bamboo and wicker furniture, and laid-back, friendly service. The frequently changing menu is short and relatively simple but everything is well done, whether it's a Moroccan couscous, a feta cheese soufflé, a plate of saffron gnocchi or a revitalising fresh salad. The choices for vegetarians are excellent. The wine choice is also small, but the bottles are well chosen.

## Vietnamese

### Saigon At Stanley

*1/F & 2/F, Stanley Beach Villa, 90 Stanley Main Street, Stanley, HK Island (2899 0999). Buses to Stanley.* **Open** noon-10.30pm daily. **Main courses** HK$80-$160. **Credit** AmEx, DC, MC, V. **Map** p95.

A modern Vietnamese restaurant with whirling fans, wicker chairs and contemporary crockery. The setting, with its view of the waterfront, is great and all the staple Vietnamese dishes are done well, from lettuce-wrapped spring rolls to succulent roast duck.

# Kowloon

## Tsim Sha Tsui

## Chinese: Beijingese

### Peking Garden

*3/F, Star House, Tsim Sha Tsui, Kowloon (2735 8211). Tsim Sha Tsui MTR (exit E)/ buses to Tsim Sha Tsui Star Ferry Pier & along Salisbury Road/Tsim Sha Tsui Star Ferry Pier.* **Open** 11.30am-3pm, 5.30-11.30pm daily. **Main courses** HK$80-$180. **Credit** AmEx, DC, MC, V. **Map** p98 B3.

Peking duck is legendary, but Beijing dumplings are a lesser known (and much more affordable) treat. Stuffed with vegetables and pork, or mushrooms, they are steamed or fried and arrive plump, juicy and piping hot. Here, they're superb, as are the Yunnan (air-dried, like Serrano) ham dishes.

## Chinese: Cantonese

### Dynasty

*4/F, Renaissance New World Hotel, 22 Salisbury Road, Tsim Sha Tsui, Kowloon (2369 4111). Tsim Sha Tsui MTR (exit E)/buses to Tsim Sha Tsui Star Ferry Pier & along Salisbury Road/Tsim Sha Tsui Star Ferry Pier.* **Open** 11am-11pm daily. **Main courses** HK$120-$220. **Credit** AmEx, DC, MC, V. **Map** p98 C3.

An elegant setting for fine Cantonese cuisine. Dim sum options go beyond the usual, and Dynasty is lauded for its barbecued meats and Portuguese-influenced dishes from nearby Macau. The higher price tags are worth it; there's less noise and more sophistication here than at your average local eaterie.

### Spring Moon

*1/F, Peninsula Hotel, Salisbury Road, Tsim Sha Tsui, Kowloon (2315 3160). Tsim Sha Tsui MTR (exit E)/buses to Tsim Sha Tsui Star Ferry Pier & along Salisbury Road/Tsim Sha Tsui Star Ferry Pier.* **Open** 11.30am-3pm, 6-11pm daily. **Main courses** HK$180-$340. **Credit** AmEx, DC, MC, V. **Map** p98 B3.

Located inside the timeless Peninsula Hotel, Spring Moon lives up to expectations. Classic and creative Cantonese cuisine is served up to a cultured crowd who don't mind working through their wallet for fine dining. From the duck to the goose, abalone and lobster, everything is magnificently done with a large helping of style.

## French

### Au Trou Normand

*63 Carnarvon Road, Tsim Sha Tsui, Kowloon (2366 8754). Tsim Sha Tsui MTR (exit B2)/buses along Nathan Road.* **Open** noon-11pm daily. **Main courses** HK$200-$280. **Credit** AmEx, DC, MC, V. **Map** p98 C1.

Probably the best French restaurant in Hong Kong that isn't located in a five-star hotel. Its façade often goes unnoticed, but people who dine here frequently return for the ambience and fine food. The menu is full of French classics, but there are often a few surprise dishes available if you ask the waiter.

### Gaddi's

*1/F, Peninsula Hotel, Salisbury Road, Tsim Sha Tsui, Kowloon (2315 3171). Tsim Sha Tsui MTR (exit E)/buses to Tsim Sha Tsui Star Ferry Pier & along Salisbury Road/Tsim Sha Tsui Star Ferry Pier.* **Open** noon-3pm, 7-11pm daily. **Main courses** HK$250-$400. **Credit** AmEx, DC, MC, V. **Map** p98 B3.

With irrepressible Brit Philip Sedgwick behind the pans, Gaddi's reputation for stellar French cuisine has only increased – so much so that there's a long waiting list for the 'chef's table' in the kitchen itself, where diners can watch the preparation of superb dishes such as steamed cod fillet larded with lemon confit and quick-fried cherrystone clams. The restaurant itself is formal in atmosphere, and the prices reach the same heights as the food.

## Fusion

### Felix

*28/F, Peninsula Hotel, Salisbury Road, Tsim Sha Tsui, Kowloon (2366 6251). Tsim Sha Tsui MTR (exit E)/buses to Tsim Sha Tsui Star Ferry Pier & along Salisbury Road/Tsim Sha Tsui Star Ferry Pier.* **Open** 6pm-2am daily. **Main courses** HK$200-$350. **Credit** AmEx, DC, MC, V. **Map** p98 B3.

Enjoying phenomenal views from its perch atop of the Peninsula Hotel, Felix has a deserved reputation as the coolest (and some say finest) restaurant in Hong Kong. The lofty-ceilinged Philippe Starck-designed interior, cocooned private rooms, opulent decor and savvy clientele are unrivalled. But the imaginative fusion food doesn't come cheap. If you prefer to settle for a (relatively) inexpensive glimpse, pop into Felix's bar for a cocktail. And if you're a man, use the toilets – the windows above the urinals offers a stunning vista, and the bizarre sensation that you are relieving yourself over Kowloon.

## International

### Mint

*122-126 Canton Road, Tsim Sha Tsui, Kowloon (2735 5887). Tsim Sha Tsui MTR (exit A1)/buses along Canton Road/Tsim Sha Tsui Star Ferry Pier.* **Open** 11.30am-12.30am daily. **Main courses** HK$90-$340. **Credit** AmEx, DC, MC, V. **Map** p98 A1.

Young trendy Chinese are flocking to this ambitious newcomer to the scene, which offers individual servings or huge portions to share – as in Cantonese restaurants, but the setting is very European. And the food is great (particularly the salmon and quail), at prices below many similar quality eateries, hence its popularity with young white collar workers.

## Italian

### Sabatini

*3/F, Royal Garden Hotel, 69 Mody Road, Tsim Sha Tsui, Kowloon (2721 5215). Tsim Sha Tsui MTR (exit C1)/203, 973 bus & buses along Chatham Road South & Salisbury Road.* **Open** noon-3pm, 6-11.30pm daily. **Main courses** HK$180-$350. **Credit** AmEx, DC, MC, V. **Map** p98 C2.

The finest Italian restaurant this side of the harbour, Sabatini attracts discerning diners. Its relaxed ambience is a world away from the urban chaos outside. Pastas and mains are authentic award-winners, desserts an irresistible indulgence and the wine list extensive.

## Japanese

### Katiga Japanese Food Shop

*G/F, Sung Oi Building, 37 Sung Kit Street, Hung Hom, Kowloon (2764 6436). Buses along Ma Tau Wai Road.* **Open** 11.30am-11pm daily. **Main courses** HK$50-$100. **Credit** MC.

Japanese restaurants can be found almost everywhere in Hong Kong, but many are on the expensive side. This tiny eatery, tucked away down a side alley is an exception, serving quality sushi, sashimi, noodle and rice dishes, not to mention great sake. The decor's not fancy, but it's always crammed with chatty diners. Try the eel, salmon and octopus.

## Seafood

### Buddy's Famous Seafood

*G/F, Kowloon Centre, 31 Ashley Road, Tsim Sha Tsui, Kowloon (2199 7998). Tsim Sha Tsui MTR (exit C1, E)/buses along Nathan Road/Tsim Sha Tsui Star Ferry Pier.* **Open** noon-midnight daily. **Main courses** HK$120-$250 (portions for 2 or 3). **Credit** AmEx, DC, MC, V. **Map** p98 B2.

American-sized servings make this place ideal for big groups, who can split lots of platters – couples may be limited to sharing just one or two. The seafood is, as you'd expect, great and, in the case of

Starck truths at **Felix**. *See p156.*

lobster, one of the best deals in town. All dishes are served simply, with a complimentary bread basket and salad, by the most enthusiastic staff around.

### Oyster & Wine Bar

*18/F, Sheraton Hong Kong Hotel & Towers, 20 Nathan Road, Tsim Sha Tsui, Kowloon (2369 1111). Tsim Sha Tsui MTR (exit E)/buses along Nathan Road/Tsim Sha Tsui Star Ferry Pier.* **Open** 6.30pm-1am Mon-Thur; 6.30pm-2am Fri, Sat. **Main courses** HK$150-$250. **Credit** AmEx, DC, MC, V. **Map** p98 C3.

As the name suggests, the reason to come here is the oysters: a dozen varieties are waiting to be shucked by chefs and whizzed to your table by attentive staff. Imported from all over the world, including Scotland and the US, they're as fresh as aviation technology allows. Plenty of mains are offered and the wine list is extensive.

### Steakhouse

#### Morton's Of Chicago

*4/F, Sheraton Hong Kong Hotel & Towers, 20 Nathan Road, Tsim Sha Tsui, Kowloon (2732 2343). Tsim Sha Tsui MTR (exit E)/buses along Nathan Road/Tsim Sha Tsui Star Ferry Pier.* **Open** 5.30-10.30pm Mon-Sat; 5-10pm Sun. **Main courses** HK$200-$300. **Credit** AmEx, DC, MC, V. **Map** p98 C3.

Probably the finest steak joint in Hong Kong. Huge slabs of mouth-wateringly tender, prime aged beef are served on giant platters, which means you have

little room for the wonderful starters and scrumptious desserts at which Morton's also excels. Not easy on the wallet or the waistline – leave your guilty conscience at the door.

### Swiss

#### Swiss Chalet

*12-14 Hart Avenue, Tsim Sha Tsui, Kowloon (2191 9197). Tsim Sha Tsui MTR (exit A2, D2)/ buses along Nathan Road & Chatham Road South.* **Open** 11am-midnight Mon-Sat; 5pm-midnight Sun. **Main courses** HK$110-$170. **Credit** AmEx, DC, MC, V. **Map** p98 C2.

The 1970s are no longer derided as the decade taste forgot – and fondue is back in fashion. And the finest cheese fondue in Hong Kong is available here. Dip your bread cubes into the simmering sauce and devour. That's not all that's on offer; there are typical French dishes as well, but the fondue is the best reason for dropping in.

### Vegetarian

#### Joyce Café

*4/F, Prestige Tower, 23 Nathan Road, Tsim Sha Tsui, Kowloon (2316 7333). Tsim Sha Tsui MTR (exit E)/buses along Nathan Road/Tsim Sha Tsui Star Ferry Pier.* **Open** 11am-7pm Mon-Sat; 11am-6pm Sun. **Main courses** HK$100-$180. **Credit** AmEx, DC, MC, V. **Map** p98 C3.

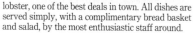

**Eat, Drink, Shop**

# Restaurants by cuisine

### Chinese: Beijingese

**American Restaurant**, Wan Chai, HKI (p150); **Peking Garden**, Tsim Sha Tsui, Kowloon (p155); **Peking Restaurant**, Jordan, Kowloon (p158).

### Chinese: Cantonese/dim sum

**Cheung Kee**, Cheung Chau (p165); **Chun Woo House**, Mong Kok, Kowloon (p158); **City Hall Chinese Restaurant**, Central, HKI (p142); **Dim Sum**, Happy Valley, HKI (p150); **Dynasty**, Tsim Sha Tsui, Kowloon (p155); **Law Fu Kee Noodle Shop**, Central, HKI (p142); **Luen Yick Restaurant**, Tai Po, New Terrs (p160); **Luk Yu Tea House**, Central, HKI (p143); **Nice Hoover Hotpot & Seafood Restaurant**, Fanling, New Terrs (p161); **Royal Park Chinese**, Sha Tin, New Terrs (p161); **Spring Moon**, Tsim Sha Tsui, Kowloon (p155); **Tung Kee Restaurant**, Sai Kung, New Terrs (p163); **Yung Kee**, Central, HKI (p143); **Zen**, Kowloon Tong, Kowloon (p160).

### Chinese: Chiu chownese

**Eastern Palace**, Tsing Yi, New Terrs (p162); **Mirage**, Clearwater Bay, New Terrs (p163).

### Chinese: Hunanese

**Hunan Garden**, Central, HKI (p143).

### Chinese: pigeon

**Han Lok Yuen**, Yung Shue Wan, Lamma (p164).

### Chinese: seafood

**Cheung Chau Eastern Court Seafood Restaurant**, Cheung Chau (p165); **Golden Lake Restaurant**, Cheung Chau (p165); **Rainbow Seafood**, Sok Kwu Wan, Lamma (p164); **Sampan Seafood Restaurant**, Yung Shue Wan, Lamma (p164).

Get to see the real Hong Kong, that of the Prada-clad *tai-tais* gathering for a gossip after a hard morning's shopping. Beyond people watching, Joyce has a reputation for serving the most delicious – and healthiest – veggie food in town: creative salads and inspired mains abound. Great juices, too.

## Yau Ma Tei & Mong Kok

### Chinese: Beijingese

#### Peking Restaurant

*1/F, 227 Nathan Road, Jordan, Kowloon (2730 1315). Jordan MTR (exit C1)/any bus along Nathan Road.* **Open** 11am-11pm daily. **Main courses** HK$30-$80. **No credit cards. Map** p110 B5.
If you really want a blow-out, opt for the ever-popular Peking duck. Served in the traditional manner, with pancakes, spring onions, cucumber and plum sauce, it's comparatively cheap here, but as good as any you find in more expensive restaurants. The garlic and soy sauce soused chicken is another excellent dish.

### Chinese: Cantonese

#### Chun Woo House

*79 Tung Choi Street, Mong Kok, Kowloon (2725 8473). Jordan MTR (exit D3)/buses along Nathan Road.* **Open** 11am-2am daily. **Main courses** HK$20-$40. **No credit cards. Map** p110 A3.
Dumpling heaven. Whether steamed or fried, the tiny bundles of dough come with a range of delicious fillings, including traditional pork and chive, as well as more exotic combinations. Basic decor.

### Chinese: vegetarian

#### Light Vegetarian Restaurant

*New Lucky House, 13 Jordan Road, Jordan, Kowloon (2384 2833). Jordan MTR (B2)/buses along Nathan Road.* **Main courses** HK$30-$50. **Credit** DC, MC, V. **Map** p110 B5.
All the mock meat treats are here, but the best dishes are those that don't pretend to be anything else, like the fried beancurd and mushroom rice. Simple, but effective.

### Indonesian/Malaysian

#### Bali Restaurant

*10 Nanking Road, Jordan, Kowloon (2708 2902). Jordan MTR (exit A)/buses along Nathan Road.* **Open** 11.30am-11pm daily. **Main courses** HK$30-$50. **No credit cards. Map** p110 A5.
The decor's tacky, but there's nothing wrong with the Indonesian/Malaysian food: the curries are good and the nasi goreng has been known to lure Hong Kong Islanders all the way to Jordan. It's also extremely easy on the wallet.

### International

#### Cinematique

*Shop H2, Prosperous Garden, 3 Public Square Street, Yau Ma Tei, Kowloon (2388 4665). Yau Ma Tei MTR (exit C)/buses along Nathan Road.* **Open** noon-10pm Mon, Sun; noon-10.30pm Tue-Sat. **Main courses** HK$70-$130. **Credit** AmEx, MC, V. **Map** p110 A4.

Eat, Drink, Shop

### Chinese: Shanghainese
**Lao Ching Hing**, Wan Chai, HKI (*p150*);
**Shanghai Hui Guan**, Kowloon Tong, Kowloon
(*p160*).

### Chinese: Sichuanese
**Red Pepper**, Causeway Bay, HKI (*p151*).

### Chinese: vegetarian
*See also* **Vegetarian. Chinese Vegetarian**,
Po Lin, Lantau (*p147*); **Light Vegetarian
Restaurant**, Jordan, Kowloon (*p158*); **Po Lin
Vegetarian**, Sheung Wan, HKI (*p164*).

### American
**The Bayou**, Central, HKI (*p142*).

### Asian
**Eating Plus**, Central, HKI (*p142*);
**Noodle Box**, Central, HKI (*p142*).

### British
**Harry Ramsden's**, Wan Chai, HKI (*p149*);
**Soho Soho**, Central, HKI (*p142*).

### French
**Au Trou Normand**, Tsim Sha Tsui,
Kowloon (*p156*); **Café Des Artistes**,
Central, HKI (*p143*); **Gaddi's**, Tsim Sha
Tsui, Kowloon (*p156*); **Le Tire Bouchon**,
Central, HKI (*p143*); **Petrus**, Central,
HKI (*p143*).

### Fusion
**Felix**, Tsim Sha Tsui, Kowloon (*p156*).

### Greek/Middle Eastern
**Bacchus**, Wan Chai, HK Island (*p151*).

### Indian
**The Chapel**, Happy Valley, HKI (*p151*);
**India Today**, Central, HKI (*p144*);
**Jo Jo Indian Restaurant**, Discovery Bay,
Lantau (*p164*); **Shaffi's Indian
Restaurant**, Yuen Long, New Terrs
(*p162*); **Taste Of India**, Kowloon City,
Kowloon (*p159*); **Toochkas**, Yung Shue Wan,
Lamma (*p164*).

▶

A culinary oasis in predominantly grubby Yau Ma Tei can be found on the same site as the excellent Broadway Cinematique cinema (*see p216*). The clean, chrome interior is a pleasingly sanitary experience and the Western food (salads, pasta dishes, risotto and steaks to name but a few) is easily the best of its kind in the area. The friendly staff are another big plus, and you can always catch a movie before or after eating.

## Japanese

### Tokyo Sushi
*566 Nathan Road, Mong Kok, Kowloon (2388 4182). Yau Ma Tei MTR (exit A1, A2)/buses along Nathan Road.* **Main courses** HK$60-$100. **Credit** AmEx, MC, V. **Map** p110 A3.
Take your pick from the plates on the conveyor belt rotating in front of you, gorge until you can eat no more, then head to the cashier to settle the bill. Surprise – the cost isn't half what you feared it might be. Tokyo Sushi is one of the cheapest sushi bars in Hong Kong – and it prides itself on its quality fish.

## Kowloon City

## Indian

### Taste Of India
*24 Southwall Road, Kowloon City, Kowloon (2716 5128). Bus 101, 104, 110.* **Open** 11am-3pm, 6-11.30pm daily. **Main courses** HK$40-$60.
**No credit cards**.

Curried seafood (be it crab, cuttlefish, eel, fish and shrimps) is what the Taste of India does best. All are smothered in aromatic spices and served with mounds of rice. Local Chinese like this place because it reminds them of Cantonese cooking.

## Thai

### Combo Thai Restaurant
*14-15 Nga Tsin Long Road, Kowloon City, Kowloon (2716 7318). Bus 101, 104, 110.* **Open** 11.30am-1am daily. **Main courses** HK$30-$50. **Credit** DC, MC, V.
If you like Thai food, Kowloon City (with its strong Thai community) has it in spades. You can choose from more than a dozen restaurants, but this one is a fine example of the no-nonsense approach Thais have to food. The tom yum gung will force you bolt upright, the fish cakes are moreish and the salads will have you reaching for the fire extinguisher.

## Vietnamese

### Wing Chun Vietnamese Restaurant
*16 & 18 Lion Rock Road, Kowloon City, Kowloon (2716 6122). Bus 101, 104, 110.* **Open** 11am-midnight daily. **Main courses** HK$25-$50.
**No credit cards**.
Tables and chairs are arranged higgledy-piggledy in this converted shop. Staff will woo you in and usher you out as fast as possible, but in between they'll serve you tasty meat and seafood dishes; those fried with chilli and garlic are the most alluring. There's also the usual spring rolls, cold glass noodle dishes and soft-shell crabs – none disappoint.

## Restaurants by cuisine (continued)

### Indonesian/Malaysian
**Bali Restaurant**, Jordan, Kowloon (p158); **Cosmopolitan Curry House**, Tai Po Market, New Terrs (p161); **Thai/Malaysian Restaurant**, Sheung Shui, New Terrs (p161).

### International
**Aqua**, Central, HKI (p144); **Bookworm Café**, Yung Shue Wan, Lamma (p164); **Cococabana**, Lamma (p164); **Café Deco**, The Peak, HKI (p148); **Café Lagoon**, Castle Peak Bay, New Terrs (p162); **Cheung Chau Windsurfing Centre & Outdoor Café**, Cheung Chau (p165); **Cinematique**, Yau Ma Tei, Kowloon (p158); **Coffee Culture**, Tsing Yi, New Terrs (p162); **EXP/2**, Kowloon Tong, Kowloon (p160); **IP Café**, Sheung Wan, HKI (p148); **Jaspa's**, Sai Kung, New Terrs (p163); **Madison's**, Central, HKI (p144); **M At The**

**Fringe**, Central, HKI (p144); **Mint**, Tsim Sha Tsui, Kowloon (p156); **Morocco's**, Cheung Chau (p165); **Oasis Bar & Café**, Ma On Shan, New Terrs (p163); **Open Kitchen**, Wan Chai, HKI (p153); **Peak Café**, The Peak, HKI (p149); **Pepperonis**, Sai Kung, New Terrs (p163); **Tapas Tree**, Sai Kung, New Terrs (p163); **The Verandah**, Repulse Bay, HKI (p154).

### Italian
**Chianti Restaurant Italiano**, Tsuen Wan, New Terrs (p162); **Fat Angelo's**, Wan Chai, HKI (p153); **Grissini**, Wan Chai, HKI (p153); **Nicholini's**, Central, HKI (p144); **Sabatini**, Tsim Sha Tsui, Kowloon (p156); **Trattoria**, Central, HKI (p144).

### Japanese
**Hello Kitty Café**, Tsuen Wan, New Terrs (p162); **Katiga Japanese Food Shop**, Hung Hom, Kowloon (p156); **Tokio Joe**, Central, HKI (p145); **Tokyo Sushi**, Mong Kok, Kowloon (p159).

## Kowloon Tong

### Chinese: Cantonese

#### Zen
*G/25, Festival Walk, 80 Tat Chee Avenue, Kowloon Tong, Kowloon (2265 7328). Kowloon Tong KCR or MTR (exit C1, C2)/2C, 203 bus.* **Open** 10.30am-11pm Mon-Sat; 9.30am-11pm Sun. **Main courses** HK$70-$125. **Credit** AmEx, DC, MC, V.
Class is not normally a word associated with dim sum restaurants, but Zen is a cut above the rest. In a stylish interior, with calming fountains and palatial decor, smart staff serve a mouth-watering array of dishes. The dim sum, including deep-fried duck tongues (which are delicious), is popular at lunchtimes, but the mains, from suckling pig to roast pigeon, are also superb.
**Branch**: LG1, The Mall, Pacific Place, 88 Queensway, HK Island (2845 4555).

### Chinese: Shanghainese

#### Shanghai Hui Guan
*UG/F, Wah Do House, 322 Junction Road, Kowloon Tong, Kowloon (2337 7829). Kowloon Tong MTR (exit A2)/buses along Junction Road & Waterloo Road.* **Open** 11am-2am daily. **Main courses** HK$40-$70. **Credit** AmEx, DC, MC, V.
Shanghainese food, sharing simplicity with its Cantonese cousin, is popular in Hong Kong. There are many expensive Shanghainese outlets, but this

unpretentious one rates highly. The pork and shrimp dumplings are delicious, especially steamed, as are the sweet and sour noodle dishes – the sauce is rich and tasty, but not cloying.

### International

#### EXP/2
*UG/23, Festival Walk, 80 Tat Chee Avenue, Kowloon Tong, Kowloon (2265 8298). Kowloon Tong KCR or MTR (exit C1, C2)/2C, 203 bus.* **Open** 11am-midnight daily. **Main courses** HK$35-$60. **Credit** AmEx, DC, MC, V.
The perfect place to stop for a quick bite. The menu features Asian, Western and fusion dishes, from basics like spicy chicken wings to more exotic choices, such as crab roe salad, ramen and risotto, served in rapid time. Its modern, fresh interior makes it a popular lunch choice with the chic office crowd.

# The New Territories

## Central New Territories

### Chinese: Cantonese

#### Luen Yick Restaurant
*Luen Yick Village, Sam Mun Tsui, Tai Po, New Territories (2664 0455). Tai Po KCR, then minibus to Luen Yick.* **Open** 11.30am-11pm daily. **Main courses** HK$40-$100. **No credit cards.**

## Mediterranean

**Lucy's**, Stanley, HKI (*p155*); **Stoep**, Lower Chueng Sha, Lantau (*p165*).

## Mexican

**I-Caramba**, Central, HKI (*p145*).

## Seafood/fish

*See also* **Chinese: seafood**. **Anthony's Catch**, Sai Kung, New Terrs (*p163*); **Buddy's Famous Seafood**, Tsim Sha Tsui, Kowloon (*p156*); **Oyster & Wine Bar**, Tsim Sha Tsui, Kowloon (*p157*).

## South African

**The Gallery**, Tong Fuk, Lantau (*p165*).

## Spanish

**Boca**, Central, HKI (*p145*); **Nico's**, Mid-Levels, HKI (*p145*); **Olé**, Central, HKI (*p145*).

## Steakhouse

**A Hereford Beefstouw**, Airport, Chek Lap Kok (*p165*); **Morton's Of Chicago**, Tsim Sha Tsui, Kowloon (*p157*).

## Swiss

**Swiss Chalet**, Tsim Sha Tsui, Kowloon (*p157*).

## Thai

**Café Siam**, Central, HKI (*p145*); **Chili Club**, Wan Chai, HKI (*p153*); **Combo Thai Restaurant**, Kowloon City, Kowloon (*p159*); **Good Luck Thai Café**, Central, HKI (*p145*); **Thai Thai**, Causeway Bay, HKI (*p153*).

## Vegetarian

*See also* **Chinese: vegetarian**. **Joyce Café**, Tsim Sha Tsui, Kowloon (*p157*); **Vegetarian International Paradise**, Causeway Bay, HKI (*p154*).

## Vietnamese

**Indochine 1929**, Central, HKI (*p147*); **Saigon At Stanley**, Stanley, HKI (*p155*); **Song**, Central, HKI (*p147*); **Wing Chun Vietnamese Restaurant**, Kowloon City, Kowloon (*p159*).

Luen Lick Restaurant is an ideal place to stop after a hot day's rural exploring. Expect solid Cantonese homecooking in a typically basic setting – restaurants don't come more traditional than this. Stick with the regulars, like chilli and garlic prawns, steamed fish and minced pigeon, and you won't be disappointed.

### Nice Hoover Hotpot & Seafood Restaurant

*G/F-1/F, Comfort Court, 2A Luen Cheong Street, Luen Wo Hoi, Fanling, New Territories (2682 0683). Fanling KCR/70, 70K, 70X, 73, 73A, 77K, 79K bus.* **Open** 7am-2am daily. **Main courses** HK$25-$50. **Credit** MC, V.

Fanling is not a tourist haven, so you won't be exactly spoilt for choice when it comes to eating. Nice Hoover, however, is clean, efficiently run and, above all, cheap. Dim sum is the main fare, but it's a mixed bag. If you don't fancy chicken feet, you can always opt for shrimp dumplings, barbecue pork buns or excellent bean curd sheet rolls in oyster sauce.

### Royal Park Chinese

*2/F, Royal Park Hotel, Pak Hok Ting Street, Sha Tin, New Territories (2601 2111). Sha Tin KCR/buses to Sha Tin.* **Open** 11am-3pm, 6-11pm Mon-Sat; 9am-3pm, 6-11pm Sun. **Main courses** HK$100-$140. **Credit** AmEx, DC, MC, V.

Sha Tin's Royal Park Chinese is something of a hidden gem, located inside a hotel patronised mainly by business travellers. All the delicacies are here, from abalone to shark's fin soup, but the simpler dim sum are delicious, especially the

steamed shrimp dumplings and steamed pork spare ribs in black bean sauce. Prices are high, but if you're a bit fazed by the local eateries, the quality is worth it.

# Indonesian/Malaysian/Thai

### Cosmopolitan Curry House

*80 Kwong Fuk Road, Tai Po Market, New Territories (2650 7056). Tai Po Market KCR/buses to Tai Po.* **Open** 11am-11.30pm daily. **Main courses** HK$50-$100. **Credit** DC, MC, V.

It's loud, busy and chaotic, but that's because this curry house serves up excellent Indonesian and Malaysian dishes to its adoring faithful. Fruit and seafood never tasted so good together – the mango prawn curry is to die for. You may have to queue if you drop in, so try to book.

### Thai/Malaysian Restaurant

*28-30 Sun Fat Street, Sheung Shui, New Territories (2673 2230). Sheung Shui KCR/buses to Sheung Shui.* **Open** 11am-11.30pm daily. **Main courses** HK$50-$75. **No credit cards.**

This no-frills restaurant in Sheung Shui (the last stop on the KCR before the border with Shenzhen and the rest of China) serves up crab, prawns and fish in spicy, creamy sauces. The seafood tastes as if it was plucked from the sea only minutes earlier (and it probably was), while the casual surroundings are perfect for avoiding embarrassment when you find yourself up to your wrists in curry sauce. Thankfully, hot napkins allow you to clean yourself up before you leave.

Eat, Drink, Shop

# West New Territories

## Chinese: Chiu chownese

### Eastern Palace
Unit 210, Maritime Square, Tsing Yi, New Territories (2751 0888). Tung Chung MTR.
**Open** 8am-11pm daily. **Main courses** HK$60-$130. **Credit** AmEx, MC, V.
If you love goose, this place is well worth stepping off the train at Tung Chung for. Slices of the bird are marinated in soy sauce and cooked to juicy perfection. Other dishes to try include the steamed chicken and barbecued pork, while the vegetable and oyster congee will satisfy non-meat lovers. It's loud and the staff are not particularly helpful, but there's nothing unusual in that in a Hong Kong restaurant.

## Indian

### Shaffi's Indian Restaurant
14 Fau Tsoi Street, off Main Road, Yuen Long, New Territories (2476 7885). Tuen Mun Ferry Pier, then 615, 610, 614 bus. **Open** 11am-3pm, 6-11pm daily. **Main courses** HK$40-$60. **Credit** AmEx, MC, V.
There's a history behind this restaurant. Owner Liaqat Ali cooked for British troops at Shek Kong army barracks (as did his uncle before him, as far back as 1972), but when the soldiers left in 1997, he was forced to set up on his own. You get exactly what you would expect at Shaffi's: creamy, spicy dishes that taste a treat.

## International

### Café Lagoon
Gold Coast Hotel, 1 Castle Peak Road, Castle Peak Bay, New Territories (2452 8888). Tsuen Wan MTR, then minibus/to Castle Peak Bay. **Open** 6am-midnight daily. **Main courses** HK$140-$220. **Credit** AmEx, DC, MC, V.
This hotel restaurant, which serves up good lunch buffets, provides a fine dining option in this remote part of the territory. Also within the Gold Coast Hotel, the Atrium does a good international dinner buffet and the Qi Chinese restaurant offers reasonable Cantonese fare.

### Coffee Culture
Shop 15-16, L1, Old Market, Maritime Square, Tsing Yi, New Territories (2880 5622). Tsuen Wan MTR, then bus/minibus to Tsing Yi. **Open** 11am-10pm daily. **Main courses** HK$25-$45. **No credit cards.**
More than a coffee shop, this eaterie offers good sandwiches, snacks and home-style favourites, such as lasagne, at reasonable prices. The quaint setting inside the old market in Tsing Yi, provides a touch of history that is so often lacking in downtown Hong Kong.

## Italian

### Chianti Restaurant Italiano
Mezzanine, 3/F, Kowloon Panda Hotel, 3 Tsuen Street, Tsuen Wan, New Territories (2409 1111). Tsuen Wan MTR/buses to Tsuen Wan. **Open** noon-3pm, 6-11pm daily. **Main courses** HK$110-$170. **Credit** AmEx, DC, MC, V.
Western fare is hard to come by in this part of the Hong Kong, but Chianti (within the Kowloon Panda Hotel) is a venerable exception. It serves a good, if predictable, array of pasta dishes, along with meat and seafood mains, plus a decent selection of appetisers and desserts. Besides hotel residents, it's popular with visitors wanting to escape the grim industrial landscape around.

## Japanese

### Hello Kitty Café
1/F, Luk Yeung Galleria, 22-26 Wai Tsuen Road, Tsuen Wan, New Territories (2414 3262). Tsuen Wan MTR/32B, 43X, 49X, 263R bus. **Open** 7.30am-10pm daily. **Main courses** HK$20-$40. **Credit** AmEx, MC, V.
Some fans love Hello Kitty, the mouthless cat, so much they eat her – and most of them are young women in their twenties (which says a lot about local culture). Imprints of the Japanese cartoon megastar are on just about everything here, from the table-

**Jaspa's:** fancy dining in Sai Kung. See p163.

cloths and crockery to the food. The Japanese noodle dishes, like chicken teriyaki udon, are better than the lame attempts at toasties and other Western snacks, but – as you'd expect – the desserts are sickly sweet.

## East New Territories

### Chinese: Cantonese

#### Tung Kee Restaurant
*96-102 Man Nin Street, Sai Kung, New Territories (2792 7453). Choi Hung MTR, then minibus 12 to Sai Kung.* **Open** 11am-11pm daily. **Main courses** HK$80-$160. **Credit** MC, V.
Watch the fishing boats come in, then head for the aquariums outside this restaurant and pick something fresher than a first-day student. You can choose how to have it cooked, but it's best to leave it up to the experienced chefs, who'll probably steam or fry it and throw some ginger, garlic, chillies and oil over the top.

### Chinese: Chiu chownese/Thai

#### Mirage
*Level 7, Silverstrand Mart, Silver Cape Road, Clearwater Bay, New Territories (2335 1323). Choi Hung MTR, then minibus to Clearwater Bay.* **Open** noon-11pm daily. **Main courses** HK$70-$150. **Credit** AmEx, MC, V.
Clearwater Bay has a few Chinese eateries near the beach, but most are nothing more than stop and go places for noodles and chicken wings. Mirage's cuisine is a notch up, like the venue, which is on the seventh floor of a shopping mall. Thankfully, it has a rooftop garden offering excellent views. The restaurant serves Chiu Chownese and Thai dishes, and the chefs will make the food as fiery or mild as you want. The Thai dishes are probably better: try the curried crab or shrimp cakes.

### International

#### Jaspa's
*13 Sha Tsui Path, Sai Kung, New Territories (2792 6388). Choi Hung MTR, then minibus 12 to Sai Kung.* **Open** 11am-11pm Mon-Sat; 9am-11pm Sun. **Main courses** HK$80-$130. **Credit** AmEx, MC, V.
If you're hungry after a hike in the countryside, but still pine for that quality restaurant feeling, Jaspa's offers fancy cuisine in laid-back surroundings. The steaks are excellent, as are the seafood dishes and heavenly desserts. Friendly staff add to the relaxed ambience.

#### Pepperonis
*18B Main Street, Sai Kung, New Territories (2792 2083). Choi Hung MTR, then minibus 12 to Sai Kung.* **Open** 10am-10pm daily. **Main courses** HK$65-$110. **Credit** AmEx, MC, V.

# Bars with food

Many of Hong Kong's bars serve food, which can range from simple bar snacks to full-blown meals. If you fancy eating in a more casual environment than a restaurant, *see chapter* **Pubs & bars**.

Hong Kong's first Pepperonis opened in Sai Kung and proved so popular that the concept has subsequently spread across the city. You'll find that all the branches are good, and always busy. The recipe for their success: big portions of old favourites like nachos, spaghetti carbonara, fried calamari and an exotic array of pizzas (try the New Orleans). The deep-fried camembert is good, too – if you're not worried about your cholesterol levels.

#### Oasis Bar & Café
*Whitehead Golf Centre, Ma On Shan, New Territories (2633 7220). University Station KCR, then free shuttle bus every 20 mins.* **Open** 11am-11pm Mon-Fri; 8.30am-11pm Sat, Sun. **Main courses** HK$140-$300. **Credit** AmEx, DC, MC, V.
Besides being a grand setting for a leisurely round, Whitehead Golf Centre has an excellent restaurant offering sea views and first-class service. The menu is high-end, including lobster Thermidor and magret de canard. But the reason to visit is for a slice of stately, almost colonial, grandeur.

#### Tapas Tree
*Shop 10A, Po Tung Road, Sai Kung, New Territories (2792 6608). Choi Hung MTR, then minibus 12 to Sai Kung.* **Open** noon-11pm daily. **Main courses** HK$80-$130. **Credit** AmEx, DC, MC, V.
Besides the tapas, this continental restaurant serves everything from steak to salads and pasta. For such diversity, the food is surprisingly good, although the wine list could be better. The terracotta walls and bamboo furnishings give it a homely feel.

### Seafood/fish

#### Anthony's Catch
*Lot 1826B, Po Tung Road, Sai Kung, New Territories (2792 8474). Choi Hung MTR, then minibus 12 to Sai Kung.* **Open** 6-10pm Mon-Thur; 6-11pm Fri-Sun. **Main courses** HK$100-$150. **Credit** AmEx, DC, MC, V.
There isn't actually a catch to this impressive eaterie, apart from the fresh fish of the day. There are always several types of fish to choose from, depending on what the boats have brought in, and all are bursting with flavour. Choices beyond fish may be a bit limited, but whether it's seafood or steak you're after, everything is tasty and the servings are huge.

**Eat, Drink, Shop**

# The Outlying Islands

## Lamma

### Chinese: pigeon

#### Han Lok Yuen
*16-17 Hung Shing Ye, Lamma (2982 0680). Yung Shue Wan Ferry Pier, then 15-min walk.* **Open** 11.45am-10.30pm Tue-Sat; 11.45am-7pm Sun. **Main courses** HK$80-$150. **Credit** AmEx, DC, MC, V.
Nicknamed the 'pigeon restaurant' after its speciality dish, this hilltop eaterie is worth the hike. The roast pigeon is the best in the city and was favoured by former Governor Chris Patten, known as *fei pang* (Fatty Patten) by the Chinese. If he can make it up here, anyone can. The minced quail eaten in rolled up lettuce leaves is delicious, as are the vegetable dishes. Ask for directions at the ferry pier.

### Chinese: seafood

#### Rainbow Seafood
*16-20 First Street, Sok Kwu Wan, Lamma (2982 8100). Sok Kwu Wan Ferry Pier.* **Open** 11am-11pm Tue-Sun. **Main courses** HK$110-$150. **Credit** AmEx, DC, MC, V.
Step off the ferry in Sok Kwu Wan and you'll immediately see a row of waterfront seafood restaurants, with lobsters, multi-coloured fish and all manner of other sea creatures clambering over each other in tanks. Pick whatever takes your fancy and it'll be cooked for you in a variety of ways – the sweet and sour sauce at Rainbow is one of the best. The view of the cement works isn't much cop, but the food is.

#### Sampan Seafood Restaurant
*16 Main Street, Yung Shue Wan, Lamma (2982 0159). Yung Shue Wan Ferry Pier.* **Open** 7am-10pm daily. **Main courses** HK$80-$150. **Credit** AmEx, DC, MC, V.
Dim sum is available in the mornings, but the real reason to come here is the seafood. Sampan is among the best of the waterfront Chinese restaurants. The fish and the crab are alive when you choose them, and taste great just minutes later when they arrive sizzling hot. Great al fresco dining.

### Indian/pub grub

#### Toochkas
*44 Main Street, Yung Shue Wan, Lamma (2982 0159). Yung Shue Wan Ferry Pier.* **Open** 10am-11pm Tue-Sun. **Main courses** HK$45-$75. **Credit** AmEx, DC, MC, V.
In the hub of the main street, Toochkas is always packed with those seeking good old-fashioned pub grub and/or Indian food. It's not haute cuisine, but it's a solid meal and a great place for sinking a beer or two with your food.

### International

#### Bookworm Café
*79 Main Street, Yung Shue Wan, Lamma (2982 4838). Yung Shue Wan Ferry Pier.* **Open** 10am-9pm daily. **Main courses** HK$30-$60. **No credit cards.**
There's no need to feel guilty if you eat here – it's cheap, healthy and spiritually satisfying. Everything is vegetarian and organic, and it's a rare place where you find simple meals like baked beans or poached egg on toast. The walls are lined with books and new age paraphernalia, but – relax – the staff don't preach.

#### Cococabana
*7 Mo Tat Wan, Lamma (2328 2138). Sok Ku Wan Ferry Pier, then 15-min walk to Mo Tat Wan/ferry or junk from Aberdeen to Mo Tat Wan.* **Open** noon-10pm Tue-Sun. **Main courses** HK$110-$180. **Credit** AmEx, DC, MC, V.
Transport yourself to a tropical paradise… well, almost. This beachside restaurant has a large terrace and is the perfect place to unwind come sundown, especially when the Cuban band plays on Saturdays. The Mediterranean food is excellent, if a little highly priced – try the scallops or fresh fish of the day. And watch out for the drinks charges, or you could end up swimming back to Hong Kong Island.

## Lantau

### Chinese: vegetarian

#### Chinese vegetarian
*Po Lin Monastery, Po Lin, Lantau (no phone). Mui Wo Ferry Pier, then bus towards the Big Buddha.* **Open** 9am-6pm daily. **Main courses** HK$60-$100. **No credit cards.**
As you might expect at a Buddhist place of worship (which has a neighbouring dairy farm run by monks), there are plenty of vegetable delights. For less than HK$100, you can gorge on beancurd, mock meat dishes and a wide range of vegetables, all very tastily cooked in everything from stir fries to soups. If you've been up the steps to the Big Buddha, you'll need the refuelling.

### Indian

#### Jo Jo Indian Restaurant
*Shop 101, 1F, Block A, Discovery Plaza, Discovery Bay, Lantau (2987 0122). Discovery Bay Ferry Pier.* **Open** noon-3pm, 6-11pm Mon-Fri; noon-11pm Sat, Sun. **Main courses** HK$60-$90. **Credit** AmEx, DC, MC, V.
Jo Jo offers hot food at cool prices. The tandoori chicken is a delight and the lamb is succulent whichever way you have it. Courteous staff attend your every need and supply plenty of Kingfisher beer to wash down the spicy dishes.

## Mediterranean

### Stoep

*32 Lower Cheung Sha Village, Lantau (2980 2699).
Mui Wo Ferry Pier, then any bus towards the Big
Buddha, alighting at Lower Cheung Sha Beach.*
**Open** 10am-10pm daily. **Main courses** HK$90-
$160. **Credit** AmEx, DC, MC, V.
Cheung Sha is one of the most beautiful stretches of
sand in Hong Kong – with a little imagination, you
could be in Thailand. Right on the sand stands this
al fresco restaurant. The location is perfect and the
food (Mediterranean-style tapas and salads) is good,
but the prices are a little high for what you get.

## South African

### The Gallery

*Tong Fuk Village, South Lantau Road, Lantau (2980
2582). Mui Wo Ferry Pier, then any bus towards the
Big Buddha, alight at Tong Fuk Village.* **Open** 6pm-
late Wed-Fri; noon-late Sat, Sun. **Main courses**
HK$80-$140. **No credit cards**.
The big draw here is the barbecue. Huge slabs of
South African meat (including delicious ostrich) are
cooked over burning coals in the open-air front of
the Gallery. Excellent wines are available and it's in
a great spot, just a steak's throw from the beach.

## Steakhouse

### A Hereford Beefstouw

*Level 8, Passenger Terminal Building, Hong Kong
International Airport, Hong Kong (2136 0695).
Airport Express terminus.* **Open** noon-11pm daily.
**Main courses** HK$180-$300. **Credit** AmEx, DC,
MC, V.
If you want a substantial meal before you fly, this
airport restaurant is worth dining in, and you won't
feel too much like you're in an airport departure
lounge. The imported prime cuts from Australia will
certainly make sure you pass up the airline food later
– fish and seafood also feature on the menu.

## Cheung Chau

## Chinese: Cantonese

### Cheung Kee

*83 Praya Street, Cheung Chau (2981 8078).
Cheung Chau Ferry Pier.* **Open** 11am-8pm daily.
**Main courses** HK$20-$40. **No credit cards**.
This 20-year-old noodle shop is famous, not just
among Cheung Chau locals, but others who take an
hour-long ferry ride just to eat the fish ball noodles
(made from a secret recipe). Other Cheung Kee trade-
marks are the deep-fried fish skin, which is crisp but
not oily, and *won ton* noodles, which – though small
– are wrapped up with just the right proportion of
meat and shrimp. Wash the latter down with a glass
of soya bean milk.

## Chinese: seafood

### Cheung Chau Eastern Court Seafood Restaurant

*1 Tung Wan Road, Cheung Chau (2981 1001).
Cheung Chau Ferry Pier, then walk towards Tung
Wan Beach.* **Open** 5.30am-11pm daily. **Main
courses** HK$50-$120. **Credit** AmEx, DC, MC, V.
Eastern Court is the most luxuriously decorated
Chinese restaurant on the island – it has three
storeys, decked out in pink, red and gold. The
restaurant opens early and closes late, serving
breakfast dim sum, Cantonese dishes and seafood.
Despite the luxurious image, the place is a bargain.

### Golden Lake Restaurant

*Pak She Fourth Lane, Cheung Chau (2981 3402).
Cheung Chau Ferry Pier, turn left on exit & walk
along the waterfront for 15 mins.* **Open** noon-
midnight daily. **Main courses** HK$40-$120.
**No credit cards**.
Located at the end of a row of waterfront seafood
restaurants, it's always enjoyable to watch the ferries and fishing boats come and go while eating al
fresco. The owners have just expanded the place and
set up their own seafood store, thus guaranteeing
diners the freshest fish possible. The restaurant also
serves up a good variety of less common Cantonese
dishes – the salty fish eggplant bowl is a must try.

## International

### Cheung Chau Windsurfing Centre & Outdoor Café

*1 Hak Pai Road, Cheung Chau (2981 8316).
Cheung Chau Ferry Pier.* **Open** noon-8pm daily.
**Main courses** HK$40-$80. **No credit cards**.
Hong Kong has one Olympic champion in its
history: windsurfer Lee Lai-shan, who scooped gold
in Atlanta in 1996. Operated as a family business,
this is where the star grew up and honed her skills
offshore. Located right on the beach, where it enjoys
fantastic views, the café has been around for more
than ten years and is packed with windsurfers every
weekend. The simple food (like omelettes) is delicious. From the ferry pier, cross over to the other
side of the island and turn right along Cheung Chau
Beach Road, which becomes Hak Pai Road.

### Morocco's

*71 Sun Hing Praya Street, Cheung Chau (2986
9767). Cheung Chau Ferry Pier.* **Open** 5pm-3am
Mon, Tue, Thur-Sat; noon-3am Sun. **Main courses**
HK$30-$50. **Credit** MC, V.
Ignore the name, this place is about as Moroccan as
a penguin. But it does serve food from everywhere
else and at prices you'd be pleased to get in a bazaar.
The maxim 'jack of all trades and master of none'
springs to mind when looking at the menu, which
covers all bases from Thai to Indian to burger and
chips. However, regulars know the staff excel at
Thai food, and the chicken hotpot induces cravings.

**Eat, Drink, Shop**

# Pubs & Bars

You can imbibe around the clock in Hong Kong's ever more trendy drinking holes – if your wallet can take the strain.

The cliché that Hong Kong was once nothing more than a barren rock certainly rings true when it comes to the metropolis's nightlife. Before the mid 1980s, drinkers couldn't really choose where to go; they went where was open. Thankfully, things have changed dramatically. Besides the long-established, after-dark zones of Central's Lan Kwai Fong and Wan Chai (on Hong Kong Island) and Tsim Tsui (at the southern tip of Kowloon), there are now world-class bars and restaurants opening up in the most unexpected of places virtually every week.

### DRINKING BY DISTRICT

**SoHo** (South of Hollywood Road, which – somewhat counter-intuitively – is uphill from said street) is by far the most exuberant new nightlife hotspot in the city. What began as a solitary restaurant by the side of the Mid-Levels Escalator, which carries workers to and from their homes, has turned into an area teeming with bars, cafés and chic eateries. Previously, the district was the preserve of Chinese ceramic shops, printers and dried-food retailers, but these are disappearing rapidly as the big bucks come in and either buy them out or force them out by pushing up rents. The current cheek by jowl existence of long-standing family businesses and western bar culture makes for a fascinating mix – if the new money wins out totally, it will be a shame.

One local legislator has come up with the hilarious idea of renaming SoHo 'the Mid-Levels Themed Dining Area'. Catchy, eh? His reason being that the name SoHo is indelibly linked with London's sleazy sex district. In a city where common sense rarely prevails, this may yet happen. A downside for night owls is that the area is part residential, so most bars have to shut at 11pm. Those that cannily located themselves outside the restricted zone can carry on until the last customer leaves (as late as 6am). Legal battles over licensing hours are expected to rage, but there's no turning back on SoHo's new identity now.

The area north of (and below) Hollywood Road, which has only been christened **NoHo** by a few, is developing in a similar vein, with bars, clubs and restaurants springing up between the vegetable and flower hawkers and butchers' shops, outside of which hang pig carcasses and

headless chickens. If you emerge bladdered from a bar as dawn breaks, you'll need a cast-iron stomach to keep the night's drink down.

Elsewhere in Central, the expat magnet of **Lan Kwai Fong** (off D'Aguilar Street) still rocks of an evening, but more with suits and tourists than Hong Kong hipsters.

Tourists often spend far too much time in the shoddy bars of **Tsim Sha Tsui**, where there's a proliferation of imitation British pubs (that are surprisingly popular with the local Chinese). While there are some good watering holes in the area, most of the best are to be found on Hong Kong Island.

In **Causeway Bay**, there are some good places around Yiu Wah Street (behind Times Square), which are popular with trendy locals; **Happy Valley** is beginning to sparkle; and parts of seedy old **Wan Chai** have steadily moved upmarket (*see p167* **Sex in the city**).

### ANATOMY OF A HONG KONG BAR

Because of their very newness, many of the bars reflect modern trends. For a good many years now, the decor of choice has been savvy New York wine bar, rather than good old London boozer. Clean lines, subtle and flexible lighting systems, and large windows letting in lots of natural light have all become the norm. Bars with steps or alleys outside (like those on Central's Pottinger Street) are invariably popular as people can sprawl onto the street. Most bars serve food and the terms 'restaurant' and 'bar' are often interchangeable, as owners seek to pay their high rents *and* reap a profit. And there, it must be said, is the rub.

### HAIL THE HAPPY HOUR

When people first arrive in Hong Kong and order a drink in a bar, the price often makes them splutter out the first sip. Drinking is expensive. But things are not as bad as they were. For several years, drink prices have remained relatively stagnant, while other international cities have seen steep rises. It's nowhere near as expensive as Tokyo, for example. Nevertheless, be warned: a serious drinking session will have you scurrying to the ATM more than once.

Thankfully, happy hours are common in Hong Kong – and most run for much more than an hour. Happy hour in Hong Kong usually means cut-price drinks, but can also mean two drinks for the price of one, so check the house policy with the bar staff before ordering. Another way of optimising value is to go for cocktails. They may cost around HK$20 more than the HK$40-$50 you pay for a spirit and mixer, but they are likely to include several shots. A local favourite is the innocuous sounding but very potent, Long Island Iced Tea (five white spirits – usually vodka, gin, rum, tequila and triple sec – topped up with coke and lemon and served in a pint glass). It tastes sweet and not particularly alcoholic, but start on these and you may not find your way home.

Hong Kong doesn't have a great reputation for beers. Both San Miguel and Carlsberg are brewed locally, but – whether on tap or in a bottle – taste chemically and can leave you nursing an almighty hangover. Tsing Tao (made at a German-modelled brewery in China) is the closest you'll come to a 'local' lager. It tastes good and is usually the cheapest beer on offer, especially in restaurants. Local micro-breweries do exist, but they are small and rare.

For example, the South China Brewing Company makes Stone Cutter's, which is available in more traditional pubs. Heineken, which is served in almost every bar, is imported from the Netherlands and is normally a safe choice. A host of other imported beers are available, but at a price.

Wine consumption soared in the late 1990s, to the extent that flash Chinese businessmen were blamed for pushing up the price of Burgundy and Bordeaux wines by buying expensive bottles in an effort to impress. In nightclubs over the Guangdong border, they even mixed pricey wines with lemonade or Coke (don't tell the French). The trend towards extravagance has subsided somewhat now, following the Asian financial crisis, but wines in bars and restaurants remain relatively expensive, and not many have a good selection by the glass. For the average punter, New World wines are a wise choice because they lack snob value and, therefore, the prices have not been ridiculously inflated.

# Sex in the city

The world of Suzie Wong – the Wan Chai prostitute immortalised in Richard Mason's novel of the same name (*see p82 & p216*) – may have changed radically over the past 40 or so years, but the district's reputation for fleshpots and sleaze still lingers. In recent years, though, Wan Chai's nightlife has been dragged by its bra straps towards a more upmarket image to ensure economic survival. And yet a simple stroll along any of the main roads suggests that the more things change, the more they stay the same.

'Hello, you like sexy girl?' is the kind of enquiry any single man or group of males is bound to hear from a 40–something Chinese woman standing under a flashing neon sign above an entrance to a girlie bar. Look behind the Mamasan, through the curtains, and you'll probably glimpse scantily clad young women (normally imported on short-term contracts from the Philippines, Thailand or mainland China) cajoling you inside. The names of these bars should tell you all need to know: Club Pussycat, Venus, Club Country…

Hong Kong's reputation for its sex industry surpasses itself. But, in reality, these bars are no more risqué than those in any major city. Inside, the women do not strip, but move around on a stage like caged lions. Dressed in underwear, they occasionally writhe against

a pole with much less enthusiasm than a performing seal, then wink at a punter in the hope he'll buy them a fancy drink at even fancier prices. The routine form here is easy to guess. As anywhere, these bars are not cheap. A standard bar drink and quick ogle may only set you back the usual HK$45, but that's not why the management want you here. Those who hang around for a longer lech get the hard sell and if you start buying a dancer drinks, you'll need more than a few hundred dollar notes in your wallet. Girlie bars are certainly not places to haggle over the bill.

These days, however, Wan Chai is not dominated by sailors and labourers on a flesh fest. Nestling among the seedy joints are some fine modern bars (*see p171*) and restaurants (*see p149*). The old-style pubs have gone too, replaced by chic theme bars. To see how things have changed, pop into the **Old China Hand** on Lockhart Road. Situated amid a row of girlie bars, it used to open 24 hours a day, serving food and drink to those dropping by before or after a long session. In 2000, the dingy pub closed, amid an outcry from those nostalgic for what it represented. The clamour had its desired effect and it reopened, but not around the clock and this time with a flashy open front and new furniture. It was a bitter irony for its devotees.

# Hong Kong Island

## Central

### Agave
*33 D'Aguilar Street, Central, HK Island
(2521 2010). Central MTR (exit D1, D2)/12M,
13, 23A, 40M, 43 bus.* **Open** noon-late Mon-Sat.
**Credit** AmEx, DC, MC, V. **Map** p66 C4.
With more than 100 tequilas imported from Mexico
and the US, Agave has the biggest choice in Asia
outside Japan. They're served in style (it doesn't
have to be just salt and lemon), while the jugs of
margaritas are the best in Hong Kong. Happy hour
runs from 5-8pm.

### Alibi
*73 Wyndham Street, Central, HK Island (2167
1676). Central MTR (exit D1, D2)/12M, 13, 23A,
26, 40M, 43 bus.* **Open** noon-3pm, 6pm-2am Mon-
Sat. **Credit** AmEx, DC, MC, V. **Map** p66 C4.
Popular with *tai tais* (the name given to Hong Kong
ladies who lunch) and those who consider themselves a cut above the rest, Alibi is pretentious but
bearable. One of the latest 'lounge bars', it has marble and glass fittings straight from New York, a few
comfy sofas and a DJ spinning chill-out and acid jazz
vibes. Upstairs, there's a restaurant serving lavish,
but not always excellent, food.

### Antidote
*15-19 Hollywood Road, Central, HK Island
(2526 6559). Central MTR (exit D2)/Mid-Levels
Escalator/12M, 13, 23A, 26, 40M, 43 bus.*
**Open** 6pm-2am daily. **Credit** AmEx, DC, MC, V.
**Map** p66 C3.
Resembling a cocoon (or a large padded cell, depending on your state of mind), Antidote's white, cush-
ioned walls, sumptuous low slung couches and
relaxed ambience are perfect for a cosy get together with friends. The young, trendy clientele is a good
mix of locals and expats.

### Après
*Shops A&B, 79 Wyndham Street, Central, HK Island
(2882 2246). Central MTR (exit D1, D2)/12M, 13,
23A, 26, 40M, 43 bus.* **Open** 7.30am-late daily.
**Credit** AmEx, DC, MC, V. **Map** p66 C4.
A portion of Après is a restaurant serving simple,
but good and reasonably priced, food all day and
evening. The rest of it is a bar, which pulls in such
large crowds that throngs gather on the cobbled
street outside on busy nights. A recent addition to
the rapidly growing Pottinger Street scene, it
attracts a trendy, mixed crowd.

### California Bar
*24-26 Lan Kwai Fong, Central, HK Island (2521
1345). Central MTR (exit D1, D2)/12M, 13, 23A,
26, 40M, 43 bus.* **Open** noon-1am Mon-Thur, Sun;
noon-4am Fri, Sat. **Credit** AmEx, DC, MC, V.
**Map** p66 C4.
This ground floor bar, restaurant and club
all-in-one has windows looking out on to the never-
less-than-busy street of Lan Kwai Fong. The well-
dressed and beautiful people come here to let their
hair down, and it's a popular haunt for singles.
Resident DJs get the place jumping after midnight
on Friday and Saturday nights.

### Club Feather Boa
*38 Staunton Street, Central, HK Island (2857 2586).
Mid-Levels Escalator/12M, 13, 23A, 26, 40M, 43
bus.* **Open** 6pm-late daily. **Credit** AmEx, DC, MC, V.
**Map** p66 B3.
The Feather Boa feels like a small room in a stately
house, which is not that surprising because it used
to be an antiques shop and the welcoming staff
make you feel right at home. Elegantly furnished
with drapes, candelabras and paintings, drinks are
served in giant, ornate glasses until the last customer goes home.

### Club 1911
*27 Staunton Street, Central, HK Island (2810 6681).
Mid-Levels Escalator/12M, 13, 23A, 26, 40M, 43
bus.* **Open** 5pm-midnight Mon-Sat; 5-11pm Sun.
**No credit cards. Map** p66 B3.
Chinese revolutionary leader Sun Yat-sen lived on
this street, many decades before it became a thriving nightlife hub. This bar's named after the year
in which he led the revolution, but the connection
ends there. In terms of atmosphere, Club 1911 is like
a scaled-down British boozer, and it's popular with
an older crowd.

### Club 64
*12-24 Wing Wah Lane, Central, HK Island
(2523 2801). Central MTR (exit D1, D2)/12M,
13, 23A, 40M, 43 bus.* **Open** 2.30pm-3am daily.
**No credit cards. Map** p66 C4.
This bar always closes on 4 June (hence the
name: 6th month, 4th day) in memory of the 1989
Tiananmen Square massacre. Not surprisingly then,
it's the favourite hangout of pro-democracy cam-
paigners, as well as a mixed crowd of gays, lesbians,
intellectuals and media types. Conversations tend to
be intense and cerebral in this down-to-earth two-
room pub, the walls of which are adorned with a
variety of works by local artists. And the drink
prices are reasonable, especially during happy hour
(5-9pm daily).

### Cyrano
*56/F, Island Shangri-La Hotel, Pacific Place Tower
Two, Central, HK Island (2877 3838). Admiralty
MTR (exit C1)/buses & trams through Central.*
**Open** 5pm-1am Mon-Thur, Sun; 5pm-2am Fri, Sat.
**Credit** AmEx, DC, MC, V. **Map** p67 F5.
The breathtaking view from this sky-high bar in the
Island Shangri-La Hotel is reason enough to visit.
Throw in the spacious, plush surroundings, irre-
sistible free snacks and live jazz, and this really is a
fine spot for a drink. There's a good choice of fine
wines and cigars, and while it may cost a little more
than most bars, it's easily worth it. *See also p237.*

Enjoy the good life at **La Dolce Vita**.

### Dublin Jack

*37 Cochrane Street, Central, HK Island (2543 0081). Central MTR (exit D1, D2)/Mid-Levels Escalator/ buses along Queen's Road Central.* **Open** noon-2am Mon-Thur, Sun; noon-3am Fri, Sat. **Credit** AmEx, V. **Map** p66 C3.

This Irish theme pub is popular with male expats, and is busy most evenings, particularly when football is showing on the big screen. It serves good pub grub too, even if the 'Dublin menu' improbably includes spring rolls alongside the more traditional pies and stews.

### Empire Bar

*11 Staunton Street, Central, HK Island (2522 2808). Mid-Levels Escalator/12M, 13, 23A, 26, 40M, 43 bus.* **Open** 3pm-1am daily. **Credit** AmEx, DC, MC, V. **Map** p66 B3.

The entrance to this gem is tucked away around the back of Staunton Street (close to New York Fitness). Its velvety decor attracts thirtysomethings, who squeeze into the snugs, but it can get a bit claustrophobic and stifling, especially for non-smokers. Happy hour runs from 4-9pm.

### The Globe

*39 Hollywood Road, Central, HK Island (2543 1941). Central MTR (exit D2)/Mid-Levels Escalator/12M, 13, 23A, 26, 40M, 43 bus.* **Open** 7.30am-1am Mon-Fri; 11am-1am Sat, Sun. **Credit** AmEx, DC, MC, V. **Map** p66 C3.

A proper local boozer, serving a good range of draught and bottled beers, and simple pub grub, with a respectable juke box. Prices are lower than most in the area and the furnishings are unpretentious, with old prints of Mercator's projection maps adding interest to the walls. Once popular with the pre-rave crowd, The Globe is now more of an after-work watering hole.

### LA Café

*G/F, Lippo Centre, Queensway, Central, HK Island (2526 6863). Admiralty MTR (exit B)/buses & trams through Central.* **Open** 11am-11.30pm Mon-Sat; 10am-10.30pm Sun. **Credit** AmEx, DC, MC, V. **Map** p67 F4.

This is a real American bar with booths, television screens visible from every seat (and the men's urinals) and a Harley Davidson behind the bar. When the US Navy ships are docked (which is not so often these days), you can't move for sailors; the rest of the time, you can normally get a seat. The menu offers a good selection of salads, fajitas and burgers.

### La Dolce Vita

*9 Lan Kwai Fong, Central, HK Island (2810 8098). Central MTR (exit D1, D2)/12M, 13, 23A, 40M, 43 bus.* **Open** 11am-late daily. **Credit** AmEx, DC, MC, V. **Map** p66 C4.

The place to see and be seen in Lan Kwai Fong, it's definitely worth a visit if you want to be gawped at by the passing masses or watch the night owls go by between bars and clubs. The bar takes up half the venue, but punters cram round its sides and teeter on the ledge outside. But drinking here is not cheap – the draft Stella Artois only comes in half-pint glasses, for the price of a full one elsewhere.

### Le Jardin

*10 Wing Wah Lane, Central, HK Island (2526 2717). Central MTR (exit D1, D2)/12M, 13, 23A, 40M, 43 bus.* **Open** noon-3am (or later) Mon-Sat. **Credit** AmEx, DC, MC, V. **Map** p66 C4.

Forever green in Lan Kwai Fong, this bar has a huge outdoor terrace, far removed from the bustling streets. Garden furniture and overhanging trees give the illusion of being out of Central. Every night is busy, but Fridays and Saturdays are heaving with a hip crowd when the weather's good. The juke box normally has the best selection in town.

Eat, Drink, Shop

**Le Jardin**'s less bucolic side.
*See p169.*

### Mes Amis

*35 Pottinger Street, Central, HK Island (2973 6167).*
*Central MTR (exit D1, D2)/buses along Queen's*
*Road Central.* **Open** noon-late daily. **Credit** AmEx,
DC, MC, V. **Map** p66 C3.

One of Central's classiest bars, Mes Amis is on what
is fast becoming the busiest street in town. Packed
seven nights a week, it is at its most crowded at
weekends as a pre-raveteria – many good clubs are
a stone's throw away. The only problem is you may
have to stand as there's limited seating. The bar of
choice for many long-term expat residents, lured by
its friendly, lively, yet sophisticated, atmosphere.
Good quality snack platters are available and there's
an extensive choice of wines by the glass. (Mes Amis
has a sister outlet on the corner of Luard Road and
Lockhart Road in Wan Chai.)

### Park Inn

*Hong Kong Park, Central, HK Island (2522 6333).*
*Admiralty MTR (exit B, C1)/buses & trams through*
*Central.* **Open** 11am-11pm Mon-Fri; 9.30am-11pm
Sat, Sun. **Credit** AmEx, MC, V. **Map** p67 E5.

Forget drinking or eating inside: the air-conditioning turns this place into a giant fridge, which is a
pity as the restaurant section overlooks a large pond
with swans gliding across it. But the large terrace is
the district's finest al fresco drinking spot. The beers
are very cheap, but the food is hit-and-miss.

### Petticoat Lane

*2 Tun Wo Lane, Central, HK Island (2973 0642).*
*Central MTR (exit D1, D2)/12M, 13, 23A, 26, 40M,*
*43 bus.* **Open** 11am-midnight Mon-Thur, Sun;
11am-2.30am Fri-Sat. **Credit** AmEx, DC, MC, V.
**Map** p66 C3.

This stylish hangout began as a thriving, mainly gay
bar and then became popular with all. However, ever
since police hassle forced the owners to take away
the high stools and tables in the lane out front, it has
been much less busy. Still, it is a comfortable place
to hang out. Food comes courtesy of the neighbouring El Pompose tapas restaurant.

### Post 97

*1/F, 9 Lan Kwai Fong, Central, HK Island (2810*
*9333). Central MTR (exit D1, D2)/12M, 13, 23A,*
*40M, 43 bus.* **Open** 8.30am-1am Mon-Fri;
8.30am-4am Sat, Sun. **Credit** AmEx, DC, MC, V.
**Map** p66 C4.

For years, this first-floor oasis of calm in Lan Kwai
Fong has been the late night hangout of the stars
and 'it' crowd. Great food, a good selection of wine
by the glass and surroundings you can flop in lan-
guorously make it the perfect chill-out after a night
of madness or for a recovery brunch. A DJ plays
jazzy sounds on Saturday nights until 3am.

### Staunton's

*10-12 Staunton Street, Central, HK Island (2973*
*6611). Mid-Levels Escalator/12M, 13, 23A, 26,*
*40M, 43 bus.* **Open** 9am-midnight daily.
**Credit** AmEx, DC, MC, V. **Map** p66 B3.

Day or night, Staunton's is always busy. Thanks to
its large windows and location right next to the
Mid-Levels Escalator, it's a perfect meeting point
and people-watching spot. Popular with twenty-
something and thirtysomething trendies, it is at its
busiest early in the evening when customers gather ready for a night on the town. Afternoons are
more relaxing: you can read the papers in comfort
and munch on good snacks, even if they are on the
pricey side.

### V-13 Vodka Bar

*13 Old Bailey Street, Central, HK Island (8208*
*1313). Central MTR (exit D1, D2)/Mid-Levels*
*Escalator/buses along Hollywood Road & Caine Road.*
**Open** 6pm-late Mon-Sat. **Credit** AmEx, DC, MC, V.
**Map** p66 C4.

If you like vodka as much as Boris Yeltsin, this is
the place to go. From choca-vodka shots to red hot
chilli ones, the choice at this hip bar is so bewildering that many just opt for plain vodka with Red Bull.
At weekends, it's standing room only and the crush
can get too much. Cheap vodka's served from 6-8pm
daily and costs HK$20 a shot all night on Tuesdays.

## Sheung Wan & Mid-Levels

### Bruce Lee Café
*22 Robinson Road, Mid-Levels, HK Island (2525 3977). Mid-Levels Escalator/3B, 12, 12M, 23, 23A, 40 bus.* **Open** noon-midnight (or later) daily. **Credit** AmEx, DC, MC, V. **Map** p66 B4.
Due to Government dithering, there is no museum to Bruce Lee (*see p219* **Bruce & Jackie**), so John Benn, a former actor in Kung Fu flicks who had on-screen fights with Lee, has created his own tribute in the shape of this bar. In reality, it's nothing more than a few film posters hanging on the wall and the atmosphere is sadly lacking, but the Asian food's worth stopping in for.

### Rice
*33 Jervois Street, Sheung Wan, HK Island (2851 4800). Sheung Wan MTR (exit A2)/buses along Queen's Road Central.* **Open** noon-3pm, 6pm-late daily. **Credit** AmEx, DC, MC, V. **Map** p66 B2.
Ostensibly a gay bar, Rice is popular with all. Located among a clutch of rice wholesalers in Sheung Wan, it has a rice cooker as its centrepiece and rice grains under the glass bar. It's well off the beaten track, but crowds of trendy young things flock here at weekends when a DJ is on hand to spin funky beats and uplifting house. Between 6pm and 9pm, it's an unbelievably cheap HK$10 for all standard drinks. *See also p224.*

## The Peak
For **Café Deco** (*see p148*) and **Peak Café** (*see p149*).

## Wan Chai & Causeway Bay

### Alfred's on the Corner
*14 Yuen Yuen Street, Happy Valley, HK Island (2575 3181). Bus 1, 19/trams to Happy Valley.* **Open** 5pm-2am daily. **Credit** AmEx, DC, MC, V. **Map** p80 D3.
This hidden gem in Happy Valley is well worth seeking out by wine connoisseurs. Tucked away up a side street off Sing Woo Road, Alfred's has a magnificent range of bottles and several tempting tipples by the glass, plus a reputation for serving great food. Hide away upstairs or grab a chair by the open front and relax.

### Brecht's Circle
*123 Leighton Road, Causeway Bay, HK Island (2577 9636). Causeway Bay MTR (exit F)/8X, 10, 26 bus.* **Open** noon-2.30pm, 6.30pm-midnight Mon-Thur; 4pm-4am Fri-Sat; 5pm-2am Sun. **Credit** AmEx, DC, MC, V. **Map** p80 D2.
Local artists have loved Brecht's Circle ever since the owners caused controversy by installing comic sculptures of Mao, Hitler and Mussolini. Westerners and locals mix happily and, although many new bars have opened nearby, this place retains its quirky charm.

### Carnegie's
*53-55 Lockhart Road, Wan Chai, HK Island (2866 6289). Wan Chai MTR (exit C)/buses along Hennessy Road.* **Open** 11am-very late daily. **Credit** AmEx, DC, MC, V. **Map** p80 A2.
This is an Irish bar without the usual Irish clichés. Attracting a wild crowd, it's busy, raucous and, to its many regulars, outrageous fun. Even at 5am, you're likely to find inebriated punters dancing on the bar, flashing flesh and having a party in the rugby club outing kind of way. It also has live music and serves food.

### Delaney's
*2/F, One Capital Place, 18 Luard Road (junction with Lockhart Road), Wan Chai, HK Island (2804 2880). Wan Chai MTR (A1, C)/buses along Gloucester Road & Hennessy Road.* **Open** 8.30am-3am daily. **Credit** AmEx, DC, MC, V. **Map** p80 B2.
Delaney's is Hong Kong's best Irish pub. Although drink prices are a bit steep, especially the draught Guinness and beers, it's large, has comfortable snugs, a big screen showing British football and a folk band on Sundays. The pub grub is good value, while the daily lunch carvery is the best in town and will have you loosening your belt, but not your wallet.
**Branch**: Basement, Mary Building, 71-77 Peking Road, Tsim Sha Tsui, Kowloon (2301 3980).

### Joe Banana's
*23 Luard Road, Wan Chai, HK Island (2529 1811). Wan Chai MTR (exit A1, C)/buses along Gloucester Road & Hennessy Road.* **Open** 11am-10pm Mon-Thur; 11am-6am Fri-Sun. **Credit** AmEx, DC, MC, V. **Map** p80 B2.

**Brecht's Circle**. No sign of Hitler.

Eat, Drink, Shop

Tango Martini.

JB's (as it's affectionately known) specialises in the sort of fun night out you associate with 18-30 holidays in the Med. The music varies from golden oldies to current pop dance hits, while suits and made-up women gyrate suggestively (or rather blatantly) on the dancefloor. As you've probably already guessed, it's popular with business gents, lonely hearts and philanderers. Door heavies refuse entry to anyone without a collar, then try and flog you a JB's rugby shirt for HK$100 to get in. Classy. But if you want a raucous time, it's to be found here.

### Tango Martini

*3/F, Empire Land Commercial Centre, 81-85 Lockhart Road, Wan Chai, HK Island (2528 0855). Wan Chai MTR (exit A1, C)/buses along Hennessy Road.* **Open** noon-3pm, 6pm-1am daily. **Credit** AmEx, DC, MC, V. **Map** p80 B2.
A martini paradise. James Bond and Pussy Galore would be happy canoodling on the Zebra-striped couches in the corner of this bar/restaurant. It's high on the price scale for Wan Chai, but the vodka and gin measures are generous, and the fruit Martinis slip down far too easily. There's no tango night, but jazz features every Sunday evening.

### Time After Time

*118 Jaffe Road, Wan Chai, HK Island (2865 0609). Wan Chai MTR (exit A1, C)/buses along Gloucester Road.* **Open** 11am-1am Mon-Thur; 11am-3am Fri, Sat. **Credit** AmEx, DC, MC, V. **Map** p80 B2.
Although not as popular as it once was, Time After Time remains Wan Chai's best bar for those in the know. Its tiny, narrow interior can accommodate more customers than you'd imagine, the music is always hip and there are games like backgammon to play on quiet nights.

### Tott's Asian Grill and Bar

*34/F, Excelsior Hotel, 281 Gloucester Road, Causeway Bay, HK Island (2837 6780). Causeway Bay MTR (exit D1)/buses along Gloucester Road.* **Open** noon-12.30am Mon-Sat; noon-10.30pm Sun. **Credit** AmEx, DC, MC, V. **Map** p80 D1.

Tott's takes kitsch to new heights, 34 floors high to be precise. Its name is an acronym of Talk Of The Town, which may be overstating it. But whether you want to sit on a bar stool, dance the night away or sink seductively into a sofa, this multi-faceted, bright venue has it all, not to mention the harbour view. A creative fusion menu makes it a good spot for lunch and dinner, too.

## South & east coast

### Beaches

*92B Stanley Main Street, Stanley, HK Island (2813 7313). Bus 6, 260.* **Open** 11am-midnight Mon-Fri, Sun; 11am-1am Sat. **Credit** AmEx, MC, V. **Map** p66.
One of the more relaxed places on Stanley waterfront, Beaches is packed every weekend with an odd assortment of expat families, young Chinese couples and Hell's Angels (OK, so they're off-duty accountants with a fetish for Harleys and leather). Simple pastas and pub grub are served.

### Black Sheep

*452 Shek O village, HK Island (2809 2021). Shau Kei Wan MTR, then 9 bus.* **Open** 5pm-midnight Tue-Sat. **No credit cards. Map** p66.
The only real bar in Shek O is a welcome find at the end of a hike or day's surfing. Combining style and friendliness, it serves a local microbrew beer, along with a good selection of bottled beers and (especially) Spanish) wines. Mediterranean food, such as tapas, is served, but the staff are happy for people to simply pull up a chair and drink.

### Smugglers Inn

*90A Stanley Main Street, Stanley, HK Island (2813 8852). Bus 6, 260.* **Open** 10am-very late daily. **No credit cards. Map** p66.
Stanley was once a common port of call for smugglers, but the Smugglers' biggest customers used to be British soldiers from the garrison stationed at the nearby fort. Post-1997, there are still large groups of men on drinking sprees, but the clientele is much more diversified and the Inn is the better for it.

# Kowloon

## Tsim Sha Tsui

If you crave US corporate familiarity, you can head for the **Hard Rock Café** (30 Canton Road; 2375 1323) or **Planet Hollywood** (Harbour City, 3 Canton Road; 2377 7888).

### Amoeba
*Basement, 22 Ashley Road, Tsim Sha Tsui, Kowloon (2376 0389). Tsim Sha Tsui MTR (exit A1)/buses along Nathan Road/Tsim Sha Tsui Star Ferry Pier.* **Open** 4pm-3am daily. **Credit** MC, V. **Map** p98 B2.
Rock fans have long adored Amoeba, despite it being a dingy dungeon. Live bands sometimes play on the minuscule stage; the rest of the time, there's local and Western music pumped out for devotees. Beer and spirits are very cheap, and the clientele is largely local.

### Bahama Mama's
*4-5 Knutsford Terrace, Tsim Sha Tsui, Kowloon (2368 2121). Tsim Sha Tsui MTR (exit B2)/buses along Nathan Road & Chatham Road South.* **Open** 5pm-3am Mon-Thur; 5pm-4am Fri, Sat; 5.45pm-2am Sun. **Credit** AmEx, DC, MC, V. **Map** p98 C1.
This tropical theme bar helped start the flourishing entertainment scene that now exists on Knutsford Terrace. A bizarre mix of faux foliage, table football and dance music was a winning combination when it opened, but its popularity has waned a little recently.

### Chemical Suzy
*2 Austin Avenue, Tsim Sha Tsui, Kowloon (2736 0087). Tsim Sha Tsui MTR (exit B2)/buses along Chatham Road South.* **Open** 6pm-4am Mon-Sat; 9.30pm-4am Sun. **No credit cards. Map** p98 D1.
Britpop lives, at least in this part of town. The clientele at Chemical Suzy is almost 100% local or Japanese, but the walls are adorned with Union Jacks, Oasis posters and the like. It's small and basic, but plays good music to a young crowd. There are also a couple of Play Stations to keep punters amused.

### Kangaroo Pub
*1/F-2/F, 35 Haiphong Road, Tsim Sha Tsui, Kowloon (2376 0083). Tsim Sha Tsui MTR (exit A1)/buses along Nathan Road & Kowloon Park Drive/Tsim Sha Tsui Star Ferry Pier.* **Open** 11am-midnight (or later) daily. **Credit** AmEx, DC, MC, V. **Map** p98 B2.
A big, no-frills Australian theme pub where you get what you expect: decent food, a range of Aussie beers on draft or in bottles, and sports fans – although it's surprisingly popular with the local Chinese, too.

### Opium Bar
*Basement, Imperial Hotel, 32 Nathan Road, Tsim Sha Tsui, Kowloon (2782 3383). Tsim Sha Tsui MTR (exit C1, E)/buses along Nathan Road/Tsim Sha Tsui Star Ferry Pier.* **Open** noon-3am Mon-Thur, Sun; noon-very late Fri, Sat. **Credit** AmEx, DC, MC, V. **Map** p98 C2.

A happening new bar that has replaced the long-standing, but tattered, Mad Dogs and injected some life back into the Tsim Sha Tsui bar scene. Catering to a youthful crowd, Opium serves Eastern and Western food, and a good range of drinks. It's comfortable but, contrary to its name, not that laid-back.

### Rick's Cafe
*53-55 Kimberley Road, Tsim Sha Tsui, Kowloon (2311 2255). Tsim Sha Tsui MTR (exit B1, B2)/buses along Nathan Road.* **Open** Mon-Thur; 5pm-5am Fri, Sat; 6pm-3am Sun. **Credit** AmEx, DC, MC, V. **Map** p98 C1.
A fun place to go if you want to get down and boogie in an unpretentious environment, Rick's is a popular place for cross-cultural fraternisation between Westerners and locals (usually Western men and local women). There's a long happy hour (5-10pm).

### Schnurrbart
*9-11 Prat Avenue, Tsim Sha Tsui, Kowloon (2366 2986). Tsim Sha Tsui MTR (exit A2, D2)/buses along Chatham Road South.* **Open** noon-1am (or later) daily. **Credit** AmEx, DC, MC, V. **Map** p98 C2.
The Germans certainly know how to brew and pour beer. If you don't mind waiting up to ten minutes for a pint to drizzle into a long thin glass, you'll get some of the finest beer on tap in Hong Kong. The schnapps are varied enough to make you sick for a week if you try them all, and the food is of the traditional sausage and spuds variety.

# The New Territories

## East New Territories

### Beach Pub
*Beach Resort Hotel, 1780 Tai Mong Tsai Road, Sai Kung, New Territories (2791 1068). Choi Hung MTR, then minibus 12.* **Open** 6pm-2am daily. **No credit cards. Map** p310-311.
A relaxing, no-frills place for a beer come sundown, and it gets livelier thereafter. Besides the ocean view, there's an affable crowd, the drink is cheap and a band plays every Saturday night.

**Chemical Suzy**: doing it for the kids.

### Cheers Sports Bar & Restaurant
*28 Yi Chun Street, Sai Kung, New Territories*
*(2791 6789). Choi Hung MTR, then minibus 12.*
**Open** 11am-3am daily. **Credit** AmEx, DC, MC, V.
**Map** p311.
Sai Kung town centre has become a lively area after
dark, especially at weekends when many bars stay
open until not far short of dawn. A large expat population, eschewing the polluted urban areas for this
rural enclave, means bars here are busy most nights,
and there's a good mix with locals. This is typical of
the more sophisticated type of bar cropping up in
the area – light, airy, with clean lines in its design
and a decent restaurant upstairs.

### Steamers
*A2-3 Kam Wah Building, 18-32 Chan Man Street,*
*Sai Kung, New Territories (2792 6991). Choi Hung*
*MTR, then minibus 12.* **Open** 9am-2am daily.
**Credit** AmEx, MC, V. **Map** p311.
One of the newest bars in the neighbourhood,
Steamers is bright, cheery and packs them in at all
times of day. An ideal place after a browse around
town or walk through the surrounding country park.

# The Outlying Islands

## Lamma

### Diesel Sports Bar
*51 Main Street, Yung Shue Wan, Lamma (2982*
*4116). Yung Shue Wan Ferry Pier.* **Open** 6pm-
midnight Mon-Thur, Sun; 6pm-3am Fri, Sat.
**No credit cards. Map** p126.
An expat hangout, Diesel's gets packed on Saturday
nights when football is on the big screen. As the
indoors is tiny, it's hard to get a good view, but most
ignore the game and spill outside, drinking happily
and heavily. Daytimes are quieter.

### Fountain Head
*18 Main Street, Yung Shue Wan, Lamma*
*(2982 2118). Yung Shue Wan Ferry Pier.*
**Open** 5pm-1am (or later) daily. **No credit cards.**
**Map** p126.
The 'tinhead' as it's known by regulars is an old-
fashioned British boozer. Many people stop here for
a lunchtime pint at the tables out front and don't go
home 'til late. Like all Lamma pubs, it can seem
intimidating, but join in the fun and everyone's
your mate.

### Island Bar
*6 Main Street, Yung Shue Wan, Lamma (2982 1376).*
*Yung Shue Wan Ferry Pier.* **Open** 6pm-1am Mon-Fri;
noon-late Sat, Sun. **No credit cards. Map** p126.
Lamma has changed since its halcyon pre-1997 days
as a traveller and hippy haven. Young professionals are moving in, and spots like the Island Bar have
benefited. It gets pretty hectic in the evenings, as
workers walking home from the ferry pier drop in
for a quiet beer (or seven).

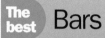

## The best Bars

### To see and be seen
**La Dolce Vita** (*see p169*) – watch the world
teeter by.

### For dancing half-naked and half-cut on the bar
**Carnegie's** (*see p171*) – where cheap
spirits lead to high spirits.

### For living-room comfort
**Club Feather Boa** (*see p168*) – a bordello
boudoir hidden behind the curtains.

### For cool surroundings, wine by the glass and funky tapas
**Boca** (*see p145*) – an extensive choice
from the old world and new.

### For rebels with a cause
**Club 64** (*see p168*) – an arty pub where
renegades hang to talk in earnest.

### For finding out where the good parties are
**Mes Amis** (*see p170*) – a favourite meeting
point for the hip crowd.

## Lantau

### China Bear
*Mui Wo Centre, Mui Wo, Lantau (2984 9720). Mui*
*Wo Ferry Pier.* **Open** noon-midnight Mon-Fri; 11am-
midnight Sat, Sun. **No credit cards. Map** p126.
A stone's throw from the ferry pier and bus terminus, this is an ideal watering hole for those who have
spent a long day exploring the island – or those too
lazy to walk more than 30 metres from the ferry pier.
Its window overlooks the sea and there's a good
range of beers, including local microbrews.

### Hippo Bar
*11 Mui Wo Ferry Pier Road, Mui Wo, Lantau (2984*
*9876). Mui Wo Ferry Pier.* **Open** 4pm-midnight
Mon-Fri; 11am-midnight Sat, Sun. **No credit cards.**
**Map** p126.
The Hippo is small, but it's always busy at weekends, when daytrippers and tourists flock over to
the Big Buddha or the island's beaches. When expat
builders working on the airport lived on Lantau in
their hundreds, Lantau bars had a reputation for
brawling drunks. Things have improved since and
the Hippo is worth stopping in for a cool beer – it
has some rare brews – but keep your wits about you.

## Cheung Chau
For **Morocco's**, *see p165*.

# Shops & Services

Don't believe the hype – but there's still plenty to delight shopaholics.

You want music? **HMV** will oblige. *See p199.*

If Hong Kong is famous for anything, it is as a shopping nirvana. As one of the busiest ports in Asia, the territory has a phenomenal range of goods, of all types and quality, both legal and otherwise. Displayed in a bewildering number of outlets, from glittering mega-malls to shifty street-corner stalls, there's enough here to tempt even the most reluctant of shoppers to dig deep into their pockets.

Yet Hong Kong today is both consumer haven and tourist trap. Unlike during the booming 1980s, when bargains were ubiquitous and prices ridiculously low, shoppers now have to wade through oceans of unexciting, standard (and rarely *that* cheap) stock to find the real deals. However, if you're after a steal, don't despair: they can still be found on the back streets of the city, as well as in the main consumer districts.

There are four main shopping areas in Hong Kong: **Tsim Sha Tsui**, at the southern tip of Kowloon, and **Central**, **Admiralty** and **Causeway Bay** on the north side of Hong Kong island. Oddly, all four are home to remarkably similar shops, yet each targets a different type of consumer.

**Tsim Sha Tsui** is trawled by tourists, to whom copy-watch selling touts cling like limpets. Follow one of these guys to a dingy back room and you'll be offered everything from a standard, sturdy Tag Heuer to a flash, fashionable Gucci. Not bad imitations, they may not be such a bad investment either, as their inner workings are often from hardy brands like Seiko and are quite likely to outlast many well-known high street brands (although they are, of course, entirely illegal).

For clothing bargains in Tsim Sha Tsui, **Granville Road**, running between Nathan Road and Chatham Road South, is a must. The shops that line this street stock everything from separates costing as little as HK$40 to designer labels – if you're lucky, tucked away at the back of a cramped maze of rails, you may even come across a little something from DKNY. Although some assume that these branded goods are imitations, most are the real thing that have found their way through the back door from a factory in Shenzhen (*see p201* **Break for the border: Shenzhen**). In general, they're either well-made seconds or excess production from last season's collection.

Across the harbour, shopping in **Central** is a little more upmarket. Customers will be seduced by classy arcades, malls, department stores and heavy duty labels, but there is also a scattering of shops that sell inexpensive clothing. And there are also 'The Lanes', which are as old as Hong Kong itself. The three narrow alleyways of Douglas Lane, Li Yuen Street East and Li Yuen Street West run parallel to each other between Des Voeux and Queen's roads – two of the three main traffic arteries that define Central. The Lanes sell pretty much everything and anything; small stalls line the alleyways selling watches, children's toys, lighters, shoes, clothes and souvenirs. They're a good place to try out your bargaining skills (*see p177* **The art of bargaining**) – even if there's a marked price, you can usually reduce it by a good few dollars.

**Hollywood Road**, which begins in Central above Lan Kwai Fong and runs west all the way to Sheung Wan, houses most of Hong Kong's reputable antiques shops. Among them, you'll be able to find everything from ancient opium beds to Ming dynasty vases, from a battered, bejewelled hair clip from the Ching dynasty to a priceless selection of arts from any given era. But there are also plenty of cheaper items and lashings of the beautiful, simple, dark wood furniture that is proving increasingly popular in the West.

In **Admiralty**, lying between Central and Wan Chai, shopping tends to be mall- and arcade-dominated. The stores here cater to every shopper's need, as they range from high street brand to designer. In general, **Queensway Plaza**, located directly above the MTR station, is the destination for shoppers looking for mid-priced goodies, while **Pacific Place** (*see p182*) – the other side of Queensway – houses lots of glossy shops and flashy department stores like Lane Crawford and Seibu. Three of the city's larger hotels, JW Marriott, the Conrad and Island Shangri-La, are all part of the Pacific Place complex, which means that tourists have easy access to some hardcore purchasing.

Unquestionably, **Causeway Bay** is one of the busiest areas in Hong Kong: it's a mob scene and shopper's dream. Extremely popular with the local Chinese who know it inside out, there are lots of smaller shops on secluded side streets that are definitely worth investigating. A good starting point, however, is the mega-store **Sogo** (*see p183*), which hogs a prime space above a main MTR exit. Once that's been explored, step outside and follow your nose on a tour of the area's alleys and arcades. If you don't fancy trekking around and would rather stick to a sure thing, **Times Square** (*see p185*), above another Causeway Bay MTR exit, is a worthwhile destination. Set over nine floors,

the place is enormous and houses a number of large department stores, plus the music stores HMV and Tower Records. Causeway Bay is also a good place to go if you're looking for original computer hardware and software.

## HOW TO AVOID BEING RIPPED OFF

If someone tries to sell you 'genuine' designer items from a push cart, then it doesn't take a genius to work out that you're being flogged a fake. Its quality might be reasonable, but, more likely, it will be poorly made and fall apart within a week. More difficult to spot are the (often Tsim Sha Tsui electronics) shops that sell you second-hand or faulty goods. The HKTB has become so worried about tourists being ripped off that it has introduced the Quality Tourism Services (QTS) scheme as a means of identifying those shops and restaurants that have proven to offer excellent service. Look for the QTS decal.

# Antiques

## Ad Lib
*59 Wyndham Street, Central, HK Island (2530 2320). Central MTR (exit D1, D2, G)/13, 26, 43 bus.* **Open** 10am-6pm Mon-Sat. **Credit** AmEx, MC, V. **Map** p66 C4.
This well set out shop has enough room to move and work your way around the wealth of merchandise. However, it isn't exactly what you'd call cheap, although it does have stock that you'd be hard pushed to find elsewhere in Hong Kong.

## Altfield Gallery
*248-249 Prince's Building, 10 Chater Road, Central, HK Island (2537 6370). Central MTR (exit H)/buses & trams through Central.* **Open** 10am-7pm Mon-Sat; 11am-5pm Sun. **Credit** AmEx, MC, V. **Map** p67 E4.
Altfield has three different outlets – Altfield Gallery, **Altfield Interiors** and **Altfield Home** (for both, *see p198*). While Altfield Gallery deals in antique Chinese furniture, it also has a penchant for ancient prints (which have their own room) and fantastic Asian maps. These date back as far as the 1500s, and come at a price.

## Arch Angel Antiques
*53-55 Hollywood Road, Central, HK Island (2851 6828). Central MTR (exit D1, D2, G)/Mid-Levels Escalator/12M, 13, 23A, 26, 40M, 43 bus.* **Open** 9.30am-6.30pm daily. **Credit** AmEx, DC, MC, V. **Map** p66 C3.
Arch Angel Antiques is an established fixture on Hollywood Road, and stocks a good range of quality Chinese antiques. It also does repairs and restorations.

## Gallery One
*G/F, 31-33 Hollywood Road, Central, HK Island (2545 6436). Central MTR (exit D1, D2, G)/Mid-Levels Escalator/12M, 13, 23A, 26, 40M, 43 bus.* **Open** 10am-6pm Mon-Sat. **Credit** AmEx, DC, MC, V. **Map** p66 C3.

Buddha-u-like at **Gallery One**. *See p176.*

If you're looking for antique jewellery, Gallery One is the shop for you. It sells a wonderful selection of necklaces, bracelets and rings, as well as Buddhist walnut carvings – you'll just have to shift through the mess to find your perfect purchase.

### Gorgeous Arts & Crafts

*Shop A, UG/F, 30 Hollywood Road, Central, HK Island (2973 0034). Central MTR (exit D1, D2, G)/Mid-Levels Escalator/12M, 13, 23A, 26, 40M, 43 bus.* **Open** 10.30am-7pm Mon-Sat; 1-7pm Sun. **Credit** AmEx, MC, V. **Map** p66 C3.

Located close to the Mid-Levels Escalator, Gorgeous Arts & Crafts can be difficult to find – although you can see its window, stacked high with stock, above Gallery One (*see p176*) on Hollywood Road. This place has a wonderful selection of Chinese antiques, selling at some of the most reasonable prices in Hong Kong. The shop assistants are usually remarkably helpful and pleasant.

### Honeychurch Antiques

*29 Hollywood Road, Central, HK Island (2543 2433). Central MTR (exit D1, D2, G)/Mid-Levels Escalator/12M, 13, 23A, 26, 40M, 43 bus.* **Open** 10am-6pm Mon-Sat. **Credit** AmEx, DC, MC, V. **Map** p66 C3.

Conspicuously located opposite Central Police Station, Honeychurch prides itself on reliability, honesty and simple courteous salesmanship. Perhaps that's why the enterprise has survived for over 30 years. Certainly, if you're not sure of what you're buying, you can trust the staff to explain the ins and outs of whatever's caught your eye. For the serious patron, it also handles English and Chinese silverware, a superb range of jewellery and a heady collection of Asian antiques.

### Martin Fung Antiques & Furniture Company

*Shop 321, Pacific Place, 88 Queensway, Admiralty, HK Island (2524 3306). Admiralty MTR (exit C1)/buses through Central.* **Open** 10am-6pm daily. **Credit** AmEx, DC, MC, V. **Map** p67 F5.

Hidden away on the top level of Pacific Place, you'll discover several arts, antique and craft stores, including this one. As this shop has no specific bent, there's a good mix of merchandise here: paintings, sculptures, furniture and porcelain are all on offer, at very reasonable prices.

### Wonder Dragon

*30 Hollywood Road, Central, HK Island (2526 8863). Central MTR (exit D1, D2, G)/Mid-Levels Escalator/12M, 13, 23A, 26, 40M, 43 bus.* **Open** 10.30am-6.30pm Mon-Sat; 1.30-6pm Sun. **Credit** AmEx, DC, MC, V. **Map** p66 C3.

# The art of bargaining

While it rarely comes easily to Western visitors, bargaining is an essential and expected part of the shopping experience in Hong Kong (as in mainland China). Haggling won't, admittedly, cut much ice in department stores or at Versace, but it's a must at markets, and is certainly worthwhile at antiques shops.

Think of it as a game of wits. And always keep a smile on your face – anger and aggression will be met by indifference. The outraged ('how much?!') smile is always a good one to kick off with, followed, perhaps, by the incredulous ('you must be joking!') smile, the more conciliatory ('that's a bit more like it, but…') smile, and finally the satisfied ('it's a deal') smile. Don't feel under any pressure – chances are that there's another stall selling exactly the same merchandise around the corner, and don't

forget that it is you, the buyer, who holds the trump card – you can always walk away.

There are no immutable rules about what to offer for goods. To a large degree you have to judge what the item is worth to you. If a stallholder asks, say, HK$100 for a shirt, then she'll not take you seriously if you offer HK$10 for it, but HK$40-50 might be a reasonable initial counterbid. You can also always use the 'I'll give you HK$100 for two' ploy. Don't fall for the 'You're-taking-food-out-of-my-children's-mouths' line – if she's not making a decent profit, she simply won't sell.

And don't underestimate the satisfaction of some good natured sparring and the eventual striking of that mutually acceptable bargain – it'll give you a genuine insight into, and interaction with, traditional Chinese life. Not something that most visitors to Hong Kong experience.

Eat, Drink, Shop

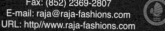
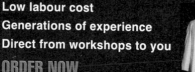

**Honeychurch Antiques.** See p177.

Wonder Dragon was established in the 1970s and is still going strong today. The interior of the store is awkward and cramped, but not only does it sell a fantastic variety of Chinese antiques, but also old stand-up phones, gramophones and typewriters. Sadly, service can be curt and somewhat haughty.

### Zee Stone Gallery
*G/F, Yu Yet Lai Building, 43-55 Wyndham Street, Central, HK Island (2810 5895/www.zeestone.com). Central MTR (exit D1, G)/13, 26, 43 bus.* **Open** 10am-7pm Mon-Sat; 1-6pm Sun. **Credit** AmEx, DC, MC, V. **Map** p66 C4.
Zee Stone Gallery deals in a sophisticated selection of Chinese works of art, as well as antique furniture and Tibetan rugs. The staff are helpful and friendly, while the shop floor is easily accessible. If you want to get a taste of its wares before dropping in, check out the website.

## Art supplies & stationery

### Angel De Capri
*18 Wo On Lane, Lan Kwai Fong, Central, HK Island (2857 7148). Central MTR (exit D1, G)/12M, 13, 23A, 40M, 43 bus.* **Open** noon-9pm Tue-Sun. **No credit cards**. **Map** p66 C4.
There are some things that can be difficult to find in Hong Kong, like straightforward, practical, clean-cut greeting cards. Look no further than Angel De Capri, which also stocks books, magazines and a small selection of CDs. *See also p226.*

### The Artland Company
*3/F, Lockhart Centre, 301-307 Lockhart Road, Wan Chai, HK Island (2511 4845). Buses & trams along Hennessy Road.* **Open** 9am-7pm Mon-Fri; 9am-5pm Sat. **Credit** MC, V. **Map** p80 C2.
In the corridors of Wan Chai's Lockhart Centre, the Artland Company sells an adequate assortment of art supplies. These include the usual stationery necessities like felt-tip pens, paints, crayons, paper and inks, all at fair prices.

### Fit Copy Equipment Co/ Da Fat Stationery
*52 Lyndhurst Terrace, Central, HK Island (2544 1917). Central MTR (exit D1, D2, G)/Mid-Levels Escalator/12M, 13, 23A, 40M, 43 bus.* **Open** 9am-7pm Mon-Sat. **No credit cards**. **Map** p66 C3.
Don't be fooled by the name, there are no copy goods for sale at this store. Instead, this tiny shop sells the simplest of stationery products – pens, Filofaxes, paper and envelopes – and deals with all your photocopying needs. Certainly it's a no-frills kind of place, which means the service is efficient and fast, just the way Hong Kong folk like it.

### PaperArt
*46 Lyndhurst Terrace, Central, HK Island (2545 8985). Central MTR (exit D1, D2, G)/Mid-Levels Escalator/12M, 13, 23A, 40M, 43 bus.* **Open** 10.30am-7.30pm Mon-Sat. **Credit** AmEx, MC, V. **Map** p66 C3.
More of a gift shop than a stationer's, PaperArt stocks rubber stamps imported from the US, handmade paper and an artsy collection of greeting cards, all at ridiculously high prices.

## Auctions

### Christie's
*Room 2203-5, Alexandra House, 16-20 Chater Road, Central, HK Island (2521 5396). Central MTR (exit J1, J2, J3)/buses & trams through Central/ Central Star Ferry Pier.* **Open** 9.30am-6pm Mon-Fri. **Credit** MC, V. **Map** p67 E4.
A branch office of the famed Christie's of London and New York, it deals in pretty much everything toting a heavy price tag. In fact, a phenomenal amount of cash passes through Christie's every year. It's an absolute must for any serious collector or dealer. *See also p204.*

**Eat, Drink, Shop**

### Sotheby's

*5/F, Standard Chartered Bank Building, 4-4A Des Voeux Road, Central, HK Island (2524 8121). Central MTR (exit J1, J2, J3)/buses & trams through Central/Central Star Ferry Pier.* **Open** *9.30am-6pm Mon-Fri.* **Credit** *MC, V.* **Map** *p67 D4.*

Sotheby's held Hong Kong's first auction of high quality Chinese art in 1973. Since then, it has sold some of the finest collections of Chinese art in the world. Its biannual sales have focused on items such as Chinese ceramics, works of art and jade carvings, modern and contemporary Chinese paintings, and postage stamps of the Far East. *See also p204.*

## Books & magazines

### Bookazine

*Shop 327-329 Prince's Building, 10 Chater Road, Central, HK Island (2522 1785). Central MTR (exit J1, J2, J3)/buses & trams through Central/Central Star Ferry Pier.* **Open** *9am-7pm Mon-Sat; 10am-6pm Sun.* **Credit** *AmEx, MC, V.* **Map** *p67 E4.*

The Bookazine stores (there are branches all over Hong Kong) stock a good selection of fiction, non-fiction and imported magazines. Unfortunately for bookworms, import taxing means that prices on overseas publications are unreasonably high, so you'd better off picking up your paperbacks before you leave home.

### Commercial Press (HK) Limited

*9-15 Yee Wo Street, Causeway Bay, HK Island (2890 8028). Causeway Bay MTR (exit E)/buses along Hennessy Road.* **Open** *11am-9pm daily.* **Credit** *AmEx, MC, V.* **Map** *p80 D2.*

Commercial Press is a large bookshop that stocks both Chinese and English literature, particularly paperbacks. It also sells collectors' stamps. **Branch**: 608 Nathan Road, Mong Kok, Kowloon (2384 8228).

### Dymocks

*Unit EP1, Central Star Ferry Concourse, Central, HK Island (2522 1012). Central MTR (exit A)/buses along Connaught Road Central/Central Star Ferry Pier.* **Open** *8am-10.30pm Mon-Sat; 9am-10pm Sun.* **Credit** *AmEx, DC, MC, V.* **Map** *p67 E3.*

There are various Dymocks outlets all over Hong Kong, of which the Star Ferry branch is probably the most accessible. The shop is small, cramped and often crowded, but it is so easy to drop into, it's worth checking out. Much like its rival, Bookazine, Dymocks stocks a good choice of US and UK magazines, fiction and non-fiction, the latter including a large assortment of coffee table books.

### Government Publications Centre

*G/F, Low Block, Queensway Government Offices, 66 Queensway, HK Island (2537 7195). Admiralty MTR (exit C1)/buses through Central.* **Open** *9am-6pm Mon-Fri; 9am-1pm Sat.* **No credit cards.** **Map** *p67 F5.*

Located beside the main entrance of Pacific Place, the Government Publications Office has the feel of a schoolroom-cum-dole office. It stocks everything

you need to know about the inner and outer workings of the region, like the annual budget or exam reference books for schools. It also sells maps of Hong Kong, which are particularly good for those interested in hiking or sailing.

### Hong Kong Book Centre

*LG/F, 25 Des Voeux Road, Central, HK Island (2522 7064). Central MTR (exit B, C)/buses & trams through Central.* **Open** *9am-6.30pm Mon-Fri; 9am-5.30pm Sat.* **Credit** *AmEx, MC, V.* **Map** *p67 D3.*

Under the same ownership as the Swindon Book Company (*see p181*), the Hong Kong Book Centre is a demure, well-stocked bookworm's haven. The stock is wide-ranging, though fiction is a forte, and there's a wide selection of international magazines.

### Kelly & Walsh

*Shop 348, Pacific Place, 88 Queensway, Admiralty, HK Island (2522 7893). Admiralty MTR (exit C1)/buses through Central.* **Open** *9.30am-8pm Mon-Sat; 11am-8pm Sun.* **Credit** *AmEx, MC, V.* **Map** *p67 F5.*

The inside of Kelly & Walsh looks a little like a stationer's, rather than a bookshop, but it does stock a fantastic mix of local and imported magazines, as well as certain overseas newspapers that can often be hard to come by in Hong Kong. Somewhat cluttered, somewhat pricey, it's always busy.

### Page One

*B1, Times Square, 1 Matheson Street, Causeway Bay, HK Island (2506 0381). Causeway Bay MTR (exit A)/63, 108, 117, 170, N170 bus.* **Open** *10.30am-10pm Mon-Thur, Sun; 10.30am-11pm Fri, Sat.* **Credit** *AmEx, DC, MC, V.* **Map** *p80 D2.*

For used books, go with the **Flow**. *See p181.*

Page One carries an extensive, comprehensive collection of fiction and non-fiction in both Chinese and English. *See also p226.*
**Branch**: Festival Walk, Kowloon Tong (2778 2808).

### Swindon Book Company

*13-15 Lock Road, Tsim Sha Tsui, Kowloon (2366 8001). Tsim Sha Tsui MTR (exit C1, E)/buses along Nathan Road/Tsim Sha Tsui Star Ferry Pier.* **Open** 9am-6.30pm Mon-Thur; 9am-7.30pm Fri, Sat; 12.30-6.30pm Sun. **Credit** AmEx, MC, V. **Map** p98 B2.
There are several Swindon Book Company shops in Hong Kong, although the Tsim Sha Tsui store is the main outlet. The store is enormous, stretching across two floors, with a wide range of titles in English. Pricing is reasonable considering that most of the stock is imported, and American paperbacks here tend to be the cheapest in town.

## Antiquarian/second-hand

### Flow

*1-2/F, 40 Lyndhurst Terrace, Central, HK Island (2964 9483). Central MTR (exit D1, D2, G)/Mid-Levels Escalator/12M, 13, 23A, 40M, 43 bus.* **Open** 12.30-8pm Tue-Sat; 12.30-7pm Sun. **No credit cards**. **Map** p66 C3.
This second-hand bookshop is a dream come true for those who read regularly and end up being bitten by the high prices of imported paperbacks. Flow will exchange your old books, CDs and videos for cash or other products – a must for any avid reader, music lover or film fanatic.

## Department stores & malls

### Beverley Commercial Centre

*87-105 Chatham Road South, Tsim Sha Tsui, Kowloon. Tsim Sha Tsui MTR (exit B2)/Buses along Chatham Road South.* **Open** noon-8pm daily. **Credit** varies. **Map** p98 D1.
This was the centre of local fashion before the Rise Commercial Building (*see p182*) stole the limelight. The two floors include outlets for second-hand jeans, bags and jewellery.

### Fashion Walk

*Paterson Street, Causeway Bay, HK Island. Causeway Bay MTR (exit E)/A11, 103, 170, N170 bus.* **Open** 10.30am-8pm daily. **Credit** varies. **Map** p80 D1.
Paterson Street used to be dominated by Japanese department stores until recent financial problems led to their disappearance. The area is now being revitalised by smaller boutiques, including shops like Tsumori Chisato and D-Mop (*see p191*).

### Festival Walk

*Tat Chee Avenue, Kowloon Tong, Kowloon. Kowloon Tong MTR.* **Open** 10.30am-8pm daily. **Credit** varies.
Resembling Pacific Place (*see p182*) in appearance, Festival Walk's target market is rather more mid market. The mall also has an ice rink, an AMC cinemaplex and some good restaurants.

The labyrinthine **Harbour City** complex.

### Harbour City

*Canton Road, Tsim Sha Tsui, Kowloon. Tsim Sha Tsui MTR (exit E)/buses to Tsim Sha Tsui Star Ferry Pier & along Salisbury Road/Tsim Sha Tsui Star Ferry Pier.* **Open** 10.30am-8pm daily. **Credit** varies. **Map** p98 A3.
Just a short walk from Tsim Sha Tsui Star Ferry, Harbour City is divided into five interconnected shopping arcades, including the massive Ocean Terminal and Ocean Centre. This gigantic mall is undoubtedly the largest shopping emporium in Tsim Sha Tsui and it's no easy task to avoid getting lost. Our advice is to pick up a guide on your way into the mall. You'll find just about everything here, from clothing brands such as Kookai to furniture outlets like Banyan Tree.

### Island Beverley

*1 Great George Street, Causeway Bay, HK Island. Causeway Bay MTR (exit E)/buses along Hennessy Road.* **Open** 11am-11pm daily. **Credit** varies. **Map** p80 D1.
In the hub of Causeway Bay, you'll find four floors of small boutiques selling mainly locally made fashion, accessories, make-up and novelty items.

### Jusco

*Kornhill Plaza 2, Kornhill Road, Quarry Bay, HK Island (2884 6888). Quarry Bay MTR.* **Open** 9.30am-10.30pm daily. **Credit** AmEx, DC, MC, V. **Map** p62.
Jusco, one of the largest department stores in Japan, set up its first Hong Kong outlet in Quarry Bay back in 1987. Although some of its outlets are showing

their age, they are all exceptionally large stores, and each is well stocked with fashion, food and household items. Notably, the prices here are low, making Jusco a far better choice than many of the other Japanese megastores.
**Branches**: G/F, Basement One, Site 5 & 6, Whampoa Garden, Hung Hom, Kowloon (2627 6688); Tuen Mun Town Plaza, Phase One, Tuen Shun Street, Tuen Mun, New Territories (2452 7333).

### The Landmark

*16 Des Voeux Road, Central, HK Island. Central MTR (exit B, C, E, G)/buses & trams through Central/Central Star Ferry Pier.* **Open** 10am-7.30pm daily. **Credit** varies. **Map** p67 D4.
Located right in the heart of Central (between Des Voeux Road and Queen's Road), the Landmark may be one of the older malls in Hong Kong, but it's still very clean, elegant and expensive looking. Inside, there's a huge central atrium and a wide range of shops, which are worth checking out for their flash window displays, even if you're not in a buying mood. Brand boutiques include Gucci, Prada, Miu Miu, Dries Van Noten and Dolce & Gabbana.

### Lane Crawford

*Pacific Place, 88 Queensway, Admiralty, HK Island (2845 1838). Admiralty MTR (exit C1)/buses through Central.* **Open** 10am-9pm daily. **Credit** AmEx, DC, MC, V. **Map** p67 F5.
One of the city's largest and oldest department stores, Lane Crawford is Hong Kong's answer to Harrods. Set over several floors, it has great beauty ranges such as Aveda, plus a blinding household section, which is worth a gander even if you're not buying. If you're a girl, the store's range of shoes and handbags will have you humming, as will the contemporary fashions. The Causeway Bay branch is pitched towards the younger market, while the other outlets are more sedate and laid-back, catering to a more mature clientele.
**Branches**: 70 Queen's Road, Central, HK Island (2118 3388); G-1/F, Times Square, 1 Matheson Street, Causeway Bay, HK Island (2118 3638); Shop 100, Ocean Terminal, Tsim Sha Tsui, Kowloon (2118 3428).

### Lee Gardens

*33 Hysan Avenue, Causeway Bay, HK Island. Causeway Bay MTR (exit F).* **Open** 10.30am-8pm daily. **Credit** AmEx, DC, MC, V. **Map** p80 D2.
Lee Gardens provides a relaxed environment in which the most prestigious (and expensive) brands congregate. Hermes, Louis Vuitton, Chanel, Cartier, Tiffany and Christian Dior are all here, as well as the likes of Costume National, Dirk Bikkembergs, Paul Smith and Prada.

### Marks & Spencer

*Central Tower, B-1/F, 28 Queen's Road Central, HK Island (2921 8303). Central MTR (exit D1, D2, G)/buses along Queen's Road Central.* **Open** 10.30am-8.30pm Mon-Fri; 10.30am-8pm Sat, Sun. **Credit** DC, MC, V. **Map** p67 D4.

This is the most accessible of Hong Kong's M&S stores. While the stock mirrors that of the UK outlets, the prices aren't quite as sound. In fact, some products cost almost double. There's a good choice of clothing, and small but adequate food and cosmetics sections. At the time of going to press, the future of M&S's overseas outlets was in some doubt.
**Branches**: Shop 822, Ocean Centre, Canton Road, Tsim Sha Tsui, Kowloon (2926 3318); Units 120 & 229, The Mall, Pacific Place, 88 Queensway, Admiralty, HK Island (2921 8888).

### Pacific Place

*88 Queensway, Admiralty, HK Island. Admiralty MTR (exit C1)/buses through Central.* **Open** 10.30am-8pm daily. **Credit** AmEx, DC, MC, V. **Map** p67 F5.
Even Pacific Place's own exit from the MTR station is sleek and chic like the four-storey mall. Well set out, open and easily accessible, its outlets (particularly the department stores Lane Crawford, Seibu and Marks & Spencer) cater for a wide range of clientele.

### Rise Commercial Building

*Granville Circuit (corner of Chatham Road South & Granville Road, behind the Ramada Inn), Tsim Sha Tsui, Kowloon. Tsim Sha Tsui MTR (exit B1, B2)/buses along Nathan Road.* **Open** noon-varies daily. **Credit** MC, V. **Map** p98 D1.
This rather rundown looking arcade is the current fashion hotspot. Tucked away from view near the factory outlets in Granville Road, the four floors of shopping target the young. Home to a number of young, lesser-known designers, you'll also find a temporary tattoo parlour, a tour bus company, fortune tellers, homewares and a flower shop. At the back, on the ground floor, the Fortune Co specialises in dancewear supplies.

### Seibu

*Pacific Place, 88 Queensway, Admiralty, HK Island (2971 3888). Admiralty MTR (exit C1)/buses through Central.* **Open** 10.30am-8pm Mon-Wed, Sun; 10.30am-9pm Thur-Sat. **Credit** DC, MC, V. **Map** p67 F5.
Seibu, which recently had a facelift, continues to be everyone's favourite megastore. Although it may have a Japanese name, it is owned by Dickson 'Harvey Nichols' Poon and is decidedly cosmopolitan. The chic four-floor store in Pacific Place stocks foodstuffs in the basement, while the other floors hold a mix of cosmetics, gifts, household items, accessories, shoes and clothes – from brands such as French Connection to the more cutting-edge styles of Vivienne Westwood and various Japanese labels. Seibu is also a good place to go for perfume and posh gifts. The Causeway Bay branch is geared towards young street fashion.
**Branch**: Windsor House, 311 Gloucester Road, Causeway Bay, HK Island (2890 0333).

### Sincere

*173 Des Voeux Road, Central, HK Island (2544 2688/www.sincere.com.hk). Sheung Wan MTR (exit E1, E3)/buses & trams through Central.* **Open** 10am-7.30pm daily. **Credit** AmEx, DC, MC, V. **Map** p66 C2.

# Hong Kong fashion designers

With a textile and garment industry that blossomed in the 1960s and 1970s, Hong Kong should have been a place to which the fashion industry looked for bright sparks. Sadly, history has proved that creative industries in Hong Kong struggle, due to general indifference, overriding commercial concerns and an underlying conservatism.

The first generation of Hong Kong fashion designers, such as **Eddie Lau Pui Kei** and **Ragence Lam**, have largely redirected their businesses from couture and ready-to-wear to manufacturing, or simply retired. Of the second wave, **Walter Ma** (see p190) is now considered the elder statesman. He was the first designer to open chain boutiques, such as Front First, Vee and Gee, stocking his diffusion lines. Initially, his retailing business boomed, but in recent years it has hit hard times. Perhaps this is not surprising: the demand for local fashion is probably just too small to justify one designer having several brands.

One of the industry's younger stars is **Barney Cheng**, whose reputation for pricey couture creations has placed him in the global spotlight. Like many Hong Kong-based designers, he has opted not to get involved in high street retailing and concentrates on running his operation from his workshop-cum-office instead, focusing specifically on the export market. Those who do set up shop usually head for spaces or malls where rents are affordable.

The local media attention on **William Tang**, the designer, is consistent, even though his work is only sold outside Hong Kong. Tang's notoriety as the 'bad boy' of Hong Kong fashion is in contrast to his role as a newspaper columnist, and food, travel and cultural critic. His house shows are often spiced up with theatrical dashes – one employed syringes as accessories – and out-of-favour faded crooners as models.

**Pacino Wan**'s fun street wear (see p188) is infinitely accessible to the general public,

while Wan himself is touted as a role model in the design arena. The high-profile **Flora Cheong-Leen**, whose work heavily employs Chinese symbolism, mostly sells her output overseas. Something of an acquired taste, it is a hit-or-miss affair. **Joanna Ho**'s luscious dresses are also reserved for an overseas clientele.

Menswear ranges are rarely produced by Hong Kong designers, for the simple fact that the market share is miniscule. Silvio Chan first opened as The Tailor, specialising in menswear, and then moved on to **37 º 2 In The Morning** (see p188), where he incorporated a women's range. His recent house show characteristically focused entirely on menswear, a daring public challenge considering the rather risque themes of gender and sexuality.

Others, like **Benjamin Lau** and **Joseph Li**, take a more low-key approach. Lau's work is delicate and expensive, with the best fabric and meticulous cuts taking precedence. **Lulu Cheung** (see p188) achieves recognition for taking her retailing business to a mainstream context, where her boutiques are housed in a department store and high-end shopping malls. **Ruby Li**, on the other hand, embraces the rhythm of the street, where she overturns the limits of function with the fusion of formal and casual wear.

Because the city is awash with imported designer clothes and budget pieces, few people in Hong Kong own the work of local designers. Those that do tend to be a younger local crowd who are interested in alternatives. Still, many fashion graduates brave the elements to expose their work, and many have set up small retail studios in arcades like **Rise** (see p182).

The Trade Development Council stages **Hong Kong Fashion Week** twice a year (in January and July) to promote Hong Kong designers. Check out the fashion section at www.tdctrade.com.

Eat, Drink, Shop

The main Sincere in Central was established over 100 years ago, making it the oldest department store in Hong Kong. Like many of its peers, it's a slick mega-store, with merchandise galore – think, all your house-hold and fashion needs set out over several floors. **Branches**: L1-L3, Lee Theatre Plaza, 99 Percival Street, Causeway Bay, HK Island (2839 9898); 73 Argyle Street, Mong Kok, Kowloon (2394 8233);

L1-L2, Grand Century Place, Mong Kok, Kowloon (2399 0688); L1-L3, Dragon Centre, 37K Yen Chow Street, Sham Shui Po, Kowloon (2708 6688).

### Sogo
*555 Hennessy Road, Causeway Bay, HK Island (2833 8338). Causeway Bay MTR (exit B, D2)/buses & trams along Hennessy Road.* **Open** 10am-10pm daily. **Credit** AmEx, DC, MC, V. **Map** p66 D2.

This Japanese store has a little bit of everything, and is an extremely popular place to shop among the local well-heeled Chinese. However, it's not quite as flush – or as well set out – as its rival, Seibu (*see p182*). In fact, it's somewhat confusing, especially if you're on your first visit. But it does have a good assortment of household accessories, such as glass, plates and vases, not to mention necessities like irons, kettles, teapots and electrical merchandise. Much of the stock is Japanese and remarkably well priced.

### Style House

*Park Lane Hotel, Great George Street, Causeway Bay, HK Island. Causeway Bay MTR (exit E)/buses along Hennessy Road.* **Open** 11am-9pm daily. **Credit** AmEx, DC, MC, V. **Map** p80 D1.
Home to the Agnès B store, this youth-slanted fashion arcade is across the road from the Causeway Bay branch of Seibu.

### Times Square

*Russell Street, Causeway Bay, HK Island. Causeway Bay MTR (exit A)/buses along Hennessy Road.* **Open** 10.30am-9pm daily. **Credit** AmEx, DC, MC, V. **Map** p80 D2.
At weekends, this sizeable mall overflows with mid-price shoppers.

### Wing On

*Wing On Centre, 211 Des Voeux Road, Central, HK Island (2852 1888/www.wingonnet.com). Sheung Wan MTR (exit A1, E1, E3)/buses & trams through Central.* **Open** 10am-7pm daily. **Credit** AmEx, DC, MC, V. **Map** p66 C2.
Wing On, fast on the heels of Sincere (*see p182*), is one of the oldest department stores in Hong Kong (founded 1907). The store's motto is 'value for money', and it delivers. Prices here are extremely reasonable, while the choice of goods is fantastic and principally aimed at the Chinese market. Merchandise includes cool cosmetics, clothing of all types, household goods and electrical items – a diversity of stock that makes Wing On a store popular with locals and those in the know.
**Branches**: Shop 301, 401, 501, Telford Plaza II, 33 Wai Yip Street, Kowloon Bay, Kowloon (2710 6288); Wing On Plaza, 62 Mody Road, Tsim Sha Tsui, Kowloon (2885 7588); 345 Nathan Road, Tsim Sha Tsui, Kowloon (2710 6288); Block C, 114 Discovery Bay Plaza, Discovery Bay, Lantau (2987 9268).

## Dry cleaners & laundries

### Goodwins of London

*Shop 27, G/F, Central Building, 1 Pedder Street, Central, HK Island (2525 0605). Central MTR (exit D1, G)/buses & trams through Central/Central Star Ferry Pier.* **Open** 8.15am-7.30pm Mon-Sat; 10.30am-6.30pm Sun. **Credit** MC, V. **Map** p67 D4.
Goodwins of London is one of those all-English, extra-refined dry cleaners that provides a reliable, careful service for cleaning clothes. Recently, the

company opened a second outlet in Pacific Place and further expansion is expected in the near future.
**Branch**: G/F (car park entrance), Pacific Place, 88 Queensway, Admiralty, HK Island (2918 1400).

### Jeeves

*Shop 2, Lobby Floor, Bank of East Asia Building, 10 Des Voeux Road, Central, HK Island (2973 0101). Central MTR (exit H)/buses & trams through Central/Central Star Ferry Pier.* **Open** 8am-7pm Mon-Sat. **Credit** AmEx, DC, MC, V. **Map** p67 D4.
One of the older dry cleaning establishments in Hong Kong, this is an upmarket place for the upwardly mobile, which means the prices are steep.

### Robinson Dry Cleaning

*73B Caine Road, Mid-Levels, HK Island (2523 8317). Mid-Levels Escalator/buses along Caine Road.* **Open** 8am-8pm Mon-Sat; 8am-6pm Sun. **No credit cards**. **Map** p66 B4.
This is an amiable, dependable dry cleaner situated outside the main hubbub of Central, so the pricing is fair – much fairer than the ridiculous cost of dry cleaning at most hotels anyway.

### The Valet Shop

*Upper Basement, Furama Hotel, 1 Connaught Road, Central, HK Island (2525 5111). Central MTR (exit J3)/buses to Star Ferry Pier/Central Star Ferry Pier.* **Open** 8am-7pm Mon-Sat. **Credit** AmEx, DC, MC, V. **Map** p67 E4.
Said to be the fastest dry cleaners in town, it will dry clean your clothes in less than four hours.

## Electronics

Tsim Sha Tsui is packed with electronics and camera shops, but your chance of being ripped off is high. For peace of mind, stick to **Fortress** or **Citicall** stores, or check out the honest dealers on Queen Victoria Street in Central.
   The **Sham Shui Po** district of Kowloon is the biggest centre for computer goods (legitimate and, more famously, pirated).
   In Causeway Bay, **Windsor House** (on the corner of Great George Street and Gloucester Road) harbours several floors of shops dedicated to Mac and PC wares. Prices are competitive, so have a look around before you buy. The pirate CD, DVD, VCD and software market still thrives in Hong Kong. One of its focuses is a crazy warren of stores packed into three floors at 298 Hennessy Road in Wan Chai. If you're lucky, a shifty looking gent will say something along the lines of 'looking for products, sir/madam?', sending you off in the direction of a short-lived, copy market, stocking all the latest gear. As this is illegal, many of the goods on offer, especially the VCDs, can be shoddy, so don't be too seduced by the low, low costs. After all, you tend to get what you pay for, and besides, the real thing isn't that much more expensive in Hong Kong.

*Eat, Drink, Shop*

### Citicall

*G/F, Hung Kei Mansion, 5-8 Queen Victoria Street,
Central, HK Island (2391 4366). Central MTR (exit
B)/buses & trams through Central.* **Open** 10am-8pm
daily. **Credit** MC, V. **Map** p66 C3.

Although Fortress hogs the main market for electronics, Citicall comes in a close second. Its three outlets sell cameras, stereos, radios, TVs, DVDs and
more, and you won't be ripped off (unlike at many of
the Tsim Sha Tsui electronics shops). Don't be put off
by the chaos inside the stores – the staff are usually
friendly and willing to give a good price.
**Branches**: 36 Jardine's Bazaar, Causeway Bay, HK
Island (2369 8822); G/F, 85-87 Fa Yuen Street, Mong
Kok, Kowloon (2391 5451).

### Fortress

*Shop 3281, Ocean Terminal, Harbour City, Canton
Road, Tsim Sha Tsui, Kowloon (2735 8628). Tsim
Sha Tsui MTR (exit C1, E)/buses to Tsim Sha Tsui
Star Ferry Pier/Tsim Sha Tsui Star Ferry Pier.*
**Open** 10.30am-7.30pm Mon-Sat; 10am-9pm Sun.
**Credit** AmEx, DC, MC, V. **Map** p98 A3.

If you're after a TV, camera, stereo, CD player, plug
or hairdryer, one of the many Fortress branches
around town will doubtlessly stock it. There's also
a small collection of CDs, DVDs and VCDs to choose
from. These, like the rest of the store's stock, are reliable and the set prices are low. Importantly, you'll
also be served by friendly, helpful staff.

### Wah Kiu Radio Co Ltd

*7 Queen Victoria Street, Central, HK Island (2522
8843). Central MTR (exit B)/buses & trams through
Central.* **Open** 9.30am-7.30pm daily. **Credit** V.
**Map** p66 C3.

Wah Kui has sat pretty on Queen Victoria Street for
decades. It's a long, lean, musty little shop, with cyn-
ical, yet honest service. It sells cameras and stereos,
as well as a large range of Swiss army knifes.

## Fashion

Hong Kong is full of fashion stores. For high-
end shopping, try Central and Admiralty;
for streetwear, go to Causeway Bay; and for
factory outlets, try Tsim Sha Tsui. The more
adventurous can head towards Temple Street
and Mong Kok for local bargains.

## Budget

### Bossini

*Shop 415, Pacific Place, 88 Queensway, Admiralty,
HK Island (2523 9847). Admiralty MTR (exit
C1)/buses through Central.* **Open** 11am-9pm Mon-
Fri; 10.30am-9.30pm Sat, Sun. **Credit** AmEx, DC,
MC, V. **Map** p67 F5.

Luckily for budget shoppers, there's a Bossini outlet on almost every street in Hong Kong (in addition
to this one in Pacific Place). In addition to well-made
basics, the store's seasonal collection is often one
that would put many high street labels to shame.

**Bossini** and **Giordano** – great for cheap kit.

### Giordano

*Shop 4, G/F, China Building, 29 Queen's Road,
Central, HK Island (2921 2028). Central MTR
(exit D1, D2, G)/buses along Queen's Road Central.*
**Open** 10am-8.30pm Mon-Sat; 11am-8pm Sun.
**Credit** AmEx, MC, V. **Map** p67 D4.

Like Bossini, Giordano offers good clothing basics,
from accessories to simply must-haves, like jeans
and T-shirts, and it has branches on virtually every
street corner. As for the pricing, it's so low it's a sin.
The only letdown is the shopping experience: the
stores are often a mess, and the crowds and noise
may grate – but there sure are bargains here.

## Children

### Crocodile For Kids

*Shop 105-107, Ocean Terminal, Tsim Sha Tsui,
Kowloon (2735 5136). Tsim Sha Tsui MTR
(exit C1, E)/buses along Chatham Road South.*
**Open** 11am-8pm daily. **Credit** AmEx, DC, MC, V.
**Map** p98 A3.

Hong Kong has several branches of Crocodile, a
Chinese label selling the Western look (trainers, T-
shirts, jeans and more) at exceptionally low prices.
This branch sells the kids' version of the adult label.

### Kingkow

*Shop 023, B/F, Ocean Terminal, Tsim Sha Tsui,
Kowloon (2317 4088). Tsim Sha Tsui MTR (exit C1,
E)/buses along Chatham Road South.* **Open** 10am-
8pm daily. **Credit** AmEx, DC, MC, V. **Map** p98 A3.

Kingkow stocks inexpensive clothes for kids (under
the age of 16 years) that suit any occasion.

# Designer: international

## Birkin

*Shop C, Causeway Bay Mansion, 42-48 Paterson Street, Causeway Bay, HK Island (2577 9323). Causeway Bay MTR (exit E)/A11, 103, 170, N170 bus.* **Open** noon-10pm daily. **Credit** AmEx, DC, MC, V. **Map** p80 D1.

Look here for the latest from Prada, Miu Miu and Gucci, all at prices more competitive than at the official outlets.

**Branch:** Basement, 50 Kimberley Road, Tsim Sha Tsui, Kowloon (2721 8837).

## Donna Karan/DKNY

*Hang Lung Centre, Paterson Street, Causeway Bay, HK Island (2970 2288). Causeway Bay MTR (exit E)/A11, 103, 170, N170 bus.* **Open** 10.30am-10pm daily. **Credit** AmEx, DC, MC, V. **Map** p80 D1.

Donna Karan and her diffusion label DKNY infiltrated the wardrobes of many Hong Kong *tai-tais* a long time ago. As with most diffusion lines, DKNY is far funkier, and cheaper, than the upwardly mobile, stiffly elegant Donna Karan line.

## Extravaganza

*Shop F-16, Fashion Island, 11-19 Great George Street, Causeway Bay, HK Island (2915 0051). Causeway Bay MTR (exit E)/buses along Hennessy Road.* **Open** noon-10.30pm Mon-Thur, Sun; noon-10.30pm Sat. **Credit** AmEx, DC, MC, V. **Map** p80 D1.

Like Birkin (*see above*), Extravaganza offers the latest designer brands at prices lower than the official outlets.

**Branch:** Miramar Shopping Centre, 1-23 Kimberley Road, Tsim Sha Tsui, Kowloon (2730 0500).

## Gucci

*G1, The Landmark, 16 Des Voeux Road, Central, HK Island (2524 4492). Central MTR (exit B, C, E, G)/buses & trams through Central/Central Star Ferry Pier.* **Open** 10.30am-7.30pm Mon-Sat; 11am-7pm Sun. **Credit** AmEx, DC, MC, V. **Map** p67 D4.

If you've got cash in your pocket and/or credit on your card, Gucci is a luxurious place to shop.

**Branch:** Shop 368 Pacific Place, 88 Queensway, Admiralty, HK Island (2524 2721).

## IT

*Sino Plaza, 255-257 Gloucester Road, Causeway Bay, HK Island (2834 4393/www.ithk.com). Causeway Bay MTR (exit C)/buses along Gloucester Road.* **Open** noon-10pm daily. **Credit** AmEx, MC, V. **Map** p66 C1.

This chain stocks brands such as Paul Smith, Helmut Lang, Vivienne Westwood, Christophe Lemaire and Comme des Garçons. The newly revamped two-storey store in Sino Plaza is decked out like an early 1980s' disco with smoked glass, mirror balls, dark furnishings and pinspots – which doesn't exactly make for a comfortable shopping experience. A section also features furniture and selected homewares.

**Branches:** 2-4 Kingston Street, Causeway Bay, HK Island (2881 1865); 8 Queen's Road, Central, HK Island (2525 2960); Harbour City, Canton Road, Tsim Sha Tsui, Kowloon (2117 0655).

## IT Sale Shop

*Shop 72-119, 3/F, Silvercord, 30 Canton Road, Tsim Sha Tsui, Kowloon (2377 9466). Tsim Sha Tsui MTR (exit A1)/buses along Canton Road.* **Open** noon-9pm daily. **Credit** AmEx, MC, V. **Map** p98 B2.

After a visit to Harbour City's IT store, cross the road to the sale outlet where surplus seasonal stocks are available at reduced prices.

## Joyce

*23 Nathan Road, Tsim Sha Tsui, Kowloon (2367 8128). Tsim Sha Tsui MTR (exit E)/buses along Nathan Road/Tsim Sha Tsui Star Ferry Pier.* **Open** noon-10.30pm Mon-Sat; noon-7pm Sun. **Credit** DC, MC, V. **Map** p98 C2.

Named after its founder, Joyce Ma, this store is a bit of an institution in Hong Kong. Several branches around the city stock designer brands such as Comme des Garcons, Dolce & Gabbana, Anna Sui and Ghost, alongside top brand shoes, accessories and cosmetics. The Tsim Sha Tsui outlet is the mainstream venue (and houses a Prada outlet), while the Central store is reserved for more upmarket brands and the Admiralty outlet is geared to the young and groovy. The Joyce Ma empire also boasts individual boutiques for Dries Van Noten, Dolce & Gabbana, Missoni (all in The Landmark; *see p182*), Jil Sander (Alexandra House, Central), Costume National, Y's by Yohji Yamamoto (both Lee Gardens; *see p182*) and Boss (Pacific Place; *see p182*). In fact, Joyce is such a fashion revelation that it even publishes its own magazine, entitled (you guessed it) *Joyce*, which is on sale at newsagents across town.

**Branches:** New World Tower, 16 Queen's Road, Central, HK Island (2810 1120); 334 Pacific Place, 88 Queensway, Admiralty, HK Island (2523 5944).

## Joyce Warehouse

*21/F, Horizon Plaza, South Horizon, 2 Lee Wing Street, Ap Lei Chau, HK Island (2814 8313). Bus 90.* **Open** 10am-7pm Tue-Sat; noon-6pm Sun. **Credit** MC, DC, V. **Map** p62.

It's label heaven at evergreen **Joyce**.

Eat, Drink, Shop

Joyce Warehouse may be hard to get to, but keen shoppers will be elated by the range and prices – womenswear is often vastly reduced.

## Overheads

*G/F, 120 Percival Street, Causeway Bay, HK Island (2881 8002). Causeway Bay MTR (exit A)/buses along Gloucester Road.* **Open** noon-9pm daily. **Credit** AmEx, MC, V. **Map** p80 D2.
This hip hop wear shop resembles a minimalist gallery: there's not much of a selection, but apparently when new stock does arrive, droves of youngsters line up to worship.
**Branch:** Abyss, 18 Yiu Wah Street, Causeway Bay, HK Island (no phone).

## Prada

*Shop 213, The Landmark, 16 Des Voeux Road, Central, HK Island (2845 6678). Central MTR (exit B, C, E, G)/buses & trams through Central/ Central Star Ferry Pier.* **Open** 10.30am-7.30pm Mon-Sat; 11am-6pm Sun. **Credit** AmEx, DC, MC, V. **Map** p67 D4.
Like many other designer stores in this city, Prada has armed security at the entrance, which is odd, because shoot outs in classy clothing shops are rare. Still, you never know.

## The Swank Shop

*Shop 103-105, The Landmark, 16 Des Voeux Road, Central, HK Island (2810 0769). Central MTR (exit B, C, E, G)/buses through Central/Central Star Ferry Pier.* **Open** 10.30am-7.30pm daily. **Credit** AmEx, DC, MC, V. **Map** p67 D4.
Don't be put off by the naff name, the Swank Shop is one of the oldest fashion stores in Hong Kong. It sells an odd, but extensive, assortment of designer labels, like Gianfranco Ferre and Valentino, for both men and women. Even if these labels aren't for you, there's a slick collection of accessories on offer.

## Versace

*Shop 108, Times Square, 2 Matheson Street, Causeway Bay, HK Island (2506 2281). Causeway Bay MTR (exit A)/63, 108, 117, 170, N170 bus.* **Open** 11am-8.30pm daily. **Credit** AmEx, DC, MC, V. **Map** p80 D2.
The Versace label has a large following in Hong Kong and, therefore, a wide choice of outlets. All are cold and crisp, topped off by service that touts a thin smile.

## Vivienne Tam

*Shop 219, Times Square, 2 Matheson Street, Causeway Bay, HK Island (2506 1162). Causeway Bay MTR (exit A)/63, 108, 117, 170, N170 bus.* **Open** 11am-8pm Sun-Thur; 11am-9pm Fri, Sat. **Credit** AmEx, DC, MC, V. **Map** p80 D2.
Sometimes you'll wander into a store selling the New York-based Chinese designer Vivienne Tam's latest collection and be wowed by her exquisite sexy silk dresses covered in intricate Chinese embroidery. Other times, you'll be appalled by the downmarket nylon fabrics and cheap looking T-shirts. Still, as one of Hong Kong's greatest design exports, Tam's something of a local treasure.

**Branches:** Hang Lung Centre, Great George Street, Causeway Bay, HK Island (no phone); Ocean Centre, Tsim Sha Tsui, Kowloon (2375 6263); Festival Walk, Kowloon Tong, Kowloon (no phone).

## W1

*Shop 3009, 3/F, New Wing, Miramar Shopping Centre, 21-27 Kimberley Road, Kowloon (2375 7969). Tsim Sha Tsui MTR (exit B1, B2)/buses along Nathan Road.* **Open** 1.30-10pm daily. **Credit** AmEx, MC, V. **Map** p98 C1.
Run by a group of fashion students and stylists, W1 carries pieces by a range of cutting-edge British designers, including Robert Carrey Williams, Jeremy Scott and 2:1.

# Designer: local

## 37 º 2 In The Morning

*11 Sharp Street East, Causeway Bay, HK Island (2838 2597). Causeway Bay MTR (exit A).* **Open** 12.30-10.30pm daily. **Credit** AmEx, DC, MC, V. **Map** p80 C2.
The growing reputation of Silvio Chan is based on his disparate men's and women's designs, which veer from the minimal, pared-down look to show pieces infused with elements of sexuality. His recent shows have garnered both media and public praise.

## Lulu Cheung

*Shop G309, G/F, Harbour City, Canton Road, Tsim Sha Tsui, Kowloon (2117 0682). Tsim Sha Tsui MTR (exit C1, E)/buses along Canton Road/Tsim Sha Tsui Star Ferry Pier.* **Open** 10.30am-8pm daily. **Credit** AmEx, DC, MC, V. **Map** p98 A2.
Cheung's designs are low-key and subtle, concentrating on a monochrome colour palate, refined cuts and detailings. She also has an outlet at Seibu in Pacific Place (*see p182*).

## Pacino Wan

*Shop 2045, Miramar Shopping Centre, 1-23 Kimberley Road, Tsim Sha Tsui, Kowloon (2375 6718). Tsim Sha Tsui MTR (exit B1, B2)/ buses along Nathan Road.* **Open** 1-10pm daily. **Credit** MC, V. **Map** p98 C1.
Wan's tongue-in-cheek creations, which include dresses printed with pictures of the Queen and instant noodle packets, have earned him attention and awards in equal measure. He also produces a children's wear label called Mimimomo. A second outlet can be found at Island Beverley (*see p181*).

## Rib Yeung

*10 Pak Sha Road, Causeway Bay, HK Island (2972 2185). Causeway Bay MTR (Exit F).* **Open** noon-10pm daily. **Credit** AmEx, DC, MC, V. **Map** p80 D2.
Yeung has a keen eye on the latest trends and a knack for translating more aggressive high-fashion styles into wearable outfits.
**Branches:** 55D Kimberley Road, Tsim Sha Tsui, Kowloon (no phone); 53-63 Peking Road, Tsim Sha Tsui, Kowloon (no phone).

# HK profiles David Tang

Businessman, bon viveur, culture vulture and cigar-chomping celebrity, David Tang, is the man who single-handedly made Chinese style chic again. His **Shanghai Tang** store in Central (*see p189*), which sells clothes, fabrics and all manner of miscellaneous objects bearing the signature 'Made By Chinese', is almost as essential to the Hong Kong tour as a ride on the Star Ferry and a tram trip up the Peak. Hillary Clinton, the late Princess Diana and many other '90s icons have created traffic havoc by stopping by with their entourage to do a little shopping.

Tang's clothes are unmistakable. They are *very* Chinese. Stylish silk suits and *cheongsams* in vivid colours, ornate embroidery and hand-woven buttons. This contemporary Chinoiserie does not come cheap and cynics are wont to trash his goods as tacky trinkets aimed at Westerners – Mao wristwatches, Mao suits, PLA caps, fortune sticks and feng shui diaries. But Tang's philosophy is very different: why should all Chinese spurn their native dress in favour of Levi's jeans and Italian suits? Shanghai Tang has stores in London and New York as well as designs on the world.

Tang himself loves the term 'Chinese-ness' and is always keen to emphasise his own. He wears hand-tailored Mandarin clothes, pyjama-like silk suits, smoking jackets and cloth slippers. Tang is as adept at marketing his products by marketing himself as is the British entrepreneur Richard Branson. He has friends in high places and holds esteem in the corridors of Beijing, Washington and Whitehall, which is no mean feat. For all that, his reputation is strongest as a man who knows how to have a good time. His trademark Havana cigar in hand (he owns the franchise to sell them in Hong Kong and the rest of Asia), Tang comes across as an affable, endearing character. He is a gregarious raconteur, seemingly loving

nothing more than holding court before distinguished guests and partying with the rich and famous.

Much of his entertaining is done at the **China Club**, located on the top floors of the old Bank of China building in Central. It's an impressive club, and one in which billions of dollars of business deals are brokered by ambitious young entrepreneurs in the mould of Tang himself. The interior is 1920s art deco, reminiscent of swinging Shanghai, with its grand staircase, ceiling fans, elaborate glasswork and marble surfaces. If every tourist visits Shanghai Tang, then every mover and shaker dines at the China Club. It is here that he often does his schmoozing, pressing of flesh and, of course, cigar smoking.

Tang has a knack of tapping into the next big thing. He opened a cigar shop in 1992 at the time the pastime was about to take-off. It is now extremely popular among Chinese businessmen, with divans and lounges filled with the aroma of burning tobacco, springing up across the city, in the same way wine bars cater for the sudden upsurge in demand for expensive red wines. Both are seen as status symbols by the Chinese nouveau riche.

Some who dismiss Tang as a showy, social butterfly point to his privileged upbringing: his grandfather was the bus tycoon and philanthropist Sir Shiu-kin Tang. Money aside, he found his own way in the world after travails through an English education, several rounds of academia in which he switched subjects three times, the corporate business culture and the legal world. Eventually he found out what he was best suited to being – an entrepreneur with an eye for the main chance. Instead of following trends, he decided to create his own. His clothing line is billed, appropriately, as 'the emperor's new clothes'. If one were to suggest a slogan for the man himself, it would surely be the new Tang dynasty.

### Ruby Li

*Shop 31-33, 1/F, Beverley Commercial Centre, 87-105 Chatham Road South, Tsim Sha Tsui, Kowloon (2375 8001). Buses along Chatham Road South.* **Open** 1-9.30pm daily. **Credit** AmEx, DC, MC, V. **Map** p98 D1. Li infuses her clothes with a young street attitude, characterised by clashing contrasts. Her evening and daywear comes together in an alluring fusion.

### Shanghai Tang

*G/F, Pedder Building, 12 Pedder Street, Central, HK Island (2525 7333/www.shanghaitang.com). Central MTR (exit D1, G)/buses through Central/Central Star Ferry Pier.* **Open** 10am-8pm Mon-Sat; 11am-7pm Sun. **Credit** AmEx, DC, MC, V. **Map** p67 D4. The money-making brainchild of local entrepreneur David Tang (*see above* **HK profiles: David Tang**),

**Shanghai Tang.** See p189.

Shanghai Tang is a favourite shopping spot for many. Trad China, with a kitsch twist, the shop sells everything from silk covered diaries to Mao clocks, and leather coats to *cheongsams*. The store also has its own troupe of tailors – some of whom are rumoured to be the original clothiers who come from Shanghai, establishing Hong Kong as a renowned tailoring centre way back when. They're certainly some of the few garment makers who can still create a real deal *cheongsam* – the *cheongsams* worn by Maggie Cheung in *In The Mood For Love* were made here. Prices range from HK$3,000 to HK$4,000 for labour, plus the cost of the fabric. If you want to learn more about the exquisite service on offer, check out the 'Imperial Tailors' section on the website.

### Shopaholic
*4 Yiu Wa Street, Causeway Bay, HK Island (2893 3293). Causeway Bay MTR (exit A).* **Open** 1-10pm daily. **Credit** AmEx, MC, V. **Map** p80 C2.
Hilda Yim's shop is relaxed and casual, a mix of street-inspired creations, vintage bags and accessories, and desirable hand-made jewellery. You'll also find hints of hip hop and black American cultural influences.

### Spy by Henry Lau
*11 Sharp Street East, Causeway Bay, HK Island (2893 7799/www.spybyhenrylau.com). Causeway Bay MTR (exit A).* **Open** 1-11pm daily. **Credit** AmEx, DC, MC, V. **Map** p80 C2.
Lau's flamboyant designs, which mix street chic with splashes of the theatrical, have made their mark on the local scene.
**Branch**: Shop 406-407, 4/F, Rise Commercial Building, 5-11 Granville Circuit, Tsim Sha Tsui, Kowloon (2366 5866).

### Walter Ma
*G/F, The Galleria, 9 Queen's Road, Central, HK Island (2840 1266). Central MTR (exit H, K)/buses along Queen's Road Central.* **Open** 11am-8pm daily. **Credit** AmEx, DC, MC, V. **Map** p67 D4.
Considered one of Hong Kong's most successful fashion designers, Ma was the first to set up diffusion lines for all his creations – they include Front First, Gee and Vee.

## Factory outlets

### Arbutus
*29B Granville Road, Tsim Sha Tsui, Kowloon (2366 5200) Tsim Sha Tsui MTR (exit B1, B2)/ buses along Nathan Road.* **Open** 11am-11pm daily. **Credit** MC, V. **Map** p98 C1.
This outlet is noted for the fact that it carries genuine items of hip sports and active brands – you'll find shops in the same street selling counterfeits.

### Granville Road & Kimberley Road
*Tsim Sha Tsui, Kowloon. Tsim Sha Tsui MTR (exit B1, B2)/buses along Nathan Road.* **Map** p98 C1.
Two parallel streets where lots of factory outlets sell competitively priced clothes.

### Lok Wah Top Place
*24A & 55 Granville Road, Tsim Sha Tsui, Kowloon (2311 3726). Tsim Sha Tsui MTR (exit B2)/buses along Chatham Road South.* **Open** 10am-11pm daily. **Credit** MC, V. **Map** p98 C1.
Lok Wah has two shops offering all kinds of factory surplus.

## Fetish/erotic

### Fetish Fashion
*The 'Cockloft', Merlin Building, 32 Cochrane Street, Central, HK Island (2544 1155). Mid-Levels Escalator/buses along Queen's Road Central.* **Open** noon-10pm Mon-Sat. **Credit** AmEx, MC, V. **Map** p66 C3.
If latex, whips and adult accessories are your thing, Fetish Fashion is bang up your alley. It sells a heady line of rubber clothes, bondage gear and accessories, as well as sex toys and books.

Dark pleasures at **Fetish Fashion**.

## Second-hand

### Dada

*Shop 108, Fortune Centre, 44-48 Yun Ping Road, Causeway Bay, HK Island (2972 2070). Causeway Bay MTR (exit F)/buses along Gloucester Road.* **Open** 1-9pm Mon-Sat; 1.30-8.30pm Sun. **Credit** AmEx, MC, V. **Map** p80 D2.
This Fortune Centre shop sells branded cast-offs that once belonged to, for example, local pop diva Kelly Chen and songwriter/celebrity Mark Lui. **Branch**: F13a, Fashion Island, Paterson Street, Causeway Bay, HK Island (no phone).

## Streetwear/clubwear

### D-Mop

*11-15 On Lan Street, Central, HK Island (2840 0822/www.d-mop.com). Central MTR (exit D1, G)/ 13, 26, 43 bus & buses along Queen's Road Central.* **Open** 11am-8pm Mon-Sat; noon-7pm Sun. **Credit** AmEx, DC, MC, V. **Map** p67 D4.
D-Mop is one of the trendier shops in Hong Kong, selling stuff no self-respecting, fashion-conscious guru would be without. Patrick Cox and Komodo woolies, Martine Sitbon and Xavier Delacour, and a

great selection of decent jeans, like good fashionable Levi's, are stocked.
**Branch**: 55 Paterson Street, Causeway Bay, HK Island (2890 6622).

### The Max Channel

*1/F, 533 Lockhart Road, Causeway Bay, HK Island (2792 4448/www.maxchannel.com). Causeway Bay MTR (exit C, D1)/buses & trams along Hennessy Road.* **Open** 10am-9.30pm Mon-Sat; 2-9.30pm Sun. **Credit** MC, V. **Map** p66 D1.
If you simply can't face the crowds of Causeway Bay, you can always check out the Max Channel online. A very cool store, it majors in sport and club-wear, and also does a line in colourful Lava lamps.

## Tailors

### The Couples

*Shop 38 & 39, G/F, Beverley Commercial Centre, 87-105 Chatham Road South, Tsim Sha Tsui, Kowloon (2317 6855). Buses along Chatham Road South.* **Open** 1-9.30pm daily. **Credit** AmEx, DC, MC, V. **Map** p98 D1.
Orders usually take a week, but rush jobs can be done in two days. Expect to pay about HK$500 for a basic design.

# HK profiles Sam the Tailor

If you want a suit made in Hong Kong, there is a choice of thousands of tailors. In the streets of Tsim Sha Tsui, touts thrust cards in your hands offering made-to-measure outfits that will be ready within hours at knockdown prices. The suits are normally pretty good, too. Bring along your favourite designer labels and copies are stitched up in no time at a fraction of the cost. It's a competitive business, yet one man manages to stand out from the crowd. From Bill Clinton to the late Princess Diana, there's only one place celebrities go – **Sam the Tailor**.

Sam is actually named **Manu Melwani**, and, walking into his tiny shop in a rundown arcade on Nathan Road, you would have no idea he was a friend to the stars. None that is, apart from the photos and letters that adorn the walls and counter of shop, reading like a *Who's Who* of the rich and famous. Skilled though his staff are, this has as much to do with the fact that Melwani is a self-publicist extraordinaire (most famous clients usually lead to a press release or leak of some sort) and his uncanny ability to be at the right hotel room at the time the most important guest shows up, just so he can introduce himself.

Born in India, Melwani was a young boy when his father set up the shop 40 years ago. Now several dozen staff are employed by Sam, who, needless to say, has become quite rich, and they are able to turn out a perfectly fitting suit or *cheongsam* in less than two hours. So many a visiting celeb who decides to don a bit of chinoiserie just hours before a glitzy function will send for Sam. No matter where they are, he'll be there in minutes and have the finished article back double quick. In fact, Sam has been flown to Washington to measure up Bill Clinton, frequently visits the Belgian royal family and holds monthly measuring sessions in London.

Melwani puts his success down to the personal touch, creating a rapport with the client. For all his brushes with grandeur, Melwani still offers a good price for Joe Public, who walks through the door of the shop in scores every day. 'Everyone who comes into my shop is treated with respect, be they a king or a passer-by,' Melwani notes. And don't be shy to ask him about his high-flying life should you call in – Sam is rightly famous for his clothes, but not for his modesty. *See p193.*

# salon Picasso

THE RITZ-CARLTON H.K. SHOP 1-2, BASEMENT 1,
3 CONNAUGHT RD., CENTRAL, HONG KONG.
TEL : (852) 2810 0123   FAX : (852) 2147 2388

### Linva Tailor

*38 Cochrane Street, Central, HK Island (2544 2456).*
*Mid-Levels Escalator/buses along Queen's Road*
*Central.* **Open** 9.30am-6pm Mon-Sat. **Credit** AmEx,
DC, MC, V. **Map** p66 C3.
This small tailor offers a friendly, reliable, well-
priced service for custom-made clothing. Linva also
does alterations.

### Sam's Tailor

*94 Nathan Road, Tsim Sha Tsui, Kowloon (2367*
*9423/www.samstailor.com). Tsim Sha Tsui MTR*
*(exit B1)/buses along Nathan Road.* **Open** 10am-
7.30pm Mon-Sat; 10am-midnight Sun. **Credit** AmEx,
DC, MC, V. **Map** p98 B1.
*See p191* **HK profiles: Sam the Tailor.**

### Sze Sze

*83C Percival Street, Causeway Bay, HK Island (2576*
*6233). Causeway Bay MTR (exit A)/buses along*
*Gloucester Road.* **Open** 10am-7pm Mon-Sat.
**No credit cards. Map** p80 D2.
Around the corner from Times Square, this traditional ladies' tailor has been around since the 1950s.
For a *cheongsam*, expect to pay HK$2,000-$3,000 for
labour and around HK$3,000 for the silk. An order
normally takes two weeks, but a rush job can be
completed in a week.

## Underwear

### Lily Co Ltd

*17 Li Yuen Street East, Central, HK Island (2810*
*7178). Central MTR (exit C)/buses & trams through*
*Central.* **Open** 10am-7pm daily. **Credit** MC, V.
**Map** p67 D3.
Concealed by the chaotic market stalls of Li Yuen
Street East, Lily Co Ltd has possibly the best selec-
tion of knickers any girl could wish for – at
good prices. Its stock includes Jockey, Wacoal and
Sloggi, alongside a clutter of more obscure and
colourful brands.

### Lingerie Café

*Shop 119, Prince's Building, 10 Chater Road,*
*Central, HK Island (2869 0039). Central MTR*
*(exit J1, J2, J3)/buses & trams through Central/*
*Central Star Ferry Pier.* **Open** 10am-7pm Mon-Sat;
noon-5pm Sun. **Credit** AmEx, MC, V.
**Map** p67 E4.
Once the Lingerie Café occupied a tiny space on the
corner of Wyndham Street. Now it's all grown up,
and has relocated into the sleek aisles in Prince's
Building. Here you'll find women's underwear to die
for, including elusive La Perla. They also do a great
range in swimwear, as well as a sideline in sexy,
saucy eveningwear.

## Fashion accessories

For a wide range of accessories and knick-
knacks, try the street stalls on Jardine's
Crescent in Causeway Bay.

### Mandarina Duck

*The Landmark, 16 Des Voeux Road, Central, HK*
*Island (2845 4898). Central MTR (exit B, C, E, G)/*
*buses & trams through Central/Central Star Ferry*
*Pier.* **Open** 10am-7pm daily. **Credit** AmEx, DC, MC,
V. **Map** p67 D4.
Every self-respecting dapper local has probably
owned a Mandarina Duck bag at some stage or
another. Their neat, compact designs, often in a hardened man-made fabric, have an almost sci-fi appearance. Although pricey, the products wear well.

### Mayfair Leather

*92 Nathan Road, Tsim Sha Tsui, Kowloon*
*(2366 2588). Tsim Sha Tsui MTR (exit B1)/buses*
*along Nathan Road.* **Open** 9.30am-11pm daily.
**Credit** AmEx, DC, MC, V. **Map** p98 B1.
Mayfair Leather is a rather sleek store that was
established over a decade ago. It stocks leather
accessories, such as handbags, briefcases and shoes.
Prices aren't too hard on the wallet, while service
comes with a keen smile.

### Renomme

*Flat B, 13/F, North Point Mansions, 702 King's*
*Road, North Point, HK Island (2522 6435). Quarry*
*Bay MTR (exit B4)/buses along King's Road.*
**Open** 10am-6pm Mon-Fri; by appointment Sat.
**No credit cards.**
Renomme is a small shop run by a group of
Filipinos, who make superb custom-made hats for
any occasion. They also allow the client as much
control over the creation as he/she likes, which
means you can bring your own materials and fabric
to help create the design.

### Samsonite

*Shop 5, G/F, Family Square, 9 Kingston Street,*
*Causeway Bay, HK Island (2972 2656). Causeway*
*Bay MTR (exit E)/A11, A12 bus.* **Open** 10am-9pm
daily. **Credit** AmEx, MC, V. **Map** p80 D1.
If you're in need of an extra suitcase to carry home
your wealth of Hong Kong purchases, Samsonite is
the place to go for robust cases, travel bags and luggage of every description.

### Style

*35 Granville Road, Tsim Sha Tsui, Kowloon (2721*
*0110). Tsim Sha Tsui MTR (exit B2)/buses along*
*Chatham Road South.* **Open** 9.30am-midnight daily.
**Credit** MC, V. **Map** p98 C1.
This trinket store stocks all kinds of cheap acces-
sories, from hairclips to wigs and feathered masks.

## Florists

### Anglo-Chinese Florist

*25 D'Aguilar Street, Central, HK Island (2845*
*4212). Central MTR (exit D1, G)/12M, 13, 23A,*
*40M, 43 bus.* **Open** 8am-11pm daily. **Credit** AmEx,
MC, V. **Map** p66 C4.
A small, recently opened florist selling wonderful
flowers fit for any event. It also has a variety of
plants to fill your home, and will deliver.

**Eat, Drink, Shop**

# Markets of Hong Kong

## Stanley Market

*Stanley, HK Island. Buses to Stanley.*
**Open** 11am-6pm daily. **Map** p95.
At one time Stanley Market was known for its rock bottom prices, but, as tourists discovered the market, they've gradually risen. However, you can still uncover some decent souvenirs, factory seconds, fake goods, trinkets and arts and crafts. The bus ride from Central is a pleasure in itself.

## Temple Street Night Market

*Jordan, Temple Street, Kowloon. Jordan MTR (exit A, C2).* **Open** 2-10pm daily. **Map** p110 A5.
After 6pm, Temple Street comes alive with market stalls, entertainers and buzzing crowds. It's a good place to give your bargaining skills a go, especially if you're interested in copy CDs, watches and bags. At the far end of the market, you'll discover fortune tellers and rows of small street shows performing Chinese opera, which are aimed more at the locals than tourists. Not far away, north of Yau Ma Tei MTR, on Tung Choi Street, are the cheap clothes and accessories of the so-called **Ladies' Market** and **Goldfish Market**.

## Lai Chi Kok Market

*Lai Chi Kok, Kowloon. Lai Chi Kok MTR.* **Open** 1-2pm Mon-Fri.
If you fancy a meander through industrial Hong Kong, trek out to Lai Chi Kok Market. Located in an area of clothing factories and wholesalers (behind the MTR station close to Wing Hong Street), this remarkably busy market sells stuff (including clothes) that probably walked out of the back door of nearby factories. This is the kind of place you'll find real bargains.

## Western Market

*Des Voeux Road Central, Sheung Wan, HK Island. Sheung Wan MTR (exit B, C)/buses & trams through Central.* **Open** 10am-7pm daily. **Map** p66 B1.
Housed in a fine red-brick colonial building (*see p75*), the pickings within Western Market are disappointingly uninspiring. A variety of kitschy nick-nacks are sold on the ground floor (although you might be able to find some second-hand designer watches), but most of the market is devoted to fabrics. There is a decent Chinese restaurant on the top floor, though.

## Jade Market

*Kansu & Shanghai streets, Yau Ma Tei, Kowloon. Yau Ma Tei MTR (exit C) or Jordan MTR (exit A, B1).* **Open** 10am-3.30pm daily. **Map** p110 A4.
The earlier you arrive at the Jade Market, the more likely you are to bag a good deal, but recognising such a deal may not be so easy. Jade is priced according to a complicated system that considers the consistency of its colour, the thickness, translucency and purity of the material. Unless you really know what you're doing, stick to cheap trinkets, or the great selection of freshwater pearls that are sold alongside the jade.

## Bird Market

*The Bird Park, off Flower Market Road, Mong Kok. Prince Edward MTR (exit B1).* **Open** 7am-8pm daily. **Map** p110 B1.
The Bird Market is surprisingly clean and pristine, particularly in comparison with the old venue of Hong Kok Street, from where it moved a couple of years ago. Stacks of cages filled with much-prized songbirds fill the air with cacophonous birdsong. Also on sale at the market are wonderfully carved wooden bird cages, which are ornaments in themselves and reasonable priced. If you're an animal lover of any sort, you'd be better to give the place a miss.

**Temple Street Night Market.**

**SoHo Bakery**: cake heaven.

## Sim's Flower Workshop

*Shop 9, 1 Lyndhurst Terrace, Central, HK Island (2542 4544). Central MTR (exit D1, D2, G)/Mid-Levels Escalator/12M, 13, 23A, 40M, 43 bus.* **Open** 9am-6.30pm Mon-Fri; 9am-5.30pm Sat. **Credit** AmEx, MC, V. **Map** p66 C3.

Sim's Flower Workshop is a long, lean shop, filled with sweet smelling flora. The service is polite and, if requested, they'll gather up a bouquet for delivery anywhere in Hong Kong.

# Food & drink

## Bakeries & pâtisseries

### The Bagel Factory

*Shop B2, 41 Elgin Street, Central, HK Island (2951 0755). Mid-Levels Escalator/26 bus.* **Open** 8am-9pm Tue-Sun. **Credit** (over HK$100) AmEx, MC, V. **Map** p66 B3.

The compact Bagel Factory serves up every kind of bagel imaginable. Choose from a wealth of cream cheeses, as well as fillings like tuna and chicken salad. There are a few tables around the shop's tiny seating area, so customers can either eat in or take out.

### SoHo Bakery

*Shop B1, 41 Elgin Street, Central, HK Island (2810 7111). Mid-Levels Escalator/26 bus.* **Open** 8am-9pm Tue-Sun. **Credit** (over HK$100) AmEx, MC, V. **Map** p66 B3.

Under the same ownership and roof as its neighbour the Bagel Factory, the SoHo Bakery supplies a fine range of cakes and pâtisserie, as well as the likes of chocolate marble cookies and apple pie.

## Chocolate & confectioners

### Frais

*11 Lyndhurst Terrace, Central, HK Island (2581 2885). Central MTR (exit D1, D2, G)/Mid-Levels Escalator/12M, 13, 23A, 40M, 43 bus.* **Open** 7.30am-7.30pm Mon-Sat; 10am-6pm Sun. **Credit** MC, V. **Map** p66 C3.

Frais specializes in delicious Belgium chocolates, and also does a tasty sideline in pastries and cakes. At HK$68 per 100g, though, the chocs don't come cheap.

### Godiva

*Shop 309-310, Lee Gardens, Hysan Avenue, Causeway Bay, HK Island (2907 4818). Causeway Bay MTR (exit F).* **Open** 10.30am-8pm Mon-Sat; noon-7pm Sun. **Credit** AmEx, MC, V. **Map** p80 D2.

The Belgian chocolatier Godiva dishes up the crème de la crème of chocolates in Hong Kong. The assortment of sweet stuff is heady, while prices are equally disconcerting.

## Coffee & tea

### Pacific Coffee Company

*Star Ferry Pier, Central, HK Island (2537 1484). Central MTR (exit A)/buses to Central Star Ferry Pier/Central Star Ferry Pier.* **Open** 7.30am-9pm Mon-Sat; 9am-7pm Sun **Credit** DC, MC, V. **Map** p67 E3.

There are so many Pacific Coffee outlets in Hong Kong that it's worth popping in to pick up a location card listing all their addresses if you're a fan. They'll often do snacks alongside their 'to go' coffees and will happily grind you a big bag of beans from their selection. Some branches have Internet access.

## Delicatessens

### Oliver's Delicatessen

*Shop 233, 2/F, Prince's Building, 10 Chater Road, Central, HK Island (2810 7710). Central MTR (exit J1, J2, J3)/buses & trams through Central/Central Star Ferry Pier.* **Open** 9am-8pm daily. **Credit** MC, V. **Map** p67 E4.

If you're after some good old European tucker, this is the place for you – Oliver's food shelves are stocked with food that is hard to find elsewhere. It also has tempting meat, fish, cheese, salad and pâtisserie counters.

## Health & organic food

### Green Cottage Shop & Co-op

*15A Main Street, Yung Shue Wan, Lamma (2982 6934). Yung Shue Wan Ferry Pier.* **Open** 11am-6pm Mon-Sat; 8am-7.30pm Sun. **Credit** MC, V.

It's only recently that people have begun to sit up and take notice of organic foodstuffs in Hong Kong. This little Lamma store prides itself on being as close to pesticide-free as you can get, which is about 80%. They have organic wine, iced Earl Grey tea and tasty sandwiches, all served with courtesy.

## Supermarkets

### Indian Provisions Store

*18 Spring Garden Lane, Wan Chai, HK Island (2572 7725). Wan Chai MTR (exit A3)/buses along Queen's Road East & Hennessy Road.* **Open** 8am-7pm daily. **No credit cards. Map** p80 B2.

Indian Provisions Store has the most extensive assortment of spices in town, stocking herbs and seasonings from Malaysia, Thailand, and of course, India. There are also a full range of other goodies you'll need to make the perfect curry.

### Park 'n' Shop

*G/F, Manning House, 38-48 Queen's Road,*
*Central, HK Island (2526 7164). Central MTR*
*(exit D1, D2, G)/buses along Queen's Road Central.*
**Open** 8am-9pm daily. **Credit** AmEx, MC, V.
**Map** p67 D3.

The biggest problem with Hong Kong's supermarkets is the selection of food, which lies somewhere between Chinese and American. But if you fancy turning out a proper stir fry or sampling some microwave dim sum, then Park 'n' Shop's the place. Don't expect much in the way of service, though.

### Wellcome

*Basement, The Landmark, 16 Des Voeux Road,*
*Central, HK Island (2529 8266). Central MTR*
*(exit B, C, E, G)/buses & trams through Central/*
*Central Star Ferry Pier.* **Open** 8am-8pm daily.
**Credit** AmEx, MC, V. **Map** p67 D4.

Much like its rival, Park 'n' Shop, Wellcome offers a mix of foods catering for local tastes. Several of the larger outlets also have excellent sushi counters.
**Branch**: 50 Stanley Street, Central, HK Island
(2849 7303).

## Tea

### Fook Ming Tong Tea Shop

*G3-4, The Landmark, 16 Des Voeux Road, Central,*
*HK Island (2521 0337/www.fookmingtong.com).*
*Central MTR (exit G)/buses & trams along Des Voeux*
*Road Central.* **Open** 10am-7.30pm Mon-Sat; 11am-
6pm Sun. **Credit** AmEx, DC, MC, V. **Map** p67 D4.

The people at Fook Ming Tong are accommodating, amicable and ready to help you with your every tea whim. They'll not only grant on-the-spot tastings, but they stock the most remarkable array of tea leaves. These can be pricey – 300g of Silver Needle Tea, which originates from China's Fujian Province, costs a scary HK$620, while 100g of Chrysanthemum Tea is a rather more accessible HK$50.
**Branches**: Shop 124, 1/F Ocean Terminal, Canton Road, Tsim Sha Tsui, Kowloon (2735 1077); B2, Sogo Department Store, 555 Hennessy Road, Causeway Bay, HK Island (2834 9978); Unit 24, Departure Hall, Hong Kong International Airport, Chek Lap Kok (2121 8180).

### Moon Garden Tea House

*5 Hoi Ping Road, Causeway Bay, HK Island (2882*
*6878). Causeway Bay MTR (exit F)/8X, 10, 26, 63,*
*108 bus.* **Open** noon-midnight daily. **Credit** AmEx,
DC, MC, V. **Map** p80 D2.

A tea drinker's dream. Not only does it run a course in tea testing (aimed at visitors), but also stocks an excellent selection of leaves for sale, such as the ever popular jasmine, rose and Chinese green tea.

## Wine, beers & spirits

### Watson's Wine Cellar

*36 Queen's Road, Central, HK Island (2147 3641).*
*Central MTR (exit D1, D2, G)/buses along Queen's*
*Road Central.* **Open** 8am-9pm daily. **Credit** AmEx,
MC, V. **Map** p67 D3.

Watson's Wine Cellar stocks a great selection of wines from around the world, as well as beers, spirits and liqueurs.
**Branches** throughout the city.

## Gifts & souvenirs

For **Shanghai Tang**, *see p189.*

### Chinese Arts & Crafts

*Star House, 3 Salisbury Road, Tsim Sha Tsui,*
*Kowloon (2735 4061). Tsim Sha Tsui MTR (exit*
*E)/buses to Tsim Sha Tsui Star Ferry Pier & along*
*Salisbury Road/Tsim Sha Tsui Star Ferry Pier.*
**Open** 10am-9.30pm daily. **Credit** AmEx, DC, MC, V.
**Map** p98 B3.

If you're looking for Chinese gifts to take home – antiques, linens, clothes, jewellery, this is a great one-stop destination. The jewellery section is one of the best in town, with an extensive collection of pearls, jade, precious and semi-precious stones, all at very reasonable prices. The shop also sells bags and embroidered goods, which are incredibly cheap considering the intricate workmanship involved.

### Craft Inn

*56 Main Street, Yung Shue Wan, Lamma*
*(2982 2120). Yung Shue Wan Ferry Pier.*
**Open** 11am-6pm daily. **Credit** AmEx, MC, V.
**Map** p126.

If you venture across the water to Lamma island, the Craft Inn is worth checking out. It's a small outlet that stocks wonderful Asian trinkets, jewellery, lampshades, mirrors and cards.

### Just Gold

*27A Nathan Road, Tsim Sha Tsui, Kowloon*
*(2312 1120). Tsim Sha Tsui MTR (exit E)/*
*buses along Nathan Road/Tsim Sha Tsui*
*Star Ferry Pier.* **Open** 11am-8pm Mon-Thur;
11am-8.30pm Fri-Sun. **Credit** AmEx, DC, MC, V.
**Map** p98 C2.

If yellow gold is your passion, this is the place for you – Just Gold produces everything from earrings to gifts in the metal, and at reasonable prices.

### King & Country

*Shop 362, Level 3, Pacific Place, 88 Queensway,*
*Admiralty, HK Island (2525 8603). Admiralty MTR*
*(exit C1)/buses through Central.* **Open** 10.30am-8pm
Mon-Sat; 11am-7pm Sun. **Credit** AmEx, DC, MC, V.
**Map** p67 F5.

Beautifully wrought Victorian-style model soldiers and scenarios. Heaven for grown up little boys.

### Mountain Folkcraft

*12 Wo On Lane, Central, HK Island (2525 3199).*
*Central MTR (exit D1)/12M, 13, 23A, 40M, 43 bus.*
**Open** 9.30am-6.30pm Mon-Sat. **Credit** AmEx, DC,
MC, V. **Map** p66 C4.

A favourite for many, Mountain Folkcraft is a tiny Aladdin's cave of a store, hidden from the bedlam of Central's busier streets, close to Lan Kwai Fong. Inside, you'll discover knick-knacks and ornaments from all over Asia.

## My House

*57 Yung Shue Wan Main Street, Lamma (8105 0044). Yung Shue Wan Ferry Pier.* **Open** 12.30-7.30pm Mon, Wed-Sun. **Credit** (over HK$200) MC, V. **Map** p126.

While My House sells hoards of kiddies' toys and accessories, it also offers a clutter of girlie bits and bobs, such as pin-boards, mirrors, ornaments and more. The staff are friendly, prices are reasonable, and stock is especially cutesy and cool, although the shop floor does feel rather too manicured.

## Oriental Crafts

*Room B, G/F, 53-55 Hollywood Road, Central, HK Island (2541 8840). Central MTR (exit D1, D2, G)/ Mid-Levels Escalator/12M, 13, 23A, 26, 40M, 43 bus.* **Open** 10am-6pm daily. **Credit** AmEx, MC, V. **Map** p66 C3.

For a gift with a difference, stop by Oriental Crafts. This tiny, jumbled shop deals (allegedly) in mammoth – as in the extinct animal –carvings. All kinds of sizes and shapes are on offer, from minute ornaments to gigantic carved boats laden by a crew of spindly skeletons.

## Vincent Sum Collection

*15 Lyndhurst Terrace, Central, HK Island (2542 2610). Central MTR (exit D1, D2, G)/Mid-Levels Escalator/12M, 13, 23A, 40M, 43 bus.* **Open** 10am-6.30pm Mon-Sat. **Credit** AmEx, DC, MC, V. **Map** p66 C3.

Vincent Sum's shop has been around for 20 years. It stocks Thai silks, Indonesian ornaments and Indian imported goods at very reasonable prices.

## Wah Tung China Ltd

*59 Hollywood Road, Central, HK Island (no phone). Central MTR (exit D1, D2, G)/Mid-Levels Escalator/ 12M, 13, 23A, 26, 40M, 43 bus.* **Open** 10am-6.30pm Mon-Sat; 11am-6pm Sun. **Credit** AmEx, DC, MC, V. **Map** p66 C3.

One of the leading reproducers of ceramics in Hong Kong, Wah Tung China has a superb range of exquisite porcelain, in all sorts of styles and size. And they're so well-made, it's impossible for the amateur to tell the difference between a copy and the real thing.

## Welfare Handicrafts

*Shop 7, Basement, Jardine House, 1 Connaught Road, Central, HK Island (2524 3356). Central MTR (exit J3)/buses to Central Star Ferry Pier/ Central Star Ferry Pier.* **Open** 9.30am-5.30pm Mon-Fri; 9.30am-1.30pm Sat. **No credit cards**. **Map** p67 E3.

Welfare Handicrafts is a charity organisation. Its outlets, for a small fee, work as an agent to charities selling crafts for funds. Most of the goods on sale, such as napkin holders, purses, and decorations, come from the Philippines, although there's also some merchandise on offer from China and Hong Kong.

**Branch**: The Red House, Salisbury Road, Tsim Sha Tsui, Kowloon (2366 6979).

## The Body Shop

*Shop B28, The Landmark, 16 Des Voeux Road, Central, HK Island (2525 5100). Central MTR (exit B, C, E, G)/buses & trams through Central/Central Star Ferry Pier.* **Open** 10am-8pm Mon-Sat; 11am-7pm Sun. **Credit** AmEx, DC, MC, V. **Map** p67 D4.

The Body Shop franchise appeared in Hong Kong in the late 1980s and now has several branches scattered through the city. Just as in other countries around the world, it promotes fair trade and recycleable containers.

**Branches**: G/F, Wing Lok Building, 14 Peking Road, Tsim Sha Tsui, Kowloon (2367 8230); Shop 33A, Carnarvon Road, Tsim Sha Tsui, Kowloon (2369 4777); Shop 121, Pacific Place, 88 Queensway, Admiralty, HK Island (2537 7072); Shop C& D, 51 Sai Yeung Choi Street, Mong Kok, Kowloon (2380 7134).

## Crabtree & Evelyn

*Shop 245, Pacific Place, 88 Queensway, Admiralty, HK Island (2523 8668). Admiralty MTR (exit C1)/ buses through Central.* **Open** 10am-8pm daily. **Credit** AmEx, DC, MC, V. **Map** p67 F5.

Sweet smelling products, including a sumptuous range of bubble baths, home fragrances and skin care goodies.

## Icon

*Hang Lung Centre, Great George Street, Causeway Bay, HK Island (2881 7333). Causeway Bay MTR (exit E)/buses along Hennessy Road.* **Open** 11am-10.30pm daily. **Credit** AmEx, DC, MC, V. **Map** p80 D1.

You can try out the products to your heart's content (without prying staff) at this cut-price cosmetics megastore, resembling an airport duty-free shop.

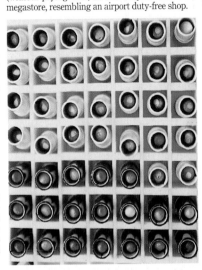

**Rainbow Cosmetic.** *See p198.*

## Professional Hair Products

*49A Wellington Street, Central, HK Island (2536 0603). Central MTR (exit D1, D2, G)/12M, 13, 23A, 40M, 43 bus.* **Open** 10am-8pm Mon-Sat. **No credit cards. Map** p66 C3.

Stocks a fantastic collection of hair care goods for stylists and ordinary punters. If you're planning to do an at-home dye job and aren't sure where to start, the staff here will set you straight.

## Rainbow Cosmetic

*Shop 3, Tem Plaza, 5 Cameron Road, Tsim Sha Tsui, Kowloon (2724 8804). Tsim Sha Tsui MTR (exit B2)/buses along Nathan Road.* **Open** 10am-10.30pm daily. **Credit** AmEx, DC, MC, V. **Map** p98 C1.

Over the past few years, a number of 'cosmetic companies' have appeared across Hong Kong at a surprising rate, but they're not your average beauty outlet, selling the usual brands in a well structured setting. They tend to be cluttered shops like Rainbow, which has everything from upmarket perfumes to the free samples you'd be handed in big department stores. The good news is that prices are low and the brands are the real thing.
**Branches:** Parker House, Queen's Road, Central, HK Island (2526 4099); 518 Lockhart Road, Causeway Bay, HK Island (2573 8282); 10 Kai Chiu Road, Causeway Bay, HK Island (2576 6287).

## Sasa Cosmetic Company

*62 Queen's Road, Central, HK Island (2521 2928). Central MTR (exit D1, D2, G)/buses along Queen's Road Central.* **Open** 9.30am-8.30pm daily. **Credit** AmEx, DC, MC, V. **Map** p66 C3.

Rainbow's major rival Sasa, with similar low prices and a wide range of merchandise, is fast taking over Hong Kong's cosmetics market – the number of outlets is staggering. Although some of the brands and lines may be limited or out of stock, all is forgiven when you see the drastically reduced prices.
**Branches:** 180 Nathan Road, Tsim Sha Tsui, Kowloon (2366 1033); see telephone directory for other branches.

## Shu Uemura Beauty Boutique

*Shop 204, Ocean Centre, 5 Canton Road, Tsim Sha Tsui, Kowloon (2735 1767). Tsim Sha Tsui MTR (exit C1, E)/buses along Canton Road/Tsim Sha Tsui Star Ferry Pier.* **Open** 10.30am-7.30pm Mon-Sat; 12.30-6pm Sun. **Credit** AmEx, DC, MC, V. **Map** p98 A2.

Shu Uemura's range of brushes and make-up is any girl's dream. This place is like a paint box dedicated to beautifying oneself, but the prices will strain the average wallet.
**Branch:** Shop B25, The Landmark, 16 Des Voeux Road, Central, HK Island (2845 3987).

## Interiors, furniture & fabrics

There are a number of fabric shops on Bowring Street, close to Jordan MTR and just off Nathan Road in Kowloon.

## Altfield Home

*220-221 Prince's Building, 10 Chater Road, Central, HK Island (2524 7526). Central MTR (exit H)/buses & trams through Central.* **Open** 10am-7pm Mon-Sat; 11am-5pm Sun. **Credit** AmEx, MC, V. **Map** p67 E4.

Dedicated to soft furnishings, Altfield promises to make your home into a cosy fantasy comfort zone. It also has a wide collection of lamps and lights, elegant cushions and reproduction furniture.

## Altfield Interiors

*223-225 Prince's Building, 10 Chater Road, Central, HK Island (2525 2738). Central MTR (exit H)/buses & trams through Central.* **Open** 10am-7pm Mon-Sat. **Credit** AmEx, MC, V. **Map** p67 E4.

Altfield Interiors is a friendly, well groomed outlet that specialises in fabrics, especially silks. It has a great tableware section with wonderful linen tablecloths. And if you're after a real touch of class, Altfield can print personalised stationery for you.

## Aluminium

*G/F, Shop 1B, Capitol Plaza, 2-10 Lyndhurst Terrace, Central, HK Island (2546 5904). Central MTR (exit D1, D2, G)/Mid-Levels Escalator/12M, 13, 23A, 40M, 43 bus.* **Open** 12.30-8pm Mon-Sat; 1-6pm Sun. **Credit** AmEx, MC, V. **Map** p66 C3.

Aluminium, which recently moved to its present location from Lan Kwai Fong, stocks some of the coolest furniture and PC accessories around (imported from Europe). It covers a colourful, space age, 1970s-esque range. If you're looking for an allusive bubble chair or a JVC Videosphere TV, this is where you'll find it.

## Banyan Tree

*2/F, 214-218 Prince's Building, 10 Chater Road, Central, HK Island (2523 5561). Central MTR (exit H)/buses & trams through Central/Central Star Ferry Pier.* **Open** 10.30am-6.30pm Mon-Sat; noon-5.30pm Sun. **Credit** AmEx, DC, MC, V. **Map** p67 E4.

Banyan Tree sells Asian furniture and accessories. While the service is friendly and helpful, the goods on offer are far from spectacular – you've probably seen most of them a thousand times before.

## Graham 32

*32 Graham Street, Central, HK Island (2815 5188). Mid-Levels Escalator/26 bus.* **Open** 11am-8pm Mon-Fri; 11am-7.30pm Sat; noon-6pm Sun. **Credit** AmEx, MC, V. **Map** p66 C3.

This recently opened outlet is one of the most classy and sophisticated shops in Hong Kong. Promoted as a style concept store, it sells hip homewares, such as dining collections and tableware, as well as a small line of easy-to-wear, around-the-house wear.

## Ito Futon

*6/F, 64-66 Wellington Street, Central, HK Island (2845 1138). Central MTR (exit D1, D2, G)/12M, 13, 23A, 40M, 43 bus.* **Open** 10am-7pm Mon-Sat. **Credit** AmEx, MC, V. **Map** p66 C3.

No matter what size, status or colour you want your futon, Ito Futon will have one for you. It also does a funky line in bed covers and Japanese lights.

### Kinari

*3-5 Old Bailey Street, Central, HK Island (2869 6827). Mid-Levels Escalator/12M, 13, 23A, 26, 40M, 43 bus.* **Open** *10am-7.30pm Mon-Sat.* **Credit** *AmEx, MC, V.* **Map** *p66 C4.*
Kinari is an Aladdin's cave of a store, stocking a wide range of products imported from Thailand and Burma. Ornate carved wooden pieces, big beds, silver Buddhas and lacquered boxes cover the shop's floor like a three dimensional carpet. However, such riches come with a high price tag.

### Tequila Kola

*Horizon Plaza, 2 Lee Wing Street, Ap Lei Chau Ind. Estate, Ap Lei Chau, HK Island (2877 3295). Bus 90B, 590.* **Open** *10am-7pm Mon-Fri; 10am-6pm Sat; noon-5pm Sun.* **Credit** *AmEx, DC, MC, V.*
Since Tequila Kola opened in the early 1990s, it has acquired a dedicated cluster of rich clients. It stocks an extensive, and expensive, melange of furniture, such as ancient teak tables, TV cabinets, great wrought iron beds and trendy mirrors.

## Music

### HMV

*1/F, Central Building, 1 Pedder Street, Central, HK Island (2739 0268). Central MTR (exit D1, G)/buses through Central/Central Star Ferry Pier.* **Open** *9am-10pm daily.* **Credit** *AmEx, DC, MC, V.* **Map** *p67 D4.*
This mega music store sells everything and anything in watching and listening form. Prices of CDs are comparable to those in the US, and cheaper than in Europe. And magazines here are almost half the price of those on sale in bookshops and at newsstands. The Tsim Sha Tsui branch is the largest.
**Branches:** 1/F, Windsor House, 311 Gloucester Road, Causeway Bay, HK Island (2504 3669); G/F-4/F, Sands Building, 12 Peking Road, Tsim Sha Tsui, Kowloon (2302 0122); Shop 408D, Level 4, New Town Plaza, Phase 1, Sha Tin, New Territories (2602 3931).

### Tower Records

*Shop 731, 7/F, Times Square, 1 Matheson Street, Causeway Bay, HK Island (2506 0811). Causeway Bay MTR (exit A)/63, 108, 117, 170, N170 bus.* **Open** *10am-10pm daily.* **Credit** *AmEx, MC, V.* **Map** *p80 D2.*
The only Tower Records outlet in Hong Kong, like its sister stores worldwide, stocks every kind of CD, from popular pop to classy classical.

## Opticians & eyewear

### Optical 88

*17 Cameron Road, Tsim Sha Tsui, Kowloon (2367 3200). Tsim Sha Tsui MTR (exit A1)/buses along Canton Road/Tsim Sha Tsui Star Ferry Pier.* **Open** *10.30am-9.30pm daily.* **Credit** *AmEx, DC, MC, V.* **Map** *p98 C1.*
This big, bright shop has opticians on hand to assess you, and assistants to see to all your eyewear needs.
**Branch:** Shop 105, Level 1, Man Yee Arcade, 50-58 Des Voeux Road, Central, HK Island (2259 5188).

### The Optical Shop

*6/F, China Building, 29 Queen's Road, Central, HK Island (2810 6022). Central MTR (exit D1, D2, G)/buses along Queen's Road Central.* **Open** *9am-7.30pm Mon-Sat; 10am-7pm Sun.* **Credit** *AmEx, DC, MC, V.* **Map** *p67 D4.*
The Optical Shop will happily test your eyes and equip you with a funky pair of bifocals, or comfy contacts. But if this is all too bright for you and doesn't suit your style, they've also got a choice collection of sunglasses on sale – DKNY, Calvin Klein, Gucci, Ray Ban, etc.
**Branch:** Shop 108, Pacific Place, 88 Queensway, Admiralty, HK Island (2845 9442).

### Senses Optik

*1/F, 28 Wellington Street, Central, HK Island (2869 5111). Central MTR (exit D1, D2, G)/12M, 13, 23A, 40M, 43 bus.* **Open** *10am-8.30pm Mon-Sat; 11am-6pm Sun.* **Credit** *AmEx, DC, MC, V.* **Map** *p66 C3.*
The Senses Optik assistants will test your eyes and kit you out with a classy pair of glasses. Alternatively, if the sun's making you squint, pick up a pair of sunglasses from the large range on offer, which run the gamut from designer to standard.

## Pharmacies

### New Pharmacy

*55 Queen's Road, Central, HK Island (2868 1038). Central MTR (exit D1, D2, G)/buses along Queen's Road Central.* **Open** *9am-7pm Mon-Sat; 9am-5pm Sun.* **Credit** *AmEx, MC, V.* **Map** *p67 D3.*
If all chemists were like this, no one would ever visit the doctor. Whatever your needs, New Pharmacy sells it, including the contraceptive pill, sleeping tablets and pain killers. The pharmacists aren't bad on simple advice, either.

### Watson's

*G/F, Melbourne Plaza, 33 Queen's Road, Central, HK Island (2523 0666). Central MTR (exit D1, D2, G)/buses along Queen's Road Central.* **Open** *9am-9pm daily.* **Credit** *AmEx, DC, MC, V.* **Map** *p67 D3.*

Ethnic treasures at **Kinari**.

**Eat, Drink, Shop**

Watson's is a mega-store of a chemist, with lots of outlets located throughout the region – check the telephone directory for your nearest store. It sells a wide range of hair products and designer make-up, and has an adequate drug counter with helpful staff.

# Photography & film processing

Stanley Street in Central has many reputable, competitive dealers. For **Fortress**, *see p186*.

### Color Point Photo Company
*140 Wellington Street, Central, HK Island (2805 2513). Sheung Wan MTR (exit E2)/buses along Queen's Road Central.* **Open** 9.30am-7pm Mon-Sat. **No credit cards.** **Map** p66 C3.
Color Point has been around for many years – it develops film and stocks a limited range of photographic accessories.

### Hing Lee Camera Company
*25 Lyndhurst Terrace, Central, HK Island (2544 7593). Central MTR (exit D1, D2, G)/Mid-Levels Escalator/12M, 13, 23A, 40M, 43 bus.* **Open** 9.30am-7pm Mon-Sat. **No credit cards.** **Map** p66 C3.
If you buy a camera in Tsim Sha Tsui, you're likely to be ripped off. Hing Lee Camera, on the other hand, will sell you guaranteed stock at a good price. The staff laid-back, honest and helpful.

### Union Photo Supplies
*13 Queen Victoria Street, Central, HK Island (2526 6281). Central MTR (exit B)/buses & trams through Central.* **Open** 9.30am-6pm Mon-Sat. **Credit** MC, V. **Map** p66 C4.
A pristine store that oozes professionalism. Its stock is extensive and well priced, while the staff are abrasively helpful, and won't rip you off.

## Shoes

### Ming Kee
*30 Bowring Street, Jordan, Kowloon (2730 4815) Jordan MTR (exit C1, C2)/buses along Nathan Road.* **Open** 11am-9pm Mon-Sat. **No credit cards.** **Map** p110 A5.
This is where local pop and movie stars have their glitzy shoes made. Orders normally take two weeks, but a rush job can be done in ten days. Bring a sketch or picture of the shoe you want copied. Prices start at HK$650, depending on the design.

### Millie's
*Shop 13, G/F, Central Building, 1 Pedder Street, Central, HK Island (2523 8001). Central MTR (exit D1, G)/buses & trams through Central/Central Star Ferry Pier.* **Open** 10am-8pm Mon-Sat; 10am-7pm Sun. **Credit** AmEx, DC, MC, V. **Map** p67 D4.
Millie's, which has been around since the 1960s, stocks a decent collection of Italian shoes and handbags. Prices are sweet and the designs flatter any modern man or woman.

### Nine West
*Shop 11-12, Central Building, 1 Pedder Street, Central, HK Island (2921 2628). Central MTR (exit D1, G)/buses & trams through Central/ Central Star Ferry Pier.* **Open** 9.30am-7.30pm daily. **Credit** AmEx, DC, MC, V. **Map** p67 D4.
Having conquered the US market and subsequently set up shop in the UK, Nine West has become every gal's favourite shoe shop. In fact, most swear by its styles and fair pricing. If you're lucky enough to be around during the sales, the store often reduces its prices by more than half.

## Sport

### Marathon Sports
*Shop 125, Pacific Place, 88 Queensway, Admiralty, HK Island (2524 6992). Admiralty MTR (exit C1)/ buses through Central.* **Open** 10am-9pm daily. **Credit** AmEx, DC, MC, V. **Map** p67 F5.
There are almost 30 Marathon Sports outlets across Hong Kong and the New Territories. The Pacific Place shop is one of the longest established, and specialises in trainers. Brands such as Puma, Adidas, Converse and Diesel are sold alongside a small line of sports clothing and accessories.

### Running Bare
*Shop 1, G/F, Wyndham Mansion, 32 Wyndham Street, Central, HK Island (2526 0620). Central MTR (exit D1, G)/13, 26, 43 bus.* **Open** 11am-7pm Mon-Sat. **Credit** AmEx, DC, MC, V. **Map** p66 C4.
Having already built up a string of clients selling sportswear from her flat, Lynn Fong Boseley decided to open this tiny store in Central. It sells her own label, plus Wahini bikinis and the Rival range.

## Tobacconists

### Cohiba Cigar Divan
*East Lobby, Mandarin Oriental Hotel, 5 Connaught Road, Central, HK Island (2825 4074). Central MTR (exit F)/buses to Central Star Ferry Pier/Central Star Ferry Pier.* **Open** 10am-9pm Mon-Sat; noon-6pm Sun. **Credit** AmEx, DC, MC, V. **Map** p67 E3.
You don't need to be a genius to realise that this is the place to pick up a Cohiba or two. Sleek and sweet smelling, the service in the divan is charming – staff have been known to offer clients an espresso while choosing their Cohiban delight.

### Davidoff
*Peninsula Hotel Lobby, Salisbury Road, Tsim Sha Tsui, Kowloon (2368 5774). Tsim Sha Tsui MTR (exit E)/buses to Tsim Sha Tsui Star Ferry Pier & along Salisbury Road/Tsim Sha Tsui Star Ferry Pier.* **Open** 10am-8pm daily. **Credit** AmEx, DC, MC, V. **Map** p98 B3.
Davidoff sells all sorts of cigars and, if you're not sure which ones to splash out on, the staff will be happy to help you make an informed choice. But be warned, none is exactly cheap.

# Break for the border: Shenzhen

Few settlements in China have experienced the sort of transformation that **Shenzhen** has over the past 25 or so years. This one-time farming village on the border with the New Territories was designated a Special Economic Zone in the 1970s, set up in deliberate competition with the then British colony. Today, Shenzhen is one of the most unrestrained and irrepressible industrial and commercial cities in China.

You wouldn't come here for its sights (although there are a number of cheesy theme parks), but Hong Kong's hardcore shoppers know that Shenzhen offers far superior bargains to anything that can be found south of the border.

Most of the stores in Shenzhen are located very near the rail station, which means they're very easy to find. The biggest of the malls is **Lowu Commercial Centre**, a mecca of shops with floors and floors of goodies, like copy bags, shoes, electrical appliances and watches. When buying, bargaining is a must. With a little skill, you can expect to cut prices by more than half in most cases.

Other than buying cheap goods, another reason for the steady influx of consumers to Shenzhen is the selection of skilful tailors, most of whom are located in the malls.

These guys can make most garments within a week, at exceedingly low prices. For example, a pair of made-to-measure trousers will only set you back around HK$60, not including the fabric. With all this in mind, you may decide to spend more than a day in Shenzhen. Most of the hotels here are relatively new, and fairly classy, although once you've got all your shopping done, there's not much else to do in the city.

## Practicalities

You will need a visa to enter Shenzhen from Hong Kong. These take about a week to process from the **China Visa Office** in Wan Chai. However, it can be quicker and cheaper to ask a travel agent to get the visa for you. Once you've got the necessary paperwork, it's fairly easy to get to Shenzhen by MTR and KCR – changing lines at Kowloon Tong station. The border is extremely busy, especially at weekends, so travel on a weekday if at all possible.

Once in Shenzhen, you are advised to change your Hong Kong dollars for renminbi (RMB), at an exchange rate of approximately HK$1 to RMB 1.06. Although almost all the stores do accept HK dollars, they will not give you change for the exact dollar difference.

## Toys, games & magic

### Mothercare

*338-339 Prince's Building, Central, HK Island (2523 5704). Central MTR (exit H)/buses & trams through Central.* **Open** 10am-7pm Mon-Sat; 10am-5pm Sun. **Credit** AmEx, DC, MC, V. **Map** p67 E4.

Like its sister stores worldwide, Mothercare in Hong Kong stocks all a child needs, from nappies, bibs and dummies to toys, all of which are well-designed, well-made and safety tested. A must for mums.

### Toys 'R' Us

*B/F, Shop 032, Ocean Terminal, Tsim Sha Tsui, Kowloon (2730 9462). Tsim Sha Tsui MTR (exit C1, E)/buses along Chatham Road South.* **Open** 10am-9pm daily. **Credit** AmEx, MC, V. **Map** p98 A3.

This huge international toy emporium is every kid's dream. Along its aisles, you'll find children's clothes, toys, games and sporting goods.

## Watches

### City Chain

*24 Des Voeux Road, Central, HK Island (2525 5259). Central MTR (exit B, C)/buses & trams through Central.* **Open** 10am-8pm daily. **Credit** AmEx, DC, MC, V. **Map** p67 D3.

There's a City Chain watch outlet on almost every street corner in Hong Kong, selling standard watches, such as Seiko, Adidas, Cat and Esprit. Don't expect anything from the service.

### Eldorado Watch Co Ltd

*Peter Building, 60 Queen's Road, Central, HK Island (2522 7155/2526 8826). Central MTR (exit D1, D2, G)/buses along Queen's Road Central.* **Open** 10am-6pm daily. **Credit** AmEx, DC, MC, V. **Map** p67 D3.

Eldorado is a gigantic store that oozes elegance and sells chic, sleek watches. As well as being the official agent for Omega in Hong Kong, it also offers Cartier, Ebel and Rolex timepieces.

### Masterpiece (by King Fook)

*Shop 216-217, Level 2, Pacific Place, 88 Queensway, Admiralty, HK Island (2845 6766). Admiralty MTR (exit C1)/buses through Central.* **Open** 10.30am-8pm Mon-Sat; 11.30am-8pm Sun. **Credit** AmEx, DC, MC, V. **Map** p67 F5.

Major brands of watch are dispensed with a smile at Masterpiece's two stores.

**Branch**: Shop 21, Central Building, 1-3 Pedder Street, Central, HK Island (2526 6733).

Eat, Drink, Shop

Some of the cheaper items on sale at Yau Ma Tei's **Jade Market**. *See p194.*

Eat, Drink, Shop

# Arts & Entertainment

| | |
|---|---|
| By Season | 204 |
| Children | 209 |
| Film | 215 |
| Galleries | 220 |
| Gay & Lesbian | 223 |
| Nightlife | 228 |
| Performing Arts | 238 |
| Sport & Fitness | 247 |

## Feature boxes

| | |
|---|---|
| Hong Kong Arts Festival | 207 |
| **HK walks** Jungles, concrete & otherwise | 210 |
| The best stuff for kids | 212 |
| Location: Hong Kong | 216 |
| Top ten HK films | 218 |
| Bruce & Jackie | 219 |
| Cruise zones | 225 |
| Local mixmasters | 231 |
| Canto-pop | 232 |
| **HK profiles** Melvis | 234 |
| Everybody salsa! | 237 |
| Local heroes | 240 |
| Chinese performing arts | 242 |
| Hong Kong beaches | 250 |
| Hong Kong Sevens | 252 |

# By Season

The best international sport and arts events, and a wealth of traditional festivals.

From a Taoist village bun festival to the best of international cinema, from endurance hikes on pristine mountain trails to dragon boats racing across the harbour, from autumn moonlit picnics to a string of performing arts festivals, Hong Kong offers a range of events that is exhilarating and dizzying in variety.

Like Hong Kong itself, the territory's calendar of events and festivals is densely crowded, brimming with contrasts and wonderfully cross-cultural. A good place to find detailed information about Hong Kong's traditional and seasonal events is the Hong Kong Tourism Board's website (www.DiscoverHongKong.com).

Traditional Chinese festivals are major highlights of the year and at times such as Chinese New Year, visitors are able to experience the rare pleasure of seeing Hong Kongers relax. Many of Hong Kong's traditional Chinese festivals are rich and poetic celebrations linked to the lunar calendar and dedicated to renewal, ancestral worship and ancient rural folklore. Although some of these festivals are celebrated with equal gusto in other parts of the Chinese world, others, such as the Cheung Chau Bun Festival are unique to Hong Kong.

Hong Kong also celebrates a number of Western holidays, and Christmas, Boxing Day, New Year, Good Friday and Easter Monday are all public holidays. The calendar is dotted with a number of annual artistic, cultural and sporting events. The Hong Kong Arts Festival, the City Festival and Hong Kong International Film Festival form an impressive cultural season at the beginning of the year, while annual football, tennis, running and horse racing events bring the year to an exciting close.

## Spring

### Credit Suisse First Boston Hong Kong Rugby Sevens

*Hong Kong Stadium, 55 Eastern Hospital Road, So Kon Po, Causeway Bay, HK Island (2504 8311/ www.hksevens.com.hk). Bus 5B.* **Date** 3 days late Mar/early Apr. **Tickets** *3-day* HK$750; HK$250 concessions. **Credit** AmEx, DC, MC, V. **Map** p80 E3.
The Hong Kong Sevens rugby tournament is the most prestigious leg of the International Rugby Board's World Sevens Series. See some of the world's finest players in action, and some wild partying from the fans. *See p252* **Hong Kong Sevens**.

### Birthday of Tin Hau

**Date** Apr/May (23rd day of the 3rd lunar month).
Tin Hau, the goddess of the sea, occupies a special place in the heart of the Harbour City. To celebrate her birthday, fishermen decorate their boats and head to temples dedicated to the goddess to pray for good catches during the coming year. Traditional birthday rites can seen at the Tin Hau Temple in Joss House Bay (in the eastern New Territories) and in the 40 other temples to Tin Hau around the territory. A birthday parade with colourful floats and lion dances also takes place in Yuen Long in the western New Territories. *See p94* **Tin Hau, sea goddess**.

### Christie's & Sotheby's auctions

**Christie's** *2203-5 Alexandra House, 16-20 Chater Road, Central, HK Island (2521 5396/enquiryhk@christies.com). Central MTR (exit J1, J2, J3)/buses & trams through Central/Central Star Ferry Pier.* **Open** 9.30am-6pm Mon-Fri. **Date** Apr, Oct. **Map** p67 E4.
**Sotheby's Hong Kong** *5/F, Standard Chartered Building, 4-4A Des Voeux Road, Central, HK Island (2524 8121/www.sothebys.com). Central MTR (exit H)/buses & trams through Central/Central Star Ferry Pier.* **Open** 9.30am-6pm Mon-Fri. **Date** Apr, Oct. **Map** p67 E4.
In spring and autumn, serious art collectors from around the world gather in Hong Kong to bid for treasures from the world's two great auction houses. Christie's and Sotheby's both showcase collections of Chinese art and ceramics, jewellery, fine wine and cigars. Auctions normally take place in a hotel but bidders are invited to look at catalogues in the Hong Kong offices of both auction houses.

### Hong Kong International Film Festival

*www.hkiff.org.hk.* **Date** 2 wks in Apr.
The best of oriental and occidental film-making is showcased in this enjoyable two-week festival (founded in 1977). Films are shown in venues around the city and are offered in four main categories: Hong Kong Panorama, Hong Kong Cinema Retrospective, Asian Cinema and World Cinema. A comprehensive festival programme booklet is available from URBTIX box offices from late February/early March. Advance postal bookings can be made to individual screenings about a month before the Festival, then the remaining seats are sold on a first-come, first-served basis through URBTIX box offices. Although screenings do sometimes sell out in advance, it is often possible to pick up single tickets for about HK$50 a few nights before a screening.

Arts & Entertainment

Children play a major role in the colourful **Cheung Chau Bun Festival**.

### Cheung Chau Bun Festival

**Date** 1 wk in Apr/May. **Map** p126.

The world's one and only bun festival takes place on the island of Cheung Chau. This week-long village festival is dedicated to peace, renewal and harmony and the dates of the festival are divined by Taoist priests (although locals note with a smile that the most colourful celebrations frequently coincide with a weekend, enabling more visitors to come to the island). During the festival, three 20-metre (66-foot) bamboo towers (representing Heaven, Earth and Man), studded with sweet buns, are raised in front of the Pak Tai Temple. The buns are stamped with auspicious pink symbols and are intended, some say, as offerings to the ghosts of pirates. In the past, young men scrambled up the towers in a mad race to collect the highest buns on each tower. This dash ended in 1978 when several people were injured scaling the towers, and nowadays buns are safely handed out to patiently queueing crowds. A highlight of the festival is a large procession that features 'floating' children who are (almost invisibly) carried on supporting poles that are hidden beneath their elaborate costumes.

### Le French May Festival of Arts

*www.frenchmay.com.* **Date** Apr-June.

This annual, approximately month-long celebration (though if often starts in April and ends in June) of all things Gallic is the biggest French festival in Asia. Expect an eclectic, high quality range of performers, shows, exhibitions and concerts across the territory.

## Summer

### Dragon Boat (Tuen Ng) Festival

**Date** June (5th day of the 5th lunar month).

The 2,000 year-old Dragon Boat ('Tuen Ng') Festival is one of Hong Kong's most exciting annual events. It features elaborately decorated 10-metre (33-foot) dragon boats with crews of 20 paddlers racing to the sounds of pounding drums and the screams of spectators. The festival commemorates the death of the popular Chinese national hero Qu Yuan, who drowned himself in protest at the corruption of the government in the 3rd century BC. Legend has it that as the hero threw himself into the river, the townspeople raced to rescue him, beating their drums to scare away fish and throwing dumplings into the sea to keep them from eating the martyr's body. Today, much enthusiastic eating of rice and meat dumplings wrapped in bamboo leaves commemorates this part of the story, while the races symbolise the attempt to rescue Qu Yuan. Dragon boat races can be seen at Aberdeen, Stanley, Sai Kung, Lamma and Lantau.

### Hungry Ghost Festival

**Date** mid/late Aug (for one lunar month).

This is the time of the year when the mouth of Hell opens and renegade spirits come looking for a place to stay. To keep spirits out of their houses, people leave offerings of food on the streets and burn paper money and gold. The festival is celebrated all over the territory but the older and more traditional neighbourhoods of Sheung Wan, Wan Chai and Cheung Chau village are fascinating places during the festival.

## Autumn

### Mid Autumn Festival

**Date** late Sept/early Oct.

As the northwest monsoon begins to cool Hong Kong, families and friends gather to watch the autumn full moon rise and to eat traditional lotus paste moon cakes. This lovely ritual commemorates a 14th-century uprising against the Mongols, when rebels slipped pieces of paper into 'moon' cakes that were then smuggled to compatriots. Six centuries

**Dragon Boat (Tuen Ng) Festival.** *See p205.*

after the uprising, the festival is a much more peaceful affair and Hong Kong's streets glow with lanterns in all shapes, sizes and colours. Mid Autumn Festival is a particularly exciting time for children, who are allowed to stay up late. Public transport runs all night and the celebration is followed by a public holiday. The most popular spots to light lanterns and picnic on moon cakes are Victoria Park, Repulse Bay, Cheung Chau's beaches and the Peak.

### National Day fireworks
**Date** 1 Oct.
To celebrate the founding of the People's Republic of China, Hong Kong puts on a spectacular fireworks display. Best viewing spots are the Tsim Sha Tsui esplanade and the much less crowded square in front of City Hall on Hong Kong Island.

### Hong Kong Chinese Arts Festival
**Date** Oct/Nov 2001 & 2003.
This three-week event held every two years showcases world-renowned artists and performing ensembles from mainland China, Taiwan, Hong Kong and overseas Chinese communities. The festival revolves around a theme and includes performances, workshops and seminars, free outdoor shows and exhibitions. Previous festivals have included exhibitions of traditional musical instruments, a Chinese music parade with professional performers and students, and a tribute to street opera. Venues include the Hong Kong Cultural Centre and New Territories town halls. Tickets range from about HK$80 to HK$200 (available from the relevant venues) and free performances also take place in the Hong Kong Cultural Centre foyer and piazza. *See also p245.*

### Cathay Pacific Championships
*Grand Hall, 5th Floor, Hong Kong Convention & Exhibition Centre, Wan Chai, HK Island (Ticket City 2805 2804/www.seniorstennistour.com). Wan Chai MTR (exit A1)/buses along Gloucester Road/Wan Chai Star Ferry Pier.* **Date** 4 days late Oct/early Nov. **Tickets** HK$250-$850. **Credit** AmEx, DC, MC, V. **Map** p80 B1.
Come to see former tennis champions and household names of years past (aged over 35) compete in the Hong Kong event on the Champions Tour.

### Hong Kong Youth Arts Festival
*(Performing arts enquiries 2877 2656/Visual arts enquiries 2802 9455).* **Date** Nov. **Tickets** free-HK$75. **Credit** AmEx, DC, MC, V.
This month-long celebration of the arts aimed at five- to 25-year-olds offers a multidisciplinary range of events taking in the visual and performing arts and literature. The festival places a stong emphasis on education and involves a number of school students in workshops and performances. Many musical and visual arts events are free, while theatre and dance tickets are HK$50-$75.

### Macau Grand Prix
*(24-hour reservation & enquiries: Macau 853 555 555; Hong Kong 852 7171 7171/ www.macau.grandprix.gov.mo/online reservations: www.kongseng.com.mo).* **Date** 3rd weekend in Nov. **Tickets** *single-day* HK$200-$400; *weekend packages* HK$350-$700. **Credit** AmEx, DC, MC, V.
Part of the Formula 3 World Championship, the Grand Prix is the biggest annual event in the former Portugese colony. As in Monaco, cars race around the city's streets, and the event attracts a huge number of visitors from Hong Kong. Tickets are available in person from the Macau Government Tourist Office (9 Largo do Leal Senado), the Tourist Information Counter at Shun Tak Centre, 200 Connaught Road, Central, Hong Kong and from the Kong Seng Ticketing Network in Macau and Hong Kong.

### Star Alliance Open
*Clearwater Bay Golf & Country Club, Clearwater Bay, New Territories (2719 1595). Bus 91/103 minibus.* **Date** Nov. **Tickets** phone for details. **Credit** AmEx, DC, MC, V. **Map** p311.
First held in 2000, it is hoped that this will become the region's premier golf tournament, pulling in many of the top Asian players and a good selection of US and European players. Limited free tickets are available from HKTB information centres.

### Trailwalker
*Start: Pak Tam Chung, Sai Kung, New Territories; finish: Immigration Service Training School, 80 Castle Peak Road, Tuen Mun, New Territories (Oxfam 2520 2525).* **Date** 3 days in Nov. **Entrance** free. **Map** pp310-311.
This popular and immensely tough charity walk takes place along the 100 kilometres (62.5 miles) of the MacLehose Trail. Walkers must finish the course (which takes in 20 hills and mountains, including Tai Mo Shan, Hong Kong's tallest) within 48 hours, which means continuing through the night.

### Hong Kong International Ballroom Dancing Championships
*Queen Elizabeth Stadium, 18 Oi Kwan Road, Wan Chai, HK Island (URBTIX 2734 9009). Buses along Queen's Road East.* **Date** 2 days end Nov. **Tickets** HK$65-$330. **Credit** AmEx, DC, MC, V. **Map** p80 C2.
This increasingly popular competition attracts competitors from more than 15 countries.

## Winter

### Hong Kong International Races

*Sha Tin Racecourse, New Territories
(www.hkjockeyclub.com/english). Racecourse KCR/
buses to Sha Tin.* **Date** 5 days in Dec. **Tickets**
varies. **No credit cards. Map** pp310-311.

The International Races is one of the 11 legs of the
Emirates World Series Racing Championship. The
races attract top horses and jockeys from around the
world and huge crowds of Hong Kong's fanatical
horse racing fans. The horse racing season runs from
September to June, with weekly races at Sha Tin in
the New Territories and Happy Valley on Hong Kong
Island. The HKTB run 'Come Horseracing' tours
to Sha Tin and Happy Valley (for info, see
www.hktourismboard.com/tours). *See also p251.*

### Christmas & New Year

Hong Kong celebrates Christmas with an amazing
display of lights and decorations. Shopping centres
are draped in baubles and tinsel and entire skyscrapers are turned into giant neon Yuletide scenes.
A past favourite was Santa riding the Star Ferry.
Taking a trip across the harbour or a stroll along the

Tsim Sha Tsui East esplanade is an exciting experience the week before Christmas. Many of the
Christmas lights are cleverly reconfigured a couple
of weeks later for Chinese New Year and Santa
miraculously becomes the God of Prosperity.
Churches are well attended over Christmas and New
Year, particularly by the territory's large community of Filippina domestic helpers.

### City Festival

*www.hkfringe.com.hk.* **Date** 3 wks in Jan.

The former Fringe Festival has been reinvented as
an enjoyable celebration of theatre, stand-up comedy, poetry, exhibitions and outdoor entertainment.
The festival brings together an eclectic range of
international and local performers and artists.
Also included in the programme are fashion
parades, music events, culinary displays and an
open-air arts fair. Tickets are available from the
Fringe Club (2 Lower Albert Road, Central; 2521
7251) and from TICKETEK outlets at the Hong
Kong Convention & Exhibition Centre (2582 8888),
the Hong Kong Academy for Performing Arts (2584
8514) and the Hong Kong Arts Centre (2582 0232),
all in Wan Chai.

# Hong Kong Arts Festival

Since its beginnings in 1973, the Arts
Festival has become the most significant
event in the Hong Kong arts calendar, and
now involves hundreds of performers from
around the world. In addition to attracting top
name international companies such as the
Royal Shakespeare Company, the Hamburg
Ballet, the Kirov Opera and the Vienna
Philharmonic, the festival also showcases
a number of specially commissioned local
and regional productions.

A chief attraction of the festival is a
tradition of ambitious fusion programmes
which feature artists of very different musical
genres performing together. Some of the
more memorable recent pairings have
included Yo-Yo Ma and the Silk Road
Ensemble, Phillip Glass and the Kronos
Quartet performing to a showing of Bela
Lugosi's film *Dracula*, John Williams playing
with the China National Symphony Orchestra
and flautist James Galway and the Beaux
Arts Trio performing with the Hong Kong
Philharmonic Orchestra.

From its inception, the festival has tended
to follow a tried and true formula that
guarantees audiences at least one major
visiting orchestra, several classical recitals
and choral concerts, a splashy opera
production, a range of dance productions and

a performance by a jazz legend. In recent
years the Tallis Scholars, Wynton Marsalis,
Jose Carreras, members of the Buena Vista
Social Club, Paco Peña and Sir Yehudi
Menuhin have taken the festival stage.

**TICKETS**

Glossy and detailed festival programme
brochures are available from early November
each year from the Hong Kong Cultural
Centre, City Hall and HKTB Centres. From
mid November to mid December, advance
tickets can be ordered via the festival
website, by fax on 2802 8160 or by post
via a form within the festival programme
brochures. From mid December, all remaining
tickets are sold at URBTIX box offices in the
Hong Kong Cultural Centre, City Hall and
the Hong Kong Arts Centre in Wan Chai.
A number of half-price student tickets
are available for all performances. These
tickets are sponsored by donations from
festival goers. Only one student ticket per
performance can be ordered when making
advance bookings. Free programmes
accompany every festival performance.
*(Programme enquiry hotline 2824 2430/
www.hk.artsfestival.org).* **Date** early Feb-early
Mar. **Credit** AmEx, DC, MC, V.

**Arts & Entertainment**

Floats parade through the city as part of the **Chinese New Year** celebrations.

## Carlsberg Cup

*Hong Kong Stadium, 55 Eastern Hospital Road, So Kon Po, Causeway Bay, HK Island (www.carlsberg.com.hk). Bus 5B.* **Date** late Jan/early Feb. **Tickets** HK$140-$380; HK$80 concessions. **Credit** AmEx, DC, MC, V. **Map** p80 E3.

Soccer is popular in Hong Kong, even if the SAR's team remains no more than a minnow, even within the Asian football world. To coincide with the Chinese New Year holidays, three international football teams compete for the Carlsberg Cup, Hong Kong's most popular annual soccer tournament. In recent years, the Czech Republic, Denmark, Japan and Mexico have battled on the field. Norway won the 2001 tournament.

## Chinese New Year

**Date** 3 days in late Jan/early Feb.

Chinese (or Lunar) New Year is the biggest festival of the year and the three-day public holiday involves great preparation and celebration. Businesses shut down, families travel across the border to be re-united, and for the one and only time in the year, street vendors shut up shop and take a well-earned rest. On the eve of the holiday, throngs of smiling people promenade on the streets. Victoria Park becomes a giant outdoor market and the flower markets in Mong Kok are packed with families buying kumquat trees, narcissus and pussy willow, which signify new beginnings, prosperity and good luck. Children and unmarried young adults receive *lai see*, gifts of freshly minted notes in red envelopes and the greeting of '*kung hei fat choi*' (prosperous wishes) can be heard as people visit relatives and friends. Although the holiday is primarily a family celebration, there's plenty for visitors to enjoy. Hong Kong's city council organises a parade of lavishly decorated floats, and a spectacular fireworks display lights the skies above Victoria Harbour on the evening of the second day of the New Year.

## Hong Kong Arts Festival

*(2824 3555/programme enquiry hotline 2824 2430/ www.hk.artsfestival.org).* **Date** early Feb-early Mar.

One of the world's premier arts festivals, this month-long feast of classical music, ballet, opera, theatre and popular performance attracts first-rank names such as Yo-Yo Ma, the Royal Shakespeare Company, Mikhail Baryshnikov and the China National Orchestra. Festival programme brochures are available in early November each year from the Hong Kong Cultural Centre, City Hall and HKTB Centres. Tickets can be ordered via the internet site, by fax on 2802 8160 or by post via a form within the festival programme booklets. *See also p207* **Hong Kong Arts Festival**.

## Standard Chartered Hong Kong Marathon

*(2577 0800/www.hkmarathon.com/www.hkaaa.com).* **Date** early Feb. **Entrance** from HK$250.

Attracting world-class competitors, the Standard Chartered Hong Kong Marathon also features a half marathon and a 10km race. All three races start at the Hong Kong Cultural Centre on the Tsim Sha Tsui waterfront and finish at the Hong Kong Convention & Exhibition Centre in Wan Chai. Runners who wish to run for the Hong Kong Sports Association for the Physically Disabled can enter as individuals or as a team.

## Spring Lantern (Yuen Siu) Festival

**Date** early Feb (15th day of lunar new year).

Sometimes referred to as Chinese Valentine's Day, the Spring Lantern Festival is a festival for lovers. Held on the 15th day of lunar new year, Yuen Siu also marks the end of the Chinese New Year celebrations and colourful lanterns in traditional designs are bought to decorate homes, restaurants and temples. Special celebrations take place in the evening in Ko Shan Road Park and the Ko Shan Theatre in Kowloon.

Arts & Entertainment

# Children

The strangeness of the city itself is Hong Kong's biggest attraction to kids.

Just try to see Hong Kong through your kids' eyes. Yes, it can be hot, wet, dirty, noisy and rammed solid with traffic; but, as a landscape, it's pure science fiction. Half the city clings to improbably steep mountain sides, and half rises from the sea. Interconnecting it all is a network of flying suspension bridges, swirling flyovers, aerial walkways, dizzying hill trails and a funicular railway. Mammoth container ships tiptoe through a harbour crowded with leaky wooden junks, tumbling hoverferries and jet-propelled hydrofoils. Dense bush (let's call it 'jungle') crowds almost to the doors of the world's most modern skyscrapers and, in the alleyways below, Hong Kong's ineffably up-to-date teenagers move in herds, wearing Japanese cartoon hairstyles and mobile phones clamped to their ears. It's a weird, fascinating place for a child, and the trick to giving your kids a good time here is to plan whole days for them to simply wander and take in the strangeness and charm of it all.

Of course, this is a city of contradictions, and you'll find these demonstrated in attitudes to children. Restaurant staff will go gooey over your younger kids, and will happily run around fetching hot water and high chairs; but breast feeding in public, for example, is emphatically not on, and, apart from in the airport, the biggest malls and branches of Mothercare, you won't find much in the way of public baby changing facilities. Many expats will tell you that Hong Kongers can be indifferent to visitors, but you'll find the opposite if you're travelling with young children. Don't expect anyone to offer you a seat on the MTR (let's not go crazy), but, in general, locals respond well to kids and will be more than keen to help shopping and travelling go smoothly for you.

Here are some ideas for great days out that should provide enough weirdness, exercise, fun and food for kids, even those who think they've seen it all.

## Hong Kong Island

### Central

There's not a whole lot to actually *do* around Central, but there's plenty to see, and kids should find the pure spectacle of all those insane space-age buildings thrilling enough.

Arts & Entertainment

Two of the major draws at the extensive **Ocean Park**. *See p213.*

Keep them craning their necks upwards, and don't miss the **HSBC Building** ('It's all inside out!') and the **Bank of China Tower** (for both, *see p69*) – startling looking outside, although inside it's, well, just a lot of offices (although it's well worth going up to the viewing gallery). Moving eastwards, they can explore the huge, linked malls of **Queensway Plaza** and **Pacific Place** (*see p182*) in air-conditioned comfort. Two shops might specifically interest kids. **King & Country** (*see p196*), on the top floor of Pacific Place, sells military models, many of them in specifically Hong Kong uniform and contexts; not toys, but the glass-cased displays are fascinating. **Loft**, on the lowest floor, offers an eclectic mix of toys, games, clothes and gadgets that should keep kids contentedly browsing for a while.

From Pacific Place, you can enter the eastern end of **Hong Kong Park** (*see p72*), a Tardis-like layered space that should provide an hour or so's rest and relaxation. The curtain-waterfall fountain at the entrance is a good place to splash feet, arms and faces while taking photos. A bit further in, you'll find the **Park Inn** (*see p170*), where kids should enjoy the Southeast Asian buffet lunch. The **Flagstaff House Museum of Tea Ware** (*see p72*) won't hold a child's attention for long: cut straight to its gift shop, purchase quality souvenirs, then keep going. There's a big children's play area further up the slope.

The heart of the park is a waterfall and pools cut from natural bedrock, and above this is the huge, excellent **Edward Youde Aviary** (*see p72*); actually a chunk of recreated forest

# HK walks Jungles, concrete & otherwise

Weekday mid-mornings are a good time to head west from Central and explore the steep streets above and below Hollywood Road. Start on Queen's Road Central, at the bottom of the **Mid-Levels Escalator** (actually a series of linked escalators). To ride up its full 792-metre (2,600-foot) length should be enthralling enough in itself, and it's worth stopping off at intervals to explore the streets on either side: either just to look around, or to buy food and drink for a picnic.

Ride the Escalator to the very top, which is on Conduit Road, then turn right. It's a pleasant, 20-minute stroll to the foot of **Hatton Road** (on your left), where you should take a break before attacking the quite challenging climb, along a tarmac path, that takes you with surprising speed into dense forest. Leave the path when you reach a junction with a pagoda and climb the stepped trail. On either side, you'll see terraces cut into the hillside that are home to (technically illegal) gardens maintained by residents from the dwellings further down. They're often quite lovely, brimming as they are with flowers and vegetables, and they're OK to explore as long as you don't pick anything. The trail eventually brings you to the **Pinewood Battery**, a disused World War II artillery station with commanding views of the western harbour. This is a great place for a picnic, as the kids can spend an hour or so playing among the ruins. Rejoin the tarmac path of Hatton Road, climbing steadily to a junction with Lugard and Harlech Roads – following either will lead you to the Peak, but the Harlech route is slightly quicker taking about 15 or 20 minutes. Take the Peak Tram back down to Central.

A second enjoyable family walk is along **Bowen Road**, above Wan Chai, starting at the Adventist Hospital on Stubbs Road (take bus 6, 15, 15B, 61, 66 or 76) and contouring west toward Mid-Levels. It's an airy ribbon of tarmac that hugs the forested hillside but seems to put you within touching distance of the skyscrapers of Wan Chai. Keep an eye on the kids as they clamber around **Lover's Rock**, a natural shrine located about 15 minutes along the path, which has some decidedly makeshift platforms and railings among its incense burners and idols. Ten minutes further on, you'll reach Wan Chai Gap. Climb steeply uphill here to visit the **Police Museum** (*see p85*) at 27 Coombe Road, an old-fashioned glass-case kind of place, where kids can widen their eyes at collected triad weaponry and the head of the last tiger to be shot in Hong Kong. From here you can continue by number 15 bus to the Peak, or head back down to Wan Chai. Bowen Road continues after Wan Chai Gap, providing more good views, and finally peters out right next to the Peak Tram line, from where you can take the tram up to the Peak or down to Central.

through which you descend on a wooden walkway, gawping at an impressively exotic quota of brightly coloured birdlife.

An equally arresting spectacle, at weekends, is the sight of massed brides, like real live dolls in identikit, rented, frilly white dresses, being photographed with their grooms near the **Garden Road Registry Office**.

Leaving the park at the western end, it's only a step to the foot of the **Peak Tram** (*see p88*), which offers a thrilling ride up to the Peak.

## The Peak

Don't rush your trip to the Peak. You can easily base a whole day around this area, with its abundant activities for children. It's all self-consciously touristy, of course, but that's not

necessarily a bad thing. In the Peak Tower itself, for example, you'll find the **Ripley's Believe It Or Not! Odditorium** (*see p88*), a franchised freak show on Level 3. Give it a miss in favour of the **Peak Explorer** (*see p88*) on Level 4, a multimedia motion simulator ride into space – and, not an educational one either. Robots and aliens abound.

Just across the road is the **Peak Galleria**, where the kids can stock up on the nastier end of the souvenir spectrum – Mao caps, pigtailed 'Chinese' hats, etc. Amid the bug-eyed shopping frenzy, don't neglect the amazing views over both sides of the island from the rooftop terraces of the Peak Tower and Galleria.

The Peak has plenty of places to eat, all of which make a point of welcoming children. **Shooters 52**, for example, on the ground floor

The towers of Wan Chai, as seen from Bowen Road.

# Stuff for kids

## Central

Gawp at Hong Kong Island from the **Star Ferry**, then relax and play in **Hong Kong Park** (*see p72*) and the **Zoological & Botanical Gardens** (*see p72*).

## Kowloon

Experience Chinese Hong Kong in the markets of **Mong Kok** or **Yau Ma Tei**, then relax on the **Tsim Sha Tsui** waterfront, before taking in the **Space Museum** (*see p102*) and the **Hong Kong Museum of Science** (*see p105*).

## The Peak

Ride the **Peak Tram**, peruse the shops and 'attractions' at the top, eat, and then take a stroll around **The Peak** admiring the stunning views en route. *See p88*.

## South coast

Spend the morning amid the rides and animal attractions of **Ocean Park** (*see p213*), followed by an afternoon in the market, on the waterfront and at the beach in **Stanley** (*see p93*).

## Outlying islands

Take the ferry to **Lamma** island, for an enjoyable boat ride, easy walking, beaches fine views and great food. *See p125*.

## New Territories

Enjoy a train ride into the **New Territories** to Sha Tin, and visit the **Hong Kong Heritage Museum** (*see p114*) and the **Ten Thousand Buddhas Monastery** (*see p114*). Then explore pristine countryside.

---

of the Peak Galleria, sells user-friendly American food and has a Little Tikes play area inside. Two recommended eating spots are **Café Deco** (*see p148*), also in the Peak Galleria, and the **Peak Café** (*see p149*), an older colonial building across the road (although, following a change in ownership in June 2001, the future of the latter is uncertain). Both look far too swanky to welcome kids, but, in fact, have great, reasonably-priced kids' menus (and free pencils to colour them in with). Watch in envy as Junior chomps through a HK$40 dollar plate of crisp, golden fish and chips, while you pick disconsolately at the minuscule lamb chop and dribble of sauce you paid a hundred bucks for.

The circular path that swings westwards along Harlech and Lugard Roads around Victoria Peak is a friendly hike for short legs, and offers outstanding views of the city and harbour. There's a nature trail to follow here, and toilets, snacks and drinks all available near the playground half way round, at the junction with Harlech and Hatton Roads.

You can also climb to the top of Victoria Peak (don't be misled into thinking that the Peak Tram terminus is at the Peak itself), a rewarding climb into a series of ascending parks and sculpted trails. If uphill does not appeal, try walking back down to Central via Old Peak Road – turn left coming out of the Peak Tower and take the narrow pedestrian path that switchbacks downhill through thick jungle. Especially thrilling after dark (it's lit, but not very well). The path eventually gives way to what must be one of the world's steepest residential streets. Grab a taxi here, or keep

going straight downhill for a few minutes and you're at the top entrance to the **Zoological & Botanical Gardens** (*see p72*), another shady hillside park where rare birds and an obese tiger can be seen in cages.

## Mid-Levels to Wan Chai

*See p210* **HK Walks: Jungles, concrete & otherwise**.

## Causeway Bay

Any child with even mild breathing problems should avoid street-level Causeway Bay, but indoors there are ace toy and model sections in **Sogo** (*see p183*) and the other Japanese department stores, and mall cruising fun to be had in **Times Square** (*see p185*). Level 8 of the latter has a nice clean children's play area and a fascinating toy shop called **Wise Kids**. There's also **Times Zone**, a well-lit and non-seedy video arcade for older children (you must be 16 or over to enter). Games change regularly, but are guaranteed to be cutting-edge and Japanese. Currently popular are games in which single or multi players mimic ever more complicated video dance routines in a cross-stepping, arm-waving frenzy, tracked by a web of motion sensors – as much fun to watch as to play. Most games cost about HK$3 per session, and change is available at the booth inside. Underneath Times Square, you'll find **CitySuper**, an upmarket supermarket devoted to edible curiosities, gadgets and compulsively fascinating Japanese bathroom products.

## South & east coast

If your kids have ever been to Disneyland or Alton Towers, it's possible they'll find **Ocean Park** (*see p92*) a disappointment. It's still basically a local attraction, no matter how hard it's trying. However, it's in a beautiful location, and it is clean and leafy within. Don't miss the sci-fi motion simulator ride at the main entrance – it's a blast. The cable car ride from the main entrance into the park proper will generate plenty of 'oohs' and 'aahs'. The rides on the headland are nothing special, but kids will like the sea lion and dolphin show. The rides in **Adventure Land** – the Mine Train, Raging River and Space Wheel – are newer and more entertaining. After these, you can head down the escalator to the **Middle Kingdom** for a dose of history and culture.

**Stanley** (*see p93*) has been transformed completely in the past year or so, and is now an excellent place to spend a whole day with children. Take the number 6 bus from Central for a stomach-churning rollercoaster ride over the top of the island. Once in Stanley, the narrow market streets will provide an hour or so of browsing for factory seconds and Chinese trinkets. Then there's the waterfront area, which now boasts new playgrounds and a large, canopied open space for sitting around and picnicking. **Murray House**, an old colonial building transplanted brick by brick from Central, has historical displays of the area in colonial times, and a branch of the excellent Chilli & Spice restaurant. Walk south through the town and you'll find the **Commonwealth War Cemetery**, which generates a reverential hush all its own, and **St Stephen's Beach**.

Hong Kong's newest museum, the **Museum of Coastal Defence** (*see p87*), is located at the north-east tip of Hong Kong island. From Shau Kei Wan MTR station, it's an uphill walk or bus ride to the restored fortress, but it's well worth the special trip. Kids will love exploring the ramparts and batteries overlooking the eastern harbour, as well as the indoor displays of weapons and uniforms.

## Kowloon

The **Star Ferry** ride between Central and Tsim Sha Tsui still costs mere pennies – making it one of the best value attractions in Hong Kong. The Tsim Sha Tsui Ferry Pier abuts the lengthy waterfront promenade in front of the **Hong Kong Cultural Centre** (*see p240*), with its stunning views across the harbour towards Hong Kong Island. Here, you'll also find the domed **Space Museum** (*see p102*); the shows in its Omnimax cinema centre

on general geographical themes (rainforests, glaciers, Everest) and offer differing levels of adrenaline rush, but kids should enjoy the experience whatever is showing.

Keep going east along the waterfront and you'll eventually reach the **Hong Kong Museum of Science** (*see p105*), a genuinely fascinating place in which children can spend hours pushing buttons and learning about everything from household appliances to computers. It's all hands-on, child-oriented stuff, and very well designed.

Riding north on the MTR from Tsim Sha Tsui will bring you to the heart of Kowloon. You can exit at Jordan, Yau Ma Tei or Mong Kok to explore the **Night Market**, **Ladies' Market** and **Jade Market** (for all, *see p194*) on foot. This is real Chinese Hong Kong – crowded, colourful, cacophonous and commercial, with no apologies to anyone. But again, beware the pollution: itching eyes and rough throats are likely after a few hours' wandering.

Better, perhaps, to change platforms at Mong Kok, catch the Kwun Tong Line to Kowloon Tong and head for **Festival Walk** (*see p181*). Hong Kong's newest, biggest mall is almost a day out in itself. On the entertainment side, there's an ice rink and cineplex, and a huge variety of shops, of which **Log-On**, with its vast range of Japanese consumer goods and stationery, offers the best browsing potential. When the kids get hungry, there's everything from McDonald's to upmarket Japanese restaurants, all perfectly child-friendly. Again, **Chilli & Spice** has wonderful staff, and your food will arrive within minutes of ordering, cutting down on fractious waiting time. If you want shopping, entertainment and food in one efficient package, then you should try the **Rainforest Café**, unequivocally a children's zone with a full-on ecological theme. Animatronic monkeys and elephants inhabit its rich undergrowth and go into various displays of chest beating, screeching or trumpeting every ten minutes, and a pretty convincing fake thunderstorm rolls through every 15 minutes.

From Festival Walk, you can descend into the Kowloon Tong KCR station and take the train north into the New Territories.

## The New Territories

Get off the KCR train at **Sha Tin** for the **Hong Kong Heritage Museum** (*see p114*) and the **Ten Thousand Buddhas Monastery** (*see p114*), both of which should appeal to children. The museum is a very well-designed space, with lively exhibits showing the history of Hong Kong. The exhibits change through the year, but examples of child-oriented activities include an interactive display where kids can design their own homes, and a room full of Hong Kong comic books through the years.

Of all the Buddhist monasteries in Hong Kong, the Ten Thousand Buddhas is most likely to seize a child's imagination. It's just so outlandish. There really are over 10,000 Buddha statues on this landscaped hilltop, and one of the temples contains an embalmed and gilded body to boot.

Sha Tin also boasts the by-now-familiar logjam of linked shopping malls. There's not much of profound interest to visiting children, but if you can get them to **ULM** (Shop A315, New Town Plaza III), they might like the range of Action Man-sized figures depicting every branch of the Hong Kong Police, including the famed Special Duties Unit (Hong Kong's SAS), and a Hawaiian-shirted Mong Kok CID officer. Also on offer are figures from well-known Hong Kong action movies, so if your kids like Jackie Chan, they can bring him home with them.

Beyond Sha Tin, sights and activities are more spaced out and harder to reach. The **Hong Kong Railway Museum** (*see p117*) at **Tai Po** doesn't look like much, but don't underestimate the mystical power of trains to enchant young minds. This is a small but hands-on place, where kids can clamber in and out of railway carriages and push buttons to make engines run. The busy market streets around it are also worth exploring.

If the weather is cool enough, and your kids are energetic enough, there are any number of short, satisfying hikes to be found all over the New Territories. **Sai Kung** (*see p123*) has wonderful beaches and a remote feel, but it can take a long time to get anywhere out here. More immediate gratification can be found in **Lion Rock Country Park**, best approached from Tai Wai KCR Station. The climb to **Amah Rock** (*see p114*) is tough but pays off with great views, and from there it's relatively easy to keep climbing up to **Lion Rock** itself.

## The Outlying Islands

Walking in wild countryside is one of the great attractions of the SAR's numerous islands (*see chapter* **Wild Hong Kong**). The easiest to reach is **Lamma** (*see p127*), a 40-minute ferry ride south of Hong Kong Island (ferries depart from Central's Outlying Islands Ferry Pier; map p67 D1). Start early. Breakfast in **Yung Shue Wan**, in one of the cafés in the narrow streets, then set off on the gentle hike (allow a couple of hours) that takes you past two decent beaches and over the hill to **Sok Kwu Wan**. Just outside the village, you can find the 'kamikaze caves' (supposedly some kind of fiendish Japanese

midget submarine base dating from World War II: use your imagination), and in **Sok Kwu Wan** you can eat again (great seafood; *see p164*) and catch a boat back to Central.

## Festivals

Hong Kong offers a variety of annual events that should interest children (*see chapter* **By Season**). They're all based on the lunar calendar, so you'll need to check actual dates with the Hong Kong Tourism Board.

**Chinese New Year** (late January/early February; *see p208*) is, at heart, a home-based family celebration, but visitors can always enjoy the big fireworks display (on the second day of the holiday) over Victoria Harbour. Avoid watching it from the packed Tsim Sha Tsui waterfront if you have young children.

At the other end of the year, the **Mid Autumn Festival** (late September/early October; *see p205*) is celebrated in the streets and parks with lanterns, candles and cake. Go out after dark and you'll see families strolling with younger children thrilled to be up so late to greet the new moon with their lanterns – a real touch of beauty. **Victoria Park** (*see p86*) in Causeway Bay is a good place to see the lights and buy battery-operated cartoon lanterns of your own. You might see older kids playing hideously dangerous games with streams of molten wax, which is apt to vaporise and ignite, causing the kind of injuries that traditionally attend Bonfire Night in the UK. Steer well clear.

The **Dragon Boat (Tuen Ng) Festival** (June; *see p205*) is a great spectacle. The shambolic races at Stanley feature a lot of expat participation and a great deal of alcohol consumption, but it's reasonably clean fun. More serious international competition can be seen at the Shing Mun River in Sha Tin.

The **Cheung Chau Bun Festival** (Apr/May; *see p205*) brings alive the little island off the coast of Lantau. Kids love the rush of music, lion dances and especially the children's parade, featuring Cheung Chau's kids riding on floats, or stilt-walking, over the crowds.

## Resources

For general queries about any aspect of visiting Hong Kong with kids, call the **Community Advice Bureau** (2815 5444; 10am-4pm daily).

### Child-minding

Most four- or five- star hotels offer a babysitting service. Private services are rare. **Rent-A-Mum** (2523 4868/2805 7559) specialises in finding nannies, babysitters and short-term child care.

# Film

The city that produced Bruce Lee and Jackie Chan has a rich cinematic heritage.

Film lovers have always regarded Hong Kong as one of the most respected and innovative centres of the cinematic world. From the martial arts classics of the legendary Bruce Lee to the modern-day international box office bonanzas enjoyed by the city's favourite son, Jackie Chan (*see p219* **Bruce & Jackie**), Hong Kong cinema has had a lasting influence on the world's leading film-makers, from Martin Scorsese to Quentin Tarantino. And now stars like Chan, and directors such as John Woo are making their own mark in Hollywood.

If there can be said to be a defining characteristic of Hong Kong cinema, it is not subtlety. Irrepressible energy, non-stop action and an almost fetishistic obsession with comic-book violence – and not an inkling of politics – are the norm. There are exceptions (the art house offerings of Wong Kar-wai being the most obvious) but they are few.

Our pick of the **Top ten HK films** (*see p218*) is a good starting point if you are new to the genre. Most of these movies date from the industry's golden years in the affluent 1980s and early 1990s. Uncertainty regarding the Handover led to much talent going overseas, and it remains to be seen whether film-making of the quality seen at that time will return to Hong Kong.

If you are interested in learning more about Hong Kong cinema, Fredric Dannen and Barry Long's book *Hong Kong Babylon* is peerless.

## MOVIE-GOING

Film watching and film making are as much a part of the local scene as the trams trundling through Causeway Bay or the junks out on Victoria Harbour. On any given day, pedestrians can find their daily commutes disrupted by film crews as they use the dramatic city as a backdrop to their latest production.

The city itself is littered with more than 60 cinemas, with modern multiplexes and dusty one-house cinemas screening everything from the latest Hollywood blockbuster to such unique local productions as the 2001 New Year release *The Human Pork Chop* (based on the real-life tale of a woman who was murdered and had her head stuffed inside a Hello Kitty doll, no less).

For visitors to the city, going to the movies Hong Kong-style can be a unique, albeit sometimes frustrating, experience. Be warned: mobile phones and pagers will go off

**Cine-Art House.** *See p217.*

incessantly, and conversations will continue to rattle on regardless of any protests.

Daily cinema listings can be found in all Hong Kong's Chinese and English-language dailies, as well as the various weekly entertainment guides that can be picked up at bars, clubs, coffee shops and newsagents all over town.

Ticket prices vary according to which cinema you pick and the time you choose to go. Generally, you can expect to pay between HK$50-$65 (plus an additional HK$7.50 if you book your ticket online or by phone). For the cost-conscious, Tuesdays give the best value as tickets are sold at a reduced price (around HK$45 or less), but get in early as the locals love a bargain and more often than not, the screenings are sold out. Bookings at all cinemas can be made up to five days in advance.

And if you want to know what you're letting yourself in for, consider the following categories by which all films showing in Hong Kong are rated. (I) means suitable for all ages; (IIA) means not suitable for children; (IIB) means not suitable for young adults and children; and (III) means over-18s only.

Wading through the list of Hong Kong cinemas can be quite tricky. Most have facilities to match anything offered across the globe, but you will occasionally still find yourself in a breezy old hall looking at a dusty screen trying to listen while the cleaner insists on starting his work ten minutes before the show is over. So here are some of the best Hong Kong has to offer, all within easy access of the city centre.

### AMC Festival Walk

*88 Tat Chee Avenue, Kowloon Tong, Kowloon (2265 8545). Kowloon Tong MTR or KCR/ 2C, 203 bus.* **Credit** MC, V.

Situated deep within one of the region's newest and largest shopping centres, Festival Walk, the AMC complex has 11 screens showing international and local features every day. The seats are new and comfortable, and provide a great break for bargain hunters. Early screenings cost either HK$30 or HK$40, so you can save yourself a few dollars here as well. And MTR access makes finding the place simple.

### Broadway Cinematique

*Prosperous Garden, 3 Public Square Street, Yau Ma Tei, Kowloon (2332 9000). Yau Ma Tei MTR (exit C)/buses along Nathan Road.* **Credit** MC, V. **Map** p110 A4.

Even though it's a little bit out of the way for those not staying in Kowloon, the Cinematique gets the nod as the best place in town – if only for the diverse range of films it shows. Here, you'll find movies from all over the place, including a great selection of Asian films and those that make the world's festi-

# Location: Hong Kong

Hong Kong first appeared in Hollywood films, at least in name, as early as 1931 (*The Girl from Hong Kong*), and sporadically throughout that decade and the 1940s, in films like *Passage From Hong Kong* (1941) and *Escape from Hong Kong* (1942). But it was during the 1950s that studios really caught the Hong Kong bug, producing a wave of films such as *Hong Kong* (1951) starring Ronald Reagan, *Target Hong Kong* (1952), *Flight to Hong Kong* (1956), *Hong Kong Confidential* (1958) and *Hong Kong Affair* (1958). Quite clearly, the name alone held a certain allure.

It's no coincidence that this trend began shortly after the Chinese revolution, at a time when the colony was going through its least secure, and consequently most exciting and self-defining, period. Even neighbouring Macau got a look in, with Robert Mitchum and Jane Russell's popular film noir *Macao* (1952) and Tony Curtis's lesser-known *Forbidden* (1953).

Although few early films used anything more than stock footage and sound stages to represent Hong Kong, there were some exceptions. In 1955, 20th Century Fox shot two big-budget films simultaneously: *Soldier of Fortune* and *Love is a Many Splendored Thing*.

*Soldier of Fortune,* starring Clark Gable and Susan Hayward, was based on Ernest K Gann's novel of the same name and featured a number of prominent locations around the city. The opening shot of the film shows Gable at the Barker Road Peak Tram station – the last stop before the Peak terminus. It's one of the few locations from that era that still remains unchanged. If you take the

number 15 bus back down the Peak and sit upstairs on the left-hand side, halfway down you can also see the Chinese mansion used as Gable's residence in the film. Although the exteriors are the real thing, the fabulous lobby of the Peninsula hotel was recreated in Hollywood, while leading lady Susan Hayward didn't come to Hong Kong at all. Her local shots were filmed by Jennifer Jones, who at the time was starring opposite William Holden in Fox's other Hong Kong production.

*Love is a Many Splendored Thing* was an adaptation of Eurasian author Han Suyin's autobiographical novel of interracial romance and showed Hong Kong at its most appealing: the bustle of Queen's Road, Kennedy Town and Aberdeen, a sleepy Kai Tak airport and a glistening Deep Water Bay. For the exteriors of the hospital in which Jones's character

Arts & Entertainment

val circuit but often don't get a look in at Hong Kong's major cinema chains. There's also a film library so locals can borrow DVDs and VCDs, a great film poster and book shop, and a cheap and handy café for before and after show snacks and drinks. Another bonus is its proximity to Temple Street Night Market (just a block away), where you can pick up everything from dim sum to dildos. Just follow the signs from the Yau Ma Tei MTR station.

### Cine-Art House
*Sun Hung Kai Centre, 30 Harbour Road, Wan Chai, HK Island (2827 4820). Wan Chai MTR (exit A1)/ A12, 18, 88, 104 bus & buses along Gloucester Road.* **No credit cards. Map** p80 B1.
This is another cinema that offers a break from the usual mainstream fare, and a good chance to grab a look at some of the wonderful movies being produced by mainland China film-makers. Zhang Yimou's

breath-taking *The Road Home* and Joan Chen's heart-breaking *Xiu Xiu: The Sent Down Girl* got their first Hong Kong runs here. It's nothing flash – the seats are a bit shoddy – but it's close to the bars and clubs of Wan Chai if you fancy making a night of it.

### JP Cinema
*JP Plaza, 22-36 Paterson Street, Causeway Bay, HK Island (2881 5005). Causeway Bay MTR (exit E)/ A11, 103, 170, N170 bus.* **No credit cards. Map** p80 D1.
Stuck in among the huge, anonymous shopping malls of Causeway Bay, JP Cinema has two large screens and concentrates mainly on the latest Hollywood releases. Recent refurbishments have brought the place up to scratch and the cinema's steep incline allows uninterrupted viewing – something a fair few of Hong Kong's older cinemas can't boast.

Han Suyin lived and worked, the film used the wonderful old Foreign Correspondents' Club building at 41a Conduit Road, in Hong Kong Island's Mid-Levels district. The Club foolishly sold the premises years ago, and it was demolished by developers. Today, the only other way to see it is in photographs, notably on the stairs of the current Club building at the top of Ice House Street in Central.

In 1958, Orson Welles arrived in the colony to shoot *Ferry To Hong Kong*, based on the trials of Hungarian-born Steven Ragan who spent ten months in the early 1950s stuck on the Hong Kong–Macau ferry because he lacked the correct visas for either port. The film offers few specific locations that can still be recognised, but gives a glimpse of the old Hong Kong–Macau ferry service, locally filmed interiors and streets around Wan Chai.

In 1960, *The World of Suzie Wong* saw William Holden return to Hong Kong and the debut of Nancy Kwan in the title role. From the opening scene aboard the Star Ferry, to the vanished neoclassical architecture of Central, from Wan Chai market to the boat yards at Aberdeen, it's a highly evocative film. The Nam Kok Hotel was supposedly located in Wan Chai, but its exterior shots were filmed on Hollywood Road, at its junction with Ladder Street. Man Mo Temple is often visible, as is the red Royal Mail post box that was replaced just before the 1997 handover. The views from the roof of the hotel were shot from a location high on the Peak. As he had done with Jennifer Jones five years earlier, Holden accompanied Kwan to the Aberdeen floating restaurant. The one shown in the film has long since disappeared, but the latest incarnation still offers a similar location and experience.

Although *The World of Suzie Wong* signalled the beginning of the end of Hollywood's love affair with Hong Kong, the 1960s saw a few other releases. In 1962, Bob Hope and Bing Crosby made *The Road To Hong Kong*, the last of their famous *Road* movies (although they never actually made it to Hong Kong). And in 1967, Charlie Chaplin's cinematic swansong *A Countess From Hong Kong*, starring Marlon Brando and Sophia Loren, had some interesting opening scenes shot in Hong Kong and touched on the little-explored theme of White Russian bar girls who once worked here. But, sadly, all the action took place at Pinewood Studios in England. In the same year, Sean Connery showed up briefly with *Ferry To Hong Kong* director Lewis Gilbert, to make *You Only Live Twice*.

In 1974, Roger Moore, who had his trademark safari suits made at Sam's Tailor on Nathan Road (*see p191* **HK profiles: Sam the Tailor**), arrived in Hong Kong to film parts of *The Man With The Golden Gun* (which featured the Macau Road topless bar Bottoms Up and the Peninsula Hotel). In *Revenge of the Pink Panther* (1978), Peter Sellers checked in to the Excelsior Hotel in Causeway Bay in hilarious, but very politically incorrect, Chinese disguise.

It seems quite likely that Hong Kong became less appealing to film makers and location scouts as the city became less attractive. Huge swathes of striking architectural beauty disappeared almost overnight in the 1970s, and were replaced by a bland and unromantic mess of concrete, steel and glass. Much of what was Hong Kong at its best remains only in the films that were made in situ during its aesthetic heyday – a sad fact that makes seeking them out all the more worthwhile.

# HK films

## Ah Ying
(Allen Fong, 1982)
Absorbing social realist docudrama –
about as far from a stereotypical Hong
Kong movie as it's possible to get

## Ashes of Time
(Wong Kar-wai, 1994)
Confusing, beautifully photographed non-
action action movie. A masterpiece to
some, pretentious nonsense to others.

## A Better Tomorrow
(John Woo, 1986)
A stock gangster tale taken to a new
level, thanks to Woo's verve and a superb
performance from Chow Yun-fat. 'The *Citizen
Kane* of Hong Kong cinema', one critic said.

## Bullet in the Head
(John Woo, 1990)
Woo's rhapsodic, bleak, deeply unsettling
answer to *The Deer Hunter*.

## Center Stage
(Stanley Kwan, 1991)
A study of victimisation and the Shanghai
film industry of the 1930s.

## A Chinese Ghost Story
(Ching Siu-tung, 1987)
Fantastic tale featuring an ancient tree
demon with a life-sapping tongue. Combines
tradition with Hong Kong energy and verve.

## Chungking Express
(Wong Kar-wai, 1994)
This art-house gem paints an unforgettable
picture of Hong Kong in the 1990s. A
beautiful, open-hearted romantic comedy.

## The Killer
(John Woo, 1989)
Exciting, stylish tale of the hunt by a 'bad'
cop for a 'good' killer, with some blacker-
than-black comic moments.

## Peking Opera Blues
(Tsui Hark, 1986)
The female actors shine in this rip-roaring
romantic action-comedy. Great stunts.

## Rouge
(Stanley Kwan, 1987)
Conjuring up Hong Kong past, this clever,
warm, funny melodrama has much to say
about the city's changing culture

## Ocean Theatre
*3 Canton Road, Tsim Sha Tsui, Kowloon (2377
2100). Tsim Sha Tsui MTR (exit C1, E)/Tsim Sha
Tsui Star Ferry Pier.* **No credit cards. Map** p98 B3.
The greatest attraction Ocean Theatre can boast is
its enormous screens. For action-packed local 'chop-
socky' productions and mega-action hits like the
*Mission: Impossible* series, it's the best place in town.

## UA Queensway
*One Pacific Place, 88 Queensway, Admiralty, HK
Island (2869 0322). Admiralty MTR (exit C1)/buses
through Central.* **No credit cards. Map** p67 F5.
The Queensway multiplex has one of the SAR's best
shopping centres right on its doorstep, and the most
modern and comfortable seats in town.

## Windsor
*Windsor House, 311 Gloucester Road, Causeway
Bay, HK Island (2882 2621). Causeway Bay MTR
(exit C)/buses along Gloucester Road.* **Credit** MC, V.
**Map** p80 D1.
Tucked away next to Causeway Bay's branch of
HMV, the Windsor cinema plays host to a number
of premières and the latest, biggest local and international features. But perhaps the greatest attraction for both locals and tourists is the back few rows'
two-seater benches, which are perfect if you fancy a
little snogging to heat up an otherwise less-than-
exciting cinematic experience.

## Resources & other cinemas

### Hong Kong Film Archive
*50 Lei King Road, Sai Wan Ho, HK Island (2739
2139). Sai Wan Ho MTR (exit A)/2A, N8, 77, 84,
99, 110, 606, 722 bus.* **Open** 10am-8pm Mon-Fri;
noon-8pm Sat, Sun. **Map** p62.
The fascinating HK$185-million Hong Kong Film
Archive was finished at the end of 2000, and is home
to several studios, an exhibition hall, film and information archives and other facilities. It contains 3,800
films and 85,000 pieces of film heritage dating to
1898, which have been collected from all over the
world. To ensure the preservation of its precious film
collection, the four-storey archive is equipped with
state-of-the-art temperature and humidity control
systems. Access to all information and materials is
gained through a computerised multi-media system.
For film buffs, there are independent viewing rooms
where you can sample all the delights. There's also
a vast collection of materials, such as publicity
posters, film photos and scripts.

### Lim Por Yen Film Theatre
*Hong Kong Arts Centre, 2 Harbour Road, Wan Chai,
HK Island (2582 0200). Admiralty MTR (exit D)/A12,
18, 88 bus.* **Credit** AmEx, DC, MC, V. **Map** p80 B2.
For fans of the obscure and those wanting to check
out the many film festivals held in Hong Kong each
year, look no further than the little-but-lovely Lim
Por Yen Film Theatre. Supported by the Hong Kong
Arts Development Council, the Film Theatre is a

# Bruce & Jackie

Although Hong Kong film makers have been part of the global scene since the silent era, and US films have been screened here since the 1920s, the local film industry really hit international headlines in the 1970s – mainly thanks to one man.

**Bruce Lee** stands tall among the very best world cinema has ever offered. He had it all: looks, charm and a seductive on-screen presence. Although born in San Francisco (on 27 November 1940), Lee starting his acting career as a little boy in Hong Kong. He soon went on to become Hong Kong's cha-cha champion, before conquering the world of kung-fu. Films such as *The Way Of The Dragon* and *Enter The Dragon* made him a household name around the globe and, when he died tragically from a cerebral oedema under mysterious circumstances on 20 July 1973 at the age of just 33, the whole of Hong Kong mourned his passing.

As yet, the Hong Kong government hasn't seen fit to erect a monument to this superstar, If you want to check out the pad where Lee lived during his last few years, be prepared for a shock. Crane's Nest, as it was called by Lee and his wife Linda Lee-Cadwell, is now a love motel (the Romantic Hotel on Cumberland Road in Kowloon Tong).

Since the passing of the legendary Bruce Lee, the title of Hong Kong's favourite son has passed to **Jackie Chan**. Born on 7 April 1954, Chan started his career with Hong Kong mega-studio Golden Harvest as a stunt man. By the time he was 20, he had

**Bruce Lee** in *Game of Death*.

made 25 films and Golden Harvest king-makers Raymond Chow, Leonard Ho and Leung Fung saw a star in the making. Chan's big break came in 1980, when Golden Harvest decided to give him top-billing in *The Young Master*. ('I think today that without Golden Harvest, there is no Jackie Chan', says Chan). His first effort (of many) at acting and directing, it hit box office pay-dirt in Hong Kong and Japan, where it was given the rare honour of a simultaneous nationwide release.

With Golden Harvest, Chan's career simply went ballistic. He now has more than 70 films under his belt and is a Hong Kong icon. He is also a man very much in charge of his own destiny. With the international box office success of *Rush Hour* (1998) and *Shanghai Noon* (2000), Chan has become one of the most bankable stars on the planet.

natty little place that has hosted a diverse selection of events, including the Hong Kong and Macau Student Film and Video Festival, a regular Hong Kong Film Forum for local productions that film-goers might have missed, as well as the more left-of-centre efforts from overseas. The theatre offers more than 30 screenings each month and its newsletter *Cinelink*, which lists screening times and ticket prices, is available at bookshops and cafés around town, or from the Arts Centre itself.

### Space Museum Theatre

*10 Salisbury Road, Tsim Sha Tsui, Kowloon (2721 0226). Tsim Sha Tsui MTR (exit E)/buses to Tsim Sha Tsui Star Ferry Pier & along Salisbury Road/Tsim Sha Tsui Star Ferry Pier.*
**Open** *museum* 1-9pm Mon, Wed-Fri; 10am-9pm Sat, Sun. **Admission** HK$24-$32; HK$12-$16 concessions. **Credit** AmEx, DC, MC, V. **Map** p98 B3.

The Space Museum shows an Omnimax production that changes roughly every three months. Screenings are in Cantonese, English, Mandarin and Japanese.

## Festivals

Hong Kong hosts a number of film festivals each year, although the timing of the events often changes. November sees the **MAX! Festival**, which concentrates on films from Germany, Austria and Switzerland. Run by the Goethe Institut (2802 0088), it kicks off with a gala 1920s-style opening party. There's also the French **Cinepanorama** in December run by the Alliance Francaise de Hong Kong (2527 7825). Generally, the best bet is to contact the Hong Kong Arts Centre (2734 2009) and ask them what's going on around town.

**Arts & Entertainment**

# Galleries

Art scene? What art scene?

A prominent European art gallery owner, familiar with the Hong Kong art scene, has said that Hong Kong 'hates contemporary art'. Strong words. To be precise, he was referring to how institutions, dealers and the market (or rather the lack of it) feel about contemporary art. For those who come here looking for art that is 'exotic' and 'foreign', there's plenty to be found in many gift-shop style galleries, but if you're searching for something that is about the 'now' in this chaotic desert hothouse, you may have to peel back the layers of the obvious and look hard.

Of course, Hong Kong art is not all mass-produced paintings of junks and sunsets or Chinese pagodas swimming in swirling clouds. Yet a swift perusal of the **Hong Kong Museum of Art** (*see below*), the government-run gallery in Tsim Sha Tsui, reveals where the city's 'officially appointed' art and culture firmly sits (or is stuck, according to some) – in the gulf between tradition and modernity. Since the museum opened a decade ago, the criticisms have rarely ceased. Its architecture, including the surrounding Cultural Centre, is seen as an eyesore, and the art communities throw daggers at its programming and administration. Art professionals who visit the museum generally agree that the presentation is poor. The Tate Modern it will never be, however hard the **Contemporary Hong Kong Art** biennial (the next will be in 2002), an open-juried art competition, tries to provide a focus for the developing visual arts scene.

The **Hong Kong Arts Centre**, a community arts complex, attempts to plug some of the gaps by hosting topical local and international exhibitions that question the role of art in the context of changing societies and cultures. The **Pao Galleries** (*see p221*) is the main space; its other showing areas are closer to holes-in-the-wall. In the same building, the Goethe Institut's small **Würth Gallery** (*see p221*), in addition to its mission of promoting German culture, is a staunch supporter of local art – and its exhibitions are generally first rate.

Established in 1984, the **Fringe Club** (*see below*), and its associated annual January **City Festival** (formerly known as the Fringe Festival; *see p207*), has been instrumental in fostering the emerging art scene, giving exposure to anyone keen to create and exhibit. The Festival's initial 'creativity for all' attitude was embraced wholeheartedly by the local arts scene, but its

recent change towards a more defined direction, adding a substantial international focus, has diminished the buzz somewhat.

The **Hong Kong Arts Festival** (every February; *see p207*), on the other hand, is a run-of-the-mill international festival with largely formulaic programming – and a minimal visual arts side.

Artist-run spaces and collectives come and go in Hong Kong, with high rents resulting in many spaces only existing for short periods of time. One of the more enduring collectives, which operates its own gallery, is run by a mature group of young artists called **Para/Site** (*see p221*). Another group called **1aspace** (*see p221*), which aims to provide a contemporary art space for Hong Kong, is particularly innovative. It has recently been re-housed in a new venue in Kowloon.

On the commercial gallery front, visitors may find the choices limiting and unchallenging. In contrast to private galleries elsewhere in the world, local dealers are predominantly interested in mainland Chinese and Asian art, with few local works in sight. The majority of local buyers and collectors favour the decorative genre or avant-garde mainland works, while local artists occupy minimal attention in the commercial market.

## Public galleries & spaces

### Fringe Club

*Montblanc & Nokia Galleries, 2 Lower Albert Road, Central, HK Island (2521 7251). Central MTR (exit K)/23A bus.* **Open** noon-10pm Mon-Sat. **Admission** free. **Map** p66 C4.
The Montblanc Gallery is a highly visible street front space, whereas the Nokia Gallery is essentially wall-space within the club's bar. Both galleries have offered exposure for many emerging artists over the years, and this is one of the key Hong Kong visual arts venues. *See also p240.*

### Hong Kong Museum of Art

*10 Salisbury Road, Tsim Sha Tsui, Kowloon (2721 0116). Tsim Sha Tsui MTR (exit E)/buses to Tsim Sha Tsui Star Ferry Pier & along Salisbury Road/ Tsim Sha Tsui Star Ferry Pier.* **Open** 10am-6pm Mon-Wed, Fri-Sun. **Admission** HK$10; HK$5 concessions; free on Wed. **No credit cards. Map** p98 B3.
Considering that this is meant to be the cultural focus of Hong Kong art, both casual visitors and art aficionados are likely to be disappointed by

**Hong Kong Arts Centre**. *See p220.*

the limitations of its works and their often un-sympathetic presentation. The antique porcelain collection is the museum's strength, and there are also interesting sections of Hong Kong art, Chinese antiquities, folk art, ink and brush *shui mo* paintings, and colonial sketches. Explanations and contexts are often frustratingly scant. The gallery shop is a mish-mash of tourists gifts, knick-knacks and books on Chinese art. *See also p104.*

### Hong Kong Visual Arts Centre

*7A Kennedy Road, Central, HK Island (2521 3008). Buses along Garden Road & Cotton Tree Drive.* **Open** 10am-9pm Mon, Wed-Sun. **Admission** free. **Map** p67 E5.
Housed in a former British army barracks, this historical building is sadly wasted in its transformation into a community visual arts complex. Although it is situated by lovely Hong Kong Park, just steps away from the Lower Terminal of the Peak Tram, the much under-utilised space is generally only booked for school and amateur art shows. Operating under the wing of the Hong Kong Museum of Art (*see p220*), the building houses a lecture/film theatre and workshop studios in screenprinting, woodwork and ceramics. Not many visitors or audiences venture near here, least of all artists.

### 1aspace

*Cattle Depot, Ma Tau Kok Road, To Kwa Wan, Kowloon (2529 0087/space1a@hotmail.com). Buses along Ma Tau Kok Road.* **Open** phone for details. **Admission** free.
Set up in 1998, this contemporary art organisation mounted satellite exhibitions after the loss of its original spacious venue in Oil Street, North Point in December 1999. However, since May 2001, courtesy of the government, 1aspace and 19 other art organisations/groups have been installed in the old Ma Tau Kok Cattle Depot. Focusing on curated exhibitions, the group is centred on discussions around contemporary art. Shows in the past have included exhibitions on Hong Kong painting, identities and fashion. One to watch.

### Pao Galleries

*Hong Kong Arts Centre, 4/F-5/F, 2 Harbour Road, Wan Chai, Hong Kong (2582 0200). Wan Chai MTR (exit A1, C)/buses along Gloucester Road & Harbour Road/Wan Chai Star Ferry Pier.* **Open** 10am-8pm daily. **Admission** free. **Map** p80 B2.
The Hong Kong Arts Centre has its own regular programme of exhibitions, but most of the time its highly popular spaces are rented out to private exhibitors. Unfortunately, because the programming of exhibitions, films, plays and dance productions often tends to be fast and furious, many of the curated exhibitions are rushed and undeveloped, with many of the same artists returning over and over, without much rhyme or reason. The same could not be said of the Goethe Institut's excellent Würth Gallery (*see below*), which is also in the centre.

### Para/Site

*2 Po Yan Street, Sheung Wan, HK Island (2517 4620). Sheung Wan MTR (exit A2)/buses along Hollywood Road.* **Open** noon-8pm Thur; noon-7pm Fri-Sun. **Admission** free. **Map** p66 A2.
This young contemporary artists' collective has struggled over the past few years to maintain the existence of its gallery space. There were bright sparks in its early shows, but the programming has been patchy in recent times.

### University Museum & Art Gallery

*University of Hong Kong, Pok Fu Lam Road, HK Island (2241 5500). Buses along Pok Fu Lam Road.* **Open** 9.30am-6pm Mon-Sat; 1.30-5.30pm Sun. **Admission** free. **Map** p62.
The old Fung Ping Shan Museum is complimented by a recent new wing, but the University gallery only occasionally presents new art exhibitions, their focus being largely on antiquities and traditional arts and crafts artefacts. *See also p79.*

### Würth Gallery

*Goethe Institut, 14/F, Hong Kong Arts Centre, 2 Harbour Road, Wan Chai, HK Island (2802 0088). Wan Chai MTR (exit A1, C)/buses along Gloucester Road & Harbour Road/Wan Chai Star Ferry Pier.* **Open** 10am-8pm Mon-Fri; 2-6pm Sat. **Admission** free. **Map** p80 B2.

**Arts & Entertainment**

This gallery is one of the best exhibition venues in Hong Kong. For most of the year, the 'white cube' space is taken up by shows promoting German arts and culture, but the gallery is equally committed to exhibiting high quality local contemporary works. The Hong Kong Arts Centre is also home to the Pao Galleries (*see p221*).

## Commercial galleries

### Alisan Fine Arts
*Shop 315, Prince's Building, 10 Chater Road, Central, HK Island (2526 1091). Central MTR (exit J1, J2, J3)/buses & trams through Central/ Central Star Ferry Pier.* **Open** 10am-6pm Mon-Fri; 11am-6pm Sat. **Admission** free. **Map** p67 D4.
Being one of the longest established dealers in town, the works on offer here are mostly in the traditional or modernist vein, encompassing a range of Chinese *shui mo* or expressionist abstractions at the high end of the market. The tiny space (in a busy shopping arcade) does not offer much of a viewing experience, but its owner, Alice King, sister of the Hong Kong Chief Executive, certainly knows what the local collectors like.

### Art Scene China
*7/F, 1 Lan Kwai Fong, Central, HK Island (2501 0211/www.aschina.com). Central MTR (exit D1, G)/12M, 13, 23A, 40M, 43 bus.* **Open** 10.30am-7pm Mon-Sat. **No credit cards.** **Map** p66 C4.
At one time, Art Scene China traded solely from its website. These days, it's also gone offline, and has a clean-cut space above the craze and chaos of Lan Kwai Fong. As the name suggests, it deals with Chinese artists, predominantly those from the mainland. Exhibits change every three weeks and are almost always high quality.

### Chouinard Gallery
*1 Prince's Terrace, Mid-Levels, HK Island (2858 5072). Mid-Levels Escalator/buses along Caine Road.* **Open** 11am-8pm Tue-Sun. **Admission** free. **Map** p66 B4.
A new addition to the circuit, this gallery specialises in contemporary art from Asia (meaning mostly from outside Hong Kong) and overseas, again mostly in the expressive abstraction category.

### Galerie Martini
*1/F, 99F Wellington Street, Central, HK Island (2526 9566). Central MTR (exit D1, D2, G)/buses along Queen's Road Central.* **Open** 11am-7pm Tue-Sat. **Admission** free. **Map** p66 C3.
Galerie Martini isn't the easiest place to find; its entrance is a discreet door slotted between some large office blocks on Wellington Street. However once you've tracked it down, you'll find yourself checking out some of the most interesting and engaging works to be shown in Hong Kong. Exhibitions change monthly, and are usually international in scope.

### Hanart TZ Gallery
*Room 202, Henley Building, 5 Queen's Road, Central, HK Island (2526 9019). Central MTR (exit H, K)/buses along Queen's Road Central.* **Open** 10am-6.30pm Mon-Fri; 10am-6pm Sat. **Admission** free. **Map** p67 D4.
The gallery is a showcase for works by mainland Chinese, Taiwanese, local and – now and again – international artists. The flavour is distinctly Oriental with a play on naïve art, while avant-garde China pop works direct the sales angle. Don't expect to find much cool minimalism here.

### John Batten Gallery
*64 Peel Street, Central, HK Island (2854 1018). Mid-Levels Escalator/buses along Caine Road.* **Open** 11am-7pm Tue-Sat. **Admission** free. **Map** p66 B3.
John Batten's small street-front space has to rank as one of the top commercial venues in town. While his taste stretches from subtle lyrical abstraction to modernist photography and Asian contemporary art, he has an equally committed interest in the local art scene.

### Schoeni Art Gallery
*UG/F, 21-31 Old Bailey Street, Central, HK Island (2869 8802). Mid-Levels Escalator/buses along Hollywood Road & Caine Road.* **Open** 10am-6.30pm Mon-Sat. **Credit** AmEx, MC, V. **Map** p67 C4.
After ten years in the arts business, Mr Schoeni, the man behind the gallery, recently opened a second studio on busy Hollywood Road (No.27; 2542 3143; 10am-6.30pm Mon-Sat). Both outlets display a diverse assortment of art, but always have oils of a humorous nature from Asia, Europe and, of course, China. Exhibits change monthly, so it's worth popping back to check out the latest works.

## Other venues/sources

### Far Out East
*9492 1560/helen@far-out-east.com.* **Open** by appointment.
Specialising in original revolutionary and propaganda posters from China from the 1950s, Helen Rigby's rare collection of printed memorabilia is modestly priced (HK$150 to HK$1,200). She works from home, so you have to phone in advance to make an appointment and for directions.

### Suite Caroline
*9049 3339/suitecaroline@hongkong.com.* **Open** by appointment.
Currently situated on Caroline Road in Causeway Bay, this private venue mounts one-day group and solo exhibitions in a small domestic environment. Its representation includes artists working in photography, installation and fashion. The works occupy the conceptual/postmodern territory, reflecting the hybrid of art, commerce, design and fashion in a critical and humorous manner. Phone for the latest location details.

# Gay & Lesbian

It's small, and imperfectly formed, but the scene is there if you know where to look.

With a slow but sure increase in social acceptance, the Hong Kong gay communities are becoming more proactive and vocal, fighting over rights and issues. However, there's still a very long way to go. The subject of homosexuality is still considered taboo in traditional Chinese society, and solidarity is often restricted to those involved in some of Hong Kong's dedicated gay groups. Although younger gays are becoming more open and accepting of their identity, you will still find much of the more mature gay crowd remains firmly in the closet. Having said that, Hong Kong-published gay pictorials are increasingly popular purchases at the street news-stands.

Hong Kong's gay scene generally focuses on bars and discos, with karaoke bars offering more limited meeting opportunities. For those who don't like to beat around the bush, the various saunas are the prime pickup joints. The best night for a party trail is Saturday, when Propaganda becomes the focus of the gay scene.

## Bars, cafés, clubs & karaokes

### Club 97
*9 Lan Kwai Fong, Central, HK Island (2186 1819). Central MTR (exit D1, D2)/12M, 13, 23A, 40M, 43 bus.* **Open** 6-10pm Fri. **Credit** AmEx, DC, MC, V. **Map** p66 C4.
This once premier (mixed) night spot is still the hangout for many local stars and celebrities, but the shine on the *Casablanca*-style decor is fast losing its patina – rather like an old Hollywood set. Every Friday evening, the suited gay brigade turn up for their pre-dinner drinks. *See also p230.*

### G Attitude
*3/F, 38 Cochrane Street, Central, HK Island (2851 7933). Mid-Levels Escalator/Central MTR (exit D1, D2)/buses along Queen's Road Central.* **Open** noon-10pm Mon-Thur; noon-midnight Fri, Sat. **No credit cards. Map** p66 C3.
In the heart of Central, this newish café is a relaxing place to hang out. The menu includes non-alcoholic drinks and desserts. Books, magazines and video CDs are available for patrons to peruse.

### G2K
*15/F, Yeung Iu Chi Commercial Building, 460-462 Jaffe Road, Causeway Bay, HK Island (2892 1391). Causeway Bay MTR (exit C)/buses along Gloucester Road.* **Open** 4pm-midnight Mon-Thur; 4pm-1am Fri-Sun. **No credit cards. Map** p80 C1.

Before the rush at **Propaganda**. *See p224.*

A small, intimate café, G2K offers light snacks, coffees and other drinks, plus a selection of magazines and books for customers to peruse, and a terminal for Internet access.

### H2O Entertainment Club
*2/F, Hop Yee Building, 474-476 Lockhart Road, Causeway Bay, HK Island (2834 6451). Causeway Bay MTR (exit C)/buses & trams along Hennessy Road.* **Open** 8pm-4.30am Mon-Thur; 5pm-6am Fri, Sat. **Credit** MC, V. **Map** p80 D1.
This friendly karaoke bar is frequented by lesbians, although guys are equally welcome.

### New Wally Matt Lounge
*5A Humphreys Avenue, Tsim Sha Tsui, Kowloon (2721 2568). Tsim Sha Tsui MTR (exit A2)/buses along Nathan Road.* **Open** 5pm-4am daily. **No credit cards. Map** p98 C2.
Decorated like an old-style pub, the New Wally Matt Lounge's clientele is almost exclusively big burly guys, but the atmosphere is pretty laid-back, if not subdued. There is an Internet terminal for all to use.

## Propaganda

*Lower G/F, 1 Hollywood Road, Central, HK Island
(2868 1316). Central MTR (exit D1, D2)/Mid-Levels
Escalator/12M, 13, 23A, 26, 40M, 43 bus.* **Open**
9pm-3.30am Mon-Fri; 9pm-6am Sat. **Admission**
*Mon-Wed* free; *Thur* free-HK$80; *Fri* HK$70-$140;
*Sat* HK$150-$220. All prices include 1 drink.
**Credit** AmEx, DC, MC, V. **Map** p66 C3.
This is the only gay disco in town. Considering the
hefty entry fees and drinks prices, and the music
served up by the resident DJs, which often veers
towards the dreary and monotonous, the local crowd
has a love-hate relationship with Propaganda. First-
time visitors, though, should be delighted by the fer-
vour and pace on a Saturday night. *See also p232.*

## Rice

*33 Jervois Street (corner of Mercer & Jervois streets),
Sheung Wan, HK Island (2851 4800). Sheung Wan
MTR (exit A2)/buses along Queen's Road Central.*
**Open** 6.30pm-2am Mon-Fri, Sun; 8pm-3am Sat.
**Credit** MC, V. **Map** p66 B2.
Out of the way in Sheung Wan, this intimate bar is
a haven for those in search of a laid-back atmosphere. The rice-themed retro interior comes courtesy
of the architect-owner, while pigeon holes in the wall
offer a message service for anyone interested. DJs
play every night except Monday. *See also p171.*

## Virus

*6/F, Allways Centre, 468 Jaffe Road, Causeway Bay,
HK Island (2904 7207). Causeway Bay MTR (exit
C)/buses along Gloucester Road.* **Open** 9pm-1am
daily. **Credit** MC, V. **Map** p80 C1.
Another karaoke bar, mainly for lesbians.

## Wally Matt Bar & Lounge

*3 Granville Circuit, Tsim Sha Tsui, Kowloon (2367
6874). Tsim Sha Tsui MTR (exit B2)/buses along
Chatham Road South.* **Open** 5pm-4am daily.
**Credit** MC, V. **Map** p98 C1.
Confusingly, this place is apparently no relation
to the New Wally Matt Lounge (*see p223*). Keen
observers will notice a quite different set of patrons:
the crowd here is largely young. The decor borders
on the tacky, but it is still worth a look. Located
behind the Ramada Hotel on Chatham Road in
Tsim Sha Tsui, you'll find the bar's entrance on
Granville Road.

## Why Not

*12/F, Kyoto Plaza, 491-499 Lockhart Road,
Causeway Bay, HK Island (2572 7808). Causeway
Bay MTR (exit C)/buses & trams along Hennessy
Road.* **Open** 9pm-4.30am Mon-Fri, Sun; 9pm-6am
Sat. **Credit** (HK$200 min) AmEx, MC, V.
**Map** p80 D1.
This once extremely popular karaoke lounge has
had its ups and downs. After 2am on Saturday, the
more subdued karaoke crooning gives way to the
fast-track limericks of Cantopop. Strictly for the
adventurous and those seeking an experience at the
grass roots of the Hong Kong gay scene.

## Works

*1/F, 30-32 Wyndham Street, Central, HK Island
(2868 6102). Central MTR (exit D1, D2, G)/
13, 26, 43 bus.* **Open** 7pm-2am Tue-Sat;
9pm-3am Sun. **Admission** HK$60 inclusive
of 1 standard drink. **Credit** AmEx, DC, MC, V.
**Map** p66 C4.

**Rice** – well worth a trip to Sheung Wan.

This bar/club occupies the old Propaganda location right on the five-way junction near Lan Kwai Fong, and the uniformly black interior is hardly able to mask the aging premises. The crowd generally frequents the bar as an early cruising spot, before moving on to Propaganda after midnight. Try Friday and Saturday nights around 11pm.

### Zip

*G/F, 2 Glenealy, Central, HK Island (2523 3595). Buses along Upper Albert Road.* **Open** 6pm-2am daily. **Credit** AmEx, MC, V. **Map** p66 C5.
High on Glenealy, Zip sports a large steel door but no visible signage (it's next to Labelle Hair Salon). Once a bustling bar with a decor worthy of a mention in *Wallpaper\**, its looks have faded away along with the gay *gweilos* who used to congregate here. Still, those in search of an al fresco venue can pay a visit to the covered outdoor patio.

## Saunas

For a place the size of Hong Kong, there is a surprisingly large number of gay saunas. The best time to visit is in the early evening, right after the end of the working day, or on weekend afternoons.

### Babylon

*2/F, Chun Lee Commercial Building, 494-496 Nathan Road, Yau Ma Tei, Kowloon (2388 5963) Yau Ma Tei MTR (exit A1, A2, B1, C, D)/buses along Nathan Road.* **Open** 2pm-midnight Mon-Fri; noon-midnight Sat, Sun. **Admission** *Mon-Fri* HK$49; *Sat, Sun* HK$70. **No credit cards.** **Map** p110 B4.
Babylon is a well-established name among the locals, where everyone seems to be on familiar terms with each other.

# Cruise zones

### Here's the pick of the pick-up places.

### Joyce

*23 Nathan Road, Tsim Sha Tsui, Kowloon (2367 8128). Tsim Sha Tsui MTR (exit E)/ buses along Nathan Road/Tsim Sha Tsui Star Ferry Pier.* **Open** noon-10.30pm Mon-Sat; noon-7pm Sun. **Map** p98 C2.
Joyce Ma's fashion empire is the store *de rigueur* for the gay and lesbian community. You can find smaller branches in Pacific Place and Admiralty, and on Nathan Road, Tsim Sha Tsui. *See also p187.*

### Kowloon Park Public Pool

*Kowloon Park, Jordan, Kowloon. Jordan MTR (exit A1).* **Map** p98 B1.
Open during the summer months, this is a hot cruising spot, along with the Victoria Park public pool (Tin Hau MTR). You can also try the Morrison Hill Public Pool (Oi Kwan Road, Wan Chai. Wan Chai MTR). The pools are closed noon-1pm and 6.30-7.30pm.

### Middle Bay Beach

*South Bay Road, HK Island.* **Map** p62.
Catch the 6, 6A, 6X or 260 bus, or a minibus at Tang Lung Street, Causeway Bay (outside We Club), to Repulse Bay Beach. Walk a short distance along South Bay Road, then take a long flight of narrow steps down to Middle Bay, Hong Kong's official gay beach. Follow your instincts and you'll find it; otherwise, consult passers-by. After the sun sets, the beach turns raunchy.

### Monmouth Park

*Corner of Monmouth Path & Queen's Road East, near Pacific Place, Admiralty, HK Island. Admiralty MTR (exit F).* **Map** p80 A2.
Fronted by a small resting area, this public convenience turns into an industrious meeting place from dusk. Lan Kwai Fong's public loo in Central is also popular.

### Pacific Place

*88 Queensway, Admiralty, HK Island. Admiralty MTR (exit C1)/buses through Central.* **Open** 10.30am-8pm daily. **Map** p67 F5.
The reigning mall for pickups or just people-spotting. Also popular are Festival Walk, Kowloon Tong; Ocean Terminal and Ocean Centre, Tsim Sha Tsui, plus the HMV stores in Central and Tsim Sha Tsui. *See also p182* and *chapter* **Shopping**.

### Tom Turk's Gym

*Citibank Tower, 3 Garden Road, Central, HK Island (2521 4547). Buses along Garden Road.* **Open** 6.30am-10.30pm Mon-Thur; 6.30am-9pm Fri, Sat; 10am-8pm Sun. **Admission** HK$200 for one-off visit before 5pm; HK$250 after 5pm. **Credit** AmEx, DC, MC, V. **Map** p67 E5.
For unknown historical reasons, this long-established gym is much favoured by gays. The indoor pool is an added bonus. Check out the premises during the off-peak daytime hours.

**Arts & Entertainment**

### CE (Central Escalator)

*2/F, Cheung Hing Commercial Building, 37-43 Cochrane Street, Central, HK Island (2581 9951) Mid-Levels Escalator/buses along Queen's Road Central.* **Open** 2pm-midnight daily. **Admission** HK$108 for 1st visit, plus discount voucher for next visit. **Credit** AmEx, MC, V. **Map** p66 C3.

This popular sauna in Central attracts a mix of local and overseas patrons.

### Chaps Fitness Centre

*G/F, 15 Ming Yuen Western Street, North Point, HK Island (2570 9339). North Point MTR.* **Open** 3.30pm-midnight Mon-Thur; 2.30pm-1am Fri; 2.30pm-4am Sat; 2.30pm-midnight Sun. **Admission** HK$118, plus 20% discount voucher for next visit. **No credit cards.**

Off the beaten track, but worth a visit because the friendly staff stage creative theme nights throughout the week. Monday is dedicated to underwear, Tuesday and Wednesday are running bare for all, and Thursday belongs to the executive set (entry costs HK$95 for those in suits). Friday is stripped down to T-backs, Saturday returns to the naked skin and Sunday is handed over to muscle guys.

### Dream Factory

*Unit E, 2/F, Ho Lee Commercial Building, 17-22 Lan Kwai Fong, Central, HK Island (2868-2786). Central MTR (exit D1, D2, G)/12M, 13, 23A, 40M, 43 bus.* **Open** 3-11pm Mon-Thur; 2pm-midnight Fri-Sun. **Admission** *Mon-Thur* HK$78; *Fri-Sun* HK$88. **No credit cards.** **Map** p66 C4.

This sauna's advertisement features a host by the name of Danny Fung, so perhaps he's the man to ask for upon your arrival.

### EM-motion@l

*26/F, Workingview Commercial Building, 21 Yiu Wa Street, Causeway Bay, HK Island (2572 1318). Causeway Bay MTR (exit B, F)/buses along Hennessy Road.* **Open** 4pm-midnight Mon-Thur; 3pm-midnight Fri-Sun. **Admission** HK$132. **No credit cards.** **Map** p80 D2.

The enthusiastic staff pride themselves on operating the cleanest sauna, and one of the most fancifully themed programmes, in town. Monday is for the young; Tuesday is underwear night; those who turn up in a business suit on Wednesday get in for HK$70; Thursday turns raunchy – everybody is nude except for their masks (provided); and Friday goes wild with rugged cavemen. If you arrive after 9pm, just click open the gate at the entrance, and enter.

### Game Boy

*2/F, 324 Lockhart Road, Wan Chai, HK Island (2369 8174). Buses & trams along Hennessy Road.* **Open** 4.30pm-midnight daily. **Admission** HK$98. **No credit cards.** **Map** p80 C2.

A favourite spot for both locals and visitors.

### HX Box

*Shop B, 9 Old Bailey Street, Central, HK Island (2810 0144/www.hxhongkong.com). Buses along Hollywood Road.* **Open** 4-11pm Wed-Sun; 4pm-5am Sat. **Admission** HK$60. **No credit cards.** **Map** p66 C4.

A new addition to the list, this is a Japanese-style enterprise that's devoted to rippling muscles and bulges from Thursday to Sunday. There are no karaoke machines or TVs, but there are two action rooms, a maze and private rooms. It's located next to Staunton Street Wine Cellar.

### Rome Club

*2/F, Chiap Lee Commercial Building, 27 Ashley Road, Tsim Sha Tsui, Kowloon (2376 0602). Tsim Sha Tsui MTR (exit A1)/buses along Nathan Road/ Tsim Sha Tsui Star Ferry Pier.* **Open** 3pm-midnight daily. **Admission** HK$118 for 1st visit, plus voucher for HK$77 entry on 2nd visit. **No credit cards.** **Map** p98 B2.

One of Hong Kong's oldest saunas, Rome Club features a nude night on Mondays. On Tuesdays, entry for those under the age of 24 is HK$48.

### We Club

*3/F, Thai Kong Building (entrance on Tang Lung Street, opposite minibus depot), 482 Hennessy Road, Causeway Bay, HK Island (2833 6677). Causeway Bay MTR (exit B)/buses & trams along Hennessy Road.* **Open** 3pm-midnight Mon-Fri; 2pm-midnight Sat, Sun. **Admission** HK$185 plus HK$20 membership fee on 1st visit, plus $180 voucher for next visit; Tue HK$120. **Credit** AmEx. **Map** p80 D2.

This sauna is at the top of many a gay list. More of a recreation club, it has a weight training area, karaoke room and small sauna.

## Shops

## Books

### Angelo De Capri

*18 Wo On Lane, Lan Kwai Fong, Central, HK Island (2857 7148). Central MTR (exit D1, G)/12M, 13, 23A, 40M, 43 bus.* **Open** noon-9pm Tue-Sun. **No credit cards.** **Map** p66 C4.

This shop sells gay and lesbian books, magazines, videos and cards. *See also p179.*

### General

*10/F, United Building, 499 Hennessy Road, Causeway Bay, HK Island (2572 0768). Causeway Bay MTR (exit B)/buses & trams along Hennessy Road.* **Open** 1-10pm Mon-Sat; 2.30-10pm Sun. **Credit** MC, V. **Map** p80 D2.

Open since 1992, this shop has a range of books, magazines, videos, toys and swimwear.

### Page One

*Shop 130, Lower G/F, Festival Walk, 80 Tat Chee Avenue, Kowloon Tong, Kowloon (2778 2808). Kowloon Tong MTR.* **Open** 11am-10pm Mon-Thur, Sun; 11am-10.30pm Fri, Sat. **Credit** AmEx, DC, MC, V.

Although this chain also has branches in Times Square (Causeway Bay) and Harbour City (Tsim Sha Tsui), its gay section is largely located in the Festival Walk store. In addition, there's a large selection of general books. *See also p180.*

**Angel De Capri.** *See p226.*

This is the best place to head if you are looking for a special outfit to dazzle at any party. Specialising in creating corporate entertainment events, it also hires out costumes for that special occasion.

## Resources & organisations

### Freemen
*PO Box 2443, Hong Kong (9106 4983/ hongkongfreemen@hotmail.com).*
This gay male social group offers group counselling and regular social activities.

### Gay Station Hong Kong
*PO Box 84366, Hung Hom Bay Post Office, Hong Kong (2333 1004/www.gaystation.com.hk).*
This bilingual gay/lesbian site has a live webcast in Cantonese from 11pm to midnight daily, as well as a chatroom, message board, personals and archive content.

### HK Blessed Minority Christian Fellowship
*2834 6601/www.bmcf.org.hk/ blessedminority@hongkong.com.*
Worship and gathering for gays and lesbians every Sunday. Newcomers should meet a member of the Blessed Minority, who will be holding a bible, at the Fountain of the Grand Millennium Plaza in Sheung Wan (exit E2 of MTR) between 3.30pm and 3.45pm every Sunday. The service is conducted in Cantonese, so ring ahead if you require simultaneous translation.

### HK Ten Percent Club
*PO Box 72207, Kowloon Central Post Office, Hong Kong (2314 8726/hkten@hotmail.com).*
**Phone enquiries** 7.30-9.30pm Tue, Thur.
The club, which publishes a quarterly newsletter, aims to raise the social and political awareness of the Hong Kong gay community.

### Horizons
*PO Box 6837, Hong Kong (2815 9268/ horizons_tongzhi@hongkong.com).*
**Phone enquiries** 7.30-10.30pm Tue, Thur.
Horizons offers counselling and social activities, including monthly hiking trips, music appreciation and other interest groups.

### Queer Sisters
*PO Box 9313, Hong Kong (hotline 2314 4348/ pager 7112 8445 a/c 1613/www.qs.org.hk).*
**Phone enquiries** 7.30-10pm Thur.
Counselling, educational workshops and social activities for lesbians are offered by Queer Sisters, and it has a gathering on the last Sunday of every month.

### Tongzhi Conference
*pager 7309 7557/tongzhi@egroups.com.*
The Tongzhi Conference, which brings together communities in Hong Kong and other Asian cities to discuss gay and lesbian issues, was previously held in 1996, 1998 and 1999. The next conference is scheduled for the latter part of 2001.

### POV
*1/F, Hong Kong Mansion, 137-147 Lockhart Road, Wan Chai, HK Island (2865 5116). Wan Chai MTR (exit A1, C)/buses along Hennessy Road.* **Open** 11am-10pm Mon-Fri; 11am-midnight Sat; 1-10pm Sun. **Credit** MC, V. **Map** p80 B2.
Primarily a film bookstore, POV boasts the best range of specialist cinema books in Hong Kong, including a generous gay section.

## Partywear & lingerie

### Fetish Fashion
*Mezzanine Floor, Merlin Building, 32 Cochrane Street, Central, HK Island (2544 1155/ www.fetishfashion.com.hk). Mid-Levels Escalator/ buses along Queen's Road Central.* **Open** noon-10pm Mon-Sat. **Credit** AmEx, MC, V. **Map** p66 C3.
Specialising in leather and rubber wear, Fetish Fashion also has a range of erotic underwear, plus playroom equipment. *See also p190.*

### Globemen
*Shop 212, Causeway Bay Centre, 15 Sugar Street, Causeway Bay, HK Island (2808 2370). Causeway Bay MTR (exit E)/buses along Hennessy Road.* **Open** 3-9pm Mon-Fri; 2-8.30pm Sat, Sun. **Credit** MC, V. **Map** p80 D2.
A small shop sells a range of body- and underwear. The mall in which it is located also has a selection of interesting shops dealing in comics and toys, film paraphernalia and second-hand CDs.

### House of Siren
*23 Staunton Street, Central, HK Island (2530 2371). Mid-Levels Escalator/12M, 13, 23A, 26, 40M, 43 bus.* **Open** by appointment. **No credit cards**. **Map** p66 B3.

# Nightlife

Hong Kong clubs are kickin', but live music is stinkin'.

## Clubs

The club scene in Hong Kong is one of the most vibrant in Asia, and is on a par with most global cities. Top international DJs drop in regularly, world-class venues are cropping up and the scene has really kicked off in recent years.

It's also a place where you can party until you drop. Clubbing through until Sunday afternoon has long been possible – and popular. But since 1997, the club scene has undergone a major transformation. What was once a hard core of a few hundred (mainly British) expatriates gathering in converted restaurants has become über-chic among the Chinese. Many thousands of young locals, including models, actors and the children of billionaires, now flock to raves. But so, too, do triad gangs.

The explosion of 'rave culture' has led to a certain amount of media hysteria over a sudden surge in recreational drug use, particularly ecstasy (which translates into Chinese as 'head-shaking pill') and ketamine. More positively, the growth has spawned more and better local DJs, a greater variety of music and a more sophisticated permanent club scene. Clubbers are a mix of the casually dressed and expensive sophisticate: if they can afford to trash it, they'll be wearing a D&G outfit.

The most disturbing trend is probably for GLO-STICKS, babies' dummies and oversized sunglasses, which shows no sign of abating. But perhaps that's not surprising in a culture that deifies the anodyne Japanese cartoon character Hello Kitty. Yes, they proudly wear the mouthless feline on their raving attire, too.

For all the diversity, progressive house and trance remain the most popular with young clubbers, with trance tending to attract the less desirable elements. Almost every week there is a big name DJ from the US, Europe or Japan in town. Get-rich-quick entrepreneurs are often the driving force behind these large parties, meaning high prices (of up to HK$600) when the likes of John Digweed are playing. To be fair, it isn't cheap to hire and install a sound system – and that's before the DJ costs are taken into account. And, anyway, clubbers tend to be fickle, meaning organisers sometimes go to great lengths only to come a cropper on the

Flash your cash with the Gucci set at **JJs**. *See p230.*

night. Venues are normally ad hoc, the old Hong Kong Exhibition Centre in Wan Chai and the Hi-Tech Industrial Centre in Kowloon being two favourites for large-scale parties.

Among the regular party organisers Way Out East dominates, guaranteeing a good turn out with a stable that includes Digweed, Sasha and Judge Jules. But other promoters, like Space and Fierce Productions, regularly put on good nights. Hong Kong is a staple on the Ministry of Sound, Renaissance and Cream international circuits. For drum 'n' bass, Cloud 9 has good monthly parties. Details of events can be seen in flyers around Lan Kwai Fong and SoHo, or in events guides such as *24/7*, *HK Magazine* and *BC Magazine*. The clubbers' bible, however, is *Absolute*, a monthly magazine.

If you're not blinded by big names, locally run parties are cheaper, feature many talented local spin doctors (*see p231* **Local mixmasters**) and can be much more fun. Club Progressive runs regular progressive house all-nighters at Kwun Tong Ferry Pier. It boasts a membership of 10,000 and has some good local DJ/producers on its books, including Tszpun, who has his own mini-album out on the Club Progressive label (download it from www.clubprogressive.co.uk).

Then there are about a dozen or so smaller party-makers who hold nights, from Funky Times ('70s disco and disco house) to the Mash Up crew's monthly drum 'n' bass fix.

In 2000, Hong Kong's first superclub, Pink, was born. With two dance floors, a host of bars, superb lighting and a great sound system (plus a vibrating floor, and many other gadgets and gizmos), Pink is by far the region's most cutting-edge club. But its location in Chai Wan (a hefty trek on the MTR or expensive taxi ride) means it has yet to reach its potential. And it may find life harder as a cluster of clubs, like Blush, Drop and Liquid, have sprung up in Central. These may be smaller, but their location means that clubbers can walk between half a dozen clubs.

Although there are some exceptions, places tend to be amazingly popular when they open and then quickly fall out of fashion. These days it is Central that is in the ascendancy, with Wan Chai and Tsim Sha Tsui struggling to compete for genuine, discerning club-goers.

In their favour, when you're up for a big night out, the Wan Chai clubs stay open later. But you have been warned: many Wan Chai bars have house bands playing Bontempi organs over records and are so high on the cringe factor that they go way beyond humorous – unless hopelessly drunk suits and off-duty hookers bumpin' and grindin' to the strains of a tacky dance tune amuse you. If you want a real club experience, you'd do best to avoid them.

As you've probably realised by now, thanks to the late opening hours, Hong Kongers party long and hard. It's not unusual to go from Friday night to Sunday afternoon in one roll. On Sunday mornings, clubs such as CE Top and Yellow Frog have been known to only stop when the punters go home.

Finally, a warning: just like anywhere else in the world, problems can occur in clubs. Triad gang fights are not unknown, weapons have been found inside venues and police sometimes switch off the music to search clubbers. However, Hong Kong still remains one of the safest cities in the world, and you would be unlucky to witness violence or trouble.

### Blush

*Shops D & E, Felicity Building, 54-58 Hollywood Road, Central, HK Island (2522 6428). Central MTR (exit D1, D2, G)/Mid-Levels Escalator/12M, 13, 23A, 26, 40M, 43 bus.* **Open** 6pm-very late daily. **Admission** *Mon-Thur, Sun* free; *Fri, Sat* HK$100 (more for special nights). **Credit** DC, MC, V. **Map** p66 C3.

Blush was created by the team behind phi-b (*see p231*), after crowds began to outgrow the original (tiny) venue. But Blush has its own identity and is designed to create 'floating energy'. Musically, it plays a full range of styles and fields the best local talent and, occasionally, international DJs. Each night has a consistent groove.

### C Club

*Basement, California Tower, 30-32 D'Aguilar Street, Central (2526 1139). Central MTR (exit D1, G)/ 12M, 13, 23A, 40M, 43 bus.* **Open** 7pm-3am Mon-Sat; 6-11pm Sun. **Admission** free. **Credit** AmEx, DC, MC, V.

Rich red velvet sofas and drapes gives this new club in Lan Kwai Fong a sumptuous, sexy feel. The crowd has a too few many suits in the week and can be a bit posey, but the music is good, especially after 11pm. Drink prices aren't cheap, but if you can grab a cosy sofa at the back, you'll want to stay for hours.

### CE Top

*3/F & 9/F, Chuang Hing Commercial Building, 37-43 Cochrane Street, Central, HK Island (2544 3581). Mid-Levels Escalator/buses along Queen's Road Central.* **Open** 7pm-late Mon-Thur; 11pm-8am Fri, Sat. **Admission** *Mon-Thur* free; *Fri, Sat* HK$100 (incl 1 drink). **Credit** MC, V. **Map** p66 C3.

A perennial late-night, early morning hangout. Hard house, trance and Goa vibes are the staples. A dilapidated lift (or staircase for the energetic) serves the two floors of the club, which is located in a narrow commercial block. The third floor is a karaoke venue during the week, but at weekends it becomes a full-on club, like the ninth floor, which also has a rooftop from where you can see the sun come up. It's cramped and popular with young miscreants, but no one seems to care as long as the music's going. Regular nights include Club Elements and Hear No Evil on Fridays.

## Club ING

*4/F, Renaissance Harbour View Hotel, Harbour Road, Wan Chai, HK Island (2836 3690). Wan Chai MTR (exit A1, C)/buses along Gloucester Road.* **Open** 7pm-late Mon-Sat. **Admission** *Mon, Tue* free; *Wed* HK$100 (incl 1 drink); *Thur* HK$160 (free for women); *Fri* HK$120 (incl 1 drink); *Sat* HK$160 (incl 1 drink). **Credit** AmEx, MC, V. **Map** p80 B1.

Stylish, upscale venue that has been through many incarnations. Popular with the Prada set, especially on Ladies' Night (Thursdays), you'll know why when you see the drink prices. Musically, it runs the gamut from pop to house, with salsa on Wednesdays (*see p237* **Everybody salsa!**). Fridays and Saturdays, when guest DJs often play, are normally best.

## Club 97

*9 Lan Kwai Fong, Central, HK Island (2810 9333). Central MTR (exit D1, D2, G)/12M, 13, 23A, 40M, 43 bus.* **Open** 8pm-3am Tue, Wed; 8pm-4am Thur; 11pm-6am Fri (6-10pm gay happy hour); 11pm-6am Sat. **Admission** supposedly members only, but non-members can pay on the door most nights. **Credit** AmEx, MC, V. **Map** p66 C4.

Club 97 is frequented by the flash and wealthy (or wannabe wealthy) set, and visiting celebrities. Small, it has a Moroccan style interior of comfy alcoves surrounding a tiny dance floor. Its door bitches are famous and drinks are expensive (HK$65 upwards), but the music, which includes jazzy house and New York garage with resident DJ Janv, is normally good. Things hot up at weekends, with house and garage, plus Afro-tribal and Latino beats. *See also p223.*

## Drop

*B/F, On Lok Mansion, 39-43 Hollywood Road, Central, HK Island (2543 8856/www.drophk.com). Central MTR (exit D1, D2, G)/Mid-Levels Escalator/ 12M, 13, 23A, 26, 40M, 43 bus.* **Open** phone for details. **Admission** varies. **Credit** phone for details. **Map** p66 C3.

New and noted by the club cognoscenti, Drop is a slick club in the tradition of Club 97 – only a lot cooler. DJ Joel Lai presides over operations, and there's a good mix of expats and locals who like funky vibes. Drinks aren't cheap, but the friendly atmosphere and consistent music policy are worth the expense.

## Home

*2/F, 23 Hollywood Road, Central, HK Island (2545 0023). Central MTR (exit D1, D2, G)/Mid-Levels Escalator/12M, 13, 23A, 26, 40M, 43 bus.* **Open** 10pm-late (very late at weekends) Tue-Sat. **Admission** free. **Credit** AmEx, MC, V. **Map** p66 C3.

Home has a great chill-out area, with low slung couches separated from the dance floor by a large island bar. Home has a no-trance policy and its nights are the most funky and soulful of all Central's clubs. Resident DJ Kulu may be 60 years old (complete with white beard), but his acid jazz/soul collection is the envy of younger DJs. If you like R&B, uplifting house and disco beats, Home is where your heart is (and soul) should be. There are also regular gay nights.

## In-V

*17/F-19/F, New World Renaissance Hotel, 22 Salisbury Road, Tsim Sha Tsui, Kowloon (2734 6640). Tsim Sha Tsui MTR (exit E)/buses to Tsim Sha Tsui Star Ferry Pier & along Salisbury Road/Tsim Sha Tsui Star Ferry Pier.* **Open** 7pm-3am Mon-Sat. **Admission** free. **Credit** AmEx, DC, MC, V. **Map** p98 C3.

More of an entertainment complex than a club, this opulent nightspot is for the well-heeled, or financially well-endowed, with live karaoke, a cigar and fine wine area, and live music courtesy of a resident band. DJs play tried and tested dance tunes and pop, depending on the crowd. Women get two free drinks on Ladies' Night (Friday).

## JJs

*Grand Hyatt Hotel, 1 Harbour Road, Wan Chai, HK Island (2588 1234 ext 6353). Wan Chai MTR (exit A1, C)/buses along Gloucester Road.* **Open** 5.30pm-3am Mon-Thur; 5.30pm-3am Fri; 6pm-4am Sat; 2.30-7pm Sun. **Admission** *Mon-Thur* HK$100 (incl 1 drink); *Fri, Sat* HK$200 (incl 2 drinks). **Credit** AmEx, DC, MC, V. **Map** p80 B1.

Dress to impress if you head here. Suits winding down after work and young Gucci-clad women hopping to attract a budding tycoon wriggle around the dance floor to covers of Latin and disco tunes cranked out by the house band, before the DJs get going with popular songs of the moment, be it Ricky Martin or a crossover dance hit. Put the tab on your corporate credit card – or don't be too flash.

## Liquid

*G/F, Winly Building, 1-5 Elgin Street, Central, HK Island (2517 3310). Mid-Levels Escalator/ 26 bus.* **Open** 6pm-late daily. **Admission** varies; members only, others can apply for temporary membership at the door. **Credit** AmEx, MC, V. **Map** p66 B3.

One of the very latest, classier additions to the burgeoning Central nightlife scene, Liquid is modelled on London's popular night haunts. The 3,000sq ft space is divided into an upstairs lounge bar and downstairs nightclub. Local, and occasionally international, DJs create different vibes for the different floors, which appeal to an ultra-cool, Western/Chinese crowd.

## Mine

*G/F, Lockhart House, 441 Lockhart Road, Wan Chai, HK Island (2267 8822). Causeway Bay MTR (exit C)/buses & trams along Hennessy Road.* **Open** 5pm-4am Mon-Thur; 8pm-6am Fri, Sat. **Admission** *Mon-Thur* HK$100; *Fri, Sat* HK$180. **Credit** AmEx, V. **Map** p80 C2.

Opened in the summer of 2000, Mine's interior is like a silver mine, sparkling at every turn. At 10,000sq ft, it's one of the largest clubs in town and has hosted the DMC DJ championships, plus a few big name DJs recently. The rest of the time it's trance, progressive house and hip hop with local turntablists. The crowd tends to be young.

# Local mixmasters

In the early 1990s, the fledgling club scene in Hong Kong served a small hardcore of clubbers, but that didn't mean there was a lack of local talent behind the decks. Until noon on Sunday the Big Apple, and, later, Neptunes, in Wan Chai were heaving sweatboxes crammed with people still going from all-night parties.

It was at these seemingly never-ending parties that DJs like **Lee Burridge** honed their skills. Burridge had a loyal following and his marathon ten-hour sets became legendary, albeit in parochial terms. Local DJs, however, always had a chance to play with the international big guns, warming up and winding down parties on the same bill as the likes of Carl Cox, John Digweed and Tony de Vit.

It was playing with Sasha and Craig Richards that Burridge earned his big break. Impressed by Burridge's mixing and ability to work the crowd, Sasha and Richards encouraged him to up sticks back to his native Britain, where they jointly set up Tyrant.

Burridge went from strength to strength, and within a couple of years was voted best newcomer by *Mixmag*, playing UK venues such as Fabric, Cream and Ministry of Sound, and Twilo in New York.

He attributes much of his success to those heady nights in Hong Kong, and his 'local boy made good' story not only provides inspiration to others plying the trade in Hong Kong, but also reveals the talent in the city.

While big names are still brought out every weekend, a visit to any local club night can be just as, if not more, rewarding. There are plenty worth hearing and the styles being played have diversified over the past two years.

Burridge's former sidekick, **Christian**, still plays long, hard sets, even though the venues and atmosphere means there is less call for them these days.

Of the Chinese DJs, **Joel Lai** has become the most celebrated. He built up his reputation during his years as a resident at Club 97 in Lan Kwai Fong. He has since left, being replaced by **Janva**, but now plays on most of the top bills in the city. Lai is in charge of music policy at Drop (*see p230*) and runs the club promotion company Way Out East, with fellow DJ **Simon Blackjack**, which has many international DJs on its books. His sets range from funky house to progressive.

There are also a few good turntablists – DJs who make an art of scratchin', fast mixing and performing at the same time. The most lauded talent is **DJ Tommy**, who was a regular winner of the local DMC DJ championships in the '90s, and once came runner-up at the world championships. Others have followed in his wake, including **Yeodie** and **Galaxy**, who are regular performers in clubs around Causeway Bay.

Among the other established and up-and-coming spin kings to watch out for when you check out line-ups at local clubs are: **Teng Boon**, who plays funky, uplifting house at most of the city's best clubs; **Eric Byron**, a young Frenchman playing funky house; **Buff**, a former resident at Manumission and Ibiza, who now plays 'sexy house' with a residency at C Club (*see p229*); **JP**, a regular at phi-b (*see p231*) and **Blush**; drum 'n' bass specialist **Johnathan**; and **DJ Kulu**, who at 60 and with a wispish white beard looks more like the stereotypical wise old Chinese man, but is undoubtedly the oldest swinger in town. Kulu moved out from the UK two years ago where he ran clubs in Leeds and London. He plays a lot of acid jazz and funky sets.

There are many more, but the best way to find out is go and see for yourself. You'll rarely be disappointed – and you might even spot the next Lee Burridge.

## New Club Star

*3/F, Chuang's Enterprises Building, 382 Lockhart Road, Wan Chai, HK Island (2574 4388). Causeway Bay MTR (exit C)/buses & trams along Hennessy Road.* **Open** 11pm-6am Fri, Sat. **Admission** HK$120 (incl 1 drink). **No credit cards. Map** p80 C2.

It's hot, sweaty and popular with those who like their music hard – trance and progressive house dominate. Still, some of the city's top DJs spin here and it really gets going after other clubs have closed.

## phi-b

*Lower basement, Harilela House, 79 Wyndham Street, Central, HK Island (2869 4469). Central MTR (exit D1, G)/13, 26, 43 bus.* **Open** 5pm-2am Mon-Thur; 5pm-5am Fri, Sat. **Admission** free. **Credit** AmEx, MC, V. **Map** p66 C4.

What should be a bar had far grander pretensions: people dance even though there really isn't room. A different DJ each night serves up everything from soul, funk and R&B early in the week to jungle, house and techno towards the weekend. You may have to settle for standing on the steps outside – along with all the visiting DJs and rock stars.

### Pink

*8 Commercial Tower, 8 Sun Yip Street, Chai Wan, HK Island (2607 8688). Chai Wan MTR, free shuttle bus from Central & Causeway Bay (phone for details).* **Open** varies. **Admission** HK$100-$450. **Credit** AmEx, MC, V. **Map** p62.

Hong Kong's first 'superclub' is a dream inside: spacious and funkily decorated with two dance floors, it has state-of-the-art sound and lighting systems. So far, it's attracted big name international DJs, but has struggled a little because of its far-flung location. Still, it's worth a trek when a DJ you like is playing.

### Propaganda

*1 Hollywood Road, Central, HK Island (2868 1316). Central MTR (exit D1, D2, G)/Mid-Levels Escalator/ 12M, 13, 23A, 26, 40M, 43 bus.* **Open** 9pm-3.30am Mon-Thur; 9pm-5am Fri; 9pm-6am Sat. **Admission** *Mon-Wed* free; *Thur* HK$80; *Fri* HK$70-$120; *Sat (before 10.30pm)* HK$120, *(after 10.30pm)* HK$220. **Credit** AmEx, DC, V. **Map** p66 C3.

Hong Kong's best-known and busiest gay club, but frequented by all. Inside, you'll find a UV-lit labyrinth and anything from hot house to progressive musically, courtesy of long-serving resident DJ, Ricky. *See also p224.*

### Queen's

*1/F, Queen's Theatre, Theatre Lane, Central, HK Island (2522 7773). Central MTR (exit D2)/buses along Queen's Road Central.* **Open** 5pm-3am Mon-Thur, Sun; 5pm-5am Fri, Sat. **Admission** HK$100 (incl 1 drink); women free. **Credit** AmEx, DC, MC, V. **Map** p67 D3.

An annexe of the old-fashioned Queen's Theatre in Central, Queen's is a large, high-ceilinged club dominated by a stage, an elevated DJ booth and a huge island bar behind which bartenders juggle cocktails. After a live band open up early in the evening, happy and funky house is played until very late. Opened in early 2001, the aim was to attract the wealthy business crowd more than the discerning clubber.

### Strawberries

*48 Hennessy Road, Wan Chai, HK Island (no phone). Wan Chai MTR (exit B1)/buses along Hennessy Road.* **Open** varies. **Admission** free (or a charge if they don't like the look of you). **No credit cards.** **Map** p80 A2.

This is the latest place to hang out in Wan Chai – until 9am. Cheesy music, drunken suits, after hours hostesses and not-to-be-stared-at punters make this a club of last resort, and yet, strangely, it can be fun, as long as you've had a skinful and no intention of going home.

# Canto-pop

For the past 25 years, local music lovers have chosen to create their own superstars, rather than adopting those of the West. The genre spawned is Canto-pop (though some label it Canto-pap). Michael Jackson, while popular, could never match the popularity of idols such as Jackie Cheung and Leon Lai here. Nor could Barry Manilow. Though judging by the cleancut Canto-pop stars churning out soppy love songs, he would have been embraced if he had been born Chinese.

Until recently, while the names of the idols changed over the years, the content always remained pretty much the same. Then, rival idols like Aaron Kwok (*pictured*) and Nicholas Tse began to introduce outrageous costumes and wild behaviour on stage in a belated attempt to stand out from the Canto-crowd. It certainly hasn't harmed sales: their records continue to shift by the shedload.

Canto-pop came about by serendipity. In the early 1960s, Hong Kong was dominated by sentimental Mandarin love songs from mainland China and western pop tunes.

Then, when television sets started popping up in every home, the theme songs to Cantonese dramas unexpectedly became hits, the most famous of which was the theme to *Mad Tides* sung by Roman Tam. As a result, popular local bands like Wynners made the switch from performing English songs to Canto-pop.

Still, it took until 1976 for the genre to become entrenched. Sam Hui's theme song to the film *The Private Eyes* was the catalyst. Suddenly, Canto-pop became the voice of Hong Kong. Featuring the extensive use of slang, Hui's songs were popular because they related to people's feelings and concerns, from love life woes to oil price rises.

In the early 1980s, patriotic songs to the motherland appeared, and in the early

*Arts & Entertainment*

## Yellow Frog

*35 Peel Street, Central, HK Island (9103 5080).*
*Mid-Levels Escalator/26 bus.* **Open** 7pm-late Tue-Sat.
**Admission** free. **No credit cards**. **Map** p66 C3.
If you want to party late, head to the Frog. This place
starts kicking after everywhere else has shut up
shop. It's tiny, dark and always a squeeze after dawn
on weekends, but for a fun and up-for-it crowd, it's
often the only place left to go in Central. However,
it's not as popular with nearby residents, who sometimes insist on curtailing the evening early. DJs spin
house, with dollops of funky disco beats, as well as
trance and progressive, and there's even a reggae
night on Fridays.

## Live music

While the club scene in Hong Kong is on a par
with most leading international cities, the live
music scene lags far behind. With a handful of
exceptions, Hong Kong just isn't on the agenda
of many global touring acts.

Besides Ricky Martin, Primal Scream and
Leftfield, 2000 was typically barren – Olivia
Newton John or Air Supply anyone? Having said
that, the likes of Whitney Houston and Tom
Jones did fly in, but only for private concerts at
the whim of wealthy corporate clients.

**Queen's**. *See p232.*

Many acts cite the lack of a suitable
venue (even though the Hong Kong Coliseum
seats 12,500), as concerts were banned at the
40,000-seater Hong Kong Stadium due to
noise complaints – at one gig, audience
members were given gloves to soften the
sound of their clapping.

1990s, when Hong Kong was worried about
the 1997 handover, Law Tai-yau made
*Queen's Road East*, a humorous, melodic
song hinting at the changes to come. But
such political posturing is rare.

And in the mid 1980s, with growing
affluence in Hong Kong, style and personality
won out over lyrical content. Although Hui
continued to sing about topical issues, like
the local craze for doll-like Japanese girls,
other stars played safe and sang Cantonese
versions of Western and Japanese classics
and hits. Megastars of this genre in the
1980s included Alan Tam, Leslie Cheung and
Anita Mui, followed by Jackie Cheung, Andy
Lau, Leon Lai and Aaron Kwok in the 1990s.

Not only did Canto-pop lack imagination,
it also became highly commercialised. So,
instead of bothering with the music, most of
the stars focused their attentions on their
face, hair and clothes. Along with songs
focusing on love, unrequited affection and
heartbreak, it was all part of a policy to target
the youth market. Commercially, it worked.

At the start of the 1990s, Jackie Cheung,
Andy Lau, Leon Lai and Aaron Kwok were
declared Canto-pop's 'Four Heavenly Kings'
by the media. All were squeaky clean, lacked
charisma and, by decadent Western pop

standards, were decidedly boring. But the four
Kings were the focus of screaming, obsessive
teenage fans, most of whom were girls.

However, following a decade of immense
success, the four have slipped into decline.
Their fading star has allowed new ones
to emerge. Beijing-born singing queen
Faye Wong has been at the forefront. Her
wild, rebellious look, with tattered clothes
and spiked hair, gives her a unique style.
Although modelled heavily on Björk and
Sinead O'Connor, Wong re-injected a dose of
creativity into Canto-pop, composing her own
songs, which sounded abstract and fresh.

Nicholas Tse, long rumoured to be her beau,
is one of the new crop that has emerged in
her wake. Others include Joey Yung and, most
recently, Edison Chan Kwun-hei. But they have
not carried forward her advances.

'Everyone is producing easy-to-sell bubble
gum,' says Kenny Bee, the former leader
of 1960s Canto-pop band Wynners. 'The
faces are all interchangeable. But it doesn't
matter, because the media will create all
the hype anyway.'

If songs can tell a folk's character, Canto-
pop reveals Hong Kongers as conservative,
safe and uncreative. But at least they have
their own idols.

The home-grown market is dominated by Canto-pop stars (*see p232* **Canto-pop**), as a local indie scene is only just beginning to emerge. Leading the latter's way is hip hop collective LMF (LazyMuthaFuckas), who've released a promising debut album. However, a sponsorship deal with a local beer company to do TV ads may damage their credibility. Others to watch out for include Paul Wong, a former guitarist with popular pop rock band Beyond. If indie is your thing, the collective gigs put on by the bands at their own expense to increase their exposure are worth a visit.

The music charts focusing on international imports are filled with boy and girl band pap, which is played ceaselessly on Asia's two satellite music channels, MTV and Channel [V]. Even they don't come and play live, though they may drop in for a signing and a 'showcase' (read three songs at a naff venue).

Only jazz aficionados and folk fans are likely to find events regularly worth going to. There's an annual folk festival late in the year and a few quality jazz venues, such as the Jazz & Blues Club and Brown, which host visiting international performers. The local scene has its own talented stars too, including singer and guitarist Eugene Pao, local chanteuse Elaine Liu, trumpeter Mark Henderson – a former US Army paratrooper who writes and plays music in the style of the classic 1950s'

and 1960s' Blue Note sound – guitarists Guy Le Claire and William Tang, and pianist Allen Youngblood. At least one of these performers is likely to be playing each night, and sometimes you'll find some of them playing together as an ensemble.

The many top class hotels that thrive in Hong Kong usually have an in-house band, which trots out segues of 1960s and 1970s hits, a few Latin and Cuban numbers, and any popular current songs. Some are good entertainment, but too many are merely travelling entertainers on the international hotel circuit.

And, unfortunately, the future does not look like brightening. Bars, restaurants and clubs may spring up all the time, but there's little evidence that things are going to improve for live music buffs.

## Major venues

### Hong Kong Coliseum

*9 Cheong Wan Road, Hung Hom, Kowloon (2355 7233). Kowloon KCR/101, 104, 110 bus.* **Box office** 24-hour bookings through URBTIX: 2734 9009. **Tickets** varies. **Credit** AmEx, MC, V. This 12,500-seat venue is the premier indoor site for pop and rock concerts, particularly of the Canto-pop variety, but it has also hosted Barry Manilow and Santana. It's not new, but it does have everything you need for a concert – you can even get out of your seat and dance if you want, which is not the case everywhere in Hong Kong.

# HK profiles Melvis

Arts & Entertainment

Unlike most world cities, Hong Kong is all but devoid of eccentrics, street entertainers and genuine oddballs. In none of the underground MTR stations or pedestrian subways will you you find a genuine busker. It is not just that the authorities put a stop to them, its simply not part of the local culture. Hang about in the entertainment world and the situation is the same – bar one. A big round of applause please for... **Melvis Kwok**.

Yes, even Hong Kong is not immune to the Elvis clone craze. If you drink in a bar around Lan Kwai Fong or SoHo, chances are you'll bump into the Elvis of the East. As talent goes, Melvis is not truly blessed – he doesn't appear to know most of the words to Elvis's songs, let alone look or sound like the King. But in terms of courage, gumption and perseverence, he's hard to beat.

Every night, Melvis dons one of his 20 home-stitched Elvis suits, puts on his Elvis shades and picks up his guitar before

heading out from his tiny flat ready to face the throngs of locals and tourists in the city's bars and crowded streets. It's part a labour of love, part a means to live.

Melvis came to Hong Kong from the mainland in 1974 and his fascination with Elvis began after he watched one of the King's movies in the 1980s. He was instantly converted. Melvis began learning the songs and quit his job on a production line to carve out his own musical career. The money he earns – a few hundred dollars on a good night – is saved to support his wife and two teenage children.

'My family don't like Elvis, and my wife didn't understand when I started, but now she sees that I earn a living she's happy with it,' he says.

After darkness falls, Melvis wanders from bar to bar playing requests. He claims to know 100 Elvis songs, but no-one has ever put him to the test. A rendition of one or two

## Hong Kong Exhibition Centre

*3-4/F, Low Block, China Resources Building, 26
Harbour Road, Wan Chai, HK Island (2827 9908).
Wan Chai MTR (exit A1)/buses along Gloucester
Road/Wan Chai Star Ferry Pier.* **Open** when event
scheduled. **Tickets** varies. **Credit** varies.
**Map** p80 B1.

It's large, charmless and has no liquor licence, but
some bands (like Primal Scream and local hip hop
band LMF) chose it because it's about the only
indoor venue where you can have a mosh pit. The
acoustics are passable – considering it's a giant, concrete exhibition room.

## Ko Shan Theatre

*Ko Shan Park, Hung Hom, Kowloon (2740 9212).
Bus 111, 101, 107, 116.* **Box office** 24-hour
bookings through URBTIX: 2734 9009.
**Tickets** varies. **Credit** AmEx, MC, V.

Air-conditioning was installed in 1996 to make life
bearable in this 1,000-capacity auditorium. With an
upgraded stage, sound and lighting system, it is
popular for collective indie gigs and smaller Canto-
pop acts.

## Queen Elizabeth Stadium

*18 Oi Kwan Road, Wan Chai, HK Island (2591
1347). Buses and trams along Hennessy Road.* **Box
office** 24-hour bookings through URBTIX: 2734 9009.
**Tickets** varies. **Credit** AmEx, MC, V. **Map** p80 C2.

This 3,500-seat venue is favoured by the likes of
Björk and Suede, but there's no mosh pit – over zeal-
ous security staff shine torches in the face of anyone
who dares stand up and wiggle their hips.

# Other rock venues

## Chasers

*2 Carlton Building, Knutsford Terrace,
Tsim Sha Tsui, Kowloon (2367 9487). Tsim
Sha Tsui MTR (exit B2)/buses along Chatham
Road South.* **Open** 9.30pm-around 5am daily.
**Admission** free. **Credit** AmEx, MC, V.
**Map** p98 C1.

Bands rotate between Chasers, Dusk til Dawn and
Insomnia, ensuring all the venues have live music
every night. The musical style depends on what
band you get, but it's all covers. Some are surprisingly good, but all become better as the ale is sunk.
The venues are rowdy and have a reputation for
being meat markets.

## China Coast Bar & Grill

*9 Cheong Tat Road, Chek Lap Kok (2286 8888).
Chek Lap Kok station.* **Open** 8.15pm-1am daily.
**Admission** free. **Credit** AmEx, MC, V. **Map** p126.

If your flight's delayed, or you're near the airport
or the Gold Coast and feel like a blast of live music,
the sounds and atmosphere of China Coast are worth
a checking out. Otherwise, it's probably not worth
the trek.

## Dusk til Dawn

*76 Jaffe Road, Wan Chai, HK Island (2528 4689).
Wan Chai MTR (exit A1, C)/buses along
Gloucester Road.* **Open** 9.30pm-around 5am daily.
**Admission** free. **Credit** AmEx, MC, V.
**Map** p80 B2.
*See* **Chasers** *above.*

songs and he is normally sent on his way with
a few coins jingling in his pocket. He doesn't
hassle those who don't pay, and he ignores
those who poke fun. In the nine years he's
been on the circuit, he's become hardened to
anything people throw at him.

'I love Elvis's music. It makes me happy
and others too. At least I'm doing something
I enjoy and bringing some fun into people's
lives,' he says.

Recently he's been hired by locals to
entertain at parties with a whole set, a
deserved reward for his indomitable spirit.

'It's a good way of earning a living and I
help keep Elvis alive,' he says.

What does he most often play for people?

'*Suspicious Minds* is popular', he says, but
the song he enjoys playing most for people is
*It's Now Or Never*, which, coincidentally, is
the one he does best. So if you see Melvis,
be generous to Hong Kong's only busker.
Just don't ask for the other 98 songs.

**Arts & Entertainment**

### Fringe Club

*2 Lower Albert Road, South Block, Central, HK Island (2521 7251). Central MTR (exit K)/23A bus.* **Open** noon-1am daily. **Credit** AmEx, DC, MC, V. **Map** p67 D4.

Everything from jazz to rock to folk to experimental dance is staged at the Fringe's Nokia Gallery. It's one of the few places local bands can get a decent stage and crowd, and punters can savour a pint while being squeezed in close to the stage. There is normally live music on Friday and Saturday nights, but phone ahead to check. *See also p241.*

### F-Stop

*17 Lan Kwai Fong, Central, HK Island (2868 9607). Central MTR (exit D1, D2, G)/12M, 13, 23A, 40M, 43 bus.* **Open** 7pm-late daily. **Admission** free. **Credit** AmEx, DC, V. **Map** p66 C4.

The narrow ground floor of F-Stop is taken up almost entirely by the bar and stage, which means that most people end up listening in the street, a beer in hand. The good news is most of the bands play their own compositions and aren't afraid to let rip with their guitars.

### Insomnia

*38 D'Aguilar Street, Central, HK Island (2525 0957). Central MTR (exit D1, D2, G)/12M, 13, 23A, 40M, 43 bus.* **Open** 9.30pm-around 5am daily. **Admission** free. **Credit** AmEx, MC, V. **Map** p66 C4.

*See p235* **Chasers**.

### Lau Ling Bar

*1/F, Furama Hotel, 1 Connaught Road, Central, HK Island (2842 7506). Central MTR (exit J3)/buses to Central Star Ferry Pier/Central Star Ferry Pier.* **Open** 6pm-1.30am daily. **Admission** free. **Credit** AmEx, MC, V. **Map** p67 E4.

With three acts nightly, this is about the only place you can hear live music non-stop all evening. Just don't expect anything other than the usual run-through of pop, rock and jazz standards.

### Pit Stop

*Harbour Plaza Hotel, 20 Tak Fung Street, Hung Hom, Kowloon (2621 3188). Kowloon KCR/101, 104, 110 bus.* **Open** 7.15pm-late Tue-Sun. **Admission** free. **Credit** AmEx, MC, V.

This venue stands out from the hotel crowd, because the management takes its music seriously, signing up bands that have – or are likely to get – recording contracts. This means they can perform both their own songs, as well as the expected covers.

### The Wanch

*54 Jaffe Road, Wan Chai, HK Island (2861 1621). Wan Chai MTR (exit A1, C)/buses along Gloucester Road.* **Open** 9pm-2am daily. **Admission** free. **Credit** AmEx, MC, V. **Map** p80 A2.

It doesn't look much bigger than a phone kiosk, but the Wanch is steeped in music history – many local indie and folk bands made their debut here. It's not as popular as it was in the early 1990s, when punters spilled into the streets, but it can still pack a punch.

**Jazz & Blues Club.**

## Jazz, blues & roots venues

The **Fringe Club** (*see above*) often features jazz, folk and world music gigs.

### Brown

*30-32 Robinson Road, Mid Levels, HK Island (2971 0012). Mid-Levels Escalator/3B, 12, 12M, 23, 23A, 40 bus.* **Open** noon-1am (jazz from 10pm) daily. **Admission** free. **Credit** AmEx, DC, MC, V. **Map** p66 B4.

This recently opened jazz venue provides a welcome home for the many local musicians on the Hong Kong circuit. Its stylish place, has a friendly, welcoming atmosphere and the line-up is usually first class.

### Jazz & Blues Club

*2/F, California Entertainment Building, 34 D'Aguilar Street, Central, HK Island (2845 8477). Central MTR (exit D1, D2, G)/12M, 13, 23A, 40M, 43 bus.* **Open** 7pm-late daily (phone for details). **Tickets** varies. **Credit** AmEx, MC, DC, V. **Map** p66 C4.

For more than a decade, the Jazz & Blues Club has been Hong Kong's leading jazz venue and it's everything you'd expect, with its comfortable seats, smoky atmosphere and waiter service. The list of past headline acts is unrivalled – everyone from BB King to George Melly has played here – and top local performers play when the international stars are resting. Besides the main room, there's also a bar with televisions showing legendary jazz sessions. Drinks are, however, on the expensive side (HK$55 for a standard drink).

## Hotel lounge bars

### Captain's Bar

*Mandarin Oriental Hotel, Connaught Road, Central, HK Island (2522 0111). Central MTR (exit F, H)/buses to Central Star Ferry Pier/Central Star Ferry Pier.* **Open** 9pm-1am daily. **Admission** free. **Credit** AmEx, DC, MC, V. **Map** p67 E3.

Given its comfortable, affluent setting within the Mandarin Oriental Hotel, the Captain's Bar gets surprisingly raucous when the resident band runs through jazz standards, and sometimes strays into pop and R&B.

*Arts & Entertainment*

## Champagne Bar

*Grand Hyatt Hotel, 1 Harbour Road, Wan Chai, HK Island (2588 1234). Wan Chai MTR (exit A1, C)/ buses along Gloucester Road.* **Open** 9.30pm-1am Mon-Sat. **Admission** free. **Credit** AmEx, DC, MC, V. **Map** p80 B1.

A jazz and blues singer is usually on hand to help you while away the evening in opulent surroundings.

## Chater Lounge

*Ritz-Carlton Hotel, 3 Connaught Road, Central, HK Island (2532 2059). Central MTR (exit J3)/buses to Central Star Ferry Pier/Central Star Ferry Pier.* **Open** 8.30pm-12.30am Mon-Sat. **Admission** free. **Credit** AmEx, DC, MC, V. **Map** p67 E4.

Known as a place to escape the maddening crowd (and for secret liaisons), this lounge has a stately feel that is warmed by a resident female vocalist.

## Cyrano

*56/F, Island Shangri-La Hotel, Pacific Place, Queensway, HK Island (2877 3838). Admiralty MTR (exit C1)/buses through Central.* **Open** 9pm-12.45am Mon-Thur; 9pm-1.45am Fri, Sat. **Admission** free. **Credit** AmEx, DC, MC, V. **Map** p67 F5.

The view is enough to take your breath away, but there's always a jazz band to get you back in the swing of a good evening. When the Latin beats kick in, there's even some dancing. *See also p168.*

## Lobby Lounge

*Kowloon Shangri-La Hotel, 64 Mody Road, Tsim Sha Tsui (2721 2111). Tsim Sha Tsui MTR (exit C1)/203, 973 bus & buses along Chatham Road South & Salisbury Road.* **Open** 8.15pm-midnight daily. **Admission** free. **Credit** AmEx, DC, MC, V. **Map** p98 C2.

Another sumptuous setting, with a resident singer to provide background entertainment while you drink or eat.

## 27 Restaurant & Bar

*Park Lane Hotel, 310 Gloucester Road, Causeway Bay (2839 3327). Causeway Bay MTR (exit C)/buses along Gloucester Road.* **Open** 10pm-1am Mon-Sat. **Admission** free. **Credit** AmEx, DC, MC, V. **Map** p80 D1.

More great views and a relaxing ambience, but the music tends to drift away from jazz standards towards pop tunes.

# Everybody salsa!

Who was it that said Asia was the continent that rhythm forgot? Anyone who has spent any time in clubs around the region would have a tough time arguing with that conclusion. No, Asia is not a continent with 'hips', although countries such as Thailand and Indonesia do have some interesting – and complicated – national dances. To its credit though, Hong Kong does offer an alternative for those who like to dance, but don't want to hang out with kids wearing 'fat pants' and nose studs or business men in suits 'at the disco'.

To many people's surprise, the city has a thriving Latin dance scene, which has gone from strength to strength in the last three years. A dedicated hard core of salseros, who probably number less than 100, regularly attend workshops, lessons and dance sessions two or three times a week. When they're joined by friends, first-timers, the curious and people who just happen to be in earshot of the music, Hong Kong's salsa parties end up being very well attended and usually pretty lively.

In fact, they're the perfect place to meet an eclectic mix of people that you would be unlikely to find in one place elsewhere in Hong Kong. You'll find the city's few Latino residents, locals, Europeans and North American expatriates, and the odd, older

dancer, who goes to salsa now that the popular ballroom dance sessions of the 1990s have fallen from fashion. It doesn't matter that they don't speak the same language, they interact by dancing.

Currently, the two main salsa club nights are on Wednesdays and Sundays. Every Wednesday night, **Club ING** (*see p230*) at the Renaissance Harbour View Hotel in Wan Chai holds concurrent dance lessons for beginners and intermediates from 8-9.30pm. The lessons are followed by dancing until about midnight. Entry costs HK$100, and covers the lesson and one standard drink. Sunday night salsa is held at a Mexican restaurant called **La Placita Restaurante y Bar** in the Food Forum on the 13th floor of Times Square in Causeway Bay (2506 3308). There is an improvers' lesson at 6.30pm, followed by a beginners' lesson an hour later. The club evening swings into action straight after the second lesson and continues until about midnight. The HK$100 cover charge includes one standard drink.

If you're interested in joining a salsa session, check out the website used by the event organisers, http://clubs.yahoo.com/ clubs/hongkongsalsa, before you leave home. It's where you'll find all the latest salsa evening information.

# Performing Arts

The best of the West, and the cream of the East.

Often dubbed a soulless city of brokers and speculators, Hong Kong is not a place that one immediately associates with the performing arts. In this financial Babylon, it is the banks, not the concert halls or theatres, that are the city's architectural showpieces. Compared with the ever-changing and imaginative commercial skyline, Hong Kong's performing arts venues look dated and self-conscious. It's easy to feel that the city's theatres and concert halls are under-utilised clubhouses that were funded in a bygone flurry of public spending. However, like most things in Hong Kong, first impressions can be very deceptive. Despite the absence of visibly dynamic arts spaces, the performing arts, both Chinese or Western, are a significant and growing part of Hong Kong's cultural landscape.

Reflecting its eclectic population and history, Hong Kong is home to an interesting collection of popular and well-funded resident performing arts companies. These include the Hong Kong Philharmonic Orchestra and the unique Hong Kong Chinese Orchestra; the Hong Kong Ballet, Hong Kong Dance Company and the City Contemporary Dance Company; long established semi-professional companies such as the Bach Choir and the Hong Kong Singers; and a number of community-based organisations devoted to the performance of traditional Chinese opera and other Asian performance art forms. The territory is also blessed with the venues and talent emerging from the world-class Hong Kong Academy of Performing Arts.

The Hong Kong arts scene is further enlivened by a colourful, hectic calendar of local and international arts festivals, and a constant flow of touring international performers. Consular support for visiting performers is strong, and touring companies often stop in Hong Kong as part of an Asian tour, or as they travel from North America and Europe to Australia. With a little knowledge of venues and events, it is possible to be culturally stimulated every week of the year in Hong Kong.

## TICKETS & INFORMATION

Tickets for most performances in Hong Kong can be obtained from **URBTIX**, a ticket agency run by the Hong Kong Government Leisure and Cultural Services Department

(www.urbtix.com). For general information on performances and reservations call URBTIX on 2734 9009 (10am-8pm daily). You can buy tickets over the counter at an URBTIX outlet or make advanced telephone bookings by providing an ID card or passport number – the tickets must then be collected within three days. A credit card is not required for telephone bookings.

URBTIX has outlets at the Hong Kong Cultural Centre in Tsim Sha Tsui, City Hall in Central, the Hong Kong Arts Centre in Wan Chai and at several venues in the New Territories, including Tsuen Wan Town Hall, Tuen Mun Town Hall, Sha Tin Town Hall and Yuen Long Theatre.

**TICKETEK** is an Australian ticket agency that has recently set up shop in Hong Kong (www.ticketek.com.hk). It operates several ticket outlets around Hong Kong, as well as in branches of the Tom Lee Music Co.

Several publications list information about upcoming performances and events. The lobbies of City Hall, the Hong Kong Cultural Centre, the Hong Kong Academy of the Performing Arts and the Hong Kong Arts Centre brim over with glossy and informative performance brochures. The Fringe Club in Lower Albert Road, Central is a good place to get information about Hong Kong's fringe theatre, folk music, cabaret and poetry performance scenes.

The weekly *HK Magazine* and monthly *BC Magazine* also provide listings of performances, workshops and lectures. Both magazines are distributed free at restaurants and bars in Lan Kwai Fong, SoHo and Wan Chai. Every Friday, the *South China Morning Post* newspaper publishes *24/7* magazine, which includes extensive listings and reviews of performances and arts events.

The Performing Arts page of the Hong Kong Government Leisure and Cultural Services Department website (www.lcsd.gov.hk/CE/CulturalService/index.html) is an extremely useful source of information for upcoming arts events and performances. The site lists cultural programmes by venue, date and type (including everything from shadow puppet shows to circuses to full-scale opera productions) and gives information about free entertainment programmes.

The **Hong Kong Philharmonic Orchestra**. See p243.

The Government classical radio station RTHK Radio 4 (FM stereo 97.6-98.9) provides frequent updates on performances with its daily Arts News and In Town Tonight bulletins. Radio 4 also previews arts events on its Saturday morning Artbeat programme.

## Major venues

### Hong Kong Academy for Performing Arts

*1 Gloucester Road, Wan Chai, HK Island (2584 8500/www.hkapa.edu). Wan Chai MTR (exit A1, C)/ buses along Gloucester Road.* **Box office** 10am-6pm Mon-Sat. **Credit** AmEx, DC, MC, V. **Map** p80 A2.
Hong Kong's second major arts venue (after the Cultural Centre; *see p240*) incorporates the terrific Lyric Theatre, the intimate Drama Theatre, a studio theatre, a small concert hall and a recital hall. These impressive venues are used to stage HKAPA student productions and performances by local and visiting companies. The HKAPA performance calendar includes Western opera and operetta, dance and recitals, and drama in Cantonese. Check the HKAPA website for the latest programme. The HKAPA stages free lunchtime concerts every Monday and frequent free 'Happy Hour' evening performances. Unique within Asia, the Academy brings together schools of Dance, Drama, Music, Television and Film, and Technical Arts under one roof. *See also p243*.

### Hong Kong Arts Centre

*2 Harbour Road, Wan Chai, HK Island (2582 0200). Wan Chai MTR (exit A1)/buses along Gloucester Road/Wan Chai Star Ferry Pier.* **Box office** 10am-6pm daily. **Credit** AmEx, DC, MC, V. **Map** p80 B2.
Housing the Shouson Theatre and McAuley Studio, the Hong Kong Arts Centre stages mainly avant-garde theatre and community productions in English and Cantonese. It is located across the road from the Hong Kong Academy of Performing Arts.

### Hong Kong City Hall

*7 Edinburgh Place, Central, HK Island (2522 9928). Central MTR (exit J3)/buses to Central Star Ferry Pier & along Connaught Road Central/ Central Star Ferry Pier.* **Box office** 10am-9.30pm daily. **Credit** AmEx, DC, MC, V. **Map** p67 E3.
Right next to the Central Star Ferry Terminal, the anonymous, uninspiring City Hall building includes a concert hall and theatre. Concerts and recitals by local and international artists take place in the concert hall (Krzysztof Penderecki conducting his own works in December 2000 was quite a coup), while the theatre is used for drama and special film screenings. There's an excellent dim sum restaurant on the second floor (*see p142*). The area near City Hall is a good place to watch traditional dancing performed by the city's Filipina and Indonesian domestic helpers on a Sunday afternoon.

Arts & Entertainment

### Hong Kong Convention & Exhibition Centre

*1 Harbour Road, Wan Chai, HK Island (2582 8888).
Wan Chai MTR (exit A1)/buses along Gloucester
Road/Wan Chai Star Ferry Pier.* **Box office** 10am-
6pm Mon-Sat. **Credit** AmEx, DC, MC, V. **Map** p80 B1.
Site of the official Handover ceremony, the main
stage of the Convention and Exhibition Centre is
used for performances at special times of the year,
such as Christmas and Chinese New Year. Pop concerts are also staged here from time to time.

### Hong Kong Cultural Centre

*10 Salisbury Road, Tsim Sha Tsui, Kowloon (2734
2010). Tsim Sha Tsui MTR (exit E)/buses to Tsim
Sha Tsui Star Ferry Pier & along Salisbury Road/
Tsim Sha Tsui Star Ferry Pier.* **Box office** 10am-
9.30pm daily. **Credit** AmEx, DC, MC, V.
**Map** p98 B3.

Straddling the Tsim Sha Tsui waterfront, the Hong
Kong Cultural Centre is perhaps the world's worst
building on the world's best location. This but-
tressed, windowless slab of cement and tiles wildly
ignores the fact that it faces one of the world's great
harbour views and has been compared with a half
gnawed block of cheese and a giant skateboard
ramp. The Cultural Centre is home to both the
Hong Kong Philharmonic Orchestra (*see p243*)
and the Hong Kong Chinese Orchestra (*see p244*),
and most of Hong Kong's Western opera (*see p244*)
is performed in its 2,100-seat Grand Theatre.
The complex also includes a smaller concert hall,
a studio theatre and an arts library. Free performances often take place in the foyer and forecourt
of the Cultural Centre on Thursday evenings
and Saturday afternoons (call 2734 2883 for details).
*See also p102.*

# Local heroes

Not many native Hong Kong composers and
performers are internationally famous, but
lack of visibility shouldn't be confused with
lack of talent. The following are some of the
brightest stars of Hong Kong's classical
music world.

## COMPOSERS

The work of **Victor Chan Wai-kwong** has
been performed at a number of composers'
festivals, including the Asian Composers'
League Festival, UNESCO's International
Rostrum of Composers, the International
Composers Festival in the Netherlands and
the Inter-Arts Contemporary Music Forum in
England. Chan's compositions include opera,
orchestral and chamber works, choral pieces
and songs. Some of his more ambitious
recent works include *Symphonic Psalms in
Three Parts* (a choral symphony for soloists,
mass choir and orchestra) and *Music for
Eleven Instruments* (a conversation between
a string quartet, a woodwind quartet
and a brass trio). Chan has written
several orchestral pieces for the Hong
Kong Philharmonic Orchestra including
*A Symphonic Prelude for Orchestra with Piano*,
*A Glimpse of Blue* and the 1997 *Symphonic
Fantasia Hui (Converge)*, composed to mark
the Handover.

 **Law Wing-fai** was an award-winning full-
time composer of popular music for film,
television, theatre and modern dance
before he began composing contemporary
orchestral works. In addition to his career as
a composer, Law has pursued a successful

career as a musical academic and was a
visiting scholar at Stanford University. In
1981, Law won the Yoshiro Irino Memorial
Award at the Asian Composers' Conference
and Festival and he represented Hong
Kong at the International Rostrum of
Composers in Paris. Recent compositions
include *Qian Si* (1994), *Ink Spirit* (1995)
and *Lin Li* (1998).

 Born in Macau and trained in Canada, the
UK and the US, **Doming Lam** has composed
a number of Western and Chinese orchestral
works. These include *Heaven's Blessing* and
*Kung Fu*, both of which have been recorded
by the Hong Kong Chinese Orchestra. Lam
is also a celebrated composer of liturgical
music, having written 24 hymns, a requiem
and an arrangement of the eucharistic prayer
in Cantonese, in the style of a Gregorian
chant for voice and organ.

 Scottish-born **David Gwilt** has lived in
Hong Kong for over 30 years and has worked
as a composer, academic, accompanist
and conductor. Recent compositions include
*A Feastly Fugue* for orchestra, *Colloquium*
(written for the Hong Kong Sinfonietta),
*Philharmonic Fanfare* for the Hong Kong
Philharmonic Orchestra, assorted chamber
pieces and a song cycle for high voice
and piano. Gwilt and Doming Lam are
honorary presidents of the Hong Kong
Composers' Guild.

 **Richard Tsang** is an active composer,
conductor, critic and broadcaster. Since
returning to Hong Kong after studying in
Britain, Tsang has composed for the HKPO

# Other venues

## Fringe Club
*2 Lower Albert Road, Central, HK Island (2521 7251). Central MTR (exit D1, G)/23A bus.*
**Box office** 10am-10pm Mon-Sat. **Credit** AmEx, DC, MC, V. **Map** p67 D4.
The Fringe Club is the place to see alternative performances in English and in Cantonese. The club has two theatres and is the chief venue for the annual City Festival (*see p207*). See also *p236*.

## St John's Cathedral
*4-8 Garden Road, Central, HK Island (2523 4157). Central MTR (exit K)/buses along Garden Road.*
**Open** 8am-6pm daily. **Admission** free. **Map** p67 E4.
Frequently stages good, free lunchtime and evening concerts by local and visiting vocal ensembles.

## Visage Free
*21 Hollywood Road, Central, HK Island (2546 9780). Central MTR (exit D1, D2)/Mid-Levels Escalator/ 12M, 13, 23A, 26, 40M, 43 bus.* **Open** 5pm-1am Mon-Thur; 5pm-2am Fri, Sat. **Admission** free. **Map** p66 C3.
This small bar right under the Mid-Levels Escalator has monthly bilingual poetry readings and impromptu musical performances. One of the bar's owners is a local actor and staff often have interesting information on alternative arts events around town.

# Venues in the New Territories

To arouse wider public interest in the arts and to cater to the demographic heart of the SAR, Hong Kong's Leisure and Cultural Services Department organises a rich selection of

and HKCO, and written several Western and Chinese instrumental and vocal pieces. In 1989, *Prelude* was premiered by the Boston Symphony Orchestra. Tsang has composed for several Hong Kong dance companies and produced works that include the full-length ballet *The Emperor and the Nightingale*.

**Chan Wing-wah** studied composition under David Gwilt, then continued his studies in Toronto, London and Germany. He has written six symphonies and composed a number of choral pieces. In 1981, Chan won first prize at the International Double Reed Society Composition Contest in the USA. His works have been performed by a diverse range of ensembles including the Kronos Quartet, the Shanghai Broadcasting Symphony Orchestra and the Klementi Trio. Symphonies 1, 3, 4, 5 and 6 have been recorded on the HUGO label. Chan is currently the music director of the Hong Kong Oratorio Society.

**Clarence Mak Wai-chu**'s work includes chamber music, electronic and multimedia music, and music for local contemporary Chinese theatre productions. His recorded works include *Butterfly* and *Plain Autumn*.

Recordings of works by many of Hong Kong's composers are available on the local HUGO label (www.hugocd.com). There is a HUGO shop at 20 Champagne Court, 16 Kimberly Road, Tsim Sha Tsui, Kowloon (2367 6827), where you can also listen to the CDs.

## PERFORMERS
Some exciting young talent is emerging from Hong Kong's performing arts world. Here are a few of the most promising performers.

Hong Kong-born pianist **Colleen Lee Ka-ling** received her training at the Hong Kong

Academy of Performing Arts and was invited to participate at the Pianofest Music Festival in the Hamptons in New York. She has won a number of local and international competitions, including the Junior Gina Bachauer International Piano Competition and the Newport International Competition for young pianists. Countries in which she has performed include Poland, the UK, Indonesia, Thailand and Australia. In addition, she has made studio recordings for the RTHK Radio 4 programme 'Young Music Makers'.

**Fuzuki Nakajima** is one of a growing number of talented dancers who has been trained at the HKAPA and shows the promise of a prestigious international dance career. Fuzuki comes from a famous line of Japanese ballet dancers and his aunt is a dancer with the Hong Kong Ballet. While studying at the HKAPA, Fuzuki reached the finals of the Asia Pacific International Ballet Competition in Japan and was awarded third prize at the Prague Dance Festival.

**Zhu Lin** began her cello studies at the age of five in Shanghai and has since performed as a soloist with the Shanghai Symphony Orchestra, Bangkok Symphony Orchestra and Ulster Symphony Orchestra. In HKAPA master classes, she grabbed the attention of Lynn Harrell and Yo-Yo Ma, and has performed with the HKAPA chamber orchestra in Austria, England, France, Italy and Spain.

Hong Kong-born **Alex Tam Tin-lok** is establishing a promising career as one of Hong Kong's finest young tenors. He has taken the lead role in many concerts, operas and operettas at the HKAPA, as well as appearing as a soloist in a number of oratorios, masses and concerts.

# Chinese performing arts

Despite Hong Kong's obvious embracing of so much that is Western within its cityscape, and the conspicuous appearance of international retail outlets, restaurant chains and corporations, much of its soul remains forever Chinese. Besides the herbal tea shops and Buddhist temples and shrines that punctuate every neighbourhood, there is a thriving traditional Chinese (and specifically Cantonese) performing arts scene.

Although the majority of events are often only modestly publicised, now and then those seriously pursuing perfection of their art come together and make a seriously big noise. In February 2001, for example, 1,000 players of the *erhu* – an ancient string instrument played with a bow – assembled along the Tsim Sha Tsui waterfront for a massed recital, attempting to get into the *Guinness Book of Records*, while promoting an interest in Chinese classical instruments.

## CHINESE OPERA

The most immediate image of Chinese performance arts, though, is usually the brightly made-up faces and vibrant embroidered silk costumes of Chinese opera. Actors go about their age-old scripts with exaggerated movements, stylised high-pitched vocals and clashing percussion that is compelling to some, and an acquired taste for others. Dating to the 13th century, choreographies are built around the Confucian principles of courage, honesty and filial piety, with liberal splashes of scandal, sword fighting and somersaulting acrobatics.

The novice may be somewhat bemused by the colour-coding of costumes, the wealth of symbolic gesture and references to Chinese legends. For those who wish to get clued up before attending their first Chinese opera, a visit to the excellent new **Hong Kong Heritage Museum** in Sha Tin (*see p118*) will provide insights into many operatic nuances.

Live at the **Fringe Club**. *See p241.*

musical and dramatic performances in the New Territories. These take place at: **Tsuen Wan Town Hall**, 72 Tai Ho Road, Tsuen Wan (2414 0144); **Tuen Mun Town Hall**, 3 Tuen Hi Road, Tuen Mun (2450 6335); **Sha Tin Town Hall**, 1 Yuen Wo Road, Sha Tin (2694 2509) and **Yuen Long Theatre**, 9 Yuen Long Tai Yuk Road, Yuen Long (2476 1029).

### Kwai Tsing Theatre

*12 Hing Ning Road, Kwai Fong, New Territories (2408 0128).* Kwai Fong MTR(Exit C)/30, A31, E32, 42, 47X, 91, 93 bus. **Box office** 10am-6pm daily. **Credit** AmEx, DC, MC, V. **Map** pp310-311. This newly-built theatre is one of the best venues in Hong Kong and has hosted some outstanding performances by local and international companies.

## Western classical music & opera

The classical music scene in Hong Kong is proudly anachronistic and rich with complex cultural contradictions. In a city driven by free-wheeling capitalism, the main musical bodies enjoy remarkably generous government funding and are administrated by civil servants, ladies' committees and society patrons. Hong Kong is known for its collective impatience, yet performances by local Western and Chinese music orchestras are broadcast in

Arts & Entertainment

Both local and touring mainland troupes have a full calendar of performances, so check the local entertainment press for details or ask in the HKTB offices. Many performances take place in theatres in non-tourist neighbourhoods, which means that visitors get more of a cultural experience. The **Ko Shan Theatre** in Hung Hom (see p145), set in a pleasant park, is very accessible and holds performances regularly.

Besides these grand productions, more informal performances take place in makeshift theatres that are hurriedly built by local community groups before certain festivals; seating is al fresco. A visit to one of these performances includes the chance to indulge in some hot and cold food from stalls and usually a few fair-type games. Productions can last for up to five hours, with people casually coming and going and having a good chat during intermissions; children usually sit near the foot of the stage.

Chiu Chow communities, in particular, erect temporary theatres annually during the **Hungry Ghost Festival** (see p205) – notably ▶

their entirety by the bilingual government classical radio station – without the convenient interruptions of commercials. Although concerts are often marred by late audience arrivals and the occasional intrusion of a ringing mobile phone, classical music audiences are well-educated and appreciative, and many of the SAR's music lovers are amateur musicians or choristers. Classical music programmes reflect Hong Kong's eclectic tastes and sentiments: in the same week and same venue, it's possible to enjoy a sensitive performance of a Britten song cycle and an *erhu* master playing odes to Chinese nationalism.

## Orchestras

Amateur and youth orchestras, such as the **Hong Kong Youth Symphony Orchestra** and the **Pan Asia Symphony Orchestra**, perform throughout the year at various venues and are often involved in the city's arts festivals.

### Hong Kong Academy of Performing Arts Orchestra

The orchestra of the Hong Kong Academy of Performing Arts, which comprises students from both its Chinese and Western music departments, performs regularly at HKAPA venues. Members of the HKAPA Orchestra tour every year and have enjoyed great success at international competitions.

The HKAPA also organises performances by the **Children's Palace Orchestra**, a children's orchestra with players as young as five years old.

### Hong Kong Philharmonic Orchestra

The Hong Kong Phil (HKPO) is the SAR's first and only full-time, professional Western classical music ensemble. The 93-piece orchestra embodies many of the SAR's cultural incongruities. It comprises musicians from a range of Asian and Western countries, is conducted by a local who received his training overseas and has a comparatively high turnover of musicians due, in part, to a short-term contract system. The HKPO plays from September to June and is currently under the baton of Samuel Wong.

The HKPO performs a wide repertoire and is frequently joined by world class soloists. In the last decade, it has toured North America, mainland China, Southeast Asia, Taiwan and Japan. The HKPO is involved in a number of school and community outreach programmes and a large number of orchestra members teach at the Hong Kong Academy of Performing Arts.

Under maestro Wong, the HKPO is committed to performing works by emerging local composers such as John Chen and Daniel Law Ping-leung. Its Sony live recording of Tan Dun's *Symphony 1997* (commissioned for the Handover) was reviewed with great enthusiasm.

The orchestra's website (www.hkpo.com) and its free quarterly magazine *Upbeat* give detailed information on the season's concert programmes.

**Arts & Entertainment**

# Chinese performing arts (continued)

in large playgrounds in Kowloon City (opposite the old airport at Kai Tak) and in Hung Hom (Chatham Road). Enclosures also go up during the festivities surrounding the **Birthday of Tin Hau** (*see p204*); one of the largest is in Yung Shue Wan on Lamma island, which regularly attracts some of Hong Kong's biggest operatic stars.

There are also some regular outdoor amateur performance spots – such as in the small park on the left side of Nathan Road, walking north from Yau Ma Tei MTR station, and at the northern end of Temple Street. Generally performed by a small troupe, without the aid of costumes or props, and enjoyed by an enthusiastic crowd of 60- to 90-year-olds, this is, quite literally, street art.

## CHINESE ORCHESTRAS
One of the largest Chinese orchestras of its type in the world, the 58-piece **Hong Kong Chinese Orchestra** (HKCO) consists of four sections of traditional and modern Chinese instruments: bowed strings, plucked strings, wind and percussion. Under the leadership of music director Yan Huichang, the orchestra is dedicated to promoting traditional and contemporary Chinese music, and to exploring new frontiers in music by experimenting with a range of techniques and styles. Its repertoire includes traditional folk music and contemporary full-scale works. The HKCO has commissioned over a thousand original compositions and arrangements, some of which have been recorded. Besides regular public concerts in Hong Kong and abroad, the Orchestra also offers free student concerts and outreach activities for all sectors of the community. For more information, go to the orchestra's website at www.lcsd.gov.hk/hkco.

Mainland and Taiwanese ensembles also regularly come to Hong Kong to perform.

## OTHER PERFORMANCES
Dance troupes from various provinces of China regularly visit the SAR, offering some

## Hong Kong Sinfonietta
The Hong Kong Sinfonietta (2836 3336) is a medium size orchestra that was formed by local musicians in 1990. Many of the ensemble were trained at the Hong Kong Academy of Performing Arts and the Sinfonietta has now become a professional bridge between the HKAPA and the HKPO. The Sinfonietta is quickly evolving into Hong Kong's second professional (western music) orchestra and, like the HKPO, is committed to performing new works by local composers.

Besides holding regular concerts, the Sinfonietta also provides accompaniment for local and international choirs, ballet companies and soloists. In recent years, they have performed with the Kirov, Bolshoi, Stuttgart and Hong Kong Ballet. Yeh Tsung is the orchestra's current music director.

## Choirs

### Hong Kong Bach Choir
Established over 30 years ago for a single performance of a Bach cantata, the Hong Kong Bach Choir now performs a wide repertoire, ranging from Palestrina to Elgar. The choir now numbers more than 80 singers and welcomes new members (see www.bachchoir.org.hk for programme and membership details).

### Hong Kong Oratorio Society
This is the oldest, largest and most active choir in the SAR. Formed in 1956, the Society has performed more than 80 oratorios and places strong programming emphasis on works from the Baroque and Classical choral canon. On average, the choir gives five performances a year. Its present music director is composer Chan Wing-wah (*see p241*). For more information, see www.oratorio.org.hk.

## Western opera
Although there is no full-time resident Western opera company in Hong Kong, it is still possible to see five or six opera productions a year. A major event in the **Hong Kong Arts Festival** (*see p207*) is the production of a grand opera by a visiting company. In past years, the Czech National Opera, Kirov Opera and Los Angeles Opera companies have performed. Innovative and smaller scale productions of lesser-known operas, by composers such as Piazzolla, Weill and Janacek, have also been highlights of past Arts Festival programmes.

### Opera Society of Hong Kong
Created in 1992 to promote Western opera, the Opera Society of Hong Kong (www.opera.org.hk) stages an annual full-scale production in the Grand Theatre of the Hong Kong Cultural Centre (*see p240*). The Society's chorus draws mainly upon local talent, but productions also feature visiting professional singers in the lead roles. The Opera Society tends to favour works with a broad popular appeal such as *La Bohème*, *Carmen* and *La Traviata*.

fascinating ancient ritualistic performances – some animalistic, others utterly graceful. The long flowing gown of the Yunnanese female dancer is in marked contrast to the brief jungle-warrior attire of her male counterpart. And, with its deep Muslim traditions, the dancers of Xinjiang province move to an Arabic musical accompaniment and look every bit the desert nomad. Provincial folk orchestras rarely play in events that do not include dance segments.

Puppet shows, China's earliest form of children's entertainment – and enjoyed by adults too – are an unusual find these days in the form of touring shows.

Visitors may be lucky enough to encounter a lion dance, accompanied by costumed drummers, commissioned by the owners of new shops or businesses. Otherwise, the best time to catch these (usually male-youth) troupes – and there are several in Hong Kong – is within the first few days of Chinese New Year, when they roam in commercial and some residential areas, chasing away the bad spirits and are rewarded with red *lai see*

envelopes containing cash. The surest way to see lion dances though, is to find out which hotels have arranged to have one, or to watch the annual Chinese New Year parade (*see p208*; check with the HKTB for details).

Also worth looking out for is the three-week **Hong Kong Chinese Arts Festival**, held every two years in October and November (*see p206*), which showcases the best of Chinese arts and culture from world-respected artists and performing ensembles from mainland China, Taiwan, Hong Kong and overseas Chinese communities from around the globe.

### VENUES
Contemporary Cantonese theatre and Chinese music performances take place at several venues around the SAR including: **Ko Shan Theatre**, 77 Ko Shan Road, Hung Hom (2740 9222); **Sai Wan Ho Civic Centre**, 111 Shau Kei Wan Road, Shau Kei Wan (2568 3721); **Sheung Wan Civic Centre**, 5/F Sheung Wan Complex, 345 Queen's Road Central, Sheung Wan (2853 2678); **Tai Po Civic Centre**, 1 On Pong Road, Tai Po (2665 4477).

## Hong Kong Academy of Performing Arts

The Hong Kong Academy of Performing Arts also stages one or two Western operas or operettas per year. These performances allow music, dance and technical arts students to collaborate in elaborately staged, playful productions.

## Dance

The dance scene in Hong Kong is surprisingly rich. Dance education has created a deep interest in – and audience for – classical and contemporary dance performances. For many years, Hong Kong has enjoyed a consistently high standard of private dance training. The establishment of the Hong Kong Academy of Performing Arts dance school in 1984 has allowed a number of talented local dancers to receive world-class tuition and to successfully participate in international competition. Many locally trained dancers have since pursued careers in the SAR's three main dance companies, while others have worked as choreographers or established their own independent companies. As the dance scene matures, a number of theme- or site-specific works have been created that embrace social and political dimensions of life in Hong Kong and challenge the way in which local audiences regard dance. Many newly-created works have

fused the traditions and techniques of Western and Chinese dance to create new and exciting local dance forms.

Dance enthusiasts in Hong Kong also enjoy a full performance calendar of touring companies. Recent productions from some of the world's best modern dance companies have brought the work of Jiri Kylian, Mikhail Barishnikov, Lloyd Newson, Marcia Haydee, John Neumeier and Peter Schaufuss to Hong Kong audiences.

### Hong Kong Ballet
The territory's only ballet company, the Hong Kong Ballet (2573 7398/www.hkballet.com.hk) performs regularly throughout the year at various venues, including the Hong Kong Cultural Centre's Grand Theatre (*see p240*). Its repertoire includes classics such as *The Nutcracker* and *Lady of the Camellias*, as well as original works created by local choreographers. Like the Hong Kong Philharmonic Orchestra, the Hong Kong Ballet maintains close ties with the Hong Kong Academy of Performing Arts. Many of the company's principal dancers are HKAPA graduates, and many choreograph and prepare HKAPA productions. The Hong Kong Ballet has toured in Europe and North America, and the company's original productions of works such as *The Emperor and the Nightingale* and the rock ballet *The White Snake* have received favourable reviews at home and abroad. Stephen Jefferies is the current artistic director.

**Arts & Entertainment**

### City Contemporary Dance Company

The CCDC (2326 8597/www.ccdc.com.hk) is Hong Kong's third major dance company and is dedicated to the development and performance of modern dance. Founded by its current artistic director, Willy Tsao, the CCDC mostly performs a repertoire created by local choreographers. The company frequently collaborates with artists from other media and the work of choreographers such as Helen Lai and Yuri Ng fuses Eastern and Western influences.

### Hong Kong Dance Alliance

The Hong Kong Dance Alliance (2584 8753/hkdalli@netvigator.com) is a federation of dance companies, teachers and student groups that is committed to promoting dance in Hong Kong. It publishes the bilingual *Dance Journal HK* and is a good source of local dance information.

### Hong Kong Dance Company

Devoted to promoting Chinese dance, the company's growing repertoire includes traditional and folk dances, as well as original dance dramas based on Chinese and Hong Kong themes. The HKDC is under the artistic direction of Jiang Huaxuan, who was trained in Chinese folk dance in Beijing. The HKDC has presented a number of original works by prominent choreographers, including the enormously popular Jade Love, regularly gives free performances, and provides an audience-building programme of visits to schools and community centres. Phone 2734 9009 for info on upcoming performances.

### OTHER COMPANIES

A number of independent and community dance companies also enrich the Hong Kong dance scene. They include **Dance Art Hong Kong**, the **Hong Kong Chinese Dance Ensemble**, the **Miranda Chin Dance Company** and the **South Asia Dance Company**.

## English-language theatre

The English-language theatre scene in Hong Kong consists of performances by resident youth and community companies, productions by touring companies, and locally produced or touring one-actor shows that are easily staged in intimate venues such as the Fringe Club (*see p241*). Most local productions of English-language dramas are performed by semi-professional companies such as the Hong Kong Players and the Hong Kong Singers. Hong Kong's English-speaking community enjoy a number of performances by first-rate visiting companies. The Royal Shakespeare Company, the Young Vic Theatre Company and Melbourne's Playbox Theatre are frequent visitors to Hong Kong.

Musicals are also popular in Hong Kong, and excellent imported productions of shows such as *Chicago* and *Miss Saigon* have recently been staged in the SAR. Lesser known and avant-garde companies also tour Hong Kong and performances of physical theatre, mime and puppetry are popular, attracting a wider audience than many text-based productions. The **City Festival** (formerly known as the Fringe Festival; *see p207*) has a strong focus on theatre and presents one-actor shows, stand-up comedy and locally produced poetry performance. A theatrical treat unique to Hong Kong is the performance of monologues by bilingual actors who alternate from English to Cantonese over different performances.

### Hong Kong Players

The Hong Kong Players is the SAR's foremost English-language community theatre group. The semi-professional Players are successors to the Garrison Players (a company that was established in colonial days) and the Hong Kong Stage Club. They mount three or four productions a year, performing a repertoire that has included works by Shakespeare, Noël Coward and Samuel Beckett. Each year, the Players also mount a Christmas pantomime at the Hong Kong Arts Centre's Shouson Theatre. For information on productions and auditions, visit www.hongkongplayers.com.

### Hong Kong Repertory Theatre

The government-supported Hong Kong Repertory Theatre was established in 1977. The company has staged nearly 180 productions, covering a wide variety of Chinese and Western contemporary and classical works. Most productions are staged in Cantonese, with some in English and Mandarin. For programme enquiries, call 2853 2634.

### Hong Kong Singers

The Hong Kong Singers are a semi-professional community musical performance group who stage cabaret and popular musicals such as *42nd Street* and *The King and I*. They have performed at various venues around Hong Kong, including the Hong Kong Academy of Performing Arts, the Hong Kong Arts Centre and the Fringe Club.

### Zuni Icosahedron

This independent cultural collective is committed to original productions of alternative theatre, multimedia performance, sound experimentation and installation arts. Performances focus on exploring a range of themes across cultures, media and art forms. The collective has formed artistic partnerships with non-profit making arts groups from Beijing, Tokyo, Taipei, New York, London, Munich and Berlin. For information on upcoming performances, phone 2893 8704 or e-mail zuni@vol.net.

## Festivals

*See chapter* **By Season** *and p207* **Hong Kong Arts Festival**.

# Sport & Fitness

Spectate or participate in Hong Kong's multiplicity of sporty events and activities.

With the amount of energy they dedicate to making money, it is surprising that Hong Kong folk have any time for more healthy pursuits. But the locals follow (and participate in) their sport with gusto – from the dawn flood of *tai chi* devotees, through daytime games of basketball and football played out on concrete courts, to the packed gyms in the evening. At the weekend things become more adventurous, and sailing, hiking and climbing take people out of the city to stupendous countryside.

The **South China Athletic Association** (SCAA; 2577 6932) and the **YMCA of Hong Kong** (*see p248*) offer a wider range of sports than we list below, and at very reasonable prices. *HK Magazine* or *BC Magazine* list the week's and month's sports events, or try *Q Times* (2807 1481/www.qtimes.com), which details some tailor-made packages of days out incorporating various sports and activities.

## Participation sports/fitness

### Athletics

Marathons are held throughout the year at different sports grounds and clubs – top of the list is the **Standard Chartered Hong Kong Marathon** (*see p208*). For a complete calendar of events and club listings contact the **Hong Kong Amateur Athletics Association** (2504 8215/www.hkaaa.com).

### Badminton

**Hong Kong Park Government Indoor Games Hall**
*29 Cotton Tree Drive, Central, HK Island (2521 5072). Buses along Cotton Tree Drive.* **Open** 7am-11pm daily. **Prices** HK$59 per hour. **No credit cards. Map** p67 E5.

### Bowling

**AMF Bowling Club**
*New East Ocean Centre, 9 Science Museum Road, Tsim Sha Tsui East, Kowloon (2732 2255). Bus 203, 973.* **Open** 10am-1am daily. **Prices** from HK$32 per game; shoe hire HK$8. **Credit** AmEx, DC, MC, V. **Map** p98 E1.
Ten-pin bowling is immensely popular in Hong Kong. AMF have bowling centres across the city. Call the above for details of others.

**California's Fitness Centre.** *See p248.*

### Kai Tak Bowling Club
*Kai Tak Old Airport, Kowloon (2382 8189/ www.kaitakbowling.com). Buses to Kai Tak Old Airport.* **Open** 10am-2am daily. **Prices** before 2pm HK$20 per game; 2-6pm HK$28; after 6pm HK$36; shoe hire HK$8. **Credit** MC, V. **Map** p62.

### Climbing

There's a huge number of die-hard climbing fans in Hong Kong, and there are some superb climbs across the territory. These include **Tung Lung Island** (Grade – French – 5-8A; volcanic rock), **Shek O** (Grade 4-6B; granite; good for beginners), **Lion Rock** (Grade 6A-7A; granite; multipitch routes) and **Kowloon Peak** (Grade 4-7C; volcanic rock). For indoor walls, try:

### King's Park
*22 Gascoigne Road, Yau Ma Tei, Kowloon (2782 6682). Yau Ma Tei MTR (exit B2)/buses along Nathan Road.* **Open** noon-10pm Mon-Fri; 10am-10pm Sat, Sun. **Prices** HK$70 before 5.30pm; HK$90 after 5.30pm. **No credit cards. Map** p110 B5.
The best venue in the city for wall climbing, but you need to take a lead climber's assessment to climb here.

### YMCA of Hong Kong
*41 Salisbury Road, Tsim Sha Tsui, Kowloon (2369 2211/www.ymca.org.hk). Tsim Sha Tsui MTR (exit E)/buses to Tsim Sha Tsui Star Ferry Pier & along Salisbury Road/Tsim Sha Tsui Star Ferry Pier.* **Open** noon-10pm Mon-Fri; 10am-10pm Sat, Sun. **Prices** non-members HK$80 per hour; members HK$40 per hour. **No credit cards.** **Map** p98 B3.

You'll have to do a half-day assessment to get a permit to climb here, but after that it is open house.

## Fitness centres

### California's Fitness Centre
*1 Wellington Street, Central, HK Island (2522 5229). Central MTR (exit D1, D2, G)/12M, 13, 23A, 40M, 43 bus.* **Open** 6am-midnight Mon-Sat; 8am-10pm Sun. **Prices** day pass HK$300. **Credit** AmEx, DC, MC, V. **Map** p66 C3.

Call for details of other branches.

### New York Fitness Club
*Kinwick Centre, 32 Hollywood Road, Central, HK Island (2543 2280). Central MTR (exit D1, D2, G)/ Mid-Levels Escalator/12M, 13, 23A, 26, 40M, 43 bus.* **Open** 6.30am-10.30pm Mon-Fri; 7.30am-9pm Sat, Sun. **Prices** classes HK$150-HK$200; workout only HK$200. **Credit** AmEx, DC, MC, V. **Map** p66 C3.

### Tom Turk's Fitness Centre
*11/F, HK Scouts Centre, 8 Austin Road, Tsim Sha Tsui, Kowloon (2736 7188). Jordan MTR (exit D)/ buses along Austin Road.* **Open** 6.30am-10.30pm Mon-Fri; 6.30am-8pm Sat, Sun. **Prices** before 5pm HK$300 per week; all day HK$500 per week. **Credit** MC, V. **Map** p110 A5.
**Branch:** Citibank Tower, 3 Garden Road, Central, HK Island (2521 4547).

## Go-karting

### Kai Tak Karting Mall
*Kai Tak Old Airport, Kowloon (2718 8199/www.kartingmall.com). Buses to Kai Tak Old Airport.* **Open** 10am-2am daily. **Prices** HK$200 per race (approx 14mins). **Credit** MC, V. **Map** p62.

This indoor course features old signs from Kai Tak airport, so you could find yourself hurtling towards immigration as you skid round the bends. The course is full of corners and is pretty tight for over-taking, but exhilarating nonetheless.

## Golf

### Jockey Club Kau Sai Chau Public Golf Course
*Kau Sai Chau, Sai Kung, New Territories (2791 3390/2791 3344/www.kscgolf.com). Buses to Sai Kung.* **Open** 7am-8pm Mon-Thur; 7am-10pm Fri-Sun. **Prices** from HK$550 per 18 holes. **Credit** MC, V. **Map** p311.

### Tuen Mun Golf Centre
*Tuen Mun Recreation & Sports Centre, Lung Mun Road, New Territories (2466 2600). Buses to Tuen Mun.* **Open** 8am-10pm daily. **Prices** HK$12 per bay per hour; HK$12 per 30 balls. **No credit cards.** **Map** p310.

## Hiking

Surprising though it may seem to some, Hong Kong is a superb place for hiking. *See chapter* **Wild Hong Kong**.

## Horse riding

Most of the horses available to ride are ex-racehorses retrained for riding schools. The most central public riding school is:

### Pok Fu Lam Public Riding School
*75 Pok Fu Lam Reservoir Road, Pok Fu Lam, HK Island (2550 1359). Buses along Pok Fu Lam Reservoir Road.* **Open** 8am-7pm Mon-Fri; 8am-6pm Sat, Sun. **Prices** HK$340 per hour. **Credit** MC, V. **Map** p62.

## Ice skating

### The Glacier
*Festival Walk, Kowloon Tong, Kowloon (2265 8888/ www.glacier.com.hk/homepage). Kowloon Tong MTR/ KCR/buses to Festival Walk.* **Open** 8.30am-10pm daily. **Prices** HK$50 per session. **No credit cards.** **Map** p62.

## Kickboxing

*See also above* **New York Fitness Club**.

### Fightin' Fit
*2/F, World Trust Tower, 50 Stanley Street, Central, HK Island (2526 6648/www.fightinfit.com.hk). Central MTR (exit D1, D2, G)/buses along Queen's Road Central.* **Open** 7.30am-9.30pm daily. **Prices** non-members HK$200 per session. **Credit** MC, V. **Map** p66 C3.

## Martial arts

Following the legacy left by Bruce Lee and continued by Jackie Chan, martial arts of all kinds are practised fanatically all over the city. All day, but especially in the morning, you'll see the poetry-smooth moves of *tai chi* in parks. You can try *tai chi* for free on the waterfront promenade in Tsim Sha Tsui (8am-9am Tue, Wed; call the HKTB for details).

Otherwise try the **YMCA of Hong Kong** (*see above*), **Fightin' Fit** (*see above*) or the **SCAA** (2830 0951/www.scaa.org.hk/ eng_index), which between them offer classes in just about every martial art that exists.

# Mountain biking

Trails in Hong Kong can get you out of the city and into some great countryside. Check out the **Hong Kong Mountain Bike Association** (2106 7035/www.hkmba.org) for routes, maps and information.

## Flying Ball Bicycle Company

*201 Tong Choi Street, Mong Kok, Kowloon (2381 3661/www.flyingball.com). Prince Edward MTR (exit B2)/buses along Nathan Road & Prince Edward Road.* **Open** 10am-8pm daily. **Credit** AmEx, DC, MC, V. **Map** p110 A2.
Possibly the best bike shop in Asia.

## Paul Etherington

*2486 2112/9300 5197/www.kayak-and-hike.com.*
Paul takes small groups out to Sai Kung Country Park and Tai Mo Shan areas. Prices are around HK$500 per day, including all equipment, transport to and from the trails and the necessary permits.

# Rollerblading/skateboarding

Although plans are afoot, there are no skating rinks or places to hire blades or skateboards yet. Happy Valley Racetrack has a track round the outside where you can blade, or join the joggers on traffic-free Bowen Road (*see below* **Running/jogging**).

# Running/jogging

**Lugard Road** is a popular 2.8-kilometre (1.75-mile) loop round the Peak, starting from close to the Upper Peak Tram Terminal. **Bowen Road** runs four kilometres (2.5 miles) from near Robinson Road to Magazine Gap Road above Happy Valley, affording spectacular views of the city. Both are traffic-free.

For organised runs contact the Wan Chai Hash (Maggie Raynolds 2559 5955/2537 8389/www.wanchaihash.com) or go to the Wanch bar, 54 Jaffe Road, Wan Chai (2861 1621), where the board tells you about their next run. The Hash runs on Sundays, starting at 4pm, for about an hour (HK$30 for women; HK$50 for men). There is usually an optional restaurant meal organised at your destination. Also, check out www.hkrunners.com.

# Sailing

Sailing is a big weekend sport in Hong Kong and there are several major races throughout the year. If you want to hitch a lift, go down to the RHKYC (or Hebe Haven) on Saturday morning and look at the board for boats looking for crew. Experienced crew is preferred. All the clubs below hold courses.

## Hebe Haven Yacht Club

*10.5 miles, Hiran's Highway, Pak Sha Wan, Sai Kung, New Territories (2719 9682/www.hhyc.org.hk). Buses to Sai Kung.* **Map** p311.

## Royal Hong Kong Yacht Club

*Kellet Island, Causeway Bay, HK Island (2832 2817/www.rhkyc.org.hk). Causeway Bay MTR (exit C)/buses along Gloucester Road.* **Map** p80 D1.

## St Stephen's Beach Water Sports Centre

*Wong Ma Kok Path, Stanley, HK Island (2813 5402/enquiries@lcsd.gov.hk). Buses to Stanley.* **Open** 8.30am-4.30pm Mon, Wed-Sun. **Map** p62.

# Scuba diving

Due to the poor quality of the water, Hong Kong isn't the best place to scuba dive in Asia, but it is better than you might imagine. The Sai Kung and Clearwater Bay peninsulas, Shek O and Po Toi island are a few of the many dive sites regularly visited, harbouring some 50 types of coral and 400 varieties of sealife. The diving season falls roughly between March and October, when shore, wreck and night dives and various courses are all on offer.

## Mandarin Divers

*G/F, Unit 2, Aberdeen Marina Tower, 8 Shum Wan Road, Aberdeen, HK Island (2554 7110). Buses to Aberdeen.* **Open** 10am-7pm Mon-Fri; 10am-6pm Sat. **Prices** 'Fun diving day out' HK$450 including two dives, equipment but no lunch. Bring your certificate. **Credit** AmEx, MC, V. **Map** p62.

## Marine Divers Sub-Aqua Club

*3E Block 18, Dynasty View, 11 Ma Wo Road, Tai Po, New Territories (2656 9399/ginge1@netvigator.com). Buses to Tai Po.* **Prices** HK$500 (air boat supervision) day trip of three dives with beach barbecue; kit hire HK$200 members, HK$300 non-members. **No credit cards**. **Map** p311.

# Surfing

Big Wave Bay (*see p96*) near Shek O is Hong Kong Island's surfer's paradise. The beach is pleasant and there's a consistent one-metre (three-foot) beach break, so it is ideal for beginners. Big Wave Bay Kiosk (2809 4933) is right on the beach and sells food and drinks (open approx 2-7pm Mon-Fri; all day Sat, Sun; board hire approx HK$200 per day).

Sai Kung's Tai Long Wan beach at Sai Kung (in the New Territories; *see p123*) is usually a foot bigger and has better shaped waves, but it's quite a trek.

**Island Wake** surf shop organises beginners' courses throughout the summer. Call Raymond Chan on 2522 9131 for details.

## Swimming

If you don't fancy any of the beaches (*see below* **Hong Kong beaches**), most hotels allow non-residents to use their pools for around HK$250, or you could venture into the overcrowded, over-chlorinated world of the public pools.

### Kowloon Park
*22 Austin Road, Kowloon Park, Tsim Sha Tsui, Kowloon (2724 3577). Jordan MTR (exit D)/buses along Austin Road.* **Open** *June-Mar* 6.30am-noon, 1-6.30pm, 7.30-9pm daily. **Admission** phone for details. **Map** p98 B1. Four pools.

### Victoria Park
*Hing Fat Street, Causeway Bay, HK Island (2570 8347).* **Open** *Apr-Oct* 6.30am-noon, 1-6.30pm, 7.30-10pm daily. **Admission** phone for details. **Map** p80 E1.

## Tennis

Tennis courts are dotted all over Hong Kong, and they're relatively cheap, at HK$42 per hour.

### Causeway Bay Sports Ground
*Causeway Road, Causeway Bay, HK Island (2890 5127). Tin Hau MTR (exit B)/buses along Causeway Road.* **Open** 6am-11pm daily. **Map** p80 E1. 6 floodlit courts.

### Hong Kong Tennis Centre
*Wong Nai Chung Gap Road, Happy Valley, HK Island (2574 9122). Bus 6, 41A, 61, 63, 66, 76.* **Open** phone for details. 17 floodlit courts.

### King's Park Sports Ground
*15 King's Park Rise, Yau Ma Tei, Kowloon (2388 8154). Bus 2C, 103.* **Open** 7am-11pm daily. **Map** p110 B4. 6 floodlit courts.

### Victoria Park
*Hing Fat Street, Causeway Bay, HK Island (2570 6186). Tin Hau MTR (exit A2)/buses along Hing Fat Street.* **Open** 7am-11pm daily. **Map** p80 E1. 14 courts.

## Wakeboarding, waterskiing & windsurfing

There are a number of sheltered bays in Hong Kong perfect for waterskiing and wakeboarding. Windsurfing suffers from lack of wind punctuated by sudden gusts but you could follow in the wake of Cheung Chau's own Lee Lai-shan who won an Olympic gold medal (Hong Kong's only ever) at Atlanta in 1996.

**Deep Water Bay Water-ski Tuition** (2812 0391; HK$580 per hour for boat, equipment and tuition) and Charles Cheung at **Wakeboard Tai Tam** (9170 4551; HK800 per hour) both offer waterskiing and wakeboarding.

### Cheung Chau Windsurfing Centre
*Hai Pak Road, Tung Wan beach, Cheung Chau (2981 8316). Cheung Chau Ferry Pier.* **Open** 10am-6pm daily. **Prices** big sail HK$120 per hour; medium sail HK$100 per hour; small sail HK$60 per hour; one-day courses HK$550. **No credit cards**. **Map** p126.

### Wave Star the Windsurfing Spirit
*Stanley Main Beach, Stanley, HK Island (Barry Ho 2813 7561/www.wakewindhkstar.com). Buses to Stanley.* **Open** *summer* 9am-6pm daily; *winter* 9am-

# Hong Kong beaches

Swimming in the ocean in Hong Kong isn't always the blissful tropical experience you imagine. Water pollution is a serious problem, and you could find yourself cresting the waves in the company of a shoal of plastic bags. However, there are some fantastic beaches if you venture a bit further afield.

The best beach for swimming, way out in the eastern New Territories at **Tai Long Wan**, has pale sand and sparkly blue water (with phenomenal phosphorescence at the right time of year). There's a noodle shack here, so camping is very popular (although beware the leavings of the local herd of cows).

On Hong Kong Island, **Big Wave Bay** (*see p96*) near Shek O is pleasant, and, although the surfers have made it their own, it is a

great place to swim, too. There's a kiosk selling food and drink, frisbies and you can hire surfboards, too. **Shek O**'s main beach (*see p95*) has more people but more facilities. **Deep Water Bay** and **Repulse Bay** (*see p93*) are popular beaches, situated side by side, just a 20-minute bus ride from Central. They're nice enough, with cafés, showers and shops selling buckets and spades. The water quality can vary, so look out for the daily reports in the newspaper. Further along the coast towards Stanley are two gay beaches at **South Bay** and **Middle Bay** (*see p225*). Middle Bay is rocky, so not great for swimming; South Bay is more favourable, and even better for celebrity spotting, as Hong Kong's stars search for somewhere off the beaten track.

Arts & Entertainment

Heading for the line at **Sha Tin Racecourse**. *See p118.*

6pm Sat, Sun. **Prices** windsurfing HK$100 per hour; two-day course HK$800; ocean kayaking HK$60 per hour; wakeboarding/waterskiing HK$600 per hour. **No credit cards. Map** p62.

## Yoga

**Yoga Studio** (Al Aqmar House, 30 Hollywood Road, Central; 2525 7415), **Yoga Central** (4/F, 13 Wyndham Street, Central; 2982 4308), **New York Fitness** (*see p248*) and **California's** (*see p248*) all offer yoga. Call for times and prices.

## Spectator sports

### Adventure sports

The **National Geographic Channel Action Asia Challenge** is a punishing one-day challenge taking participants through the rugged terrain of the New Territories, testing their skills in kayaking, jungle trekking, orienteering, rock scrambling, trial running and more. For details, see www.actionasia.com and www.NGC-AAChallenge.com.

### Athletics

For the **Standard Chartered Hong Kong Marathon**, *see p208* and *p248*.

### Dragon boat racing

The **Dragon Boat (Tuen Ng) Festival** on the last weekend of June features races all over Hong Kong. Stanley's contribution has racers paddling a gruelling 500 metres (1,640 feet) towards the beach while the junks moored up to each other along the side heave with supporters, most considerably the worse for wear for alcohol. The party outside the row of bars and restaurants on Stanley Main Street lasts all night. *See p205.*

### Football

World Cup qualifying games are being played in Hong Kong Stadium in So Kon Po for the first time for the 2002 competition. January sees international teams flying into town to compete in the **Carlsberg Cup** tournament (*see p208*).

### Golf

The annual **Star Alliance Open** (Nov/Dec; *see p206*) is one of the top golfing events in Asia, bringing in top players from around the world.

### Horse racing

Horse racing is huge here. Thousands pack into the two racecourses at **Happy Valley** on Hong Kong Island (every Wednesday) and **Sha Tin** in the New Territories (weekends; *see p118*) every week from September to June to gamble their earnings away. This is racing Hong Kong style, with floodlit pitches and flashing information boards. Among the major meetings are the **Hong Kong Derby** in March, the **Queen Elizabeth II Cup** in April and the **Hong Kong International Races** in December, all at Sha Tin (*see p207*). For details, see www.hkjockeyclub.com. *See also p87* **Will Hong Kong lose its shirt?**

#### Happy Valley Racecourse

*Happy Valley, HK Island (1817/www.hkjockeyclub. com). Trams to Happy Valley.* **Open** varies; see website or phone for racing calendar; closed July/Aug. **Admission** HK$10. **No credit cards. Map** p80 D3. An evening at Happy Valley is a must. The entry fee is cheap, as are the food and drinks inside, and minimum bets are low, too (HK$10). Bets can only be made at the Jockey Club counters inside the stand. It's a simple process – there are leaflets explaining the various betting options and officials will help with any questions. Large screens display the odds

# Hong Kong Sevens

In March every year the Rugby Sevens returns to the place of its invention: Hong Kong. First played in 1975, the **Credit Suisse First Boston Hong Kong Sevens** (*see also p204*) features more than 50 games of rugby in less than 72 hours. During the day, the city grinds to a standstill while its population stampedes into the stands and corporate boxes of the 40,000 capacity Hong Kong Stadium to cheer players from some 24 different countries.

The international giants such as Australia, New Zealand and Fiji are the tournament's royalty, and each participating team strains every muscle to knock them from their thrones. This is high-intensity, no-holds-barred sport at its best. Meanwhile, in the south stands, high-intensity, no-holds-barred chaos reigns. Support for the Hong Kong team, from both locals and expats, is fanatical. During the three days, the costumed, chanting and plain crazy supporters in the furthest quarter of the stadium hold the biggest party of the year. Around 200,000 litres of beer is slurped, thrown (and vomited), over 18,000 meat pies are devoured, launched (and sat on), while over 900 staff try to keep the crowds watered, fed and under some semblance of control.

The same characters and rituals star year after year – the humungous pie-man lumbers up and down the rows, as the crowd screams 'Who ate all the pies?' The guy dressed as a slice of pizza gets passed round the stands on the tips of everyone's fingers. Someone's phone goes and everyone chants 'Who's the wanker on the phone?' and missiles of pies

and beer follow. It is impossible not to get caught up in the frenetic enjoyment and enthusiasm of the day.

But it's not the end of the party when the Rugby finishes. No way – it's just the wallpaper that changes. Straight after the last ball is hurled and the last triumphant wave disappears into the changing rooms, there's more partying to be had. There's Lan Kwai Fong and Wan Chai of course, but just opposite the stadium the huge annual Valley Big Top Marquee blasts into life. While the bands play, the crowds keep the enthusiasm high as they drink, eat and dance into the small hours. Friendships are made and broken, trousers and shorts are torn off and abandoned, jugs of drink are hurled onto the marquee roof… You've got to be crazy to go, but you'd be even crazier to miss it.

and show the races in progress. There is seating in the stands and a standing-only area looking directly onto the track. This is the most exciting place to be during the race as you can feel the horses thunder past as the roar of the crowd rises in the stands behind. Race events are usually held on Wednesday evenings (although the race calendar is not entirely regular) throughout the September-June season. The first race is usually at 7.30pm. The HKTB also runs a 'Go Racing' tour, complete with meal. Despite Happy Valley's 55,000 capacity, punters are sometimes turned away at the busy meetings.

## Rugby

The famous annual Rugby Sevens tournament transforms watching rugby into short chapters of intense competition interrupted by beer, fights and general pandemonium in the stands. *See above* **Hong Kong Sevens**.

Look out also for the **E-Kong Women's Rugby Sevens & Asia Championship** on the Thursday and Friday of the Sevens weekend (www.hkwomensrugby.com). The **Hong Kong Tens** focuses on the best teams from New Zealand, Australia and the UK as well as many others, and takes place on the Wednesday and Thursday prior to the Sevens weekend (www.hongkongtens.com).

## Tennis

Three annual tournaments pull in current champions and crowd favourites from the past. The **Salem Open** at Victoria Park starts the season off in October, followed by the **Cathay Pacific Championships** in the Convention & Exhibition Centre in November (*see p206*) and, in late November/early December, comes the **Watson's Water Challenge** in Victoria Park.

# Trips Out of Town

| Macau | 254 |
| Guangzhou | 267 |

## Feature boxes

| Cash to burn? | 264 |
| Rough trade | 275 |
| Hey, good looking! | 276 |
| A rock icon(oclast) | 279 |
| Chinese characters | 280 |

# Macau

When the chips are down, see a few sights or bask on a beach.

Most visitors drawn to the small mainland peninsula of Macau are coming for one thing – a roll of the dice. And that's a shame, because the Macau Special Administrative Region, as it is officially known, has so much more to offer than just the crazy-quilt colours and jingle-jangle cacophony of a casino. Macau (its name is a corruption of 'A-Ma-Gau', meaning 'Bay of A Ma', a reference to the A Ma temple on the Inner Harbour) is a vibrant place that straddles the wide psychological divide separating Asia and Europe. Its fine European architecture (at least, what's left of it), its extraordinary dialect (although it's rarely heard these days) and much of its East-West mentality hark back to more than four centuries as a Portuguese colony, while its ancient temples and the hustle and bustle of its street life are an open window into Chinese life. At the same time, its restful islands – Taipa and Colôane – offer a blissful retreat from the hectic world of modern Hong Kong. And it's all less than 70 kilometres (45 miles) away.

Macau is the alpha and omega of Western colonisation in Far East Asia, being both the first area east of Malaysia to be settled by

Europeans and the last to be released. The first recorded Portuguese navigator to visit China was Jorge Alvares, who reached Lintin, an island in the Pearl River estuary in 1513. Even though he spent ten months on the island, he did not establish a long term base.

It was not until 1557 that the Portuguese were given permission by the local magistrate at Heung Shan (in modern Zhuhai) to settle permanently on the Macau peninsula – reportedly in return for assistance in driving away pirates. Macau, therefore, became the Portuguese headquarters for trade in this part of Asia.

As the Chinese had banned Japanese traders from entering their ports (which had been ravaged by Japanese pirates for centuries), the Portuguese became crucial intermediaries in the trading of copper and silver and raw silks. By the early 1600s, Macau was a thriving city that was home not just to traders but also Portuguese missionaries determined to convert the Asian communities to Catholicism.

However, Macau's golden era did not last long. In 1637, Japan entered a self-inflicted period of exclusion and the Portuguese no

The **Largo do Senado**: the old colonial heart of Macau. *See p257.*

longer had a role to play in Far East Asian trade. In addition, within a matter of years, Portugal's domination of world trade was threatened by the Dutch, who took the Portuguese port of Malacca (on Malaysia's west coast) and set up ports in (what is now known as) Sri Lanka to rival Goa. As a result, Macau's prosperity suffered and the city became a complete backwater.

But it still retained its international flavour, with a community that included Portuguese traders, Chinese merchants, Japanese Christians, and slaves from Portuguese colonies in Africa, India and Malaysia. As there were few European women, the Portuguese men tended to marry Asians (who had converted to Catholicism), resulting in the distinctive Macanese people. In addition, a local patois developed combining Portuguese, Malay, Japanese and Cantonese elements, but it is now more or less extinct, only ever being spoken by those aged 80 or more. Other elements of the Macanese culture, such as dress, were also derived from Malacca and elsewhere, and until the early 20th century, many elderly Macanese women still wore *sarong kebaya* (traditional Malay dress) and lived relatively secluded lives.

Although Macau did experience something of a resurgence from the mid 18th century onwards, when it was used as a base by many Europeans and Americans trading with Canton (as Guangzhou was then known), it was not really until the mid 20th century that Macau discovered its raison d'être – and long-term prosperity. Licensed gambling now accounts for 40 per cent of the government's revenue and forms the backbone of the economy.

In 1887, although they had already been in Macau for over 300 years, the Portuguese finally formalised their presence in the city by securing a concession of sovereignty from the Chinese. At times, however, their control of Macau has been somewhat reluctant. Following a revolution in Portugal in 1974, for example, the Portuguese attempted to withdraw from Macau, as they did elsewhere in their empire at that time. Yet despite years of anti-colonial rhetoric, the Chinese asked them to remain. Portugal agreed to remain in name, but withdrew its remaining troops and declared Macau a Chinese sovereign territory under Portuguese administration. The Sino-Portuguese Joint Declaration – signed in 1987 – finally provided for Macau's return to Chinese administration in 1999.

After the signing of the Declaration, Macau experienced a few years of unsustained property boom, similar to that experienced by Hong Kong in the early 1990s. During this time, massive land reclamation schemes

were undertaken, completely changing the peninsula's appearance. For all the apparent modernity, however, there is still a lot of old Macau to be found, much of which has been beautifully restored in recent years. Otherwise, the transition to an SAR has been fairly seamless – and certainly smoother than that of Hong Kong. For although there were outbreaks of violence, as the local and mainland Chinese triads flexed their muscles and staked their claims to various pieces of 'business', items such as passports were never an issue – Lisbon granted passports to all those who had been born in Macau prior to 1980, as well as their children.

## Sightseeing

Macau is divided into three very separate sections: the area that is joined to mainland China, and the two islands of Taipa and Colôane. The heart of the city, with most of the sights and most of the action, is to be found in the mainland section, while the two islands – particularly the more distant Colôane – offer a more peaceful respite.

## Central Macau

Central Macau's famous waterfront avenue, the **Avenida da Praia Grande**, is an excellent place to start a tour of the city. The grand street once extended in a graceful banyan-lined crescent from the ramparts of São Francisco Battery and Gardens, along the coast to the fortress of Bom Parto, around the cliffs towards the fortress of Barra, eventually reaching the Porto Interior (Inner Harbour). Lined with magnificent buildings, the Praia Grande was one of Macau's renowned beauty spots, described by one author as an 'elegant crescent of Latin architecture facing the waterfront, beyond which rise the low domes and towers of seminaries and churches, the whole creating that uniquely unexpected European view which is Macau's greeting to every visitor from the sea'. Sadly, extensive reclamation has diminished the beauty of the Praia Grande in recent years, though the southern end of Avenida de República, beyond Santa Sancha, the Governor's Residence, still gives a tangible echo of what it once looked like.

Walking down Avenida de Praia Grande, one of the first significant sights is the **Jorge Alvares Monument**. Alvares was the first Portuguese explorer to make his way to China. His historic journey to Lintin (where he later died) was marked by two relatively recent memorials, one in Macau and the other in Hong

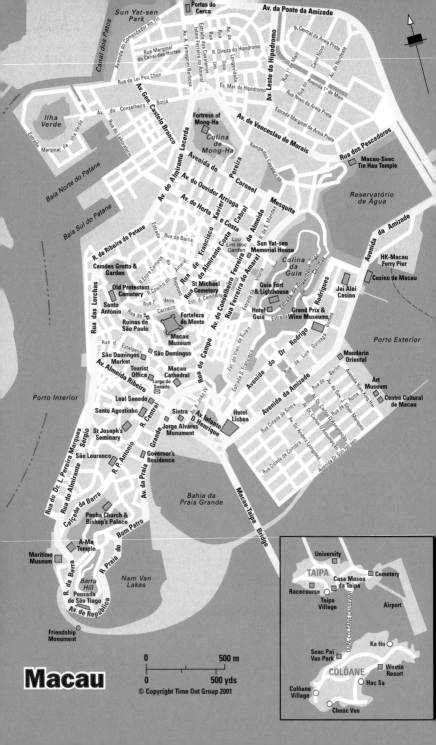

# Macau

© Copyright Time Out Group 2001

0      500 m
0      500 yds


Sun Yat-sen Park
Portas do Cerco
Av. da Ponte da Amizade
Canal dos Patos
Avenida do Comandador Ho Yin
R. Central da Areia Preta
Canal Novo
Av. do Nordeste
Estrada Marginal do Canal das Hortas
Rua Marginal do Canal das Hortas
Estrada A. Tamagnini Barbosa
Rua A. Tamagnini Barbosa
Estrada Ferreira do Amaral
Av. da Longevidade
Av. de Cavaleiros
R. Direita do Hipodromo
Uln
Dois
Es. Mar. do Hipodromo
Av. 1 de Maio
Avenida 1ª de Maio
Av. 49
Rua Nova da Areia Preta
Estrada Marginal da Areia Preta
Rua de Lei Pou Chon
Av. Gen. Castelo Branco
Borja
Av. do Conselheiro
Av. de Venceslau de Morais
Ilha Verde
Estrada Marginal da Ilha Verde
Rua da Ilha Verde
Rua do Laboratorio
Rua dos Pescadores
Macau-Seac Tin Hau Temple
Fortress of Mong-Ha
Colina de Mong-Ha
Avenida do
Coronel
Mesquita
Reservatório de Água
Baía Norte do Patane
Av. do Almirante Lacerda
Pereira
Av. do Ouvidor Arriaga
Av. de Horta Xavier e Costa
Cabral
Baía Sul do Patane
R. de Ribeira do Patane
Estrada
Rua da Barca
Lou Lim Ieoc Garden
R. S. Mendes
Avenida da Amizade
HK-Macau Ferry Pier
Camões Grotto & Garden
R. Entra Campos
Amaral
Sun Yat-sen Memorial House
Colina da Guia
Casino de Macau
Old Protestant Cemetery
R. Coelho do Amaral
Ramoso
Jai Alai Casino
R. das Lorchas
Rua de B.
Veira
St Michael Cemetery
Guia Fort & Lighthouse
Rodrigues
Santo António
Carneiro
Estr. d. Cemitério
Estrada da Vitoria
Hotel Guia
Grand Prix & Wine Museums
Porto Exterior
Ruínas de São Paulo
Rua d.
Estalgens
Fortaleza do Monte
Rua do Campo
Estrada do Engenheiro Trigo
Mandarin Oriental
São Domingos Market
São Domingos
Macau Museum
Estr. do Visc. de Sulan
Estrada do Eng.
Gonzaga Gomes
Av. Almeida Ribeiro
Tourist Office
Macau Cathedral
Largo do Senado
Estrada S. Francisco
Dr. Rodrigo
Av. de Luis Gonzaga Gomes
Art Museum
Porto Interior
Leal Senado
Avenida do
Centro Cultural de Macau
Santo Agostinho
R. Central
Sintra
Av. Infante D. Henrique
Hotel Lisboa
Avenida da Amizade
St Joseph's Seminary
Grande
Jorge Alvares Monument
Rua Cidade de Sintra
R. de Av. de Berlim
Av. de Av. de Gov.J
Roma
Avenida Xian Xing Hai
Rua do Dr. L. Pereira Marques
Sergio
R. P. Antonio
Governor's Residence
Al. Dr. Carlos D'Assumpção
Rua de Silver Marques
São Lourenço
Rua do Almirante
Av. da Praia
Al. St. Anders's. Lingostrad
Rua Cidade de Coimbra
Avenida Dr. Sun Yat-sen
Penha Church & Bishop's Palace
Bom Patro
Bahia da Praia Grande
Macau-Taipa Bridge
A-Ma Temple
Calçada da Barra
Maritime Museum
R. da Barra
Barra Hill
R. Praia do
Nam Van Lakes
Pousada de São Tiago
Av. de República
Friendship Monument

**Inset map (Taipa & Coloane):**

University
TAIPA
Casa Museu de Taipa
Cemetery
Racecourse
Taipa Village
Airport
TAIPA-COLOANE CAUSEWAY
Ka Ho
Seac Pai Van Park
Westin Resort
COLÔANE
Colôane Village
Hac Sa
Cheoc Van

**Ruinas de São Paulo**: symbol of Macau.

Kong. Here, Alvares is remembered by a stone statue that was first unveiled in 1953. It depicts him as a stocky bearded figure in a medieval tunic and long cape, holding a sheathed sword with the *padrão* (marker stone) he erected at Lintin standing behind him, his arm raised in greeting. (*See also p7.*)

Turn left off Avenida da Praia Grande onto Avenida de Almeida Ribeiro and you will reach the buildings of the **Leal Senado** (Loyal Senate; *see p259*). Built in classic Manueline style in 1784, it stands on the site of a much older, open-sided Chinese pavilion dating from the very first Portuguese settlement in Macau. It was here that the Red Guards gathered to express their anger during the riots of December 1966. They caused extensive damage to the public library on the second floor, as well as to other parts of the city (and prompted a Portuguese offer of complete withdrawal from Macau, which was refused by the Chinese). Today, the building houses the Municipal Council.

Opposite the Leal is the **Largo do Senado** (Senate Square), the symbolic heart of Macau. It is surrounded by a number of lovely colonial structures including the General Post Office and the charitable foundation **Santa Casa da Misericordia**. Well-preserved architecture abounds here, the **Edificio Ritz**, which now houses the tourist office, being a good example.

A short walk through the square to Rua São Domingos, on its northern side, will bring you to the church of **São Domingos** (St Dominic's; *see p260*), also known as Santa Rosa. Next to it is the **São Domingos Market**, also known as **Central Market**, and one of the busiest in

Macau. Closed for renovation in 1994 and splendidly restored, it has recently reopened.

From near here, Rua de São Paulo leads to the Jesuit Collegiate Church of Madre de Deus, more commonly known as the **Ruinas de São Paulo** (Ruins of St Paul; *see p259*). For many, this is quite simply *the* symbol of Macau – the elaborate stone façade has featured on postcards since the 19th century. The original church was built by Japanese Christians, who had fled persecution in their homeland. (By the early 1600s, Portuguese missionaries had converted more than 100,000 Japanese to Christianity, and their swelling numbers, combined with concerns about their potentially mixed allegiances, led to gradual anti-Christian suppression within Japan. The Portuguese were repeatedly asked not to bring any more missionaries from Macau, but, in open defiance of the ban, every ship that arrived at Nagasaki carried more priests. Eventually, the Japanese responded with anti-Christian violence, that sent many Japanese Christians on the run to Macau.) Unfortunately, much of their handiwork on the church no longer exists as the entire building, with the exception of the stone façade, was destroyed by fire in 1835. At that point it was being used as a barracks, as the Jesuits had been expelled from Macau along with all other religious orders.

Perched on a hill directly above the Ruinas de São Paulo, the **Fortaleza do Monte** (*see p259*) provides the strongest connection between modern Macau and its colonial roots. Also built by the Jesuits, construction of the fortifications began in 1616. This was the first home of the Portuguese settlers. Dug into the hillside near the fortress is the **Macau Museum** (*see p259*), which tells the history of the peninsula.

From the Ruinas de São Paulo, it's a short walk to **Santo António** (St Anthony's; *see p259*). A place of worship has stood here since the mid 16th century, which makes the modern structure on the site today the oldest church in Macau – by association. Churches here are ill-fated, having burned down on several occasions.

Next to Santo António stand the tranquil **Camões Grotto and Garden** (*see p258*), where many locals come to relax. On the eastern edge of the garden is the no longer used **Old Protestant Cemetery** (*see p259*). Established in 1821 to provide for the burial needs of the non-Roman Catholic foreign community (most Portuguese residents were Catholic), the cemetery was badly needed as tenets of Catholicism forbade the burial of non-believers in consecrated soil (which effectively meant there was no place to bury Protestants in Macau).

About a 15-minute walk from the Old Protestant Cemetery is the lovely **St Michael**

**Trips Out of Town**

Cemetery. This large Catholic cemetery on Estrada do Cemitério is filled with statues of angels and features some beautiful, elaborate tombs. From the cemetery, walk north along Avenida Do Conselheiro Ferreira De Almeida (which is lined with historic buildings) to the peaceful **Lou Lim Ieoc Garden** (*see p259*), with its ornate mansion and shady gardens. Early in the morning, you'll find people here doing *tai chi*, practising their traditional Chinese instruments or strolling with their birds in cages. Just around the corner from the Garden is the **Sun Yat-sen Memorial House** (*see p260*) – although he never lived in this house, Sun practised medicine in Macau before deciding to become a revolutionary.

From here, it's a short walk along Avenida Sidónio Pais to the **Flora Garden**, the largest of Macau's gardens, and one of the most beautiful, which is home to a miniature zoo, landscaped grounds and a pond. The Governor of Macau's summer house once stood in the gardens, but it burned down in the 1920s, after an explosive accident at a nearby fireworks factory. This is also the place to catch the cable car up to Guia Hill (a single journey costs MOP$3, a return MOP$5; it's open 7.30am-6.30pm daily). At the top, you'll find the **Guia Fort and Lighthouse** (*see p259*) – the fort has stood watch over Macau since 1638.

Wander down Guia Hill and along Estrada De Cacilhas in the direction of the harbour if you wish to visit the Grand Prix and Wine museums, which are both housed in the Macau Forum. The **Grand Prix Museum** has lots of information on the local Grand Prix (if you've just been on Estrada De Cacilhas, you've walked along part of the race circuit), while the **Wine Museum** houses information for oenophiles, most specifically on Portuguese wines.

Further east, in among the waterfront development, stands the **Centro Cultural de Macau** (Macau Cultural Centre).

### Camões Grotto and Garden
*Praca Luis de Camões, Macau.* **Open** 6am-9pm daily. **Admission** free. **Map** p256.
The grotto and its gardens are dedicated to 16th-century Portuguese poet Luis Vaz de Camões, who is beloved in Macau, despite the fact that little is known about him locally – and there is no hard evidence he ever actually lived here. (Macau residents firmly believe that he did, and that he penned one of his most famous works, *The Lusiads*, here.)

### Centro Cultural de Macau
*Avenue Xian Xing Hai, Macau (700 699/ www.ccm.gov.mo).* **Box office** 11am-7pm daily. **Credit** AmEx, DC, MC, V. **Map** p256.
The Macau Cultural Centre hosts an interesting programme of music, opera, dance, theatre and film. The annual **Macau Arts Festival** in March attracts a number of good regional and international performers. Tickets for Macau Cultural Centre performances can be bought in Hong Kong through the Kong Seng ticket selling network (7171 7171).

Trips Out of Town

Guarding money-spinning Macau: the **Guia Fort and Lighthouse**.

## Fortaleza do Monte

**Open** *May-Sept* 6am-7pm daily; *Oct-Apr* 7am-6pm
daily. **Admission** free. **Map** p256.

The fort was built around the early settlement here,
so its walls became those of the city. It was built with
such extensive storage space that it was believed
residents could have withstood a two-year siege. It
did not take long before the settlers found out just
how strong the walls of the fort really were. In 1622,
the Dutch attacked Macau, but were ultimately
defeated by artillery fired from the fortress, as
the settlers huddled inside. After the military were
withdrawn in 1966, the grounds were opened to the
public, and today the fort is more public park than
public protector. On a clear day the view from Monte
takes in much of Macau and affords a good view
across to the neighbouring Chung Shan (formerly
Heung Shan) district, and as far north as Zhuhai.

## Grand Prix and Wine Museums

*Macau Forum, Macau (798 4108).* **Open** 10am-6pm
daily. **Admission** *Grand Prix* MOP$10. *Wine*
MOP$15. *Both* MOP$20. **No credit cards.**
**Map** p256.

The Grand Prix Museum is home to lots of interesting exhibits from the local Formula 3 Grand Prix,
including a number of cars. There are also simulators
that test your driving skills and TV monitors that let
you see what it's like to drive around the Macau race
circuit. The Wine Museum, displaying (predominantly Portuguese) wines and wine-making tools, is
not as impressive. Tastings are sometimes possible.

## Guia Fort and Lighthouse

*Estrada de Cacilhas, Macau.* **Open** 9am-5.30pm
daily. **Admission** free. **Map** p256.

Built as on the highest point of the peninsula, the
fort overlooked the border with China. Its prime
position meant that, after its early days as a fortress,
it was soon adapted into a more benign role as a
lookout post. In the 1830s, it started a third life as a
lighthouse – the oldest on the China coast. (To enter
the lighthouse, you need permission from the Marine
Department, which has offices on site.) The lovely
chapel on the site was built in the 17th century as
Our Lady of Guia, and its bell tower was used to
warn residents of incoming storms.

## Leal Senado

*Largo do Senado, Macau.* **Open** 9am-9pm daily
(gallery closed Mon). **Admission** free.
**Map** p256.

Here, Chinese and Portuguese officials met to
discuss trade and other issues relating to the
Portuguese presence in Macau. The name came
about as a result of the Macau Senate refusing to
accept the so-called dual kingdom of Spain and
Portugal. From 1580, until the countries were separated again in 1640, it was the Portuguese flag – not
the Spanish one – that flew in Macau. As a result of
this, in 1654 the city was rewarded with the title
*Cidade de Nome de Deus, Não Há Outra Mais Leal*
(City of the Name of God, There is None More Loyal).

It's worth popping in to admire the fine colonial
architecture and the gallery, which houses regularly changing shows of local interest.

## Lou Lim Ieoc Garden

*Avenida Do Conselheiro Ferreira De Almeida,
Macau.* **Open** dawn-dusk daily. **Admission**
MOP$1; free on Fri. **No credit cards.** **Map** p256.

This garden, and the ornate house that stands in it
(which is now a school), used to belong to a wealthy
Chinese family. While there are huge shady trees
reminiscent of European gardens, there are also
twisting pathways and ornamental mountains
representing traditional Chinese landscape paintings, as well as lotus ponds and bamboo groves.

## Macau Museum

*Citadel of São Paulo do Monte, Macau.* **Open** 10am-
6pm Tue-Sun. **Admission** MOP$15. **Map** p256.

Getting to the museum is actually more fun than
being inside, as it is reached by way of an escalator
near the Ruinas de São Paulo. Its extensive, educational exhibits begin with the early colonial years
and continue through to modern times, and feature
multi-media displays, CD-ROMs and videos.

## Old Protestant Cemetery

*Praca Luis de Camões, Macau (inside the Camões
Garden).* **Open** 9am-6pm daily. **Admission** free.
**Map** p256.

Many American and European Protestants lived in
Macau in the early part of the 19th century, prior to
the establishment of Hong Kong as a British colony.
Among them was George Chinnery, the well-known
China Coast painter, who is buried here; as is Dr
Robert Morrison, the first Protestant missionary to
China. The cemetery fell into disrepair after its
closure to burials in the 1860s, when the new
Protestant Cemetery at Mong Ha was established.
However, it was gradually restored and extensively
documented from the 1950s to the 1970s by the Vice-
Chancellor of Hong Kong University, Sir Lindsay
Ride, and his wife Lady May, both of whom took on
the job as a hobby.

## Ruinas de São Paulo

*Rua de São Paulo, Macau (358 444).* **Open** 9am-
5pm daily. **Admission** free. **Map** p256.

The first Western theological college established in
the Far East, São Paulo trained missionary priests,
such as Matteo Ricci, before they headed off to work
in mainland China and Japan. Constructed between
1602 and 1638 of wood with a stone façade, most
of the stone carving was completed by Japanese
Christians fleeing persecution in their homeland in
the 1630s. All but the façade burned down in 1835.

## Santo António

*Rua de Santo António, Macau.* **Open** 8.30am-
5.30pm. **Admission** free. **Map** p256.

The first chapel, built in 1558, burned down.
Construction of the church that replaced it – the
frame of which still stands today – was completed
in 1638, but that also fell victim to fire in 1809.

Rebuilt in 1810, it went up in flames again 64 years later. Although it was repaired, another fire in 1930 necessitated further restoration, and more work was done on the façade and tower in 1940.

## São Domingos
*Largo do Domingos, Macau.* **Open** 10am-6pm daily. **Admission** free. **Map** p256.
This enormous place of worship was built in 1587 by the Spanish Dominicans, which accounts for its distinctively Spanish look. However, it's worth noting that, not long after the church was completed, Portuguese friars took over from the previous Spanish incumbents. Upstairs is a small museum of ecclesiastical items, some centuries old and made in Macau. A convent was formerly attached to the church, but this was closed along with all the others in the Portuguese realm in the 1830s, during a suppression of religious influence in Portugal.

## Sun Yat-sen Memorial House
*Avenida Sidónio Pais, Macau.* **Open** 10am-1pm, 2.30pm-5pm Mon, Wed-Sun. **Admission** free. **Map** p256.
This monument to Sun Yat-sen (a former resident of Macau and the founder of the Chinese Republic) was once home to his discarded first wife. The house contains a collection of flags, photos and other relics.

## Southern Macau

There are a few attractions on the southernmost tip of Macau that are worth visiting if you are staying for more than a day.

Walk south along the Avenida da Praia Grande, passing the headquarters of the Government of the Macau SAR on the right, until you reach a stunning colonial building at the point where the road becomes the Avenida da República. This used to be the famous **Bela Vista Hotel**, but is now home to the Portuguese consul in Macau.

Continuing along this road, you will pass Santa Sancha, the **Governor's Residence**. Behind it stands **Barra Hill**, on which a fortress was built in 1629. Although it no longer exists, a hotel called the **Pousada de São Tiago** (which is worth taking a peep at; *see p265*) has been built within its ruined walls. You can also walk round the hill, which is a designated park area.

On the westernmost tip of Macau, there is a world-class **Maritime Museum** (*see below*) and, opposite it, the **A-Ma Temple** (*see below*). A motorised junk moored next to the museum takes tourists on rides around the harbour on weekends and Mondays.

## A-Ma Temple
*Rua de São Tiago da Barra, Macau.* **Open** 8am-5pm daily. **Admission** free. **Map** p256.
This temple is dedicated to A-Ma, more commonly known to the Chinese as Tin Hau, but who came to

be known by the Portuguese as A-Ma-Gau, and thus gave her name to the colony. Although the temple has several Ming shrines, they are probably 'recent' additions, as a temple is thought to have stood on this spot since before the Portuguese arrived and that the present building dates to the 17th century.

## Maritime Museum
*Rua de São Tiago da Barra, Macau (595 481).* **Open** 10am-5.30pm Mon, Wed-Sun. **Admission** MOP$5. **No credit cards. Map** p256.
The museum is home to a number of ships, including a flower boat, a tugboat, a Chinese fishing vessel and a dragon boat (that is still used for racing). It also has lots of artefacts that are of relevance to Macau's seafaring past.

## Taipa

If you've flown into Macau, **Taipa** will have been your first port of call, as the airport is built on reclaimed land attached to the island. You can reach Taipa from mainland Macau by one of two bridges, the original (imaginatively named) Macau–Taipa Bridge, and the newer Friendship Bridge.

The highlight of the island, which is fast becoming a modern sleeper town for mainland Macau, is the traditional village of Taipa (on the southern side of the island). It is home to the **Casa Museu da Taipa** (Taipa House Museum; *see below*). Although engulfed by high-rise housing blocks, life goes on much as it long has in the two-storey colonial buildings that line the village's narrow lanes and alleys.

## Casa Museu da Taipa
*Avenida de Praia, Taipa, Macau (853 827 088).* **Open** 9.30am-1pm, 3-5.30pm Tue-Sun. **Admission** free. **Map** p256.
One of five colonial buildings lining the street, the Casa Museu combines both European and Oriental designs. The rooms, which include a large living and dining room,and a games room are all filled with period furniture, paintings, art and personal artefacts that reflect a dual heritage.

## Colôane

Connected to Taipa via a causeway that has been enlarged by reclamation, the less-developed **Colôane** offers a little peace and quiet away from the bustle of Macau. There's not much in terms of 'sights' here, but there are some good beaches and large expanses of greenery.

The best beaches are **Cheoc Van** and **Hac Sa** on the southern side of the island. Both have lifeguards on duty (in the summer), surf boards for hire and public swimming pools nearby that are open late. Hac Sa is also home to the renowned restaurant **Fernando's** (*see p261*). If you want to take a walk on the green side, then head for **Seac**

**Pai Van Park** on the western side of the island, where there are plenty of hiking trails and 'sights' (such as an aviary and botanical garden).

Otherwise, you could visit the village of Colôane, which has been subjected to less development than that of Taipa. Certainly more picturesque, the village focus is a small, tiled square, at the end of which is the **Chapel of St Francis Xavier**. Built in 1928 and dedicated to Asia's most famous missionary, it even contains some of his bones. Built in classic Portuguese style, it is decorated with Chinese artworks.

### Seac Pai Van Park

*Estrada de Seac Pai Van, Colôane, Macau (870 277).* **Open** 8am-6pm Tue-Sun. **Admission** free. **Map** p256.
This large expanse of greenery is home to a walk-in aviary, hillside trails, Chinese-style pavilions, a small botanical garden, a children's playground and a picnic area.

## Where to eat & drink

## Restaurants

When it comes to dining out, Macau offers all the variations Hong Kong can boast – and then some. The rich Portuguese influence has enabled chefs to blend Eastern and Western cuisine to create a unique Macanese style. And it all comes at a much, much cheaper price than you'll find yourself paying in Hong Kong.

### A Lorcha

*289 Rua do Almirante Sergio, Macau (313 193). Bus 5, 9, 10, 10A, 11.* **Open** 12.30-3.30pm, 7-11.30pm Mon, Wed-Sun. **Main courses** MOP$25-30. **Credit** AmEx, MC, V. **Map** p256.
Portuguese influences run high at A Lorcha, and it boasts Macanese-style food at its finest. It is also perhaps the best value-for-money restaurant in Macau. Signature dishes include the ever-popular African chicken (a local speciality), salt cod and giant prawns of quite frightening dimensions. A great stop-off for day-trippers, as it's right next to the Maritime Museum and close to the A-Ma Temple *(see p260)*. The best nod A Lorcha gets, though, is that the locals love the place. Expect to pay around MOP$200 per head (including wine).

### Estrela do Mar

*11 Travessa do Paiva, Macau (322 074).* **Open** 11.30am-11.30pm daily. **Main courses** MOP$25-30. **Credit** MC, V. **Map** p256.
Close to Avenida da Praia Grande, this small and relatively inexpensive restaurant serves Portuguese food and is popular with the locals – always a good sign. Soups, salads, African chicken, Macau sole, curries and steak all pop up on the menu, but you can always opt for a smaller meal, such as a sandwich or omelette.

### Fernando's

*Hac Sa Beach, Colôane, Macau (882 531). Bus 26.* **Open** noon-9.30pm daily. **Main courses** MOP$25. **No credit cards.** **Map** p256.
For some people, no trip to Macau would be complete without a jaunt across to the island of Colôane and lunch or dinner at Fernando's. It's Portuguese dining at its best – fresh, simple salads, handsome main courses (try the jumbo shrimp for size) and plenty of cheap, but very good, wine. Situated right next to Colôane beach, Fernando's has drawn such illustrious visitors as French actor Gerard Depardieu, spied quaffing some red over chicken with the host. It's a Macau institution, and consequently draws the crowds. Transport can be a problem due to its remoteness, so you may have to wait for a taxi, but the staff will call one for you. Expect to pay around around MOP$200 per head.

### Long Kei

*78 Largo do Senado, Macau (573 970).* **Open** 11am-10.30pm daily. **Main courses** MOP$25-30. **Credit** AmEx, MC, V. **Map** p256.
Long Kei, with over 350 items on the menu, has long been one of Macau's favourite Chinese restaurants.; don't be put off by the bright overhead lights and sparse decor – the staff are friendly and the food is excellent. It serves up all the usual Chinese dishes, plus a few specialities such as shark's fin, bird's nest and abalone, as well as dim sum – if you're still hungry.

**Fernando's**: a Macanese institution.

Trips Out of Town

### Mezzaluna

*Mandarin Oriental Hotel, 956-1110 Avenida da Amizade (567 888). Bus 3, 11, 26, 26A, 28A.* **Open** 11am-3pm, 6.30-11.30pm daily. **Main courses** MOP$45. **Credit** AmEx, DC, MC, V. **Map** p256.

The Mandarin Oriental's recent refurbishments have meant the place has become even more popular as a getaway. And in Italian restaurant Mezzaluna, it also boasts one of Macau's more relaxed and interesting dining experiences. Intimate dining is assured, and the menu boasts some exquisite signature pasta dishes. Prices vary, but generally set you back around MOP$400 per head (including wine).

### Robuchon a Galera

*3/F, Hotel Lisboa, 2-4 Avenida de Lisboa, Macau (577 666).* **Open** noon-2.30pm; 6.30-11pm daily. **Main courses** from MOP$300. **Credit** AmEx, DC, MC, V. **Map** p256.

Deep within the Hotel Lisboa lies Robuchon a Galera, Macau's best and most expensive restaurant. At the helm is super-chef Joël Robuchon, who was voted Chef of the Century by the Gault-Millau restaurant guide, so you can expect a dining experience to remember. Despite this, the restaurant still comes in far cheaper than its equivalents in Hong Kong, and boasts a menu and wine list to rival anything in Asia. The cuisine is an intoxicating mix of Continental and Portuguese. The surroundings are opulent and Robuchon a Galera provides a perfect excuse to spend a bit of cash.

---

# Bars & nightlife

A common complaint in Macau's pre-Handover era was that the enclave had no central bar district like, say, Hong Kong's Lan Kwai Fong. And that basically meant that going out for a drink outside the main hotels and resorts was something of a lottery; you just never quite knew what you were getting or quite who you were going to run in to. Then the docks or waterfront area, also known as the ZAPE reclamation, Wong Chiu or Dynasty Plaza (just to keep things simple), was developed between the Mandarin Oriental Hotel and the Hotel Lisboa, and the bars started springing up almost overnight.

Avenida Dr Sun Yat-sen is where it all happens, one reason being that the bars have great sea views. Within months of the first bar opening, 17 establishments had popped up and people were flocking here in droves. The area is totally laid-back, and attracts a wide cross-section of those living in and visiting Macau. Generally, the crowds don't start to gather until mid evening, and then you'll find that they quite happily come and go from door to door.

For better or worse, depending on what you're after, Macau has always been labelled the Wild West of the East when it comes to nightlife. But things have certainly calmed down a bit since the enclave returned to Chinese sovereignty in 1999. The tourism industry was quietly quaking in its boots in the lead up to the 1999 Handover, as Macau's local triad factions came to blows on more than one occasion creating a lot of bad publicity for the city. But this period of unrest proved to be more a case of muscle flexing and posturing than the descent into violence that was first feared, and although you will definitely see more than your fair share of shady characters around town at night, they generally keep to themselves and don't bother with tourists.

What keeps the crowds flocking into Macau week in, week out is the excitement that the city generates. And with its blend of European and Oriental influences, Macau provides a unique experience on every visit. The nightlife all over Macau varies from hostess and karaoke bars, through to the stock standard 'old English pub', live music and trendy clubs. Many of the larger hotels also boast above-average bars and clubs, some of which are among the most popular in town. However, you'll find that the Portuguese influence means the bars and club don't usually begin filling up until the evening is already quite old, following a late supper. There are cheap eats available as well, and generally you'll find a bar to suit every taste.

### Embassy Bar

*G/F, Mandarin Oriental Hotel, 956-1110 Avenida da Amizade, Macau (567 888). Bus 3, 11, 26, 26A, 28A.* **Open** 5pm-1am Mon-Thur, Sun; 5pm-late Fri, Sat. **Credit** AmEx, DC, MC, V. **Map** p256.

The Embassy has long been an early evening meeting place for Macau's finest, before they head off for a bit of dinner or dancing. It's close proximity to the waterfront has given the bar a new lease of life, too. There's even a separate cigar bar, and a house band kicks in around 9.30pm every night. Standard drinks come in at around the MOP$30 mark, but there's also an extensive wine and cocktail list.

### Macau Jazz Club

*Avenida Dr Sun Yat-sen, Macau (596 014). Buses to the Waterfront.* **Open** 7pm-late Wed-Sun. **No credit cards**. **Map** p256.

In its old home, deep in the centre of town on the Rua das Alabardas, the Macau Jazz Club was distinctly tricky to find. But things have changed over the past two years, thanks to Macau's redeveloped waterfront. The Jazz Club now takes pride of place on the promenade that looks over the Kun Iam statue. There's live music from 9.30pm until late, Wednesday to Sunday. And drinks come at regular prices. As well as their own headliners, artists touring Asia have dropped by for a jam and the club hosts the Macau Jazz Festival every May. But don't be surprised to hear Celine Dion on the stereo if there's no live performance…

**Sanshiro** – a cool late-night haunt.

### Opiarium Café

*Avenida Dr Sun Yat-sen, Macau (750 975).*
*Buses to the Waterfront.* **Open** varies.
**No credit cards. Map** p256.

Another one of the first bars to open in the water-front district, the Opiarium Café's open spaces, out-door tables and cosy upstairs couch area were an instant hit. As were the live bands featuring the best in local session players. It has closed, inexplicably, a few times, but always seems to reopen without much delay. Things get lively after around 10pm, and drinks start at around MOP$30.

### Sanshiro

*Avenida Dr Sun Yat-sen, Macau (752 552).*
*Buses to the Waterfront.* **Open** 6pm-4am daily.
**Credit** AmEx, MC, V. **Map** p256.

The later, the better is the general rule with Sanshiro. It's a great 'drop-by' bar, which sees punters come and go constantly from about 10pm until very late. Cool music and plenty of space to hide away and chat are its main selling points – that and the Portuguese live-and-let-live attitude. And the drinks are cheap, starting at about MOP$25 for standards.

### Signal Café

*Avenida Dr Sun Yat-sen, Macau (751 052).*
*Buses to the Waterfront.* **Open** varies.
**No credit cards. Map** p256.

Macau's hippest hangout provides some excellent views out over the harbour from its first-floor vantage point. It's cool ambience brings in plenty of the younger brigade, as do the DJs who play every night. There are comfortable couches to chill out on, and, while drinks come in at around the regular MOP$30, a dive into the cock-tail list (impressive, it must be said) won't leave you with much change.

## Shopping

If you're after a bargain, Macau is a good place to find one – prices tend to be around 25 per cent lower than in Hong Kong. The two items, in particular, that many hunt down here are clothes and 'antiques'.

Knitwear manufacturing is a major local industry, so expect to find lots of great clothes (usually over-runs, discontinued lines and seconds with recognisable, if not designer, labels) at good prices. The best clothing shops and stalls are found in Largo do Senado and the market on Rua São Domingos.

Macau is also well-known for its 'antiques', although you'll have to decide for yourself whether or not the piece on which you've set your heart is really old, as many of the shop owners will certainly try and pass reproductions off as 'the real thing'. You'll also have to decide whether it's worth the price being demanded by the vendor. If in doubt, treat buying 'antiques' here a bit like gambling – you certainly should not pay more for something then you're prepared to lose on the casino tables.

A great place to browse for artefacts both old and new is **Rua de São Paulo**. Try **Wa Fat Trade Company** at No.11 for Ming dynasty-style furniture, **Mobilias e Antiquidades Lu Va** at No.23 for really beautiful, but expensive antiquities, **Iok Nagi** at No.31 for classical Chinese furniture, and **Mobilias Soi Cheong Hong** at No.38 for leather and wooden boxes. In between, you'll find lots of shops selling curios such as bamboo bird cages, carved walking sticks and butterfly-shaped kites. If you do decide to buy something, bargain hard (business has been bad since the 1999 Handover) and don't worry about your luggage weight limit: large pieces, such as furniture, the shop owners can always arrange for them to be shipped home for you.

Other items to look out for in Macau include competitively priced electrical goods and gold jewellery (which you'll find in the shops lining Avenida Almeida Ribeiro), and – for their novelty value – Chinese herbs and medicine. Of course, you can always take a gamble and buy (mainly gold jewellery) from one of the many pawn shops clustered around the casinos, but do be cautious if you decide to go down this route, and bargain hard.

If you're the kind of person who's happier buying in a department store or smart mall, then head for New Yaohan next to the ferry terminal (which has all the usual department store offerings, including a food hall) or Central Plaza and The Landmark, both brimming with trendy designer shops.

# Cash to burn?

For the majority of visitors to Macau, the place has one attraction, and one attraction only: gambling. The Chinese like nothing more than a good punt and in Macau, you can flutter away to your heart's content, 24 hours a day, seven days a week. The selection of gambling venues available to those who make the jaunt across the Pearl River Delta is as varied as the bets they have to offer. From casinos to horse and greyhound racing, there are countless ways to win (or lose, as is more likely) vast amounts of cash.

## CASINOS

Macau has long been regarded as the playground of business bigwig Dr Stanley Ho, and his influence reaches deep into the country's gaming industry. At least until 2001, Ho's Sociedade de Turismo e Diversoes de Macau operated all the casinos in Macau under Government franchise. And it's no wonder Macau's 'God Of Gamblers' leads such a charmed and revered life – casino tax payments account for five billion patacas, or 57 per cent of Government budget revenue. According to the Macau Government Tourist Office, every hour, three million or more patacas in bets are placed.

There are nine casinos operating in Macau, and they range from the glitzy to the down-right dodgy. There's no entry fee, of course, but foreigners have to be aged over 18 (locals over 21). There's also no real dress code, but you'd hardly expect to be allowed to enter in your bathrobe and slippers, so smart casual is probably always best.

Apart from the usual casino fare of baccarat, blackjack and roulette, you can try your luck at the distinctive Chinese games of *fantan* and *dai siu* (but you'll be hard pressed to get anyone to explain them to you). No photos can be taken inside any of the casinos, and the bets are usually set at

a minimum of MOP$50. If you do get lucky, you're not obliged to tip the croupiers, but be wary; they normally skim ten per cent of your winnings as a matter of course. And for those expecting casinos that are all Vegas-like smiles and free drinks, think again. Macau's casinos give you action, but they also give you smoked-filled rooms, and a lot of pushing and shoving.

## Hotel Lisboa

*2-4 Avenida de Lisboa, Macau (577 666/ 377 666). Free shuttle bus from pier/buses from pier.* **Open** 24 hours daily. **Credit** AmEx, DC, MC, V. **Map** p256.

Dr Stanley Ho's landmark Lisboa Hotel is perhaps the most recognisable building in Macau. Resembling a Salvador Dali-inspired pepper shaker, it juts upwards from its vantage point, just in front of the old bridge to Taipa. It houses the busiest and smokiest casino in town, more than 966 rooms and 74 suites, including five presidential suites, 18 restaurants, a nightclub, and two floors that are entirely given over to regular punters.

As well as casino betting, wagers can be placed on sports such as English Premiership football. The Lisboa is also one of Macau's notorious fleshpots, with ladies of the night stalking each and every corridor.

## HORSE RACING

Long seen as the poor cousin to the big-spending, internationally regarded Hong Kong Jockey Club, the Macau Jockey Club (also a subsidiary of the Sociedade de Turismo e Diversoes de Macau) has been lifting its game over the past years, upgrading facilities and improving the standard of horse flesh in action. Macau also boasts perhaps the most internationally diverse jockeys' room in the world, with riders coming from as far afield as the West Indies and Japan to ply their trade.

## Where to stay

Macau has a wide range of hotel options, from the luxurious to the very basic, as well as from the typical city property to the beach resort. At the expensive end, a number of well-known chains have hotels in Macau; they include the **Hyatt Regency Resort** (830 195) on Taipa and **Holiday Inn** (783 333) between the ferry terminal and downtown Macau. Due to the great number of hotels in the city, it is never difficult

to get a room – except in late November when the Formula 3 Grand Prix takes place – but booking in advance is always a good idea to make sure you get exactly what you want.

### East Asia Hotel

*Rua da Madeira 1-A, Macau (922 433).* **Rates** MOP$300-400 single; MOP$400-500 double. **Credit** AmEx, MC, V. **Map** p256.

In the heart of old Macau, the East Asia is one of city's best bets when it comes to cheaper accommodation. Over 60 years old, but recently renovated, most of the is very modern with spotless rooms. If you want a harbour view, ask for a room on the fifth (top) floor.

Free shuttle buses run to the racecourse from the ferry pier at the Hotel Lisboa on race days, starting one hour before the first race and stopping one hour after the start of race two. Race meetings are held every week, either on Wednesday or Thursday evenings, and at weekends, but this can vary due to public holidays, so give the club a call just to be sure. Entrance fee is usually around MOP$5, and you can also get a members' stand pass if you flash your passport.

### Macau Jockey Club

*Est.Gov. Albano da Oliveira, No.2014 RC, Taipa (821 188). Bus 11, 22, 28A, 33, 38, AP1.* **Races** Wed or Thur, Sat or Sun. **Admission** MOP$5. **No credit cards**. **Map** p256.

### GREYHOUND RACING

Macau also boasts Asia's only greyhound racing club, which happens to be one of the largest and best in the world. Set on the site of what was once the Macau national football stadium, the Macau club is almost 40 years old and is still going strong. There are two recently renovated grandstands, private boxes, a VIP lounge and coffee shop, and a healthy 14 races on each card. Meetings are held on Tuesdays, Thursdays and at weekends, with racing starting from 8pm. Entrance to the Canidrome costs MOP$2, but if you're prepared to pay another three patacas, you can get into the members' stand.

### Macau (Yat Yuen) Canidrome

*Avenida General Castelo Branco S/N, Macau (221 199). Bus 1, 1A, 3, 4, 5, 16, 26A, 32, 33.* **Races** Tue, Thur, Sat, Sun. **Admission** MOP$2; *members' stand* MOP$5. **No credit cards**. **Map** p256.

large rooms have bathrooms and windows; if you can't live without either, make sure you ask for a room with both when you make your reservation.

### Hotel Guia

*Estrada do Engenheiro Trigo 1-5, Macau (513 888). Free shuttle bus from ferry terminal and Hotel Lisboa.* **Rates** MOP$500-600 single/double. **Credit** AmEx, MC, V. **Map** p256.
Not surprisingly, given its name, this hotel is located on the slopes of Guia Hill. Although surrounded by traditional colonial architecture, the hotel itself

### Hotel Lisboa

*2-4 Avenida de Lisboa, Macau (577666). Free shuttle bus from ferry terminal and airport.* **Rates** MOP$1,000-1,700 single/double. **Credit** AmEx, DC, MC, V. **Map** p256.
The Hotel Lisboa is something of a landmark in Macau, thanks to its distinctive architecture and central location. Although not particularly stylish, it is home to one of the oldest casinos in town, the Crazy Paris Show and the best restaurant in town.

### Mandarin Oriental

*956-1110 Avenida da Amizade, Macau (751 052). Free shuttle bus from ferry terminal and airport.* **Rates** MOP$1,300-1,650 single/double. **Credit** AmEx, DC, MC, V. **Map** p256.
A sister hotel to the Mandarin Oriental in Hong Kong, this is a very exclusive hotel – although the prices are cheaper this side of the Pearl River Delta. While it used to sit right on the water's edge, the waterfront reclamation has left it landlocked, with fewer views and more noise. Still, the Portuguese-inspired interior remains stylish and the service impeccable.

### Pousada de São Tiago

*Avenida da República, Fortaleza de São Tiago da Barra, Macau (378 111). Free shuttle bus from ferry terminal and airport.* **Rates** MOP$1,400-1,700 single/double. **Credit** AmEx, DC, MC, V. **Map** p256.
The Pousada is charming and will make you feel like you are in a former Portuguese colony – or Portugal itself. Built within the ruins of a 17th century fort, it has some dramatic design features, as well as lots of imported Portuguese furniture and tiles. Although not in the most convenient location, its more remote setting makes it perfect for a romantic break.

### Sintra

*Avenida de Dom João IV, Macau (710 111). Free shuttle bus from ferry terminal.* **Rates** MOP$700-1,000 single/double. **Credit** AmEx, DC, MC, V. **Map** p256.
Although built in 1975, the Sintra looks almost new thanks to a mid 1990s renovation programme. Moderately priced, it offers real value for money in Macau, given its central location and large rooms, some of which have partial harbour views.

### Westin Resort

*1918 Estrada de Hac Sa, Colôane, Macau (378 111). Free shuttle bus from ferry terminal, airport and Hotel Lisboa.* **Rates** MOP$2,000-2,250 single/double. **Credit** AmEx, DC, MC, V. **Map** p256.
This is Macau's most luxurious resort hotel, boasting landscaped gardens, two outdoor swimming pools, an indoor pool, tennis courts, a health club and an 18-hole golf course. It also overlooks Hac Sa, one of Macau's best beaches. Of course, it's far from the centre of the action, but if you're booking into the Westin, you're probably in search of a little exercise or relaxation rather than the roll of the dice.

**Trips Out of Town**

# Resources

## Getting there & around

### By air

Most of the flights into Macau's airport on Taipa island are from China, Taiwan, Singapore and Korea. On arrival, there are free shuttle buses from the airport to all the leading hotels, as well as paying buses downtown, to the ferry terminal and the border crossing. In addition, there are plenty of taxis.

The 22 helicopter flights per day from Hong Kong also land at Macau's international airport; the flight time is 20 minutes. The cost of a one-way flight is MOP$1,205 on weekdays, MOP$1,309 on weekends/holidays. For more information, call East Asia Airlines's Dial-A-Ticket-Hotline (853) 727 288.

### By sea

A number of ferries (jetfoils, turbo-cats, jumbo-cats and hover ferries) operate more than 100 sailings daily between Hong Kong and Macau, with jetfoils operating around-the-clock services. The jetfoil also provides the quickest sea-borne method of making the 60-km (38-mile) journey, taking just 55 minutes. There are two ferry terminals in Hong Kong serving Macau: the China Ferry Terminal in Tsim Sha Tsui and the larger Macau Ferry Terminal on the waterfront west of Central on Hong Kong Island.

The Hong Kong Yau Ma Tei Ferry company operates catamarans from the China Ferry Terminal to Macau; fares start at HK$113. For more information, call 726 301 in Macau or 2516 8581 in Hong Kong. Weekends and holidays tend to be busy, so book in advance.

On arrival in Macau, there are free shuttle buses from the ferry terminal to all the leading hotels, otherwise check with the Tourist Information desk in the terminal for public transport facilities to your destination. If in doubt, take a taxi.

### Visas

All visitors require a valid passport. Citizens of the US, UK, Canada, Australia, South Africa, New Zealand and most European countries do not require a visa for a stay of 20 days or less. All other visitors entering Macau must have a passport or other travel document that is valid for at least 30 days after the date of their arrival. Visas are issued for 20 days on arrival, and cost MOP$100 for an individual (MOP$50 for children under the age of 12 years); MOP$200 for a family visa that is valid for children under the age of 12 years; and MOP$50 per member of bona fide groups of ten or more.

### Getting around

However you arrive in Macau, you will probably either hop into a hotel shuttle bus, paying bus or taxi to your final destination. Buses cover virtually every corner of the city, are frequent and fares low, while all taxis are metered and are also inexpensive.

Alternatively, once you are in the centre of town, you can use your own two feet, as most places are within walking distance. But if you do find yourself getting tired, then why not try the traditional method of getting around town, a two-seater pedicab? They cost about MOP$25 for a short trip, or MOP$100 for an hour if you want one to give you a guided tour of the sights – just make sure you negotiate the fare before you get on board.

Once you get out onto the islands of Taipa and Colôane, you might want to consider hiring cycles, which cost about MOP$40/hour, from near the Municipal Council Building in Taipa.

## Tourist information

### Macau Government Tourist Office

*PO Box 3006, 9 Largo de Senado, Macau (315 566/ 513 355/fax 510 104/mgto@macautourism.gov.mo).* The MGTO also has information counters at the following locations: Guia Fort and Lighthouse (569 808; 9am-5.30pm daily), Centro Cultural de Macau (751 718; 9am-6pm daily), Ferry Terminal (726 416; 9am-10pm daily), International Airport (861 436; 9am-6pm daily) and Ruinas de São Paulo (358 444; 9am-6pm daily). Alternatively, you can always try the Tourist Assistance Hotline (340 390; 9am-6pm daily).

And if you are in Hong Kong and want information before you depart, then visit the MGTO at Counter 3B, Meeters & Greeters Hall, Passenger Terminal Building, Chek Lap Kok International Airport – 2769 7970/2382 7110 or at 336 Shun Tak Centre, 200 Connaught Road Central – 2857 2287/2559 0147.

### Language

The official languages are Mandarin, Cantonese and Portuguese, but English is widely understood.

### Money

Macau's official currency is the pataca (usually symbolised by MOP$), which is divided into 100 avos. It is indexed to the Hong Kong dollar, which is widely accepted in Macau, at a rate of MOP$103.20 to HK$100. Just remember that if you do pay in Hong Kong dollars, you will receive your change in patacas.

Macanese money comes in the following denominations: bank notes of 20, 50, 100, 500 and 1000 patacas; and coins of 1, 5 and 10 patacas, as well as 10, 20 and 50 avos.

Foreign currency and travellers' cheques can easily be changed in hotels, banks and at authorised money-changers, which are located throughout Macau. Alternatively, you can withdraw money from one of the city's many ATMs. Credit cards are accepted in many hotels, shops and restaurants.

### Telephones

Local calls are free from private phones, but cost MOP$1 from public phones. You can buy phone cards to the value of MOP$50, 100, 150 and credit card phones are found in busier areas.

To call abroad from Macau, dial 00 + country code + local number (omitting the 0 of the area code if there is one), except when calling Hong Kong, dial 01+ the eight-digit number. International calls from Macau are very expensive.

To call directory enquiries in Macau, dial 181 or, for overseas enquiries, 101. The international code for Macau is 853.

# Guangzhou

Prepare for a sensory overload in southern China's most dynamic city.

Guangzhou is what Hong Kong would be today, if it were not for drugs and gunboats. In fact, had there been no Opium Wars (*see p10*), it's more than likely there would be no Hong Kong at all, and Guangzhou would be on the cover of this guidebook.

Formerly known as Canton, this southern Chinese city – and the surrounding province of Guangdong – is the hereditary home of 90 per cent of the world's 'overseas Chinese'. And several million of them did not get further than Hong Kong. In Hong Kong, it's their language you hear on the streets, their food you eat and even their water you drink – one of the reasons that the British handed back Hong Kong Island is that it has no fresh water supply.

The main difference between Hong Kong and Guangzhou is that the latter simply has not caught up yet. The road system is chaotic. The pollution can be all but incapacitating – on bad days, carbon monoxide hangs off the flyovers like an untucked bed sheet. The noise of construction sites, car horns, squealing brakes on cranky buses, haggling street vendors, mobile phones ringing, people shouting into mobiles, beepers, goes on and on… and, like this list, never stops. It is dirty. It is half demolished and half built. Glistening glass office towers back onto truck stops that double as markets on waste ground that only yesterday was a shanty town. It is, in a word, chaos.

But Guangzhou has something intangible that Hong Kong has lost. There is something about the place that grabs you – and doesn't let go. There is an energy, an enthusiasm for life, for work and for pleasure, and a genuineness and warmth about its 11 million inhabitants that you will not find in any other mainland Chinese city – at least not in a Han Chinese one, like Beijing or Shanghai. And the locals have none of the (post-)colonial chippiness of Hong Kongers. If they do have a chip about something, it is that they have had to struggle through a socialist planned economy while their Hong Kong cousins have been free to take the capitalist road. They are now doing everything they can to catch up.

There is a traditional Chinese saying, quoted so often that it has become a cliché: 'Heaven is high above and the Emperor is far away.' In other words, Guangzhou gets on with its own affairs and does not pay too much attention to central government. That attitude has changed recently.

Pets? Or for the pot…?

It had to, in fact, when Beijing appointed a non-Cantonese provincial governor for the first time in many years. But that has not dampened the city's innate enthusiasm too severely. The benefits of paying central dues can be seen in improved roads, better national transport links and support for a Pearl River Delta trade zone that is supposed to subsume Hong Kong. More open supervision has also revealed bad eggs like the GITIC (Guangdong International Trade and Investment Corporation), a local government-backed corporate dinosaur from the days when only the government could trade, which crashed ignominiously in 1999.

So Guangzhou is on the up. It is not getting the support and encouragement from Beijing that Shanghai enjoys in its bid to become the financial, economic and cultural centre of the Far East by sometime next week. But Guangzhou does not need it. As it always has done, it will take care of itself, thank you. And when it gets there, it will be the better for it.

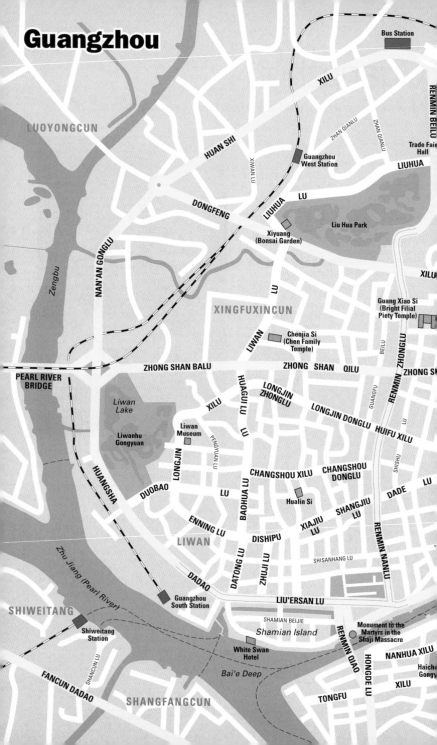

# Guangzhou

LUOYONGCUN

Zengbu

NAN'AN GONGLU

PEARL RIVER
BRIDGE

Liwan
Lake

Liwanhu
Gongyuan

HUANGSHA

DUOBAO

LONGJIN LU

ENNING LU

LIWAN

DADAO

Zhu Jiang (Pearl River)

SHIWEITANG

Shiweitang
Station

SHANCUN LU

FANCUN DADAO

SHANGFANGCUN

HUAN SHI

DONGFENG

XIWAN LU

Guangzhou
West Station

LIUHUA LU

Xiyuang
(Bonsai Garden)

ZHAN QIANLU

ZHAN QIANLU

XILU

Bus Station

RENMIN BEILU

Trade Fair
Hall

LIUHUA

Liu Hua Park

XILU

Guang Xiao Si
(Bright Filial
Piety Temple)

XINGFUXINCUN

LIWAN

Chenjia Si
(Chen Family
Temple)

ZHONG SHAN BALU

ZHONG   SHAN   QILU

RENMIN ZHONGLU

BEILU

ZHONG S

Liwan
Museum

XILU

HUAGUI LU

PENGYUAN LU

LONGJIN
ZHONGLU

LONGJIN DONGLU

HUIFU XILU

GUANGFU

SHISHU

CHANGSHOU XILU

CHANGSHOU
DONGLU

Hualin Si

SHANGJIU
LU

DADE LU

BAOHUA LU

LU

XIAJIU
LU

DISHIPU

ZHUJI LU

DATONG LU

SHISANHANG LU

Guangzhou
South Station

DADAO

LIU'ERSAN LU

SHAMIAN BEIJIE

Shamian Island

White Swan
Hotel

Bai'e Deep

RENMIN QIAO

RENMIN NANLU

Monument to the
Martyrs in the
Shaji Massacre

NANHUA XILU

Haich
Gongy

HONGDE LU

XILU

TONGFU

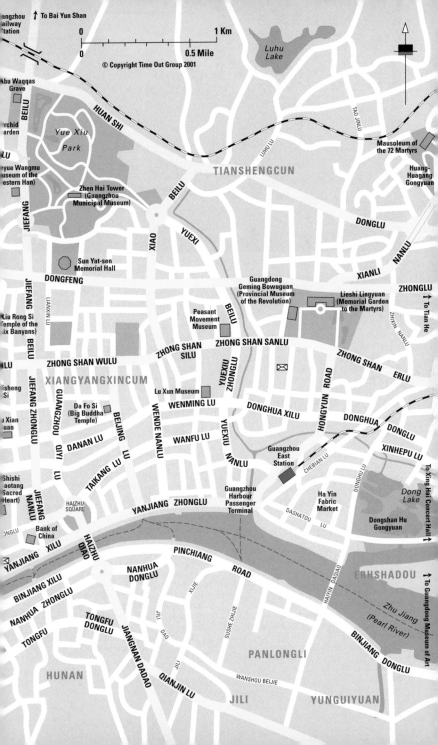

**Shamian Island**: once home to foreign traders in old Canton.

## Sightseeing

'Sights' in China, by local reckoning, must obey the following cardinal rules to be worth seeing: they must be man-made, covered in bright flags and ideally involve a ride in a cable car. The Great Wall is a perfect example. Guangzhou's equivalent is Bai Yun Shan (*see below*); ignore the knick-knack booths at the top, because the views from the summit of this sizeable hill are quite stunning on a clear day. Wandering the few remaining old streets of the Liwan district or Shamian Island (*see below*), where traditional Cantonese life just about survives, fit more into the Western mould of sightseeing. There are also some small temples tucked away around the city, where that distinctly Cantonese version of religion, praying for luck and wealth, is actively practised. However, to really 'see' Guangzhou, you could do worse than find a streetside food stall and watch the world go by.

### BY AREA

The two natural landmarks of Guangzhou are the **Zhu Jiang** (Pearl River), which cuts through the city from east to west, and **Bai Yun Shan** (White Cloud Mountain), which dominates the city from the north. The large hill is dressed up in pleasant parkland, popular with weekend walkers and topped by temples. There are a couple of restaurants with fantastic panoramic views. Hike, or take a taxi or cable car. The main man-made arteries are Huanshi Lu, Zhongshan Lu and Dong Feng Lu, all of which traverse the city east-west.

South of the river is known as, and literally translates as, **Hunan** (the same characters as, but nothing to do with, the province). Not much goes on here to attract visitors. It is the home to

Zhongshan University and the Zhou Tou Zi Pier, where the hydrofoil from Hong Kong comes in, and from where it is a short hop across the river to the city proper.

The traditional heart of the city lies in the westerly **Xiguan** and **Liwan** districts, tucked into a crook of the Pearl River. Much of the traditional housing that once crowded these areas is being demolished to make way for high rises, but there are enough quaint alleyways in which to get lost for a day or two. The once unforgettably atmospheric **Qing Ping Market**, a long-standing focal point of the area, has sadly been moved into a modern block in Liwan. The street market was infamous, especially among Western visitors, for its exotic wildlife – intended not as pets, but for the pot. The history of Liwan is documented in the **Liwan Museum** (*see p272*).

Stuck on the riverside edge of Xiguan, across a man-made dyke, is **Shamian Island**. The island is covered by Western-style buildings, which once housed (or, rather, confined) the first foreign merchants and their wares. The 'Flower Boats' that once tied up for the gentlemen's entertainment are long gone, but the aura lingers. This is the setting for Timothy Mo's novel *The Monkey King*, an excellent account of the period. Shamian is a haven of calm in an otherwise frenetically bustling metropolis. Wandering the island's tree-lined streets is the perfect antidote to the stress of first-time China travel.

Between **Liu Hua Park** and the enormous **Yue Xiu Park**, north of Xiguan, you'll find the China Hotel and the Dong Fang Hotel facing the **Trade Fair Hall**, a place to avoid during the fair itself (*see p275* **Rough trade**), but otherwise home to some good bars and restaurants. The parks provide some respite from the carbon monoxide that cloaks the streets. The main train station is just to the north, the stepping off point for destinations upcountry.

Within Yue Xiu Park is the 14th-century **Zhen Hai Tower**, which houses the **Guangzhou Municipal Museum** (*see p273*). Also in the park is a swimming pool, boating lake, open-air cinema, sports ground, and a range of eating and drinking options.

Just south of the park stands the **Sun Yat-sen Memorial Hall** (*see p273*), built in 1931 as a tribute to the man universally regarded as the father of modern China. Qing Quan Lu, the street tucked behind, is the haunt of the best local fortune tellers.

A kilometre or so south of here stands **Da Fo Si**, otherwise known as the Big Buddha Temple (*see below*). Close by are two other temples worthy of a visit: **Guang Xiao Si** and **Liu Rong Si** (for both, *see p272*). Not far away, you can brush up on your revolutionary history at the **Peasant Movement Museum** (*see p273*).

Towards the east, Huanshi Dong Road, in the area of the Friendship Store, is a centre of activity. Expat bars, hotels, some good restaurants and the Windflower Music Pub (*see p276*), the hottest bar/club in the city, are here. Taojin Road, which runs north up the side of the Guangzhou Friendship Store (*see p277*), is a lively little street that leads to some big clubs on the apex of Heng Fu Road.

Further out to the east, **Tian He** is the city's new business district, dominated by the vast Citic Tower. The area houses some major shopping malls and Computer City, just the place to pick up some software courtesy of Captain Blackbeard. Trains from Hong Kong arrive at the East Station just up the road. The city Sports Stadium sits in the middle.

For concerts and culture, trek out to **Er Sha Dao** (Ersha Island), a grassy knoll in the Pearl River that is home to the **Xing Hai Concert Hall**, where major international classical stars often appear, and the **Guangdong Museum of Art** (*see below*).

### Da Fo Si
*21 Cha Xin Zhong Street, Hui Fu Dong Lu, Guangzhou (8333 5678).* **Open** 8am-5pm daily. **Admission** free. **Map** p269.
Da Fo Si (Big Buddha Temple) is a haven of peace. Having been fully restored, its monks can be seen leading and coaxing people through rites that have long been forgotten. Enter from the alley off Hui Fu or through the gate on Beijing Road.

### Guangdong Museum of Art
*38 Yan Yu Lu, Er Sha Dao, Guangzhou (8735 1468 ext 8402).* **Open** 9am-5pm Tue-Sun. **Admission** RMB15; RMB7 concessions. **No credit cards. Map** p269.
A modern edifice beside the Xing Hai Concert Hall on Er Sha Island. Built in 1997, the museum holds regular exhibitions of both ancient and modern art, and is well worth a visit.

A quiet corner of the extensive **Yue Xiu Park**.

## Guang Xiao Si

*109 Guang Xiao Lu, Guangzhou (8108 1961).*
**Open** 8am-5pm daily. **Admission** RMB2.
**No credit cards**. **Map** p268.
The ancient 'Bright Filial Piety' Temple, dating originally from the second century BC when it was a royal palace, has maintained an aura of almost magical calm within one of the world's least calm cities. The equally ancient trees that fill the large complex block out the 'view' of the surrounding low-rise blocks. Buddhist services are held regularly.

## Liu Rong Si

*87 Liu Rong Lu, Guangzhou (8339 2843).*
**Open** 8am-5pm daily. **Admission** RMB1.
**No credit cards**. **Map** p269.
Hua Ta (Tall Flower Pagoda), which has recently been restored, is the major attraction at the Liu Rong Si (Temple of the Six Banyan Trees). Groups of Americans come here with their recently adopted Cantonese children to go though the motions of the traditional Buddhist adoption ceremony.

## Liwan Museum

*84 Feng Yuan Bei Lu, Long Jing Xi, Guangzhou (8193 9917).* **Open** 8.30-11.30am, 2-5pm daily.
**Admission** RMB5; RMB1 concessions.
**No credit cards**. **Map** p268.
The district of Liwan, one of the oldest surviving parts of Guangzhou, has narrow streets lined with wooden fronted houses. The museum is located inside a 1912 house that was built for a Hongkong Bank manager and is bursting with local history.

**Guang Xiao Si...**

... and **Liu Rong Si**, two of Guangzhou's most atmospheric temples.

## Peasant Movement Museum

*42 Zhong Shan Si Lu, Guangzhou (8333 3936).*
**Open** 8-11.30am, 2-5pm Mon-Fri; 9.30am-4.30pm
Sat, Sun. **Admission** RMB2. **No credit cards.**
**Map** p269.
Set in beautiful temple grounds, this is the place to
mug up on your *Revolutionary History of Various
Countries*, as taught by Mao Zedong and Zhou Enlai.
It carries a tribute to the dedication of the young ide-
alists – a moving gallery of those who lost their lives
is on display – who hoped to build a socialist paradise.

## Sun Yat-sen Memorial Hall

*Dong Feng Zhong Lu, Guangzhou (8355 2430).*
**Open** 8am-5.30pm daily. **Admission** RMB5-10.
**No credit cards.** **Map** p269.
This beautiful piece of symmetrical Chinese archi-
tecture houses a theatre, where acrobatic shows tend
to be staged for tourists. It also houses some Sun
Yat-sen memorabilia.

## Zhen Hai Tower/Guangzhou Municipal Museum

*Yue Xiu Park, Guangzhou (no phone).* **Open** 9am-
5.30pm daily. **Admission** RMB6; RMB3
concessions. **No credit cards.** **Map** p269.
The tower, a 14th-century gate, is all that remains
of the old city wall. It now houses the Guangzhou
Municipal Museum, which covers the period from
the Nan Yue kingdom, the first southern Chinese
dynasty, to the days of the foreign concessions on
Shamian Island.

# Where to eat & drink

## Restaurants

Dining in Guangzhou is much like eating
in Hong Kong – only there are no decent
'international' restaurants to speak of. On
the upside, the local restaurants are far
cheaper, and the staff are generally much
more friendly and helpful, though you should
watch out for their 'recommendations', which
are often quite simply the most expensive
dish on the menu. Dim sum (*see p149*) or *yum
cha*, which translates literally as 'taking tea',
and refers to a selection of small eats, is a
must. If you thought Hong Kong's dim sum
restaurants were noisy, you'll be dreaming
of them as havens of peace and quiet once
you've screamed through a meal in Guangzhou.
Seafood and fish feature highly – make sure
you see them live first, to be sure they are fresh.
Snake is a staple delicacy too, and should also
be checked for life before it is cooked, either in
a stew or deep fried. Thanks to low costs and
high aspirations, some really rather smart
restaurants are springing up across the city,
including Xiang Guan Cun (*see p274*). They are
well worth checking out and will not cost half
as much as a similar place in Hong Kong.

## Banana Leaf

*1/F, Broadcasting & Television Hotel, 8 Lu Hu Lu,
Guangzhou (8359 1288 ext 3118).* **Open** 11am-
midnight daily. **Main courses** RMB25-45.
**Credit** AmEx, DC, MC, V. **Map** p269.
The Banana Leaf, which serves Southeast Asian
food, is almost always packed with a very mixed
crowd. A Guangzhou institution, the über-congenial
owner manager, Thomas, does insist on taking a
snap of every *gweilo*, which can test the patience.

## Flory City

*40 Jian Shi Liu Ma Lu, Guangzhou (8383 3299).*
**Open** 5.30pm, 5pm-3am daily. **Main courses**
RMB30-40. **Credit** AmEx, DC, MC, V.
A higher – if not entirely high – class, well-known
Cantonese restaurant, not far from the city centre
action. Authentic in that there are no English lan-
guage menus, diners should make the effort to under-
stand the manager's 'Chinglish' – the food is worth it.

## Matsubaya

*5/F, Gitic Office Tower, 339 Huan Shi Dong Lu,
Guangzhou (8331 1888 ext 70518).* **Open** 11.30am-
2.30pm, 4.30-11pm daily. **Main courses** RMB50-80.
**No credit cards.** **Map** p269.
Friendly staff, a multilingual menu and cheap prices
set Matsubaya apart from the usual expensive
Japanese standards.

## Milano's

*1-103, Xin Cheng Bei Street, Tian He Dong Lu,
Guangzhou (3881 0594).* **Open** 11am-midnight daily.
**Main courses** RMB40-60. **No credit cards.**
This pizza joint, tucked away in Tian He, is run by
an enterprising and hospitable expat who employs
bilingual staff. If you need something solid after a
few drinks, the thick pizzas are the best in town.

## My Home

*19 Tao Jin Lu, Guangzhou (8559 2101).*
**Open** 11am-10.30pm daily. **Main courses** RMB20-
40. **No credit cards.** **Map** p269.
Hunanese food in convivial surroundings. The manager has been catering to international clients for
years, so you'll be well looked after. Check out the
dry-fried spicy french beans.

## Pu Li Chuan

*744 Dong Feng Lu, Guangzhou (8730 0619).*
**Open** 11.30am-2.30pm, 5-9.30pm daily. **Main
courses** RMB20-40. **No credit cards.** **Map** p269.
Fiery Sichuan restaurant with messy hotpot downstairs and 'fine' dining above. The hotpot does a
good value buffet, and you can test your mettle on
*lazi ji*, deep-fried chicken pieces buried in a mountain of dried chillies.

## Rong Hua Tea House

*712 Long Jing Dong Lu, Guangzhou (8184 7255).*
**Open** 6am-midnight daily. **Average** RMB20.
**No credit cards.** **Map** p268.
Nothing prepares you to beat off a hangover quite
like a full on dawn dim sum breakfast. Rong Hua is
very, very busy though, so get there early.

**Trips Out of Town**

### Xiang Cun Guan

*23 Xian Lie Nan Lu, Guangzhou (8778 9888 ext 86128).* **Open** 10am-2am daily. **Main courses** RMB20-40. **No credit cards.**

Rustic Hunanese cuisine in a very cosmopolitan setting. The smart set frequent Xiang Cun Guan for obvious reasons: it oozes style, and the food ain't bad at all.

### Xi Gong

*Yanjiang Lu, Guangzhou (no phone).* **Open** 5pm-midnight daily. **Main courses** RMB20-50. **No credit cards. Map** p269.

This is a strip of riverside seafood restaurants that were recently cleaned up, but they still manage to maintain something of their original, chaotic character. The beautiful touts will physically drag you into their restaurant if you look at all uncertain. As they're all much of a muchness, you need not worry, but do try and get an upstairs balcony table. Ordering is easy: point.

### Yun Xiang Shi Jie

*342 Dong Hua Dong Lu, Guangzhou (8777 6057).* **Open** 6am-1am daily. **Main courses** RMB15-30. **No credit cards. Map** p269.

The advantage of this bustling Cantonese restaurant is that the dim sum is wheeled around on trolleys, making the point and shoot method of ordering all the easier.

## Bars & nightlife

Guangzhou nightlife is the epitome of all that is energetic and frenetic about the city. Guangzhouren party hard and late, and then move on to a street stall to yak until the morning. The night of the week is irrelevant. Nightlife is also a moving target. To get into a club or bar, you'll have to fight through a crowd of youngsters passing on the latest party venue by mobile phone. Inside, clattering dice games and the booming beat created by the in-house DJ raise the volume of conversation to shouting pitch. There are a couple of expat hang-outs, but generally it's a mix of all-comers – except perhaps for the karaoke lounges, reserve of the rich and the well connected.

### African Bar

*2nd Floor, Zi Dong Hua Building, 707 Dong Feng Dong Lu, Guangzhou (8778 2433 ext 621).* **Open** 7pm-2am daily. **No credit cards.**

A long-standing institution. Once the 'in' spot, then the gay hang-out, now a bit of everything. Music is, you've guessed it, heavily African influenced.

### Café Elles

*2nd Floor, Hua Xin Building, 1 Shui Yin Lu, Guangzhou (3760 4909).* **Open** 7.30pm-2am daily. **Credit** AmEx, DC, MC, V.

This is as international as you get in Guangzhou. French/Cantonese run, it has live music plus

Top Hunanese tucker at **Xiang Cun Guan**.

pumping weekend dance nights. A cool, laid-back mix of expat teachers and locals pack it out on Fridays and Saturdays.

### Catwalk

*Basement, China Hotel, Liu Hua Lu, Guangzhou (8666 6888 ext 3068).* **Open** 9pm-2am daily. **Credit** AmEx, DC, MC, V. **Map** p268.

Sophisticated, but you'll pay for it. Live music in the innards of the China Hotel, put on by a resident band that is normally not bad.

### D & D

*98-100 Heng Fu Lu, Guangzhou (8350 8316).* **Open** 8pm-6am daily. **No credit cards.**

The home of hardcore techno, head-shaking, platform-soled young trendies, this is the place for a low down look at Guangzhou nightlife. Dancing girls included.

### Face Club

*Basement, International Bank Tower, 191 Dong Feng Dong Lu, Guangzhou (8388 0688).* **Open** 5pm-3am daily. **No credit cards.**

This bar has been through a couple of incarnations and locations, but it's now settled down with a weekend live band (English) and regular guest DJs. Run by a very with-it local crew, it attracts the pretty people.

### Gipsy King Bar

*Basement, West Tower, Pearl River Building, 360 Huan Shi Dong Road, Guangzhou (8387 5177).* **Open** 6pm-2am daily. **No credit cards. Map** p269.

Expat post-work watering-hole and late-night chat-up joint. Pleasantly decked out in gypsy frippery, it throws some popular parties.

# Rough trade

There used to be only one reason to visit
Guangzhou: trade. The city was the first
Chinese port to be opened to foreign trade
in the 19th century. And those early traders,
if they managed to escape the confines of
Shamian Island, where they were holed up
for the limited season, would have probably
been surprised to find down a backstreet the
oldest surviving Arab minaret in the world,
according to the locals. It was erected in
AD627 by some of the earliest traders to
find their way to southern China. (For well
over a thousand years, the tower was the
tallest building in Guangzhou.)

Jumping ahead to the 'modern era',
in 1956, a mere seven years after the
Communist takeover, Guangzhou was again
nominated by the central government as the
only avenue for trade with the outside world.
It retained that exclusivity until 1978.

The trading was limited, however, to
two fortnight-long trade fairs, one in spring
(generally the last two weeks of April) and the
other in autumn (usually the last two weeks
of October). The fairs were major earners for
the city, not just for the hotels (which still
double their prices for the fairs), because
revenues from all the business had no
alternative but to pass through the city.

Officially known as the **Guangzhou Export
Commodities Trade Fair**, the business
bonanza is held in a monstrous hall on
Liu Hua Lu. Next door is the original
1950s building, about an eighth of the
current venue's size. Thanks to modern
communications, loosening of trade
regulations and the fact that just about
every city in China has a trade fair nowadays,
the Guangzhou event has diminished in
significance, but it maintains a certain
cachet. The local government would even
have you believe that it is still growing year
on year. Their benchmark is the number of
contracts signed at the fair. The deals are
in fact saved up from the previous six
months and symbolically inked at the

event. 'Metaphorically' would be more
accurate. One of the convenient vestiges
of a planned economy.

In the good old bad old days, exhibitors
at the fair were the great and the good of
the state-owned enterprises, along with their
import–export corporations, without whom
they could do no business with the outside
world. An endless array of identical booths
beckoned the buyers. In each, behind a
folding table, sat an export manager, his
rolled up trouser leg tucked underneath and
at his side a pretty secretary, his interpreter.
The interpreters often wore smiles that were
very open to misinterpretation. On the table
you could find a sample of mineral ore, a bag
of medicinal powder or a couple of swathes
of cloth. On the strength of those samples, a
trader had to book his six-month contract, go
home and hope the right stuff turned up on
his door. To get into the Fair, you needed an
invitation from a Chinese sponsor (chopped
by countless bureaux), enough passport
photos to plaster a wall and, of course,
to pay a fat registration fee.

Today, many of the great and good are
bankrupt or banged up in jail for misuse
of public funds. Private and semi-private
enterprises, with well-made and marketed
goods, aggressive sales plans and
multilingual management have taken over. A
foreign trader has to be constantly aware that
in the middle of his bid, New York might ring
up the Chinese guy's mobile and book his
year's output before you can say 'Big Apple'.

The Fair has also taken on the look of a
bazaar, with many small-scale companies
that produce everyday household goods
clogging the aisles with carpets, antique
furniture, tableware, repro art works,
Christmas decorations – for which there
seems to be a massive market. You name it,
you can find it. And you can buy much of it on
the spot. For the last two days of the fair,
Guangzhou's expat wives flock in to snap
up bargains that the exhibitors cannot be
bothered to ship back to their rural factories.
You can fit out an entire household at half
the normal price. Next thing, they'll be doing
wedding lists. All you need now to get in is
RMB100, though in the final scrummage you
can probably bluff it for free. If you bargain
hard, you'll be amazed what you walk out
with. Just try not to buy the factory.

# Hey, good looking!

It is quite possible that you might be approached on the streets of Guangzhou – or in a bar – by someone asking you if you are interested in being a model. No, they have not confused you for Claudia Schiffer or Brad Pitt. You could have a face like an ocean-going tadpole for all they care. The thing is: non-Chinese is cool.

Despite the centuries-engrained idea in China that all foreigners are barbarians, have big noses and smell like a cow's udder (it's the dairy diet we are brought up on that's to thank for that), Western mugs sell. One can only assume it has something to do with imported products generally being considered superior to local ones. You will notice buses and billboards are plastered with faces of Mr and Ms Average Foreigner. Local resident Russian dancing girls make good pocket money from the sideline.

There is a catch, however. The touts are looking to save themselves money, too. Quite often they will tell you that they can barely cover your expenses. They will promise you everlasting fame as fair compensation. If you think you can live with yourself in underpants overlooking a busy street junction for the next six months, go ahead and take the fame. The going rate is more like RMB5,000 yuan a day for a Mr/Ms Normal. They'll also tell you they only need you for an hour or so. Quadruple it.

On the up side, some expats make a good supplementary income from grinning in ads for bathrooms, washing powder, toothpaste or even the odd part in a Chinese play. If you live here, and pretend to have a serious career, then it can get embarrassing, but if you are only passing through, why not? Magazine covers have regular slots for anonymous big noses. Makes a change from sending a postcard home.

### Hard Rock Café

*Basement, China Hotel, Liu Hua Lu, Guangzhou (8666 6888 ext 3050).* **Open** 11.30am-2am daily. **Credit** AmEx, DC, MC, V. **Map** p268.
If you really have to. Complies to standard Americana principle of restaurant with T-shirt shop attached.

### Hill Bar

*367 Huan Shi Dong Lu, Guangzhou (8333 3998).* **Open** 11am-2am daily. **No credit cards.** **Map** p269.
No night of utter debauchery is complete without a final stop at the Hill Bar. Seediness in extremis, but a great central location and cheap booze. Emerge to dawn *tai chi* on the doorstep; remove your beer goggles and get rid of him/her.

### Shui Bian Bar

*Room 102, Block 15, Ji Nan Garden, Shi Pai Dong Lu, Guangzhou (3889 9695).* **Open** 2pm-2am daily. **No credit cards.**
Well off the beaten track, but well worth the effort. Owner Jiang Nan Li Guo is a standard bearer for local culture, particularly salon theatre and local music. He also serves a delicious pot of warm plum wine on a mini stove at your table. Rustic, yet remarkably un-kitsch, decor.

### Take Five Jazz Café

*11 Tao Jin Street, off Tao Jin Lu, Guangzhou (8359 6681).* **Open** 8pm-2am daily. **No credit cards.**
Occasional live jazz, but as they get complaints from the neighbours the volume is kept low. Otherwise, an excellent collection of CDs in this quiet back street bar.

### Windflower Music Pub

*387 Huan Shi Dong Lu, Guangzhou (8358 2446).* **Open** 6pm-4am daily. **No credit cards.** **Map** p269.
The hottest bar in town for the 'in' crowd – and it's been that way for two years now. Cosy back rooms, plus a perma-tented main bar area with foreign/local DJs and occasional live music. A must visit.

## Shopping

You might be upset to discover that the Versace outfit you re-mortgaged your house for back home is going for a tenth of the price in Guangzhou. Get used to it. Copying does not just extend to clothes. Cigarettes, toothpaste, even Coca-Cola are ripped off in mainland China. Not long ago HMV, only it was not HMV, opened a megastore to great press acclaim. It subsequently had to change its name, but it's kept the original colours and is now a perfectly good local record store. Restaurant owners have even complained of being sold fake fish – work that one out. If you want genuine stuff, then stay local and natural. Guangzhou is great for herbs and traditional Chinese medicines, 'antique' knick-knacks and silks.

### Daily Living

*2 Hua He Road, Guangzhou (8382 6907).* **Open** 10am-6pm daily. **No credit cards.**
Expat deli where you can stock up on a few treats for that 36-hour train ride to Xinjiang, or create a simple picnic for the grassy slopes of Bai Yun Shan.

Trips Out of Town

### Guangzhou Friendship Store

*369 Huan Shi Dong Lu, Guangzhou (8357 6628).*
**Open** 9.30am-9.45pm daily. **Credit** AmEx, DC, MC,
V. **Map** p269.
Once the only type of store in China where you could
buy imported goods (like milk), Friendship Stores
are now temples to international fashion brands and
some good quality local ones.

### Huasheng Furniture Art Centre

*1-8 Sector, Hai Yi Building, Seashore Garden,*
*South Luo Xi Bridge, Guangzhou (8450 9875).*
**Open** 10.30am-6pm daily. **No credit cards**.
There seems to be an endless supply of antique
furniture in the surrounding province of Guangdong
that inevitably finds its way into one of many
antiques stores in Guangzhou. This shop is set
out like a traditional home (rather like a museum),
which makes it great for a browse, but you can
buy the artefacts, too. Buses run here from the Gitic
Hotel (*see p277*).

### Tian He Book Centre

*123 Tian He Lu, Guangzhou (8759 4208).*
**Open** 9.30am-9.30pm daily. **Credit** AmEx, DC,
MC, V.
A multi-storey bookshop with some surprises up in
the gods. Good art, such as woodblock prints, at
keen prices and some music CDs of local bands that
are hard to find anywhere else.

### Wu Lu Furniture

*523 Teem Plaza, Tian He Lu, Guangzhou*
*(8559 0541).* **Open** 10am-9.40pm daily.
**No credit cards**.
It might look genuine, but it isn't. Nonetheless the
furniture here is well made, and of course cheaper
than the real antique thing. For that, you are best to
tap into the local expat wife scene – any woman over
40 drinking coffee with another blue rinse – they'll
delight in telling you where to get a bargain, but it
will be outside the main city.

### Yue Ya Tang

*170 Wen De Bei Lu, Guangzhou (8334 9901).*
**Open** varies. **Cards** AmEx, DC, MC, V.
One of the few downtown 'antiques' shops that deals
in the real McCoy (mostly from the Qing dynasty –
around 100 years old) as well as a decent range
of repro stuff.

## Where to stay

All Guangzhou hotels will give you a
discount, sometimes a major one, off their
rack rates – all you have to do is ask. This
is due to the fact that there's a glut of hotel
rooms that is rarely full. The only times
when you'll never get a discount are during
the spring and autumn trade fairs (*see p275*
**Rough trade**), when massive premiums
are charged. The days of foreigners being
limited to certain hotels – 'for their safety' –

are almost entirely over, thankfully. It was
simply a ploy to justify a ridiculous mark
up on prices, anyway. Some very 'local' hotels
might still blanch at taking in foreigners,
but generally they ignore the colour of
your passport. A decent room in the city
can cost as little as RMB150.

### Garden Hotel

*368 Huan Shi Dong Lu, Guangzhou (8333*
*8989/www.gardenhotel-guangzhou.com).*
**Rates** RMB1,160-1,490 double; RMB3,740-
RMB16,600 suite. **Credit** AmEx, DC, MC, V.
**Map** p269.
A classy traders' truck stop, the Garden has been
around forever. After a recent refit, the lobby bar
has become a pleasant – if expensive – place to hang
out, particularly to view the 'wallflowers' who line
the bar in the evening. The rooms are gradually
being upgraded, too, which means rates are on the
up. Given that the prices listed above are subject to
a 20% government tax and service charge, it's only
really an option if you are seriously splashing out.
Hotel shuttle buses run from the East Station and
the airport.

### Gitic Hotel

*339 Huan Shi Dong Lu, Guangzhou (8331 1888/*
*www.gitic.com.cn).* **Rates** RMB1,162-1,411 double;
RMB1,826-21,580 suite. **Credit** AmEx, DC, MC, V.
**Map** p269.
Also known locally as '63', thanks to the number
of its floors, the Gitic is one of the original hotels
set up for the business traveller, especially the
trade fair businessman. Hence, it demands ridiculously high prices twice a year and spends the rest
of it wondering where all its business has gone.
Good rooms though, in the centre of town. The
prices listed, as at the Garden Hotel, are subject to
a 20% surcharge.

### Heng Fu Hotel

*41 Heng Fu Lu, Guangzhou (8359 0868).*
**Rates** RMB199 double. **No credit cards**.
Little known and hard to find – tell the taxi driver
it's opposite the Golden Times Disco, inside the hospital grounds and you should get there. With a garden swimming pool, quiet and comfortable rooms at
a keen price and a very central location, it's hard to
beat for value and convenience.

### Shamian Youth Hostel

*2 Shamian Si Lu, Guangzhou (8188 4298).* **Rates**
RMB100 single; RMB170 double; RMB230 triple.
**No credit cards**. **Map** p268.
A popular budget option on Shamian Island (once
the 'Cantonment' for foreign traders), where dorm
rooms and decent doubles are available. Facing
the grand White Swan hotel, it is surrounded by
classic Concession Era buildings, once known as
'godowns', where the traders stored their dope and
tea. The streets are lined with plane trees and locals
practising *tai chi*.

**Trips Out of Town**

## Yuanyang Hotel

*6 Long Kou Dong Lu, Tian He, Guangzhou (8759 6988/www.yyanghotel.com).* **Rates** RMB368 single; RMB418 double; RMB448 triple; RMB688-988 suite. **Credit** AmEx, DC, MC, V.

Bog standard, but comfortable, business hotel stuck a bit out of town in Tian He, but benefiting from a lively neighbourhood. A warren of tiny alleys runs off a night market popular with local students. Around the corner is the Shui Bian Bar (*see p276*). Prices are subject to a 15% surcharge.

# Resources

## Getting there & around

### By air

Flights from Hong Kong land in Guangzhou almost before they have taken off. It's a 20-minute hop, hardly worth the effort of getting out to the airport – which takes twice as long as the flight itself – and through customs. About the only advantage must be the duty-free selection at Chek Lap Kok.

### By sea

The high-speed catamaran takes two hours to reach Guangzhou (Zhou Tou Zi Pier) from Hong Kong's City Pier and is a great way to see something of Hong Kong harbour. Departures leave at 7.30am and 2pm daily.

### By train

The fastest and most convenient option. Non-stop express trains leave from Kowloon's Hung Hom Station four times a day. Allow about 20 minutes for customs. The journey time is around two hours. One-way tickets cost HK$250. You arrive at Guangzhou East Station, a ten-minute taxi ride from the city centre.

Alternatively, a slower and cheaper option is to take the KCR (Kowloon–Canton Railway) up to the Lo Wu border crossing, which costs HK$32 from Kowloon (either board the KCR at Hung Hom or the metro interchange at Mong Kok). Once over the border, catch a local train for about RMB70 from Shenzhen station, right outside the border crossing point. Total travelling time is about three hours.

From Lo Wu/Shenzhen, there are buses that leave from the car park beside the train station every ten minutes. Tickets cost RMB60 and the trip to Guangzhou takes just over two hours. Where you end up in Guangzhou can be a bit of a lottery, but most buses pass the main train station. Return buses leave from opposite the China Hotel, again every ten minutes. Some go straight through to Hong Kong itself.

If you are really stuck, in a mad rush or have some friends to share the cost with, there are always Guangzhou taxis in Shenzhen looking for a fare back to the city. You can get them down to around RMB400 one way.

### Visas

Non-Hong Kong residents must obtain a visa for China. You can go in person to the Chinese Visa Office, 5/F, Lower Block, China Resources Building,

26 Harbour Road, Wan Chai (2585 1794; open 8.30am-4.30pm Mon-Fri; 8.30am-12.30pm Sat), but it's much simpler (and can even be cheaper) to ask a travel agent to get the visa for you. A popular agent for regular China travellers is **Time Travel** (16/F, Chungking Mansions, Nathan Road, Tsim Sha Tsui, Kowloon; 2723 9993). They can even arrange a six-month multi-entry business visa in a day, should you need one. *See also p288.*

### Getting around

**Bicycles** can be rented outside the Shamian Youth Hostel (*see p277*), the backpacker hang-out. A fun, if hairy, way to see the city.

Don't bother with the **buses**, unless you have a local friend to help. Drivers rarely speak any English and destinations are only indicated in Chinese script. If you do happen to need one to get out into the suburbs or surrounding area, get on a full one – empty ones drive around in circles for ages until they fill up.

By far the easiest way for visitors to get around Guangzhou is by **taxi**. They're cheap, plentiful and pretty efficient. Their meters start at RMB7, and clock an extra RMB1 for every 250 metres (270 yards) travelled after the initial three kilometres (two miles). You'll need to have your destination written in Chinese to show the driver, unless, of course, you're taking one from a major hotel, in which case the doorman will tell the driver your destination.

## Tourist information

The days of the national tourist agency CITS (China International Travel Service) are numbered. Once the only bureau for foreign travellers, its efficacy expired long ago. You are much better off dropping into the nearest decent hotel, where an in-house agency will be able to meet all your needs, in fluent English and with a smile. Commissions are negligible and ticket prices competitive. The international hotels also all run English-language tours of Guangzhou and its environs, if getting on a bus with the blue rinses is your idea of adventure travel. If you require air or train tickets, then head for a local hotel for assistance.

Some of the better hotel agencies are at the **Gitic Hotel** (*see p277*), **Garden Hotel** (*see p277*) and **White Swan Hotel** (1 Sha Mian Da Street; 8188 6968). A couple of locally run agencies that are used to dealing with foreigners may be better able to meet the needs of independent travellers. They are: **Xpat Travel Planners** (Flat E, 20/F, Regent House, 50 Taojin Lu, Guangzhou; 8358 6961/xpats@public.guangzhou.gd.cn) and **Jennifer & Mei Travel** (13/F, East Tower, Zhu Jiang Building, 360 Huanshi Dong Road, Guangzhou; 8386 5575/jmtravelagency@yahoo.com).

### Language

Cantonese is the lingua franca of the city. Most natives also speak Mandarin, while English is spoken at all major hotels and Western-style bars. Watch out for young locals wanting to practise

# A rock icon(oclast)

Mainland China's indigenous rock scene is pretty limp. Rip-offs and straight mimicry of western bands vie for prominence with the Beijing-based disaffected 'dongbei' (northeast) young grunge bands. Every other band calls itself 'punk', even if their sound is more akin to the Shadows than the Sex Pistols.

But in Guangzhou, away from the mainstream – in fact deliberately avoiding it, because that would mean selling out and moving to Beijing – there's one guy fighting a campaign for originality and a sound that one day could be known as the root of real 'Chinese' rock.

**Wang Lei** actually comes from Sichuan in the west. Trained as a classical opera singer and dancer from a young age, he happened to win a dancing competition in Guangzhou 12 years ago and has been here ever since. In the meantime, he has learned to play guitar, released five albums and established himself as a beacon for all southern Chinese musicians. At one stage, all were welcome to experiment and record at his own tiny studio that abutted his ramshackle house, then (in 1998) he opened a bar called Unplugged that acquired legendary status for its unbridled jam sessions.

Bands with names like Punk God, Cavesluts and Monkeys in Raincoats flocked to the first ever venue where they could do their stuff without having to apply in triplicate to the Cultural Bureau beforehand. In a city where

the wildest music gets is *Bohemian Rhapsody* on the karaoke machine, Unplugged shook things up so much that it soon attracted official attention. Barely a year after opening, it was demolished by the municipal government as part of a clean-up campaign. Apparently, the structure was unsafe, or in the way of a traffic light, or something. Wang Lei saved the demolition men some effort. When they turned up at dawn on the appointed day, they found five punk bands (all members shirtless and drunk) had already done half the job for them – and were still at it.

Wang Lei, and south China rock, are still homeless, but he does play the odd concert around town and it is well worth seeking one out to witness some raw Guangzhou energy – and the only live music in town worthy of the name. The **Shui Bian Bar** (*see p276; pictured above*) sells his CDs and can tell you where it's going down.

their English. Some can be incredibly helpful and will happily act as a tour guide just for the chance to speak with you; some can be a pain; and some are just plain touts.

## Local English-language media

The official *Guangzhou Morning Post* (no relation to the *South China Morning Post*) offers anodyne business news and the odd titbit of cultural info. *That's Guangzhou* (www.thatsguangzhou.com), a free monthly city mag available at most international bars and hotels, has comprehensive listings and some good feature articles. *South China City Talk*, a less dense rag, is very much expat orientated. The website www.chinanow.com recently launched a Guangzhou section.

## Money

The basic unit of Chinese currency goes by two names: the **yuan** and the **Renminbi** (RMB). One Hong Kong dollar is roughly equivalent to one Renminbi. Although some places in Guangzhou

may accept Hong Kong dollars, you'll certainly need to change some money into Renminbi. Tourist hotels, branches of the Bank of China and major entry points all have such facilities and rates vary very little. There are a few ATMs around Guangzhou that accept international cards, but don't rely on them. Top end hotels accept credit cards, but most establishments don't. You shouldn't have any problems changing Renminbi back to Hong Kong dollars in Hong Kong.

## Telephones

To dial abroad from Guangzhou, dial 00 (not 001 as in Hong Kong), followed by the country code and local number (omitting the 0 of the area code if there is one). It is easiest to find phones that accept IDD calls in the big international hotels, but be aware that you'll pay heavily for the privilege. Calls from Guangzhou to Hong Kong are considered international, but are cheap. The international code for China is 86, while the area code for Guangzhou is 20.

**Trips Out of Town**

# Chinese characters

**Guangzhou**
廣州

**SIGHTSEEING**
**Ban Yun Shan**
白雲山
**Da Fo Si**
大佛寺
**Er Sha Dao**
二沙島
**Guangzhou Friendship Store**
友誼商店
**Guangzhou Trade Fair**
廣州出口商品交易會
**Guangdong Provincial Museum**
廣東省博物館
**Guang Xiao Si**
光孝寺
**Liu Hua Park**
流花公園
**Liu Rong Si**
六榕寺花塔
**Peasant Movement Institute**
農民運動講習所
**Shamian Island**
沙面
**Sun Yat-sen Memorial Hall**
孫中山紀念堂
**Tian He**
天河
**Yue Xiu Park**
越秀公園
**Zhu Jiang (Pearl River)**
珠江

**RESTAURANTS**
**Banana Leaf**
蕉葉風味屋
**Flory City**
花城海鮮酒家
**Matsubaya**
松葉屋
**Milano's**
米蘭意大利西餐廳

**My Home**
我家
**Pu Li Chuan**
普利川大酒樓
**Rong Hua Tea House**
榮華餐廳
**Xiang Cun Guan**
湘村館
**Xi Gong**
西貢
**Yun Xiang Shi Jie**
雲香食街

**BARS & CLUBS**
**African Bar**
非洲巴
**Café Elles**
木子巴
**Face Club**
菲私俱樂部
**Gipsy King Bar**
大蓬車酒巴
**Hard Rock Café**
硬石餐廳
**Hill Bar**
小山巴
**Shui Bian Bar**
水邊巴
**Take Five Jazz Café**
藍調咖啡

**HOTELS**
**Garden Hotel**
花園酒店
**Gitic Hotel**
廣東國際大酒店
**Heng Fu Hotel**
恒福賓館
**Shamian Youth Hostel**
省外辦招待所
**White Swan Hotel**
白天鵝賓館
**Yuanyang Hotel**
遠洋賓館

# Directory

| | |
|---|---|
| Getting Around | 282 |
| Resources A-Z | 286 |
| The Language | 298 |
| Further Reference | 299 |
| Index | 302 |

## Feature boxes

| | |
|---|---|
| Key phone numbers | 289 |
| Weather | 296 |

# Directory

## Getting Around

### By air

**Hong Kong International Airport** (www.hkairport.com) has rightly dubbed itself 'Asia's Super-Hub'. Situated on the levelled island of Chek Lap Kok, just north of Lantau island, the new airport is one of the largest and most modern in the world – it replaced Kai Tak (one of the most notoriously difficult airports for pilots to land at) in 1998. The airport is around 32 kilometres (20 miles) west of Kowloon and Hong Kong Island.

On arrival, transport to Kowloon, Hong Kong Island, the New Territories and Lantau, as well as to Macau and China, is available from the four-level Ground Transportation Centre. Follow the relevant signs.

The quickest (though most expensive) public transport link into the city is the **Airport Express** train to Kowloon and Central on Hong Kong Island, which takes just 23 minutes to reach downtown. Trains run every ten minutes from 6am to 1.30am daily. A one-way adult fare to Kowloon is HK$80 (HK$140 return) and to Hong Kong Island (Central) is HK$90 (HK$160 return). The service is operated by the MTR Corporation (2881 8888).

Free Airport Express shuttle buses run from Kowloon and Central stations to and from the major hotels, Hung Hom KCR Station and the China Ferry Terminal (6am-11pm daily; every 20mins).

The A-prefixed airbuses offer express **bus** services to Hong Kong Island (A11, A12; HK$40-$45 one way), Kowloon (A21, A22; HK$33-$39 one way) and the New Territories (A31, A35, A41, A41P, A43; HK$17-$28 one way). Services operate from 6am to midnight (after this time, the N11 bus goes to Hong Kong Island, the N21 to Kowloon and the N31 to the New Territories). You can buy tickets in the Meeters & Greeters Hall of the Arrival Hall or, if you have the exact fare, when you board the bus. Buses take 35 to 45 minutes to reach Kowloon and another 10 or so minutes to Hong Kong Island, but be aware that traffic congestion in the city can be horrific.

**Taxis** are the most expensive way to travel to and from the airport (not least because of the various road tolls). Expect to pay anything between HK$300 and HK$400 depending on your destination and traffic conditions. Red taxis serve Hong Kong Island and Kowloon, green ones serve the New Territories, and blue ones serve Lantau island. Taxis are located on the left-hand ramp as you leave the arrivals hall.

A **ferry** (2987 7351) runs from the airport to Tuen Mun in the New Territories. It leaves every 20 to 40 minutes, takes nine minutes and runs from 6am to 11pm daily, HK$15 one way.

**Car parks** (2286 0163/ 2949 1083) have pick-up and drop-off zones; and offer complimentary 30-minute parking for departing/arriving passengers. Parking spaces close to the terminal are reserved for the disabled.

If you intend to travel directly on to Macau or mainland China, onward coach services are provided by CTS (2764 9803), Global Express (2375 0099) and Airport Chinalink (9747 1202).

On leaving Hong Kong, and before boarding the Airport Express or the express bus service, you can check in your luggage (up to 90 minutes prior to take off) at the City Check-In Halls in Kowloon and Central.

**AIRPORT ENQUIRIES**
**Hotline**: 2181 0000.
**Multilingual hotline**: 2508 1234.
**Check-in**: 2183 1334.
**Arrivals**: 2182 1559.

**AIRPORT FACILITIES**
(Free) porter services are available in the baggage reclaim hall.

In the Meeters & Greeters Hall, there are service counters for hotel reservations and pick-ups, private limousine services, the Macau Government Tourist Office, China Travel Service (for visa applications to China) and ferry/train reservations. There is also a left luggage counter (*see p290*).

There are banks (with ATMs) and foreign exchange outlets located in arrival and departure areas – the banks tend to offer better rates. HKTB Visitor Information Services can be found in the Buffer Halls and Transfer Area T2.

Public payphones, courtesy phones and 24-hour help phones are located throughout the terminal.

In-terminal electric vehicles are available in the East Hall, and there is an Automated People Mover, a driverless tram, in the basement of the passenger terminal that travels between the East and West Halls every three minutes between 6am and midnight.

In the Check-In Hall, there is a Police Report Centre (East Hall; 2106 7020; open 24 hours daily); in the Departure Hall, an instant photo kiosk and a post office; and in the East and West Halls, post-boxes.

Skymart has duty-free shops, Chinese speciality stores and books/gift shops. Food courts offer fast food, sandwich counters, Chinese delicacies and restaurants.

As befitting a modern airport, Hong Kong's is well wired for the 21st century. Multimedia lounges provide 24-hour free broadband access to email and the Internet, and visitors with PCs and PC-LAN cards can also access the Internet from almost anywhere in the terminal, with charges being based on time online. In addition, the CyberMall Cyber Break Café (2928 6421), with 16 iMac terminals, provides up unlimited free Internet access and free refreshments.

For those requiring a full range of business services, there is a Business Centre at PO83 (2883 3871).

For frequent flyers and business travellers, several airlines operate dedicated lounges. They include The Wing for Cathay Pacific, South African Airways and Swissair passengers (2747 7072), China Airlines' Dynasty Lounge (2261 1801) and Singapore Airlines' Silver Kris (2769 7833). Meanwhile, the Plaza Premium Lounge on Level 7 of the West Hall offers Internet access, massage, shower and business facilities, food, music, movies and magazines for those prepared to part with HK$250. The Plaza Group also runs a Hair and Beauty Centre and a Oriental Massage Centre.

For smokers, there are two dedicated lounges – one at boarding level, the other on the arrivals level – which are comfortable and equipped with ionizers and fresheners.

Special needs facilities for the physically, visually and hearing impaired are provided in the form of restrooms, telephone access, escalators, elevators, car parks, drinking fountains, wheelchairs, a people mover, no level changes, and tactile guide paths to help find phones, the Airport Express train and Information Centre.

Other facilities at the airport include a Medical Centre at room 6T-052; general and emergency services (2261 2626); nursing rooms with changing and feeding facilities; children play areas; and a Lost and Found Room at 6T-056 (2181 0000).

## By rail

Trains from mainland China arrive at Hung Hom Station in eastern Kowloon. Taxis are available outside the station, otherwise directions to bus services are well marked and the Hung Hom ferry is a ten-minute walk away.

If you wish to travel by train to mainland China (for which you'll need a visa; see p288), tickets can be purchased at Hung Hom Station or in advance from either of the two China Travel Services branches listed below.

### China Travel Services
*1/F, Alpha House, 27-33 Nathan Road, Tsim Sha Tsui, Kowloon (2315 7188). Tsim Sha Tsui MTR (exit C1, E)/buses along Nathan Road/Tsim Sha Tsui Star Ferry Pier.* **Open** *9am-5pm Mon-Fri; 1-6pm Sat; 9am-12.30pm, 2-5pm Sun.* **Map** *p98 C2.*
*G/F, CTS House, 78-83 Connaught Road, Central, HK Island (2853 3888). Sheung Wan MTR (exit E4)/buses along Connaught Road Central.* **Open** *9am-5pm Mon-Sat.* **Map** *p66 C2.*

## By sea

The various ferry services to and from Macau (*see also p264*) dock either at the **Hong Kong–Macau Ferry Terminal** in the Shun Tak Centre, Sheung Wan, Hong Kong Island (map p66 B1) or the **China Ferry Terminal**, China HK City, Canton Road, Tsim Sha Tsui, Kowloon (map p98 A1). The latter is also the arrival point for ferries from China.

At the Hong Kong–Macau Ferry Terminal, taxis are available at exit level, while buses are at street level. Sheung Wan MTR station is just a short walk away.

At the China Ferry Terminal, taxis and buses are available on street level, while both the Star Ferry and MTR are 15 minutes away on foot.

Tickets for the ferries can be purchased at the terminals. Fares vary according to the type of vessel and class. If you wish to travel on a weekend or public holiday, it's advisable to book in advance – and consider buying a return fare.

## By road

Although unlikely, you may arrive in Hong Kong by road from mainland China. There's currently a CTS bus service operating between Guangzhou and Hong Kong, while Citybus routes link the Shenzhen economic zone and Hong Kong.

## Public transport

Hong Kong has a reliable, affordable, clean and safe public transport system that makes use of buses, minibuses, trams, ferries and a metro (Mass Transit Railway or MTR). Because of the compact nature of Hong Kong, you can reach most parts of it within an hour using public transport. That is, as long as you don't get caught in rush hour traffic

**Directory**

(8-10am or 5-7pm) or delayed by an accident or road works. All buses, minibuses and taxis and long haul ferries are air-conditioned.

## Fares & tickets

Visitors who are planning to use public transport frequently over a week or more can buy an '**Octopus**' stored-value smart card. Available from MTR stations, it can be used on virtually all public transport systems. You pay a deposit of HK$50 for the card, which is refunded on its return, and then add as much value to the card as you think you will need – you can always add more value at the machines located in public transport systems or at 7-Eleven stores all over Hong Kong. Place the Octopus card on the machine displayed in the buses, trams, ferries and minibuses to log in the fare. If you reach your destination before the end of the bus route, place the card on the machine again when alighting, so that you're not charged more than necessary.

## Buses

Buses run regularly – and frequently during the rush hour. Bus stops display the bus numbers and routes they serve, as well as the fares. If you don't have an Octopus card (*see above*), make sure you have the exact fare ready, which can vary between HK$2 and HK$15 depending on your destination and the type of bus on which you travel.

Yellow minibuses with red stripes do not always ply fixed routes, and passengers can get on or off anywhere (except in restricted zones). Fares can be much higher than on buses, as they are dictated by the whim of the driver, but usually range from HK$2 to HK$20. The same yellow minibuses, but with green stripes, are called

maxicabs and they travel specific routes with fixed fares. They, too, can be flagged down anywhere and called to a halt near your destination as they have no bus stops. A quick shout (of '*lee doe*') should be enough to alert the driver that you wish to get off the bus.

## Ferries

Ferries sail between Hong Kong Island and Kowloon, and to the outlying islands, Macau and mainland China. The Star Ferry provides services to Central, Wan Chai and North Point on Hong Kong Island, as well as to Tsim Sha Tsui, Hung Hom, the Gold Coast and Discovery Bay on Lantau. A five-minute walk from the Central Star Ferry Pier, services to Lamma, Cheung Chau, Peng Chau and Lantau operate from the Outlying Islands Ferry Piers. In addition, there are inter-island ferries for island hopping, as well as a number of small ferries plying their trade between Aberdeen and the outlying islands.

## MTR (metro)

The **Mass Transit Railway** (**MTR**) is clean, fast and efficient. It runs along the north coast of Hong Kong Island, and travels beneath the harbour to Kowloon, the New Territories and Lantau. Trains run from 6am to 1am, and the maximum fare is HK$26 for an adult single journey. For more information, call 2881 8888.

The network is made up of four interconnected lines: the blue **Island Line** runs along the north side of Hong Kong Island from Sheung Wan in the west to Chai Wan in the east; the red **Tsuen Wan Line** runs from Central, Hong Kong Island under the harbour to Tsuen Wan in the New Territories; the green **Kwun Tong Line** starts at Yau Ma Tei, Kowloon, looping around

to the east and crossing the harbour to terminate at Quarry Bay on Hong Kong Island; the yellow **Tung Chung Line** runs all the way from Central to Tung Chung on Lantau in the west.

## Rail services

Aside from the Airport Express, Hong Kong has two rail systems. The **Kowloon–Canton Railway (KCR) East Rail** runs from Hung Hom in Kowloon to the boundary with mainland China at Lo Wu. All trains, with the exception of the Special Express trains to Guangzhou (*see p279*), terminate there. You need a visa (*see p288*) and special ticket to travel to Lo Wu station and into Shenzhen. KCR trains run every three to ten minutes from 5.30am to 12.20am, and the maximum fare is HK$33. For more information, call 2602 7799.

The **Light Rail (LR)** connects the New Territories towns of Tuen Mun and Yuen Long. It runs from 5.40am to 12.30am daily, with fares from HK$4 to HK$5.80. For more information, call 2468 7788.

## Trams

Double-decker trams run along the north side of Hong Kong Island from Kennedy Town to Chai Wan, with a flat fare of HK$2. Enter the tram at the rear and exit at the front, paying the fare before alighting (trams should soon be able to accept Octopus cards; *see above*). Tram stops are in the middle of the main road, splitting the two-way traffic.

The famous **Peak Tram** (*see p88*), which is over 100 years old, travels to the Peak from Garden Road. It affords a panoramic view of Hong Kong on a clear day and is a thrilling ride up a very steep slope. Adult fares are HK$20 one way, HK$30 round trip.

# Taxis

Taxis are plentiful in major areas and fares are reasonable. You will find red taxis on Hong Kong Island and Kowloon, green in the New Territories and blue on Lantau, but all will go to the airport. Taxis stop at designated areas and hotels, in bays, side lanes and along unmarked roads, but never near a single or double yellow line. Although many taxi drivers do speak some English, it is advisable to have your destination written down in Chinese to avoid confusion.

Fares vary according to the colour of the taxi: the basic flagfall on a red one is HK$15 (and HK$1.40 for every additional 200 metres); on a green one, it is HK$12.50 and on a blue one HK$12 – both adding HK$1.20 for every additional 200 metres). There are extra charges for tunnel tolls, the driver's return toll and luggage placed in the trunk (carry your bags with you to avoid this). Tipping of about HK$5-$10 is optional, but appreciated.

If you want to book a taxi, try **Chan's Motors** (2334 6105) or **City Motors** (2887 2163/2566 8368).

# Cycling

Don't even think about cycling in the car-dominated canyons of Central or Tsim Sha Tsui. In contrast, cycling on the islands or in the New Territories can be immensely enjoyable. For information on cycling, contact the **Hong Kong Cycling Association** (2573 3861) or the Hong Kong Tourism Board (2508 1234).

## Bicycle hire

### Siu Kee Bicycle
*1 Pak She Road, Cheung Chau (2981 1384/www.hongkongbikes.com). Cheung Chau Ferry Pier.* **Rates** HK$10-$15/hour. **No credit cards**.

# Driving

Road congestion and pollution are major problems in Hong Kong. This, combined with the relatively cheap, efficient and extensive public transport system, all but eliminates any incentive to drive. If you do, however, hire a car, the following information will be of use to you:

• vehicles drive on the right side of the road
• signs are in Chinese/English
• stopping by a double or single yellow line is illegal except in side lanes, bays or at designated areas and times
• the use of seat belts in cars and taxis is mandatory
• the speed limit is 80kmph (50mph), unless otherwise indicated
• 50 milligrams of alcohol per 100ml of blood warrants prosecution for drunk driving
• the use of mobile phones is not allowed while driving
• an international driving licence is required by visitors.

## Breakdown services

### HK Automobile Association
*2304 4911/insurance: 2739 5273.*

## Fuel stations

### Mobil Oil
*1 Lockhart Road, Wan Chai, HK Island (2865 3563).* **Open** 24 hours. **Credit** AmEx, DC, MC, V. **Map** p80 A2.

## Insurance

Third party insurance is compulsory by law.

## Parking

Parking is available on some streets with meters for 30 minutes or two hours. Cards for meters can be bought at 7-Eleven stores and post offices. Meters operate from 8am to midnight. Parking is expensive

in malls and office buildings, but some restaurants and hotels offer complimentary valet parking.

On Hong Kong Island, there are car parks in Central at the Star Ferry Pier, Murray Car Park, Rumsey Street and City Hall; in Causeway Bay in the basement of a number of department stores; and in Tsim Sha Tsui at Ocean Terminal and Middle Road (behind the Sheraton Hotel). Charges are HK$20-$25 per hour. Minimum stay is two hours.

## Vehicle hire

### Toplink
*Flat F, 20/F, 23 Greig Crescent, Quarry Bay, HK Island (2880 0616).* **Rates** HK$230/hour, for a minimum three hour limousine hire in the city, four fours in the New Territories (excluding tunnel tolls and petrol). **No credit cards**.

### Avis
*Bright Star Mansions, 85-91 Leighton Road, Causeway Bay, HK Island (International rentals 2890 6988/www.avis.com).* **Rates** (for a Toyota Corolla) HK$720/day; HK$2,200/week. **Credit** AmEx, DC, MC, V. **Map** p80 D2.

# Walking

There are plenty of hazards to walking on the built-up north side of Hong Kong Island and Kowloon. The primacy of the car means that an often baffling series of walkways is the only way to traverse the fume-choked major roads. Additionally, as soon as you've walked a few minutes inland in Central or Wan Chai, you'll find the ground starting to slope steeply upwards, so a good pair of lungs and stout footwear are recommended.

In contrast, walking in the New Territories and on the outer islands is one of Hong Kong's little known delights (*see chapter* **Wild Hong Kong**).

# Resources A-Z

## Addresses

Written in standard style: name, apartment/house number, name of building, road/street and area. There is no post/zip code. Taxi drivers know most addresses, but you'd be wise to get hotels to write them in Chinese, just in case.

You'll also find the relevant floor of the building an intrinsic part of most Hong Kong addresses. G/F (ground floor) is the floor at street level; 1/F (1st floor) is the next one up, etc. Variations you might see include G-29, which will be room 29 on the ground floor, and 702, being flat number 2 on the 7th floor.

## Age

Drinking, driving, sex and smoking are restricted to those aged 18 and over.

## Attitude & etiquette

Hong Kong Chinese are used to having foreigners around and are non-intrusive. They are sometimes perceived as being abrupt and rude, but it is only a manner, nothing personal. Hong Kong is a cosmopolitan city, but Chinese etiquette presides. Respect for local customs and beliefs, particularly the importance of family is evident.

Surnames are written first. Elders and men are introduced first. If you want to give a gift, chocolates and money are suitable, but not clocks or watches.

As in China, keeping face is of paramount concern – to such a degree that it can sometimes seem quite traumatic for a Hong Kong citizen to admit to common errors. If you cause someone to lose face, you, too, will be perceived negatively. Losing your temper in front of others is seen as loss of face for you and others. *See chapter* **HK Culture & Customs**.

## Business

Business cards are usually written in English on one side, and Chinese on the other. Many hotels will print them within 24 hours. They should be presented with both hands to a Chinese person, and received similarly, and you should take care to read them.

Business meetings and entertainment engagements require suits. Wait for the host to initiate drinking any beverage on offer. No business is conducted during Chinese New Year (*see p208*).

## Business centres & office hire

### Harbour International Business Centre

*Room 2802, Tower 1, Admiralty Centre, 18 Harcourt Road, Central, HK Island (2529 0356). Admiralty MTR (exit A)/buses along Harcourt Road.* **Map** *p67 F4.*
Harbour International offers secretarial help and office rentals.

### Plaza Business Centre

*35/F, Central Plaza, 18 Harbour Road, Wan Chai, HK Island (2593 1111). Wan Chai MTR (exit A1)/buses along Gloucester Road & Harbour Road.* **Map** *p80 B2.*
Plaza has 35 fully serviced executive office suites and offers a full range of secretarial services.

## Conventions & conferences

International conventions, conferences and exhibitions are always being held in the Hong Kong Convention & Exhibition Centre. Bookings are accepted years in advance.

### Hong Kong Convention & Exhibition Centre

*1 Expo Drive, Wan Chai, HK Island (general 2582 8888/ info 2582 1818/sales 2582 7919/ www.hkcec.com.hk). Wan Chai MTR (exit A1)/25A, 25C, 961 bus.* **Map** *p80 B1.*

## Couriers & shippers

### DHL

*Central MTR station (exit F) (2877 2848).* **Map** *p67 D3.*
*Tsim Sha Tsui MTR (exit D1/D2), (2722 0501).* **Map** *p98 C2.*
*Head Office, 11/F, Trade Square, 681 Cheung Sha Wan Road, Kowloon (2765 8111).*

### Dyna Trans

*5/F, 152 Queen's Road, Central, HK Island (2851 6120). Sheung Wan MTR (exit A2, E2)/buses along Queen's Road Central.* **Map** *p66 B1.*

### Federal Express

*Shop 43, 1/F Shopping Arcade, Admiralty Centre, Queensway, Central, HK Island (2730 3333). Admiralty MTR (exit C1)/ buses through Central.* **Map** *p67 F4.*

### Jupiter Air

*Suite 1701, Tower 1, China HK City Building, 33 Canton Road, Tsim Sha Tsui, Kowloon (2735 1946/47). Tsim Sha Tsui MTR (exit A1)/buses along Canton Road/ Tsim Sha Tsui Star Ferry Pier.* **Map** *p98 A1.*

## Translators & interpreters

### Language Line

*Flat 1B, 163 Hennessy Road, Wan Chai, HK Island (2511 2677). Wan Chai MTR (exit A2, A4)/ buses along Hennessy Road.* **Map** *p80 B2.*
Language Line can deal with European/Asian translation.

### Polyglot

*Flat 14B, Times Centre, 53 Hollywood Road, Central, HK Island (2851 7232). Central MTR (exit D1, D2)/Mid-Levels Escalator/ 12M, 13, 23A, 26, 40M, 43 bus.* **Map** *p66 C3.*
Polyglot offers a wide range of translation services.

## Useful organisations

### American Chamber of Commerce
*Room 1904, Bank of America Tower, 12 Harcourt Road, Central, HK Island (2526 0165/amcham@amcham.org.hk).* Map p67 F4.

### Australian Chamber of Commerce
*4/F, Lucky Building, 39 Wellington Street, Central, HK Island (2522 5054/austcham@hk.astanet.net.hk).* Map p66 C3.

### British Chamber of Commerce
*Room 1201, Emperor Group Centre, 288 Hennessy Road, Wan Chai, HK Island (2824 2211/bcc@britcham.com).* Map p80 C2.

### Canadian Chamber of Commerce
*Suite 1003, Kinwick Centre, 32 Hollywood Road, Central, HK Island (2110 8700/canada@cancham.org).* Map p66 C4.

### Chinese General Chamber of Commerce
*4/F, 24-25 Connaught Road, Central, HK Island (2525 6385/cgcc@cgcc.org.hk).* Map p67 D3.

### HK General Chamber of Commerce
*22/F, United Centre, 95 Queensway, Admiralty, HK Island (2529 9229/aihkgcc@attglobal.net).* Map p67 F5.

### HK Stock Exchange
*Exchange Square, Central, HK Island (2524 6452).* Map p67 D3.

### HK Trade Development Council
*36/F, Office Tower, Convention Plaza, 1 Harbour Road, Wan Chai, HK Island (2584 4333/fax 2824 0249/www.tdc.org/hktdc@tdc.org).* Map p80 B1.
The HK Trade Development Council advises business newcomers on all aspects of doing business in the SAR.

### Japanese Chamber of Commerce
*38/F, West Wing, Hennessy Centre, 500 Hennessy Road, Causeway Bay, HK Island (2577 6129).* Map p80 D2.

## Consumer

The Consumer Council in Hong Kong is an independent public organisation that protects the rights and interests of consumers, tests products in the market to establish the claims made by manufacturers and retailers, and publishes a journal with the results of its findings. Visitors and residents alike can call the hotline number listed below for help with any shopping problems – there are also a number of Advice Centres dotted all over the city.

### Consumer Council Hotline
*Head office: 22/F, K Wah Centre, 191 Java Road, North Point, HK Island (2929 2222).* **Open** *phone* 9am-5pm Mon-Fri; 9am-noon Sat.

### Central & Western Consumer Advice Centre
*G/F, Harbour Building, 38 Pier Road, Central, HK Island (2921 6228). Sheung Wan MTR (exit E4)/buses along Connaught Road Central.* **Open** phone for details. Map p67 C4.

### Tsim Sha Tsui Consumer Advice Centre
*Room 126, 1/F, Tung Ying Building, 100 Nathan Road, Kowloon (2926 1088). Tsim Sha Tsui MTR (exit B1)/buses along Nathan Road.* **Open** phone for details. Map p98 C1.

## Customs

At the time of going to press, visitors were allowed to bring the following items into Hong Kong duty free:

• 200 cigarettes or 50 cigars or 250 grams of tobacco
• one litre bottle of wine or spirits.

A doctor's prescription is essential if you are bringing in personal medication in any quantity. Bottles of perfume must be for personal use only.

The following may not be imported into Hong Kong:

• animals, plants or soil
• firearms/weapons (must be declared and handed into custody until departure)
• narcotics.

The following must be declared and duty paid:

• trade or import goods
• any amount of alcohol, cigarettes, tobacco or cigars in excess of duty free allowances
• perfume/cosmetics
• cars.

## Disabled

The Hong Kong government is aware of the need to improve accessibility for people with mobility and sensory disabilities. Space being precious, every inch is utilised, so shops, offices, restaurants, theatres and malls are located on every level of a building accessible by elevator, escalator or stairs.

HKTB's free brochure *HK Access Guide For Disabled Visitors* gives information on how to read signs for getting around and who to call for assistance. Call the places you wish to visit ahead of time to determine accessibility, such as ramps, turning space, door and corridor clearance, and inquire about parking, seating, telephones, fitting rooms, toilets and other facilities. Generally, bus and taxi drivers are helpful.

If you feel you are being denied access, complain to:

### Equal Opportunities Commission
*Room 2002, 20/F, Office Tower, Convention Plaza, 1 Harbour Road, Wan Chai, HK Island (2511 8211).*

## Drugs

Drugs like heroin and ecstasy (and also, strangely, the horse tranquiliser ketamine) are a big problem among young people in Hong Kong, as teenage children are vulnerable to triad drug pushers. As a result, the police patrol areas where there are big parties and schools do random drugs testing. Expatriates caught with drugs have to leave the territory or could face imprisonment.

### Narcotics Bureau Hotline

*2860 2888.* **Open** *phone 24 hours daily.*

### Anti-Drug Abuse Line

*2366 8822.* **Open** *phone varies.*

## Electricity

The voltage in Hong Kong is 220 volts 50 cycles. Most hotels provide adaptors, or you can buy one from an electrical shop for about HK$18-$25.

## Embassies & consulates

### Australian Consulate

*21F-24F, Harbour Centre, 25 Harbour Road, Wan Chai, HK Island (2827 8881/fax 2585 4457/ webmaster@australia.org.hk). Wan Chai MTR (exit A1)/buses along Gloucester Road.* **Open** *8.45am-5pm Mon-Fri; immigration 9.30am-1.30pm Mon-Fri.* **Map** *p80 B1.*

### British Consulate & Trade Commission

*1 Supreme Court Road, Central, HK Island (2901 3000/fax 2901 3066/ information@britishconsulate.org.hk). Admiralty MTR (exit C1)/buses along Queensway.* **Open** *8.45am-noon, 2-4.30pm Mon-Fri.* **Map** *p67 F5.*

### Canadian Consulate

*11F-14F, One Exchange Square, 8 Connaught Place, Central, HK Island (2847 7555/fax 2847 7493/ www.canada.org.hk). Central MTR (exit A)/buses along Connaught Road Central.* **Open** *8.30am-5pm Mon-Fri; immigration 8-11.30am Tue, Thur, Fri.* **Map** *p67 D3.*

### Irish Consulate

*6/F, Chung Nam Building, 1 Lockhart Road, Wan Chai, HK Island (2527 4895/fax 2520 1833). Wan Chai MTR (exit C)/buses along Hennessy Road.* **Open** *10am-noon, 2-4.30pm Mon-Fri.* **Map** *p80 A2.*

### New Zealand Consulate

*Room 6501, Central Plaza, 18 Harbour Road, Wan Chai, HK Island (2525 5044/fax 2845 2915/*

*nzcghk@netvigator.com). Wan Chai MTR (exit A1)/buses along Gloucester Road/Wan Chai Star Ferry Pier.* **Open** *8am-1pm, 2-5pm Mon-Fri; immigration 9am-1pm, 1.30-3pm Mon-Fri.* **Map** *p80 B2.*

### US Consulate General

*26 Garden Road, Central, HK Island (2841 2219/fax 2147 5790/ www.usconsulate.org.hk). Buses along Garden Road.* **Open** *8.30am-12.30pm, 1.30-5.30pm Mon-Fri.* **Map** *p67 E5.*

## Visas for China

### China Visa Section

*5/F, China Resources Building, 26 Harbour Road, Wan Chai, HK Island (2585 1794). Wan Chai MTR (exit A1)/buses along Gloucester Road.* **Open** *8.30am-4.30pm Mon-Fri; 8.30am-12.30pm Sat.* **Map** *p80 B1.* You can apply in person for a visa for travel to mainland China at this office (it should take about a week), although it is much simpler and quicker (and sometimes even cheaper) to ask a travel agent to arrange it for you. Try **HYFCO**, which has branches all over Hong Kong, including Room 1909, Lane Crawford House, 70 Queen's Road, Central (2526 5305) and Shop B3, Basement, Starhouse Plaza, 3 Salisbury Road, Tsim Sha Tsui, Kowloon (2730 8608). *See also p278.*

## Emergencies

### General emergencies

*999.*

### Free ambulance service

*2576 6555.* For non-emergencies.

### 24-hour crime hotline

*2527 7177.* For lost passports, credit cards and complaints against taxis.

### Complaints against the police

*2574 4220.*

## Gay & lesbian

*See chapter* **Gay & Lesbian**.

## Health

Ensure that you have adequate personal medical insurance prior to travelling to Hong Kong.

Vaccinations against typhoid, influenza, Hepatitis A and B are precautionary. Routine polio, tetanus, mumps, measles and diptheria updates are recommended. Check with your doctor about immunisation prior to travelling.

For further information, take a look at the website www.healthinasia.com.

## Accident & emergency

For the **Hospital Authority One Stop Enquiry Service**, phone **2300 6555**.

A full range of accident/ emergency medical services are provided 24 hours a day at the following places:

### Caritas Medical Centre

*111 Wing Hong Street, Sham Shui Po, Kowloon (2746 7911). Lai Chi Kok MTR (exit B1)/buses along Castle Peak Road.*

### Prince of Wales Hospital

*30-32 Ngan Shing Street, Sha Tin, New Territories (2623 2211). Bus A41, 73A, 80K, 85A.*

### Queen Mary Hospital

*102 Pok Fu Lam Road, Pok Fu Lam, HK Island (2855 3838). Buses along Pok Fu Lam Road.*

### St John Hospital

*Cheung Chau Hospital Road, Tung Wan, Cheung Chau (2981 0378). Cheung Chau Ferry Pier.*

## Complementary medicine

### Natural Health Association of HK

*GPO 8268, Hong Kong (http:// members.xoom.com/natureheal).* Contact the Natural Health Association for general information and details of local practitioners.

### The New Age Shop

*G/F, Old Bailey Street, Central, HK Island (2810 8694). Central MTR (exit D1)/buses along Hollywood Road & Caine Road.* **Open** *11am-7pm; 10am-6pm Sat; 1pm-6pm Sun.* **Credit** *AmEx, MC, V.* **Map** *p66 C4.*

# Key phone numbers

**Police, fire, ambulance**
999 (free)
**24-hour crime hotline**
2527 7177 (for theft
of passports, credit
cards, etc)
**Free ambulance** (St John's)
2576 6555 (HK Island);
2713 5555 (Kowloon);
2639 2555
(New Territories)

**Directory enquiries**
(local) 1081
**Directory enquiries**
(international) 10013
**Collect telephone calls**
10010
**Community Advice Bureau**
2815 5444
(advice in English on any
aspect of living in or visiting
Hong Kong).

## Optimum Health Centre Alexander Yuan
*2/F, Prosperous Commercial Building, Jardine's Bazaar, Causeway Bay, HK Island (2577 3798). Causeway Bay MTR (exit F)/buses along Hennessy Road.* **Open** 9am-7pm Mon-Fri; 9am-4pm Sat. **Map** p80 D2.
Homeopathy and naturopathy.

## Stuart Bradshaw Health Consultancy
*Room 1204, Luk Yu Building, 24-26 Stanley Street, Central, HK Island (2523 7121). Central MTR (exit D1, D2, G)/buses along Queen's Road Central.* **Open** 9am-6pm Mon-Fri; 9am-1pm Sat. **Map** p66 C3.
Homeopathy and naturopathy.

## Contraception & abortion
For advice, call the **Family Planning Association** (Kowloon: 2711 9271; Wan Chai: 2575 4477).

## Dentists

### Dr Eric Carter
*Room 1103, Century Square, 1-13 D'Aguilar Street, Central, HK Island (2525 4285). Central MTR (exit D1, G)/12M, 13, 23A, 40M, 43 bus.* **Map** p66 C4.

### Dr James Woo & Associates
*Room 1631A, Star House, 3 Salisbury Road, Tsim Sha Tsui, Kowloon (2735 6008). Tsim Sha Tsui MTR (exit E)/buses to Tsim Sha Tsui Star Ferry Pier & along Salisbury Road/Tsim Sha Tsui Star Ferry Pier.* **Map** p98 B3.

## Doctors
There are travel clinics at the Adventist and Matilda hospitals; *see below.*

### Dr Nicholson & Partners
*Room 402, New World Tower, 18 Queen's Road, Central, HK Island (2525 1251). Central MTR (exit D1, D2, G)/buses along Queen's Road Central.* **Map** p67 D4.

### Dr Orum & Partners
*Room 1003, Bank of America Tower, 12 Harcourt Road, Central, HK Island (2525 1730). Central MTR (exit J3)/buses to Central Star Ferry Pier/Central Star Ferry Pier.* **Map** p67 F4.

## Hospitals
For hospitals with 24-hour accident and emergency wards, *see p288.*

Good quality medical care is widely available, thanks to a large number of foreign-qualified local and expatriate practitioners. The private hospitals listed below have English-speaking staff. Facilities include dental and maternity clinics, travel clinics for advice on immunisations, healthcare for women, Well-Woman Clinics, related information and courses for health maintenance. All operate outpatient departments at the following (approximate) times: 8.30am-4pm Mon-Fri; 8.30am-12.30pm Sat.

## Adventist Hospital
*40 Stubbs Road, Happy Valley, HK Island (2835 0566/2574 6211/www.hkah.org.hk). Bus 6, 15, 15B, 61, 66, 76.* **Map** p80 C3.

## Baptist Hospital
*222 Waterloo Road, Kowloon (2337 4141). Kowloon Tong MTR/KCR/buses along Waterloo Road & Cornwall Street.*

## Canossa Hospital
*1 Old Peak Road, Mid-Levels, HK Island (2522 2181). Bus 3B, 12, 12M, 23, 23A, 40.* **Map** p66 C5.

## Matilda Hospital
*41 Mount Kellett Road, The Peak, HK Island (2849 0111). Bus 15, 15B/hospital shuttle from City Hall every 20 mins.*

## Opticians
*See p199.*

## Pharmacies
Over the counter medicines for colds, headaches, fever and minor ailments are available in pharmacies, such as the Mannings and Watson's chains (*see p199*), located in malls and most shopping areas.

Doctor's clinics are licensed to sell prescription drugs, but if you do go to a pharmacy, be aware that only prescriptions from Hong Kong-based doctors will be accepted. Shops with dispensaries display a red-cross sign.

The Adventist (*see above*) and Queen Mary hospitals (*see p288*) have pharmacies that are open 24 hours a day; those in other hospitals are usually open between 10am and 6pm daily.

## STDs, HIV & AIDS

### AIDS Counselling Service
*2780 2211, then press 2.* **Open** 24hrs daily.

### HIV Education Centre
*2501 0653.* **Open** *phone varies.*

**Directory**

## Women's health

There are Well-Woman Clinics located within the **Adventist** (2574 6211) and **Matilda** (2849 0373) hospitals; see p289.

## Helplines

The following helplines are all manned by English-speaking operators. For the **AIDS Counselling Service**, see p289.

### Alcoholics Anonymous

2522 5665. **Open** phone 6-7pm daily.
There is a weekly Alcoholics Anonymous meeting at 6-7pm, at G/F, 12 Borrett Road, HK Island.

### Community Advice Bureau

2815 5444. **Open** phone 10am-4pm daily.
This excellent organisation can offer advice on any aspect of Hong Kong, both for residents and for visitors.

### Kely Support Group

2521 6890/9032 9055/9032 9096. **Open** phone 2-10pm daily.
Kely Support Group offers counselling for young people.

### Rape Crisis/Shelter

2572 2733, then press 3. **Open** phone 24hrs daily.

### St John's Ambulance

2576 6555 (HK Island); 2713 5555 (Kowloon); 2639 2555 (New Terrs). **Open** phone 9am-12.45pm Mon-Fri; 9am-noon Sat.

### The Samaritans

2896 0000. **Open** phone 24hrs daily.

### SER Foundation Drug Rehabilitation

2988 1771. **Open** phone 9am-11pm daily.

## ID

Visitors are officially 'advised' to carry their passport or other photo ID with them at all times while staying in Hong Kong. The police sometimes do random street checks and if found without any ID, then you are liable for a fine.

## Insurance

Make sure you have adequate travel and health insurance prior to arrival in Hong Kong, as the territory has no reciprocal arrangements with other countries.

## Internet

The number of cybercafés in Hong Kong is steadily increasing (although there aren't as many as might be expected in a city that has embraced technology – in the form of mobile telephony – so wholeheartedly), and terminals can also be found in cafés, beauticians and barber shops. The HKTB (see p296) offers free Internet access at the airport and at its various centres. Many hotels provide Internet access in their business centres (at a charge) and some allow access from their rooms.

## Internet access

### Arts Library of Hong Kong

Podium Level, Administration Building, Hong Kong Cultural Centre, 10 Salisbury Road, Tsim Sha Tsui, Kowloon (2734 2042). Tsim Sha Tsui MTR (exit E)/buses along Salisbury Road/Tsim Sha Tsui Star Ferry Pier. **Open** 10am-7pm Mon-Thur; 10am-9pm Fri; 10am-5pm Sat, Sun. **Rates** free for one hour; call ahead to make a reservation. **Map** p98 B3.

### Kublai's Cyber Diner

3/F, One Capital Place, 18 Luard Road, Wan Chai, HK Island (2529 9117). Wan Chai MTR (exit B2)/buses along Hennessy Road. **Open** phone for details. **Rates** use of the two terminals is free for diners; HK$48 per half hour including one drink for non-diners. **No credit cards**. **Map** p80 B2.

### Pacific Coffee Company

Shop 1022, Level 1, Southern Retail Podium, International Finance Centre, Harbour View Street, Central, HK Island

(2868 5100). Central MTR (exit A)/buses through Central. **Open** phone for details. **Rates** free. **Map** p67 D3.

Shop 404, Queensway Plaza, Queensway, Admiralty, HK Island (2861 2302). Admiralty MTR (exit C1)/buses through Central. **Open** phone for details. **Rates** free. **Map** p67 F5.

3/F, City Super, Gateway, Canton Road, Tsim Sha Tsui, Kowloon (2117 0950). Tsim Sha Tsui MTR (exit A1)/Tsim Sha Tsui Star Ferry Pier. **Open** phone for details. **Rates** free. **Map** p98 B2.
This coffee shop chain offers access in some of its locations, free of charge and for an unlimited time period (as long as there are no queues).

### Shadowman Cyber Café

Karlock Building, 7 Lock Road, Tsim Sha Tsui, Kowloon (2366 5262/www.shadowman.com.hk). Tsim Sha Tsui MTR (exit C1, E)/buses along Nathan Road/Tsim Sha Tsui Star Ferry Pier. **Open** 7.30am-11pm daily. **Rates** 1st 20mins free with the purchase of a drink or food, HK$10 per 15mins thereafter. **No credit cards**. **Map** p98 B2.

### Xyberia Interactive

China Bear, Mui Wo Centre, 3 Ngan Wan Road, Mui Wo, Lantau (2984 7618). Mui Wo Ferry Pier. **Open** phone for details. **Rates** HK$40/hour. **No credit cards**. **Map** p126.

## Language

English and Cantonese are the official languages (see p298 **The Language**), but moving away from business, shopping and expat-frequented areas, English is less widely spoken. If you want to go anywhere off the beaten track, ask your hotel concierge to write out the destination in Chinese.

## Left luggage

There are no left luggage facilities in any of the public transport terminals – except at the airport.

### Airport

Meeters & Greeters Hall (2868 3190). **Open** 6am-1am **Rates** HK$35/piece up to 3 hours; $50/piece per day.

## Legal help

For help in finding a lawyer and basic information on Hong Kong law, call 2521 3333/2522 8018.

## Libraries

The **Urban Council** runs a network of libraries with a good selection of books, newspapers, magazines, videos, cassettes, records, slides and microfilm – the largest UC library is listed below.

### Urban Council Library
*City Hall Public Library, 2-5/F & 8-11/F, City Hall High Block, Central, HK Island (2879 5565/ www.uc.gov.hk/ucpl).* **Open** 10am-7pm Mon-Fri. **Map** p67 E3.

### Alliance Française
*123 Hennessy Road, Wan Chai, HK Island (2527 7825). Wan Chai MTR (exit B1)/buses along Hennessy Road.* **Open** 9am-9pm Mon-Fri. **Map** p80 B2.

*52 Jordan Road, Jordan, Kowloon (2730 3257). Jordan MTR (Exit A)/buses along Nathan Road.* **Open** 9am-9pm Mon-Fri. **Map** p110 A5. French music CDs, DVDs, magazines and books.

### British Council Library
*1 Supreme Court Road, Central, HK Island (2901 3000). Admiralty MTR (exit C1)/buses along Queensway.* **Open** noon-8pm Mon-Fri; 10.30am-5.30pm Sat. **Map** p67 F5. Located in the same building as the British Consulate, it stocks books, magazines, DVDs and videos.

### Goethe Institute
*14/F, Hong Kong Arts Centre, 2 Harbour Road, Wan Chai, HK Island (2802 0088). Wan Chai MTR (exit A1)/buses along Gloucester Road.* **Open** phone for details. **Map** p80 B1. The place to come for German books and audiovisual materials.

### US Foreign Commercial Service
*21/F, St John's Building, 33 Garden Road, Central, HK Island (2521 1467). Buses along Garden Road.* **Open** by appointment only 9am-noon, 2-5pm Mon-Wed; 9am-noon Thur, Fri. **Map** p67 E5. Stocks reference material on Hong Kong as a market place, a directory of US companies and US trade publications.

## Lost property

Call **2860 2000** if you lose anything in the city and you'll be told which police station to contact to retrieve your property if it's been found.

## Airport
*See p282.*

## Buses
**Citybus** *2873 0818.*
**Kowloon Motor Bus (KMB)** *2745 4466.*
**New World First Bus** *2136 8888.*

## Ferries
**Discovery Bay Ferries** *2987 7351.*
**New World Outlying Islands Ferries** *2131 8181.*
**Star Ferry** *2366 2576.*

## Taxis
**HK taxis** *2574 7311.*
**Kowloon taxis** *2760 0411.*

## Trains
**MTR** *Admiralty Station (hotline 2881 8888).* **Open** phone 7.30am-10.30pm daily. **Map** p67 F4.
**KCR** *2602 7799.*
**LR** (within the New Territories) *2468 7788.*

## Trams
**HK Tramways** *2548 7102.*
**Peak Tramways** *2522 0922.*

## Media

### Newspapers

Since the Handover, Hong Kong's freedom of speech has been closely monitored – and generally hasn't suffered as badly as expected from Beijing's influence. However, self-censorship is becoming increasingly and worryingly widespread as some publications' owners tread carefully to protect their Chinese interests.

Of the two main English speaking newspapers, the *South China Morning Post* (www.scmp.com) boasts the biggest circulation and wields the heaviest clout. Known as a pro-China paper, it usually toes the Beijing line, while the *Hong Kong iMail* (www.hk-imail.com), formerly the *HK Standard*, is generally considered to be closer to being the voice of the people. The tabloid style *iMail* with its big, bold and brash whole front-page pictures and screaming headlines certainly give Kongers a visually punchy wake up call.

The Chinese language newspapers – three of the most popular are *Apple Daily*, *Oriental Daily News* and *Sing Tao Daily* – go a step further in their efforts to shock Hong Kongers awake. Sensationalist pictures full of blood and guts are spread across the front page on a daily basis. If there is any sex and violence to be had, the Chinese paparazzi are on the scene snapping away before the blood has stopped trickling along the pavement.

### Magazines

As you'd expect from the financial hub of Asia, there are piles of locally-based magazines reporting on business and finance, including the *Far Eastern Economic Review, Time Asia, Asiaweek* and the *Asian Wall Street Journal*.

Society magazines *HK Tatler* and *B International* are full of pictures of glossy *tai-tais* attending glossy launches of even glossier international fashion gurus. *Home Journal* takes a peek at their multimillion dollar residences on the Peak, and *Talkies* spreads the latest local and international gossip. There are literally hundreds of Chinese publications, some with

'You've just got to buy me, even though you can't read me' titles like *Cheez!* and *Amoeba*.

*HK Magazine* has its weekly finger on the pulse of the Hong Kong entertainment world, including info on film, art, clubbing, bars and restaurants, as well as illuminating articles on life in the SAR. *BC Magazine* is bi-monthly and does roughly the same thing, but in a smaller, glossier package. Both can be picked up for free in bars, restaurants and shops around town.

Major international magazines are available, too – at a huge mark-up.

## Radio

**Radio Television Hong Kong (RTHK)**, once government-run, is now publicly funded and editorially independent. Despite being attacked by a pro-China big cheese, it still continues to criticise the government and airs public opinions without restraint on its talkback programmes. **RTHK3** (567AM, 1584AM) is the main English programme provider of news, finance and current affairs. **RTHK4** (97.6-98.9FM) plays Western and Chinese classical music. **RTHK6** (675AM) broadcasts BBC World Service. **Metro Plus** (1044AM) is a local station with news and music.

## TV

If you believed the terrestrial channels of **ATV World** and **TVB Pearl**, the English-speaking population of Hong Kong is almost exclusively interested in programmes on nature, cooking and horse racing – oh, and lengthy commercials advertising Miracle Foot Repair. Luckily, **Star TV**, Hong Kong's satellite TV station, and **Cable TV** step in to provide some badly needed entertainment.

## Money

The **Hong Kong dollar** is pegged to the US dollar. At the time of going to press, £1 = HK$11.2, US$1 = HK$7.8, AUS$1 = HK$4, 1 Euro = HK$7.

Hong Kong dollar notes come in denominations of 1,000, 500, 100, 50, 20 and 10, while coins come in 10, 5, 2 and 1 dollar and 50, 20 and 10 cent pieces.

There is no central mint. Bank notes are issued by the HSBC, Bank of China and Standard Chartered Bank, and are interchangeable. Most banks have automated teller machines (ATMs) and offer a wide range of services, including telephone banking.

Exchange bureaus and banks charge a fee (enquire as to what it is before you make a transaction) for changing money and cashing traveller's cheques – unless you take the latter to the issuing bank.

## ATMs

There are ATMs on virtually every street corner in Hong Kong. Some of the most conveniently located are at the airport, the Star Ferry terminals and in the MTR stations.

## Bureaux de change

Foreign exchange facilities are plentiful, though the best rates are usually offered by the banks.

## Credit cards

Credit cards are widely accepted in the city (though, unsurprisingly, hardly at all in rural areas). Most large shops, department stores, restaurants, travel agents and hotels take all the major cards.

## Lost/stolen credit cards

**American Express** *2811 6122.*
**Diners Club** *2860 1888.*
**MasterCard** *2511 6387.*
**Visa** *2810 8033.*

## Natural hazards

Hong Kong's subtropical climate is at its most oppressive during the summer (*see p297*). July to September is typhoon season, and two forms of storm signals are used to indicate the severity of the rain and wind. Although they are given out on TV and radio channels, you can also call 2835 1473 for cyclone information.

An **amber** rainstorm warning means that in excess of 30 millimetres (1.2 inches) of rain in an hour is expected; a **red** warning is for 50 millimetres (1.9 inches) of rain and over; while a **black** rain signal warns of rainfall in excess of 70 millimetres (2.8 inches) in an hour. If the latter comes into effect, you can expect roads to become flooded, landslides to take place and public facilities to be closed down.

**Typhoon Signal 1** indicates that a tropical cyclone is within 800 kilometres (500 miles) of the city; **Typhoon Signal 3** means that winds of up to 62 kilometres per hour (39 miles per hour) are expected across Hong Kong; **Typhoon Signal 8** is serious news, with storm-force winds of up to 117 kilometres per hour (73 miles per hour) and gusts of up to 180 kilometres per hour (112 miles per hour); **Typhoon Signal 9** means that the winds are increasing further; **Typhoon Signal 10** is as bad as it gets – a 'direct hit' hurricane is on its way with winds higher than 117 kilometres per hour (73 miles per hour) and destructive gusts

**Directory**

as fierce as 220 kilometres per hour (137 miles per hour). From Signal 8 upwards, you should stay indoors – most of Hong Kong's buildings can withstand such winds, but there's a serious danger of being hit by flying debris and street signs. However, only about 12 maximum severity typhoons have hit Hong Kong in the last 50 years.

There are no flies, but some mosquitoes, which may leave you itching in parks and green areas during the summer months. As a deterrent, repellent is recommended, but if you do get bitten, try locally made Tiger Balm (available in all drugstores) to calm the itching. For suggested vaccinations and health precautions, *see p288*.

## Opening hours

Generally, office hours are 9am to 6pm Monday to Friday (with lunch usually at 1pm to 2pm) and 9am to 1pm on Saturday.

Major banks, however, are open 9am to 4.30pm Monday to Friday and 9am to 12.30pm Saturday.

Government departments are open from 9.30am to 5pm Monday to Friday and 9.30am to noon Saturday.

Most shops open 10.30am to 6.30pm every day. However, in major shopping areas like Causeway Bay and Nathan Road, Kowloon, shopping goes on until 9pm or later at the weekends. During Chinese New Year (*see p208*), everything shuts down for around three days.

Opening hours vary for bars and restaurants, depending on their location and the type of restaurant, but happy hours tend to be 5pm to 8pm.

## Police

The Hong Kong police are still largely run and staffed as they were under the British, and are proud of their reputation as one of Asia's best forces.

Officers wear an olive uniform in summer and a dark blue one in winter. English-speaking policemen wear a red strip under their shoulder badge. Organised Crime and Triad Hotline: 2527 7887.

### Police stations

**Hong Kong HQ** *Arsenal Street, Wan Chai, HK Island (2860 2000). Wan Chai MTR (exit B1)/buses along Hennessy Road.* **Map** p80 A1.

*Hollywood Road, Central, HK Island (2841 6311). Central MTR (exit D1, D2, G)/Mid-Levels Escalator/12M, 13, 23A, 26, 40M, 43 bus.* **Map** p66 C3.

**Kowloon HQ** *190 Argyle Street, Mong Kok, Kowloon (2761 2228). Mong Kok MTR/buses along Nathan Road & Argyle Street.* **Map** p110 B2.

## Postal services

The Hong Kong postal service (www.hongkongpost.com) is generally reliable and efficient.

Airmail letters/postcards to Zone 1 countries (all parts of Asia except Japan) cost HK$2.50 for 20 grams (0.7oz) or less – delivery time is three to five days; to Zone 2 (all other countries) cost HK$3.10 for 20 grams or less – delivery time is five to seven days. Local mail costs HK$1.30 – delivery time is one to two days. International (Speedpost) and local courier services are also available.

## Post offices

### General Post Office

*2 Connaught Place, Central, HK Island (2921 2222). Central MTR (exit A)/buses along Connaught Road Central/Central Star Ferry Pier.* **Open** 8am-6pm Mon-Sat; 8am-2pm Sun. **Credit** (minimum HK$300) AmEx, DC, MC, V . **Map** p67 E3.

### Post Office

*10 Middle Road, Tsim Sha Tsui, Kowloon (2366 4111). Tsim Sha Tsui MTR (exit E)/buses along Nathan Road/Tsim Sha Tsui Star Ferry Pier.* **Open** 8am-6pm Mon-Sat; 8am-2pm Sun. **Credit** (minimum HK$300) AmEx, DC, MC, V. **Map** p98 C3.

## Poste restante

The poste restante service operates out of the General Post Office (*see above*) by the Star Ferry Pier in Central. You can collect poste restante mail from 8am until 6pm Monday to Saturday; don't forget to take your passport with you.

## Public holidays

New Year's Day (1 Jan); Chinese Lunar New Year (three days Jan/Feb); Good Friday; Easter Monday; Ching Ming Festival (5 Apr); Tuen Ng Dragon Boat Festival (May/June); Labour Day (1 May); Buddha's Birthday (11 May); HKSAR Day (1 July); Day after Mid Autumn Festival (Sept/Oct); China National Day (1 Oct); Chung Yeung (25 Oct); Christmas Day (25 Dec); Boxing Day (26 Dec).

## Religion

### Anglican

**St John's Cathedral** *4-8 Garden Road, Central, HK Island (2523 4157). Central MTR (exit K)/buses along Garden Road.* **Services** 7am, 6pm daily. **Map** p67 E4.

### Baptist

**Kowloon English Baptist Church** *300 Junction Road, Kowloon (2337 2555). Kowloon Tong MTR or KCR/Lok Fu MTR/buses along Junction Road.* **Services** 7.30pm Wed; 8.20am, 11am, 6pm Sun.

### Catholic

**St Joseph's** *37 Garden Road, Central, HK Island (2522 3992). Central MTR (exit K)/buses along Garden Road.* **Services** 7.45am, 6pm Mon-Fri; 6pm Sat; from 7am (and every hour thereafter) Sun. **Map** p67 E5.

### Interdenominational

**Union Church Interdenominational** *22A Kennedy Road, Wan Chai, HK Island (2522 1515). Wan Chai MTR (exit A3)/buses along Queen's Road East.* **Services** 10.30am, 6.30pm Sun. **Map** p80 B3.

**Directory**

### Islamic

**Kowloon Mosque & Islamic Centre** *junction of Nathan Road & Cameron Road, Tsim Sha Tsui, Kowloon (2724 0095). Tsim Sha Tsui MTR (exit A1)/buses along Nathan Road.* **Services** phone for details. **Map** p98 B2.

### Jewish

**Ohel Leah Synagogue** *70 Robinson Road, Mid-Levels, HK Island (2549 0981). Bus 3B, 12M, 13, 23, 23B, 40.* **Services** Minyan daily; Kabbalat Shabat, Shabbatot and festival services Fri. **Map** p66 B4.

### Lutheran

**Church of All Nations** *8 South Bay Close, Repulse Bay, HK Island (2812 0375). Buses to Repulse Bay.* **Services** 10.15am Sun. **Map** p62.

### Methodist

**English Methodist Church** *271 Queen's Road East, Wan Chai, HK Island (2575 7817). Wan Chai MTR (exit A3)/buses along Queen's Road East.* **Services** 7.45am Wed; 8.15am, 11am Sun. **Map** p80 B3.

### Mormon

**Mormon Church** *7 Castle Road, Mid-Levels, HK Island (2559 3325). Buses along Caine Road or Castle Road.* **Services** phone for details. **Map** p66 A3.

## Safety & security

For a city of its size, Hong Kong is remarkably safe – both during the day and at night. Violent crime is very rare, and almost entirely confined to triad disputes and domestic incidents. The biggest danger is pickpocketing, and even that is not widespread. However, all the normal city precautions apply (particularly in the main tourist areas): don't flash large wads of cash around, don't leave bags where you can't see them (hanging from the back of seats, etc), keep wallets/cash in front pockets, and don't put anything valuable in your backpack.

Sexual harassment is rare, and many well-travelled female residents claim that this is the safest city they've ever

lived in. Although you will come across touts anxious to lure you into their shops in some well touristed areas, they are rarely persistent.

## Smoking & spitting

Smoking is considered anti-social. Many restaurants, theatres, offices and malls are smoke-free, as is public transport. Hawking and spitting in the street is common in the rest of China, but less so in Hong Kong. Spitting is, in fact, strictly forbidden in public areas and a four-figure fine is imposed on defaulters for both.

## Study

Hong Kong has seven universities offering degree programmes in a wide variety of subjects, both academic and vocational. Student unions are visible and active. The Hong Kong, Chinese and Open Universities also offer continuing education programmes.

The **YMCA of Hong Kong** (2369 2211), **YWCA** (2522 4291), **Island School** (2526 5884) and **Sha Tin College Evening Institute** (2696 3193) run informal courses on a variety of topics, including elementary Cantonese and Mandarin.

### Universities

#### Chinese University of Hong Kong

*Sha Tin, New Territories (2609 6000/fax 2603 5544/ www.cuhk.edu.hk).*

#### City University

*83 Tat Chee Avenue, Kowloon Tong, Kowloon (2788 7654/fax 2778 1167/www.cityu.edu.hk).*

#### Hong Kong Baptist University

*Kowloon Tong, Kowloon (2339 7400/fax 2338 7644/ www.hkbu.edu.hk).*

#### Hong Kong Polytechnic University

*Yuk Choi Road, Hung Hom, Kowloon (2766 5111/fax 2764 3334/www.polyu.edu.hk).*

#### Hong Kong University

*Pok Fu Lam Road, Mid-Levels, HK Island (2859 2111/fax 2858 2549/www.hku.hk).*

#### Open University of Hong Kong

*30 Good Shepherd Road, Ho Man Tin, Kowloon (2711 2100/fax 2761 3935/www.ouhk.edu.hk).*

#### University of Science & Technology

*Clearwater Bay, Kowloon (2358 6000/www.usthk.edu.hk).*

## Tax

Hong Kong is a duty-free port; import duty is only payable on alcohol, cosmetics, tobacco and cars (*see p287*).

No tax is levied on purchased merchandise or in restaurants, but hotels do charge tax.

There is an airport departure tax for adults of HK$50 (included in the ticket price), while the tax for leaving Hong Kong by boat or ferry (about HK$25) is also included in the ticket price.

## Telephones

### Dialling & codes

The international code for Hong Kong is 852, so to call Hong Kong from abroad, you dial the international access code (00 in the UK, 011 in the USA and Canada, 0011 in Australia), then 852 and the eight-digit local number. There are no area codes within Hong Kong.

To call abroad from Hong Kong, dial the international access code 001, then 44 for the UK, 1 for the USA/Canada, 61 for Australia, 64 for New Zealand and 353 for Ireland, then the local area code (omitting the initial 0 if there is one) and the local number – you'll probably have to precede all this with the digit 9 if you are calling from a hotel.

Long-distance IDD calls are the cheapest in Asia, but only if you are calling from a public payphone – many hotels tend to charge an excessive surcharge.

## Public phones

Local calls from public coin boxes cost HK$1 for each five minutes (phones accept HK$1, HK$2 and HK$5 coins). Local calls from private homes, restaurants, offices and shops are free, but hotels (as they do almost everywhere in the world) make an extra charge for both local and international calls. If you want to call abroad from a public phone, then you'll need to purchase a phone card from HKTB Visitor Information & Services Centres (see p296), the Star Ferry piers, machines by some phones and from convenience stores. These cards come in denominations of HK$50, HK$100, HK$200 and HK$300. Some public phones accept credit cards.

## Operator services

**Local directory assistance** *1081.*
**International inquiries** *10013.*
**Reverse-charge/collect calls** from any private or public phone: *10010.*

The Home Direct system allows direct access to an operator in the country being called, making collect calls cheaper or allowing you to charge the call to your home phone card. The Home Direct access numbers from Hong Kong are:

**Australia** *800 96 0161.*
**Canada** *800 96 1100.*
**UK** *800 96 0044.*
**USA** *800 96 1111* for AT&T; *800 96 1121* for MCI; *800 96 1877* for Sprint.

## Telephone directories

Directories are provided in most hotel rooms and by some public phones. There are Yellow Pages (with business listings by category) and White Pages (with both business and residential numbers listed alphabetically). To access both these directories online, go to **www.hkt.com**.

## Mobile phones

Hong Kong people love their mobile phones. In fact, the SAR boasts the world's highest per capita usage of pagers and mobiles. If you're visiting Hong Kong, you can rest assured that your dual-band phone will work.

If you want to hire a phone while in Hong Kong, you'll find good rental packages (for a minimum of one week) on offer from **HKT** shops. On Hong Kong Island, these include 455 Queen's Road West, Central; 102A One Exchange Square, Central; 3 Hennessy Road, Wan Chai; 94 Johnston Road, Wan Chai; 290 Shau Kei Wan Road, Shau Kei Wan; 256 King's Road, Quarry Bay. In Kowloon, they include 2A Prat Avenue, Tsim Sha Tsui; 10 Middle Road, Tsim Sha Tsui; 31 Jordan Road, Tsim Sha Tsui; 83 Argyle Street, Mong Kok.

For general enquiries, call 2888 2888; for information about mobile rental, call 2888 1010.

## Faxes

Most hotels are willing to accept incoming faxes for their guests.

Faxes can either be sent from hotels or (generally, more cheaply) from photocopying shops (see below). The charge is about HK$10 (local) or HK$75 (international) per page.

### Xerox

*Shop 3, 33 Canton Road, Tsim Sha Tsui, Kowloon (2736 6011). Tsim Sha Tsui MTR (exit A1)/buses along Canton Road/ Tsim Sha Tsui Star Ferry Pier.* **Open** 9am-6pm Mon-Sat. **Credit** (minimum HK$300) AmEx, DC, MC, V. **Map** p98 B2.
*47 Pitt Street, Yau Ma Tei, Kowloon (2780 4884). Yau Ma Tei (exit A2)/buses along Nathan Road.* **Open** 9am-7pm Mon-Sat. **Credit** (minimum HK$300) AmEx, DC, MC, V. **Map** p110 A3.
*New Henry House, 10 Ice House Street, Central, HK Island (2524 9799). Central MTR (exit H)/buses & trams through Central.* **Open** 9am-6pm Mon-Sat. **Credit** (minimum HK$300) AmEx, DC, MC, V. **Map** p67 D4.

## Telegrams

Telegrams can be sent from any HKT shop (see above **Mobile phones**). There is a standard charge of HK$25, and then HK$3.60 per word.

## Time

Hong Kong does not have Daylight Saving Time. Time differences:

| | |
|---|---|
| Chicago | -13hrs |
| London | -7hrs |
| (-8hrs during DST) | |
| Los Angeles | -15hrs |
| New York | -12hrs |
| Sydney | +2hrs |

## Tipping

Tipping isn't a part of Chinese culture, but Westerners have been in Hong Kong so long that it is widely expected. A standard ten per cent service charge is added to the bill at most restaurants and hotels. Where there is no service charge, tipping is at your discretion, but ten per cent is the usual amount given. Small tips of HK$3-$20 may be given to taxi drivers, bellboys, doormen and washroom attendants.

**Directory**

# Weather

| | Temperature | Rainfall |
|---|---|---|
| January | 14-19°C | 23mm |
| February | 14-19°C | 48mm |
| March | 17-21°C | 67mm |
| April | 20-25°C | 162mm |
| May | 24-29°C | 317mm |
| June | 26-30°C | 376mm |
| July | 27-32°C | 324mm |
| August | 26-31°C | 392mm |
| September | 26-30°C | 300mm |
| October | 23-28°C | 145mm |
| November | 19-24°C | 35mm |
| December | 15-21°C | 27mm |

## Toilets

Toilets in parks, malls, hotels, restaurants, bars, cafés and department stores are usually clean. Toilets in some parks/beaches have no toilet paper and in the more Chinese areas, be prepared to squat.

## Tourist information

The official tourist organisation, the **Hong Kong Tourism Board (HKTB)** produces excellent maps and well-written brochures on eating, shopping and sightseeing, which are available free. It also sells souvenirs. A red junk sticker in the windows of shops and restaurants denotes that the establishment meets HKTB standards and is reliable.

The award-winning website (www.DiscoverHongKong.com) is well worth checking prior to arriving in Hong Kong.

### Hong Kong Tourism Board

*The Center, 99 Queen's Road, Central, HK Island (visitor hotline 2508 1234/www.DiscoverHongKong. com).* **Open** 8am-6pm daily. **Map** p66 C2.

There's another HKTB office in the Tsim Sha Tsui Star Ferry Pier in Kowloon.

## Visas & immigration

All foreigners entering Hong Kong for employment, business, education or training purposes (as well as their dependents) require a visa. The only exceptions are those born in Hong Kong and those holding a permanent identity card, HKSAR or BNO passport.

In addition, nationals of the UK and British Commonwealth Dependent/Protected countries do not require a visa for a visit of less than three months; neither do American and South African visitors for less than a month's visit, and other nationalities for a stay of less than eight days; but check to make sure.

Entry permits/visas can be obtained from a Chinese consular mission in your country: apply prior to arrival.

For visitors, a visa is valid for a month, though it can be extended, but employment of any kind is not permitted during visits.

Visitors are not allowed to change their status after they've arrived in Hong Kong, except in exceptional cases.

For frequent visitors, a pass or multiple entry visa can be obtained.

### HK Immigration Department

*7 Gloucester Road, Wan Chai, HK Island (2824 6111/fax 2877 7711/ www.info.gov.hk). Wan Chai MTR (exit A1)/buses along Gloucester Road.* **Open** 8.45am-4.30pm Mon-Fri; 9-11.30am Sat. **Map** p80 B2.

## Water

Tap water in Hong Kong conforms to UN World Health Organisation standards and it is considered safe to drink from taps. However, residents tend to filter or boil their water before drinking it, not quite trusting the condition of the pipes in their buildings. If in doubt, local and imported bottled water is available everywhere.

Beaches are given a daily pollution rating, as many are below WHO standards, ocean pollution being a serious problem.

## Weights & measures

Hong Kong has adopted the metric system, although you will still sometimes see pounds and ounces in use in supermarkets, as well as a Chinese measurement of weight, the 'catty' (600 grams/21 ounces).

1 kilometre = 0.621 miles
1 metre = 1.093 yards
1 centimetre = 0.3937 inches
1 kilogram = 2.2046 pounds
1 gram= 0.0352 ounces
1 litre= 0.2642 imperial gallon
0 degrees = 32 degrees fahrenheit

## What to take

Everything you're likely to need can be bought in Hong Kong, although some items may be more expensive than they would be back home, but it is wise to bring all essentials with you. Important medication may not, however, be available.

## When to go

Hong Kong has a subtropical climate and there are times of the year when its high humidity can be seriously debilitating, making a visit to the city distinctly uncomfortable.

A summary of what temperatures, humidity and general weather conditions to expect during the year follows, but do bear in mind that the weather in Hong Kong can be very unpredictable.

**Spring** (March to mid May) is often pleasant, with temperatures from 18°C to 27°C (64-80°F), but humidity is often high (82 per cent on average). You should bring a light jacket or sweater for the evenings, which can be cool.

**Summer** (late May to mid September) is hot and stiflingly humid; temperatures range from 26°C to 33°C (78-91°F) and humidity can reach a crippling 90 per cent. Ironically, you'll probably still need to bring an extra layer for when you're indoors, as shops, restaurants, bars and hotels tend to crank up the air-conditioning to icy levels. This is also typhoon season (*see p292* **Natural hazards**) and rainfall is at its highest.

**Autumn** (late September to early December) is the usually the best time to visit; temperatures are a comfortably warm 18°C to 28°C (64-82°F), but humidity levels drop to a bearable average of 72 per cent. Sunny days and clear skies are relatively common.

**Winter** (mid December to February) can also be a good time to visit Hong Kong; with temperatures of 14°C to 20°C (57-68°F) and humidity of around 72 per cent. It can get chilly, windy and cloudy, though, so you'll need to bring a few extra layers.

For daily weather reports and three-day advance forecasts, contact **HK Observatory** 2926 8200 or **Dial-a-Weather** (in English; 187 8066). Also, the website www.underground.org.hk features a massive range of detailed information about current and predicted weather conditions in Hong Kong.

## Women

Women in Hong Kong are active and visible, holding high profile jobs in private and government sectors – the most prominent example is Anson Chan, Chief Secretary for Administration (second in command to the Chief Executive) at the time of the Handover.

Besides volunteer associations and charities, there are several business and professional groups run by women for networking and socialising.

For helplines (rape, shelter, etc), *see p290*.

### Organisations & resources

#### American Women's Association
*C7, Monticello, 48 Kennedy Road, Mid-Levels, HK Island (2527 2961/fax 2865 7737/www.awa.com.hk).*

#### Association of Business & Professional Women
*GPO Box 1526, Hong Kong (2535 9198/fax 2904 0788/ annafang@netvigator.com/ www.hkabpw.org).*

#### Federation of Women Centres
*2386 6256/fax 2728 0617.*

#### Safetalk Support Group for Women
*2603 7815.*
Safetalk offers emotional and practical support group for women in abusive relationships.

### St John's Cathedral HIV Education Centre
*4-8 Garden Road, Central, HK Island (2501 0653/ 2523 0531/fax 2523 1581/ sjhivctr@asiaonline.net).* Buses along Garden Road. **Open** 10am-6pm Mon-Fri; 10am-1pm Sat. **Map** p67 E4.

### Women in Publishing Society
*Judy Love Eastham, GPO Box 7314, Hong Kong (9756 5972/ judy@accomasia.com).*
For journalists and editors.

### Women's Corona Society
*GPO Box 8151, Hong Kong (2792 4109).*
The Women's Corona Society is a social support group for English-speaking women.

## Working in Hong Kong

Prior to 1997, British citizens didn't need work visas to get a job in Hong Kong, but it has now become more difficult for all foreigners to work in the SAR. Immigration requires proof of local unavailability of skills before issuing work visas to foreigners. Spouses holding a dependent visa can pursue employment.

### Work permits

To work in Hong Kong, it is necessary for a sponsor/ employer to apply for a work visa for you. This application is reviewed by immigration for its validity before a work visa is issued. Sometimes, work visas can take from six to 12 months to be processed.

In general, it is best to apply for a work visa prior to arrival in the SAR.

### Useful addresses

#### Professional Overseas Postings
*(2791 9907/fax 2791 9908/ www.hongkongvisas.com/ pops.asia@netvigator.com).*

# The Language

Cantonese, English and (since 1997) Mandarin are the official languages of Hong Kong.

**Cantonese** is the dialect of the southern Chinese province of Guangdong, from where most Hong Kongers originate and is, therefore, the SAR's lingua franca, being spoken in 89 per cent of households. Three decades ago, it was considered rather low-brow and many Western sinologists predicted that it would fade away after the Handover, as Mandarin came to dominate, but it looks set to stay for good.

Cantonese is very difficult for foreigners to learn, because of the seven tones involved, each of which can change the meaning of a word. For example, the word 'gai', when said in different ways, can mean either chicken, street or prostitute. Even for the Chinese, the various tones only avoid confusion up to a certain point: complete understanding is gained from the context.

As it is very difficult to master, many foreigners never bother to learn more than a few essential words of Cantonese – however long they live in Hong Kong. They do get by without it, but with a fair degree of frustration, because – despite the fact that it is an official language – many locals do not speak English.

**Mandarin**, as the Beijing dialect is known in the West, is not widely spoken in Hong Kong. However, a standardised form of it, **Putonghua**, is promoted by the Chinese government as the national language and is, therefore, spoken by 70 per cent of those living on the mainland.

Mandarin was the dialect used by government officials (or mandarins, hence its name) to communicate with each other in days gone by. Putonghua translates as 'the language that can be used everywhere', because it is common to so many of the mainland Chinese. The same – or at least a very similar – language is called Guoyu (national language) in Taiwan and Huayu (Chinese people's language) in Singapore. The differences between these languages are minor, and can be compared with the distinctions between the English language spoken in Britain and that of the US.

What all Chinese dialects have in common is an ingeniously flexible system of non-phonetic writing. In other words, Chinese characters can be read by all Chinese people, whichever dialect they speak.

**Hanyu pinyin**, the official romanisation of Chinese characters, is used in major Chinese cities on street signs (alongside Chinese characters). This is useful for foreigners who cannot read the characters, as it indicates the Chinese pronunciation, but is also confusing because it does not indicate the tones that must also be used.

Any attempt by foreigners to talk Chinese using pinyin is therefore likely to be unintelligible to the locals. If you are really keen to impress, the only way is to pick up a Chinese dictionary (be it Mandarin or Cantonese), because it also indicates the correct tones of characters.

Having said all that, here are some words and phrases, with approximations on how they should be pronounced in Cantonese: even if your attempt at communication is unintelligible, you will be applauded for trying…

## Phrases

| | |
|---|---|
| how are you? | nei ho ma? |
| fine, thank you | gay ho nei yau sum |
| good morning | jo sahn |
| good night | jo tau |
| goodbye | joy gen |
| hello! (on phone) | wai! |
| how much does it cost? | gaydo cheena? |
| too expensive | tei gway |
| I'm sorry (excuse me) | m'ho yi si |
| yes | hai |
| no | mm hai |
| please & thank you (for a service) | m'goy |
| please (invitation) | cheng |
| thank you (for a gift) | doh jeh |
| you're welcome | m'sai m'goy |

## Restaurant & bar phrases

| | |
|---|---|
| beer | beh jau |
| water | soi |
| English tea | lai tcha |
| bill | my dan |
| telephone | deen wah |

## Taxi directions

| | |
|---|---|
| street/road | gai/do |
| turn right | chin yau |
| turn left | chin jo |
| straight on | yat jik hui |
| hurry | fai dee |
| stop | teng |
| wait here | tang hai nee dow |

## Geographical features

| | |
|---|---|
| beach | wan |
| mountain | shan |
| harbour | o |
| headland | tau/kok |
| island | chau |
| village | tsuen |
| rock | shek |

(Shek O is, therefore, named after its rocky harbour.)

## Numbers

| | |
|---|---|
| one | yat |
| two | yih |
| three | sahm |
| four | sei |
| five | ung |
| six | lok |
| seven | chat |
| eight | baht |
| nine | gau |
| ten | sahp |
| zero | ling |

# Further Reference

If you consider its size, a disproportionate number of books have been written about Hong Kong. Most of these are of an historical nature, but there's a handful of novels as well.

## Non-fiction

The Government Publications Centre (*see p180*) sells a wide range of guides to Hong Kong's countryside, flora and fauna, as well as maps. *See also p36.*

**Magnus & Kasyan Bartlett**
*Over Hong Kong*
A pictorial record of Hong Kong since it became a Special Administrative Region of China.

**Austin Coates**
*Myself A Mandarin*
A fascinating insight into life in Hong Kong in the 1950s, when Austin Coates was a Special Magistrate in South Kowloon and the New Territories. Many of the cases he tried in his office on Nathan Road make fascinating, funny and enlightening reading.

**Maurice Collis** *Foreign Mud*
An account of the shameful history of the Opium Wars.

**Fredric Dannen & Barry Long**
*Hong Kong Babylon*
Superb insight into the world of Hong Kong movies, with interviews, plot summaries and film ratings.

**Jonathan Dimbleby**
*The Last Governor*
The author, a close friend of Chris Patten, had unrivalled access to the last governor and, as a result, this book provides a compelling narrative of the government side of the final chapter in Hong Kong's colonial history.

**GB Endacott**
*A History of Hong Kong*
A classic account of the colony's history, written in 1958.

**Jonathan Fenby**
*Dealing With The Dragon*
A year (1999) in the life of Hong Kong and the author, who was then editor of the *South China Morning Post*, provides a valuable and entertaining insight into life in post-Handover HK and its effect on his newspaper.

**Patricia Lim**
*Discovering Hong Kong's Cultural Heritage*
The first half of this book is dedicated to the cultural heritage of Hong Kong and, in particular, the New Territories. The second half is more akin to a guide, giving detailed information on 12 places of interest in the New Territories and outlying islands.

**Jan Morris**
*Epilogue to an Empire: Hong Kong*
Morris presents an insightful and comprehensive study of the fascinating enigma that is Hong Kong. A charming travel book, it is full of interesting information about past and present-day HK.

**David Newman, Bruce Bueno de Mesquita & Alvin Rabushka**
*Red Flag over Hong Kong*
This book discusses the future of Hong Kong and, because it is an intrinsic part of it, China too. Unfortunately, the authors' view is not a particularly positive one, worrying as they do that Hong Kong will gradually lose its economic vitality and the residents their individual liberties.

**James O'Reilly, Larry Habeggar & Sean O'Reilly** (editors)
*Hong Kong*

This collection of almost 50 tales by a wide range of travel writers – including stars of the genre such as Bruce Chatwin, Paul Theroux and Jan Morris – provides a delightful and entertaining insight into Hong Kong and all its idiosyncrasies.

**Christopher Patten**
*East and West*
In June 1997, over a century and a half of British rule in Hong Kong came to an end. Chris Patten wrote this book about his experiences as the last governor of the British colony, explaining why he adopted the stance that he did, and how he fought his battles.

**Russell Spurr** *Excellency (The Governors of Hong Kong)*
Provides a riveting look at the lives of the men – 28 British governors and two Japanese generals – who ruled Hong Kong for more than 150 years.

**Han Suyin**
*A Many Splendoured Thing*
The greatest literary success in Han Suyin's career, this book describes her love affair with Ian Morrison, a foreign correspondent for *The Times* – an affair that was brought to a brutal end by Ian's death while reporting on the Korean War. In 1955, the book was made into a movie called *Love Is a Many Splendoured Thing*, which won two Oscars.

**Frank Welsh**
*A History of Hong Kong*
A comprehensive history of Hong Kong, from the early days of British trade to Canton to the 1997 Handover.

**Michael Yahuda** *Hong Kong*
This book (written a year before the Handover) analyses the serious problems and real opportunities that the return of Hong Kong poses to China's international status.

## Fiction

### John Le Carré
*The Honourable Schoolboy*
George Smiley is chief of the British Secret Service when the betrayals of a Soviet double agent riddle the spy network. In order to exact revenge and return stability to the Service, Smiley travels to Hong Kong.

### James Clavell *Noble House*
The Noble House hong is in trouble and, as rival taipans seek revenge for blood feuds over a century old, Hong Kong itself becomes a deadly playground of the CIA, the KGB and the People's Republic of China.

### James Clavell *Taipan*
In the mid 19th century, Dirk Struan is determined to make the newly acquired Hong Kong the jewel in the British Empire and, in so doing, become taipan – the most powerful man in town. Although dull, it's always been a popular read.

### Austin Coates
*City of Broken Promises*
This 18th-century historical novel is based on the true story of a love affair between a Chinese orphan called Martha Herop and the son of the British founder of Lloyd's.

### Richard Mason
*The World of Suzie Wong*
Written in the 1950s, Mason's novel paints an unusually frank picture of the lives of Wan Chai's bar girls.

### Timothy Mo
*An Insular Possession*
Set in 19th century Hong Kong, Canton and Macau, this doorstop of a novel documents the lives of foreign traders.

### Timothy Mo
*The Monkey King*
This (often humorous) novel follows the marriage of Wallace, a young man of Portuguese and Cantonese descent, who marries into an important Hong Kong Chinese family in the 1950s.

### Paul Theroux *Kowloon Tong*
The worries of expats on the brink of the Handover.

### Nury Vittachi
*The Feng Shui Detective*
Mystery, comedy and Zen mysticism combine in this book about a travelling *feng shui* man – and solves a few mysteries on the way. Written by one of Asia's best-loved journalists, it's highly entertaining.

## Macau

Charles Ralph (CR) Boxer is an authority on Macanese history and has written a number of books on the subject, most of which – unfortunately – are out of print.

### WH Auden & Christopher Isherwood
*Journey To A War*
Auden and Isherwood travelled to China in 1938, when the country was ravaged by civil war and being invaded by Japan. This book, which resulted from their travels, includes a few interesting snapshots of life in Macau at that time.

### Luiz Vaz de Camões
(translated by William C Atkinson) *The Lusiads*
The translation of Camões's epic poem, at least part of which may have been written in Macau, tells the story of Vasco da Gama's voyage via southern Africa to India. If you can get past the flowery prose, this is a classic.

### Austin Coates & Cesar Guillen-Nunez
*A Macau Narrative*
A concise history of the former Portuguese colony.

### Leila Hadley
*Give Me the World*
In the 1950s, as a 25-year-old divorcee with a six-year-old son in tow, the author gave up on the rat race and headed for Asia, where she enjoyed a riotous few years of travel that included a few unexpected events in Macau.

### Jill McGivering
*Macau Remembers*
This book was published to commemorate Macau's return to China on 20 December 1999, after more than 450 years of Portuguese administration. It consists of interviews with 30 different people, representing most of Macau's unique mixture of races, creeds, classes and traditions.

### Lindsay & May Ride
(abridged, with additional information by Jason Wordie)
*The Voices of Macau Stones*
There are stones, statues and memorials dotted all over Macau that help trace its history from the days of the first Portuguese navigators in the 16th century to the events of more recent times. Unnoticed by almost all who pass them, this book documents their importance, revealing Macau's rich and colourful history.

## China

### David Bonavia
*The Chinese*
Bonavia's book is an excellent introduction to every aspect of the Chinese.

### Jonathan Spence
*The Search For Modern China*
The definitive work on contemporary China.

### Tiziano Terzani
*Behind The Forbidden Door*
A fascinating account by an Italian journalist of life in Communist China, where he lived in the early 1980s before being expelled for his increasingly critical writing.

## Film

For a run-down of some of the best indigenous films, *see p218* **Top ten HK films**. For a feature on international films shot in Hong Kong, *see p216* **Location: Hong Kong**.

## Music

For information on Hong Kong-based classical composers, *see p240* **Local heroes**. For the low-down on Hong Kong's own brand of pop music, *see p232* **Canto-pop**.

## Websites

**BC Magazine**
*www3.netvigator.com/ bcmagazine/index.html*
Online version of the free mag that is distributed through bars in HK: detailed listings and interesting articles.

**The Chinese University of Hong Kong**
*www.cuhk.edu.hk/hkwww.html*
One of the SAR's larger universities provides a site brimming with links to lots of other Hong Kong sites.

**Food4HongKong**
*www.food4hongkong.com/home*
A database of Hong Kong's restaurants, which allows you to make reservations online.

**Foreign & Commonwealth Office**
*http://193.114.50.10/travel/ countryadvice.asp?HK*
Travel warnings and information sheets from the British Government.

**Funhongkong.com**
*www.funhk.com*
Loads of different things to do in Hong Kong, with a special section on what to do if you're travelling with kids.

**Health in Asia**
*www.healthinasia.com*
Lists the medical bits and bobs you should take with you to Asia, as well as all the possible diseases you can catch – perhaps you should read this section on your return…

**HKevents.net**
*www.hkevents.net*
A useful guide to the performing arts, sport and festivals taking place in the SAR that allows you to reserve tickets online.

**Hongkongcalling.com**
*www.hongkongcalling.com*
This site provides a thorough A to Z of what Hong Kong has to offer with regard to living, working and socialising.

**Hong Kong Dolphin Watch**
*www.zianet.com/dolphins*
Dedicated to Hong Kong's unique pink dolphins, with details of trips to visit them and how to help the campaign to save them from extinction.

**Hong Kong Economic and Trade Office USA**
*www.hongkong.org*
Useful source of information for those (primarily in the United States) seeking to do business in Hong Kong.

**Hong Kong International Airport**
*www.hkairport.com*
If you're in transit at Chek Lap Kok, or simply want to know how to make a speedy airport escape, this site's for you.

**Hongkongnet.net**
*www.hongkongnet.net*
Great site for scooping deals on all sorts of holiday packages, but particularly for finding cheap hotel rates.

**Hong Kong SAR of the People's Republic of China**
*www.info.gov.hk*
Lots of facts and figures on the SAR straight from the horse's mouth: interesting for some, deadly dull for others.

**Hong Kong Trade Development Council**
*www.tdc.org.hk*
Stacks of information about Hong Kong for those interested in doing business in the SAR.

**Hong Kong Tourism Board**
*www.discoverhongkong.com*
The award-winning tourism board site is definitely worth a surf prior to departure.

**HotelsTravel.com**
*www.hotelstravel.com/ hongkong.html*
Detailed hotel and basic tourist info, with the ability to book online.

**iMail**
*www.hk-imail.com*
With its tabloid format, Hong Kong's other English-language newspaper tends towards the sensationalist: expect the same from the website.

**Macau Government Tourist Office**
*www.macautourism.gov.mo*
An overload of information and far too many website gimmicks from the Macau SAR's official tourist board.

**The No.1 Expat Site in Asia**
*www.asiaxpat.com.hk*
Lots of information relevant to residents and travellers – with the opportunity to post queries and (hopefully) receive answers from those in the know.

**South China Morning Post**
*www.scmp.com*
The site of Hong Kong's leading English-language newspaper provides all the latest local news.

**That's Guangzhou**
*www.thatsguangzhou.com*
As much for residents, as for visitors, this website provides a comprehensive guide to what is happening in Guangzhou.

**Time Out Hong Kong**
*www.timeout.com/hongkong*
The online version of this guide, with up-to-the-minute listings of current events.

**Totally HK**
*www.totallyhk.com*
A fact-packed e-zine with information relevant to residents and visitors, from the publishers of the SCMP.

**US Department of State**
*http://travel.state.gov/ hongkong.html*
Travel warnings and consular information sheets on the SAR.

**Weather Underground of Hong Kong**
*www.underground.org.hk*
Perfect for finding out what's in store for Hong Kong weather-wise, both short and long term.

**Directory**

# Index

**Note:** Numbers in **bold** indicate key information on a topic; *italics* indicate photographs.

## a

Aberdeen 15, **91-92**, *91*
Aberdeen, Lord 8
accommodation **40-53**
best hotels 47
by area
Central & Mid-Levels 40-43
Cheung Chau 53
Hong Kong Island 40-45
Kowloon 45-53
Lantau 53
New Territories 53
Tsim Sha Tsui 45-51
Wan Chai & Causeway Bay 43-45
Yau Ma Tei & Mong Kok 51-53
cheap 43, 44-45, 49, 52-53
deluxe 40-44, 46-47
expensive 43, 44, 47-48
guesthouses 45, 49-51
hostels 45, 53
moderate 44, 48-49, 51-53
youth hostels 52
Admiralty **72**, 176
*Ah Ying* 218
air, arriving by 282-283
Airport Express (train) 65, **282**
airport, Hong Kong International (Chek Lap Kok) 25, **282**
airport, Kai Tak 23, 282
Airport Core Programme Exhibition Centre 120, **122**
Alvares, Jorge **7**, 254
Amah Rock **114**, 214
Amherst Mission 25
antiques 76
arriving in Hong Kong 282-283
Arrow War 12
Art Museum, Chinese University 115, **118**
arts, Chinese 32
arts & entertainment **203-252**
Arts Festival, Hong Kong **207**, 208
Arts Festival, Hong Kong Chinese **206**, 245
Arts Festival, Hong Kong Youth 206

*Ashes of Time* 218
astrology, Chinese 33
athletics 247, 251
auctions, Christie's & Sotheby's 204
Aviary, Edward Youde 72, **74**, *74*, 210

## b

badminton 247
Ballroom Dancing Championships, Hong Kong International 206
Bank of America Tower *60*
Bank of China Tower *60*, 65, *68*, **69**, 210
bargaining 177
bars *see* pubs & bars
Basic Law 25
bath-houses, public 14
beaches 95, 125, 128, 130, 132, 136, **250**
Beijingese cuisine 150
*Better Tomorrow, A* 218
bicycles & bicycle hire 285
Big Buddha, Lantau 132-133, *134*
Big Wave Bay **96**, 250
Bird Market 108, *108*, **194**
blues music venues 236
books
further reading 299-300
shops 180-181
gay & lesbian 226-227
Bond, Alan 72
Bonham, Sir George 8
Boundary Street 15, **111**
Bowen Road 65
Bowen, Sir George F 8
bowling 247
Bowring, Sir John 8
Bowrington Road Market 85
Boxer Rebellion 19
Bride's Pool 123
British East India Company **10**, 25
Buddhism 29
*Bullet in the Head* 218
Bun Festival, Cheung Chau **205**, *205*, 214
burial customs 136
Burridge, Lee 231
buses 284
business 286-287
centres & office hire 286
conventions & conferences 286
couriers & shippers 286
translators & interpreters 286
useful organisations 287

## c

Caine, William 8
Cameron, Major-Gen NG 8
Canton trade 10
Cantonese cuisine 148
Cantonese people 28
Canto-pop 232-233
Carlsberg Cup (football) **208**, 251
Carnarvon, Lord 8
cars *see* driving
carvings, Bronze Age 96
Castle Peak Monastery 122
Cathay Pacific Championships (tennis) **206**, 252
Causeway Bay **81-87**
accommodation 43-45
for children 212
pubs & bars 166, 171-172
restaurants 149-154
shopping 176
Causeway Bay Typhoon Shelter 86
Center, The *61*
*Center Stage* 218
Central *60-61*, **63-74**
accommodation 40-43
development of 12
for children **209-211**, 212
pubs & bars 168-170
restaurants 142-147
shopping 176
Central Market 11, **72**
Central Plaza *58*, **82**
Chan, Jackie 219
Chan, Wai-kwong Victor 240
Chan, Wing-wah 241
Chang, Hsueh-liang (Young Marshal) 20
Chang, Tso-lin (Old Marshal) 20
Chater Garden 69
Chater, Sir Paul 8
Chau, Kai-bong & Brenda 70
Che Kung 29
Che Kung Temple, Tai Wai 114, *116*, **117**
Chek Lap Kok (Hong Kong International) Airport 25, **282**
chess, Chinese 32
Cheung Chau 135-136
accommodation 53
Bun Festival 135, **205**, *205*, 214
pubs & bars 174
restaurants 165

Cheung Kong Centre *60*, **69**
Cheung Sha beach, Lantau 132
Cheung Sha Wan 113
Chi Lin Buddhist Nunnery 112, **113**
Chiang Kai-shek 20
children **209-214**
best stuff for 212
child-minding 214
clothing shops 186
resources 214
toy shops 201
walks 210-211
China Club 189
Chinese chess 32
Chinese Christian Cemetery 112
Chinese Civil War **23**, 25
Chinese cuisines 141, **148-151**
*Chinese Ghost Story, A* 218
Chinese medicine 33, **75**, **76**
Chinese New Year **208**, 214
Chinese opera 242-244
Chinese orchestras 244
Chinese University Art Museum 115, **118**
Chinese University of Hong Kong 115
Ching Chung Koon Temple 120, **122**
Ching Ming festival 30
Chiu Chownese cuisine 150
Christianity 30
Christmas 207
Chuen Pi, Convention of **10**, 25
Chuen Yun festival 30
Chuk Lam Shim Yuen Monastery 120, **122**
*Chungking Express* 101, *101*, **218**
Chungking Mansions 49, 51, **101**
Cinepanorama 219
Citic Tower *59*
City Contemporary Dance Company 246
City Festival 207
classical music (Western) 242-244
Clearwater Bay 124
Clementi, Sir Cecil **18**, 19
climbing 247-248
Clock Tower 99, *99*
clubs 228-223
gay & lesbian 223-225
girlie 81, 167
coffee culture 155

Commonwealth War Cemetery 213
Community Advice Bureau 214
comprador class 16
Conrad Hong Kong Hotel **40**, *59*, *60*
consumer 287
*Countess from Hong Kong, A* 217
Court of Final Appeal 69
Credit Suisse First Boston Hong Kong Rugby Sevens 204, 252
cruising 225
Cultural Revolution 23
culture and customs **28-33**
customs regulations 287
cycling *see* bicycles

D'Aguilar, Major-General Charles 8
Dairy Farm Building 71
dance 244-246
Davis, Sir John F 8
Deep Water Bay **93**, 250
Dent's 10, 11
dim sum 149
disabled information 287
Discovery Bay, Lantau 130
Disneyland, Lantau 130
DJs, local 231
dolphins, pink 35
Dragon Boat (Tuen Ng) Festival **205**, *206*, 214, 251
Dragon's Back Trail **36**, 95
drinking *see* pubs & bars
driving 285
  breakdown services 285
  car hire 285
  car insurance 285
  parking 285
  petrol stations 285
drugs 287-288

Edward Youde Aviary 72, **74**, *74*, 210
electricity 288
Elgin, Lord 8
Elliot, Captain Charles 10
embassies & consulates 288
emergencies 288
English, pidgin 21
entertainment *see* arts & entertainment
*Escape from Hong Kong* 216
etiquette 286
Exchange Square *61*, **65**
Executive Council 18
expats 124-125

face, saving and losing 30
Fanling 117
Far East Finance Centre *59*, *60*, **72**
Farrell, Terry 89
fashion designers, Hong Kong 183
fashion shops 186-193
faxes 295
*feng shui* **31-32**, 69
ferries 284
*Ferry to Hong Kong* 217
Festival Walk **181**, 213
festivals 204-208
  film 219
  for children 214
  Hong Kong Arts Festival 207
  Hong Kong Chinese Arts Festival **206**, 245
  Hong Kong Youth Arts Festival 206
  traditional 32
Filipinos 29
film **215-219**, 300
  cinemas 216-217
  festivals 219
  Hong Kong International Festival 204
  Hong Kong film locations 216-217
  resources 218-219
  top ten films 218
Finger Hill, Peng Chau 137
fire brigade, Lamma 128
fitness *see* sport & fitness
Flagstaff House Museum of Tea Ware 32, 72, **74**, 210
*Flight to Hong Kong* 216
flora & fauna 36-37
Flower Market 108
football 208, **251**
Foreign Correspondent's Club 71
Foster, Norman 69
French May Festival of Arts, Le 205
French Mission Building 69
Fringe Club 71, **220**, 240
Fringe Festival 207
Fun Lau Trail, Lantau 133
Fung Wong Shan (Lantau Peak), Lantau 132
Fung Ying Sin Koon Temple, Fanling 117

galleries **220-222**
  commercial 222
  other venues 222
  public 220-222
gambling 87, **264-265**
Garden Road Registry Office 210

gay & lesbian **223-227**
  bars, cafés, clubs & karaokes 223-225
  resources & organisations 227
  saunas 225-226
  shops 226-227
General Post Office *61*, **65**
General Strike of 1925 18, 19, 25
Gin Drinker's Line 20
*Girl from Hong Kong, The* 216
girlie bars/clubs 81, 167
go-karting 248
Goldfish Market **108**, 194
golf 206, 248, 251
Government Bacteriological Laboratory 14
Government Civic Hospital 15
Government House, former 11, 22, 69, *71*, **71**
Grand Hyatt Hotel **43**, *58*
Grand Prix, Macau 206
Grantham, Sir Alexander 22
Granville, Lord 8
Granville Road 175
Great Eagle Centre *58*
Guangzhou **267-279**
  accommodation 277-278
  Bai Yun Shan 270
  bars & nightlife 274-276
  Da Fo Si 271, **271**
  eating & drinking 273-274
  Er Sha Dao 271
  getting there 278
  Guang Xiao Si 271, **272**, *272*
  Guangdong Museum of Art 271-272
  Guangzhou Export Commodities Trade Fair 275
  Guangzhou Municipal Museum 271, **273**
  Hunan 270
  Liu Hua Park 270
  Liu Rong Si 271, **272**, *272*
  Liwan Museum 270, **272**
  music 279
  Peasant Movement Museum 271, **273**
  Qing Ping Market 270
  Shamian Island 270, *270*
  shopping 276-277
  sightseeing 270-272
  Sun Yat-sen Memorial Hall 271, **273**
  Tian He 271
  tourist information 278
  trade fair 275
  Trade Fair Hall 270
  Xiguan 270
  Xing Hai Concert Hall 271

Yue Xiu Park 270, *271*
Zhen Hai Tower 271, **273**
Zhu Jiang (Pearl River) 270
guesthouses *see* accommodation
Gwilt, David 240

Hakka people 12, 28
Handover (1997) **24**, 25
happy hours 166-167
Happy Valley **86**, 166
Happy Valley Racecourse 86, **251-252**
Harbour Centre *58*
Harbour City 99, **181**, *181*
Harbour Plaza 104
Harcourt, Sir Cecil 8
Hart, Sir Robert 8
Hau Wong Temple 112
health 288-290
  accident & emergency 288
  complementary medicine 288-289
  contraception & abortion 289
  dentists 289
  doctors 289
  hospitals 289
  pharmacies 289
  STDs, HIV & AIDS 289
  women's health 290
helplines 290
Hennessy Road 81
Hennessy, Sir John Pope 8, **17**
High Island Reservoir 124
hiking **34-37**, 248
Hinduism 30
history, Hong Kong **7-25**
HMS *Tamar* 71
Hoklo people 28
Holden, William 216
Hollywood Road **76-78**, 166, 176
Hollywood Road Park 78
Hollywood Road Police Station 76
*Hong Kong* 216
Hong Kong Academy for Performing Arts *59*, 83, **239**, 243, 245
*Hong Kong Affair* 216
Hong Kong Arts Centre *58*, 83, **221**, 239
Hong Kong Arts Festival **207**, 208
Hong Kong Bach Choir 244
Hong Kong Ballet 245
Hong Kong Chinese Arts Festival **206**, 245
Hong Kong Chinese Orchestra 244
Hong Kong City Hall *60*, 65, **239**

Hong Kong Club *60*
*Hong Kong Confidential* 216
Hong Kong Convention &
  Exhibition Centre *58, 81*,
  82, **239-240**
Hong Kong Cultural Centre
  102, *102*, 213, **240**
Hong Kong Dance Alliance
  246
Hong Kong Dance
  Company 246
Hong Kong Dolphinwatch
  35
Hong Kong Film Archive
  218
Hong Kong Heritage
  Museum 114-115, **118**,
  212, 213, 242
Hong Kong history **7-25**
Hong Kong Housing
  Authority 23
Hong Kong International
  Airport *25*, **282**
Hong Kong International
  Ballroom Dancing
  Championships 206
Hong Kong International
  Film Festival 204
Hong Kong International
  Races 207
Hong Kong Island **63-74**
  accommodation 40-45
  acquisition of 10-11
  derivation of name 11
  for children 209-213
  pubs & bars 168-172
  restaurants 142-155
Hong Kong Museum of Art
  32, 102, **104-106**,
  220-221
Hong Kong Museum of
  Coastal Defence **87**, 213
Hong Kong Museum of
  History 104, **106**
Hong Kong Museum of
  Medical Sciences 14, **78**
Hong Kong Museum of
  Science 104, **106**, 212
Hong Kong Oratorio
  Society 244
Hong Kong Park 72, *72*,
  **74**, 210, 212
Hong Kong Philharmonic
  Orchestra *239*, 243
Hong Kong Players 246
Hong Kong police 23
Hong Kong Racing
  Museum 86, **87**
Hong Kong Railway
  Museum 117, **118**, 214
Hong Kong Repertory
  Theatre 246
Hong Kong Rugby Sevens,
  Credit Suisse First
  Boston 204, 252
Hong Kong Sinfonietta 244
Hong Kong Singers 246
Hong Kong Space Museum
  102, **106**, *106*, 212, 213

Hong Kong Today **26-27**
Hong Kong Tourism Board
  99
Hong Kong Trail **35**, 90,
  95
Hong Kong University 78
Hong Kong Visual Arts
  Centre 221
Hong Kong Yacht Club
  86
Hong Kong Youth Arts
  Festival 206
Hong Kong Zoological &
  Botanical Gardens 72,
  *72*, **74**, 212
Hopewell Centre *59*, 83
horse racing 207, 251
horse-riding 248
hostels *see* accommodation
hotel lounge bars 236-237
hotels *see* accommodation
HSBC Building *60*, **69**,
  210
Hung Hom 15, **104**
Hung Shing Temple, Ping
  Shan 121
Hung Shing Temple, Wan
  Chai 83
Hung Shing Ye, Lamma
  128
Hungry Ghost Festival
  **205**, 243
Hutchison House *60*

ice-skating 248
Independent Commission
  Against Corruption
  (ICAC) **23**, 25
Indian population 29
Inner Line 20
insurance 290
International Finance
  Centre *61*
Internet 290
Islam 30
Island Shangri-La Hotel
  **40**, *59*, *60*
Islands, Outlying
  **127-138**

Jackson, Sir Thomas 69
Jade Market 108, **194**
Jamia Masjid Islamic
  Centre 104
Japan & China 20
Jardine House *61*, **65**, *68*
Jardine Matheson 8, 10, 11,
  65
jazz music venues 236
jogging 249
'Joint Declaration' **24**, 25
Judaism 30
Jumbo Floating Restaurant
  91

**k**
Kadoorie Farm & Botanic
  Garden 37, **119**
Kai Tak airport 23, 282
kaifongs 16
Kam Fa 29
Kam Tin 19
Kamikaze Caves, Lamma
  129
Kang Yu-hwei 19
karaokes, gay & lesbian
  223-225
Kennedy, Sir Arthur E 8
Kennedy Town 76
kickboxing 248
*Killer, The* 218
Kimberley, Lord 8
Knutsford Terrace 104
Knutsford, Lord 8
Ko Shan Theatre **243**,
  245
Kowloon **97-107**
  accommodation 45-53
  acquisition &
    development of 12
  for children 212, **213**
  pubs & bars 173
  restaurants 155-160
Kowloon–Canton Railway
  (KCR) 99, **284**
Kowloon City, restaurants
  159
Kowloon Park 104
Kowloon Tong, restaurants
  160
Kowloon Walled City 113
Kowloon Walled City Park
  112
Kuan Tin Temple 77
Kun Ting Study Hall 121
Kuomintang 18, 19
Kwai Tsing Theatre 242
Kwan Kung 30
Kwan Kung Pavilion,
  Cheung Chau *28*
Kwun Tong 23
Kwun Yum 30

**l**
Ladies' Market **108**, 194
Lai Chi Kok Market 194
Lai, Joel 231
Lam, Doming 240
Lamma **127-129**
  fire brigade 128
  for children 214
  pubs & bars 174
  restaurants 164
Lan Kwai Fong **71**, *71*, 166
Landmark, The 71, **182**
Lane Crawford 182
'Lanes, The' 71, 176
language 298
Lantau **130-134**
  accommodation 53
  pubs & bars 174

restaurants 164-165
Lantau Peak 130, **132**
Lantau South Country Park
  132
Lantau Trail 35
Law, Wing-fai 240
Lee, Ka-ling Colleen 241
Lee, Bruce 219
left luggage 290
legal help 291
Legislative Council 17, 18,
  25, 26
Legislative Council
  Building 69
Lei Cheng Uk Han Tomb
  Museum 113
Lei Yue Mun 112
lesbian *see* gay & lesbian
Leung Kwok-hung *see*
  'Long Hair'
Li, Ka-shing 69
libraries 291
Lin, Tse-hsu **10**, 25
Lin, Zhu 241
lion dance 245
Lion Rock Country Park
  214
Lippo Centre *60*, *68*, 72
Lo Hon Monastery, Lantau
  133
Lo So Shing, Lamma 129
Lo Wai 117
Lockhart, James Stewart 8
Lok Ma Chau 117
'Long Hair' 105
Long Ke Wan 124
lost property 291
*Love is a Many Splendored
  Thing* 216
Lover's Rock 210
Lugard, Sir Frederick 8
Lung Yuek Tau Heritage
  Trail 117

**m**
Ma Liu Shui 116
Ma Wat Wai 117
Ma, Joyce 187
*Macao* 216
Macartney mission 25
Macau 9-10, **254-266**
  accommodation 264-265
  A-Ma Temple 260
  Barra Hill 260
  bars & nightlife 262-263
  beaches 260
  Camões Grotto and
    Garden 257, **258**
  Casa Museu de Taipa
    260
  casinos 264
  Centro Cultural de Macau
    258
  Colôane 260-261
  eating & drinking
    261-262
  Edifício Ritz 257
  Flora Garden 258

Fortaleza do Monte 257, **259**
gambling 255, **264-265**
getting there 266
Governor's Residence 255, 260
Grand Prix 206
Grand Prix Museum 258, **259**
greyhound racing 265
Guia Fort & Lighthouse 258, *258*, **259**
history 254
horse racing 264-265
Hotel Lisboa 264
Jorge Alvares Monument 255
language 266
Largo do Senado 257
Leal Senado 257, **259**
Lou Lim Ieoc Garden 258, **259**
Macau (Yat Yuen) Canidrome 265
Macau Jockey Club 265
Macau Museum 257, **259**
Maritime Museum 260
money 266
Old Protestant Cemetery 257, **259**
Ruinas de São Paulo 257, *257*, **259**
St Michael Cemetery 257-258
Santa Casa de Misericordia 257
Santo António 257, **259-260**
São Domingos 257, **260**
São Domingos Market 257
Seac Pai Van Park 261
shopping 263
sightseeing 255-261
Sun Yat-sen Memorial House 258, **260**
Taipa 260
telephones 266
tourist information 266
visas 266
Wine Museum 258, **259**
MacDonnell, Sir Richard 8, 15, 16
MacLehose, Sir Murray 23, 25, 34
MacLehose Trail **34-35**, 120
Madame Tussaud's 89, **90**
magazines 291-292
mah jong 32
Mai Po Marshes 37, 117, **121**
Maio people 28
Mak, Wai-chu Clarence 241
Man Mo Temple 76, *77*, **79**
Man Mo Temple, Tai Po 117
*Man With The Golden*

*Gun, The* 217
Mandarin Oriental Hotel 41, *61*
Marathon, Standard Chartered Hong Kong **208**, 251
markets 194
  Bird 108, *108*, **194**
  Bowrington Road 85
  Central 11, **72**
  Flower 108, *108*
  Goldfish **108**, 194
  Jade 108, **194**, 213
  Ladies' **108**, 194, 213
  Lai Chi Kok 194
  Reclamation Street 108, *108*
  Sham Shui Po 113
  Stanley 93, **194**
  Tai Po 117
  Temple Street 32, 108, **194**, 213
  Western 75, *78*, **194**
martial arts 248
Mass Transit Railway (MTR) 25, **284**
Matheson *see* Jardine Matheson
MAX! Festival 219
May 4th Movement 20
media 291-292
medicine, Chinese 33, 75, **76**
Melvis 234-235
metro (MTR) 284
Mid Autumn Festival **205-206**, 214
Middle Bay 250
Mid-Levels Escalator 76, 210
Mid-Levels 12, **75-80**
  pubs & bars 171
  restaurants 147-148
Mirador Mansions 49, **51**
money 292
Mong Kok **108-111**
  accommodation 51-53
  restaurants 158-159
Moore, Henry 65
Mount Collinson 36
Mount Davis 76
Mount Gough 90
Mount Stenhouse, Lamma 129
mountain biking 249
Mui Fat Buddhist Monastery 120, **122**
Mui Wo, Lantau 130-132
Murray House **94**, 213
museums
  Chinese University Art Museum 115, **118**
  Flagstaff House Museum of Tea Ware 32, 72, **74**, 210
  Hong Kong Heritage Museum 114-115, **118**, 212, 213, 242
  Hong Kong Museum of

Art 32, 102, **104-106**, 220-221
  Hong Kong Museum of Coastal Defence **87**, 213
  Hong Kong Museum of History 104, **106**
  Hong Kong Museum of Medical Sciences 14, **78**
  Hong Kong Museum of Science 212, 104, **106**
  Hong Kong Racing Museum 86, **87**
  Hong Kong Railway Museum 117, **118**, 214
  Hong Kong Space Museum 102, **106**, *106*, 212, 213
  Lei Cheng Uk Han Tomb Museum 113
  Police Museum 85, **87**, 210
  Sheung Yiu Folk Museum 124, **125**
  University Museum & Art Gallery 78, **79**, 221
music 301
  Chinese opera 242-243
  choirs 244
  hotel lounge bars 236-237
  jazz, blues & roots venues 236
  live 233-237
  local composers & performers 240-241
  orchestras 243-244
  venues 234-236
  Western classical 242-244
  Western opera 244-245

Nakajima, Fuzuki 241
Nanking, Rape of 20
Nanking, Treaty of 10, 25
Napier, Lord William John 10, 25
Nathan Road *97*, 99
Nathan, Sir Matthew 8
National Day Fireworks 206
Nepalese population 29
New Kowloon 15, **112-113**
New Territories **114-125**
  accommodation 53
  acquisition of 111
  for children 212, **213-214**
  leasing of 17
  performing arts venues 241-242
  pubs & bars 173-174
  restaurants 160-163
New Year 207
New Year, Chinese **208**, 214

newspapers 291
Ng Choy 17
Ngong Ping, Lantau 132-133
Night Market, Temple Street 32, 108, **194**, 213
nightlife **228-237**
Nim Shue Wan beach, Lantau 130
NoHo 166
Noon Day Gun 86

### o

Ocean Park **92**, *92*, **209**, 212, 213
Old Wan Chai Post Office 85
1aspace 221
opening hours 293
opera, Chinese 242-244
Opera Society of Hong Kong 244
opera, Western 244-245
opium trade 10, 25
Opium (Anglo-Chinese) War, First **10**, 25
Opium (Anglo-Chinese or Arrow) War, Second **12**, 25
orchestras, Chinese 244
outlying islands **127-138**

### p

Pacific Place 72, 176, **182**, 210
*padrão* 7
Pak Sing Ancestral Hall 77
Pak Tai Temple, Cheung Chau 135
Pak Tam Chung 124
Pak Tam Chung Visitor Centre 124
Pak Tso Wan beach, Cheung Chau 136
Pao Galleries 221
parks
  Hollywood Road 78
  Hong Kong 72, *72*, **74**, 210, 212
  Kowloon 104
  Lantau South Country 132
  Plover Cove Country 117
  Tai Mo Shan Country 120
  Victoria **85**, *86*, 214
*Passage from Hong Kong* 216
Pat Sing Leng Nature Trail 123
Patten, Chris **24**, *24*, 25
Peak, the 15, *61*, 65, **88-90**
  for children 211-212
  pubs & bars 171
  restaurants 148-149
Peak Explorer 211
Peak Galleria 89, 211
Peak Tower *61*, **89**

Peak Tram 15, *16*, 88, **90**, 211, 212
Pedder Building 71
Pedder, Lieutenant William 8
Peel, Robert 8
Pei, IM 69
Peking, Convention of 17
*Peking Opera Blues* 218
Peng Chau 130, **137-138**, *137*
Peninsula Hotel *45*, **46**, 65, *99*, 102
performing arts **238-246**
  Chinese 242-246
  festivals 246
  Hong Kong Arts Festival 207
  Hong Kong Chinese Arts Festival **206**, 245
  Hong Kong Youth Arts Festival 206
  local composers and performers 240-241
  tickets & information 238
  venues 238-242
pidgin English 21
Pinewood Battery 210
Ping Chau 116
Ping Shan Heritage Trail 120-121
pink dolphins 35
plague **14**, 77, 78
Plover Cove 123
Plover Cove Country Park 117
  Visitor Centre 123
Po Lin Monastery, Lantau 29, *131*, 132-133, **134**
Po Toi 138
Pok Fu Lam Country Park 90
police 293
Police Museum 85, **87**, 210
Portuguese & South China trade 9
Portuguese in Kowloon 12
Possession Point 11
postal services 293
Pottinger, Sir Henry 8
Prince of Wales Building *59*, *60*, **65**
public holidays 293
public transport 283-284
pubs & bars **166-174**
  best 174
  gay & lesbian 223-225
  girlie 167
  top five in SoHo 79
  with food 163
Pui O Wan, Lantau 132
Punti people 28

Qu Yuan 205
Queensway Plaza 176

radio 292
rail, arriving by 283
rail services 284
Reclamation Street 12
Reclamation Street Market 108, *108*
religion 29-30, 293-294
Repulse Bay **93**, 250
restaurants **141-165**
  Asian 159
  American 142, 159
  best 144
  British 142, 149-150, 159
  by area
    Causeway Bay 149-154
    Central 142-147
    Cheung Chau 165
    Hong Kong Island 142-155
    Kowloon 155-160
    Kowloon City 159
    Kowloon Tong 160
    Lamma 164
    Lantau 164-165
    Mong Kok 158-159
    New Territories 160-163
    Peak, the 148-149
    Sheung Wan 147-148
    South & east coast 154-155
    Tsim Sha Tsui 155-158
    Wan Chai 149-154
    Yau Ma Tei 158-159
  Chinese: Beijingese **150**, 155, 158
  Chinese: Cantonese 142-143, **148-149**, 150, 155-156, 158, 160-161, 163, 165
  Chinese: Chiu Chownese **150**, 158, 162, 163
  Chinese: Hunanese 143, 158
  Chinese: pigeon 158, 164
  Chinese: seafood 158, 164, 165
  Chinese: Shanghainese **150-151**, 159, 160
  Chinese: Sichuanese **151**, 159
  Chinese: vegetarian 147-148, 158, 159, 164
  dim sum 149, 158
  floating 91
  French 143, 156, 159
  fusion 147, 156, 159
  Greek/Middle Eastern 151, 159
  Indian 144, 151-152, 159, 162, 164
  Indonesian 158, 160, 161
  international 144, 148-149, 153, 154, 156, 158-159, 160, 162, 163, 164, 165

Italian 144, 153, 156, 160, 162
  Japanese 145, 156, 159, 160, 162-163
  Malaysian 158, 160, 161
  Mediterranean 155, 161, 165
  Mexican 145, 161
  seafood 156-157, 161, 163
  snacks 154-155
  South African 161, 165
  Spanish 145, 161
  steakhouse 157, 161, 165
  Swiss 157, 161
  Thai 145-147, 153, 159, 161, 163
  vegetarian 154, 157-158, 161
  Vietnamese 147, 155, 159, 161
*Revenge of the Pink Panther* 217
Revolution, Chinese 19
Ripley's Believe It Or Not! Odditorium 89, **90**, 211
Rise Commercial Building 182
Ritz-Carlton Hotel **43**, *60*
Riva, Remo 65
road, arriving by
*Road to Hong Kong, The* 217
Robinson, Sir Hercules 8
Robinson, Sir William 14
rollerblading 249
*Rouge* 218
Rudolph, Paul 72
rugby 252
Rugby Sevens, Credit Suisse First Boston Hong Kong 204, 252
running 249
Russell's 10

safety & security 294
Sai Kung 123, *123*, **124-125**
Sai Kung Peninsula **116**, 214
Sai Wan, Cheung Chau 136
sailing 249
St John's Cathedral 12, *69*, 71, **74**, 240
St Stephen's Beach, Stanley **95**, 213
Salisbury, Lord 8
salsa 237
Sam Tung Uk Museum 120, **122**
Sam's Tailor 191
saunas, gay & lesbian 225-226
scuba diving 249
sea, arriving by 283
season, Hong Kong by **204-208**
Seibu 182

services *see* shops & services
Sevens, Hong Kong 204, 252
sex clubs 81, 167
Sha Tin **114-115**, 213, 214
Sha Tin Racecourse 115, **118-119**, *251*
Sham Shui Po 15, **20**
Sham Shui Po Market 113
Sham Wan, Lamma 129
Shanghai Tang 72, **189**
Shanghainese cuisine 150
shark's fin trade 75
Shek Kip Mei 23
Shek O 36, **95-96**
Shek Pai Wan, Lamma 129
Shek Pik Reservoir 132
Shenzhen 25, 117, 175, **201**
Sheung Cheung Wai 121
Sheung Shui 117
Sheung Wan & Mid-Levels 12, **75-80**
  pubs & bars 171
  restaurants 147-148
Sheung Yiu Folk Museum 124, **125**
Shing Mun reservoirs 19
Shing Mun San Tsuen 19
shops & services **175-201**
  antiques 176-179
  art supplies & stationery 179
  auctions 179-180
  books 180-181
    antiquarian & second-hand 181
    gay & lesbian 226-227
  department stores & malls 181-185
  dry cleaners & laundries 185
  electronics 185-186
  fashion 186-193
    accessories 193
    budget 186
    children 186
    designer: international 187-188
    designer: local 188-190
    factory outlets 190
    fetish/erotic 190
    gay & lesbian
      partywear & lingerie 227
    second-hand 191
    streetwear & clubwear 191
    tailors 191-193
    underwear 193
  florists 193-195
  food & drink 195-6
    bakeries & pâtisseries 195
    chocolate & confectioners 195
    coffee & tea 195
    delicatessens 195
    health & organic food 195

supermarkets 195-196
tea 196
wines, beers & spirits 196
gifts & souvenirs 196-197
health & beauty 197-198
interiors, furniture & fabrics 198-199
music 199
opticians & eyewear 199
pharmacies 199-200
photography & film processing 200
shoes 200
sport 200
tobacconists 200
toys, games & magic 201
watches 201
Sichuanese cuisine 151
sightseeing **55-138**
Signal Hill Garden 102
Silvermine Bay, Lantau 130
Silverstrand Beach 125
skateboarding 249
smoking 294
Sogo 85, **183-184**, 212
SoHo 71, **78-79**, 166
SoHo, top five bars 79
Sok Kwu Wan, Lamma 127, **128-129**, 214
*Soldier of Fortune* 216
South & east coast **91-96**
pubs & bars 172
restaurants 154-155
South Bay 250
South China Athletic Association 247
Special Administrative Region (SAR) 25
spitting 294
sport & fitness **247-252**
adventure sports 251
fitness centres 248
participation sports 247-251
shops 200
spectator sports 251-252
Spring Lantern (Yuen Siu) Festival 208
Standard Chartered Hong Kong Marathon **208**, 251
Stanley 12, 22, **93-95**, 212, 213
Stanley Cemetery 94
Stanley Fort 95
Stanley, Lord 8
Stanley Main Beach 95
Stanley Market 93, **194**
Stanley Old Police Station 94
Star Alliance Open (golf) **206**, 251
Star Ferry **63**, 65, 99, *100*, 212, 213
Star Ferry riots 23
Star House 99
Statue Square 15, **65**
street names 8

Stubbs, Sir Reginald E 8
Sui Tsing Pak Temple 77
Sun Hung Kai Centre *58*
Sun Yat-sen, Dr **19**, 25
Sun Yat-sen Historical Trail 78
surfing 249-250
Suyin, Han 216
swimming 250
Swire House *61*

*tai chi* 32
Tai Fu Tai 117, **119**
Tai Long Wan 250
Tai Mei Tuk 123
Tai Mo Shan 120
Tai Mo Shan Country Park 120
Tai O, Lantau 133, *133*
Tai Ping Shan 14, **76-78**
Tai Po **116-117**, 214
Tai Po Market 117
Tai Tau Chau 96
Tai Wai 114
Tai Wan To, Lamma 128
Tam, Tin-lok Alex 241
Tang Ancestral Hall 121
Tang Chung Ling Ancestral Hall 117, **119**
Tang, David 189
Tanka people 28
Taoism 29
Tap Mun Chau 116, **138**
*Target Hong Kong* 216
tax 294
taxis 282, **285**
telegrams 295
telephones 294-295
Temple Street Night Market 32, 108, **194**, 213
temples 76, *77*, 79, 83, 86, *93*, 94, 108, 112, 114, 117, 120, 125, 135
Ten Thousand Buddhas Monastery 114, *115*, **119**, 212, 213
tennis 206, 250, 252
theatre, English language 246
Tiananmen Square massacre **24**, 25
TICKETEK 238
time 295
Times Square 85, 176, **185**, 212
Tin Hau 29, 86, **94**
Tin Hau, birthday of **204**, 244
Tin Hau Temple
Causeway Bay 86
Clearwater Bay 125
Stanley *93*, 94
Tai Po 117
Tap Mun Chau 116, 138
Yau Ma Tei 108
tipping 295
toilets 296

Tolo Harbour 123
Tong Kok Wai 117
tourist information 296
Trailwalker 35, **206**
trams 69, **284**
Trappist Monastery, Lantau 130, 132
trips out of town **253-279**
Tsang, Richard 240-241
Tsang Tai Uk 114, *118*
Tsim Sha Tsui **99-107**, *100*
accommodation 45-51
development of 12
pubs & bars 166, 173
restaurants 155-158
shopping 175
Tsuen Wan 23, **120**
Ts'z, I 15
Tuen Mun 120-121
Tuen Ng (Dragon Boat) Festival **205**, *206*, 214
Tung Chee-hwa *24*, 25, 31, 69
Tung Chung, Lantau 132
Tung O, Lamma 129
Tung Wah Hospital **15**, 25
Tung Wah Hospital Committee 16
Tung Wan beach, Cheung Chau 136
television 292

universities 294
University of Hong Kong, Chinese 115
University Museum & Art Gallery 78, **79**, 221
Urban Council 14
URBTIX 238

Versailles Peace Conference 20
Victoria Gap 89
Victoria Harbour *9*
Victoria Park **85**, *86*, 214
Victoria Peak *61*, **89-90**, 212
Victoria Peak Garden 89-90
Victoria Prison 76
Vietnamese population 29
Visage Free 241
visas 288, 296
vistas, top five 65
Voeux, Sir William Des 8

wakeboarding 250-251
walks 285
Dragon's Back Trail **36**, 95
for children 210-211
Peak 90
*see also* hiking

Wan Chai *58*, **81-87**, *211*
accommodation 43-45
pubs & bars 166, 167, 171-172
restaurants 149-154
Wang Lei 279
waterskiing 250-251
weather 296
websites 301
Weddell, Captain 9
Weihaiwei 17, 19
Wellington, Duke of 8
Western Market 75, *78*, **194**
Whampoa 104
wildlife **34-37**
windsurfing 250-251
Wing On 85, **185**
Wishing Tree 116
women 297
Wong Shek 124
Wong Tai Sin 29
Wong Tai Sin Temple 112, **113**
Wong, Suzie 77, **82-83**, 167
working in Hong Kong 297
*World of Suzie Wong, The* 77, 81, **82-83**, 217
World War II 20
Wu Ting Fang 17
Würth Gallery 221-222

Xavier, St Francis 9

Yao people 28
Yau Ma Tei **108**
accommodation 51-53
restaurants 158-159
Yim Tin Tsai 123
YMCA of Hong Kong 247, **248**
yoga 251
*You Only Live Twice* 217
Young, Sir Mark 22
Youth Arts Festival, Hong Kong 206
youth hostels *see* accommodation
Yu Kiu Ancestral Hall 121
Yuen Siu (Spring Lantern) Festival 208
Yuen Yuen Institute 120, **122**
Yung Shue Wan, Lamma **127-128**, 214

Zuni Icosahedron 246

# Advertisers' Index

Please refer to relevant sections for addresses
and telephone numbers

Raja Fashions                                    **IFC**

## In Context

International Agenda                                **4**
Time Out Magazine                                  **6**

## Accommodation

Kowloon Shangri-La                                **38**
Furama Hotel                                      **42**

## Sightseeing

i-D Magazine                                      **54**
Trattoria Restaurant & Bar                        **64**

## Restaurants

Yung Kee Chinese Restaurant                      **140**
Ruth's Chris Steakhouse                          **146**

## Shops & Services

Raja Fashions                                    **178**
Sam's Tailor                                      **184**
Salon Picasso                                     **192**

## Maps

Time Out City Guides                             **312**

Sam's Tailor                                     **IBC**

| | |
|---|---|
| Place of interest and/or entertainment . . . . . . . | ▢ |
| Railway station . . . . . . . . . . . . . . . . . . . . . . . . . | ▢ |
| Park . . . . . . . . . . . . . . . . . . . . . . . . . . . . . . . . . . . | ▢ |
| Hospital/university . . . . . . . . . . . . . . . . . . . . . . | ▢ |
| Post office . . . . . . . . . . . . . . . . . . . . . . . . . . . . . | ⊠ |
| MTR station . . . . . . . . . . . . . . . . . . . . . . . . . . . | Ⓜ |
| MTR station exit. . . . . . . . . . . . . . . . . . . . . . . | ③ |
| Area . . . . . . . . . . . . . . . . . . . . . . . . . . . CENTRAL |
| Tram route . . . . . . . . . . . . . . . . . . . . . . . . . . . | — |
| Elevated walkway . . . . . . . . . . . . . . . . . . . . . . . | ░░░░ |

# Maps

| | |
|---|---|
| **Hong Kong** | **310** |
| **Hong Kong, Macau &** | |
| **Guangzhou** | **313** |
| **Street Index** | **314** |
| **Rail Transport** | **316** |

See page 62

# The **Time Out City Guides** spectrum

Available from all good bookshops and at www.timeout.com/shop

www.timeout.com     www.penguin.com

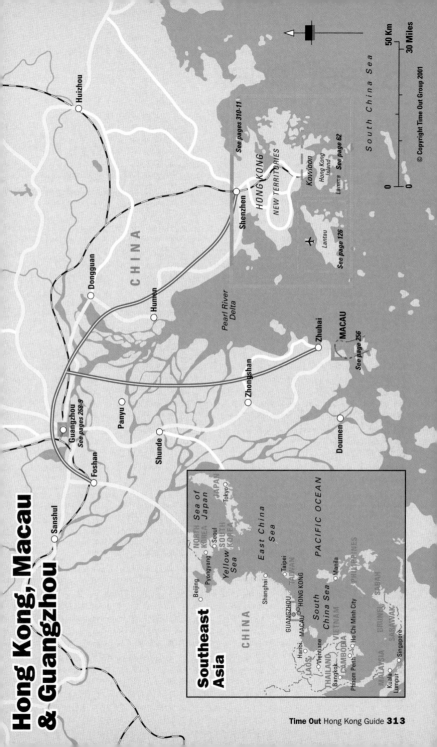

# Hong Kong, Macau & Guangzhou

South China Sea

© Copyright Time Out Group 2001

50 Km
30 Miles

*See pages 310-11*

HONG KONG

NEW TERRITORIES

Kowloon

Hong Kong Island  *See page 62*

Lamma

Huizhou

Shenzhen

CHINA

Dongguan

Humen

Pearl River Delta

Lantau  *See page 126*

Zhuhai

MACAU

*See page 256*

Guangzhou *See pages 268-9*

Panyu

Zhongshan

Doumen

Shunde

Foshan

Sanshui

## Southeast Asia

Sea of Japan

NORTH KOREA

JAPAN

Tokyo

Beijing

Pyongyang

Seoul

SOUTH KOREA

East China Sea

PACIFIC OCEAN

Yellow Sea

Shanghai

Taipei

TAIWAN

CHINA

GUANGZHOU

MACAU

HONG KONG

South China Sea

PHILIPPINES

Manila

Hanoi

Vientiane

LAOS

VIETNAM

THAILAND

CAMBODIA

Ho Chi Minh City

Bangkok

Phnom Penh

MALAYSIA

SABAH

BRUNEI

SARAWAK

Kuala Lumpur

Singapore

# Street Index

Aberdeen Street -
p66-7 B3/C2-3
Aberdeen Tunnel - p80 C3
Albany Road - p66-7 C4-5
Amoy Street - p80 B2
Anton Street - p80 A2
Arbuthnot Road - p66-7 C4
Argyle Street - p110 A2-C2
Arran Street - p110 A2
Arsenal Street - p80 A2
Arthur Street - p110 A4
Ashley Road - p98 B2
Austin Avenue - p110 B5
Austin Road - p110 A5-C5

**Bank Street** - p66-7 E4
Battery Path - p66-7 D4/C4
Battery Street - p110 A4-5
Blenheim Avenue - p98 C2
Blue Pool Road - p80 D3
Bonham Road - p66-7 A3
Bonham Strand East -
p66-7 B2
Bonham Strand West -
p66-7 A1-2
Boundary Street -
p110 A1-C1
Bowen Drive - p80 A2-3
Bowen Road - p80 A3-C3
Bowring Street - p110 A5/B5
Bowrington Road - p80 C2
Braga Circuit - p110 B2/C1-2
Breezy Path   - p66-7 A3
Bridges Street - p66-7 B3
Bristol Avenue - p98 C2
Broadwood Road - p80 D3
Bullock Lane - p80 B2
Burd Street - p66-7 B2
Burrows Street - p80 C2
Bute Street - p110 A2

**Caine Lane** - p66-7 A3
Caine Road -
p66-7 A3/B2-3/C4
Cameron Lane - p98 C1
Cameron Road -
p98 C1-2/D1
Canal Road East - p80 C2
Canal Road West - p80 C2
Cannon Street - p80 D1
Canton Road - p98
A1-2/B2-3 - p110 A2-5
Carnarvon Road - p98 C1-2
Caroline Hill Road -
p80 D2-3/E2-3
Castle Road - p66-7 A3/B3
Castle Steps - p66-7 B3-4
Causeway Road - p80 E1-2
Cedar Street - p110 A1
Chancery Lane - p66-7 C4
Chater Road - p66-7 D3/E4
Chatham Road - p110 C4-5
Chatham Road South - p98
C2-3/D1-2 - p110 C5

Cheong Wan Road - p98 E1 -
p110 C5
Cheung Sha Wan Road -
p110 A1
Chi Wo Street - p110 B5
Chiu Lung Street - p66-7 D3
Chun Yi Lane - p110 B3-4
Chung Hau Street - p110 C3-4
Cleveland Street - p80 D1
Cleverly Street - p66-7 B2
Club Street - p66-7 E3-4
Cochrane Street - p66-7 C3
Conduit Road -
p66-7 A3-4/B4-5
Connaught Place - p66-7 E3
Connaught Road Central -
p66-7 B1-2/C2/D2-3/E3/F4
Connaught Road West -
p66-7 A1/B1
Convention Avenue - p80 B1
Cornwall Avenue - p98 C2
Cotton Path - p80 E2
Cotton Tree Drive -
p66-7 D5/E5
Cox's Road - p110 B5
Cross Harbour Tunnel -
p80 C1/D1 - p98 E1-3
Cross Street - p80 B2
Cumberland Road - p110 B1

**D'Aguilar Street** -
p66-7 C4/D4
Des Voeux Road Central -
p66-7 B2/C2-3/D3-4/E4
Des Voeux Road West -
p66-7 A1
Douglas Lane - p66-7 D3
Douglas Street - p66-7 D3
Drake Street - p66-7 F4
Duddell Street - p66-7 D4
Duke Street - p110 B1
Dunbar Road - p110 C2
Dundas Street - p110 A3/B3

**Eastern Hospital Road** -
p80 E2-3
Edinburgh Place - p66-7 E3
Electric Road - p80 E1
Electric Street - p80 A2
Elgin Street - p66-7 B3-4/C4
Embankment Road -
p110 B1
Expo Drive - p80 B1
Expo Drive Central - p80 B1
Expo Drive East - p80 B1
Expo Promenade - p80 B1

**Fa Yuen Street** -
p110 A1-2/B2-3
Fat Hing Street - p66-7 A2
Fat Kwong Street - p110 C3-4
Fenwick Pier Street - p80 A1
Fenwick Street - p80 A1-2
Ferry Street - p110 A3-5

Fife Street - p110 A2
Fleming Road - p80 B1-2
Flower Market Road -
p110 B1

**Gage Street** - p66-7 C3
Garden Road - p66-7 D5/E4-5
Gascoigne Road - p110 B5/C5
Gilman Street - p66-7 C2
Gilman's Bazaar - p66-7 C2
Glenealy - p66-7 B5/C5
Gloucester Road - p80
A2/B2/C1-2/D1-2/E2
Gough Street - p66-7 B3/C3
Graham Street - p66-7 C3
Granville Road - p98 C1/D1
Great George Street - p80 D1
Gresson Street - p80 A2
Gutzlaff Street - p66-7 C3

**Haiphong Road** - p98 B2
Hamilton Street - p110 A3
Hankow Road - p98 B2-3
Hanoi Road - p98 C2
Happy View Terr - p80 D3
Harbour Drive - p80 B2/C1-2
Harbour Road - p80 B1/C1
Harbour View Street -
p66-7 D2-3
Harcourt Road - p66-7 F4 -
p80 A2
Hart Avenue - p98 C2
Hau Fook Street - p98 C1
Hau Man Street - p110 C3-4
Hau Tak Lane - p80 C3
Haven Street - p80 C2
Heard Street - p80 C2
Hennessy Road - p80 A2/B2
Hillier Street - p66-7 B2
Hillwood Road - p110 B5
Hing Fat Street - p80 E1
Ho Man Tin Hill Road -
p110 B3-4/C3
Ho Man Tin Street - p110 B3
Hoi Ping Road - p80 D2
Hollywood Road - p66-7
A2/B2-3/C3
Hong Chong Road - p98 E1 -
p110 C5
Hornsey Road - p66-7 B5/C5
Humphreys Avenue - p98 C2
Hung Hing Road - p80 C1/D1
Hysan Avenue - p80 D2

**Ice House Street** - p66-7
D3-4
Ichang Street - p98 B2
Irving Street - p80 D2

**Jackson Road** - p66-7 E3-4
Jaffe Road - p80 A2/B2/C1-2
Jardine's Bazaar - p80 D2
Jardine's Crescent - p80 D2
Jervois Street - p66-7 B2

Johnston Road –
p80 A2/B2/C2
Jordan Path - p110 B5
Jordan Road - p110 A5/B5
Jubilee Street -
p66-7 C2-3/D2
Justice Drive - p80 A2

**Ka Ning Path** - p80 E2
Kadoorie Avenue -
p110 B1-2
Kai Chiu Road - p80 D2
Kansu Street - p110 A4
Kau U Fong - p66-7 B2/C2-3
Kennedy Road -
p80 A2-3/C3
Kennedy Street - p80 B3
Ki Lung Street - p110 A1
Kimberley Road - p98 C1/D1
Kimberley Street - p98 C1
King's Park Rise - p110 B4
Kingston Street - p80 D1
Knutsford Terrace - p98 C1
Ko Shing Street - p66-7 A1-2
- p80 D1
Kowloon Park Drive -
p98 A1/B1-3
Kui In Fong - p66-7 A2-3
Kwong Yik Lane - p80 A2

**Ladder Street** -
p66-7 A3/B2-3
Lai Chi Kok Road -
p110 A1-2
Lambeth Walk - p66-7 F4
Lan Fong Road - p80 D2
Lan Kwai Fong - p66-7 C4
Landale Street - p80 A2
Lau Li Street - p80 E1
Lau Sin Street - p80 E1
Lee Garden Road - p80 D2
Lee Tung Street - p80 B2
Leighton Road - p80 C2/D2
Li Chit Street - p80 A2
Li Yuen Street East -
p66-7 D3
Li Yuen Street West -
p66-7 D3
Link Road - p80 D2
Lock Road - p98 B2
Lockhart Road - p80
A2/B2/C2/D1
Lok Ku Road - p66-7 B2
Lower Albert Road -
p66-7 D4-5/E5
Lower Lascar Row - p66-7 A2
Luard Street - p80 B2
Luen Wan Street - p110 B2
Lugard Road - p66-7 A5
Lun Fat Street - p80 A2
Lung King Street - p80 A1
Lung Wui Road - p66-7 F3 -
p80 A1
Lyndhurst Terrace - p66-7 C3

**Man Cheung Street** -
p66-7 D2 - p110 A4-5
Man Fuk Road - p110 C2
Man Kwong Street - p66-7
C1-2/D1-2/E2
Man Po Street - p66-7 D2/E2
Man Wa Lane - p66-7 B2
Man Ying Street - p110 A5
Man Yiu Street - p66-7 E2-3
Maple Street - p110 A1
Market Street - p110 A4
Marsh Road - p80 C1-2
Matheson Street – p80 D2
Mercer Street - p66-7 B2
Middle Road - p98 B3/C3
Min Street - p110 A5
Minden Avenue - p98 C2
Minden Row - p98 C2
Mody Lane - p98d2/E2
Mody Road - p98 C2/D2/E1
Mody Square - p98 D2
Mong Kok Road - p110 A2
Monmouth Path - p80 A2
Monmouth Terrace - p80 A2
Moreton Terrace – p80 E2
Morrison Hill Road - p80 C2
Morrison Street - p66-7 B2
Mosque Junction - p66-7 B4
Mosque Street - p66-7 B4
Murray Road - p66-7 E4

**Nanking Street** - p110
A5/B5
Nathan Road - p98 B1/C2 -
p110 A1-4/B4-5
Nelson Street - p110 A3/B2
New Market Street -
p66-7 A1/B1
New Street - p66-7 A2
Ngan Mok Street - p80 E1
Ning Po Street - p110 A5/B5

**O'Brien Road** - p80 B2
Observatory Road -
p98 C1/D1
Oi Kwan Road - p80 C2
Old Bailey Street -
p66-7 C3-4
On Lan Street - p66-7 D4
On Wan Road - p110 C5

**Pak Hoi Street** - p110 A4
Pak Sha Road - p80 D2
Palm Street - p110 A2
Parkes Street - p110 A5/B5
Paterson Street - p80 D1
Peace Avenue - p110 B2-3
Peak Road – p80 A3
Pedder Street - p66-7 D3-4
Peel Street - p66-7 B3-4/C3
Peking Road - p98 B2
Pennington Street - p80 D2
Percival Street - p80 D1-2
Perkins Road - p80 E3
Perth Street - p110 C2
Pier Road - p66-7 C2
Pilkem Street - p110 B5
Pitt Street - p110 A3/B3
Playing Field Road -
p110 A1
Po Hing Fong - p66-7 A2-3

Po Yan Street - p66-7 A2
Po Yee Street - p66-7 A2
Poplar Street - p110 A1
Portland Street - p110 A1-3
Possession Street -
p66-7 A2
Pottinger Street - p66-7 D3
Pound Lane - p66-7 A2-3
Prat Avenue - p98 C2/D2
Prince Edward Road West -
p110 A1-2/-C1
Prince's Terrace - p66-7 B4
Princess Margaret Road -
p110 C2-4
Public Square Street -
p110 A4
Pui Ching Road -
p110 B3/C3

**Queen Street** - p66-7 A1-2
Queen Victoria Street -
p66-7 C3/D-3
Queen's Road Central -
p66-7 B2/C2-3/D3-4/E4
Queen's Road East -
p80 A2/B2-3/C2-3
Queen's Road West -
p66-7 A2/B2
Queensway - p66-7 E4/F4-5 -
p80 A2

**Reclamation Street** -
p110 A2-5
Robinson Road -
p66-7 A3-4/B4/C5
Rodney Street - p80 A2
Rozario Street - p66-7 A3
Rumsey Street - p66-7 C2
Russell Street - p80 C2/D2

**Sai Street** - p66-7 A2
Sai Yee Street -
p110 A1-2/B2-3
Sai Yeung Choi Street North
- p110 A1
Sai Yeung Choi Street South
- p110 A2-3
Saigon Street - p110 A5
St Joseph's Path - p66-7 D5
Salisbury Road -
p98 B3/C3/D2-3/E1-2
Salvation Army Street -
p80 C2
Science Museum Road -
p98 D1/E1
Seymour Road -
p66-7 A3/B3-4
Shanghai Street - p110 A2-5
Shantung Street -
p110 A3/B3
Sharp Street East - p80
C2/D2
Shek Ku Street - p110 C2
Shek Lung Street - p110 A2
Shelley Street -
p66-7 B4/C3-4
Shelter Street - p80 E2
Sheung Foo Street -
p110 C2-3
Sheung Lok Street -
p110 C2-3

Sheung Shing Street -
p110 C2-3
Shing Wong Street -
p66-7 B3
Ship Street - p80 A2/B2
Shiu Fai Terrace -
p80 B3/C3
Soares Avenue - p110 B2
Soy Street - p110 A3/B3
Sports Road - p80 C3/D3
Spring Garden Lane -
p80 B2
Square Street - p66-7 A2/B3
Stanley Street - p66-7 C3
Star Street - p80 A2
Staunton Street -
p66-7 B3/C3-4
Staveley Street - p66-7 C3
Stewart Road - p80 C2
Stone Nullah Lane -
p80 B2-3
Stubbs Road - p80 B3/C3
Sugar Street - p80 D2
Sun Chun Street - p80 E2
Sun Street - p80 A2
Sung Tak Street - p80 C2
Sung Yin Lane - p80 C2
Supreme Court Road -
p66-7 F5
Swatow Street - p80 B2

**Tai Hang Road** - p80 E2-3
Tai Hang Tung Road -
p110 B1
Tai Nan Street - p110 A1
Tai Ping Shan Street -
p66-7 A2-3
Tai Wo Street - p80 B2
Tai Wong Street East -
p80 B2
Tai Yuen Street - p80 B2-3
Tak Hing Street - p110 B5
Tak Yan Street - p80 C2
Tamar Street - p66-7 F4
Tang Lung Street -
p80 C2/D2
Tank Lane - p66-7 A3/B2-3
Tat Chee Avenue - p110 B1
Temple Street - p110 A4-5
Theatre Lane - p66-7 D3
Thomson Road - p80 B2
Tim Wa Avenue -
p66-7 F3-4
Tong Mi Road - p110 A1-2
Tonnochy Road - p80 C1-2
Triangle Street - p80 B2
Tsing Fung Street - p80 E1
Tun Wo Lane - p66-7 C3
Tung Choi Street -
p110 A1-3/B3
Tung Lo Wan Drive -
p80 E2
Tung Lo Wan Road - p80 E2
Tweed Road - p110 C2

**Upper Albert Road** -
p66-7 C4/D4-5
Upper Lascar Row -
p66-7 A2/B2
Upper Station Street -
p66-7 A2-3

**Ventris Street** - p80 D3
Victoria Park Road -
p80 D1/E1
Victory Avenue - p110 B2-3

**Wai Ching Street** -
p110 A5
Wan Chai Gap Road -
p80 B3
Wan Chai Road - p80 B2/C2
Wan Shing Street - p80 C1
Warren Street - p80 E2
Waterloo Road -
p110 A4/B2-4/C1-2
Wellington Street - p66-7 C3
Western Fire Services Street
- p66-7 A1
Wing Cheung Street -
p80 C2
Wing Fung Street - p80 A2
Wing Hing Street - p80 E1
Wing Kut Street - p66-7 C2
Wing Lee Street - p66-7 B3
Wing Lok Street -
p66-7 A1-2/B2
Wing Shing Street -
p66-7 C2
Wing Wah Lane - p66-7 C4
Wing Wo Street - p66-7 C2
Winslow Street - p110 C5
Wo Fung Street - p66-7 A2
Wong Chuk Street - p110 A1
Wong Nai Chung Road -
p80 C2-3/ D2-3
Wood Road - p80 C2
Wun Sha Street - p80 E2
Wylie Path - p110 BC4-5
Wylie Road - p110 B3-5
Wyndham Street - p66-7 C4

**Yat Sin Street** - p80 C2
Yee Wo Street - p80 D2
Yim Po Fong Street -
p110 B2-3
Ying Fai Terrace -
p66-7 B3-4
Yiu Wa Street - p80 C2/D2
Yu Chau Street - p110 A1
Yuk Choi Road - p110 C5
Yun Ping Road - p80 D2

**Zetland Street** - p66-7 D4

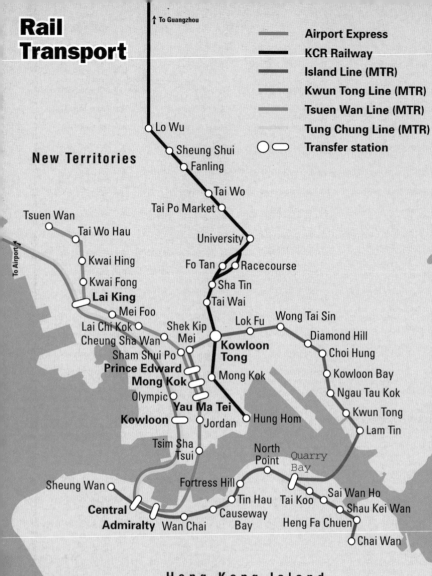

# Rail Transport

**Airport Express**
**KCR Railway**
**Island Line (MTR)**
**Kwun Tong Line (MTR)**
**Tsuen Wan Line (MTR)**
**Tung Chung Line (MTR)**
**Transfer station**

↑ To Guangzhou

**New Territories**

Lo Wu
Sheung Shui
Fanling
Tai Wo
Tai Po Market
University
Fo Tan
Racecourse
Sha Tin
Tai Wai

Tsuen Wan
Tai Wo Hau
Kwai Hing
Kwai Fong
**Lai King**
Mei Foo
Lai Chi Kok
Cheung Sha Wan
Shek Kip
Mei
Sham Shui Po
**Kowloon Tong**
Lok Fu
Wong Tai Sin
Diamond Hill
Choi Hung
Kowloon Bay
Ngau Tau Kok
Kwun Tong
Lam Tin

To Airport ↗

**Prince Edward**
**Mong Kok**
Olympic
**Yau Ma Tei**
**Kowloon**
Mong Kok
Jordan
Hung Hom

Tsim Sha
Tsui

North Point
Quarry Bay
Fortress Hill
Sheung Wan
Tin Hau
Tai Koo
Sai Wan Ho
Shau Kei Wan
**Central**
**Admiralty**
Wan Chai
Causeway Bay
Heng Fa Chuen
Chai Wan

**Hong Kong Island**

# TimeOut

## Hong Kong
### Please let us know what you think

Visit Time Out's website at **www.timeout.com**
or email your comments to **guides@timeout.com**

(FIRST EDITION)

---

**About this guide...**

**1. How useful did you find the following sections?**

| | Very | Fairly | Not very |
|---|---|---|---|
| In Context | ☐ | ☐ | ☐ |
| Accommodation | ☐ | ☐ | ☐ |
| Sightseeing | ☐ | ☐ | ☐ |
| Eat, Drink, Shop | ☐ | ☐ | ☐ |
| Arts & Entertainment | ☐ | ☐ | ☐ |
| Trips Out of Town | ☐ | ☐ | ☐ |
| Directory | ☐ | ☐ | ☐ |
| Maps | ☐ | ☐ | ☐ |

**2. Did you travel to Hong Kong...?**

Alone ☐
As part of a group ☐
On business ☐
With a partner ☐
With children ☐
On vacation ☐
To study ☐
I live here ☐

**3. How long was your trip to Hong Kong?** (write in)

_____ days

**4. Where did you book your trip?**

*Time Out* Classifieds ☐
On the Internet ☐
With a travel agent ☐
Other (write in) ☐

_____

---

**5. Where did you first hear about this guide?**

Advertising in *Time Out* magazine ☐
On the Internet ☐
From a travel agent ☐
Other (write in) ☐

**6. Is there anything you'd like us to cover in greater depth?**

_____
_____

**7. Are there any places that should/ should not* be included in the guide?**
(*delete as necessary)

_____
_____
_____
_____
_____

---

**8. How many other people have used this guide?**

none ☐  1 ☐  2 ☐  3 ☐  4 ☐  5+ ☐

**9. What city or country would you like to visit next? (write in)**

_____

### About other Time Out publications...

**10. Have you ever bought/used *Time Out* magazine?**

Yes ☐   No ☐

**11. Have you ever bought/used any other Time Out City Guides?**

Yes ☐   No ☐

If yes, which ones?
_____

**12. Have you ever bought/used other Time Out publications?**

Yes ☐   No ☐

If yes, which ones?
_____

---

**About you...**

**13. Title (Mr, Ms etc):**
First name:
Surname:
Address:

P/code:

Email:
Nationality:

**14. Date of birth:** ☐☐/☐☐/☐☐

**15. Sex:** male ☐  female ☐

**16. Are you...?**
Single ☐
Married/Living with partner ☐

**17. What is your occupation?**

**18. At the moment do you earn...?**

under £15,000 ☐
over £15,000 and up to £19,999 ☐
over £20,000 and up to £24,999 ☐
over £25,000 and up to £39,999 ☐
over £40,000 and up to £49,999 ☐
over £50,000 ☐

☐ Please tick here if you do not wish to receive information about other Time Out products.

☐ Please tick here if you do not wish to receive mailings from third parties.

**Time Out Guides**

FREEPOST 20 (WC3187)
LONDON
W1E 0DQ

**Penguin Direct**
**Penguin Books Ltd**
Bath Road
Harmondsworth
West Drayton
Middlesex
**UB7 0DA**

AFFIX
STAMP
HERE